The Letters
of
John Greenleaf Whittier

Volume II

John Greenleaf Whittier

Engraved by A. C. Warren, 1848–1849, after A. G. Hoit's portrait of 1846

The Letters
of
John Greenleaf Whittier

Edited by
John B. Pickard

Volume II

1846-1860

The Belknap Press of
Harvard University Press
Cambridge, Massachusetts
and
London, England
1975

Contents

Illustrations

1846 Whittier published *Voices of Freedom*, a collection of reform and abolitionist poems. Opposed Mexican War and began correspondence with John P. Hale.

1847 Became corresponding editor for the *National Era*, an abolitionist weekly in Washington. Published most of his prose and poetry in this paper for the next ten years. Printed ninety-three prose pieces and fifteen poems during this year in the *Era*. Published *Supernaturalism of New England*.

1848 In February visited Washington and was present when John Quincy Adams died. Supported John P. Hale for the Free Soil presidential nomination and then reluctantly backed Martin Van Buren as the Free Soil candidate. Published fifty-eight prose pieces and thirteen poems in the *Era*.

1849 Issued an edition of his collected poems, *Poems by John G. Whittier*, and ended main period of prose writing with the publication of *Margaret Smith's Journal*.

1850 In May printed "Ichabod" as a response to Daniel Webster's defense of the Fugitive Slave Law. During the summer persuaded Charles Sumner to run for senator and supported a coalition of Free Soilers and Democrats to defeat the Whigs in Massachusetts. Published *Old Portraits and Modern Sketches* and *Songs of Labor*. Friendships with Grace Greenwood and Bayard Taylor.

1851 Charles Sumner elected abolitionist senator. Was very ill during the spring.

1852 Supported John P. Hale as the Free Soil candidate for president.

1853 Published *The Chapel of Hermits, and Other Poems* in February. Friendship with Lucy Larcom.

1854   Aroused by the passage of the Kansas-Nebraska
                bill and the return of Anthony Burns, a fugitive
                slave, from Boston. Worked for the formation
                of a new abolitionist party and supported the
                resulting national organization of the Republican
                party.

1854–1855 Published "Maud Muller" and "The Barefoot
                Boy" and increasingly turned to New England
                legend, history, and scenery for poetic subjects.
                Wrote few reform or political poems after 1856.

1856   Published *The Panorama and Other Poems*, hop-
                ing to influence the coming presidential election.
                Shocked by the assault on Sumner in the Senate.
                Actively supported John C. Frémont, the first
                Republican party candidate, by writing cam-
                paign songs.

1857   Fields issued his *Poetical Works* (the "Blue and
                Gold" edition). Assured of a wide reading public
                with the founding of the *Atlantic Monthly* and
                published "Skipper Ireson's Ride" in the Decem-
                ber number. Whittier's mother died on Decem-
                ber 27.

1858   Elected to the Board of Overseers of Harvard
                College.

1859   Began writing for the New York *Independent*.
                Visited Philadelphia in April and May and re-
                newed friendship with Elizabeth Lloyd Howell.
                The relationship deepened into a mature love
                and marriage was considered. By late summer
                decided against marriage.

1860   The *National Era* ceased publication. In July
                published *Home Ballads and Poems*, a collection
                of his best poetry from the 1850's, which secure-
                ly established him as the poet of New England.
                Voted for Lincoln and was a member of the
                Electoral College. Friendships with Gail Hamilton
                and Annie Fields.

Part Six

National Era and Free Soiler

1846-1848

National Era and Free Soiler

1846-1848

"The Reformer," a poem written in 1846, aptly character-
izes Whittier's moral vision and reform activities during this
period. The grim and wrathful reformer of the poem demol-
ishes church temples, art treasures, and state institutions,
seemingly wreaking havoc for its own sake. The reformer,
however, rebuilds on the ruins of the old and leaves behind
him opened prison doors, fruitful grains on former battlefields
and ploughshares instead of chains. Optimistically Whittier
concludes that the reformer's acts are part of eternal progress,
for:

> God works in all things; all obey
>   His first propulsion from the night:
> Wake thou and watch! the world is gray
>   With morning light!

As Whittier's newspaper communications and his extensive
correspondence with John P. Hale, Joseph Sturge, Henry
Bowditch, and Charles Sumner demonstrate, politics and practical reform remained his overwhelming concern. New correspondence dealt almost entirely with abolitionist matters
and little, if any, time was allotted for personal correspondence with old friends or relatives. A mature, dedicated
Whittier pursued the goals formalized in 1840 when Whittier
and other abolitionists vowed to create an abolitionist third
party. At the same time he continued to broaden his reform
interests, commenting on all events that affected mankind:
the Irish famine, the French Revolution, utopian communities, world peace, reform bills in Parliament. Whittier's reform
writings show an increasing dependence on religious faith
and an awareness that outward social reform could be mean-
ingful only if accompanied by inward moral change—ideas
which were characteristic of his later life and writings.
  Whittier's appointment as corresponding editor for the

National Era in 1847 significantly affected his personal and literary life. Under the editorship of Gamaliel Bailey this new abolitionist weekly at Washington became a national, self-supporting paper which stressed congressional matters and the abolitionist third party movement. The *Era* also had a definite literary emphasis. From 1847 to 1857 it published nearly all of Whittier's prose and poetry, printed original works by Hawthorne and Harriet B. Stowe (her *Uncle Tom's Cabin* appeared serially in the *Era* before book publication), and solicited pieces from new writers like Alice Cary, Gail Hamilton, and Lucy Larcom. Whittier's position guaranteed him enough income to support himself and his family. Before 1847 Whittier's income had been derived from various editorial positions throughout the northeast and from small sums paid by abolition organizations. With little return from his books or poetry, Whittier had never earned more than $500 a year and on three occasions had accepted financial assistance from Joseph Sturge. Another benefit of the position was his freedom from policy decision or practical editorial tasks; he remained at Amesbury within the circle of his family, able to write whenever he wanted.

The extent of Whittier's involvement with the *Era* can be gauged by his contributions of 151 prose pieces and twenty-eight poems in 1847 and 1848 (in the next ten years he was to write only 100 prose pieces). For a typical issue he averaged two contributions, but on some occasions, as on July 31, 1847, he printed two short poems, a commentary on Daniel O'Connell's life, a burlesque account of a sea monster reported near Nahant beach, and an article on the qualities needed in a presidential candidate. Whittier sent to the *Era* biographical sketches, fictional pieces, prose essays, antiquarian articles, and literary reviews as well as miscellaneous letters. A group of biographical portraits of seventeenth-century Puritans and Quakers highlighted the attributes of successful reformers. In the winter of 1847 Whittier also wrote a series of five letters from the East which covered a variety of topics from the Mexican War and New Hampshire elections to book reviews and the speeches of Daniel Webster. Relaxed and informal, Whittier commented about Caleb Cushing's role with the Massachusetts Volunteers for Mexico: "During his late Oriental Embassy, he had ample opportunity to study the military tactics of the Chinese and will doubtless be prepared to oppose Santa Anna, after the manner of that redoubtable people, by turning upon him the muzzles of pickle jars, and gallipots, setting up scarecrows, and issuing highsounding proclamations." Furthermore, Whittier contributed a series of literary reviews, calling Longfellow's *Evangeline* an answer to British objections about the lack of a native American poetry, praising Holmes's new poems, and finding Lowell's "Above and Below" one of the finest lyrics in our literature. In his literary notices he lauded the writings of new authors like Bayard Taylor, Lucy Larcom, and Grace Greenwood—all of whom became close personal friends. Finally the *Era* published in serial form *Margaret Smith's Journal*, Whittier's longest fictional piece and his closest approach to a novel.

Politically Whittier continued as a "humble and toiling member of that party of reform and progress," the Liberty party, and performed his usual chores in committees and at conventions. National events cast an increasingly large shadow over all political efforts. The Mexican War, especially, brought a sense of urgency to the local and state Liberty organizations, for only votes could challenge southern dominance of Congress and national politics. With a bitterness rare in his letters Whittier railed against the war: "I am heartsick with this miserably wicked Mexican War. The love which I bear my country makes me sad in view of her disgraceful position. Only think of Massachusetts—after being kicked and cuffed and spit upon by Slavery—being called upon to raise three regiments of her sons to conquer more territory for new slave states." However, the election to the Senate of John P. Hale from nearby New Hampshire as an independent abolitionist raised Whittier's depressed spirits and led him to hope that slavery's hold over the northern voter had been finally broken. Throughout 1846 and 1847 Whittier advised Hale to separate himself completely from both Whig and Democratic factions and to publicly affirm his allegiance to abolitionist principles. Whittier urged a radical stance toward the Constitution since southern politicians had used it for a defense of slavery. "We must take it out of the custody of slavery," Whittier wrote, "and construe it in the Light of Liberty. . . . At all events, with the Constitution or without the Constitution, *Slavery must die.*"

Originally Whittier had believed that the Liberty party must remain sternly exclusive and overthrow the old parties with a platform of abolitionism alone. He feared that the broadening of its scope to include such issues as tariff and finance would dilute the basic strength of the party. However, when events showed the necessity for such moves, Whittier acquiesed and, like many others, helped direct the Liberty party toward a national coalition with the Free Soil party. Whittier began by working with independents like Hale and then with the aboli-

tion Whigs of Massachusetts: Charles Francis Adams, Stephen
Phillips, and especially Charles Sumner. Whittier appreciated
Sumner's learning and eloquence, responded to his moral
principles, and recognized his political capabilities. Praising
one of Sumner's early speeches on abolition, Whittier said that
he hoped God would give Sumner "the strength and nerves
and patience for the practical acting out of that word."
Whittier clearly saw that such practical action must take place
outside the Whig party and so counseled Sumner. In 1848
Whittier bluntly told Sumner that he would only "stultify"
himself by remaining a Whig and that it was his charge to
help "awaken into vigorous life all that remains of manhood
in the north. Kindle up the latent enthusiasms of the Yankee
character—call out the grim fanaticism of the Puritan. *Dare,
dare, dare,* as Danton told the French: that is the secret of
successful revolt. Oh for a man! there is the difficulty after all.
Who is to head the movement?" As events later turned out,
Sumner became that man, but in 1848 Whittier still hoped that
Hale would lead an aroused North as the Free Soil presidential
candidate. Yet when the Buffalo Free Soil convention of
Liberty men, independent Democrats, and abolition Whigs
bypassed Hale to nominate ex-president Martin Van Buren,
Whittier suppressed his personal disappointment and doubts
in the interests of broader national support. Van Buren
amassed nearly 300,000 votes, a sufficient number to deprive
the Democrats of election and foreshadow the coming demise
of the Whig party. The labors of fifteen years had produced
national results and with the commitment of men like Sumner,
Hale, Van Buren, Giddings, and others to the Free Soil movement, Whittier felt that the tide had finally turned. Still,
Whittier's main political feat lay before him: the drafting
and election of Charles Sumner as a Free Soil senator from
Massachusetts.

Significantly, Whittier's final six letters in 1848 were to
James T. Fields about the coming book edition of *Margaret
Smith's Journal*. These brief notes, dealing entirely with
matters of revision, page setting, insertion of new material,
and proof corrections, set a pattern for an increasing portion
of Whittier's correspondence in the 1850's. They also indicated the role that Whittier was soon to assume as a man of
letters and poet of New England. For the present, however,
Whittier remained a reformer poet. His new 1846 volume
of poems was appropriately titled *Voices of Freedom*, and
most of the forty-six poems he published during these years
were inspired by politics or reform. Whittier's writing at

this time well merited James Russell Lowell's commentary
in his *Fable for Critics*:

> "Our Quaker leads off metaphorical fights
> For reform and whatever they call human rights,
> Both singing and striking in front of the war,
> And hitting his foes with the mallet of Thor.
>
> ***************************
>
> Who was true to The Voice when such service was hard,
> Who himself was so free he dared sing for the slave
> When to look but a protest in silence was brave."

468. To Ann Elizabeth Wendell

Lynn, January 6, 1846

Dear Cousin Ann:

Elizabeth and I are detained here by a storm, and I embrace
the occasion to drop thee a line, to let thee know of my
whereabouts and to speak of one or two matters of personal
interest to myself. I spent the night I left at William J.
Allinson's very pleasantly, and took the 1st train to Borden-
town, where I waited for the nine o'clock train from Philad.[1]

I spent 6th day in N. Y. and left on seventh day at 4 P.M.
for Boston. I found Elizabeth much as when I left her, with a
bad cold which I fear is to be attributed to her imprudence.

I left in my room sundry papers and so forth among them
some MS. of my own rhymes belonging to *Th. S. Cavender*,
which I wish thee would put up in a package and send to the
office of the American Citizen in 5th Street between Arch
and Market, directed to him.[2] Lyddon Pennock says he
intended the Daguerreotype for myself, as he has another
copy. It is at Langenheim's.[3] I had another taken: but it was
a dark day and I was compelled to sit so long that I became
tired and nervous, and doubt whether it is as good as the
other. If thee has any wish for such an image thee can have it
by sending for it. Isaac could tell which is the best likeness.
Perhaps, however, it would be as well to leave it where it is.
'Tis a poor thing at best.

One word for thyself and those present on a particular
evening which thee will remember. *Do not speak of what I
said of a certain person in Boston to any one*. Margaret
[Wendell Maule] and Elisha [Maule], of course will be discreet
about it. What I said was *in confidence*, and must be regarded
as sacred.

I shall want to see a copy of E. Lloyd's poem when it is out. It will be got up I hope in a style worthy of its beauty of thought and language.

In thinking over my late visit to Philad. I fear I was too idle in my conversation while with you. I was excited somewhat and said many foolish things which I have no doubt I have ample reason to be sorry for but I felt the freedom to *act myself* out while with you which I should not have felt in other circumstances. I have no wish that my friends should think better of me than I deserve and my only anxiety is that I may not injure others by any folly or indiscretion of my own: and that whatever degree of influence I may possess may not be exerted unfavorably on the friends whom I love, and on testimonies and principles which I hold dear. Elizabeth sends her best love to thee and all the family, and to her other friends and acquaintance[s], especially to E. Nicholson and E. Lloyd. —She hopes to see you all soon. As ever thy aff. cousin,

J. G. W.

P. S. If thee needs an *umbrella* thee will find one at your back door. I have another in Washington, and of course shall not need it!

Source: Snyder, "Whittier's Letters to Ann Elizabeth Wendell," pp. 82–84.

1. Whittier was then returning to Boston after his visit to Washington in early December 1845 to present the anti-Texas remonstrance to Congress.

2. This reference to a manuscript of rhymes for Thomas S. Cavender indicates Whittier's preparation for a new collection of his poetry, *Voices of Freedom*, which was published by Cavender in August 1846. Whittier later claimed that the volume was published without his knowledge or consent (see Currier, *Bibliography*, pp. 58–60, for further comment).

3. Frederick Langenheim (1810?–1879) and William Langenheim (1807?–1874) ran a daguerreotype shop in Philadelphia and were among the first to produce photographic pictures on glass.

469. To Moses Austin Cartland

Amesbury, January 18, 1846

Dear Cousin,

I write thee a hasty line just to tell thee that I have visited Phila. and seen all our old friends there. They all inquired after thee, and I was sorry I had not seen thee for so long a time, and was consequently unable to tell them much about thee. They expect thee to be there this Spring: and one object of my note is to enquire if thee have a prospect of this kind. Elizabeth wishes to visit P. and would like thy company if thee think of going. She however does not wish to leave before the 1st of 3rd Mo. or later. I am myself desirous of going in

season to attend the Y. M. which will be an occasion of great
interest owing to the division of sentiment and feeling so
strongly apparent in Philad. Y. M. But, it is very uncertain in
regard to myself.[1] If thee can, do write us a line to let us know
how you are getting on—thee Moses, Jonathan, Anna and
Phebe—I saw Jonathan's name at the Liberty Convention. Ann
Wendell is just as ever—better in health. Margaret do.—Would-
n't it be better for thee to take a ride over here to see us? Do
come! 'Tis but a short ride. Elizabeth and myself wish to be
kindly remembered to Jonathan and Anna.

Ever thy aff. Cousin

John G. Whittier

P. S. Say nothing in reference to the letter etc. we talked of
when I was at your house, to anyone. "Come over and see us"
Elizabeth says to Anna.

Manuscript: Harvard University. Published: Shackford, ed., *Whittier and the
Cartlands*, pp. 36–37.
1. The Whittiers, however, did not make a spring trip to Philadelphia. Both had
colds and Aunt Mercy, who had been sick that spring, died on April 11.

470. To Frederick Palmer Tracy

Amesbury, January 18, 1846

Dear Tracy:
Thy letter I found on my return from Washington and
Philada and I [take] an early opportunity to answer it briefly.
I am glad to know of thy prospect. It is just the thing. I only
wish I were better able to aid thee.[1] I know very few Editors
or Publishers. I enclose a line to Ed of "The Tribune" and give
thee leave to refer to me to any extent, if my poor authority
is worth anything! I would, it seems to me, go to N. York at
once. Greeley will introduce you to his Editorial friends, and
perhaps employ thee himself. Write me and let me know if I
can aid thee in any other way, remembering that I too am
essentially tabooed in good society.

Ever thine

J. G. Whittier

Elizabeth and I remember thy visit here with much satisfaction.
P. S. I have written a line to H. Greeley. So if thee cannot go
to N. York the way is open for thee to write.

Source: Handwritten copy, Essex Institute, Salem, Massachusetts. Published,
in Part: Mordell, *Quaker Militant*, p. 307.

1. Tracy was still acting as a Methodist minister, but in the late 1840's went to California where he became a lawyer (see Letter No. 326, *Recipient*).

471. To Thomas Tracy

Amesbury, January 21, 1846

My dear friend:—

I send thee herewith a copy of the "Bridal of Pennacook,"[1] for thy friend Dempster[2] —if I had time this morning I would copy for thee the "Song."

Elizabeth and I have been away most of the winter which will in some degree account for the delay in returning thy books. We have read the "Crescent and the Cross" with a great deal of pleasure.[3] We are now reading Carlyle's "Cromwell"—entering however many a silent *protest* as we read.[4]

We inclose also Prescott's new volume, in the hope that you have not yet seen it.[5]

Is it too late for the compliments of the season? If not, let us wish thee and thy dear Ann many years of health and happiness.

Very truly thy friend
John G. Whittier

Manuscript: Swarthmore College.

1. "The Bridal of Pennacook" had been completely printed in the June number of the *United States Magazine and Democratic Review*. The "Song" referred to in this sentence is the "Song of Indian Women" from Part VIII of the poem. Dempster set the song to music and published it in a book, *Dempster's Original Ballad Soirees* (Boston, 1847) and later separately issued the piece as "The Dark Eye Has Left Us" in 1848.

2. William Richardson Dempster (1809–1871), an English poet, had edited a selection of Scottish and English songs and ballads in 1842. He wrote ballads and songs himself and set many of Burns's songs to music.

3. Eliot Warburton's *The Crescent and the Cross* (London, 1845) was a romantic account of travels in Syria, Palestine, and Egypt. Warburton (1810–1851) was an Irish lawyer and writer.

4. *Oliver Cromwell's Letters and Speeches, with elucidations* (1845). For an account of Whittier's response to Carlyle (1795–1881), the Scottish historian and essayist, see Roland H. Woodwell, "Whittier and Carlyle," *Memorabilia of John Greenleaf Whittier* (Hartford, 1968), pp. 42–46.

5. Probably *History of the Conquest of Mexico*, which had been published in three volumes in 1843. William H. Prescott (1796–1859), the famous American historian, was then engaged in writing his *History of the Conquest of Peru*, which was published in 1847.

472. To Joshua Leavitt

Amesbury, January 24, 1846

Dear Friend Leavitt:—

I was glad to see in the last Emancipator the call of the State Committee for a Convention of the Liberty party of Massachusetts at Boston on the 25th of next month. I was especially pleased to see also that it was to be emphatically a meeting for the transaction of business. We have had quite too much of random *talk* in our Conventions: and far too little plain common-sense preparation for *doing*. Eloquent anti-slavery appeals are well enough in their place but they are well nigh wasted in Boston. The amount of speech-making in the country which has been lost upon the city, would very probably have doubled our vote in Massachusetts.

Our object then in meeting together next month it seems to me should be in the first place to consult and enquire as to the actual state of the cause in all sections of the State; and secondly to devise and take measures to carry into practice, a plan for a thorough and systematic organization of the Liberty party; and for disseminating in a judicious and effective manner our views and principles among all classes of our fellow citizens; by promoting the circulation of Liberty papers, by lecturers, and the distribution of such tracts as that excellent one just published by Prof. Cleveland—the address of the "Southern and Western Liberty Convention."[1] We want therefore a full representation of all sections of the State —a delegation of the *workers* in the cause. Essex County I hope and trust will not be found wanting.

I notice in the last Emancipator a note of warning relative to the movement for an *anti-slavery League*. That there are men who would gladly break down the Liberty party; and who would join with any thing that might have the remotest tendency to do this, I cannot doubt. But against such enemies the Liberty men of Massachusetts need no warning. They have been tried as by fire, and have proved at once their sagacity and inflexible integrity, under circumstances of temptation stronger than any which can at present be brought to bear upon them. The proposal for an Anti-slavery League of all persons really opposed to slavery, was made by a highly respected member of the late Texas Committee, and was cordially concurred in by all the Liberty men present. The entire action of the Committee had been so harmonious, so conciliatory, so earnest and honest, that we felt a desire to see a similar union of all parties on a broader scale—a union for one or two specified and well-defined objects—leaving each member free to act in other respects according to his own convictions of duty. What measures have been taken, if any, to this effect I cannot say, as I was unable to attend the preliminary meeting. I trust however that the proposal will be carried into practice; and, that one of its first fruits will be a better understanding and a kinder feeling towards each other among all classes of professed abolitionists.

Keep the subject of the Convention before the people. It is of vital importance. I will do what I can for my own neighborhood. The Liberty party of Massachusetts must not be content with merely keeping pace with the other parties; as in New Hampshire and Vermont it must be the *"party of progress."*

Thine truly,
John G. Whittier

Source: The *Emancipator*, January 28, 1846.
1. The full title was "The Address of the Southern and Western Liberty Convention Held at Cincinnati on June 11 and 12, 1845."
Charles Dexter Cleveland (1802–1869) was a professor of Latin and Greek at Dickinson College in 1832 and later at the University of New York City. He also taught in Philadelphia and served as consul to Wales from 1861 to 1867. He published many texts and compendia of literature, besides editing Milton's complete works with a concordance.

473. To Waite, Peirce and Company

Amesbury January 26, 1846

Friend Peirce.

Wilt thou oblige me by sending copies of the "Stranger in Lowell" to

> Martin Farquhar Tupper, Esq.[1]
> The "Examiner"[2]   } London
> Charles Dickens Esq
>
> Prof Wilson—Edinburgh[3]
> Dublin University Magazine—Dublin[4]

Please forward them by next Steamer. If there is any house in London where the books can be sent, they can be distributed from thence.

I am collecting my poems and hope to see thee soon with reference to them.[5]

Truly thy friend
John G. Whittier

Manuscript: Harvard University.

Recipient: Waite, Peirce and Company of Boston published Whittier's prose volume, *The Stranger in Lowell*, in July 1845.

1. Martin Farquhar Tupper (1810–1889), a British poet, was the author of *Proverbial Philosophy* (1838–1842), a book of commonplace maxims and reflections which attained great popularity throughout the 1840's and 1850's.

2. The *Examiner*, a weekly paper on politics, literature, music, and the fine arts, was published in London from 1808 to 1881.

3. Charles Wilson (1809–1882), an art teacher and author, directed a school of art in Edinburgh and later a school of design in Glasgow. He lived in Florence after 1869.

4. *The Dublin University Magazine* was published in Dublin from 1833 to 1877 and then became the *University Magazine, a literary and philosophical review*, published in London.

5. *Voices of Freedom* was published that summer in Boston by Waite, Peirce and Company and in Philadelphia by Thomas S. Cavender.

474. To Henry Ingersoll Bowditch

Amesbury January 26, 1846

My Dear Doctor.

Our very worthy young friend Robt. Davis being on the eve of returning to Boston, I drop thee a hasty line. I was not able (very much to my regret) to be at the meeting last week with reference to our proposed A. S. League: and have had no information with respect to it. I hope however there was encouragement to persevere. It is at least worth while to make an effort to unite once more the broken and divided abolitionism of the North. In the next Emancipator I shall have a letter speaking of the League Movement.[1] I do not so much wonder at Leavitt's fear: as I think he supposed the matter to have originated with certain Whig politicians for other objects than the abolition of Slavery.

The Liberty men of New Hampshire and the reformed Democrats or Hale party have united upon a candidate for Governor.—a very worthy and excellent man—Judge Berry of Hebron; and there is a fair prospect of his election (by the Legislature).[2] The Granite State will be the first to take a decided stand for Liberty.

Has thee read Giddings' speech.—Is it not stern truth? It is the boldest speech ever made on the floor of Congress. Giddings is very much a *man*.[3]

Cordially and heartily thy friend
John G. Whittier

Robt. Davis speaks very gratefully of thy kindness to him. He is a young man of fine talents, with a warm heart. I hope his health will not seriously impede his studies.

W.

Manuscript: Library of Congress.

1. See Letter No. 472.

2. Nathaniel S. Berry (1796–1894), a Democratic judge, became an abolitionist and ran on the Liberty party ticket for governor in 1846. He received a sufficient popular vote to throw the election to the legislature where he was defeated. He ran unsuccessfully from 1847 to 1850. After working for the Free Soil and Republican parties he was finally elected governor of New Hampshire from 1861 to 1863.

3. On January 5, 1846, Giddings had denounced the attempt to gain more Oregon territory and blamed the agitation with England on the proslavery members of Congress.

475. To Joseph Sturge

January 1846

Thy kind note by the last steamer has reached me. I had looked to the arrival of that steamer with intense interest. The tone of President Polk's message in relation to Oregon was a source of great regret, even to those who, like myself, believe that the American title to that territory is a good one. War, at this day, and between two nations of highly professing Christians, would be an awful absurdity. I am glad to see that the whole tone of the English press is peaceful—the bravado of the message appears to be pretty well estimated. In Congress, on our side the water, a debate is going on which looks at times rather warlike; but I can assure thee that a great deal of the ferocity is assumed by the speakers, and for *home* effect. It looks *patriotic* to eulogise ourselves and abuse the British. Among our Indians it is customary to set up a log or post, painted so as to have some faint resemblance of a warrior of a hostile tribe; and each young savage marches bravely up to it and smites it with his tomahawk, in this way giving proof of his manhood. It is very much so with our new members of Congress. They belabor the British lion *in the abstract* just as the Indians do the painted log.[1]

Source: Richard, *Memoirs of Joseph Sturge,* p. 404.

1. In his first annual message to Congress on December 2, 1845, Polk claimed the whole of Oregon and recommended the ending of the old English-American convention governing the territory. His unyielding attitude toward Great Britain was backed by expansionist cries of "Fifty-four forty or fight." A resolution for terminating joint occupation passed both houses and was signed by Polk on April 27, 1846. Fortunately the British ministry adopted a conciliatory approach and Lord Aberdeen submitted a compromise proposal that the territory be divided between Britain and the United States at the 49th parallel. This division along with some other provisions was accepted on June 15, 1846, as the Oregon Treaty (see Letter Nos. 477 and 485).

476. To the Independent Democrats of New Hampshire

Amesbury, Mass., March 18, 1846

Gentlemen:

I have just received your invitation to attend a meeting of the Independent Democrats and others, to be held in Manchester on the 20th inst. It is not in my power to comply with it, but from my heart I thank you for the opportunity it affords me to join my congratulations with yours, on the result of the late election.[1] I am not a native of your State; but I have lived all my life in view of her hills. I am allied to her citizens by ties of kindred and friendship, and I shall not suffer my joy in your triumph to be checked by the reflections that New Hampshire is taking a prouder position than Massachusetts in the cause of Human Liberty.

All who love and honor true Republicanism rejoice with you. The most ultra Democrat in the land, who comprehends the first great truth of Democracy with regard to the sanctity and the paramount importance of *Personal Rights*, cannot but sympathize with you. *Honest* Radicalism the world over, errs, if it errs at all[,] on the side of Liberty. Its very excesses are pardonable, for they grow out of humanity and its hatred of oppression. Let us beware how we wrong the Radicalism of Freedom by confounding it in the slightest degree, with the Radicalism of Slavery.

May you in all your proceedings manifest a generous and magnanimous spirit. The great body of the State really love liberty, and will not fail to sustain its friends so long as they pursue an open and manly course. The hearts and consciences of many who voted against you, are, after all, on your side. Many voted wrong because they were deceived as to the real issues of the contest. Abroad, in every section of the Free states, thousands of honest Democrats are rejoicing over the returns of your elections. When I was at Washington during the past winter, one of the leading members of the Democratic Delegation in Congress, said to me on the very day, when under the party drill, he gave his vote for Slavery and Texas, "Hale is right. He is making a noble effort, and I hope to God he will demonstrate by his success that it is safe to be honest."

He *has* succeeded! and his success has broken the spell which has hitherto held reluctant Democracy in the embraces of Slavery. The tide of Anti-Slavery feeling, long held back by the dams and dykes of the party, has at last broken over all barriers, and is rushing down from your Northern mountains upon the slave-cursed South, as if Niagara stretched its foam and thunder the whole length of Mason and Dixon's line. Let the first wave of that Northern flood as it dashes against the walls of the Capitol, bear thither for the first time an Anti-slavery Senator. Your friend in the cause of freedom.

John G. Whittier

Source: Newspaper clipping, Haverhill Public Library, with the notation from "the Worcester County Gazette." Introduced by the following: "The Allied Victory was celebrated at Manchester, N. H., on the 20th ult., by a Public Supper, got up by the Independent Democrats, at which the following among other letters from invited guests were read by the Chairman, and their sentiments heartily responded to:"

1. In the election on March 10, 1846, the proslavery Democratic candidate for governor, Jared W. Williams (1796–1864), failed to achieve the number of votes needed for his election. The Whig candidate received over 17,000 votes and the Liberty party candidate, Nathaniel Berry, obtained over 10,000 votes. This threw the election to the House where the Whig candidate, Anthony Colby, was elected governor. The Independent Democrats and Liberty party men supported Colby with the understanding that Whig votes would then put John P. Hale into the United States Senate. This was done and on June 9, 1846, Hale was selected as the New Hampshire senator and he began his term in March 1847. The entire election marked a signal defeat for proslavery supporters in New Hampshire.

477. To Joseph Sturge

March 1846

I have seen with no slight degree of interest that the friends of peace in Great Britain are actively engaged in the good work of repressing the war feeling. We are doing what we can here. I hope our friends will act on the suggestion thrown out by Sir Robert Peel in his interview with English Friends.[1] I have hopes that our Meeting for Suffering in New England will act. The tone of many members of Congress, and of a portion of our editors of public papers, is as vindictive and warlike as the enemy of all good could well wish; but the great body of both Congress and people are in favor of peace. Nobody here expects war. Our Government has evidently never expected it, for they are wholly unprepared for it. For my own part, I think there is every reason to believe that the offer on the part of your Government of the 49° boundary would be accepted by our own.[2]

Source: Richard, *Memoirs of Joseph Sturge*, pp. 404–405.

1. Throughout the dispute over Oregon Sir Robert Peel and then Lord John Russell maintained a calm and conciliatory approach.

2. Ultimately this offer was made and accepted.

478. To John Gadsby Chapman

Amesbury, April 14, 1846

Respected friend.

Thy kind and flattering letter came to hand while I was watching by the bedside of a dear friend to whom I have just paid the last offices of affection.[1] I am not a little proud of thy favorable estimate of my rhymes; and would be gratified to see my name associated with one so gifted in a work worthy of thy genius.

But, my "Songs of Labor" are but begun; I am so situated as regards health and leisure that I cannot undertake to finish them in a given time. A work of the kind thee propose, would require some 10 or 15 songs:—only 4 are written, and I can promise nothing as to the rest. So that for the present the thing must be deferred.

I send thee herewith a copy of my "Bridal of Pennacook"— which is at least an *American* poem, if nothing else. I have had proposals for publishing it but have hitherto declined. Look it over and see if it does not afford a fine field, for illustration. If it could be got out by the 15th of July—(the time for the White Mountain travel) it would I think be an acceptable offering.[2] Pardon the suggestion and believe me very truly and with respect thy friend

J. G. Whittier

P. S. I recd a line also from my friend H. T. Tuckerman on the same subject. Please thank him for his kind remembrance and assure him of my esteem and friendship.[3]

W.

Manuscript: Swarthmore College

Recipient: John Gadsby Chapman (1808–1889), an American painter and illustrator who had studied in Europe, held his first successful exhibition in 1831 and became a member of the National Academy in 1836. He was noted for his illustrations and etchings. He illustrated the Harper Bible in 1846 and in 1847 published a popular drawing book. After 1848 he lived in Rome.

1. Chapman had written to Whittier on April 6, 1846, asking if he could illustrate Whittier's "Songs of Labor" in a book form. He planned to illustrate each page and dedicate the book to the working class (letter, Essex Institute, Salem, Massachusetts).

Mercy Hussey, Whittier's aunt who lived most of her life with the Whittier family, died on April 11, 1846.

2. Nothing came of Whittier's suggestion.

3. Tuckerman had written Whittier on April 7, 1846, about Chapman's abilities and urged Whittier to do the book on "Songs of Labor" (letter, Essex Institute, Salem, Massachusetts).

479. To Moses Austin Cartland

Amesbury, 7th day Mg [before April 26, 1846]

Dear Cousin

Thine from Weare has been duly recd: and we would gladly accept thy invitation were it in our power. The sickness and death of our Aunt Mercy Hussey, have left us all very much worn with watching, fatigue and colds. Under other circumstances we should have taken special pains to be present at so important and interesting an affair as the one thee announced in thy letter.

As it is, God bless you both!—You have done right, and His blessing is always with the right. I see I shall be left alone in my old bachelorship. I wish it could be otherwise: but as it is, I make the best of it.

I have a plan to propose. Tackle the old horse and take Mary over here and spend a day with us.[1] Elizabeth joins me in the request. Now, don't hesitate, but come at once.

New Hampshire has done gloriously. I was half tempted when I heard of her triumph to take off my Quaker hat, and "Hurra for Jack Hale!" My love to Joseph[,] Jonathan, Anna and Phebe and believe me thine truly

J. G. Whittier

Elizabeth wishes to be remembered to all. Tell Joseph that we expect to see him at Quarterly Meeting.

Manuscript: Harvard University. Published: Shackford, ed., *Whittier and the Cartlands*, pp. 38–39.

1. Mary P. Gove (1823–1860) married Moses Cartland on April 26, 1846. The Cartlands had five children: Caroline, Mary, Charles, Ellen, and Jane.

480. To Elizur Wright

Amesbury, May 12, 1846

My Dear Friend:

I send herewith an "Address to the Citizens of the U. S.," adopted at a meeting of the Birmingham (Eng.) Peace Society on the 10th ult., which has been forwarded to my care.[1] Such "Olive Leaves" as this afford one of the most cheering evidence of the progress of practical Christianity. They confirm our faith in the beautiful promise of prophesy, that the time shall come when "men shall beat their swords into ploughshares, and their spears into pruning-hooks."[2]

Truly thy friend,
John G. Whittier

Source: The *Chronotype*, May 14, 1846.

1. Printed with the letter was the following:

"To The Citizens of the United States Of America:

"There has been so little apprehension felt by the inhabitants of Birmingham of a war taking place between your country and our own, that it has not been deemed needful to convene a meeting here to give a public expression to the friendly feelings they entertain towards the citizens of the United States of America.

"Although this is the largest manufactory of firearms in the world, the determination of the people in favor of Peace has recently been very strikingly manifested. A public meeting was lately held in the Town Hall here, consisting of at least 5000 persons, to oppose a contemplated Government measure for enforcing service in the militia, at which the following sentiments were unanimously adopted as the opinions of those present, viz: 'that while there is a large and increasing number of our countrymen who hold that war in every shape is contrary to the spirit and precepts of the Gospel, it is our conviction that the people in general are opposed to military establishments both as a vast unnecessary expense and a great moral injury to the nation—that at a time when the principles of peace are so much more widely recognized than in former years and the nation is anticipating the extension of friendly commercial relations all over the world, they deprecate the withdrawal of men from the occupations of productive industry, and especially for the purpose of learning the arts of war and destruction, and therefore urge that a clause may be inserted in all treaties with foreign powers, rendering it obligatory in every disputed case to submit it to the arbitration of some neutral party or parties.'

"Unhappily in this country, in common we believe with yours a large portion of the legislative body consists of individuals in the profession of arms. A legislature so constituted can never be safely entrusted with the guardianship of their country's peace, inasmuch as their personal interests and tendencies must ever lean on the side of war: but we can with the greatest confidence assure you that should the occasion require it, the inhabitants of Birmingham, whose population is estimated at about 190,000, will be ready in their collective capacity to convey to you their anxious wish for the preservation of peace, and should different feelings unhappily prevail in the Government of this country, we are persuaded that the people at large will desire to prevent if possible any act on the part of Great Britain which should give to the United States just cause of complaint, much less any ground for an appeal to arms.

"We transmit you this in the hope that these sentiments will be responded to by you, and with an earnest desire that our two countries may be henceforth united in the bands of perpetual amity.

> John Atkins Perry, }
> Arthur John Naish, }   Secretaries.
>
> James Stubbin,   Corresponding Secretary.

Birmingham
    10th April, 1846."

2. Isaiah 2:4.

481. To Elizur Wright

[Amesbury, before May 14, 1846]

It has occurred to me while reading the remarks of British Statesmen and British editors with reference to the uses of what Sir R. Peel calls the "India Corn," that it would be well for some enterprising publisher to get up a new edition of Barlow's poem on Hasty Pudding, and dedicate it to the

Government Commission, now busily occupied in collecting information as to the best means of cooking the Yankee bread stuff.[1] The old ladies who constitute said commission would need no further information. This poem, written by our countryman while at Chamberry, in Savoy, engaged in an effort to unite the Swiss cantons with the French Republic, in the summer of 1793, is by far the best specimen of his poetical powers. It has reason as well as rhyme in it. In the first Canto, wherein he apostrophizes the "India Corn," a very good idea of the cooking process is conveyed by the following lines—

> Some tawny Ceres, goddess of her days,
> First learned with stones to crack the well-dried maize,
> Through rough sieve to shake the golden shower,
> In boiling water stir the yellow flour:
> The yellow flour bestrewed and stirred with haste,
> Swells in the fluid and thickens into paste.
> Then puffs and wallops, rises to the brim,
> Drinks the dry knobs that on the surface swim,
> The knobs at last the busy ladle breaks,
> And the whole mass a firm consistence takes.[2]

For a more elaborate and minute description of the mystery of Pudding-making, Mrs. John Bull would do well to consult the Third Canto.

                                                    J. G. W.

Source: The *Chronotype*, May 14, 1846. Printed with the caption, "Hasty Pudding."

1. This note was occasioned by the debate in Parliament concerning the repeal of the "Corn Laws." These laws, which regulated the import and export of grains, imposed heavy duties on corn and caused a hardship for the poorer working class of Britain. They were finally repealed in June 1846.

2. Joel Barlow (1754–1812) was a minor American poet and statesman. The quotation is from "The Hasty Pudding," Canto I, lines 37–46, with some changes.

482. To Henry Ingersoll Bowditch

                                          [May 27, 1846][1]

My dear friend:

The enclosed $9.00 I have collected for the monument. It is to be appropriated for that and the funeral expenses *solely.*[2] The widow of poor Torrey will, under the circumstances, be comfortably well off and I hardly look upon it as the duty of abolitionists to do more for her than they have already done, at least for the present.[3] She ought not to ask it at our hands; and Dr. Ide ought not to throw his daughter unnecessarily upon the charity of strangers.[4] We are all of us here living on far less income than he does. Pray see to it that there is no more begging in behalf of the family: but, let the funeral expenses be paid, and a suitable monument erected; and if any surplus remains let it do some anti-slavery work.

I am heart-sick with this miserably wicked Mexican War. The love which I bear my country makes me sad in view of her disgraceful position. Only think of old Massachusetts— after being kicked and cuffed and spit upon by Slavery—being called upon to raise three regiments of her sons to conquer more territory for new slave-states. By "my country" I for one mean Massachusetts—I confess no sympathy for, I acknowledge no allegiance to the murderers of Torrey and Lovejoy.—

In haste thy friend.
J. G. W.

Manuscript: Swarthmore College.

1. C. Marshall Taylor (1884–1957), a Whittier collector and New York businessman, in his personal papers dates this letter as May 27, 1846. Certainly it is about that date since Bowditch answered Whittier on May 30 thanking him for his contribution of $9.00 (letter, Essex Institute, Salem, Massachusetts).

2. Charles Torrey had died on May 9, 1846, in a Baltimore prison and was given a martyr's funeral in Boston on May 18 from the Tremont Temple and buried in Mt. Auburn cemetery. Whittier wrote a long editorial in the *Essex Transcript* on May 14 entitled "The Prisoner is Free" in which he said: " 'When my blood is shed let it, oh Lord, have a voice afterwards!' was the prayer of Henry Vane, who like Torrey, died for the cause of freedom. So let it be with our brother. Let his martyrdom have a voice afterward terrible to the oppressor and cheering to the oppressed!"

3. May Ide (1817–1869) had married Charles Torrey in 1837 and had two children. She later published a book, *City and Country Life* (Boston, 1853), which Whittier reviewed in the *National Era* of July 14, 1853.

4. Jacob Ide (1785–1880) served as pastor in West Medway, Massachusetts, for over fifty years. He helped train Torrey for the ministry before Torrey's marriage to his daughter.

483. To Evert Duyckinck

Amesbury June 2, 1846

I have been expecting to see a proof sheet of my little book for some time; I am now anxious to know *when* I may expect it, as I am absent from home a good deal this summer.[1] I would like to hear in order to make my arrangements to attend to the proofs without delay.

Very truly thy friend
John G. Whittier

Manuscript: Swarthmore College.

Recipient: Evert Duyckinck (1816–1878), an editor and writer, edited the New York *Literary World* from 1847 to 1853, which was the leading weekly literary review of the period. With his brother George Duyckinck he edited the *Cyclopaedia of American Literature* in 1855 and 1866, as well as many other periodicals and books.

1. Whittier had sent Duyckinck an expanded version of his series of articles on "The Supernaturalism of New England," which had been published in 1843 in the *Democratic Review*. Duyckinck had written Whittier on March 13, 1846, that Wiley and Putnam would publish it, but apparently had done nothing about. He gave Whittier's letter of June 2 to the firm and they replied on June 10 to Whittier that the book would be put to press in a few months as business was poor (letters, Essex Institute, Salem, Massachusetts). The book was finally published in January 1847.

484. To the Northwestern Convention at Chicago

Amesbury, Mass., June 13, 1846

Dear Friends:—

Your note, inviting me to be with you at the Liberty Convention of the 24th inst., should be answered in *person*, were it in my power to do so. I have long wished to see your Great Valley, its sea-like lakes, noble rivers, broad prairies and new built cities. Yet believe me, it would be still more gratifying to look upon a Convention of true hearted friends of equal rights at the North and West—to clasp the hands of men of whose praises and sacrifices I have long heard, and feel the strong pulsations of that bold and generous enthusiasm which I have admired in the Western character. As it is, I can only give you a hearty God-speed.

You will assemble at a time, and under circumstances of peculiar and painful interest. The *re-establishment of Slavery* over large territories where it had been extinguished by the laws of Mexico, is now in progress. To the vast country of Texas, every rod of which is given over to Slavery, we have added the entire Northern valley of the Rio Del Norte. That boundary too, is passed, and our flag is now waving on the southern banks of the river,—our armies are pushing their way into the heart of Mexico. The land before them is consecrated to personal freedom; behind them they leave slavery;—the clank of chains mingles with the music of their march: the *plaza* of every conquered Mexican village becomes a market-place for human flesh;—whip-driven slave gangs take the place of free laborers, whose blood, shed in defense of home and liberty, moistens the corn and cotton fields of Tamaulipas. All wars are wicked—but in name of humanity, what shall we say of wars for Slavery? When the Revolutionists of France proclaimed their determination to aid any people who were struggling for liberty, and sent abroad over astonished Europe their battle-cry of *"War to the palace,—peace to the cottage,"* a noble and just motive atoned in some measure for the horrors of their sanguinary mission; and, wherever the French army moved, the chains of the serf fell off. But Christian America, thanking God that she is not like other nations, even these French infidels, goes out, Bible in hand, to enslave the world! The Church looks on complacently: the great political parties vie with each other in their zealous encouragement of the war. The Liberty party, as yet, remains true to the Declaration of Independence, and the honor and highest interests of the country. It dares to utter its protest against the Texas iniquity in the hour of its triumph—to call even successful robbery by its right name. Its mission is to vindicate the holy truths of Christianity and Democracy from the dishonor and disgrace brought upon them by slaveholding priests and politicians. To hold up the old standard of Liberty; and rally around it all who have eyes to see and hearts to appreciate, and courage to put into action the great principles of the Declaration of Independence. To overthrow the system of slavery, and thereby to put our country so decidedly in the "right," that we may bear no more the duty of sustaining her in the "wrong." Defeat with such a party is better than triumph with any other. But we cannot be defeated. Every remonstrance which we utter, every vote which we cast against the wrong, is a positive victory. We are told that every plant which our Heavenly Father has planted shall be rooted up. Who then doubts the doom of slavery? God has decreed its destruction, and with Him the future already *is*. Take courage then, brethren. The thunder of the cannon which announced the election of an anti-slavery Senator from New Hampshire, has but just died away among our granite hills. If Slavery has gained Texas, Liberty has gained New Hampshire—one of the "Old Thirteen!" May we not hope that the tidings of a similar triumph will ere long reach us from the West? May we not be encouraged to listen for the long, loud shout of an enfranchised people, which, sweeping over your lakes, and across the Alleghanies, shall tell us that you have sent the noble-hearted Lovejoy, sprinkled with the blood of his brother's martyrdom, to speak for Liberty in the Halls of Congress?[1]

You will, I trust, pardon me if I express the hope that the "One Idea" of the Liberty party may be preserved in its simple integrity. I, for one, am willing to be branded as a fanatic for adhering with stern exclusiveness to that idea. Let us not be discouraged by our slow growth as a party, and resort to hazardous and doubtful experiments for the purpose of winning over those who are not abolitionists. I agree with Gerrit Smith that those men who are attracted to us by our positions on Finance and Tariff, and who, but for such attractions, would still vote with their old parties, would prove accessions of weakness and corruption, instead of strength and purity. Let us press forward as we have begun, requiring no new test of our members, content with our simple anti-slavery creed, leaving individuals to the free exercise of their own judgment as to what consistency requires of them in other matters. We have no good cause for discouragement—none for impatience. Look back ten years, and note the mighty progress of our cause! Ten years more will bear witness to still greater advances. No labor is lost: no honest effort made in the cause of humanity fails of its effect. Let us labor, then, like men in earnest.

> "Onward! standing still is folly
> Going back is crime;
> Who would patiently endure
> Any ill that he can cure
> Onward! keep the march of time!"

Brethren of the West! if Eastern abolitionism is not strongly represented in your Convention, be assured it is from no lack of sympathy and fraternal feeling on our part. Standing by the grave of Torrey, we remember that Liberty's first martyr sleeps on the bank of your great river; and we stand in readiness to repeat the vow which we feel assured will be made by your Convention, as from one heart, of renewed and more earnest devotion to the cause of Freedom and Humanity. God bless and prosper you!

Your friend,
John G. Whittier

Source: The *Essex Transcript*, July 23, 1846.

1. Owen Lovejoy (1811–1864) was present at the death of his brother, Elijah Lovejoy, and served as pastor of the Congregational Church in Princeton, Illinois, from 1838 to 1856, besides being active in abolitionist work throughout the state. In 1854 he was elected to the Illinois legislature and then served in Congress from 1857 until his death in 1864.

485. To Joseph Sturge

Amesbury June 15, 1846

My Dear friend.

I cannot let this Steamer go without congratulating thee and all peace-loving Englishmen, on the happy termination of the dispute in relation to Oregon.[1] I have just learned that the propositions of Pakenham have been approved by the Senate, to which body the President submitted them some days ago.[2] My heart is full of thankfulness at this result.

The joy which true lovers of peace and freedom feel on this occasion is subdued and chastened by the war which our government has provoked with Mexico.[3] Thee will learn the horrid particulars by American papers. It is a war for Slavery, and plunder.

Two anti-Slavery Senators, John P. Hale and Col. Cilley, have just been chosen from New Hampshire.[4] I enclose a hasty sketch of Torrey's funeral.[5] Our worthy friend Burritt goes out in this vessel. Blessings of the peace maker go with him!

My sister is still very ill—Aff.

John G. Whittier

Manuscript: Swarthmore College.
1. The treaty had been signed on June 15, 1846.
2. Richard Pakenham (1797–1868), the British minister to the United States, had conducted the treaty arrangements for his government.
3. War had been officially declared on May 13, 1846.
4. Joseph Cilley (1791–1887), an abolitionist since 1820, had been nominated by the Whigs for governor in 1845, but declined. He was elected to the United States Senate to fill the vacancy left by the resignation of Levi Woodbury and served from June 1846 to March 1847, when John P. Hale became senator.
5. Probably the account which Whittier wrote for the *Essex Transcript* on May 21, "The Funeral of Torrey."

486. To the Essex Transcript

[Amesbury, June 25, 1846]

Questions for the Clergy of the U. S.

1. Is the Gospel of Jesus Christ designed to make men better and happier in this life?—to overthrow all wrong and oppression and to uproot every plant which the hand of the Heavenly Father has not planted?

2. Is Slavery consistent with this Gospel?

3. If so, should not its ministers in the United States stand forth clothed in its divine authority, and rebuke the enslavement of one sixth part of our countrymen?

4. And in order to do this, should not the professing ministers and churches of Christ be themselves free from this
crime?

5. Does the Bible sanction Slavery?—Does the written record of Christianity justify and sanctify the act of reducing
human beings to articles of merchandise?

6. If it does so, is it the Word of God?—and wherein is the
Book better than the Koran? And does not humanity cry out
against sending forth missionaries, Bible in hand, To Enslave
The World?

7. If one Christian may seize upon another, whip, fetter
and exhaust him with unrequited toil, hunt him with dogs, or
shoot him should he attempt to escape, sell his daughters to
prostitution, and compel his sons to scourge their mother;—
and at the same time retain his standing as a good christian
preacher or church-member, and be welcomed and caressed
as a worthy brother in Christ and his conduct defended as
scriptural and evangelical, wherein so far as this life is concerned, is Christianity to be preferred to Paganism, and what
should save it from the abhorrence of mankind?

These queries are not put forth lightly. They express in plain
terms, the feeling which to a greater or less extent, is agitating
every portion of the Christian World. They must be met. They
cannot be evaded. And the sooner those professed expounders
of christian doctrine who are not themselves directly impli-
cated in slave-holding, come to a decision with regard to them,
the better it will be for themselves and the community. Let
the questions be met. If Slavery is practical christianity, say
so, and let the Northern churches continue to hug to their
bosoms those who came among them red and reeking with its
abominations. But, if it is anti-christian, anti-scriptural—if God
and humanity cry out against it,—let the truth be told, let
Christianity be vindicated, and its purity preserved by an
entire separation from the accursed thing.

J. G. W.

Source: The *Essex Transcript*, June 25, 1846.

487. To the Essex Transcript

Amesbury, July 1 [1846]
Decidedly the best speech made at the late Boston Anni-
versaries was that of George S. Hillard, Esq., before the American Unitarian Association.[1] I have often read with pleasure
reports of the polished and beautiful speeches of that gentle-

man, on ordinary literary topics; but, in that now before me
the scholar and the elegant rhetorician seem to have given
place to the earnestness and soul-felt convictions of the man.
I know not how in so brief a compass, a more clear, and vivid
exposition of the necessity of a union between christianity
and politics—of making the Law of Love the rule of citizen-
ship, could have been given. Speaking of the Oregon debates
in Congress, he enquires:

"In the debates of Congress on this subject, what elevated
Christian sentiment has been uttered?—Who has ventured to
suggest that some respect was due to the precepts of Jesus of
Nazareth, in international relations? On the contrary, we
have heard sometimes sentiments of the most odious ferocity,
and sometimes of the most sordid rapacity. We have heard
men avowing sometimes the motives of pirates, and sometimes
those of peddlers; but never those of Christian statesmen and
legislators."

He thus alludes to our relations with Mexico:

"I am not going to unfold the record of our shame; it
would be a long tale and a sad one. I contend that our course
towards Mexico is not warranted, even by that inferior and
selfish code which is laid down by writers on public law, and
it is as far below the Christian standard, as the earth is below
the heavens. We have happily blended therein the robber,
the tyrant and the bully. Yet is there any public man that
gives utterance to a sentiment of Christian reprobation of our
conduct? Is there any one who sounds out with a voice of
power the noble word, duty, in the ears of our people? In a
moment Congress votes millions of money to carry on this
wicked and most unchristian war, but how slowly does a
measure, which has for its object the diffusion of truth [to]
men, toil and lag through that body!"

After speaking in terms of sorrow and indignation of the
sad lack of moral courage on the part of our public men, he
says:

"The race of public men is sadly degenerated. We must
introduce a nobler stock. I wish to see men in office, who will
turn towards the tyranny of a majority with the same resolute
countenance with which Paul met the embodied majesty of
Rome at Caesarea, and so reasoned of righteousness, temperance, and judgment to come, that Felix trembled[2] —who
will meet the roar of popular madness with the calm soul of
Geo. Fox, who records of himself, that when placed in the
dock to be tried as a felon, the spirit of the Lord so came
upon him, that when he arose, the judge and jury became as

dead men under his feet; who will see a scoffing, hissing majority, as so many dead men under their feet, if the path of duty should lie through them and over them."

Here is a significant paragraph, which goes far to explain the cause of our political Atheism as a nation.

"The great problem for the christian world now to accomplish is to effect a closer union between religion and politics. They have too long been estranged and at variance. There is a sort of division of labor in society, which is anything but satisfactory or encouraging. *We have one class of men to carry on government, another to transact the common business of life, and another to do our religion and morality.* Hence our wise men are not good, and our good men are not wise."

I give one other extract which will commend itself for its beauty, as well as for the wisdom of its sentiment:

"We must entrust the work of government to cleaner hands and purer hearts. We must rebuke the doctrines whether directly maintained, or indirectly sanctioned, that the morality of the gospel is too fine for use. We must bring about a union between wisdom and goodness. We must dedicate the most vigorous faculties of man to the highest ends. We must enlist the passions in the cause of truth and virtue. We must make men do good and be good, with that energy and intensity with which they now pursue wealth or political distinction, or make love, or seek revenge. We must have men to rule over us who will hate the cowardice of doing wrong.

My thoughts are haunted with the vision of a Christian Commonwealth, in which every man, whatever be his function or office, shall feel himself to be an anointed priest of the Lord, and infuse into his daily life the spirit of purity and devotion, in which the different sects of the Christian world shall lay aside their theological wrangling, and enter into a noble strife to see who shall most resemble, in life and spirit, Him, after whose name they are called, in which the rent fragments of Christ's garment shall be woven again into a web of wholeness and beauty. Then the earth will become a temple, and the roar and hum of daily life will go up like a chorus of praise and thanksgiving. Brethren, is this a dream and no more? are the tares ever to grow in the field of the Lord? are the faint and bleeding hosts of truth never to forgo their wasting conflict, and are the meek never to inherit the land that is promised to them?"

I would like to see this speech published in a tract form and scattered broadly over the land. Even Doctors of Divinity

and Missionary Boards would do well to listen for once to a
layman and a lawyer, who naturally looks more at the conduct
of Christians than at their creeds.

And now the question arises where and how shall the
work of reformation, suggested by this speech, begin? If such
men as its gifted author, and Charles Sumner and S. C.
Phillips, and Charles Allen[3] and C. F. Adams[4] and others I
could name, continue to give their support to a political
party wholly without moral principle, as a party, which has
just manifested the guilty cowardice of voting in Congress on
the side of oppression and atrocious wrong, and of sustaining
the unconstitutional usurpations of a political enemy,
because of the Slave Power demands it,—what hope is there
that the beautiful "vision" of our orator of a Christian
Commonwealth is near its realization?—Oh! that these men
could shake from their limbs the shackles of party and rise up
to the full stature of Christian citizens. Such as they must
do it, if it be done at all. May God put it in their hearts to
try the experiment without further delay!

J. G. W.

Source: The Essex Transcript, July 2, 1846. Printed with the caption, "Christianity in Politics."

1. The American Unitarian Association, as well as many other organizations like the American Peace Society and the Massachusetts Bible Society, held annual meetings in Boston during May 1846.

2. Acts 24:25.

3. Charles Allen (1797–1869) had been appointed a judge after serving for many years in the Massachusetts Senate. He became active in the Free Soil movement and was elected to Congress in 1848. From 1859 to 1867 he was chief justice of the Massachusetts Superior Court.

4. Charles Francis Adams (1807–1886), the son of John Quincy Adams and a lawyer in Boston, had been serving in the Massachusetts legislature. In 1848 he was nominated as the vice-presidential candidate on the Free Soil ticket. He became a congressman in 1858 and was reelected in 1860. He served as minister to England from 1861 to 1868, where his diplomacy won him wide recognition.

487A. To John Neal

67 Franklin St. [Portland, Maine] July 21 [1846][1]
My Dear friend Neal.

I find myself really too ill today, from the effect of a
severe cold which for several days has been accumulating
upon me, to enjoy the pleasure of a visit to thy house this
evening. I hope to have it in my power to take tea with thee,
in company with Friend Giddings on his return from
Bangor.[2]

Cordially and truly thy friend
John G. Whittier

Manuscript: Swarthmore College.

1. Whittier had been visiting his brother Matthew Franklin, who was then living in Portland with his second wife, Jane Vaughan (1820–1895), and their two young children, Charles and Elizabeth. Neal married a cousin of Whittier.

2. Whittier met with Giddings to discuss support for the Liberty party in the coming elections and was hopeful that Maine would vote for the abolitionists. (See Letter No. 488).

488. To Henry Ingersoll Bowditch

Amesbury July 31, 1846

Dear Doctor.

A friend of my Sister's, Mrs. Morris of N. York.—has spoken to her in high terms of a Dr. Vandermeer [Vanderveer] of Flatbush, L. I. who has for a long time specially devoted himself to cases similar to hers.[1] I wish thee would do me the favor to endeavor to ascertain something about him. Mrs. M. referred my sister to Mrs. D. Wayland and other ladies—[2]

I have just returned from Maine, where I met J. R. Giddings, M. C. There will be an effort, and I hope successful to carry Maine for Freedom this year. There are good elements to work with. John P. Hale has promised to come into the state, whenever there is a fair opening, which will soon be afforded. What shall we do for old Mother Massachusetts? I told Giddings and he fully agreed with me, that we were in a worse condition on this question in Masstts. than they are in any other N. E. State.

Are there no honest democrats who will unite with Whigs— (anti-Slavery Whigs I mean) and Liberty men to place the Old Bay State in a better position?—and will such men as C. F. Adams etc meet such democrats cordially and kindly, and forget that they are Whigs, while endeavoring to act as becomes Massachusetts *men*? Do see them and talk with them, and if possible let us *New Hampshirize* Massachusetts. I am ashamed of my mother State. If we could get 20 Liberty or independent Whigs and democrats into the Legislature we could elect a Governor who would act worthy of the best days of the Commonwealth. Can it not be done?—Who would not like to see such a man as Sewall governor?

Affectionately and truly
Thy friend
John G. Whittier

Manuscript: Yale University.

1. Adrian Vanderveer (1796–1857) had been practicing medicine since 1819 and was appointed a health officer for New York in 1832. In 1838 he aban-

doned general practice and became a specialist, achieving an international reputation with patients visiting him from all over the country and abroad.

2. This may be Hepsy S. Wayland, the second wife of Francis Wayland, then president of Brown University, whom Whittier knew.

489. To Henry Brewster Stanton

Amesbury, August 4, 1846

Dear Stanton.

I am not going to write a letter more, but just to say that I am fully aware that I did a very foolish thing in troubling thee with my letter the other day.[1] I was wrong too, to hurt thy feelings in anyway, as I fear I did although I scarcely remember what I wrote. Pray consider it *unwritten*: and let the whole thing go forever.

What shall we do to turn over Massachusetts and bring Anti-Slavery atop?—I fear the disaffected Whigs will do nothing. The passage of McKay's Tariff has put new life into the Whig party.[2] They were just on the point of taking Giddings A. Slavery ground, as a matter of policy; but now they have got the watchword of "Repeal of McKay's Tariff," and they have no occasion for the anti-Slavery alternative. See if it isn't so.

Can thee not sound Sumner and Hillard?—I would like to know whether there is any hope of them heading off as "Independent Whigs." If not, *our* duty is plain. We must begin to rally again for election: indeed we have no time to lose. "Once more unto the breach!"[3]

When I see thee or Mrs. S. again I hope I shall be in better spirits. In the mean time may God abundantly bless you both—

Aff. and truly

John G. Whittier

Dear S. The foregoing was written some days ago. I have just got a line from thy wife, in which she says thee was aggrieved by my letter the other day. She certainly misunderstands me: and misjudges me on many points. In regard to the past: but let it pass—I only wish she could see me as I am and discriminate between weakness and indecision and deliberate wrong.

Dear S. We have been friends in sun and shade too long to be disturbed now. Let us strike hands anew and defy the Arch Mischiefmaker to get us at loggerheads. I am sorry Mrs. S. regards me so unfavorably, but, if the most earnest desire to live arightly can avail anything neither she, nor any one

else, shall have occasion to exercise toward me greater charity
than our common humanity every where requires.

Affecty

J. G. Whittier

Manuscript: Library of Congress.
 1. This letter has not been recovered.
 2. James I. McKay (1792–1853) served in Congress from 1831 to 1849 as a
representative from North Carolina. He had sponsored one tariff bill in 1843 which
was defeated, but his Walker Tariff bill, a moderate protective tariff, was passed
in 1846.
 3. *Henry V*, III, i, 1.

490. To Joseph Sturge

Amesbury (Ms), August 28, 1846

My dear Friend,—

Since I last wrote, the Congress has adjourned, and the
political elements are comparatively quiet. The elections
which have just taken place in Illinois and Indiana indicate a
decided anti-slavery progress. In one congressional district in
Illinois the vote for liberty was this year, 2,386; last year,
1,337. We have some hope that Maine this fall will follow the
example of New Hampshire, and take anti-slavery ground.[1]
The election is early next month.

One very cheering event I must notice. Last year an attempt
to exclude Slavery from the Oregon territory was defeated. This
year, just at the close of the session when the bill establishing
a territorial government was before the House, a clause pro-
hibitory of slavery was introduced by a large majority.

On the last day of the session the president sent a message
to Congress, asking an appropriation for the purpose of facili-
tating and promoting an adjustment of the Mexican controversy, and paying an equivalent for such territory as Mexico
might cede to us.

The Chairman of the Committee on Foreign Relations
accordingly reported an appropriation of two millions, when
a member [from] Pennsylvania, an ultra-democrat, who had
heretofore voted with slave-holders, offered a proviso that
slavery should be excluded from any territory obtained
under a treaty with Mexico. The slave-holders rallied, threatened, and implored; *but the proviso was carried by a decided
majority*. The entire North, (with few exceptions,) Whig and
Democrat, voted for it.[2] The bill was sent to the senate just
as that body was about to adjourn, and Senator Davis of
Massachusetts, having the floor, spoke up to the moment of

adjournment, and thus prevented a vote upon it. This is much to be regretted. But the vote in the House is significant of Liberty's coming triumph. For the first time since the fatal Missouri struggle in 1819–20, the Free States stood shoulder to shoulder for the limitation of slavery. The *Anti-slavery Reporter*, which I presume friend Tappan sends thee, will give an idea of what is doing in the religious world in this respect. The project of a paper at Washington is still before the Anti-slavery Society Committee.[3] Did I mention to thee in my last that at the late North-western Liberty Convention a committee was appointed for a meeting at Washington? There may be danger in the attempt; but I am inclined to think it should be made, and that, too, without delay.

I have now with me in Essex County, a young fugitive slave, Milton Clark, of Kentucky. He is intelligent and a good speaker, and is doing good.[4] I was greatly disappointed on the sugar question in Parliament. I fear the consequence will be an increase of the traffic in human beings.[5]

As ever, affectionately thy Friend and Fellow-Laborer.

John G. Whittier

Source: The *Anti-Slavery Reporter*, October 1, 1846.

1. The fall vote in Maine showed an increase of nearly 4,000 Liberty party votes and was regarded as a great victory by Liberty papers.

2. James J. McKay, chairman of the Ways and Means Committee, not the Foreign Relations Committee, had submitted a bill which would appropriate two million dollars for the President to which this proviso or amendment was added. Proposed by David Wilmot (1814–1868), a congressman from Pennsylvania, this amendment became known as "Wilmot's Proviso." The amendment was passed in the House by an 83 to 64 vote and adopted on August 8, 1846. However, the bill was lost in the Senate on August 10 by its adjournment. The amendment was reintroduced in the next session, again passed by the House, but defeated in the Senate. A new Senate bill granting a three-million-dollar appropriation was finally accepted by the House without any proviso concerning slavery. However, a bitter national debate was occasioned by the proviso and helped lead to the formation of the Free Soil party.

3. The *National Era* (see Letter No. 505, note 4).

4. Milton Clarke, a former slave from Kentucky, spoke in Amesbury on August 23 and remained in Essex County during September, attending conventions and giving speeches. He and his brother Lewis published an account of their slave lives, *Narrative of the Sufferings of Lewis and Milton Clarke Among the Slaveholders of Kentucky*, in 1846.

5. Thomas Clarkson had written a petition to Parliament, requesting that the British government should not allow sugar to be imported from colonies with free labor and countries with slave labor under equal terms. He feared that open competition would stimulate the slave trade in many of these countries which used slave labor. After some discussion on July 27, 1846, his petition was tabled.

491. To Charles Sumner

Amesbury, September 8 [1846]

Dear friend,

There is to be a mass meeting of the people at New Market
N. H. called by the united parties in Rockingham Co. on the
12th inst. Hale and others who have borne their part in the
late victory in N. H. will be there. Now it strikes me that thou
couldst do well to step into the cars and join us.[1] Thou
wouldst have a good opportunity to counsel with John P Hale
relative to a visit to Boston.[2] Apart from that, I have no
doubt the meeting will be well worth attending.

Tell friend Hillard to accompany thee. The trip will do you
both good after such a fortnight of intolerable heat. I hope
the weather will be cooler before Seventh day.

I send herewith a copy of the Bangor Gazette to show that
the democrats are moving in the right direction.

Very truly thy friend
John G. Whittier

Manuscript: Harvard University.
1. Sumner probably did not attend the meeting, since he was not mentioned
in Whittier's account of the meeting, "The Democracy of Freedom," published in
the *Essex Transcript*, September 17, 1846. (Letter No. 494).
2. Hale was to speak in Faneuil Hall on September 18, 1846.

492. To the Essex Transcript

Amesbury, September 10, 1846
Liberty Convention

The Liberty men of District No. 3, are invited to meet in
Convention at Haverhill, on the 17th inst., at 10 o'clock,
A. M., for the purpose of nominating a candidate to represent
this District in Congress.[1]

The importance of this Convention cannot fail to be appreciated. It has for its object the selection of a candidate, who,
if elected, shall carry with him over the threshold of the
Capitol the free principles, the moral courage, the manly
integrity, the devout recognition of accountability to God,
and the earnest aspiration for Human progress, which should
characterize the statesmen of a christian republic. The representative of a free people, should have some higher qualifica-
tion than a shrewd regard for the interests of capital and
traffic. It is time for the merely mercenary idea to give place
to that of philanthropy. Humanity has its claims; the rights

of persons should be held, at least, as sacred as those of property. And where should the needed reform in our national representation commence, if not in Massachusetts—whose hill-tops are crowned with church spires,—whose whole surface is dotted with school-houses,—whose sons are descendants of those christian republicans of the seventeenth century, who in Parliament and General Court were not ashamed to acknowledge their allegiance to the paramount Law of God!

Our call is issued in the name of the Liberty Party, but we cordially invite the attendance and cooperation of all who unite with us in the Great Idea upon which that party is based. Caring nothing for names, and anxious only for the success of our principles, we throw wide open the door of our Convention to all, whatever may have been their party relations, who now, in truth and sincerity are prepared to repudiate all political connexion with slaveholders and to join with us in the watchword of "Liberty First, Finance Afterward!" Justice Before Expediency!—Humanity Before Party.

> Wm. Carruthers,[2]
> B. F. S. Griffin, } Dist. Liberty Com.
> John G. Whittier

Source: The Essex Transcript, September 10, 1846.

1. Whittier called the meeting to order on the 17th, served as chairman of the business committee, and moved to make unanimous the nomination of Chauncey L. Knapp, who had been a coeditor of the Middlesex Standard with Whittier in 1845–1846.

2. William Carruthers (1804?–1860), a native of Scotland, had been active in temperance and reform work, besides being a Liberty party candidate in 1841. He was friendly with the Whittier family and Whittier wrote a personal tribute to Carruthers on his death, "Tribute to Dea. Wm. Carruthers," which was printed in the Villager, March 8, 1860 (see Letter No. 926).

493. To John Parker Hale

[Amesbury] September 16, 1846

I see, by the papers that thy lecture in Faneuil Hall takes place on the 18th.[1] There is one point which I wish to call thy attention to. We want some common ground for all who love Liberty and abhor Slavery to unite upon. May it not be found in the following:—

1. Abolition of slavery the leading and paramount political question.

2. No voting for slaveholders.

3. No voting for men who are in political fellowship with slaveholders.

Why can we not have a great League of Freedom, with the above for its watchwords and rallying cry? We have eighty thousand Liberty voters to begin with, and a majority of both the old parties are well-nigh ready to join in such a movement. Think of it. I notice that the English Liberal papers, Birmingham "Pilot," London "Non-Conformist," etc., have an eye on the New Hampshire movement, and think of it as a most encouraging fact in favor of the Rights of Man. In the late meeting of the British Anti-Slavery Society, Joseph Sturge, the President of the Free Suffrage Union, alluded to thy course with great satisfaction. The Editor of the "Democratic Record" has spoken of Sturge as the noblest and purest of the democracy of England.

Source: Pickard, *Life*, pp. 311–312.

1. Hale had been invited to speak to the citizens of Boston by Sumner, Howe, and other abolition Whigs in the hopes that Hale would influence the Whigs before their coming state convention. His speech was well received, but the Whig convention failed to pass any antislavery resolutions.

494. To the Essex Transcript

Amesbury, September 17, 1846

I had the satisfaction of attending the meeting of the Liberty men and Independent Democrats of the 1st Congressional District in New Hampshire, which was held at New Market on the 12th inst. I had a strong desire to see the old and tried advocates of Freedom, and their younger allies of the Independent Democracy sitting in council together for the first time.

The large meeting house was well filled with a fine looking delegation of the yeomanry of Strafford and Rockingham counties. A few ladies graced the meeting with their presence. In the cause of Liberty and Humanity when was the sympathy of woman appealed to in vain?

The choice of officers of the Convention having been made, a thin, worn, carelessly dressed man, apparently between fifty and sixty years of age, lame and leaning on his staff, with a black shade over his left eye, passed up the aisle to take the President's chair. It was the Hon. Joseph Cilley from his mountain home in Nottingham, the first Liberty Senator in Congress. He has a mild, calm face, full of benevolence and kindness, yet at the same time indicating latent firmness and energy. He is still suffering from the effects of wounds received in the last war with Great Britain.

Perhaps there is no man at this time so universally popular in the Granite State, as Col. Cilley. No man questions his integrity, patriotism and philanthropy; and especially fitting is it that such a man should be the first representative of the Liberty Party in the Senate of the United States.

After the appointment of a business committee and some other preliminaries, in obedience to reiterated calls, a gentleman, apparently from thirty-five to forty years of age, fresh, clear-eyed, vigorous, in form and feature giving assurance of a man strong alike in body and intellect, rose to speak.

It was John P. Hale, U. S. Senator elect—the Liberator of New Hampshire from the control of slaveholders—the bold and indomitable leader of the Independent Democracy of the North. He was greeted with loud cheers; and spoke with great ease, fluency and effect for a few minutes. When he sat down there was a call for another friend of Liberty who was understood to be present. A young man, with a countenance strongly marked by intellectual effort, and indicating a nervous and energetic temperament answered to the call. It was Henry B. Stanton—who in 1834 revolted from Lane Seminary because the Faculty of that College attempted to silence students on the subject of Slavery; and who, in the six years following as an eloquent advocate of Freedom made his name a familiar one from Illinois to Maine.—literally crowding the work of a life-time into that brief period. He spoke in his earnest and impassioned manner amidst the reiterated applause of the audience. In the afternoon, resolutions of a decided Liberty stamp, were introduced by the Business Committee. They were drawn up by Amos Tuck, Esq., one of the right hand men of Hale in the late political Revolution.[1]   He is a man of great moral worth; and his pertinent and well-chosen remarks on introducing the resolutions, were such as became a christian politician and a sincere advocate of Liberty. He was followed by John P. Hale in a powerful speech of more than an hour. Among those who followed in brief remarks, was Moses A. Cartland, one of the earliest and ablest abolitionists of New Hampshire. Although clad in the sober garb of the Society of Friends, one has only to look at his fine intellectual face, glowing with the fire and enthusiasm of genius, as if to use Carlyle's description of the face of Camille Desmoulins, "a naphtha lamp burnt within it,"[2] to understand that so long as there is a wrong to be redressed, or the cause of Humanity needs an advocate, he is not likely to become what is called "a quiet Quaker." Among those who were present, and manifesting evident sympathy with the objects of the meeting, was the Hon. Wm. Plumer, Jr., of Epping, a gentlemen of refined taste and cultivated intellect, who represented New Hampshire in Congress during the Missouri struggle and signalized himself by an able speech against the iniquitous "compromise." Such a man can scarcely do otherwise than give his sympathies and his influence to the present Liberty movement.[3]

The Resolutions, when published will show that the Liberty men and Independents of New Hampshire, are one in feeling and action; and they so fully define the position of John P. Hale, as to preclude all doubt or cavil. May the God of Freedom enable him so wisely and firmly to bear his part in the great struggle before him, as to confound his enemies and those of freedom; and realize the hopes, and justify the confidence of the friends of Liberty and true Democracy!

W.

Source: The *Essex Transcript*, September 17, 1846. Published with the caption, "The Democracy of Freedom."

1. Amos Tuck (1810–1879), an abolitionist and lawyer from Exeter, New Hampshire, supported Hale after the Democratic party had disowned him. He was elected to Congress on the Liberty party ticket in 1847 and twice reelected. Later he served as a member of the Republican conventions of 1856 and 1860.

2. *The French Revolution: A History* (New York, 1903), I, 136. Camille Desmoulins (1760–1794) was a French journalist and revolutionist.

3. William Plumer, Jr. (1789–1854), a New Hampshire lawyer and writer, served in Congress from 1819 to 1825.

495. To John Gorham Palfrey

Amesbury, September 21, 1846

Respected friend.

I have read with no small degree of interest thy numbers on "The Slave Power" in the Whig. I see the last number has reached the all-important query "what is to be *done*!"[1]

In my view nothing can be done until a union is formed of all who love liberty in the three parties in the free states. That such a union can be effected I fully believe. In order to fix upon some common ground for such a rally, allow me to suggest the following:

1. The *Abolition* of *Slavery*[:] the leading and paramount political object.

2. No voting for slave-holders[.]

3. No voting for men in political fellowship with slave-holders.

I believe that this, and this alone can form the basis of a *League* efficient for the overthrow of Slavery. The 80,000

Liberty voters will join it, and a large portion of the Whigs and Democrats will unite with them.

Excuse this hasty hint, and believe me respectfully thy friend.

John G. Whittier

Manuscript: Harvard University.

Recipient: John Gorham Palfrey (1796–1881), a Unitarian minister and historian, taught at Harvard from 1831 to 1839 and edited the *North American Review*. After serving in the Massachusetts legislature in the 1840's, he was elected to Congress as a Whig and abolitionist in 1847. He was later noted for his *History of New England*, which was published in five volumes.

1. Palfrey was then publishing a series of twenty-four essays on slavery in the Boston *Daily Whig*. The series began on July 1, 1846, and concluded on September 22. On September 17 Palfrey published Essay XXII, "What Should the Free States Do About It," and on September 19, Essay XXIII, "What Can the Free States Do About It."

496. To Nathaniel Peabody Rogers

Amesbury, September 26, 1846

My dear bro. Rogers.

I am deeply pained to learn of thy severe illness; and, were my own health at this time better than it is, I would visit thee in person rather than by letter.[1] I hope thee are now more comfortable, than when I last heard of thee. Rest assured my dear friend of my love and sympathy, and of my earnest prayers for thy restoration to health. Thousands will join me in this prayer. Our good friend George Bradburn spent the night with me yesterday;[2] he wishes much to see thee. He has a good and warm *heart* as well as a good *head*. After all—talk as we will of great intellects and great men—the *heart* is the great thing. Without it all is hollow and cold.

I am called away: and can only invoke for thee the blessing of Him who has said inasmuch as we have done good unto one of the least of His suffering brethren we have done it unto Him.[3]

Ever Affy.
John G. Whittier

Manuscript: Haverford College.

1. Rogers and Whittier had been estranged for many years, but Whittier had written Rogers a letter of sympathy in the late spring of 1846 upon hearing that Rogers was in ill health. Rogers replied to this now lost letter on June 8, 1846, saying: "I am striving to get me an asylum of a farm. I have a wife and seven children, every one of them with a whole spirit. I don't want to be separated from any one of them, only with a view to come together again. I have a beautiful little retreat in prospect, forty miles north, where I imagine I can get potatoes and repose. . . . Why can't I have you come and see me? You see, dear W., I don't want

to send you anything short of a full epistle. Let me end as I begun, with the proffer of my hand in grasp of yours extended. My heart I do not proffer,—it was yours before,—it shall be yours while I am N. P. Rogers" Whittier, *Works*, VI, 242–243). See also Whittier's tribute to Rogers, Letter No. 504, and his article, "Nathaniel Peabody Rogers" (Whittier, *Works*, VI) for further comments on Rogers.

2. George Bradburn had been lecturing on the abolitionist question throughout Essex County.

3. Matthew 25:40.

497. To Charles Sumner

Amesbury, September 26, 1846

Dear Sumner.

I have just read the proceedings of your Whig Convention and the lines enclosed are a feeble expression of my feelings.[1] I look upon the rejection of S. C. P's resolution as an evidence that the end and aim of the managers of the Convention was to go just far enough to save *the party*, and no further. We shall have another doughface in the Senate for six years. As for Webster—thy hopes and wishes notwithstanding— he is I fear no better on this question than "a colossal coward."

All thanks for the free voices of thyself, Phillips, Allen and Adams. Notwithstanding the result you have not spoken in vain.

If thee think well enough of these verses send them to the Whig or the Chronotype.[2] Remember me kindly to friend Hillard, and believe me truly thy friend,[3]

John G. Whittier

Manuscript: Harvard University. Published, in Part: Pickard, *Life*, pp. 316–317.

1. Enclosed with the letter was the poem, "The Pine Tree," which asked:

"Where's the man for Massachusetts? Where's the voice to speak her free?
Where's the hand to light up bonfires from her mountains to the sea?
Beats her Pilgrim pulse no longer? Sits she dumb in her despair?
Has she none to break the silence? Has she none to do and dare?"

The Massachusetts Whig convention met in Faneuil Hall on September 23, and Stephen C. Phillips, supported by Charles Sumner, Charles Francis Adams, and Charles Allen, offered a series of resolutions which made opposition to slavery the main aim of the Whig party. After much debate the resolutions were defeated by a 137 to 91 vote. Daniel Webster's presence at the convention prevented the abolition Whigs from getting the resolutions adopted.

2. The poem was printed in the Boston *Daily Whig*, September 29, 1846.

3. Sumner responded to the letter on September 26: "We do not despair. We are all alive to wage the fight another day, and feel that more was done than we had hoped to do. Our vote was strong; but it was at an hour when many had gone home by the early trains, whose presence would have made it stronger. Many who were present did not vote, and they were moderately with us. The ball has been put in motion; it cannot be stopped. Hard words are said of us in State Street. I am grateful to you for your note of encouragement. The poem is beautiful, and must be printed" (Pierce, *Memoir and Letters of Charles Sumber*, III, 128).

498. To Joseph Sturge

[Amesbury] September 27, 1846

I see your Evangelical Alliance has shipwrecked itself on the slavery question.[1] Why is it that humanity and orthodoxy must needs be divorced from each other? I think I should as soon unite myself with Popery as with a Protestant alliance of slaveholders and pro-slavery preachers? When will men learn that there can be "no compromise" between right and wrong?

Source: Richard, *Memoirs of Joseph Sturge*, pp. 381–382.

1. The Evangelical Alliance, an organization of various Christian denominations throughout the world, held its first World's Convention in London, August 1846. Sturge, who was one of the leaders in the alliance, had wanted its members to exclude those Christians who directly participated or acquiesced in the guilt of upholding slavery. American church members, however, objected to such a provision and after bitter debate left the slavery question up to the disposition of the individual countries represented. Sturge himself wrote to Whittier that "thou wilt see by the papers what a mess the Evangelical Alliance has made of the slavery question, and I fear upon the whole they have done it great harm" (Richard, *Memoirs of Joseph Sturge*, p. 381).

499. To Alden Bradford Morse

Amesbury Mills, Thursday Mg. [September] 28 [1846]

Dear friend,

I enclose a call for a Caucus tomorrow night.[1] Please write out one or two and put them up at suitable places; and try and get some of your folks out to the caucus. We are doing well here—our vote will be large at this end of town.

John G. Whittier

Manuscript: Pierpont Morgan Library, New York.

1. Enclosed with the letter was a clipped notice from the newspaper which read: "Caucus. All Free Soil voters in Amesbury are requested to meet in the Academy on Friday Evening at 7 o'clock to choose delegates to attend the County Convention at Ipswich Oct. 6th and the District Convention at Lawrence Oct. 4th. A full attendance is requested. Per order of Town Committee. Amesbury, Sept. 28, 1846."

500. To the Essex Transcript

[Amesbury, before October 1, 1846]

The following which I have recently received from my venerable friend, Chief Justice Hutchinson of Vermont, will I doubt not be read with interest.[1] Trusting that the writer will pardon the liberty, I am induced to publish it for the purpose of showing the estimation which our candidate for this district is held in his native State. And I cheerfully embrace this occasion to add my own testimony to that of Judge Hutchinson. I have known friend Knapp for more than ten years as a gentleman of unblemished character and strict integrity, as an able writer and speaker, and as a clear-sighted and unwavering advocate of Freedom. To no person could I give a Liberty vote with more pleasure than to Chauncey L. Knapp.

John G. Whittier

Source: The *Essex Transcript*, October 1, 1846.
1. Titus Hutchinson (1771–1857), a Vermont lawyer, served as the United States attorney for Vermont from 1813 to 1823, became a judge of the Vermont Supreme Court in 1826, and was made chief justice in 1830.
A letter from Justice Hutchinson of September 23, 1846, in which he praises Knapp as the former secretary of state in Vermont who left his office rather than abate his abolitionist zeal, was published after this introductory note.

501. To Joseph Sturge

[October 1846] [1]

For me I do not see that your preachers and ministers in England and Scotland are one whit more abolitionized than their brethren on this side the water. The exhibition which they made of themselves in the Evangelical Alliance has satisfied me that, if they should take up their residence in Slave States, nine in ten of them would in five years either become slaveholders or open defenders of slavery. This is my deliberately-formed opinion; I should rejoice to be able to think otherwise.

Source: Richard, *Memoirs of Joseph Sturge,* p. 382.
1. Richard placed this letter after the one of September 27, 1846, with this introductory comment: "Again, a month later, he [Whittier] refers to the question."

502. To Charles Sumner

Amesbury, November 3, 1846

My Dear Sumner.

I am not surprised under the circumstances at thy declining the nomination made in thy absence.[1] But I am nevertheless sorry, although I fear I might have done the same. Yet you will not I trust abandon the idea of bearing your testimony against War and Slavery at this Election. Let me implore you

41

to *act*—it is all important that you should do so. For myself
I care more for the Senator election this Winter than for the
Election of Governor or even of members of the Lower House
of Congress. Ought you not though through the Whig and
Chronotype to sound the alarm on this point?—I cannot bear
the thought that for some years more a man deaf and dumb
to the cause of Humanity shall represent my beloved Mother
State.

I thank thee from my heart for thy P. B. K. Oration.[2] It is
a noble word for the Right. May God give thee strength and
nerve and patience, for the practical *acting out* of that word.

Pardon this hasty note and believe me with hearty sympathy

thy friend
John G. Whittier

Manuscript: Harvard University.

1. On October 29, 1846, a group of citizens nominated Sumner as a candidate
for Congress to oppose Robert Winthrop, who had voted for the Mexican War.
Sumner was at this time absent in Maine giving a lyceum lecture and when he
returned to Boston he withdrew his name from nomination. Samuel Gridley Howe
was substituted for Sumner and lost by a large margin.

2. Sumner's Phi Beta Kappa oration was delivered on August 27, 1846, at the
First Church in Cambridge. As a tribute to four famous graduates of Harvard,
John Pickering, Joseph Story, Washington Allston, and William Ellery Channing,
it also included some comments on slavery and war. It was one of his best orations
and widely praised for its eloquence and learning.

503. To William James Allinson

Amesbury, November 10, 1846

My dear William

I hasten to thank thee for thy kind interest in my welfare
and to assure thee that the injury sustained by the accident
was trifling. I took pains to have it kept from the papers but
it unfortunately got in, in spite of me. It occasioned me some
pain but is now well. The shot did not penetrate the bone
but glanced on it and passed out. I happened to stoop to pick
up something at the moment and the heavy part of the charge
passed over me. It was certainly a narrow escape and furnishes
occasion for gratitude and thankful acknowledgement of
renewed obligation to Infinite Goodness in sparing an unfaith-
ful servant yet a little longer.[1]

I was glad to hear from thee and thy dear wife and aunts—
and also from the venerable John Cox.[2] Do remember me
most affectionately to him; and tell him I shall never forget
his kind words of sympathy and encouragement in the cause

in which I was engaged when in yr part of the country. I am very sorry I could not see him when I was at Burlington last winter.

I enclosed [for] thee some autographs, and a note from the ever to be remembered Clarkson to his friend—the last work of his pen—which he did for the Philada Fair.[3] Please hand them to Elizabeth Nicholson—agreeably to J. Sturge's request.

I have been rather more than usually unwell this fall; and at this moment am scarecely able to write a long letter. My sister's health is also very poor. She and mother desire to be affectionately remembered. Please say a kind word for me to all who are our mutual friends, and believe me as ever, thy affectionate friend,

John G. Whittier

Source: Handwritten copy, Haverford College. Published: The *American Friend*, February 16, 1899, p. 150.

1. Whittier had been working in the garden behind his house when a bullet accidently shot by Philip A. Butler, the young son of Whittier's neighbors, passed through his cheek. Not wanting to alarm his mother or sister, Whittier bound the wound up with a handkerchief and had Dr. Sparhawk dress the wound. Elizur Wright when he heard of the incident was much amused, stating that Whittier was the only Liberty party man who received wounds during the Mexican War.

2. John Cox (1753?–1847), an orthodox Quaker minister, lived near Burlington, New Jersey.

3. The second annual Liberty Fair in Philadelphia sold autographs, articles of clothing, art work, and so on, with all the proceeds going to the cause of abolition. The fair was held in December and January and netted well over a thousand dollars. Joseph Sturge solicited and obtained many autographs and articles from England to be sold at the fair.

504. To the Essex Transcript

[Amesbury, November 12, 1846]
Nathaniel P. Rogers

The death of a man like Nath'l P. Rogers calls for something more than the poor common-place of an ordinary obituary notice. A man of genius, clear, sparkling, refreshing, as one of the mountain rivulets of his home, and more than this, a friend of humanity, a real lover of Freedom, and Truth, and Justice, has just left us, to return no more forever. He died at his residence in Concord, N. H. on the 16th of last month, after a long and painful illness. A lover of all things beautiful, in his last moments he turned towards the window, [so] that his latest glance might fall upon the saddened loveliness of an October landscape. Calling his young and lovely family around him, he requested them to sing the beautiful lines of the Irish poet Lover, "The Angel's Whisper."[1] And, as the sweet, sad melody died away, the pure and generous, the "frolic and the gentle" spirit passed with it. The clear eye was sealed, and the fine ear closed forever.

Since the commencement of the anti-slavery struggle in this country we have been called to mourn the loss of many of our fellow-laborers. Shipley, Lundy, Lovejoy, Benson, Follen, Holley, Channing, Torrey,—and now Rogers!

> "Like clouds which rake the mountain summits,
>   Like waves which know no guiding hand,
> How swift has brother followed brother,
>   From sunshine to the sunless land."[2]

No one who had privilege of a familiar acquaintance with Rogers could do otherwise than love him wholly and heartily. I shall never forget a delightful visit which I made him, in company with George Thompson, at his mountain retreat on the banks of the Pemigewasset, in the autumn of 1836. How beautiful, how genial was the welcome he gave us!—How our hearts glowed at his eloquent words, his alternate bursts of pathos, and of indignant feeling in view of wrong and oppression, his keen satire, his beautifully apposite references and illustrations, his sunny-heartedness, and irresistable wit and humor! Who has not when reading the charmed page of Charles Lamb, envied those who had the privilege of his familiar acquaintance?—Well, just such a man was Rogers;—he had all of Lamb's wit and exquisite humor, and in addition he had what Lamb's strongest admirers feel the want of—a deep and intense interest in humanity—a most earnest and self-sacrificing spirit. His end was quiet and peaceful. He but once expressed any anxiety to recover, and then only that he might comfort his aged mother in her declining years. He had some years before in deep disgust at the want of humanity and charity and love, in the established churches, withdrawn from them, and it is said, placed little dependence upon their dogmas. Yet he lived like a christian. He sought not his own. Of him the recording angel might have written as he did of Abou Ben Adhem, *"He loved his fellowmen."*[3]

W.

Source: The *Essex Transcript*, November 12, 1846.
1. Samuel Lover (1797–1868), an Irish poet, novelist, and painter who achieved popular success with his depictions of Irish life.
2. William Wordsworth, "Extempore Effusion upon the Death of James Hogg."
3. Leigh Hunt (1784–1859), "Abou Ben Adhem," line 14. The line should read, "Write me as one that loves his fellow men."

505. To Joseph Sturge

Amesbury, November 28, 1846

My dear friend

Thy kind letter of the 1st of the month is received. I hasten to say that the arrangement I had contemplated had been
given up before the arrival of thy letter, as the owner of the
estate has sold a part of it and his price for the residue is
higher than it is prudent to give. I hope before Spring however
to find some other place which will answer our purpose; and
should I do so, will be glad to avail myself of thy kind proposal.[1]

The vote for Liberty in Massachusetts is this year as near
as I can gather it from the returns, a little rising 10,000, a gain
of about 20 pr. ct. We have elected 6 members of the State
Legislature. This however is not as well as I had hoped. But,
the now dominant party (the Whigs) have been compelled by
the rising tide of abolition to move with it; and some of their
leading men are almost with us. Among them are Chas.
Adams, son of the Ex. President, and Charles Sumner, a young
lawyer, of great promise, who has signalized himself as an
ardent friend of Peace, the Abolition of Cap. Punishment. His
address to the citizens of Boston last year on the "4th of July
Anniversary" has I believe been printed on your side of the
water. Friend Burritt knows him well.[2] I send thee herewith
a copy of his letter to R. C. Winthrop[,] the Boston representative in Congress.[3]

The disgraceful Mexican War still drags on. I rejoice to be
able to say that it has no popular favor in this section. Two
requisitions or calls for troops have been made upon Massachusetts and though our Governor backed the first with his
Proclamation, not a soldier has left our soil to do the work of
a human butcher. Why are your English papers, loud as they
are in condemnation of us, so silent as to the actual cause and
motive of this abominable War? *The extension of Slave-
territory* is the end and aim. I enclose thee an extract to this
effect from the Charleston (South Carolina) Courier of the
2nd of this month. If thee art in correspondence with such
papers as the News, the Patriot, or Birmingham Pilot, do
induce the Editors to speak out on the *real issue* of the War.

Our Washington paper edited by Dr. G. Bailey—assisted by
Amos A. Phelps and myself, will make its appearance on the
1st of the year.[4] Everything looks favorable. Lewis Tappan is
working nobly: he is a *strong* as well as a *good* man. Why
should George Thompson attack the British and F. A. S. Soci-

ety? I cannot comprehend his motives in so doing. As to the Evangelical Alliance, [it] is a sad spiritual farce; and the sooner such good men as John Angel James, and Dr. Wardlaw get out of it the better for them and for the slave.[5]

I am in receipt of a letter from Anna Richardson which I have been too busy to answer as yet.[6] I have not forgotten her request however, and so far as I can will comply with it.

My Sister's health is for the past four days more comfortable. My own much as it was when I last wrote.

I expect to start tomorrow to procure subscribers to our paper in N. H. and Maine.

Aff. thy friend
John G. Whittier

Manuscript: University of Virginia.

1. Sturge had sent Whittier money at various times and wrote again on November 18, 1846, inquiring about Whittier's accident and asking if he could pay expenses for anything that would aid Whittier's comfort. The reference in this paragraph is apparently to one of Whittier's periodic attempts to buy a farm which would provide him with some income. Nothing ever came of these attempts, even though Sturge offered to finance him.

2. Elihu Burritt was then in England advocating world peace.

3. Robert C. Winthrop (1809–1894), a Whig lawyer, had served as speaker for the Massachusetts House before serving in Congress. He was appointed to the United States Senate in 1850 to replace Webster, but in 1851 was defeated for the Senate by Charles Sumner. He later served as president of the Massachusetts Historical Society.

Sumner had criticized Winthrop's vote in Congress to support the declaration of war against Mexico by a series of articles during the summer of 1846, and then in a public letter of October 25, 1846, had declared: "Such, sir, is the Act of Congress to which by your affirmative vote the people of Boston are made parties. Through *you* they are made *to declare unjust and cowardly war, with superadded falsehood, in the cause of slavery.* Through *you* they are made partakers in the blockade of Vera Cruz, the seizure of California. . . . Let me ask you to remember in your public course the rules of right which you obey in private life. The principles of morals are the same for nations as for individuals. Pardon me, if I suggest that you have not acted invariably according to this truth" (Pierce, *Memoir and Letters of Charles Sumner,* III, 135).

4. The *National Era* was published from 1847 to 1860 at Washington by Gamaliel Bailey. Whittier and Phelps were listed as "Corresponding Editors," but actually served more as regular contributors. Whittier had nothing to do with editorial policy and no specific assignments, but sent most of his prose and poetry for the next ten years to the *Era.* In all he contributed 109 original poems and 275 articles or communications. The salary from this editorship was Whittier's principal source of income during these years.

5. Ralph Wardlaw (1779–1853), a Congregational minister in Scotland, was noted for his preaching and theological writing. He was also an active abolitionist.

6. Anna Richardson (1806–1892), an overseer and elder in her Quaker meeting, was active in many reform movements, worked in the prisons, and attended the Peace Congress of 1849 in Paris. During the middle 1840's she along with others helped Frederick Douglass, then an escaped slave, purchase his freedom.

506. To John Parker Hale

Amesbury December 18, 1846

We are about starting our "National Era" at Washington, and should be glad of a note of encouragement from thee. Is it asking too much to request thee to drop me a line, as one of the editors, to this effect? We shall have similar letters from others for our first number.[1] We mean to make the paper worthy of the best of causes,—the cause of humanity, the Democracy of the New Testament. So the pro-slavery Democrats have troubles yet in their Israel. Who is Esquire Marston?[2] Is he a man to stick to his point and show fight? [. . .] Webster and his two hopeful sons, I see, are going for the war.[3] Your New Hampshire Whigs were in too much of a hurry to nominate him.

Source: Pickard, *Life,* pp. 317–318.

1. Whittier also wrote to John Quincy Adams requesting a similar letter, but neigher Adams nor Hale had a letter in the first number. The only printed letter was one from Moses A. Cartland, most probably solicited by Whittier.

2. Gilman Marston (1811–1890), a New Hampshire lawyer, had left the Democratic party in 1846 to support Hale and the abolitionists. He served thirteen terms in the state legislature from 1845 to 1889, was twice a Republican member of Congress, and fought in the Civil War. In 1889 Marston served four months as a United States senator.

3. Edward Webster (1820–1848), a Boston lawyer, had joined the Massachusetts regiment organized for the Mexican War as a captain and died in Mexico.

Fletcher Webster (1813–1862), a lawyer, was surveyor of the Port of Boston from 1850 to 1861 and served as a colonel during the Civil War, in which he was killed.

507. To John Quincy Adams

Amesbury, December 19, 1846

Respected Friend:

Our new paper the "National Era" will be issued at Washington on the 1st. of next mo. As one of its Editors I should be glad of a line from thee—even if it were but a line—of sympathy and encouragement. We mean to do our best to make the paper worthy of the holy cause of Freedom; and such an one, as the enemies of Slavery of all classes and of all parties, can unite in countenancing.

I rejoice to learn that thy health for which I have felt much solicitude is improving. God grant that thy life may be spared to see the West and East united in setting their feet upon the neck of Slavery!

With respect and esteem I am truly thy friend

John G. Whittier

Manuscript: Massachusetts Historical Society.

508. To the Essex Transcript

Amesbury, December 24, 1846
The National Era

Those persons in this and adjoining towns who wish to subscribe for this new Liberty paper at the Seat of Government,
can hand in their names to the undersigned, or to Dr. G.
Bailey at Washington. The first number will be issued on the
1st of the year. Terms $2, always in advance.

I take this occasion, as one of the corresponding Editors to
say, that its originators wish to draw no support for this paper
from other anti-slavery publications. All are worthy of the
continued and steady support of their old patrons, as well as
of that of new converts to the principles of freedom. We
believe that the time has come for the establishment of a free
paper at Washington; and we confidently trust that the effect
of its publication will be so to strengthen and deepen the anti-
slavery sentiment throughout the country, as to be the means
of an increase rather than a diminuation of local interest in the
papers already established. Our undertaking is a great and difficult one, and in our labors to make it successful we trust that
the kind co-operation and cordial sympathy of our friends will
cheer and sustain us.

J. G. Whittier

Source: The *Essex Transcript*, December 24, 1846.

509. To Gamaliel Bailey

Amesbury, December, 1846
My Dear Friend:

In looking over, a day or two since, some fragments of the
poetry of England in the middle ages, I was struck with the
following animated and really beautiful apostrophe to Freedom, by John Barbour, archdeacon of Aberdeen, author of
"The Bruce," a poem which has many fine passages of description, and which has been very closely imitated in Walter
Scott's "Lord of the Isles."[1] This little fragment deserves an
honorable place among our Liberty mottoes:

"Ah! Fredome is a nobill thing!
Fredome mayse man to haif liking!

Fredome all solace to man gives;
He levys at-ease who freely levys.
A nobill heart may haif nane ease
Nor nocht els that may him plese,
Gif Fredome failyth: for free liking
Is yearnet for ower all othir thing.
And he, that ay hase levyt free
May nocht know weill the properte
The angyr, nor the wretchyt doome
That couplyt is to foule thraldome!"

Honor to the brave old ministrel-monk of Aberdeen! Luckily, there was no vigilance committee of democratic slaveholders in the "dark ages," to expurgate the archdeacon's
rhymes, or we should have had them sent down to us as completely divest of such "perilous stuff," as was the American
Reprint of Howard Hinton's History of the United States.[2]

Thou wilt see, by the Boston Atlas and Advertiser, and by
the speeches of Daniel Webster over his dinner and to the
volunteers for the Mexican war, that all due care is taken to
let the Southern wing of the Whig party understand that the
Whigs of Massachusetts are "sound on the subject of Slavery,"
and the war now waged for its extension.[3] The old pledge
made by Daniel Webster, in 1840, "under the October sun,"
at Richmond,[4] was beginning to be looked upon, like the
United States Bank, as "an obsolete idea," and recent anti-
slavery demonstrations of C. F. Adams and his friends seemed
to render a new explanation and exculpation necessary. Our
Southern friends must not, however, take these interested
statements without a good deal of allowance. The truth is, a
powerful anti-slavery party appears now to be slowly evolving
itself from the two great parties at the North. In Massachusetts, the movement is mainly confined to the Whigs, although
there are many in the Democratic party thoroughly sick of
their present position, and ready to welcome any change
which shall place them in an attitude of hostility to the Slave
Power.

The issue made up between John P. Hale and the long-
dominant party in New Hampshire, was a most unfortunate
one for the "peculiar institution." The complete triumph of
Hale has had its effect upon the Democracy of the North and
West, as seen in the Wilmot and Brinkerhoff resolution of the
last session. So successful an example of the safety of doing
right cannot fail to find imitators among those Northern Democrats who have long been restive under the party collar.
Henceforth, the "natural allies" even are not to be depended

upon. The spell is broken.

When the excellent Elliott was endeavoring to christianize the wild natives of New England, the Powahs succeeded in frightening back to idolatry many of his weak disciples.[5] Their sacred "medicine bag," with its charmed contents of feathers, claws, and human hair, had more power over the rude converts than the good missionary's Bible itself. At length, a brave-hearted Indian, Hiacoomes, of Martha's Vineyard, ventured publicly to test the spell of the medicine-man, by trampling it under his feet.[6] The natives watched the experiment of the rash Iconoclast, and, when they saw that he was not stricken down at once for his temerity, they raised a shout of joy, each one hastened to give a kick to the "medicine," and the poor Powah was chased out of the village, with the squaws and the children clamoring at his heels.

Hale's experiment was, in its way, quite equal to that of old Hiacoomes. Slavery had come to be regarded as a very sacred and democratic institution, to interfere with which was to incur political death. Hale had rudely touched it, and still lives; and now other feet are profaning it, and the chances are that it will ere long share the fate of the Powah's "medicine bag."

At the late Democratic Convention in New Hampshire, this same "medicine bag," sadly the worse for the buffetings of Hale and the Liberty men, was solemnly laid before the delegates by Hon. Isaac Hill, acting as Grand Powah on the occasion. But to the great grief and chagrin of that venerable Pagan, one of those who had been selected to do it honor had the audacity to kick it over in his presence. The consequences of that last kick are now developing themselves in a manner which betokens nothing but disaster to the pro-slavery Democracy of New Hampshire.

The anti-slavery resolutions of George Barstow, at that Convention, were indeed clamored down and refused a consideration, but their proper effect has not been lost.[7] Their author, a young lawyer of fine talents, favorably known as the writer of the "History of New Hampshire," and whose really democratic principles and character are unquestioned, has taken the field in defense of his abolitionism, and resolutely appeals to the people from the decision of the party managers. He is fully equal to the emergency. As a speaker, he is one of the best in the State. He addressed a large audience in Concord on the 4th instant, and, as I learn, with great effect.

Cordially thy friend,
J. G. W.

Source: The *National Era,* January 7, 1847. Printed with the caption, "Letters from the East—No. 1."

1. John Barbour (1320?–1395), the most noted of early Scottish poets, wrote these lines in *The Bruce,* Book I, lines 225–236.

2. John Howard Hinton (1791–1873), an English clergyman, published his *History and Topography of the United States* in 1830–1832 and it was reissued at Boston in 1834.

3. Daniel Webster spoke at a testimonial dinner in Philadelphia on December 2, 1846, and severely criticized Polk for precipating war by advancing troops into a contested area. In that speech he also defended the right of Congress alone to declare war. Webster's own son Edward had joined the Massachusetts volunteers as a captain and eventually died in Mexico from an illness.

4. In October of 1840 while campaigning for the Whigs Webster spoke at Richmond and promised the South that no power in the government or Congress could interfere in the slightest degree with the institutions of the South.

5. John Eliot (1604–1690), an English-born missionary, was the first to preach to the Indians in their native tongue. He printed many books on the Indian language and Indian customs.

6. Hiacoomes (1610?–1690), one of the first American Indians to become a Christian, began preaching in 1653 and was ordained a minister in 1670.

7. George Barstow (1812–1883) published his *History of New Hampshire* in 1842. At the Democratic convention on October 15, 1846, Barstow, as one of the committee on resolutions, asked for the abolition of slavery in the District of Columbia and opposed the division of Texas into any more slave states.

510. To Gamaliel Bailey

Amesbury, December, 1846

Dear Friend:

Dr. Holmes's new poem is lying before me, in the elegant dress of Ticknor and Co.[1] It has for its title "Urania, a rhymed lesson, delivered before the Boston Mercantile Library Association."[2] In ease and beauty of versification, its author is, beyond question, unsurpassed by any American Writer, and this poem is perhaps the best specimen of his powers. Its general tone is playful and humorous, but there are passages of great tenderness and pathos. Witness the following from a description of the city church-goers. The whole compass of literature has few passages to equal its melody and beauty:

"Down the chill street, which winds in gloomiest shade,
What marks betray yon solitary maid?
The cheek's red rose, that speaks of balmier air,
The Celtic Blackness of her braided hair;
The gilded missal in her kerchief tied,
Poor Nora, exile from Killarney's side!
Sister in toil, though born of colder skies,
That left their azure in her downcast eyes,
See pallid Margaret, labor's patient child,
Scarce weaned from home, a nursling of the wild,
Where white Katahdin o'er the horizon shines,

And broad Penobscot dashes through the pines:
Still as she hastes her careful fingers hold
The unfailing hymn book in its cambric fold,
Six days at drudgery's heavy wheel she stands,
The seventh sweet morning folds her weary hands.
Yes, child of suffering, thou mayst well be sure
He who ordained the Sabbath loved the poor!"

There are many other fine passages, showing that the author is capable of moving the heart, as well as of tickling the fancy. There is no straining for effect; simple, natural thoughts are expressed in simple and perfectly transparent language. The writer's views of God's design in the creation of man, are given with great clearness and force:

"Thought, conscience, will, to make them all thine own,
He rent a pillar from the eternal Throne!
Made in His image, Thou must nobly dare
The thorny crown of sovereignty to share;
With eye uplifted, it is thine to view,
From thine own centre, Heaven's o'erarching blue;
So round thy heart a beaming circle lies,
No fiend can blot, no hypocrite disguise,
From all its orbs one cheering voice is heard,
Full to thine ear it bears the Father's word,
Now, as in Eden, where His first born trod,
'Seek thine own welfare, true to Man and God!' "

In noticing Dr. Holmes's poetry, I am reminded of a small volume, published a few months since, entitled "War Songs and Ballads from the Old Testament, By William Plumer, jun."[3] It consists of free translations of three original Hebrew Poems, viz: "The Song of Moses and Miriam"; "The Song of the Bird," and "Deborah and Barak," with two additional poems, "Absalom" and "The Witch of Endor." The task of the writer seems not to have been that of a translator alone; figures and passages, selected from different parts of the sacred writings, are added to those of the original poems, shaped into new forms and applied to new uses. In this way, he has well preserved the general tone and coloring of the old Hebrew poetry, and presented a striking and vivid picture of Jewish thought and feeling. In some instances, he has, perhaps, overloaded his pieces with rich oriental decorations—gorgeous images follow each other in too rapid succession. The form of versification which he has chosen, although in his opinion, best adapted of all others to the free introduction of Scripture names, is not sufficiently terse and vigorous

for the Hebrew war ballad. It sounds more like the sweet
music of the harp and dulcimer, at the vintage and the sheep
shearing, than the trumpet-prelude to Joab's onset, or the
shout of David's spearmen, rushing down from their mountain fastnesses of Engedi; yet, as a whole, the author's design
has been very successfully executed. I have marked several
passages for quotation, but, as they would exceed my limits,
I will cite two strikingly opposite in character and imagery.
The first is an extract from "The Witch of Endor:"

> "They came, the Elohim! as if opening earth
> Evoked, from her caverns had given them birth,
> The Weird Woman started, the King stood aghast,
> As dim in the distance, like shadows they passed!
> They came in the darkness, with low sounds between,
> Dim seen in the distance—felt rather than seen.
> An old man is with them, an old man is there,
> With broad mantle covered, and white flowing hair!"

The second extract is from "Absalom," describing young
Zilpah, the mistress of the rebel Prince. It has the warm coloring of the royal poet's "Song of Songs":

> "her dark tresses twine
> Like grapes in rich clusters 'mid bowers of the vine
> Half hid in dark tresses, and whiter than snow
> Her bosom heaves fondly in passion's warm glow.
> The snow-flake of Carmel less pure than the white
> Of Zilpah's soft bosom, less dazzling to sight.
> Her eyes, like turtle's, where love hath its birth,
> Now languish in fondness, now sparkle in mirth,
> The long silken lashes that soften their fire
> Shade gently, yet quench not, the flames of desire.
> Like treads of rich scarlet her lips, and between
> Like sheep from the washing, her white teeth are seen;
> And warm are her kisses, as wine when the cup
> Is spiced for the banquet that monarchs may sup,
> As wine that so softly the senses can steep,
> Its flavor the dreamer tastes e'en in his sleep."

The author, a son of the venerable ex-Governor Plumer,[4]
has lived for many years in retirement, on the fine old homestead at Epping, New Hampshire. In 1819-'20, he was one of
the Representatives of the State in Congress, and distinguished
himself by an able speech against the admission of Missouri
as a slave State. He has since taken little interest in political
affairs; but the anti-slavery movement seems now likely to

call him from the seclusion of his study, and furnish a fitting occasion for the exercise of his fine talents. I find, in my late New Hampshire papers, the report of a speech delivered by him, a few weeks since, at Dover. One or two extracts will show its character. Speaking of the compromises of the Constitution, he says:

"The slave States, as might have been foreseen, took the Representatives, but paid little or nothing of the taxes. For nearly forty-eight years, the slaves have been represented, and helped to govern us all that time; but they have been taxed only three years! Such were the terms and conditions of this famous compromise, and such its fulfillment. Perpetual representation on the one side, with three years' taxation on the other. And yet we are told that slavery is a State concern, with which we have nothing to do. A State concern! Sir, it is a United States concern; and if we do not look to our rights on this subject, and stop the further extension of this slave power, we shall deserve the chains which [they] are forging for us. Chains are forged, not for the black alone; every link which is fixed, at the one end, on his neck, is fastened round ours at the other; and the slaveholder has one hand on this chain, and grasps the whip in the other."

The Legislature of New Hampshire, at its last session, enacted a law with respect to this subject, which provides, that any public officer of the State or private citizen, who shall arrest, or aid in the arrest, of an alleged fugitive slave, shall forfeit a sum not exceeding $1,000 nor less than $500, or be imprisoned in the county jail not more than twelve nor less than six months. This act, signed by John P. Hale, as speaker of the House, and approved by Governor Colby,[5] the Hon. Isaac Hill, of the New Hampshire Patriot, is publishing, enclosed in *black lines*, under the head of "Outrage Upon The Holy Compromises Of The Constitution, And Sacrilege To the Memory Of The Fathers Of That Institution!" The Granite Freeman very appropriately answers the Patriot's denunciations, by publishing the names of forty Democratic members who voted for the act; and the Boston Whig still further troubles the venerable defender of "the holy compromises," by informing him, that an act identical, or nearly so, with this same "black disunion law," was adopted in Massachusetts, three years ago, by the only Democratic Legislature which has existed for the last twenty years. It was passed unanimously, in both branches and signed by Governor Morton and by Frederick Robinson, then President of the Senate, and now Democratic candidate for district

No. 4.[6] It was the first of the kind adopted, but similar enact-
ments have been since carried through the Legislatures of all
the other New England States, save Rhode Island. Taking
Governor Hill's word for it then, the Massachusetts Democrats are guilty of setting the sad example of the first violation
of the "holy compromises" of constitutional negro catching.
From all which, it appears that the Governor, in his zeal for
slavery, has committed what Talleyrand called "worse than a
crime"—a blunder.[7] He had blown up his own friends, and
enabled us to realize the

> "Sport to see the engineer
> Hoist with his petard."[8]

J. G. W.

Source: The *National Era*, January 14, 1847. Printed with the caption, "Letters from the East.—No. 2."

1. Oliver Wendell Holmes (1809–1894) gained poetic popularity with "Old Ironsides" in 1830 and published a group of witty poems in 1834, but devoted his main talents to his medical career. He served as professor of anatomy and physiology at Harvard from 1847 to 1882 and published important medical works. He continued to write poetry and Whittier reviewed an 1848 collection of his poems in the *National Era* of January 11, 1849, saying: "Holmes writes simply for the amusement of himself and readers; he deals only with the vanity, the foibles, and the minor faults of mankind, good naturedly and almost sympathizingly suggesting excuses for the folly which he tosses about on the horns of his ridicule." Whittier's friendship with Holmes began in 1854 and Whittier followed Holmes's writing in the *Atlantic Monthly* with interest and praise. Holmes's essays, "The Autocrat of the Breakfast Table" (published in book form in 1858), won him and the *Atlantic Monthly* national fame for their wit and literary qualities. Similar essays and reflections followed, as well as collections of poetry, throughout the rest of his life. On Whittier's seventieth birthday Holmes named him the "wood-thrush of Essex" and throughout the 1870's and 1880's they became increasingly intimate, exchanging visits and frequent letters which commented wryly on their fame, infirmities, and the loneliness of old age. Whittier wrote four poems of tribute about Holmes ("O. W. Holmes on his Eightieth Birthday," "Our Autocrat," "To Oliver Wendell Holmes," and "Dr. Holmes") and his last written poem was to Holmes:

> "Beloved physician of an age of ail!
>   When grave prescriptions fail
> Thy songs have cheer and healing for us all
>   As David's had for Saul."

After Whittier's death Holmes wrote a poetic tribute to Whittier "In Memory of John Greenleaf Whittier," in which he called him "best loved and saintliest of our singing train."

2. The correct title was "Urania: A Rhymed Lesson. Pronounced before the Boston Mercantile Literary Association." Holmes delivered the poem on October 14, 1846, and it was published October 31, 1846.

3. *Lyrica Sacra, or War-Songs and Ballads from the Old Testament* (Boston, 1846).

4. William Plumer (1759–1850), a lawyer from Epping, New Hampshire, served as governor of New Hampshire from 1812 to 1813 and from 1816 to 1819, after a career in the state legislature and the United States Senate.

5. Anthony Colby (1795–1873), a New Hampshire businessman, served in the state legislature and was governor from 1846 to 1847.

6. See Letter No. 120, note 6. Frederick Robinson, then a warden in the Massachusetts State Prison, ran for Congress on the Democratic ticket in 1847 and lost.

7. Charles Maurice de Talleyrand-Périgord (1754–1838), the French statesman and diplomat, was noted for his wit and epigrams.

8. *Hamlet*, III, iv, 207. The correct phrasing is: "For tis sport to have the engineer/Hoist with his own petar."

511. To the National Era

Amesbury, Mass., January 13, 1847

Our Legislature, now in session, have had the war question thrust upon them, by the proposition of Caleb Cushing, of Newburyport, to appropriate the snug little sum of $20,000, from the State Treasury, for the benefit of the new volunteers, who have been lately drummed up in Boston and vicinity. By a vote of 177 to 61, the proposition was laid on the table; but, a petition to the same effect being subsequently received, the subject was referred to a select committee, of which our late Chinese Minister is chairman. He will, of course, report in favor of the petition; but, however cogent may be his arguments, and however urgent may be his appeals to "patriotism," there seems at present, very little probability that Massachusetts will open her strong box to pay the grog and cigar bills of those interesting young gentlemen who have been, for the past six weeks, making preparations to "revel in the halls of the Montezumas."[1] Among those who voted with the war-hawks, I noticed the name of Fletcher Webster, son of Daniel Webster.[2]

I see, by the Chronotype of yesterday, that one of the sergeants of Captain Wright's company has been arrested for burglary, and that several other "patriotic" volunteers are in jail in Leverett street for prematurely commencing operations, and mistaking Boston for Mexico.

Apart from the office holders, and expectants among the Democrats, and a small but not uninfluential portion of the Whigs, this miserable war is thoroughly detested in Massachusetts. The vote in the Legislature on Cushing's proposition shows this. The falling off of the Democratic and the increase of the Liberty vote, at the general election, are indications not to be mistaken, that the moral sense of Pilgrim Land revolts at this atrocious scheme of carving out with the sword new territory for slavery. A large portion of our people regard the proposition now before our Legislature in very much the same light in which they would a proposal on the part of the State to furnish the outfit of a private vessel from Long Wharf.

A new Democratic paper has been started in Boston, taking the ground of Preston King and Wilmot, in relation to slavery. It is another sign of the times.

The election to Congress of such a man as Dr. Palfrey affords cheering evidence of the progress of anti-slavery feeling. He belongs, in reality, to the Independent Whigs, openly declaring the question of slavery to be the first importance— a question paramount to that of trade, or finance, or President-making. Still, he received the support of the Whigs, with some few exceptions, and will probably, on matters apart from the slave question, act in unison with the party. Whether he can be drawn into the support of a slaveholding candidate for the next Presidency, remains to be seen. Fears on this point alone withheld from him the votes of the majority of the Liberty men of his district. As it was, the defection of the anti-Abolition Whigs, was, at the last trial, more than compensated by Liberty votes in his favor. I have the most entire confidence in Dr. Palfrey, as an honest and conscientious man; and whatever anti-slavery pledges may be fairly deduced from his past professions and practice, I have no doubt he will be prompt to redeem them in Congress. The Liberty candidate in the same district, Hon. James G. Carter, is a gentleman no wise inferior to Dr. P. in ability, and has long been known as a hearty and thorough Abolitionist. Hon. Frederick Robinson, the Democratic candidate, favorably known as the humane and liberal-minded Warden of our State Prison, has always professed hostility to slavery and to the annexation of Texas as a slave State. The truth is, no man of any party, now dares go before the people of Massachusetts as a candidate for office, otherwise than as an enemy of slavery in some sort. To this result, the steady perseverance of the Liberty party has greatly contributed.

A late number of the Democratic Review, which has just fallen under my notice, contains an article upon "Slaves and Slavery," which seems to have been made up by a pretty equal intermingling of the two classes of facts described by Dr. Witherspoon, as "facts which do and facts which do not exist."[3] The oppressive servitude which still obtains in some portions of Europe and Asia is enlarged upon with much apparent relish, preparatory to the following dulcet description of that remarkable Americanism, known to delicate ears as "the peculiar institution." Acquitting all intelligent Southerners of its authorship, I have scarce a doubt that it is the fancy sketch of some unfortunate Yankee office-seeker, making a dead set for Governmental patronage:

"In the United States, the slavery which exists is not that of conquered owners of the soil, ground under the exactions of invading rulers, but of the descendants of imported laborers, *enjoying the same personal liberties as the free laborers in the British Islands*, and always receiving the *full measure of their wants in respect to food and rainment*; not as the scanty surplus remaining, after yielding up the products of their toil to taskmasters, but as the object first to be cared for; and until they are satisfied there remains no surplus for the profit of the master."

In the same article, we are told that there are 800,000 of the natives of British India held in personal slavery. The writer quotes, in proof of this, from a work published some eight years ago, by Professor Adam.[4] He seems not to have been aware, or to have chosen to forget, the act of the Legislative Council of India, April 7, 1843, which renders it impossible for Briton, Mussulman, or Hindoo, to hold a human being *legally* as a slave. Here is the act:

"1. *It is hereby enacted and declared*, That no public officer shall in the execution of any decree or order of court, or for the enforcement of any demand of rent and revenue, sell or cause to be sold, any person, or the right to compulsory labor or services of any person, on the ground that such person is in a state of slavery.

"2. *And it is hereby declared and enacted*, That no rights arising out of an alleged property in the person and services of another, as a slave, shall be enforced by any civil or criminal court or magistrate within the territories of the East India Company.

"3. *And it is hereby declared and enacted*, That no person who may have acquired property by his own industry, or by the exercise of any art, calling, or profession, or by inheritance, assignment, gift or bequest, shall be disposessed of such property, or prevented from taking possession thereof, on the ground that such person, or that the person from whom the property may have been derived, was a slave.

"4. *And it is hereby enacted*, That any act which would be a penal offence, if done to a freeman, shall be equally an offence, if done to any person on the pretext of his being in a condition of slavery."

It will be seen at once that this act divests the slaveholder of his right of property in his slave; of his right to compulsory labor; of his right to detain in bondage for an instant a single human being; and that, whilst it thus denudes the slave-holder of his alleged property in the person and the services of his

slave, the law confers it on the slave; and, what deserves to be
particularly remarked, it not only declares his right to any
property he may lawfully acquire in the future, but secures to
him that which he possessed, by sufferance of his master,
when in a state of slavery. The fourth article entitles the slave,
thus emancipated, to the protection of the general laws of
British India.

That there are many of the servile class in the remote prov-
inces of British India, who are still in the condition of slaves,
is doubtless true, but their slavery is contrary to law, and
can exist only through the ignorance of the subjects of it, or
the culpable negligence of the public functionaries.

I would be the last to screen Great Britain, or the East
India Company, from the responsibility of their actual sins,
which are neither few nor small; but I am unwilling to have
even their good deed misrepresented or denied, for the purpose of furnishing an excuse for wrong doing on this side of
the water.

Our Liberty vote by the official count proves to be—for
Governor 9,997; for Lieutenant Governor and Senators
10,134; average 10,068. Last year our vote was 8,316. The
Eufala (Ala.) Democrat makes a great mistake in saying that
the Abolition strength of Massachusetts has been transferred
to the Whigs. Equally erroneous is the statement of the
National Intelligencer, that an unusually small number of
Abolitionists are elected to the Legislature. Last year we had
only three; this year six. The Liberty men of Massachusetts
were never firmer or more deeply impressed with the importance of independent action than at this moment. Some few
of them indeed voted for John Quincy Adams and for John
G. Palfrey; neither of whom are relied upon as thorough Whig
partisans, and both of whom have been openly or covertly
opposed in their anti-slavery position by that portion of the
party represented by the Daily Advertiser and Atlas newspapers. The latter gentleman, I see, failed of re-election yesterday in the House, as Secretary of State, unquestionably
from this very cause.

I have been absolutely shocked by the language made use
of by Henry Clay, at the dinner at New Orleans recently.[5]
An old man, broken in health, and trembling on the threshold
of the grave, he regrets that he cannot join the army of invad-
ers in Mexico; and takes pleasure in the thought that, old and
feeble as he is, he might possibly "capture or slay a Mexican."
It is mournful, pitiful; and I now allude to it only with a feel-

ing of sorrow. How poor a thing is intellect divorced from goodness! How mean is merely selfish ambition! Looking back upon the past with a thankful heart, I rejoice more than ever that my vote in 1844 was withheld alike from Henry Clay and his successful competitor. What friend of Liberty and Peace, who at that time was alike faithful to his convictions of duty, does not rejoice with me?

J. G. W.

Source: The National Era, January 21, 1847. Printed with the caption, "Letters from the East.—No. 3."

1. The two Aztec rulers of Mexico: Montezuma I (1390?–1464) and Montezuma II (1480?–1520), who ruled at the time of the Spanish conquest.

2. Fletcher Webster had served with Caleb Cushing in China.

3. John Witherspoon (1722–1794), a leading Presbyterian minister, was president of Princeton from 1768 until his death.

4. William Adam, a British missionary to India, wrote Law and Custom of Slavery in British India in 1840.

5. Henry Clay spoke in New Orleans on December 22, 1846, at a dinner honoring the Pilgrims' first landing. In reply to a complimentary toast he is reported to have said: "And when I saw around me tonight, General Brooke and other old friends, I felt half inclined to ask for some little nook or corner in the army, in which I might serve to avenge the wrongs to my country. I have thought I might yet be able to capture or slay a Mexican. I shall not be able to do so, however, this year, but hope that successes will still crown our gallant arms and the war terminate in an honorable peace" (Essex Transcript, January 14, 1847). Clay's remarks were probably in jest and perhaps ironical since he opposed the Mexican War as unnecessary and aggressive.

512. To the National Era

Amesbury, Mass. January 18, 1847

Since my last date, the proposition of Caleb Cushing, in the Legislature, to commit the State to the support of the Mexican invasion, has been rewarded by the choice of that gentleman as colonel of the new regiment. Of his peculiar qualifications for such a post, no one can doubt. During his late Oriental embassy, he had ample opportunity to study the military tactics of the Chinese, and will doubtless be prepared to oppose Santa Anna,[1] after the manner of that redoubtable people, by turning upon him the muzzles of pickle jars, and gallipots, setting up scarecrows, and issuing high-sounding proclamations. As there is no chance of his raising the $20,000 outfit from Massachusetts, and as it is understood that the General Government, in supplying its soldiers with food and clothing, has actually outdone the economy of a Yankee slaveowner, it will scarcely be necessary to look beyond his own regiment for scarecrows. As to the matter of proclamations, and the flying artillery of words, our new military chieftan might be very fairly matched against Grand Commissioner Lin himself.

Seriously, it is a poor compliment to the civilization, religion, and humanity of our age, that a man like Caleb Cushing, with a mind highly gifted by nature, enriched by varied learning, and capable if rightly directed, of exerting a healthful influence upon his country and the world, is able to find no better employment than that of leading off a company of denuded unfortunates thousands of miles, to shoot men with whom *they* at least have no quarrel, or to be shot by them; and this, too, without the plea that the welfare of the country requires or its true honor demands it. And, when we consider that it is manifestly the design of the promoters of this war to extend the curse of human slavery over whatever territory our arms may conquer, there really seems very little to be said in favor of transforming one's self into a mad Berserker, and, tucking up the sleeve of one's Christian garb, to do gratuitous butcherwork, in its behalf. I remember a spirited reply which Cushing once made in Congress to the ridiculous threat of some exasperated member, that the law of slavery should be extended over the free North: "You may destroy," said he, "our manufactures, you may cripple our commerce, raze our cities to the dust, and lay our whole land waste; but you cannot, you shall not, introduce slavery into the heart of the North!" Is it possible that he is now prepared to do himself the very thing which he then so strongly deprecated, and to aid in introducing slavery into the heart of a free country?

After several trials, Dr. Palfrey has been re-elected Secretary of the Commonwealth. The attempt to proscribe him on account of his abolitionism, if such was the object of the opposition to him, has therefore signally failed. Had it succeeded, Dr. Palfrey's rival would have had peculiar reasons for appending to the State's official documents the customary prayer of "*God save the Commonwealth of Massachusetts.*"

J. G. W.

Source: The *National Era*, January 28, 1847. Printed with the caption, "Letters from the East.—No. 4."
1. Santa Anna (1795–1876), the Mexican president and commander of the Mexican armies.

513. To the National Era

Boston, January 20, 1847

Agreeably to the call of the State Central Liberty Committee, the friends of Freedom are now in session in time-honored Faneuil Hall. Even at this early hour, (11 o'clock A. M.) the spacious area is well filled with sturdy and substantial citizens of the Bay State, who have gathered here from the mountain land of Berkshire, from the farmer-homes of Worcester, and the stormy seaboard of Essex, Plymouth, and Bristol.

It is indeed a noble assemblage, to appearance, the largest and most imposing which the Liberty cause has yet called together in Massachusetts.

The committee on the nomination of officers have reported the names of the following persons:[1]

For President.—Hon. Jas. G. Carter, of Lancaster.

For Vice Presidents.—Hon Wm. Jackson, Rev. A. B. Eggleston, Hon. A. Bliss, S. P. Andrews, Esq., James Ford, Esq., Rev. Giles Pease, Col. Mason Stone, Martin Torrey, Esq., Charles Churchill, Esq., and Dr. Ebenezer Hunt.

For Secretaries.—Richard Hildreth, John G. Whittier, and Rev. W. H. Brewster.

Dr. Swan, of Easton, chairman of the State Central Liberty committee, has made a full report of the action of the committee for the past year—a report full of sound sentiments, animated, and full of hope.[2] The large increase of the Liberty vote, in all places where Labor was bestowed previous to election, is made the occasion for an earnest and effective appeal for increased zeal and activity.

Henry Bibb, of Michigan, the eloquent young self-emancipated colored man, has just made some spirited and deeply interesting remarks.[3] He is a good speaker, and has an air of entire candor and truthfulness.

Rev. Jos. C. Lovejoy is now speaking, eloquently and forcibly.[4] New accessions are constantly pressing into the hall. The business committee have reported a series of resolutions, which will be acted upon this afternoon.

In the State Legislature, the Liberty member from Woburn is to be heard to-day in favor of his motion of inquiring into the course of Governor Briggs on the Mexican War. The motion is as follows:

"That the Governor be requested to furnish to the House a statement of the number of volunteers enrolled in this Commonwealth for the Mexican war, and the number mustered into service; the warrants under which they were enrolled, and the authority for the same; the agency of any State officers in the enrollment and muster, and the authority under which they acted; the form of the commissions, if any, given to officers of the volunteers, and the law of Massachusetts authorizing such commissions; the expenses incurred, by whom authorized, under what law, and to whose account they now stand charged."

Mr. Giles, of Boston, is now speaking in the House, in reply to Caleb Cushing.[5] He speaks with a great deal of force and spirit.

I have no leisure to write more, being somewhat closely occupied with the Convention. Depend upon it, however, that the cause is right onward in Massachusetts.

Truly, thy friend,
John G. Whittier

Source: The National Era, January 28, 1847. Printed with the caption, "Massachusetts Liberty Convention."

1. Identifications for the following list are: Alden B. Eggleston, a minister from Franklin County; Abel Bliss from Hampden County; Stephen P. Andrews (1812–1886), an abolitionist and writer, who worked in Texas to free slaves; James Ford from Plymouth County; Giles Pease (b. 1804?), a Congregational minister, who was an agent for the abolitionists in Sandwich, Massachusetts; Mason Stone, from Bristol County; Martin Torrey, a deacon; Charles Churchill, a colonel from Berkshire County; Richard Hildreth (1807–1865), a writer and abolitionist who founded the Boston *Atlas* in 1832 and later wrote a six-volume history of the United States; and William H. Brewster, a minister from Lowell, Massachusetts.

2. Caleb Swan (1793–1870), a physician from Easton, Massachusetts, joined the Liberty party in 1840. He ran for Congress on the Free Soil ticket and later served in the Massachusetts state legislature.

3. Henry Bibb (b. 1815), an escaped slave from Georgia, had come to Detroit in 1842 and lectured for several years for the Michigan Anti-Slavery Society. In 1847 he lectured in the East. He published *A Narrative of the Life and Adventures of Henry Bibb, an American Slave* (New York, 1849) and later worked in Canada.

4. Joseph C. Lovejoy (1805–1871) worked as a pastor at Cambridgeport, Massachusetts, from 1843 to 1853. With another brother, Owen, he published a memoir of his martyred brother Elijah in 1838.

5. Joel Giles (1804–1882), a lawyer from Townsend, Massachusetts, served in the Massachusetts House for many terms and was also a member of the Constitutional Convention of 1853.

514. To the National Era

[Boston, January 20, 1847]

I write from the midst of the evening session of the great convention. The noble hall is thronged to overflowing, and Joshua Leavitt is speaking with great force and pertinency in defence and exposition of the principles and action of the Liberty party. He has spoken of the patience and long suffering with which Abolitionists for many years endeavored to obtain anti-slavery action in Congress and elsewhere from the candidates of the two great political parties. The utter folly of this, he illustrated by the case of Caleb Cushing, urging on the Mexican war, and of Daniel Webster making his obeisance to slavery under the "October sun." His remarks are upon a series of resolutions defining the views of the Liberty party. He has just closed an efficient speech. He is followed by Wm. F. Channing, (a worthy son of the lamented Dr. William Channing,) in favor of an amendment of the resolutions.[1]

We have next a series of resolutions on the Mexican war, drawn up by Samuel E. Sewall, Esq., our Liberty candidate for Governor.[2]

21st 1st mo.

I was not able, on account of ill health, to remain until the Convention closed last evening, but a friend has handed me the following sketch of the proceedings, after the reading of the resolutions on the Mexican war:

Mr. Lovejoy of Cambridge, said he wanted to support these last resolutions. He had heard of a farmer, who came to the city and went into a store to buy a catechism, but by mistake, bought a work on military tactics. He carried it home, and, in the evening, directed his son, John, to commence it aloud; but, instead of "What is the chief end of man?" he began, "Right about face! forward march!" "Stop, John!" said the farmer, "that aint catechism; but I am thinking it's just what my family ought to do, for we have gone the wrong way long enough!" Now, he (Mr. L.) thought that such a portion of *catechism* would do good if it were read in every family, from Mr. Polk's down to the humblest in the land. Mr. L. then asked, "Does the 'one idea' of this Convention comprehend the subject of the Mexican war?" He thought it did.

(Some dozen of the Mexican volunteers here pushed into the hall, commenced interrupting the speaker. The chairman told them at least the civil power was above military misrule, and called upon them to desist. This being disregarded, there was a sudden movement of the assembly, betokening a determination to take prompt measures for ejecting them from the hall; the police interposed, and quiet was restored.)

Mr. L. then went on to speak of the disgraceful nature of the war, having for its end neither glory nor profit, but the mere accession of slave territory.

Mr. Innis of Salem, added a few remarks, and was followed by Mr..Bibb, who took the stand amid loud cheers, and commenced by singing a few stanzas of a liberty song.

Mr. Bailly, of Newbury, was then introduced to the audience, as having recently joined the Liberty party.[3] On rising, he said: "My friend Bibb has told you that he is a fugitive. I, too, am a fugitive from slavery! Last fall I was a member of the Whig Convention! I now stand here to represent the Liberty party of West Newbury! It was the course of that convention that changed my views, and induced me to leave the Whig party forever. Always a friend to the abolition of slavery, I trusted to Whig promises, till I found that I was connected with a body as pro-slavery in its tendency as the Democratic party itself.

(A voice from the audience here asked, "What have the Whigs done that is so bad?")

"Some gentleman asks, 'What have the Whigs done that is bad?' I would ask what have they ever done that is good? I left them, for I had no confidence in their leaders. Old Massachusetts, God bless her! God forbid that she should be in the rear in the cause of Liberty and Freedom! But what do we see? Maine and New Hampshire are outstripping her! God grant she may not suffer this long, but may she stand forth, as she ought, the foremost and the leader! One word in relation to our organization. Do not allow the Whigs to frighten any of you from it. They call us 'partisans!' What then? So long as we are on the right side, what matters it?

"I have said that I am a fugitive from slavery! I am so, and I have found refuge in the broad and free principles of the Liberty party, and I pray that others may do the same!"

Mr. Cummings [Cummins] next occupied a short time in support of the resolution.[4] He said it was the duty of Christians to endeavor to stop the war at once, and to act decidedly, so as, if possible, to destroy the effect of precedent that has been furnished by the Government.

Mr. Osgood followed, on the same resolution.[5] He deplored the effects of the war, here and through the land—a war, the effect of which was to extend and perpetuate slavery. He had taken hold of Abolition when it was small; but, thank God, it had increased and grown until its branches overspread the whole land.

Mr. Bibb followed in some eloquent remarks; and the meeting closed at about half past 10 o'clock.

In the afternoon session of the Convention, the sum of One Thousand and Fifty Dollars was raised in cash and subscriptions, to carry on the cause in Massachusetts.

A letter from a friend in Washington, announcing his satisfaction at the appearance of the National Era, was read to the Convention, and was received with hearty applause.

J. G. W.

Source: The *National Era*, January 28, 1847. Printed with the caption, "Massachusetts Liberty Convention."

1. William F. Channing (1820–1901), after receiving a medical degree in 1844, had worked with Dr. Henry Bowditch in editing *Latimer's Journal* in 1843–1844. He became an active Free Soiler and in later years was noted for his scientific inventions, one of them being a fire alarm system.

2. Whittier, along with Richard Hildreth and W. H. Brewster, wrote a series of resolutions which were approved by the convention. The resolutions on the Mexican War said that the war was unjust and inhuman, that it was a citizen's duty not to aid such a war, and that Congress should refuse to vote supplies and require the President to withdraw the troops and offer peace.

3. Perhaps Ebenezer C. Baily (1818–1881), a shoe manufacturer from Newbury.

4. Hiram Cummins (b. 1794), a minister from Duxbury, served as a general agent for the Massachusetts Liberty party.

5. Nahum Osgood (b. 1806), a butcher from Salisbury, Massachusetts, was noted for his strength and eccentric personality. He later became an enthusiastic supporter of the Republican party.

515. To the National Era

Amesbury, Mass., February 1, 1847

The resolution appropriating $20,000 for the benefit of the volunteers of the Massachusetts regiment, has at length been *rejected* in our Legislature, by a vote of 191 to 47.

In the Boston Daily Whig of the 28th ultimo, is the report of an able argument by Charles Sumner, before the Supreme Court of Massachusetts, against the validity of enlistments in the volunteer regiment.[1] It was made on the 25th; and the next day the Court decided in favor of one of its points, viz: that a minor or ward could not be held in the regiment.

Immediately after the adjournment of our late Convention, the State Liberty Committee, therein chosen, met together, and made arrangements for a thorough organization of the friends of liberty throughout the Commonwealth. A general agent (Hiram Cummings [Cummins], who has long been engaged in the service) was selected, and an agency committee, consisting of Dr. Swan, Wm. F. Channing, and Henry B. Stanton, appointed, to confer with and advise him, and to authorize persons in the several counties, who are capable of rendering efficient service to the cause, to act as local agents and lecturers. The general agent is to make monthly reports to the committee. Under this arrangement, we hope to call out, at the next election, a greatly increased vote. Certainly, our prospects were never so good as at the present time. A

strong anti-slavery feeling pervades the community. Thousands
are almost persuaded to act with us. At all events, we feel that
all who really love liberty, abhor slavery, and fervently seek
the well being of their fellow men, although, as yet, their practice may not, in our apprehension, conform to their faith,
are, in truth, with us. Our political action is only one mode of
working out the anti-slavery feeling—a translation of the
thought of liberty into a deed. One of the resolutions adopted
by the late Convention in Boston presents our movement in
its true light:

Resolved That the Liberty party was framed by men who
had devoted themselves to the abolition of slavery, and who
had pledged themselves to do all that is lawfully in their
power for this object; and the design of the Liberty party was
not to supersede or dispence with any moral, or religious, or
personal efforts, but to add to them all the power of combined and organized political action; in a word, to supply the
hand to break the chains, as the other means shall have disposed the heart of the nation to do justice.

During my stay in Boston, I attended a meeting for public
worship in the Washingtonian Hall, Bromfield street. While in
search of it, I blundered upon a congregation of freethinkers,
and leaving them, came near taking my seat in a hall consecrated to Mormonism. What I might have discovered next in
the city of "notions," had not a friend directed me to the
place sought for, I can only conjecture. The speaker at Washingtonian Hall was William H. Channing, who has long been
known as a zealous advocate of human liberty.[2] After reading
a portion of scripture, he spoke for an hour or more earnestly
and eloquently. He dwelt upon the special opportunities which
the world, at different periods, had enjoyed of realizing the
ideal of Christianity—the seasons of refreshing, of revelation,
and outpouring of the Divine Spirit, which it had suffered to
pass, without permanent benefit. The present time he regarded
as more full of hope and promise than any which had ever
gladdened the heart of humanity. The light of a long prophe-
sied millennium was kindling the world's horizon. The age
begetting a faith without love, as that of cold philosophy and
earthward-looking skepticism, had passed away, and the
brotherhood of man, the paternal relations of God, and the
beautiful humanities of the Gospel of Christ, were beginning
to be recognized as the foundation of a true faith and a holy
practice. The world's heart had been touched and softened.
The literature of the age was no longer scoffing and skeptical;
it was becoming reverent and devout, and at the same time

deeply imbued with the benign element of charity and good
will to man. The Holy Spirit was moving once more upon the
waters; a miracle was vouchsafed to us in this latter day. He
closed with an earnest exhortation to his hearers to be "mind-
ful of the heavenly vision," to put in practice their faith in
Providence and Grace, and *live* the commandments of the
Beloved Son of God, who taught his disciples to love one
another, even as he loved them.

I was struck by the speaker's eulogium upon a class of men
who have been heretofore everywhere spoken against—the poor
Anabaptists of the Reformation. He claimed for them the
merit of having seen clearly the truth which Luther and Calvin
did not always practically admit—that Christianity was intended to bless this world as well as the next; that it discounten-
anced alike the spiritual depotism of the Pope and the temporal
tyranny of Protestant nobles.

William H. Channing is well known as a disciple of Charles
Fourier, and a strenuous and sincere advocate of social reorga-
nization.[3] His influence over his friends and associates cannot
but be of a salutary kind. He clearly perceives that the only
hope of the world's redemption from its sin and sorrow, its
public and social evils, is in the Gospel of Christ—the good
tidings foretold by prophets and announced by angels. There
was a deep significance in the remark of the excellent Legh
Richmond,[4] when he visited the establishment of the philanthropic Owen,[5] at New Lanark. Admitting the benevolent
intentions of its projector, he expressed his belief that the
scheme would fail, for *"there was no Christ in it."*

The news by the late arrival, of suffering and actual starvation in Ireland, is of the most distressing nature. Can there
not be something done in this country to assist the liberal and
generous-hearted in Great Britain, in relieving this vast and
terrible want? The details of the dreadful calamity—sickness,
hunger, nakedness, actual starvation—as I find them in my file
of English papers, are almost incredible. The London Friend
of the last month contains an affecting account of the labors
of a deputation of Friends, who are now traversing the suffering districts, and affording such relief as they are able to offer.
To save the lives of the starving thousands is the first duty;
but the British Government is imperatively called upon to
take prompt and decisive measures for preventing a recurrence of this miserable state of things. Three centuries of mis-
government and oppression have made the Irish peasant
what he is—alternately a terror and a burden to the Government—his very existence hanging upon the contingency of a

favorable season for his potato patch. There is a taint of blood on the landed estates of Ireland. Founded in robbery and violence, they have been held in succession by reckless, extravagant, absentee landlords. Sharman Crawford, one of the worthy and generous exceptions to this remark, in a letter to Lord John Russell,[6] traces every evil in the present condition of Ireland to the unnatural and unjust relations between landlord and tenant, established by the proprietors of the forfeited estates of the original Irish landowners, and continued down to the present time by their successors. In the true spirit of a Christian philanthropist, he remarks; "If we, the landlords of the present day, have by inheritance the estates of our forefathers, and enjoy the rights and privileges attached to the possession of landed property, we cannot throw off the responsibility attached to their misdeeds. I, for one, shrink not from a full acknowledgement of that responsibility." He goes on to propose the enactment of laws *making the property and estates of the country responsible for the employment of all its laborers.* This proposition is not without its precedent. Just previous to the reign of Elizabeth,[7] the disorganization of society and lawless outrage, from want of employment, existed to as fearful an extent in England as they now do in Ireland. The law of 43 Elizabeth was enacted; the estates became directly responsible for the employment or feeding of the people, and the suffering and disorder gave place to comparative comfort and quiet.

J. G. W.

Source: The *National Era,* February 11, 1847. Printed with the caption, "Letters from the East.—No. 5."

1. Sumner's argument was reprinted in his collected works as "Immorality of Enlistments in the Massachusetts Regiment of Volunteers for the Mexican War."

2. William H. Channing (1810–1884), a nephew of William Ellery Channing, was a Christian socialist. He spent a few months at Brook Farm, became a convert to Fourierism and headed the Boston Religious Union of Associationists in 1847. He edited many socio-religious magazines and wrote memoirs of his uncle and Margaret Fuller.

3. Charles Fourier (1772–1837), a French social reformer, influenced many groups in the United States with his ideas on social harmony and communal living.

4. Legh Richmond (1772–1827), an English clergyman and writer, achieved popularity in the early nineteenth century with his tales of village life.

5. Robert Owen (1771–1858), an English businessman and social reformer, introduced educational and social reforms for his mill workers at New Lanark, Scotland.

6. John Russell (1792–1878), an English statesman then serving as Prime Minister.

7. Elizabeth I (1533–1603) ruled as queen of England from 1558 to 1603.

516. To the National Era

Amesbury, Mass., February 5, 1847

The proposition of Senator Cilley to withdraw the troops of the United States from Mexico, was an excellent one; but I am sorry to see his *explanation* of it.[1] Something of allowance must undoubtedly be made for the habits of thought and feelings of a military man; but, as a member of the Liberty party of the North, I cannot do otherwise than utterly repudiate the suggestion of drilling and disciplining our armies on the borders of Mexico, for the purpose of a more successful invasion than the present promises to be. The view of Joshua R. Giddings seems to me the true one: Withdraw our armies from Mexico, not by way of preparation for a more murderous onslaught hereafter, but for the purpose of opening the way to a peaceable adjustment of the questions at issue between the two nations. In such a course, on the part of the United States—successful as the American arms have been in every contest, and with the American flag already floating over half the territory of Mexico; and taking into consideration the immense superiority of our land and naval forces, and of our resources for carrying on the war—there could be no disgrace and no concession incompatible with true honor. On the contrary, it would be in the highest degree magnanimous and praiseworthy. It would do more to make our Government and democratic institutions respected and honored throughout the world, than fifty Palo Alto and Monterey victories. The Boston Whig says, and I fear very justly, that "Senator Cilley has yielded to the war-storm." Certain it is that he can look for no response to his sentiments from the anti-slavery men of the North.

A Senator is to be chosen by our Legislature at its present session—the term of Governor Davis expiring this year. I have some faint hope that the person selected may, in a degree at least, represent the rising feeling on the subject of slavery. There are hearty friends of freedom in the Legislature, who, although nominally Whigs, are not disposed to follow their party in a wrong direction. Out of it, there are many who sympathize with them. Whether they will be able to make an advance step in the election of Senator, is certainly very doubtful. The great overshadowing interests of trade and manufactures, blight and dwarf the humanity of Massachusetts. Here as elsewhere, the greed of Gain, the intense selfishness of Traffick, have a natural aversion to the doctrine that the Rights of Persons are more sacred than those of Property. There are noble, and generous, and liberty-loving men among the merchant princes and corporation lords of our metropolis; but far too many seem disposed to verify the sarcasm of McFingal's assertion that there are:

> "Merchants, who for Satan's aid
> Would make him partner in their trade;
> Hang out their sign, with goodly show,
> Inscribed with Beelzebub and Co."[2]

Massachusetts needs, as her rightful representative at this time, in the United States Senate, men of "sterner stuff" than I fear she is likely to have—men not likely to talk to death a Wilmot proviso,[3] or to pledge the North against Liberty, "under an October sun"—men, in short, whom the skilfullest manipulators of your great Congressional kneading-trough at Washington could never work up into dough-faces.

Last night, a great meeting was held in Faneuil Hall, by those in favor of the recall of our troops from Mexico.[4] Addresses were made by Charles Sumner, Judge Williams, Theodore Parker, and others.[5] The meeting was shamefully disturbed by the riotous conduct of a large body of the "volunteers," who interrupted, and, in some instances, entirely drowned the voice of the speakers. Colonel Cushing has a courage of which Falstaff could not boast, if he is willing to "march through Coventry" with such a graceless set of vagabonds as are collected in the "Massachusetts regiment."[6]

I see by the People's Journal (London) that the emancipated blacks in British Guiana have been setting a good example to white laborers everywhere. Large numbers have made themselves free-holders, through co-partnership or association; and instead of toiling on as hired laborers on the old estates of their former masters, have become proprietors themselves, either in partnership or on the principle of the Fourier associations in this country. The editors of the Journal copy from a list printed by order of the Government, extending over twenty pages of foolscap paper, such instances as the following: "*Perseverance* estate, of 470 acres, purchased by 63 associated laborers; *Littlefield* estate, of 500 acres, by 12 partners; *Lovely Lass* estate, 500 acres, by 14 associated laborers; *North Brook* estate, 500 acres, by 84 laborers." These estates, judging from the prices, from $1,700 to $10,000, were those which had been worn out by improvident cultivation.

The Committee of the British and Foreign Anti-Slavery

Society have issued an address strongly recomending the principle of abstinence from the products of slave labor. They say that "it must be obvious to all reflecting minds, that it is the demand which exists for slave produce, which is the chief support of slavery. It is this which keeps open the slave markets. May it not, therefore, be said, that to the commission of a great amount of crime, and the infliction of unparalleled suffering on a large portion of mankind, do the consumers of slave produce, however unintentionally, furnish the motive?"

They regard the late removal of the duties on slave-grown sugar as a measure directly calculated to increase the slave trade, and strengthen slavery.

J. G. W.

Source: The *National Era*, February 18, 1847. Printed with the caption, "Mr. Cilley—Senator from Massachusetts—Public Meeting in Boston—British Guiana."

1. Senator Cilley had asked that United States troops be withdrawn from Mexico and in clarification of his proposal stated that the invasion was dispersing our forces too much and that we should withdraw to reorganize and better train our troops. He hoped that such a move would cause Mexico to ask for peace.

2. From Canto 1 of John Trumbull's mock-heroic *M'Fingal* (1776). The correct quotation is:

> "Merchants who, for his friendly aid,
> Would make him partner in their trade;
> Hang out their signs in goodly show
> Inscribed with Beelzebub and Co."

3. A reference to John Davis, the Massachusetts senator whose address to the Senate in its final hours prevented a consideration of the Wilmot proviso in 1846. Davis was, however, reelected to serve a six-year term in the Senate.

4. Held on February 4, 1847.

5. John M. Williams (1780–1868) served as chief justice of the Court of Common Pleas and was then commissioner of insolvency, serving from 1844 to 1856.

Theodore Parker (1810–1860), a Unitarian clergyman who became a Transcendentalist, devoted himself not only to religious education, but to social and economic problems. He made fiery speeches against slavery and throughout the 1850's participated in attempts to free fugitive slaves in Boston.

6. *I Henry IV*, IV, ii, 39.

517. To Joseph Tinker Buckingham

Amesbury, February 8, 1847

The condition of the people of Ireland at this time is well known doubtless to all thy readers. The melancholy details of the extreme of human suffering, need no comment. The head is sick and the heart is faint in view of this dreadful apocalypse of woe.

By the last packet, appeals are made in this country for aid in rescuing thousands from actual starvation,—from that slow death of hunger which endured by Eugulino and his children, has made Pisa's tower of Famine a horror to the world.[1]

Benevolent men and tenderhearted women, who have tasked
to the utmost their own ability to relieve the distress around
them, have appealed to the sympathy of the men and women
of the United States. In the name of our common humanity,
they beg us to unite with them in succoring those who are
ready to perish.

That the fearful responsibility rests upon the government
of Great Britain of much of the suffering of Ireland, is undoubtedly true.

Wise legislation in the past might have prevented this great
calamity, by placing the laboring population of Ireland in a
position to bear without actual starvation, the temporary
failure of a potato crop. But our duty to relieve present suffering is none the less imperative. If we have the hearts of men—
if our Christianity is not a mere cloak for selfishness—we *must*
respond to the agony of supplication which comes to us from
a people actually wasting away from the face of the earth.

Allow me to suggest the propriety of calling a public meeting of the citizens of Boston, for the purpose of raising money
for this object. Let that meeting send out an appeal to the
people of the country towns to co-operate with those of
Boston. My word for it, they will do it, cheerfully, promptly.
Whatever is done must be done speedily. If suitable measures
are taken, from $50,000 to $100,000 can be raised in Massachusetts before the packet of the 1st of next month sails.[2]

Lest any fear should be entertained that the funds so raised
might be misapplied, I would state that a deputation of the
Society of Friends, headed by William Forster, a man whose
character commands universal respect, and in whom a heart
of benevolence is combined with sound judgment and great
prudence, are now engaged in the work of distribution in
Ireland, and supplies entrusted to their care would be certain
of a judicious and careful application. At any rate, by a little
inquiry, it will be easy to find a suitable channel for whatever
is contributed.

In the hope that my suggestion may accord with thy own
view, and with those of the benevolent and liberal citizens of
Boston, I am truly thy friend,

John G. Whittier

Source: The Boston *Courier*, February 9, 1847.
1. See Dante's *Inferno*, Canto XXXIII.
2. Whittier made a similar appeal in the *National Era* on January 28 and March
4, 1847. His Amesbury Friends Meeting raised fifty dollars for the relief of victims
and similar appeals throughout the country raised nearly two million dollars.

518. To the National Era

Amesbury, February 12, 1847

Since my last date, the election of United States Senator has taken place in our Legislature. Gov. Davis was re-elected by a small majority. Joshua Leavitt, the Liberty candidate, received seven votes.

The election in New Hampshire is now near at hand; and great exertions are made by all parties, in their triangular warfare. The old pro-slavery managers of the Democratic party are denying their own acts of infamy in voting for the gag rule in Congress, and for slavery resolutions in the State Legislature. They studiously endeavor to keep in the background the real question at issue. The Whigs, having been foolish enough to nominate Daniel Webster for the Presidency, get little credit for their professions of anti-slavery. The Liberty men and Independents, as far as I can learn, act in entire harmony, and I confidently expect that they will largely increase their vote.[1]

I learn with deep regret, by the last arrival from England, of the death of Joseph John Gurney, of Norwich.[2] He was a generous, warmhearted philanthropist, and an active member of the British and Foreign Anti-Slavery Society. He was a brother of the celebrated Elizabeth Fry.[3]

J. G. W.

Source: The *National Era*, February 18, 1847.
1. See Letter No. 523 for an account of the election.
2. Gurney died on January 4, 1847.
3. Elizabeth Fry (1780–1845), a Quaker minister, was noted for her reform work with prisoners in London.

519. To Ann Elizabeth Wendell

Amesbury February 21, 1847

My dear Cousin,

I ought to have answered thy letter at once; and intended to do so, but some people intervened and the matter was deferred like duties of more vital importance to "a more convenient season."[1] I have since been able to write but little, and that mostly for the papers, and I have scarcely answered a letter for a month past. I dread to touch a pen. Whenever I do, it increases the dull wearing pain in the head which I am scarcely ever free from. So do not think that I have undervalued thy kind epistle. Far from it.

I was sorry to hear of thy mother's severe illness. She really seemed quite comfortable last winter when I left Philadelphia, but she has been very feeble for a long time. I hope she may be spared to you yet longer.[2] She has been a kind, good mother, and has I believe earnestly sought to promote the temporal and spiritual welfare of her family. Mother! how much there is in that word! Oh! If there is one earthly blessing for which more than another I feel thankful, it is that she is still spared me to whom I can apply that endearing name.

My deepest sympathy has been called out by hearing of the pecuniary embarrassment and business trials of thy father and brother. I hope they have surmounted them. Thy father has had a hard life-work; and has deserved success. I was at Dover this winter; and had the pleasure of hearing him spoken of in the kindest manner, in a circle of the most respected citizens, as a generous hearted and worthy man, whose misfortune had been to trust too much to the honor and honesty of others; and whose wish was to help and do good to all. It was at Daniel Osborne's.[3]

What a sad state of things in Ireland! We have been trying to do something in this region. Our little meeting here has raised about $50. The people of other denominations are also moving. The cheerfulness with which almost everybody contributes to this object looks well for human nature. Oh, surely there is good in all—the hardest heart is not wholly stone. The heart that can sympathize with human suffering and yearn to relieve it, cannot be wholly depraved. The longer I live I see the evil in myself in a clearer light, and more that is good in others: and if I do not grow better, I am constrained to be more charitable. I shudder sometimes at my own fierce rebukes of wrongdoers, when I consider my own weaknesses, and sins of omission as well as commission.

Elizabeth is now at Boston in the care of Dr. Channing. She is much as she has been for a year past. Mother is quite comfortable; she does not get out much this winter except in very pleasant weather.

Our paper at Washington will doubtless succeed. I should have gone on this winter, but for the state of my health and the difficulty of leaving home on my mother's account. I write but little for it and have not been able to revise or correct even that little. But, if in the Providence of God I am not to do much more for the cause of freedom, I am deeply grateful for the privilege I have enjoyed of giving the strength of my youth and manhood to it. The cause is destined to triumph; and present appearances indicate that the triumph is near.

The action in the Pa. Legislature in relation to fugitive

slaves is most gratifying.[4]   The exertions of the Committee
of the Meeting for Sufferings undoubtedly contributed much
to this result. Oh! that our Friends generally would feel their
great responsibility in this matter. They have influence sufficient to change the whole legislation of the country, if it was
only fully exerted.

I am glad to have such favorable accounts of thy health.
Abby Newhall says thee seems really well;[5] it must be a great
satisfaction to thee to be able to wait on thy mother in her
illness. I almost fear to ask about Margaret's child; it was very
sick I understood from Abby N.[6]

I have not yet seen Jos. Cartland since his return from P. I
had a letter from Moses the other day. I fear he will be disowned for his marriage, which, considering all things, will be
really hard.

With love to all and especially to thy mother, in which
my mother joins me, I am as ever thy aff cousin

J. G. Whittier

Remember me kindly to all who may take the trouble to inquire after me.

J. G. W.

What a sudden thing is the death of J. J. Gurney? He is
spoken of as one of the best and most benevolent of men. I
do hope that whatever errors of doctrine he may have entertained will now be forgotten and that Friends will now only
cherish the remembrance of the life of a good man.

Manuscript: University of Virginia. Published, in Part: Pickard, *Life*, pp. 318–319.

1. Acts 24:25, modified.
2. Anna Wendell died on March 9, 1847.
3. Daniel Osborne married Caroline Cartland, the sister of Moses Cartland, in August 1840.
4. During its session the Pennsylvania legislature passed a series of resolutions fining anyone for attempting to recapture a fugitive slave and prohibiting judges from handling fugitive slave cases.
5. This is probably Hannah J. Newhall. See Letter No. 196, note 5.
6. Margaret Wendell Maule lost three of her children during the 1840's.

520. To the National Era

Amesbury, Mass., February 24, 1847

I notice that one of the South Carolina Representatives, in
a speech against the Wilmot proviso, attributes the abolitionism of Thomas Jefferson to the influence which his French
associates and correspondents exerted upon him. Our Northern pro-slavery democrats, of the New Hampshire school, will

scarcely thank him for it, as they had always maintained that
abolitionism is entirely of British growth; an offshoot from
the "Royal Oak of England," and not a slip from the liberty
tree of Revolutionary France. Will all due deference to them
however, I have little doubt of the correctness of the view
taken by the South Carolina gentleman, so far as Jefferson is
concerned. His most intimate and valued friends among the
revolutionists of France were warm Abolitionists, and many
of them members of the famous society of the "Friends of the
Blacks." The philosophic Condorcet, the Bishop of Chartres,
Lafayette, Mirabeau, Robespierre, Petion, the good Duke of
Rochefoucauld, Necker, Vergniaud, the Abbes Raynal and
Sieyes, and the enthusiastic leader of the Girondins, Jean
Pierre Brissot, were all Abolitionists, in theory and in practice.[1] Lafayette, on coming into possession of slaves in the
West Indies, emancipated them; and George Washington warmly commended him for his benevolence of heart in so doing,
adding that he intended never to purchase another slave. The
same champion of freedom in America as well as Europe
assured Thomas Clarkson, at his last interview with him, that,
had he supposed America would have encouraged the growth
of slavery, as she had done, he would never have lifted his hand
in her behalf.

One of the most active and efficient members of the Society of "Friends of the Blacks" was Brissot[2] —a man who has
scarcely had justice done him by historians. He was not a
brilliant orator; he sought no laurels in the battle field; he
owed the great influence which he unquestionably exerted
more to the sincerity of his faith in Democracy, and his steady
consistency in maintaining it, than to any of those qualities
of person or intellect which captivate the affections of the
multitude. Clarkson, in his History of the Abolition of the
Slave Trade, gives a picture of him, which I have no doubt is
strictly just. He says the last person he saw, on leaving France
to return home from his anti-slavery mission, was Brissot,
who accompanied him to his carriage. He speaks of him as a
man of plain and modest appearance, of gentle domestic
habits: "In his own family, he set an amiable example as a
husband and father. On all occasions he was a faithful friend.
He was particularly watchful over his private conduct. From
the simplicity of his appearance, and the severity of his morals, he was called 'the Quaker' in all the circles which I fre-
quented. He was a man of deep feeling; charitable to the poor,
as far as his slender income permitted. But his benevolence
went beyond usual bounds. He was no patriot in the ordinary

sense of the word; for he took the habitable globe for his
country, and wished to consider every foreigner as his brother."[3]

This is exalted praise, and from an unimpeachable source.
It is not generally known that Brissot visited this country in
1788. He was then a young man, an enthusiastic admirer of
free institutions; and, desirous of seeing them in practice, he
appears to have travelled through the principal States of the
Union. At Philadelphia, he was delighted with the society
of the excellent Warner Mifflin—one of the truest and noblest
men of any age or country; and it is not improbable that
from him he derived that abhorrence of slavery, in all its
forms, which he so strongly manifested while the leader of the
pure and philanthropic republicans of France. He visited
George Washington, and gives, in his journal published in 1791,
an interesting account of his interview with that great and
clear-sighted man. He conversed freely with him on questions
of slavery, and mentions the anti-slavery societies which were
formed in Pennsylvania: "This great man," says M. Brissot,
"said to me, that he *rejoiced at what was doing in other States
on the subject, and that he sincerely desired the extension of it
to his own.*" Brissot suggested the expediency of forming an
anti-slavery society in Virginia. "*He told me that* He Desired
The Formation Of Such A Society, And That He Would Second It."[4]

The Father of his Country does not seem from this to have
regarded chattel slavery as the corner stone of the republican
edifice. And in these days of "Progressive Democracy," one
fairly shudders at the audacity of a foreign Abolition emissary
undertaking to get up an anti-slavery society in Virginia, and
actually getting the promise of a slaveholding President to
aid in such a project!

I am happy to learn by the last arrival, that Sweden has
abolished slavery in her island of St. Bartholomew, the only
place where it existed. This is a good movement. Holland will
soon follow; some of her ablest men are discussing the question. France is slowly but certainly approaching the same consummation. Slavery is doomed everywhere.

I have just received a letter from James Richardson, the
anti-slavery traveller in Africa, of whose noble and daring
efforts in the cause of humanity I have spoken in a late number of the Era.[5] He is about to return to the scene of his
heroic labors in the Great Desert; and inquires of me for a
young and devoted American Abolitionist who would be willing to accompany him. He wishes him to be an educated man.

I cannot forbear quoting a single paragraph from his letter:

"It is a painful lesson of Providence, that, whilst liberty fled from the Old World, to find a refuge for herself in the New, the end of it should be the building up of the most gigantic system of slavery on your free shores the world ever saw! It does immense injury to liberty in the world. Many of us have been awakened from our dreams of universal rights and universal suffrage by the horrors of the slave system, under the influence of the democracy of the slave States of the South."

I see that William Howitt, in his People's Journal, proposes the getting up of a remonstrance against American slavery, to be signed by three millions of citizens of Great Britain, and forwarded to the President of the United States. Let not our astute sentinels of American institutions [sniff] the danger from afar of an attempt to injure anything that is really republican and worth keeping among us. William Howitt is a Quaker and a Democrat. A few years ago, he sat with five others in a room in Manchester, and there he proposed a national petition to Parliament, praying the right of suffrage for the British adult male population; and he afterwards betook himself to solitude, to frame the prayer of the British people to their rulers. A few months afterwards, and he saw that petition borne down to the House of Commons upon the shoulder of *sixteen* sturdy men—the monster petition banded around with thick ropes—signed by *three million and a half* of the British people—cheered by the assembled multitude as it passed along—obliged to be parted in twain ere it could be passed through the doors of the House of Commons, (a full House of members had assembled to receive it,) and, though they granted not its prayer, still, within and without the doors of that House it created a conviction and a power which have imperceptibly swayed the subsequent work of peaceable and just legislation.

He would now like to see a remonstrance against slavery, addressed to the American people, signed by *three millions* of the British people!

The accounts from Ireland, I see, are becoming, if possible, more afflicting. A nation is starving. Thou wilt see that Boston has responded to the call of your great Washington meeting.[6] The impulse is reaching the small country towns, and the press and pulpit are everywhere speaking out in behalf of our perishing brethren on the other side of the Atlantic. The steamer which leaves on the 1st of next month will carry out large sums of money.

The measures for *immediate* relief, proposed by Lord John Russell at the opening of the Parliament, are liberal and efficient. The policy of the Government in relation to the employment of the destitute on public works is to be abandoned, and present relief afforded to the suffering, through local committees, without exacting work in return. The laborers are thus to be left.free to work on their own patches or for the farmers, and thus prepare for the next harvest. Lord Brougham[7] estimates the expense of this relief, for the year to come, at from £10,000,000 to £15,000,000. £50,000 is to be loaned to the landlords for seed for the new crop. In his plans for the permanent relief of Ireland, the Premier has omitted the only things which can possibly save that afflicted country from a recurrence of the dreadful destitution which now shocks the world. The soil of Ireland should be made to support its poor. The estates should be held responsible for the employment of all the laborers. The plan of Lord John Russell is, in reality, one for the relief of the landlords, and not of the laborers. The latter have a rightful claim upon the soil—a claim stronger and more sacred than the grants of Elizabeth or the sequestrations of the Long Parliament. A change, radical and revolutionary, must be made in the tenure of landed property. Now is the time, when the terrible necessity overlooks all conventionalisms and old usages, to effect this change peaceably; for peaceably, or, as in France, with the smoke of burning mansions and the blood of aristocracy, it must sooner or later be made.

> "Slowly comes a hungry people, as a lion, creeping nigher,
> Glares at one who nods and winks behind a slowly-dying fire."[8]

J. G. W.

Source: The *National Era*, March 4, 1847. Printed with the caption, "Abolition of French Origin—Brissot and George Washington—Abolition of Swedish Slavery—Richardson, the African Traveller—Monster Petition—Ireland."

1. All these men were noted French Revolutionary leaders and thinkers, many of whom died during the French Revolution for their beliefs: Marquis de Condorcet (1734–1834) was a mathematician and philosopher; Jean Baptiste-Joseph de Lubersac (1740–1822) served as bishop of Chartres from 1780 to 1790; Lafayette (1757–1834) fought in the American Revolution; Maximilien François Marie Isidore de Robespierre (1758–1794) was the leader of the Jacobin party during the Revolution and instituted the "Reign of Terror"; Jerome Petion de Villeneuve (1753–1794) was the first president of the National Convention; Duc de Rochefoucauld (1747–1827) was a French philanthropist who was exiled in 1792; Jacques Necker (1732–1804) served as minister of finance; Pierre Victurnien Vergniaud (1759–1793) was an orator and revolutionist; Guillaume Raynal (1713–1796) was a French philosopher and historian; Emmanuel Sieyes (1748–1836) was

a revolutionary writer who also served under Napoleon; and Jacques Pierre Brissot (1754–1793) was the leader of the Girondist faction during the French Revolution.

2. Brissot founded the Society of the Friends of the Negro in 1788 and traveled to the United States to investigate slavery. He was finally executed for his opposition to the excesses of the Jacobins.

3. From Clarkson's *History of the Rise, Progress, and Accomplishments of the Abolition of the African Slave-Trade by the British Parliament* (London, 1808), II, 165–166.

4. *New Travels in the United States of America; Performed in 1788* (London, 1794), pp. 245–247.

5. James Richardson (1806–1851), an English abolitionist, traveled throughout Africa investigating the cause of and suggesting remedies for the slave trade. He had published a series of letters on his explorations and travels and, after his death, his wife, J. E. Richardson, published a number of books from his journals and writings.

Whittier had written an article on Richardson entitled "The Heroism of Philanthropy" in the January 14, 1847, *National Era* and had also written a poem, "Song of Slaves in the Desert," based on one of Richardson's letters (*National Era*, January 21, 1847).

6. A meeting of United States senators, representatives and supreme court judges, along with the vice-president, George M. Dallas, was held on February 9, 1847, in Washington to gather funds for the relief of famine in Ireland.

7. Henry Peter Brougham (1778–1868), Scottish jurist and statesman.

8. Alfred Tennyson, "Locksley Hall," lines 135–136.

521. To the National Era

Amesbury, Mass., March 1, 1847

The able conductors of "The Harbinger," the organ of the Associationists near Boston, I perceive, in their last paper take exceptions to a paragraph in one of my late letters, in which I allude to a remark of Legh Richmond, in relation to Robert Owen's establishment at Lanark.[1] This, our friends of the Harbinger characterize as "cant," and "the faded and tattered remnants of a strong and rigid fanaticism, well enough in its day and its way." Our Association friends have been themselves often charged with dealing in "cant:" but far be it from me to retort upon them the unkindness and misrepresentations of those who cannot comprehend their earnest enthusiasm, and who refuse to give the credit of sincerity to their profession of entire faith in the "new and strange" theories of the French Philosopher. Honoring as I do their devotion, self-sacrifice, and warm sympathy with suffering humanity, I shall not take offense at their criticism. The remark of Legh Richmond, and certainly my own endorsement of it, are to be understood in a general sense, as applicable to all schemes for the amelioration of the condition of society, which are not founded upon the perfect morality of the Gospel of Christ. I have never joined in the popular clamor against those who are so unfortunate as to doubt or disbelieve the divine origin of that Gospel; I have on all occasions, and at some

cost, vindicated their rights of free speech and fair hearing;
and have, at the risk of misapprehension and obloquy, rebuked
the intolerance and bitter spirit of some of their assailants,
who had undertaken to be God's avengers in the matter.
Fully sympathizing with the free and hopeful spirit of the
age, a humble and toiling member of that party of Reform
and Progress, which is the germ of the great Free Party of the
Future, I cannot, even for courtesy's sake, admit the correctness of the charge preferred against me, of clinging to the
"tattered remnants of a strong and rigid old fanaticism." I
reverence whatever is good and true and heroic in the past,
not because it is old, but because it brings with it the freshness
and newness of an immortal life, and it is not merely a part
of the past, but of the present and future also. And hence,
while I agree with Milton, in his terrible rebuke of those who
"go searching among the verminous and polluted rags dropped
overworn from the toiling shoulders of time, with which,
deformedly, to quilt and interlace the entire, the spotless, and
undecaying robe of Truth, the daughter, not of Time, but
of Heaven," I am constrained to believe, with him, that Truth
which can alone cure the ills of humanity is "bred up between
two grave and holy nurses, the doctrine and practice of the
Gospel of Christ."[2] If this is "fanaticism" and "cant," I am
content to bear the reproach of it, regretting only that I am
not more worthy to do so.

The last number of the Newburyport Herald contains a
letter from Hon. Robert Cross, of Marshall, Michigan, formerly a resident in Amesbury, giving a detailed account of an
unsuccessful attempt to recapture a family of fugitive slaves
in that place.[3] It seems that the family, consisting of a man,
his wife, and four children, had lived in the village for about
three years, and had a fair reputation for industry and sobriety. Four "hunters of Kentucky," headed by a lawyer belonging to Carroll county, in that State, attempted to break into
the house of the fugitive family, whereupon, an alarm was
raised, a black man was mounted on a horse, and sent through
the town, ringing a bell, and calling on the people to come to
the rescue of the family; and, in a brief space of time, the
people assembled to the number of several hundreds. The correspondent of the Herald, who was on the spot, says:

"The best-looking of the assailing party, who, as it afterwards appeared, was a lawyer by profession, and the grandson
of the alleged owner of the family, stood in the midst of the
throng. What he said was delivered in courteous and conciliatory terms, but it did not seem to meet the acquiescence
of his auditors. 'Fellow citizens,' said one of the multitude,

and he was one whose word would be taken for thousands, 'I move, as the sense of this meeting, that Crosswhite is a citizen of a Free State, and, as such must not be molested without our consent.' 'Ay' was the prompt reply. 'I also,' said the stranger, 'crave leave to submit a motion, and it is this: that the law of the land, whatever it is, be allowed to go into operation, without obstruction or confusion.' 'No,' was the loud whoop with which the proposal was answered. 'I move,' said another citizen, older than him who spoke first, and quite as high in public estimation, 'that, however the law may run, these gentlemen be made to understand, that we shall not allow one of our members to be carried away, by any persons or person, against his consent.' 'Ay,' was again the prompt shout of concurrence."

In the meantime, Crosswhite, the fugitive, had obtained a warrant against the assailants for breaking open his door; and another colored man, Hackett, for an assault made upon him by the Kentuckians, with Bowie knives and revolving pistols. The Justice declared, that in Michigan every man was presumed to be free; and that his house was his unassailable castle, and therefore fined the defendents one hundred dollars and costs. They were also adjudged guilty on the complaint for assault, and compelled to [recompense] for their appearance at the circuit court. After making provision for the indemnification of their sponsors, they mounted their horses, thankful for their escape from imprisonment, and moved off southerly, making no secret of their determination never to enter the State again on a similar errand. The correspondent of the Herald, an able lawyer, and who, while a resident of Massachusetts, was regarded as decidedly hostile to the antislavery party, says:

"The sympathy with the Crosswhites was universal, running through Whigs and Democrats, Yankees and Irish.

"This conflict between the sentiment of freedom and the law of the land was direct and palpable, unobstructed by the interposition of a single pretense or circumstance. The family were undoubtedly the slaves of the claimant. The wife has been the nurse of the younger of the party; he addressed her as an old familiar, and called her 'mother.' Crosswhite did not pretend that he had ever been manumitted, or that his escape from his master was in any way known or consented to. Nor was there any mistake as to the law; for, at the outset of the matter, not less than half a dozen lawyers were present, and stated the substance of it repeatedly. Nevertheless, in the minds of the people, there seemed no doubt as to the course which they were determined to pursue. Clergymen, lawyers, doctors, men of substance and men without a dollar seemed to accord in opinion, that the law of nature was of more binding efficacy than the statute of the Union.

"After the close of the judicial inquiry, the lawyer of the party expressed a wish to address the audience, and not the least extraordinary of these proceedings were his remarks, considering the position in which he stood. He avowed himself to be hostile to the system of slavery; claimed sympathy for its burdens and inconveniences; expressed a hope that it might soon be extirpated from Kentucky; and urged, as an apology for its continuance, that it was the work of their forefathers, and not the present generation. I know not, if similar feelings would have been exhibited by our people a year ago."

After speaking of the growing jealousy of slavery in the free States, the position of [Preston] King, of New York, and the unanimous passage of a resolution against the extension of slavery in the popular branch of the Michigan Legislature, he concludes with the suggestion that it "may be that this new distrust of the South will become a basis on which the whole population of the free States may unite, in a new and triumphant party. Such a party would have a noble corner stone, an hostility to the extension of the area, or, to speak in English, the 'threshing floor!' of slavery. And such a fundamental principle would draw to it the sympathies of all; would identify the party with those who have been distinguished in all the glorious periods of history, and conciliate for it the applause of the civilized world."

I am happy to see that the Liberty men of Southern Ohio have an able organ of their sentiments. The Herald, under the care of Stanley Matthews, is an admirable paper.[4] All its leading editorials evince the vigor and freshness of a strong and healthy mind. I sincerely hope the Liberty men of Ohio will give it the support which it deserves, and which the welfare of their cause demands. The Emancipator, thou wilt see, has made some valuable accessions to its editorial strength. J. C. Lovejoy, Henry B. Stanton, and S. E. Sewall, are to be contributors.

Our Legislature have adopted, by unanimous vote in both Houses, resolutions against the extension of slavery, and deprecating it as a moral and political evil, etc.

One of the saddest jokes of the season has been the presentation of a sword to Colonel Cushing, on the eve of his departure to aid in the invasion of Mexico, by such men as John A.

Bolles,[5] Esq., author of the Prize Essay on Peace, and Robert Rantoul, jun., member of the Peace Society, and President of the Society for the Abolition of Capital Punishment. How much more important to the cause of truth is the testimony of a life, than that of tongue and pen! Both of the gentlemen, above mentioned, I have not the slightest doubt, regard aggressive war as wicked and detestable; both abhor slavery; yet, as political partisans, they give their countenance to both. "I am puzzled," says Henry Beecher, in his Lectures to Young Men, "to know what will happen at death to the politic Christian, but most unchristian politician. Will both of his characters go heavenward together? Or shall he be sundered in two, as Solomon proposed to divide the contested infant?"[6]

J. G. W.

Source: The *National Era*, March 11, 1847. Printed with the caption, "The Harbinger—Slave Case in Marshall, Michigan—Liberty Papers—Peace and War Men."

1. The *Harbinger* was edited by George Ripley (1802–1880) from 1845 to 1849 as a successor to the *Dial*. It was published to spread the associationalist ideas of Charles Fourier. See Letter No. 515 for Whittier's initial comments.

2. John Milton, "Of Prelatical Episcopacy," *Complete Prose Works of John Milton* (Yale University Press, 1953–), I, 639.

3. See Letter No. 72, "*Recipient*."

4. Stanley Matthews (1824–1889), an Ohio lawyer, helped edit the *Ohio Morning Herald* from 1846 to 1849 in Cincinnati. He became a judge, served in the Civil War, was appointed to the United States Senate from 1877 to 1879, and was a member of the Supreme Court from 1881 until his death.

5. John A. Bolles (1809–1878), a Boston lawyer, served as Massachusetts secretary of state under Governor Morton in 1843. He later became active in the Free Soil party.

6. Henry Ward Beecher (1813–1887) in his *Seven Lectures to Young Men* (Cincinnati, 1844). The quotation, somewhat changed, is from lecture IV, "The Portrait Gallery," no. VII, "The Party Man," page 130. Beecher, a popular speaker, was appointed in October 1847 as minister to the Plymouth Church in Brooklyn. For the rest of his life he served this church, becoming the most popular pulpit minister of his day. His involvement in a parish scandal during the 1870's severely damaged his reputation.

522. To the National Era

Amesbury, Mass., March 10, 1847

The emancipation of slaves seems to be the settled policy of the world. Uruguay has decreed the final abolition of servitude; Mehemet Ali is said to have given freedom to his personal slaves;[1] and a petition has been adopted in the Danish Assembly, praying "that his Majesty lay before the States, at the next meeting, a project of a law, based on careful local inquiry, for a complete emancipation of the slaves in the Danish West India colonies." The speech of the President, Professor Clausen,[2] on putting this petition to vote, is worthy of a Christian statesman, and, as the following extract will show, presents a striking contrast to those of Colquitt,[3] and Cass, and Ingersoll,[4] in our own National Legislature:

"There are certain relations maintained; the existence of which is so diametrically opposed to the first principles of Christian right and equity, the first requisites of Christian civilization, that no one can be brought to tolerate them, but by averting thought and eye—were it possible for him to do so—from the degradation of human nature on the one hand, and the violation of Christianity on the other, that lie at the bottom of these relations. It appears to me, that one may be very free from everything that may be or is accounted as sickly sentimentalism, and yet seriously entertain the opinion, that a State, when it has once arrived at a certain point of well being, (so that it can procure the conditions of a dignified and even a pleasurable existance,) is stringently bound to rectify such relations; and that no great significance can be attached to that civilization on which it would pride itself, or to the Christian name which it would not willingly renounce, were it to suffer the continuance of a system, which I know not how to designate by any other epithets than those of sinful and ungodly."

The number of slaves in the Danish colonies is said to be about twenty-four thousand. The committee who reported the above petition recommended the appropriation of two million Danish dollars for the compensation of the masters. This was rejected, as it was urged that the finances of the country would not bear such an appropriation; that the real value of the slaves had not been ascertained; and that finally, the slave owner had no right to compensation, as there could be no valid title to property in man. The vote on the compensation clause was forty-four against to twelve in its favor. Capt. Herforth made a motion, that no petition be presented on the subject, which was rejected by a close vote of thirty to twenty-six.[5] The late Joseph John Gurney visited Denmark, with his sister Elizabeth Fry, in 1841, with special reference to the anti-slavery cause; and to their labors of love and humanity, I have little doubt, this movement owes its origin.

The last number of the British and Foreign Anti-Slavery Reporter contains a testimonial from the Haytien Government to the memory of the venerable and beloved Thomas Clarkson, signed in behalf of President Riche,[6] by A. Larochel: "Ministre de la Justice, de la Instruction Publique, et des Cultes," addressed to the British and Foreign Anti-Slavery Society. I append an extract from it, which evinces the gratitude of an emancipated people towards their benefactor and friend:

"There are, gentlemen, some men whom Providence has raised up for the especial purpose of carrying out his great designs in reference to mankind. The mission of the venerable Thomas Clarkson was clearly pointed out to him; and that devoted man performed his duty with all the fidelity and zeal of an apostle. Even in this world his perseverance and his virtues found their reward; and after a long series of labors and trials he was permitted to enjoy the sweet satisfaction of seeing the slave trade abolished, liberty proclaimed throughout the whole length and breadth of the British empire, and the spirit of emancipation struggling for the deliverance of the people yet afflicted with the leprosy of slavery. He was allowed to anticipate the time when, from one end of the earth to the other, all men shall be Free. He was allowed to die in peace, giving glory to his Creator, who had designated him to be the means of so much happiness and security to a class of men who, for so long a period, had been devoted to the most degrading slavery.

"But if anything can mitigate the sorrow felt at so great a loss, it is the fact that His Excellency The President feels, in common with all Haytiens, that the work of the venerable Thomas Clarkson is ably carried on by the society over which he presided, and in whose labors he took a part more active than his advanced age would have seemed to allow. All of you, the Haytiens well know, are animated with the same fervent zeal as the virtuous man whom we now regret. He has often aided you with his counsels and his experience; he has often talked to you of better times to come for the African race. That the wishes of this holy apostle of emancipation may be realized we fervently hope. Both blacks and whites, we all will work for the accomplishment of this end, each one in his own circle; for the cause of liberty is the cause of God. You will labor for the completion of that noble temple, which the venerable Thomas Clarkson desired to raise to the honor of God, who had so often assisted him in his painful exertions, by the destruction of slavery in every country where it has raised its execrable head. In the dwelling place of the just made perfect, whence Thomas Clarkson now contemplates your philanthropic effort, he will take delight in remembering that he has left behind him disciples worthy of himself, and worthy to fulfill the mission he had undertaken in the spirit of love.

"His Excellency The President of Hayti has ordered me

further to express to you, gentlemen, the high opinion he entertains of you personally, and the interest that he takes in your labors. His Excellency regards, with an attentive eye, the progress of this great and noble question, and his heart sincerely rejoices at each new triumph that the cause to which you have so generously devoted yourselves obtains."

J. G. W.

Source: The *National Era*, March 18, 1847. Printed with the caption, "Abolition in Denmark—Haytien Tribute to Thomas Clarkson."

1. Mehemet Ali (1769–1849) ruled as viceroy of Egypt from 1805 to 1848 and was noted for his liberal reforms.

2. Henrik Nicolai Clausen (1793–1877), a Danish theologian and statesman, was the leader of the Danish legislative reform in 1840 which revised the Danish constitution.

3. Walter T. Colquitt (1799–1855) served in the Senate from 1843 to 1848 after five years in the House. He opposed the abolitionists and favored the annexation of Texas.

4. Charles Jared Ingersoll (1782–1862), a Pennsylvania lawyer, served in Congress from 1812 to 1814 and 1840 to 1849. He opposed the extreme abolitionists.

5. Probably Christian Herforth (1818–1892), a lawyer and businessman who held the rank of captain from his student days.

6. Jean Baptiste Riché (1780?–1847) was the president of Hayti from 1846 to 1847.

523. To the National Era

Amesbury, Mass., March 12, 1847

The election in New Hampshire, which took place on the 9th instant, has, as far as I can learn, resulted in the success of the Democratic candidate for Governor;[1] and it is more than probable that a majority of Democratic members of the Legislature are chosen. Gen. Peaslee, the Democratic candidate for Congress in district No. 2, is said to be elected.[2]

In some respects, I regret this result; but it is not wholly unexpected. Many voted the Independent ticket last year through personal sympathy with John P. Hale, and a desire to rebuke the party which had proscribed him; and, having affected their object in his election as United States Senator, have now fallen back into their accustomed places in the ranks of the old party. The vote of the Liberty and Independent Representatives for the Whig candidate for Governor, in the House, was intelligently condemned by some and greatly misunderstood by others. The language of the Whig papers, claiming the result of the last year's election as a Whig victory, and New Hampshire as a Whig State—the utter folly of the Whigs themselves, at some of their Conventions in the State, in nominating a man for the Presidency who disclaims any sympathy with the principles which they profess to hold on the subject of slavery—had a marked and unfavorable influence. The remarks of Col. Cilley, in the United States Senate, were not calculated to inspire Liberty men with confidence; and his vote with the Whigs, for the expulsion of the editor of the Union, had a tendency to alarm those who, although strongly inclined to act with the Abolitionists, were suspicious of Whig influence and policy, and prepared to believe the charges of "bargain" and "coalition" preferred by the Democratic press.[3] The fear of "Federalism" overcame the antislavery scruples of hundreds, and induced them to vote for the candidate of the successful party. Believing, and with good reason, that the Whig party, as a party, is as hostile to Abolitionism as the Democratic, they were told that, to vote for the independent ticket was virtually to vote for the former. I regret that they did not discriminate more clearly, and perceive that there was no necessary connection whatever between the two old parties and an anti-slavery political organization, but I am by no means surprised at their course.

One thing this election shows, I think, conclusively, viz: that, so long as the Whigs of the free States maintain their political connection with those of the slave States, they can never carry the people with them by mere professions of anti-slavery principles. More than this—these very professions, to which their practice at every Presidential election gives the lie, do more to retard the progress of liberty than the open hostility of the other party.

The Democrats have succeeded in carrying the election in New Hampshire, but, in doing this, they have been compelled themselves to do homage to the rising spirit of freedom. Let it be known throughout the country, let the South and West know, that *the now dominant party in New Hampshire stands solemnly pledged against the extension of human slavery*. This, of itself, is a great advance in the right direction; and, in the end, it will matter little to the cause of Liberty, whether a Whig or a Democrat occupies the gubernatorial chair.

J. G. W.

Source: The *National Era*, March 18, 1847. Printed with the caption, "Election in New Hampshire—Triumph of the Democrats—The Reason."

1. Jared Williams, the Democratic candidate, was elected governor and re-elected in 1848. The Liberty party vote for governor dropped by over a thousand votes.

2. Charles H. Peaslee (1804–1866), a New Hampshire lawyer, served in the House from 1847 to 1853. He was an adjutant general in the state militia.

3. A resolution had been introduced into the House to exclude the reporters

of the Washington *Union* from the floor for false and scandalous reporting. The move seemed to be a political one and the resolution was withdrawn. On February 13 the Senate adopted a resolution to exclude the editor, Thomas Ritchie, from the floor of the Senate by a vote of 27 to 21, with Cilley voting for it.

523A. To Thomas Tracy

Amesbury May 6, 1847

My dear friend Tracy.

I return the Book with my thanks, both for myself and Elizabeth, who is at Haverhill. We have been delighted with "Holy George Herbert."[1] Some of his conceits are not agreeable to our taste, and we cannot always sympathise with his Church eulogies. But there is enough beside to make us love him.

I send herewith a few pieces which I have recently written for the Washington Era. Of course Bunyan is a favorite of thine.[2]

There are some sketches publishing in the Knickerbocker— called the "St. Leger papers" which have more than once reminded me of thee: and I have been supposing that they are from thy pen. At all events, the passages I have read are well written with a quiet power and beauty which have interested me in them. I will thank thee to return the Era pieces, as I have no other perfect copy of them. My kind regards to thy excellent lady. The weather to-day seems more promising. Truly as Christabel hath it:—"The Spring comes slowly up this way."[3]

Thy sincere friend
John G. Whittier

I wanted to send you, but find my sister has carried with her, the "Cadet de Colobrières" by Madame Ch. Raybund[4] —a pure, chaste and really beautiful French story, illustrative of the life and manners of the old *noblesse* of the latter part of the last century. Do get it. I know you will like it: it is refreshing to meet with such a book in the literature disgraced by the Sues and Victor Hugos and George Sands of the modern Satanic school.[5]

Manuscript: Swarthmore College.

1. George Herbert (1593–1633), an English poet, was noted for his religious lyrics.

2. Whittier had published two articles entitled "John Bunyan" in the *National Era* on April 1 and 8, 1847. During the month of April he published an additional eleven articles, including three on Quaker slaveholding.

3. Samuel Taylor Coleridge, "Christabel," line 22.

4. Henriette Étiennette Fanny Reybaud (1802–1871), the wife of Charles

Reybaud (1801–1864), a French writer, wrote a number of novels. *The Cadet de Colobrières: A Tale of the Old Convents of Paris* (Philadelphia) was published in 1847.

5. Eugéne Sue (1804–1857), Victor Hugo (1802–1885), and George Sand (1804–1876) were all noted French novelists and writers.

524. To Gamaliel Bailey

[Amesbury, May 14, 1847][1]

Dear friend Bailey.

Wilt thou be good enough to ascertain whether any, and if so *what* celebration or notice was taken in Washington on the arrival of the news of the Revolution of the Three days in Paris in 1830?—I am especially desirous to know about it. It was stated that the Presidential Cabinet walked or rode in procession to celebrate it.[2] "Hereby hangs a tale."[3]

Thine truly
John G. Whittier

Look well to the proof of the Buena Vista poem.[4]

Manuscript: Boston Public Library.
1. Dated by postmark. Sent along with the letter were Whittier's articles, "Dancing and Sabbath Breaking" and "Sound Doctrine," which were printed in the *National Era*, May 20, 1847.
2. Whittier used the information about a grand procession of the President, the heads of departments, and other public functionaries to celebrate the French Revolution of 1830 in his article "The Two Processions," printed in the *National Era* June 24, 1847. The article contrasted the official procession for liberty with the herding of slaves to a slave market in Washington.
3. *As You Like It*, II, vii, 26.
4. "The Angels of Buena Vista," printed in the *National Era* on May 20, 1847.

525. To Moses Austin Cartland

Amesbury. First day Afternoon [May 1847][1]

Dear Cousin

I was not well on Fifth day, and was obliged to stay at home, and did not get thy kind note until today. I was really glad to hear from thee. I would be very glad to spend a week or two with thee this summer, and hope I may be able to, but, there is at present such an uncertainty about my movements that I cannot make any decided calculations upon it. If my health will allow me I must go to Washington, and relieve Dr. B. for a few weeks, this summer. Then, the continued illness of Elizabeth has confined me at home a great deal. She is rather better, at present, but not I fear permanently. She would I doubt not greatly enjoy a visit to Weare: she frequent-

ly speaks of it. I am half inclined to think one or both of
us will be at Weare sometime in the course of the summer.

I am glad thee think favorably of the "Era." What I have
written for it has been in most cases a sick man's task-work.
I have dreaded the sight of pen and paper all this spring. But,
never mind; while I am alive I mean to act as much like a live
man as possible.

As to the N. Y. resolution thee speak of: everyone to his
taste. *I* don't like *mobs* and never courted martydom,
although were it to come upon me, in the sober prudent discharge of duty, I would try and do no dishonor to the good
cause. Garrison always talks as if mobs were if not good in
themselves, the *cause* of good. He denounced us all when he
came to Philadelphia, as tame and cowardly etc.[,] said that
we needed a mob to wake us up—and then when the mob
did come, went off at midnight twenty miles into Bucks Co.
to escape it. I do not, for one, care a straw for the resolution.[2]

Don't despair of N. H. All is well, if the Liby and Ind stand
firm in the Legislature and out of it. All things considered, I
would as soon have a Loco as a Whig for Governor.[3] There
is serious mention of Hale for candidate for President. If he
stands firm this coming winter in Congress *he will be the man*,
provided the Convention is deferred till next May.[4] I want to
see Hood and Wetmore and others,[5] and half inclined to run
up soon and have a talk with them. If I do, I shall not stop
long, as I cannot leave home well at this time. Shall thee be in
Concord this week?—It is barely possible that I may be there.

Elizabeth sends her love to thee and Mary, and says she
would like much to accept your invitation. I see thee occasionally favor Hood with an article. Why not send something
to the Era?

[Signature cut out]

Manuscript: Harvard University.

1. Dated by reference to resolutions of the American Anti-Slavery Society in
May 1847.

2. The American Anti-Slavery Society held its annual meeting in New York,
May 11–13, and an account of the meeting was published in the *National Era*
on May 20 as a letter from "J. E. S.," who included the following resolution condemning the *National Era* along with his own comments:

"Resolved, That a paper located in the District of Columbia, in the capital of
the country, at the headquarters of the slave traffickers, and surrounded by slave
prisons and slave auctions, and ostensibly by name and position the grand organ
of the Anti-Slavery movement in the United States, yet conducted in such a
doubtful, cool, and pointless manner as to elicit no outbreak of slaveocratic feeling in any quarter, not even a single animadversion from the Washington Union,
(the national organ of the slave power,) not the slightest expression of alarm
or indignation in all the slaveholding regions, but on the contrary commendation
from the Southern press for its lack of all the characteristics of unadulterated

Abolitionism—is a paper which neither represents the Anti-Slavery cause, nor deserves the patronage of real Abolitionists: and such is the *National Era*, published under the auspices of the American and Foreign Anti-Slavery Society."

The writer of the letter then went on to quote Garrison:

"Indeed Mr. Garrison declared in so many words, that '*such* a paper was worse than no paper at all'; and further that had you (yes, *you*, Dr. Bailey, don't flinch) not failed to do your duty—that, had you done it, as in 'the earlier part of your career,' the second number of the National Era never would have appeared by consent of the mob. In other words, that the fact you have not stirred up the vengence of the populace around you, proves that your paper is not faithful to the cause."

3. The Democrat candidate, Jared W. Williams, had been elected governor of New Hampshire. See Letter No. 523.

4. Hale was, however, nominated as the presidential candidate for the Liberty party in October 1847 at Buffalo. See Whittier's letters to Hale, Nos. 528, 529, and 530.

5. Joseph Edward Hood (1815–1871), a native of Amesbury, had been the editor and publisher of the *Essex Transcript* in 1842–1843. From 1845 to 1848 he edited the *Granite Freeman* and *Independent Democrat*. He later worked on the staff of the Springfield *Republican*.

Robert C. Wetmore (1822–1853) of Rochester, New Hampshire, started and edited the *Independent Democrat* from May 1845 to February 1846, a paper which supported Hale's candidacy. Whittier may also be referring to Nathaniel Downing Wetmore (b. 1810), Robert's brother, a wealthy businessman in Rochester, New Hampshire, who contributed money to Hale's campaign and who served in the New Hampshire legislature from 1846 to 1848.

526. To Joseph Sturge

June 6, 1847

The American branch of the Evangelical Alliance has refused to exclude slaveholders.[1] There never was a more foolish and wicked compromise with villainy than that of the ministers of Great Britain in this matter.[2] They have done more mischief to practical Christianity by that act than they would repair were their lives prolonged a century, and crowded with good works. Let them repent deeply, heartily, if they would save their evangelical Protestantism from the contempt of the world.[3]

Source: Richard, *Memoirs of Joseph Sturge*, p. 383.

1. A meeting of the American Branch of the Evangelical Alliance was held during the first week in May in New York City. At the meeting the delegates debated the question of excluding slaveholders from membership; they finally resolved to oppose slavery in general as a terrible evil, but to keep membership open to all those wanting Christian union and brotherhood.

2. However, the British branch of the alliance, once the American group had withdrawn, voted to exclude any slaveholder from membership.

3. Whittier wrote an article on this subject for the *National Era*, on July 8, 1847, entitled "Ecclesiastical Hair-Splitting."

527. To Samuel Fessenden

Boston. July 26 [1847]

My dear friend Fessenden.

This will be handed thee by our friend A. W. Thayer Esq. of the Liberty paper at Northampton Ms.

He will explain to thee the result of our late conference in this city in respect to the affairs of the Liberty Party, and the candidates for our coming convention.[1]

I think the nomination of Hale would combine all the scattered fragments of anti Slavery in the country. He avows his entire concurrence in the principles and meaning of the Lib Party. Our friends here have been desirous of using thy name: and in this I heartily concurred; but Leavitt and Stanton now feel persuaded that the nomination of Hale would be best under our peculiar circumstances.

In haste
Affectionately thy friend
J. G. Whittier

Manuscript: Swarthmore College.
Recipient: Samuel Fessenden (1784–1869), a Maine lawyer, had served in the Maine legislature from 1825 to 1826 and was considered one of the outstanding lawyers in Maine. He was the Liberty candidate for Congress and governor throughout the 1840's in Maine. He had attended the meeting of the national committee of the Liberty party in Boston that July when it was officially decided to hold a National Liberty party convention on October 20, 1847, at Buffalo. At this meeting the Liberty party intended to nominate candidates for the 1848 presidential election.
1. On July 24 Whittier, Stanton, Leavitt and others met with John P. Hale in East Boston to discuss the presidential nomination at the Buffalo convention. At this meeting they questioned Hale with regard to his Liberty party position and decided to present him as a presidential candidate. Fessenden had been invited to the meeting, but apparently was unable to attend (see Letter No. 528).

528. To John Parker Hale

July 30, 1847

Inclosed is a letter prepared and signed by a committee chosen at our conference the other day at East Boston. Farther reflection has convinced me that so far from throwing obstacles in thy way in the Senate the nomination would give a much stronger position, and besides it would have the effect to set at rest the stories of the Radicals and the fears of some of the Independent Democrats in other States, that thou art playing into the hands of the Whigs; and thus thou wouldst be able to act more effectively upon the people, irrespective of party. As for the Whigs, depend upon it they will have no cause of dissatisfaction, if they see that thy new position enables thee more effectively to act upon the pro-slavery Democracy. Show them this, and they will not complain. I am naturally anxious that thy answer should be such a one as shall render the vote for thee in our convention entirely unanimous. It will not be published, but will be used at the convention, and sent in manuscript to a few of our leading friends in other States.[1]

Pardon me for a suggestion or two. It is important that it should be understood that thou art disconnected entirely from the two old parties; at the same time it would be right and proper for thee to avow thy Democratic faith in the doctrines of Jefferson, Leggett, and Sedgwick[2] —and true and righteous democracy of Christianity. In regard to thy anti-slavery views: Perhaps if thou wast to copy the principal resolutions of the New-market convention, held a year ago, as expressive of thy sentiments, it would be well.[3] Thee might close by avowing these as thy principles, and that if they coincide with those of the gentlemen addressing thee, and their friends generally, they are at liberty to use thy name at the convention. I take it for granted that thy answer will be favorable. The whole West will be shaken by thy nomination. Dr. Bailey is sure of great accessions from the Democratic and Whig ranks. We will try for twenty thousand votes in Massachusetts alone, and unless all indications are fallacious shall get them. If agreeable to thee, I will ride over to Dover with friend Tuck, at such time as may suit thy convenience—only let it be soon as possible—and we can see thy answer, and perhaps make some suggestions previous to its being sent. Or, I will meet thee at the Cartlands' at Lee; or, still better, wilt thou not ride over to Amesbury? [. . .] The Whigs of New Hampshire, if they are looking for anything better than a slaveholder for candidate, will be disappointed. Taylor will be urged by the hurrah boys of both parties, at the North and by the entire South.[4] I have more hope of the Democrats than of the Whigs in the coming election. They are bolder, freer, and less influenced by conservatism. Still the young Whigs of Massachusetts and Ohio will unquestionably vote the Liberty ticket, with thee as the candidate.

Source: Pickard, *Life*, pp. 319–321.

1. This summation of Hale's political position which Whittier requested was probably for use at the coming Liberty party convention in Worcester, September 1, 1847. At this Massachusetts convention a resolution praising the actions of John P. Hale was passed, but the convention decided not to nominate Hale for president. In an article in the *Era*, September 23, 1847, entitled "Massachu-

setts," Whittier gave an account of the convention and noted that "it is by no means certain that J. P. Hale will consent to stand as a candidate."

2. Probably Theodore Sedgwick (1780–1839), a lawyer and abolitionist from western Massachusetts, who gave a public address against slavery in 1831. Whittier might also be referring to the father, Theodore Sedgwick (1746–1813), who was an outstanding legislator and jurist.

3. See Letter No. 494.

4. Zachary Taylor (1784–1850), the twelfth President of the United States.

529. To John Parker Hale

[November 2, 1847] [1]

Ere this I suppose the result of the convention at Buffalo has reached thee.[2] If not already, thou wilt soon be offi-cially informed of it, when it will be expected of thee that thy position will be defined. In thy case, the boldest course is the safest. The Whigs are training Corwin and McLean to go as far as possible towards Liberty principles without actually reaching them.[3] They will strive to make it appear that they are more ultra than the anti-slavery candidate himself. On the other hand, the New York and western Democrats are pre-paring to bring out either Benton or C. C. Cambreleng, or John A. Dix, as the opponent of slavery extension. The two latter are prepared to go great lengths in denunciation of slavery. The Whigs of New Hampshire will as readily go for an ultra-abolitionist, as a half one, while they would be glad of the excuse for going for Corwin or Judge McLean, [if] they were ready to go farther than thyself in opposition to slavery. A bold, thorough-going letter at this time from thy pen would awaken too deep an interest and enthusiasm among all classes of anti-slavery men to be set aside by the stratagems of the two old parties.[4] I trust thee will not permit thyself to be troubled with "constitutional" difficulties. The Constitution has been a mere ruse of war in the hands of Slavery for half a century. It has been made to say and be just what the South wished. We must take it out of the custody of slavery, and construe it in the light of Liberty,—"as we understand it." We must bring it up out of the land of bondage, just as David did the ark from the Philistines to Obed-Edom.[5] At all events, with the Constitution, or without the Constitution, *Slavery must die*. If, however, on full reflection, thou art not prepared to take the difficult and trying position proffered thee, I would not ask thee to accept the nomination. If it seems on the whole better and wiser for thee to enter the Senate entirely independent of all parties, I would not urge thee to take upon thyself the responsibility we offer thee. I am sorry the nomination was made this fall. At our Essex County meeting, held the week before, I procured the passage of a resolution suggesting that deference should be had to the opinion of our friends in New Hampshire and Ohio in respect to deferring the nomination, and wrote the convention to that effect, being unable to attend. I have volunteered this hasty letter from motives which I trust thou wilt appreciate. Were I not confined by ill health to my house, I should try to see thee. As it is, I could do no less than drop thee a line expressive of my feelings. Thy letter will be looked for with great interest. If it is, as I trust it will be, bold, pointed, and explicit,—if it not only sustains the Wilmot Proviso, but, looking beyond that temporary measure, aims at the life of slavery itself, and points out the duty of the Free States in this crisis, to make the antislavery question first and paramount,—it will rally a mighty host of true hearts around thee as Liberty's standard-bearer. If it fall short of this, it will be greatly to be regretted, and by no one more sincerely, both as respect thyself and the cause, than by thy sincere friend.

Source: Pickard, *Life*, pp. 321–323.

1. Dated by Pickard as October 2, 1847, but this is clearly incorrect as the Buffalo convention met October 20–22, 1847.

2. The Liberty Party convention nominated John P. Hale as its presidential candidate and Judge Leicester King of Ohio as its vice-presidential candidate.

3. Thomas Corwin (1794–1865), the former governor of Ohio, was then serving in the United States Senate where he openly denounced the Mexican War as unjust. From 1850 to 1853 he was secretary of the treasury and during the Civil War was minister to Mexico.

John McLean (1785–1861) had served in Congress and as postmaster general and had been appointed to the Supreme Court. He was often mentioned as a presidential candidate.

4. Hale did not officially accept the nomination until January 1, 1848, and even then his acceptance was hesitant and provisional. He announced in his letter that if a broader-based antislavery coalition party was formed, he would gladly step aside.

5. II Samuel 6:10–12.

530. To John Parker Hale

[November 8, 1847] [1]

I wrote thee a hasty line the other day with reference to the Buffalo nomination. I sincerely hope thou wilt not feel thyself called upon to decline that nomination. Since I wrote thee I have had letters from New York and elsewhere, all highly animated, and encouraging as to the prospect of a large vote in 1848. Everywhere the nomination is received with enthusiasm by the Liberty men; and many influential Whigs

and Democrats are regarding it with favor. The "Era" of
last week contains an article originating in a Democratic
paper in New York, and which has been copied into several
other prints of the same stamp, suggesting that it would be
well for the Democracy of the North to rally under thy
nomination.[2] Everything, in short, looks favorable, beyond
our hopes. Our election took place to-day. When I left the
polls the governor vote was not declared. That for representative in Amesbury stood, Liberty 103, Whig 99, Democratic
87. The Cushing vote will be small.[3]

Source: Pickard, Life, pp. 323–324.
1. Dated by Pickard as "11th, 8th mo," which clearly is a mistake for November 8, 1847.
2. In an editorial, "General Convention of the Liberty Party at Buffalo," the
Era of November 4, 1847, printed an article from the Mercury of Potsdam, New
York.
3. Whittier wrote an account of the election for the Era, "Massachusetts Election," on November 18, 1847. Governor Briggs, the Whig candidate, was reelected,
defeating Caleb Cushing, the Democratic candidate, by nearly 14,000 votes. The
Liberty party vote was smaller than in previous years.

531. To Gamaliel Bailey

[Amesbury, December 3, 1847][1]

Dear friend.

Illness which has obliged me to give over reading and writing in a great measure must excuse my irregular communications—

I should like to visit W. this winter and shall do so, if my
health improves.—I think thy extracts from Southern papers
and comments thereon excellent. I hope to give something
better ere long than my late pieces.[2]

J. G. W.

Manuscript: University of Texas.
1. Dated by postmark.
2. Whittier had published "Massachusetts Elections," "Elihu Burritt—English
Dissenters," and a "Review of Evangeline" in the National Era on November 18
and 25. With this letter was sent "The Huskers," which was printed in the National
Era on December 16, 1847.

532. To Charles Sumner

Amesbury January 7, 1848

My dear friend.

If my poor notice of thy addresses has given thee a tythe of the pleasure which their perusal afforded me, I shall look upon it with more favor than I did when it came to me in the Era, sadly disfigured by errors of the press and omissions.[1] Believe me, I have at least spoken sincerely and from the heart.

I wish thee would write to John P. Hale, an encouraging and at the same time suggestive letter. It would do him good. He needs the support and counsel of all who love freedom. He is fearless and willing to do his duty: but his position is a very difficult one. I have been desirous of writing him at length, but the state of my health has obliged me to abandon writing and study almost entirely. I find it difficult to answer my letters.

Was thee aware that Calhoun has been prodigiously frightened by Dr. B's article in the Era some time ago suggesting the cessation of all hostilities on our part, and the offer to the several Mexican states to come into our Union on an equal footing with our own?—[2]

Hast thou not something occasionally to say which would be read and felt widely through the columns of the Era? I need not say that thy communications would be most welcome.

Cordially thy friend
John G. Whittier

Manuscript: Harvard University.

1. Whittier had written a review of Sumner's "Fame and Glory" address in the December 30, 1847, *Era*. In the article Whittier commented on other addresses of Sumner and praised him as one who ventured "to do homage to unpopular truths, in defiance of the social and political tyranny of opinion." He went on to conclude that Sumner "has boldly and at no small cost grappled with the great social and political wrong of our country, Chattel Slavery."

On January 5, 1848, Sumner wrote to Whittier: "I cannot let you off without thanks for your most kind and flattering testimony for the little that I have been able to do. I value your word very much and esteem your notice a sprig of true laurel.

"I wish I could see hope for the country, but I cannot. The war and slavery will continue to tear our vitals. Thank God! at last we have a voice in the Senate. Hale has opened well. His short speeches have been proper premonitions of what is to come. Every word from him will resound through the country. I hope you will encourage him to make thorough work in the Senate. I wish to see him discuss the war in its relation to slavery. Then I hope he will find occasion to open the whole subject of slavery constitutionally, morally, politically, economically" (Albree, ed., *Whittier Correspondence*, p. 96).

2. Bailey's editorial of August 19, 1847, "United States and Mexico—Plan of Pacification and Continental Union."

533. To Charles Sumner

Washington February 23, 1848[1]

My dear Sumner,

Ere this thou hast doubtless heard of the sudden illness of the venerable Adams.[2] At a late hour last night he was still living—but sinking fast. I have not heard this morning. His death will be the fitting end of such a glorious life. Falling at his post—dying with his harness on in the capital so often shaken by his noble battle for freedom! My eyes fill with tears—but the emotion is not unmingled with a feeling of joy that such a man should *thus* pass from us.

A few days ago I had a deeply interesting conversation with him. All his old vigor seemed to reanimate him when he touched the subject of Slavery. I shall never forget that interview.

Even, if now living, he cannot survive through the day.

An election will of course take place in his district. There is a general feeling among our friends here that his place should be worthily filled. Who so proper then as his son—our friend Chas Francis Adams. He is virtually a resident of the District. Think of it dear S.—think what a glorious thing it would be to see the vacant seat of the elder Adams so well filled.[3]

My friend Dr. Bailey is doing nobly here. But he needs help; and would be more than grateful for an occasional contribution from thy pen. Can thee not give him something—literary, historical, anti-Slavery—anything from thee would be welcome? I wish thou wouldst think of this.

Affectionately
J. G. Whittier

Look at the article in the Era of this week on Yucatan. I have had an opportunity to acquaint myself fully with the object of the Yucatan Commissioner. Cannot the fact of the rejection of his overtures for the admission of a *free* state be used in favor of liberty and against the dough faces of the North?[4]

Manuscript: Harvard University. Published, in Part: Pickard, *Life,* p. 329.

1. Whittier had been in Washington since February 10, 1848, with Henry B. Stanton. He stayed most of the time with the Baileys, who gave a reception in his honor.

2. Adams had been stricken on February 21 in the House of Representatives and died on the evening of February 23.

3. Charles Francis Adams, however, was not elected to his father's seat.

4. The article was "Yucatan and the United States," *National Era*, February 24, 1848. Justo Sierra (1814–1861), the commissioner from Yucatan, submitted a proposal from his government that Yucatan be annexed to the United States, but since its constitution forbade slavery or any distinction on the grounds of race or color, the administration was opposed to the idea.

534. To Henry Wadsworth Longfellow

Boston March 8, 1848

My dear friend.

Too ill and fatigued by my journey from Washington to visit Cambridge, I write a line to ask a great favor of thee. I do it, however, with less hesitation, from the fact that I ask it not for myself, but for a cause dear to us both.

The National Era is now entering upon its second volume. It has been our aim to make it acceptable to the best minds and hearts of our country. Its course has been, we believe, firm but kindly and courteous and its rapidly increasing circulation in both the free and slave States encourages us to hope that our efforts have not been in vain. It has about 12,000 subscribers and has acquired a reputation which we shall find it difficult to sustain without help. The undertaking has been an arduous and expensive one; and we need the sympathy and aid of all the friends of freedom. Can thee not do us a great service by giving us something in prose or verse from thy pen: Anything of thine however brief would be welcome. Is there nothing in the death of Adams to call for some expression of thine? How glorious of the brave old man to die at his post!

Do, if possible let us have something. If thou canst, comply with my request, send to me at Amesbury.

I recd. a note from thee some time since. In reference to it I can only say that I should have been false to myself and truth had I withheld from thy poem the poor tribute of which thy note speaks.[1]

Excuse this hasty scrawl. I write half blind with headache.

Very truly thy friend
John G. Whittier

Manuscript: Harvard University.

1. Whittier had reviewed Longfellow's "Evangeline" in the November 25, 1847, *National Era* and then gave it a longer review ("Evangeline—The Puritans") in the issue of January 27, 1848. In his earlier review Whittier commented: "Eureka! Here, then we have it at last,—an American poem, with the lack of which British reviewers have so long reproached us. . . . The author has succeeded in presenting a series of exquisite pictures of the striking and peculiar features of life and nature in the New World. The range of these delineations extends from Nova Scotia on the northeast to the spurs of the Rocky Mountains on the west and the Gulf of Mexico on the south. Nothing can be added to his pictures of quiet farm-life in Acadie, the Indian summer of our northern latitudes, the scenery of the Ohio and Mississippi Rivers. . . . It is not merely a work of art; the pulse of humanity throbs warmly through it."

535. To Charles Sumner

Amesbury March 26, 1848[1]

My dear Sumner.

Can'st thou procure for me the 10th and 11th Vols. of the *Retrospective* Review?[2] If so, and they could be left for me at the office of the *Amesbury Express*, *"Batchelder's* Express" Eastern R. R. No. 7 State St. I will take care to return them in a few days and will feel under great obligation to thee.

H. Mann's letter is a noble one.[3] I do not know him personally. Is he really all that his letter indicates? The speech of Root is very good—isn't it?—[4]

Affectionately and truly
Thy friend
John G. Whittier

The friends of Clay will make a very strenuous effort to procure his nomination: it will fail, I think. For my part I would quite as readily vote for Taylor as for Clay; and I am sorry to see our friend Giddings virtually pledging himself to the latter.

W.

Manuscript: Harvard University.

1. The date may be March 21, 1848. The number is hard to distinguish in the manuscript.

2. *The Retrospective Review, and Historical Antiquarian Magazine* was published in London from 1820 to 1828. Volumes X, pp. 328–343, and XI, pp. 174–195, contained an essay on Andrew Marvell's works which Whittier used for his article "Andrew Marvell," printed in the *National Era*, May 18, 1848.

3. Horace Mann, then secretary of the Massachusetts Board of Education, had been nominated as a candidate by the Whigs to succeed John Quincy Adams in Congress. Mann at first refused, but finally accepted the nomination, stressing the point that education is dependent on freedom. In his letter of acceptance Mann stated: "So far as personal preferences are concerned, I infinitely prefer remaining in my present position, with all its labors and its thanklessness, to any other office in the gift of the people. I had hoped and intended, either in a public or private capacity, to spend my life in advancing the great cause of people's education. The enactment of laws which shall cover waste territory, to be applied to the myriads of human beings who are hereafter to occupy that territory, is a work which seems to precede and outrank even education. Whether a wide expanse of country shall be filled with human beings to whom education is permitted, or with those to whom it is denied—with those whom humanity and the law make it a duty to teach, or with those whom inhumanity and the law make it a *legal* duty not to teach, seems preliminary to all questions respecting the best systems and methods for rendering education effective" (E. I. F. Williams, *Horace Mann, Educational Statesman,* New York, 1937, p. 281).

4. Joseph M. Root (1807–1879), an Ohio lawyer, served as a Whig in Congress from 1845 to 1851. He later became a Republican and served as United States attorney for northern Ohio in 1861. On March 15 Root addressed the House on the annexation of territory from Mexico and proposed that the Wilmot Proviso be applied to any new acquisitions.

536. To Charles Sumner

[March 1848] [1]

My dear Sumner:

I thank thee for the favor of the Volumes of the Ret. Review herewith returned.

What glorious changes in the Old World! I feel, almost like going to France myself, and would if I could do anything more than gratify my feelings by so doing. The position of Lamartine, Arago and their colleagues is a sublime one, but its responsibility is terrible.[2] My friend Joseph Sturge of Birmingham, who has just returned from a visit to Paris, places great confidence in them; he writes me that they are determined to put an end to Slavery at once. He found them, busily at work, greatly worn and exhausted by their severe and protracted labors. The sympathies of all friends of Liberty should be with them.

I am glad to hear thy report of H. Mann. I hope he will equal thy hopes.

I wish our Legislature, in its congratulations of France, would especially allude to their abolition of Slavery. I have not seen whether the resolves reported have passed or not. "Hale's proviso" ought to be attached to them.[3]

Affectionately and truly
thy friend
John G. Whittier

Manuscript: Harvard University. Published, in Part: Pickard, Life, p. 330.

1. Dated in another hand as "March." Since it refers to the letter of March 26, 1848, it is placed here.

2. During the crises of 1848 Lamartine, along with others like Francis Arago (1786–1853), the celebrated French astronomer and natural philosopher, formed a provisional government. Arago acted as minister of war for a few months.

3. When the United States Senate was considering a resolution congratulating France on securing a republican form of government, Hale proposed that a clause be inserted commending the French for "manifesting the sincerity of their purpose by instituting measures for the immediate emancipation of the slaves in all the colonies of the republic" (Pickard, Life, pp. 330–331). Hale's resolution was defeated by an overwhelming vote.

537. To Gamaliel Bailey

Amesbury [March 1848] [1]

Dear Doctor,

I have done my best to say the needed word in this piece; at all events I have thrown my heart and soul into it. Would to God I could present the Crisis to my countrymen as it appears to me.[2]

Be careful of the proof—the proper names especially.

Very truly thine

J. G. W.

Source: Typewritten copy, private papers of T. Franklin Currier.

1. Dated by reference to the poem, "The Crisis," which was published in the *National Era*, March 30, 1848.

2. The poem concerned the disposition of the territory ceded by Mexico to end the Mexican War. Whittier asks the nation to decide whether the territory will be slave or free.

538. To Charles Sumner

Amesbury. June 20, 1848

My dear Sumner.

I am sorry I cannot be with you tomorrow; but I hope to be at the Convention on the 28th.[1]

In the mean time what will the barnburners do?[2] Is there no hope of uniting with them, and erecting on the ruins of the old parties, the great party of Christian Democracy and Progress?—Why try to hold on to these old parties even in name? Wilson's letter is excellent.[3] What course will H. Mann take? Of Palfrey I have no fear.

It strikes me that it would be best not to make a nomination at Worcester but to appoint delegates to a General Convention of the friends of Freedom and Free Soil without distinction of party, the time and place of which to be fixed after consultation with friends of the movement in other states.

Don't stultify yourselves by boasting of your Whiggery. That died when Taylor was nominated. Judge Allen is right.[4] The Whig party is dissolved. Let your emancipated friends now rise to the sublime attitude of men who labor for the race, for humanity. Send out from your Convention if you will, a long and careful statement of the facts in the case, but with it also an Appeal to the people which shall reach and waken into vigorous life all that remains of manhood in the North. Kindle up the latent enthusiasm of the Yankee character—call out the grim fanaticism of the Puritan. *Dare, dare, dare,* as Danton told the French: that is the secret of successful revolt.

Oh for a *man*! There is the difficulty after all. Who is to head the movement? Hale has many of the essential qualities of a leader. He is honest and bold, has tact, and discretion also. As a stump-orator he is second only to John Van Buren,[5] who by the by, I would far rather see in nomination for the Presidency than his father, or Judge McLean. It would be folly and suicide to nominate a shrinking conservative, whose heart is not with you, and whom you must drag up to your level by main force. Look just now at Webster, and Tom Corwin! Flat on their faces, like Eastern Slaves, before Taylor and Slavery. In what a noble contrast stand Hale and Van Buren the younger! You must have a new and bold man—one to whom old notions and practices on the question of slavery are like threads of tow, breaking with the first movement of his limbs.

But this advice, however well-meant on my part, is doubtless not needed. You have strong and noble men. Adams, Howe,[6] Phillips, Wilson, Hoar, Allen, and others. I only wish you had the power of the French Provisional Government. I would answer for the wisdom of your decrees.

Cordially thy friend.

John G. Whittier

Manuscript: Harvard University. Published, in Part: Pickard, *Life*, pp. 331–332.

1. Sumner and other antislavery Whigs were to hold a meeting of all Whigs who protested General Taylor's nomination by the Whig party at Worcester on June 28, 1848. Whittier attended the meeting.

2. The Barnburners were a group of New York antislavery Democrats who protested the nomination of Lewis Cass for President.

3. Henry Wilson had been one of the Whig delegates to the Philadelphia Whig convention who protested Taylor's nomination. Upon his return from the convention he published a letter stating his position.

4. Charles Allen, another Whig delegate at the Philadelphia convention, announced his determination to oppose Taylor and declared at the convention that from this day forth the Whig party was dissolved, since Taylor did not represent the party or the principles of liberty.

5. John Van Buren (1810–1866), the son of Martin Van Buren, had been a power in New York politics from 1836 to 1848. He broke with the Democratic party after its nomination of Lewis Cass. He was considered a natural leader for the Free Soil party but instead threw his support to his father and secured for him the nomination at the Buffalo convention. He returned to the Democratic party after the failure of the Free Soil party in 1848.

6. Samuel Gridley Howe (1801–1876), a doctor, had served in the Greek Revolution for six years. He directed the Massachusetts School for the Blind, which became the Perkins Institution and Massachusetts School for the Blind, for forty-four years. In 1846 he ran for Congress against Winthrop and was defeated. Whittier's poem, "The Hero," praised Howe's early actions for Greek liberty and said of his later life:

> "The Cadmus of the Blind,
> Giving the dumb lip language,
> The idiot-clay a mind."

539. To Charles Sumner

Amesbury, June 23, 1848

My dear friend.

It is not in my power to be with you to-morrow, although it is my wish to do so.

In regard to thy query touching the Liberty men taking a part in the organization of the Convention, I cannot speak with authority, but will simply give my opinion.[1]

The case as I understand it is just this. The Liberty Party,— at first small and proscribed, has fought a hard battle for seven years, and has grown to be at least 80,000 strong. Pressed upon all sides, it has a compact form and organization and is strong in the indomitable will of its members, who have been tried as by fire. The men ask nothing but the privilege of fighting the battle of freedom on the ground they have heretofore maintained. They believe their position the right one, and *standing there* they are ready and anxious to cooperate with Conscience Whigs and Independent Democrats,—nay more, they are willing that the latter shall be leaders and standard-bearers, while they fall into the ranks of the common soldiers of freedom. (I see by the by that my figures are getting somewhat military.)

To show our feeling in this district, our Convention last fall nominated J. P. Hale—an Independent Democrat,—as our candidate for Presidency. For this some of our other friends greatly censured us, and have withdrawn from our organization. We nominated Hale, not only because he was eminently worthy of it, but because we wished therby to show to anti-slavery Whigs and Democrats that we were willing to meet them in a fraternal spirit, and not as mere partizans. Against his inclination, Hale consented to be a candidate. Under these circumstances, the Liberty men must be passive and let events shape themselves, in the hope that at the coming election they may be able to cooperate fraternally with all who are hostile to slavery. We cannot, as honest men, abandon Hale, who has stood up so nobly for our principles, so long as he remains in his present relation to us. Should he decline, in view of a general movement of all anti-slavery men, the case would be different.[2] But even then, for one I cannot consent after a life long struggle in this cause, to be instrumental in *lowering down* the standard of the Liberty party. I don't ask that the candidate shall be a member of that party, but I do insist that he shall be a decided and resolute anti-slavery man. In this matter the Liberty men have but one

voice. I do not believe it is in the power of myself or Dr.
Bailey or Stanton or Chase, Lewis, Tappan, Fessenden, etc.,
even could we be induced ourselves to undertake it, to carry
the Liberty party in favor of any other than a thorough,
hearty abolitionist.[3] They would cast us off, and move
onward.

As to Hale himself, he has no wish to stand as a candidate,
unless by so doing he can promote the cause. He is no parti-
zan—he has no other ties, than that of sympathy in a common
object, to bind him to the Liberty men.

Dr. Bailey has, I know, a good deal of faith in Judge
McLean. He is a worthy respectable man, but he has never
been known as abolitionist. Some of his decisions too are bad
on this very subject. His range of vision is narrow. He is the
slave of yesterday,—the victim of precedents. He is not even
"available." There are ten hearts in the country that leap
faster at the name of Hale, or John Van Buren, or J. R.
Giddings, to one that does so at that of McLean. The time
for old, worn petitioners has gone by. The party of the people
must have a man fresh and strong from the people themselves.

Not knowing therefore what is contemplated by you, in
respect to a nomination, it would hardly be best for Liberty
men to take *responsible* stations in the organization of the
Convention. At least, such is my feeling. If I cannot wholly
go with you, I wish to encourage you onward in what you
regard as duty, unembarassed by my own scruples and difficulties. In heart and soul I am with you in every honest word
and work for freedom. I rejoice to hear of Judge Allen's reception. A prominent democrat here tells me he shall go with
the party of freedom. The Whigs will lose the very flower of
their party. God bless you, and guide you.

John G. Whittier

Excuse the haste of this letter. I have no time to see what I
have written.

W.

Manuscript: Central Michigan University. Published: Albree, ed., *Whittier Correspondence*, pp. 97–100.

1. The Worcester convention was attended by 5,000 people and signalized the
beginning of the Free Soil movement in Massachusetts. The convention chose
six delegates with Charles Francis Adams as their leader to attend the Buffalo convention. Sumner was considered as a delegate, but desired that someone else
be sent in his place. He did, however, attend the Buffalo convention.

2. Hale finally declined and this opened the way for Liberty support of the
Free Soil ticket.

3. Salmon P. Chase (1808–1873), an Ohio abolitionist, presided over the
Buffalo convention. He was elected to the Senate in 1849, served as governor of
Ohio from 1856 to 1860, and was secretary of the treasury under Lincoln. In
1864 he was appointed chief justice of the Supreme Court.

Samuel Lewis (1799–1854), an Ohio educator, had reformed the Ohio public school system and served as Ohio's first superintendent of common schools. Along with Chase and others he helped form the original Liberty party in 1840.

540. To William Stevens Robinson

[June] 1848[1]

Dear Friend,—

I heartily congratulate thee on thy emancipation from the Taylor party.[2] Is it not time that a district-meeting were called for the choice of delegates to the Buffalo Convention? I find Liberty men disposed to join heartily in the new movement, provided they do not surrender thereby *principles* which Barnburners and Conscience Whigs admit to be just and right. They will not contend about *men*. The Buffalo Convention ought to take its ground boldly and strongly; the bolder the better. Nothing is to be gained now by compromise and evasions.[3] The entire divorce of the government of the United States from slavery is the only consistent platform of action.

Cordially thy friend
John G. Whittier

Source: Harriet J. Robinson, *"Warrington" Pen Portraits: A Collection of Personal and Political Reminiscences from 1848 to 1876 from the Writings of William S. Robinson* (Boston, 1877), p. 37.

Recipient: William Stevens Robinson (1818–1876) had been the editor of the Lowell *Courier and Journal* until his caustic remarks on Massachusetts politics and defense of abolitionism caused his resignation. After editing the Boston *Whig*, he worked for the Free Soil party and became a Republican. In 1856 he began printing for the Springfield *Republican* his "Warrington Pen Portraits," letters dealing with Massachusetts politics. From 1862 to 1873 he was clerk for the Massachusetts House and exercised great power in the state.

1. Robinson had resigned from the Lowell *Courier and Journal* on June 12, 1848, so the letter is probably of June.

2. The Whig convention in Philadelphia that June nominated Taylor as its presidential candidate, which caused Conscience Whigs like Sumner, Allen, Adams, and others to desert the Whig party.

3. The Buffalo convention to be held on August 9, 1848, was to include Liberty party men, Van Buren Democrats, antislavery Whigs, and others for the purpose of forming a coalition party to oppose the Whig and Democratic nominations. At this convention the Free Soil party was formed.

541. To William Francis Channing

July 1, 1848

Providence permitting, I will be with you on the 9th.[1] In the mean time I can add that I cannot vote for Van Buren in his present attitude, yet I greatly fear that the Buffalo convention will affirm his nomination, and that Hale will decline, as indeed he has a right to do when his party abandons him. What can be done? Van Buren is too old a sinner to hope for his conversion. Had the Barnburners nominated John Van Buren, I would have gone for him, for he is not bound to vindicate his consistency in evil, and he is a man of *progress*. Even now, if the Conscience Whigs so will it, he might be substituted for his father, and thus all parties might unite. I see no other way. As things now stand we are likely to lose our candidate, for self-respect alone and self-preservation would induce him to withdraw his name from a divided and dissolving party.

Would it not be well for some one—I think thee are the very person to do it—to address an earnest letter to Martin Van Buren, stating the strong desire felt to effect a union of all parties opposed to the usurpations of slavery—putting the question plainly to him whether he is willing and prepared to stand at the head of such a movement, and give his sanction to all legal and constitutional means for the limitation and overthrow of slavery. Write to him in behalf of eighty thousand Liberty voters. It is important that we should know positively how he stands.[2] The Whigs generally, I think, will prefer Van Buren to Hale, strange as it may seem. For one, I cannot and will not go blindly and rashly into the support of such a candidate as Van Buren—let Conscience Whigs and Western Liberty men do as they will.

Source: Pickard, *Life*, pp. 333–334.

1. August 9 was the date of the Buffalo convention. Channing was an alternate delegate from Boston to the convention.

2. Channing wrote such a letter to Van Buren, but received no reply.

542. To Charles Sumner

Amesbury July 10, 1848

Dear friend.

The following paper has been signed in this place by 120 of our citizens, Whigs, Democrats and Liberty men.

"Free Soil and Free Labor

The undersigned citizens of Amesbury and Salisbury being in favor of the extension of the Anti-Slavery Ordinance of 1787[1] over the territory acquired from Mexico and for Union of the people of the Free States of all parties to effect that object, hereby write to Chas Sumner Esq. of Boston to address them on the subject as soon as his convenience will permit."

It is proper to state that nearly all to whom the paper was shown signed it without hesitation, and there can be no question but that two-thirds of our legal voters in the two towns would unite with it.

Will thou not drop me a line informing me when thou canst come? Fix if possible an *early day*. The cars run up here from Boston just in season for an evening meeting, and go out again in the morning early enough to take thee back before business hours.

Very cordially thy friend
John G. Whittier

Come directly to my place, I want to talk with thee about the present posture of matters.[2]

J. G. W.

Manuscript: Harvard University.

1. The Northwest Ordinance of 1787 established policies for the development of the lands northwest of the Ohio River. The ordinance insured the rights of worship, trial by jury, and freedom of the press, and prohibited slavery in the states to be developed from these lands.

2. Sumner, however, wrote to Whittier on July 12, stating that he could not come until after the Buffalo convention. In his letter he went on to say: "Things tend to Van Buren as our candidate. I am willing to take him. With him we can break the slave-power. That is our first aim. We can have a direct issue on the subject of slavery. We hope that McLean will be Vice-President, Van B. and McL! that is a strong Free-Soil ticket" (Albree, ed., *Whittier Correspondence*, p. 101).

543. To Moses Austin Cartland

Amesbury. July 27, 1848

My dear Cousin.

Thy letter from the old homestead was most welcome.[1] I am right glad thee are established there. I should have been over to see you ere this had I not been called off in the Boston direction often, and been much of the time too unwell to visit.

I would like to go to the Buffalo Convention, but my health forbids the idea. What will be done there? I could go for V. B. if Hale declines, if he would come out in favor of abolition in the District of Columbia. But I will never vote for him until I know that he has taken a new position on that point. How we should look, if V. B. were elected by our votes, and should veto a bill to abolish the most infernal *Slave-market* this side of Tophet! No. No. I will vote alone before I will stultify myself and disgrace the cause. I give V. B. all due credit for his stand against the *extension* of Slavery; but, if we may judge by his own letter, while all the world has been making progress in liberal principles, he remains just where he was in 1836. If the Buffalo Convention is wise they will nominate John P. Hale; or if not compel V. B. or his friends for him to define his position. After having been brayed in the mortar of Slavery he must be stupider than Solomon's fool if he is still disposed to act the part of "a Northern man with Southern principles."

The free soil movement—the *animus* of it—the spirit and life which it infuses into the people—is indeed glorious. I hope much from it. And I will do all I can to urge it forward.

How nobly Hale behaves! His last speech is spoken of as admirable in the N. Y. papers. I wish the Barnburners could be induced to go for him.[2]

Your Convention comes off at Exeter on fourth day next. I would go over, did I not wish to attend our District Convention at Lowell.

Why don't some of you ride over here? We should rejoice to have you.

E and I intend paying you a visit ere long. I hope thee will go to the Buffalo Convention: if so we shall wait till thy return.

Love to Joseph and Jonathan, and all the folks. Thine ever and truly

John G. Whittier

What has become of "Long Jim"?[3] Why don't he redeem his pledges to thee and others? I wish thee would write him a rousing letter urging him to throw himself bravely into the great movement.

Manuscript: Harvard University. Published: Shackford, ed., *Whittier and the Cartlands,* pp. 39–40.

1. Cartland had written a letter from Lee, New Hampshire, on July 19, urging Whittier to attend the Buffalo convention.

2. Hale, who had not wanted the Liberty party nomination, had repeatedly in private letters expressed his willingness to resign the candidacy in order to secure a broader base of voters for the coming Free Soil convention. The Barn-burners supported Martin Van Buren and eventually secured his nomination at the Buffalo convention.

3. James Wilson (1797–1881), a New Hampshire Whig politician, was famed as a stump orator. He was a general in the state militia.

544. To Thomas Wilson Dorr

Amesbury Mass. July 28, 1848

My dear friend.

It is a long time since I have seen or heard directly from thee, but the lapse of years has in no wise abated my respect and esteem for one with whom I have heretofore acted in the cause of freedom and humanity, and with whom in his later sufferings in a kindred cause I have deeply sympathized.[1]

My single object in troubling thee with a line at this time, is to inquire how thou art disposed to regard the mighty movement now going on in favor of the *limitation of human Slavery.* I hope and believe thy hearty sympathy is with the Free Soil Democracy.

Hast thou any objection to let me know thy position on this question? I would be glad to hear from thee, but do not wish to urge thee, or to tax thy time by my queries.[2]

Believe me truly thy friend,
John G. Whittier

Manuscript: Brown University.

1. Dorr had been imprisoned from 1844 to 1845 for his attempts to claim the governorship of Rhode Island and reform its outdated constitution.

2. Dorr did not reply until November 6, 1848, and then he wrote:

"I shall effectually assure you that I have and can have nothing to do with the 3rd. party . . . [which] tends to, if it do not design the overthrow of the national democracy. When you express the hope that my sympathy is with 'the free soil democracy,' I must reply by saying that I know of no such democracy. There is a party heterogeneously compounded, without any principle of cohesion and aiming at an impossible object, which is now conflicting with the old democratic organization and to some extent jeopardizing its success. But I can have no sympathy with such a party; because I believe it the duty of all democrats to assist in maintaining the integrity and efficiency of their democratic party; and because all desirable reforms can be best accomplished through its agency; and because this neo-movement can have no other effect if it have any than to restore to power the Whigs" (letter, Brown University).

545. To Henry Ingersoll Bowditch

Amesbury. July 31, 1848

My dear friend.

I wish it was in my power to comply with thy request as respects the Marseillaise Song of Liberty. But, the truth is I have had so much correspondence etc. to attend to that I am quite worn down—and am, wholly unequal to such a task. If I only had the physical strength and energy for it I would try, but it is out of the question, at present. I have been laboring hard in a *private way* to make this glorious movement of the people all that it should be. My article in the Era was intended as a warning of the danger of losing this noble opportunity to lay the foundation of a great and permanent party of Freedom.[1] In revolutions like this *boldness* is all important. The very way to insure defeat would be for the Buffalo Convention to take a half-way, undecided position. Nothing would suit the Cass and Taylor folks better than to see the party which goes to the death for freedom in California, make the maintenance of Slavery in the District of Columbia a part of its creed, and object. If V. B. is nominated at the B. Convention, (as he now is understood to stand) we shall next see the Taylor Whigs of Massachusetts and the Cass democrats of New Hampshire passing resolutions at their local meetings this fall in favor of the abolition of Slavery in the District of Columbia, and deprecating the election of the candidate of the Free Soil party, who is pledged to veto a bill for that object! This would certainly put us in a ridiculous predicament. For one, I have made up my mind. If V. B. stands where he did in 1836 as respects Slavery in the District and the Buffalo Convention nominates him notwithstanding I will not abide that nomination. It will all end in failure and utter disgrace, and I wash my hands of it.

I hope, however, better things. I hope the Convention will take the consistent ground of opposition to the *continuance* as well as to the extension of Slavery in territory under the exclusive legislation of Congress. On this platform alone we can stand firmly. If V. Buren accepts the nomination of the Convention, and adopts its sentiments all will be well, and I could cheerfully vote for him.[2]

I hope thou wilt attend the Buffalo Convention. The very frail state of my health alone prevents me from going. I long to see the people rising up in their majesty to set bounds to the infernal aggressions of Slavery. By all means, my dear friend, go to the Convention. Such another opportunity may not occur in a long life.

With many thanks for thy kind remembrance I am heartily and truly thy friend

John G. Whittier

Our District meeting comes off on the 2nd of August (Wednesday) at Lowell. It will be a good gathering if the weather is favorable. I hope to be there with some forty more from our place. Why not come up and join us? It is said that John V. Buren, Samuel Lewis and Judge Allen are to be there.

W.

P. S. Hast thou any good *English* version of the Hymn of the Marseillaise? I do not remember of seeing any. I wish thou wouldst confer with our friends in Boston in respect to the views I have so hastily thrown out as to the position of Van Buren. I *know* that the old Hunkers are waiting for his nomination to come down upon him as the pledged opponent of the abolition of Slavery and the horrible slave-traffic of the District.

Manuscript: Yale University.

1. "The Buffalo Convention," *National Era*, July 20, 1848. In the article Whittier expressed his fears that the convention might not accomplish anything and even be the "greatest farce in which earnest and honest men ever engaged."

2. Whittier's hopes were realized and in two articles in the *Era* after the convention ("The Turn of the Tide," August 31, and "Bygones—Martin Van Buren in 1847," September 7) Whittier enthusiastically supported the actions of the convention and pledged his support for Van Buren.

546. To William Stevens Robinson

[August 18, 1848] [1]

Dear friend.

At thy urgent request I send thee a copy of my *Crisis*. It was written before the great uprising of the people against the slave-extension, but it is applicable to the present time.

I thank thee for thy paper containing the article on the Buffalo Convention.[2] I like the spirit of that article. I wait with anxiety to get the doings of the Convention. Thus far it looks better than I feared.

Cordially thy friend.

J. G. W.

Manuscript: Yale University.

1. Dated by postmark.

2. The Buffalo convention met on August 9, 1848, with thousands of dele-

gates in attendance. Van Buren was nominated for President and Charles Francis Adams for vice-president.

547. To an Unidentified Correspondent

August 21 [1848]

We must do the best we can with the nomination. [. . .] Our Co. Convention meets at Ipswich and great pains have been taken to get out a large delegation. Now, the wish has been earnestly expressed that thee would come out, and talk to us a little on the policy of the ind. nomination. We shall have some new men there—just committeed to us, and anxious to learn the whys and wherefores of our movement. We want just such a speech as thou wouldst give us. If the mere Whigs and Van Buren lawyers of Boston, could visit the country in all directions last year, let us have Abolition lawyers this year.

Source: Clipping of a letter offered for sale by Barnet J. Beyer of New York in 1936, private papers of T. Franklin Currier.

548. To the National Era

Boston, September 8, 1848

Our State Convention is just over. It was altogether the largest and most spirited political meeting ever held in Boston. The proceedings were characterized by harmony and enthusiasm. Hon. S. C. Phillips, of Salem—a great and good man, universally respected—was nominated for Governor, and Hon. John Mills, of Springfield, a distinguished member of the *late* Democratic party, for Lieutenant Governor.[1] An electoral ticket, headed by Samuel Hoar and William Jackson, was also nominated.

Among the speakers were Hon. S. C. Phillips, Judge Allen, Hon. John C. Park,[2] John Van Buren, Ex-Governor Morton, Hon. J. A. Bolles, Joshua Leavitt, Charles Sumner, and George Bradburn. An efficient State Committee were appointed, who will do their whole duty. The address, from the pen of Dr. Palfrey, is, I need not say, worthy of the cause.

J. G. W.

Source: The *National Era*, September 14, 1848. Printed with the caption, "Massachusetts Free Soil Convention."

1. John Mills (1787–1861), a lawyer from Springfield, had served in the Massachusetts Senate and was United States district attorney from 1825 to 1840. He presided at the Free Soil meeting in Boston. He later served in the Massachusetts House.

2. John C. Park (1804–1889), a Boston lawyer, was also a colonel in the state militia.

549. To Thomas Wentworth Higginson

[September] 1848[1]

Thy address here was liked well, not withstanding thy misgivings.[2] Courage. Go on and prosper.

Yours truly,
J. G. W.

Source: Higginson, *Whittier*, p. 44.

Recipient: Thomas Wentworth Higginson (1823–1911), then a Unitarian minister at Newburyport, was already dedicated to abolitionism and woman suffrage work. His radical ideas displeased his parishioners and in 1852 he accepted a post in Worcester, Massachusetts. He participated in the attempt to free the fugitive slave Burns at Boston in 1854 and during the Civil War served as colonel of a Negro regiment in South Carolina. Throughout his lifetime Higginson wrote extensively for leading journals and sponsored new writers like Emily Dickinson. He wrote biographies of both Whittier and Longfellow.

1. The date is conjectural, but Higginson places it during the Free Soil rallies of the summer and fall of 1848 and before an October 27, 1848, letter from Whittier.

2. Higginson prefaced this brief excerpt in his biography with these remarks: "I, taking some personal part in the contest, as a novice, and speaking at 'Free Soil' meetings which Whittier attended, remember that he watched me very closely, criticising and when he could, commending; indeed, usually overrating the little efforts of young speakers, as non-speakers are apt to do. Thus he wrote me after my very first effort, when I emerged with difficulty from the formidable ordeal of following the mighty Sumner" (Higginson, *Whittier*, p. 44).

550. To Thomas Wentworth Higginson

Amesbury, October 20, 1848

Dear Sir

Our people are determined to have a demonstration at *East Salisbury*, on the Evening of Friday of next week (Oct 27th) at early candle lighting. *Will you be there*, my dear Sir. It is about a mile or so from Newburyport. We hope to have two or three speakers, though of that we are not certain. We hope you will find it convenient to be there and address us. Sound the tocsin at yr place and let us have a large delegation, if possible from Newburyport. The meeting will be held at the E. Salisbury Methodist Church.

Yours etc.
D. O. Quimby[1]

We hope thou wilt aid us in this movement as we wish to make a good demonstration.

I hear a fine report of thy labor in W. Amesbury and Haverhill. *Good was done.*[2]

J. G. Whittier

Manuscript: Huntington Library, San Marino, California. Published: Higginson, *Whittier*, pp. 44–45.
1. Daniel Osgood Quimby (1821–1894), a lawyer and teacher in Amesbury, was the principal of the Norwich Academy in Connecticut in the late 1840's and then taught for many years in New York. He later went into business around Boston.
2. Only these two sentences of the note are in Whittier's hand.

551. To Joseph Liddon Pennock

Amesbury, October 20, 1848

My dear friend,
    Thy note informing me of the withdrawal by our Heavenly Father of a beloved member of your family circle, has [induced] me into deep sympathy with you.[1] Your loss is very great. Knowing in some measure the worth of her who has been called away so early and so suddenly, what can I say which will not aggravate your sorrow? I can only in spirit sit down with you in your diminished circle, silently pondering the great mystery of death, and bowing in reverent submission to the dispensation of an All-wise Providence.
    Yet when I think of her who has been removed from you, my feelings are not those of sadness. Death is the common allotment, and as the result of laws ordained by a good and merciful Being cannot be an evil in itself. I think of her as she was when I last saw her; all that we loved in her remaining unchanged. With the calm brightness of the golden autumnal day upon which her eyes closed, and the tranquil moonlight which shone upon her slumber, she is associated in my mind, —a beautiful and gentle remembrance of whatsoever is pure and lovely in the human spirit and in outward nature.

> "The mildest herald by our gate allotted
>   Beckoned, and with inverted torch did stand
> To lead her with a gentle hand
>   Into the silent land."[2]

    There is a beautiful thought of Charles Follen on the loss of friends, "it is," said he, "the enduring nature of true sorrow which forms the connexion between Time and Eternity; it is the burden of its Divine appointment to induce us to seek in Heaven that which we have lost on earth."
    With love to all and with sincere thanks for your remem-

brance of me in the season of your bereavement, I am

Very truly thy friend,

John G. Whittier

Source: Sellers, David Sellers, Mary Pennock Sellers, pp. 83–84.

1. Joseph's sister, Sarah Pennock had died on October 14, 1848.

2. "Song of the Silent Land," a song by Johann Gaudenz Von Salis-Seewis, translated by Henry Wadsworth Longfellow.

552. To the Beacon of Liberty[1]

Amesbury [before October 28] , 1848

The Convention of freemen and opponents of Slavery have selected in this District Hon. Chauncy L. Knapp of Lowell, as their candidate for Congress. It is every way an excellent nomination; and one which cannot fail to call out the entire Free Soil vote of the district.

The gentleman thus selected, has been for several years a resident in this District. He is a native of Vermont,—a practical printer—and at an early period in life his talents and his integrity gave him an honorable position in his native State. While the Editor of the leading Whig paper of the State published at Montpelier,[2] he entered boldly into a discussion of the Slavery question, and to his exertions it is in no slight degree owing that Vermont now stands in advance of her sister states on this question. He was elected Secretary of State, an office which he held until his decided refusal to support pro-slavery men and measures, and his unflinching perseverance in discussing the subject of slavery, brought down upon him the proscription of the managers of the Whig party. His prospects of promotion at this time were equal to that of any man in the party, and he had only to acquiesce in the general policy of that party, to retain its support and approval. A true and honest man he did not hesitate. He stood firm by his settled convictions, and retired from office, carrying with him the respect and esteem even of men who from motives of party policy proscribed him.

He has now been a resident of this District for some years, pursuing his occupation as a Printer. In the election of 1846, he was the Liberty candidate for Congress, and, if we rightly recollect ran ahead of the ticket generally. He was one of the three delegates from this District to the Buffalo Convention, chosen by the Free Soil Convention held at Lowell the past summer.

Of his qualifications for the office no one who knows him

can doubt.—I have rarely known any man better acquainted with political history, or more thoroughly conversant with the principles and practice of our government. He is a clear, vigorous writer, and a ready speaker. In all his habits and principles he is republican—a man of the people—exemplifying in his daily vocation the dignity of Labor—a man of intellect and refinement cheerfully earning his daily bread by the sweat of his brow.

I have known him intimately for many years, I have had the amplest opportunity to understand him thoroughly, and I hesitate not to say, that a truer friend of freedom, a worthier representative of the new and glorious movement of the Free Democracy or a more upright and honest man in all the relations of life could not have been selected. I shall vote for him with the full confidence that if elected he will do honor to the District and good service to that cause of Human Liberty to which he has made many generous sacrifices, and to which through good report and evil, he has always been true.[3]

John G. Whittier

Source: The *Beacon of Liberty*, October 28, 1848.
1. The *Beacon of Liberty*, a Free Soil campaign paper, was published at Newburyport, Massachusetts, during September and October 1848.
2. The *State Journal*, which Knapp edited during the 1830's.
3. The Whig candidate, J. Duncan, won the election, but Kanpp finished second, ahead of the Democratic candidate.

553. To Joseph Sturge

[October] 1848[1]

I trust the American papers have kept thee informed of the progress of things here. The adhesion of ex-president Van Buren, once a decided opponent to the liberty platform, bringing with him a host of able and influential men, the very flower of the democratic party, is an event of signal importance. Our vote will be more than four-fold what it was last year, unless I greatly miscalculate.[2] The enclosed report of the Pennsylvania and Delaware Society gives a condensed and unexaggerated picture of the state of things in this country as respects the slavery question. The discussion has penetrated into all the slave states—Kentucky, Missouri, Maryland, and Virginia are moving. A Free-soil Association has been formed in the district of Columbia. Delaware will, I trust, be a free state this winter. [. . .] If thou couldst be here now, I know it would gladden thy heart to witness the great change that has taken place. Instead of a few abolitionists here and there, as when thou wert here, the whole community is discussing the question. I am filled with thankfulness in view of the great moral revolution.

Source: Richard, *Memoirs of Joseph Sturge*, pp. 363–364.

1. Richard introduced the excerpt with "In 1848 he writes."

2. Van Buren and Adams obtained nearly 300,000 votes as compared with the 60,000 or so that Birney gathered in 1844. While Van Buren failed to carry a single free state, the Free Soil vote in New York gave Taylor the state and thus the election.

554. To Thomas Wentworth Higginson

Amesbury, November 3, 1848

My dear friend,

Will it be in thy power to visit us on Seventh day Evg (the 4th)[1] and be able [?] to address us. Rev. G. Pierce will also speak.[2] I understand there is a young man (A. A. Sargent) who is a good speaker.[3] He has a brother[4] in N. P. [Newburyport] and I am told is to be there tomorrow. If so, we should be glad to have him come up with thee.

We want now an appeal to the conscience rather than the pocket. The great interests of humanity—the law of love rather than anything of a selfish or sectional nature.

We can now have the Baptist House in our village and can fill it. Write me at once what thee can do.

Thine ever

John G. Whittier

The Whigs here hold meetings every night, but they cannot get ahead much. The workmen in the factories are appealed to on the ground of their "bread and butter," but there are many brave fellows whose god is *not* their belly and who hold that "man does not live by bread alone,"[5] who despise petty considerations. The Whigs may succeed—Genl Taylor may be elected—but their triumph may be their defeat in the end. Their situation reminds me of Cowley's description of his hope

> "which ruined is
> Alike if it succeed and if it miss,
> Whom good and ill do equally confound
> And both the horns of Fate's dilemma wound!"[6]

Manuscript: University of Virginia.

1. There is no record of Higginson's giving a talk in the local papers, although he was to address a Free Soil rally in Salisbury on November 6.

2. Perhaps George Pierce (1794–1871), a graduate of Andover Theological Seminary and a Congregational minister, who was president of Western Reserve from 1834 to 1855.

3. Aaron Augustus Sargent (1827–1887) had been born and worked in New-buryport, but in 1847 went to Philadelphia as a printer. He was then serving as a secretary to a member of Congress in Washington. In 1849 he went to California, where, after editing and becoming a lawyer, he served as a Republican representa-tive to Congress for three terms and was elected to the Senate from 1872 to 1879. He was considered a very able debater.

4. Moses H. Sargent (1825–1897) ran a bookstore in Newburyport for most of his life and during the Civil War cared for wounded soldiers near the front lines.

5. Matthew 4:44, modified.

6. From "Against Hope" by Abraham Cowley (1618–1667), an English poet. The first line should read "Hope, whose weak being ruin'd is."

555. To James Thomas Fields

Amesbury Tuesday Evening [December 12, 1848] [1]
My dear Fields.

I send thee herewith the engraving of R. Rawson taken after her abandonment by her husband.[2] She was about 21 when married, and about 35 when she died. The picture rep-resents her at the latter age. As an authentic picture of the heroine of the Journal, it might be well to have it in the book.[3]

I begin to have some fears that the Capitals will be a little too thick for a handsome page. It was not an invariable rule to use them at that time—in fact there was no rule about it. You can scarce find two books of the middle of the 17th century alike in spelling and lettering.[4]

Just get a proof of one or two pages, and see how it looks. If it is likely to disfigure the page, strike out most of them, let us have only the more important words capitalized.

Thine truly
J. G. Whittier

P. S. Please let me know soon what you think of the picture.[5]

Manuscript: Huntington Library, San Marino, California. Published, in Part: Pickard, *Life*, p. 340.

1. So dated by Pickard.

2. Rebecca Rawson (1656–1692) was the daughter of Edward Rawson, (1615–1693), a prominent member of the Massachusetts Colony and secretary of the Colony. She made a disastrous marriage to Thomas Rumsey, a young man from England who pretended to be the son of the Lord Chief Justice of England, Sir Thomas Hale. After the wedding trip to England, Rumsey stole all her belongings and abandoned her. Whittier made her the heroine of his longest piece of fiction which appeared serially in the *National Era* from June to November 1848 under the title "Stray Leaves from Margaret Smith's Journal in the Colony of Massachu-setts."

3. The firm of Ticknor, Reed, and Fields was in the process of publishing Whittier's narrative and issued it in February 1849 under the title *Leaves from Margaret Smith's Journal in the Province of Massachusetts Bay.* For this reprinting in book form Whittier added about fifteen new pages, including the ballad "Kath-leen."

4. As originally printed, the "Journal" employed all the mannerisms of seventeenth-century writing, use of italics, erratic capitalization, the substitution of "ie" for "y," and added letters. These devices were somewhat regularized for the reprinting.

5. Some early copies of the book have two engraved portraits inserted, one of Edward Rawson and another, the one mentioned here, of Rebecca Rawson. However, the pictures were not used in the regular edition of the book (see Letter No. 558).

556. To James Thomas Fields

Amesbury December 13, 1848

My dear Fields

I sent thee last night R Rawson's picture and a note about the *Capitals*. I am more and more inclined to think we had better omit about one half of them, applying them to the most important names only—such as the names of natural objects, animals, the passions, etc. Such I find to be the general course of the writers of that time. Exact regularity and uniformity is not desirable: and would defeat its object by wearing the appearance of care and design. If therefore the pages left with thee could be printed agreeably to the above direction I will take care that the rest of the book is all right before going to the printers.

I will send more copy tomorrow morning by the Express.

Very truly thy friend
J. G. Whittier

Manuscript: Huntington Library, San Marino, California.

557. To James Thomas Fields

[Amesbury] December 14 [1848]

Dear Fields.

I send another portion of Margaret. It will be seen that I have not marked all the names for Caps.

What does thee think of the Picture. I am no judge of the matter.

I have, a second impression from the Plate better done, and more finished wh I recd. today. I am not sure as it would be of any service. I think the face good—and the quaint dress noteworthy.

Thine ever
J. G. W.

The lettering of the plate does not suit me. I should prefer to

have no name, and give the particulars of it in the editorial
note or preface.[1]

Manuscript: Huntington Library, San Marino, California.
    1. This engraving had been published in the *New England Historical and Genea-
logical Register* for October 1849. Below the picture was "Rebecca Rawson. Born
in Boston 1656 Died at Port Royal (Jamaica) 1692. Engraved from the original
Portrait in the Possession of R. R. Dodge, East Sutton, Mass."

558. To James Thomas Fields

                                     Amesbury December 15 [1848]
Dear Fields
    Well let the Picture go. If you see any unnatural Latinized
words, let me know for Margaret is *Saxon*, or ought to be. It
reads better in proof than I feared. It is bound to go I think if
it can be got out in season.
    Say to friend Whipple that I am gratified by his notice of
my poor efforts in his Review.[1] I plead guilty to the exceptions which he takes, and would fain hope that his favorable
estimate is not wholly undeserved. As Burns' Macpherson
says, "I've led a life of strut and strife" and have had no leisure
when in tolerable health for any polishing of my rhymes.[2] I
suppose under such circumstances I ought not to have made
any, but *I could'nt help it.*
    Put the Book through the Press as soon as possible
                                              Thine truly
                                              J. G. Whittier
The enclosed MS. is to follow after that sent yesterday,
marked A in the leaf written at Agamenticus. It should have
been sent with the other sheet.

Manuscript: Swarthmore College.
    1. Edwin Whipple (1819–1886), an author and critic, had achieved consider-
able reputation for his reviews which appeared in the *North American Review* and
other journals. A collection of his articles was published as *Essays and Reviews*
(New York, 1848) and he continued to write essays and criticism for the rest of
his life. Whittier reviewed Whipple's next book, *Lectures Connected with Literature and Life* (Boston, 1849), in the *National Era*, November 1, 1849, calling it
one of the "most brilliant and fascinating volumes which has ever issued from the
American press. . . . His style is remarkably direct and energetic, a fitting medium
[for] his clear and sharply defined conceptions." In 1887 Whittier wrote an introduction for the posthumous printing of Whipple's *American Literature and Other
Papers.*
    In his *Essays and Reviews* Whipple reprinted a review of Griswold's *The Poets
and Poetry of America*, written in 1844, in which he called Whittier our most

characteristic poet, one who wrote with joy and pride of soul. He criticized Whittier's excessive fluency, excitable sensibility and the hasty composition which prevented him from displaying his full genius.

2. "Macpherson's Farewell."

559. To James Thomas Fields

[Before December 28, 1848] [1]

Dear Fields.

I like the page much, but the heading of the 1st page does not please me. As you use modern type in the body of the work, it strikes me that it is best to use it there also. But, suit yourselves.

I got the Transcript.[2] It is your wicked way and I wash my hands of it. As to the Gold, a little of it would not come amiss, and as the fools will be likely to spend their diggings for "that which profiteth not,"[3] they may as well buy Margaret as anything else.

When do you want the picture plate?

J. G. W.

Send the proof by *Mail*—or I can't get it til 5 o clk in the Evening. I return it by the Express before light in the Morning. The proof put in the Mail at night will reach me at 1/2 past 10 in the morning.

Manuscript: Huntington Library, San Marino, California.

1. Dated approximately by Whittier's instruction about sending the proof. In the December 28, 1848, letter (No. 560) to Fields, Whittier mentions receiving proof.

2. In the Boston *Transcript* for December 12, 1848, appeared the following:

"Remarkable Book Promised. One of the most striking literary novelties of the season, a literary friend assures us, will be a work purporting to be the Diary of a young girl residing in the Colony of Massachusetts during a length of time commencing with the year 1678. Some of the leaves from this diary have appeared in the columns of the National Era published at Washington, where they attracted great attention, both for their beauty of style and graphic pictures they present of every day life at an early period in New England. The manner in which this precious document—this waif of the olden time—was discovered is a curious incident in literary history. We may predict that 'Margaret Smith's Journal' will be widely read and as widely admired. We are indebted to Messrs. Ticknor and Company, the publishers, for an early glance at the proof sheets, from which we make a brief extract showing the charming style in which the journal is written. The extract is from a leaf dated, 'Ipswich, near Agawam, May ye 12th, 1678.'"

3. A variant of a phrase which is repeated many times in the Bible.

560. To James Thomas Fields

Amesbury December 28 [1848]

Dear Fields.

I have just this moment got a proof sheet, which is all right to this: 108th page, when I find that *eight pages of the copy with some MS. appended, have been omitted*. It is possible that the copy has been lost in some way. If so let me know at once. I sent it last week together with a proof-sheet. I shall send this proof back tonight with the residue of the copy.

Thine truly,

J. G. W.

Manuscript: Huntington Library, San Marino, California.

Part Seven

Literary Reputation and Charles Sumner

1849-1852

Literary Reputation and Charles Sumner

1849-1852

Near the end of 1849 Whittier humorously complained about a relative's request for an autograph with an "Et tu, Brute?" saying that he had lent his name more often than an exchange merchant. He added that two other autograph requests had come in the same mail. These solicitations suggest his growing literary reputation and are certainly far removed from the usual requests he received to attend conventions, write liberty songs, or serve as secretary on a local abolitionist committee. During this period the main emphasis in Whittier's life was literary. The year 1849 opened with the publication of Whittier's complete poems in a large octavo volume, beautifully printed, neatly bound and illustrated with steel engravings. The volume met with an unexpectedly large sale and a second and third edition were printed. In February Ticknor, Reed, and Fields published in both a cloth and paperbound edition, *Leaves from Margaret Smith's Journal, in the Province of Massachusetts Bay*, Whittier's longest piece of sustained fiction. The work not only displayed Whittier's antiquarian knowledge and historical skill, but, through the eyes of a sensitive and likable young English girl, imaginatively recreated the spirit and distinctive qualities of the Puritan world. All the chief tenets of Whittier's life—his love of old New England, deep Quaker faith, hatred of wrong, interest in folklore—are here blended and subordinated to the larger portrait of colonial times. By the summer Whittier was corresponding about the publication of a group of biographical sketches which were printed in 1850 as *Old Portraits and Modern Sketches*. Following this in August came a new volume of poetry, *Songs of Labor, and Other Poems*, "simple lays of homely toil" which tried to invest labor with a degree of beauty.

The sixteen letters written to James Fields in 1849–1850 show the deepening of a conventional editor-author relationship into one of easy intimacy and lasting friendship. Whittier accepted Fields's critical comments, joked about his Yankee rhymes, and increasingly depended upon Fields to correct "his sadly disfigured" proofs. Whittier's constant revision and alterations must have taxed Fields's patience for even Whittier had to comment: "Pray get out the book as soon as possible for yr. own sake. I have a terrible propensity after it is too late to see something which I ought to have seen before." Along with publication matters Whittier gossiped about literary subjects, commented on political events and in one casual aside about Fields's recent marriage remarked: "Were I autocrat, I would see to it that any young man over 25 and any young woman over 20 was married without delay. Perhaps, on second thought, it might be well to keep one old maid and one old bachelor in each town, by way of warning, just as the Spartans did their drunken Helots." Much of his incidental correspondence also concerned literary matters. He consulted with Rufus Griswold about a preface, introduced the Cary sisters to Longfellow, paid Hawthorne for a story in the *Era*, and established a correspondence with Grace Greenwood. He so enthusiastically reviewed Bayard Taylor's travel books in the *Era* that Taylor visited Whittier at Amesbury and began a close friendship that lasted until Taylor's death. Although the seven short notes to Emerson in 1851–1852 mainly concerned details of Emerson's lyceum lectures in Amesbury, Emerson stayed overnight with the Whittiers, leaving behind his personal copy of the Bhagavad-Gita. Whittier found the book exciting and wonderful and wrote Emerson that it would be returned only when Emerson came again.

After 1849 Whittier's prose contributions to the *Era* diminished. He still wrote occasional fine pieces, like his two historical sketches of Indian raids, an essay on the New England celebration of Guy Fawkes Night, or the humorous account of a rumored Redcoat invasion of Ipswich during the Revolution, but his main prose writing was now finished. At the same time his poetic interests moved away from reform and abolitionist subjects. Of the forty-five poems from this period, an increasing number dealt with religious problems, portrayed rural scenery or conveyed an appreciation of natural beauty. Although distrustful of beauty by itself and disposed to moralize about nature, Whittier began to write freely about "the unsung beauty hid life's common things below." Eschewing tricks of art, Whittier simply and directly expressed his appreciation of the Merrimack region and in his rural pieces attempted to capture the melodious charm of English poets like Spenser and Sidney. With characteristic honesty Whittier noted the distance between his attempts and their poems and described his own poetic deficiencies:

> "The rigor of a frozen clime,
> The harshness of an untaught ear,
> The jarring words of one whose rhyme
> Beat often Labor's hurried time,
> Or duty's march through storm and strife, are here."

But even this criticism concludes that his best gifts had been laid on freedom's shrine. His dedication to freedom's cause brought poetic returns; the years of ostracism and vilification had pared away some of his sentimental tendencies, toughened his derivative phrasings, and given him control of his emotions. Many of his reform poems from this time have a moral intensity and prophetic manner that transcended their historical occasion. The passage of a more stringent Fugitive Slave Law especially incensed Whittier and called forth poems like "In Evil Times," "Moloch in State Street," and "The Sabbath Scene," poems which reminded America of the distance between what she hoped to be and actually was. The last poem was published in papers throughout the country, reprinted in leaflets and pamphlets, and distributed by the thousands in a broadside printing. "Ichabod," his one anti-slavery piece that claims poetic immortality, was occasioned by Whittier's grief, surprise, and prescience of evil when he read Daniel Webster's speech in support of the Fugitive Slave Law. As a terse, tightly knit philippic, the poem perfectly blends Biblical allusions, light-dark imagery, and a modulated elegiac tone to mourn the loss of freedom's defender.

Though less of Whittier's correspondence concerned reform and political matters, his interest in these areas had not waned. The election of John P. Hale to the Senate in New Hampshire, the success of the Free Soil party in 1848, and the increasing popular support in northern states heartened the abolitionists, but Whittier pragmatically appraised the situation in 1849: "But we are all now abolitionists; it is as difficult to find an open pro-Slavery man now as it was in '33 to find an anti-Slavery one; yet, I have scarcely charity enough to suppose that this marvelous conversion is altogether genuine and heart-felt." However, in Massachusetts a coalition of Free Soilers and Democrats, building on public support for abolitionism, planned to upset the dominant Whig party in the 1850 elections. The coalition's object was twofold: to prevent the Whig gubernatorial candidate from obtaining a majority vote and to secure control of the legislature to elect a Democratic governor and a Free Soil senator. Despite personal reservations about working with the Democrats, Whittier supported the coalition and, more importantly, consulted with Charles Sumner about his being the Free Soil senator. In the summer of 1850 Whittier visited Sumner at his beach house and persuaded a reluctant Sumner to be the candidate. Initially all went as planned. The coalition gained control of the legislature and elected a Democratic governor. But as Whittier had feared and warned Henry Wilson, after gaining what they wanted, the Democrats did not fulfill their bargain. A group of them, led by Caleb Cushing, refused to vote for Sumner.

Without their votes Sumner could not gain House approval for his nomination and so the long process of twenty-six ballots spaced over a four-month period began in January 1851. During these difficult months, Whittier advised and wrote Sumner, suffering with him through the agony of near election and despondent attempts to withdraw. Finally on April 24, Sumner was elected by a majority of one and the large plan Whittier had shaped for Sumner on a summer evening was fulfilled. Sick in bed, Whittier heard the guns celebrating the event and, Quaker that he was, rejoiced in the sound. As he wrote to Sumner: "My heart is full of gratitude to God. . . . Thy triumph is such a direct rebuke to politicians, hoary with years of political chicanery and fraud;—that unpledged, free and without a single concession or compromise thou art enabled to take thy place in the U. S. Senate." The full extent of their intimacy and agreement can be gauged by Sumner's remark that "I distrust myself when I differ from you" and by Whittier's freedom in listing the people Sumner should see on his way to Washington.

This relationship must have been one of Whittier's main consolations during the debacle of the Free Soil movement in the 1852 Presidential campaign. Although not as active as in previous campaigns, Whittier had hoped for better results. Whittier's life and correspondence had now fallen into a pattern. Since his poems revealed his feelings on most national issues, he wrote few letters on these events, while leadership in national abolitionism fell on the shoulders of new men like Sumner, Chase, Hale, and others who would build the Republican party from the ruins of the Free Soil movement. A group of new literary acquaintances assumed greater importance in his personal correspondence, but to all his friends Whittier's letters were shorter, less revealing of his inner self and more contained, perhaps due to his increased literary fame and stature as a national figure. Certainly, at forty-five Whittier felt that his active reform days were over and he looked forward to the quiet hours removed from such conflict. For the next few years his books and poems better tell the story of his emotional and religious life. These years ended as they had begun, with Whittier once more engaged in publishing a new volume of his poems, *The Chapel of Hermits, and Other Poems.*

561. To James Thomas Fields

[Amesbury] January 3, 1849

That rascally old ballad occurred to my mind last evening, and it struck me that it wanted something, although already too long.[1] The following verses might do to follow (I quote from memory) the verse

"'He tore his beard so gray;
But he was old and she was young,
    And so she had her way'—

"Sure that same night the Banshee howled
    To fright the evil dame,
And fairy folks who loved Kathleen
    With funeral torches came.

"She watched them gleaming through the trees,
    And glimmering down the hill;
They crept before the dead-vault door,
    And then they all stood still!

"'Get up, old man! the wake-lights shine!'
    'Ye murthering witch,' quoth he,
'So I'm rid of your tongue I little care
    If they shine for you or me!'"

I think there is a touch of nature—old Adam's—in the last verse, but if it is too late let it pass. [. . .] The weather this morning is cold enough for an Esquimaux purgatory—terrible.

Source: Pickard, *Life,* p. 341.
    1. For the book publication of *Margaret Smith's Journal* Whittier added an episode of the wandering schoolmaster, O'Shane, who writes a ballad, "Kathleen." The three stanzas written here were composed as an afterthought, but were included in the final version of the poem as it appeared in the book.

562. To James Thomas Fields

[Before February 18, 1849]

My dear Fields.

The Volume is got up in fine style: but as it forms no part of the Bill of Lading of a California rig out, I fear it will not go well in these times.[1] It is really very neat.

Please send the enclosed books in your Philadelphia bundle. I noticed *Holmes* at some length in the Era and shall also Kennard.[2]

Cordially thy friend
John G. Whittier

Please send the note to J. T. Buckingham, with a copy of *Margaret.*

Manuscript: Swarthmore College.
1. An allusion to the California gold rush then in process.
2. Whittier reviewed *Poems* (Boston, 1849) by Oliver Wendell Holmes on January 11 in the *National Era* in an article entitled "Mirth and Medicine." Whittier commented that Holmes's poems cured by laughter, but that he was "capable of moving the heart as well as of tickling the fancy."
Whittier briefly mentioned *Selections from the Writings of James Kennard, Jr.* (Boston, 1849) in the *Era* on May 20, 1849. James Kennard (1815–1847) had been an invalid confined to bed for twenty years in Portsmouth, New Hampshire.

563. To James Thomas Fields

Amesbury, February 18, 1849

My dear Fields

I ought to have before this acknowledged the receipt of thy note in answer to my questions, and containing an exquisite little poem. I think it is a perfect gem—simple, and beautiful, and what is more—*good*. Is it imaginary or was [it] a real occurence?—[1]

I am glad to hear of thy Vol. forthcoming.[2]

I am obliged to thee for thy pains in sending me what is said of my little book.

I must not, I fear, think of purchasing Wilk's Ex. for the present.[3] Yet the copy is a cheap one, which you offer. We are talking of a Library in our village sometime—perhaps it will be one of our selections.[4]

I see the papers say that "Margaret Smith" was probably suggested by "Lady Willoughby."[5] I never read a half page of the latter, and only saw the book twice, once at a periodical store in State Street, and the second time, in your own store, when I showed thee the copy of Margaret. But let that pass.

I notice in the Republican a second notice of "Margaret."[6] Who wrote it?—

Has Layford's work on "Nineveh" reach this country? I see a notice of it in the Living Age from an English Review—full of interest.[7]

Thee need not answer this save at thy leisure.

Cordially thy friend
John G. Whittier

Manuscript: Huntington Library, San Marino, California.

1. This probably refers to Fields's poem, "The Tempest," which Whittier called in his review of Fields's poems an "exquisite little ballad," containing "whole folios of metaphysics and philosophy." It contained the famous lines:

> "Isn't God upon the ocean
> Just the same as on the Land?"

2. Whittier reviewed *Poems* (Boston, 1849) by James T. Fields in the *National Era*, April 12, 1849. Whittier said of the volume: "The Friends of the author—and we know of no one who has more or warmer, or who better deserves them—will be gratified by the publication of these pleasant and unambitious passages from the 'snatched leisure' of an active business life. They are characterized by chaste simplicity and healthful sentiment, and reflect the sunny warmth and hopefulness of the heart of the writer."

3. Charles Wilkes (1798–1877) performed extensive explorations and surveying for the United States navy during the period 1838–1842. He published an account of his explorations and discoveries in five volumes: *Narrative of the United States Exploring Expedition. During the Years 1838, 1839, 1840, 1841, 1842* (Philadelphia, 1844).

4. The Public Library in Amesbury was not formally opened until 1856 when Whittier served as one of its trustees.

5. *So Much of the Diary of Lady Willoughby as Relates to Her Domestic History and to the Eventful Period of Charles the First* (London, 1844–1848). A fictional diary by Hannah M. Rathbone (1798–1878), it was published in two parts, Part I in 1844 and Part II in 1847. In 1848 the two parts were combined and published as one volume.

6. On February 16, 1849, the Boston *Daily Republican* printed the following notice: "A pleasant happy book. . . . These leaves are live history, accurate as an old chronicle, and romantic as the life of genius always finds things. He who lives to-day and sees to-day, is the only one fit to see the past, and picture its life. All do not see, all look. Poets see. In this book we look out upon the past through a poet's eyes." The review goes on to further praise the book and identify its author as Whittier.

7. Austin Henry Layard (not Layford, 1817–1894), a British travel writer and amateur archaeologist, published *Nineveh and its Remains* (London) in 1849. It was reviewed in *Littel's Living Age* in the February 24, 1849, issue, pp. 358–367.

564. To Moses Austin Cartland

[February 1849][1]

Dear Moses,

I send thee herewith Margaret dressed up by the Boston milliners.

I wish Joseph or thee or Jonathan would contrive to come over and see us.

Affectionately
John G. Whittier

Manuscript: Harvard University. Published: Shackford, ed., *Whittier and the Cartlands*, p. 40.

1. Merely dated as 1849 by Shackford in *Whittier and the Cartlands*. Since *Margaret Smith's Journal* was published in February, I have placed the letter in this month.

565. To William James Allinson

Amesbury March 2, 1849

Dear William.

If thou hast read Macaulay's Histy thou hast doubtless been pained by the studied effort of the author to reverse the decision of nearly two centuries with respect to William Penn and to represent him as a weak vain sycophant and the tool of a cruel tyrant.[1]

It is important for the truth's sake that this calumny should be met fully and decidedly and put down as I think it can be.

Who will do it? Enoch Lewis?[2] It will require a great amount of reading and laborious research, and to be read it must be presented in a garb as attractive if possible as the pen of Macaulay has made the libel.

I almost felt myself like undertaking it but I have no access here to books and documents and my health is not equal to any serious effort. If answered at all it must be done thoroughly—mere contradiction and abuse of the historian will not answer—the facts must be presented plainly, clearly, impartially. If there *is* any thing indefensible in W P's connexion with James II[3] it must be frankly admitted and the proper apology for it given. By the by the character of Jas II is as deeply misrepresented, I think as is W P's. Do talk with thy bro., S. Rhods and Enoch Lewis about it.[4] My best love and that of my mother and sister to thee and thine. Remember me kindly to dear Stephen Grellet and to all enquiring friends.[5]

Affectionately
John G. Whittier

Source: Handwritten copy, Haverford College. Published: The American Friend, February 16, 1899.

    1. Thomas Macaulay (1800–1859), the great English historian, had just published the first two volumes of his History of England in 1848. Various parts of the history provoked refutations, since Macaulay was not always reliable in the evidence he used. Whittier himself reviewed the work in the National Era on March 1 and April 12, 1849.

    2. Enoch Lewis (1776–1856), an influential Pennsylvania Quaker, taught mathematics at Westtown School and in his own private school for nearly fifty years. He published many tracts on Quakers and from 1847 until his death he edited the Friends' Review.

    3. James II (1633–1701) ruled as king of England from 1685 to 1688.

    4. Samuel Rhoads (1806–1868), a Philadelphia Quaker and abolitionist, founded the Philadelphia Free Produce Association which tried to prevent the purchase of products of slave labor. He also edited the Non-Slaveholder and the Friends' Review.

    5. Stephen Grellet (1773–1855) was a Quaker missionary whose travels throughout Europe and America made him famous. He came to America in 1793 from France and after 1823 lived in Burlington, New Jersey, the home of William Allinson. One of Grellet's most noted trips was his visit to Russia from 1818 to 1820 when he helped institute reforms in the Russian school system. Whittier commemorated Grellet's tour in a poem, "The Christian Tourists," which appeared in the National Era, March 15, 1849.

566. To James Thomas Fields

March 9, 1849

My Dear Fields.

    Many thanks for the proofs of thy book. I like the Post of Honor exceedingly.[1] The politician's letter is admirable, likewise the country parson, waiting a louder call.[2]

    Dost thou have an opportunity to send to England often?— I want to send some of my books there—the Poems and Margt. Mussey I suspect has not sent any, and if thou couldst see him about it he would be glad to have thy advice as to whom it would be expedient to send.[3] I want William and Mary Howitt to have a copy of both the poems and Margt. Also Dr. Bowring (if he is in London),[4] Prof. Wilson of Edinboro, Douglass Jerrold,[5] and the Editors of the Examiner, and the Non-Conformist papers in London, and to such others as thee may think best. I would like to have them sent as soon as may be. In the Poems are some provoking errors of the press, as well as of the author, but they are too numerous to

correct.
[Remainder of letter missing]

Manuscript: Huntington Library, San Marino, California.

1. In his review of April 12, 1849, in the *Era* Whittier singled out "The Post of Honor" as having "graceful play and fancy, and depth of feeling and sentiment."

2. The politician's letter is either "Life at Niagara: An Epistle from the Falls," or one of the sections from "The Post of Honor" dealing with a politican's false sense of honor. The "country parson, waiting a louder call" is a section from "The Post of Honor," which reads:

> "The country curate, quoting Greek for gold,
> Sees it resplendent o'er some distant fold;
> His reverend locks, just turned twenty-two,
> Need other perfumes than a Cape Ann dew;—
> Her ampler arms a City church extends,
> He'll be more useful there, he tells his friends;
> He feels distressed, he goes with many a tear,
> But yearns to practice, in a wider sphere,—
> Which, to interpret in a carnal sense,
> Means a receipt of pounds instead of pence."

3. Benjamin B. Mussey (1804–1857), a Boston publisher and bookseller, was also an active Free Soiler. He published an edition of Whittier's poems in 1849, *Poems by John G. Whittier*, which remained a standard edition until 1857.

4. John Bowring (1792–1872), an English linguist and writer, edited the *Westminister Review*, besides writing poems and hymns. He also served in Parliament and had many diplomatic posts.

5. Douglass Jerrold (1803–1857), an English playwright and essayist, was noted for his wit and contributions to *Punch*. He started and edited many newspapers and journals.

567. To William James Allinson

Amesbury March 18, 1849

My dear William

I have to thank thee for two letters in answer to my note and for the interest thee manifested in the matter upon which I consulted thee. I was exceedingly pleased with thy bro's views—and it has seemed to me that he would be a suitable person in connection with E. Lewis to investigate the matter and set it right. He writes I have always noticed with a force and vigor which may go far to atone for the lack of some of the graces and ornaments of rhetoric. As for myself, I fear it is not in my power to do anything just now. I have been unable to read or write at all most of the time for the last six weeks and now see no prospect of amendment save in absolute rest. If I can I shall write for the Era a brief article on the 2nd Vol of M., vindicating as I believe truth requires W. P.[1] I am sorry to hear that the health of Enoch Lewis is so feeble. Nothing could give me more pleasure than to be able to look over this whole matter with him and thyself and bro., but I am not now able to read a page without suffering and writing is especially irksome.

I enclose for thee a notice of Macaulay from the pen of C. Sumner—as I believe.[2] The Unitarian Christian Examiner briefly defends Penn from the charges of M.[3]

I am truly sorry to hear of thy illness and hope thou didst not exert thyself too much in writing to me. Thou wilt infer from what I have already said that it is not in my power at present to do anything requiring study and labor. I leave the matter reluctantly. If Providence permits I may one day take it up in earnest.

The truth is what we want. If the character of W. P. will not abide the test of investigation let it fall—I thank thee for thy kind offer of house and home. With aff remembrance to thy household and our mutual friends etc.

J. G. W.

Why cannot E. Lewis take up the matter in the Review? He can do it justice if any one can and there are others who would assist in ascertaining facts. I think he would do well to write to Macaulay through J. Pease agreeably to thy suggestion. Why not write thyself to J. P.?[4]

Source: Handwritten copy, Haverford College. Published: The American Friend, February 16, 1899.

1. Published as "England under James II" in the Era, April 5, 1849.

2. No such review is listed in Sumner's Complete Works.

3. The Christian Examiner was published in Boston from 1824–1869.

4. Joseph Pease (1799–1872), an English Quaker and philanthropist, was an influential mine owner and became the first Quaker to be a member of Parliament.

567A. To Jonathan Law

Amesbury, April 2, 1849

My dear friend,

Do not conclude by the long delay of my answer to thy kind letter that I was not right glad to hear from thee, and to know something of thy history. Believe me I entered into a feeling of deep sympathy with thee, for I too can bear testimony to the excellence of the dear one to whom attention is made, and can in some faint degree estimate the extent of thy bereavement.[1]

I rejoice to learn that thy health has again become comfortable. It is a great blessing at thy time of life.

I have lived a long life since I saw thee, have thought, felt and suffered and enjoyed much. Ill health has not prevented me from active and I feverently hope not altogether useless efforts for the benefit of my fellow men.

I do not know as I know exactly the location of Cheshire—did we not see it from the top of [the] mountain in our pleasant excursion to the Hanging Hills, afar off in the valley? —If I remember rightly the place looked exceedingly pleasant.

My mother is still living in tolerable health. My sister's health is very poor. My own just now, is as good as common, with the exception of a nervous pain in the head and eyes which for the last three months has compelled me to forgo writing or reading to any extent; and which must excuse the brevity of this letter.

Remember me kindly to Dr. [John] C[rane] when thee see him.

I enclose for thee a rough proof of an engraving of my face. Years have changed it greatly from what it was when I was at Hartford, but the *heart* has not grown old. This was taken last winter, and is a tolerable likeness.

Cordially and affectionately thy friend

John G. Whittier

Manuscript: University of Florida.
1. Mrs. Stella Law had died in 1841 and in 1844 Law had moved from Hartford to his birthplace in Cheshire, Connecticut, where he lived until his death in 1856.

568. To Grace Greenwood

[Amesbury] May 10, 1849

We have had a dreary spring—a gray haze in the sky—a dim, beam-shorn sun—a wind from the northeast, cold as if sifted through all the ices of frozen Labrador, as terrible almost as that chill wind which the old Moslem fable says will blow over the earth in the last days.[1] The birds hereabout have a sorry time of it, as well as "humans." There are now, however, indications of a change for the better. The blossoms of the peach and cherry are just opening, and the arbutus, anemones, and yellow violets are making glad and beautiful the banks of our river. I feel daily like thanking God for the privilege of looking upon another spring. I have written very little this spring,—the "Legend of St. Mark" is all in the line of verse that I have attempted.[2] I feel a growing disinclination to pen and ink. Over-worked and tired by the long weary years of the anti-slavery struggle, I want mental rest. I have already lived a long life, if thought and action constitute it.

I have crowded into a few years what should have been given to many.

Source: Pickard, *Life*, pp. 335–336.

Recipient: Sarah Jane Clarke (1823–1904), who went by the pen name of Grace Greenwood, was a popular essayist and verse writer during this period. She and Whittier corresponded from 1848 and he wrote a number of favorable reviews of her work for the *National Era.* Her best known works were *Greenwood Leaves* (1850) and *Haps and Mishaps of a Tour in Europe* (1854). Many of her pieces were originally published in the *Era*, and she lated edited a journal for juveniles with her husband. Her abolitionism caused her to be dropped from *Godey's Lady's Book* in 1850 and occasioned Whittier's satire, "Lines on the Portrait of a Celebrated Publisher," which humorously portrayed Grace Greenwood as a "Guy Fawkes, in petticoats."

1. Grace Greenwood had written the Whittiers on April 11, 1849, commenting on the beauty of spring in Pennsylvania. She praised Whittier's *Margaret Smith's Journal* and asked his advice on a title for her new book (letter, Essex Institute, Salem, Massachusetts).

2. Published in the *National Era*, May 3, 1849.

569. To William Plumer, Junior

Amesbury May 22, 1849

My dear friend.

This will be handed to thee by my friend and late neighbor, Charles H. Chase, who is about to remove to your village, and in whom thou wilt find an agreeable and worthy neighbor, a friend of freedom and temperance.[1]

I should ere this have acknowledged the receipt of thy kind note, and pamphlets, but, illness so severe and protracted as to compel me to virtually abandon pen and paper, and books, for several weeks must be my excuse. I have read thy speech with great pleasure—I read it however when I was a boy of twelve or fourteen. If I were in thy place I would not forgo the honor of that early advocacy of freedom for the highest office in the gift of President or people.[2]

Please remember me kindly to thy neighbor John Dow,[3] and believe me very cordially thy friend

John G. Whittier

Manuscript: New Hampshire State Library, Concord, New Hampshire.

1. Charles H. Chase (perhaps 1825?–1895) was listed as a printer in the 1854 edition of the Concord *Directory.*

2. Plumer had written to Whittier on February 8, 1849, sending him a copy of his speech against the Missouri Compromise in 1820 and asking if the *National Era* would like to publish sections of it (letter, Essex Institute, Salem, Massachusetts). Whittier had commented on Plumer's recent book, *Lyrica Sacra* (Boston, 1846), in a letter printed in the *Era*, January 14, 1847.

3. John Dow (1770?–1862), a Quaker and abolitionist, worked as a machinist in Concord.

570. To Lewis Tappan

Amesbury July 14, 1849

My dear friend.

I have been spending some weeks in the Northern part of N. H. and thy kind note relative to our fd S.'s proposition, receives my earliest notice on my return.[1] I wish it were possible for me to avail myself of so generous an offer: but in my present very weak state of health, I could be of no real service to the cause without making exertions to which my strength is inadequate. If I could visit Europe as a mere looker on, careless and indifferent in respect to the great questions which agitate it, I might possibly be benefited by it. But this I cannot do, and I can ill bear any additional excitement. But, believe me I feel none the less grateful to our dear and generous friend Sturge, and to thyself for your kindness.

I am glad to hear that thou art now a "free laborer" in the cause of freedom, and peace, and humanity. I have often marvelled at the vast amount of labor performed by thee in addition to thy daily and engrossing business, in behalf of these objects: and for thy sake, as well as for theirs, I am glad thou art able to leave what Chas Lamb calls "The dull drudgery of the Desk's hardwood."[2]

Thou wilt, I apprehend, find no lack of occupation. The church is not yet right on the question of Slavery. The nominal orthodoxy of the land has sorely suffered through the conduct of its leaders in opposing the cause of practical righteousness. No man can do more than thyself to change this state of things. The Free Mission movement has already done immense good; the old Boards will all be compelled soon to take the same ground and maintain it.

Then in the matter of political action, strong as is my confidence in the good intentions of the great mass of Free Soilers, and well satisfied as I am with the result of their labors thus far, I am not without fear that they may be drawn into some unworthy compromise. We need all thy vigilance and wisdom, to keep us straight in the line of principle. I do not fear for the integrity of the old Liberty men—the mob-tried church-censored confessors of '35—and 6. They may get off the track now and then but their instincts will set them right. But we are all now abolitionists; it is as difficult to find an open pro-Slavery man now as it was in '33 to find an anti-Slavery one; yet, I have scarcely charity enough to suppose that this marvellous conversion is altogether genuine and heart-felt. The responsibilities of the cause, never rested heavier on the genuine old fashioned abolitionist than at this time. I feel extremely anxious about the result of the attempt to unite the Barnburners with the old Hunkers in yr State. If they can come together on the basis of the Vermont resolutions I shall hope for the best.[3]

The next Congress will settle the California and N Mexico question. I look forward with hope not wholly unmingled with fear.[4] Can thee not spend a few weeks at Washington this winter?—Depend upon it there would be ample opportunity for the profitable exercise of all thy powers. Dr. Bailey is confined to his office; there needs to be some one always there to supply the members with necessary facts, for they are all sadly ignorant in this matter.

But alas, I am laying out work for others while I am myself well nigh powerless! What Providence has in store for me I know not, but my heart is full of thankfulness that I have been permitted to do something for the cause of humanity, and that with all my sins and errors I have not been suffered to live wholly for myself.

Affy thy friend.
John G. Whittier

I saw the Rogers family at Plymouth. They spoke of thee with affectionate warmth. Kind, gifted, amiable, they have all the pleasant traits of their father; but the conduct of some of the church and clergy in respect to him, has made them skeptical and prejudiced them against the forms of religious observances.

Manuscript: Library of Congress. Published: Pickard, *Life*, pp. 336–339.

1. Sturge had written to Whittier on April 20, 1849, urging him to attend the coming Peace Congress to be held in Paris in August 1849 (Richard, *Memoirs of Joseph Sturge*, pp. 432–433). Sturge had also written to Tappan that he would be glad to pay the expenses of the trip for Whittier.

2. Charles Lamb's poem, "Work." See Letter No. 273, note 2.

3. The Vermont resolutions were a series of resolutions against slavery ultimately passed by the Vermont legislature in the fall of 1849 and sent on to each Vermont senator and representative, as well as being introduced into Congress. They held: (1) slavery was a crime against humanity; (2) congressional powers could be used to stop the extension of slavery in new territory and to abolish slavery in the states themselves; (3) congressmen should resist any extension of slavery in new territory; (4) congressmen should support the extinction of slavery in the District of Columbia; and (5) New Mexico and California should be admitted to the Union as free states.

4. Ultimately California was admitted as a free state and New Mexico as a territory without any restriction on slavery.

571. To James Thomas Fields

Amesbury, July 30, 1849

My dear Fields,

Thy suspicions are by no means correct. My doubt is not anent the *Jews*, but the *jewels* whether they are genuine or paste. I can't yet make up my mind: but will let thee know in the course of the next ten days, definitely.[1] As for a title, this will nearly express the contents of the Vol. "*Old Portraits and Modern Sketches.*" by etc.[2]

Has our friend Grace visited Boston yet? When she does be good enough to remind her of her promise to visit Amesbury.[3]

I shall send the "*documents*" for thy inspection at any rate. I have a mass of material, but it's like Chaos without form, and what is worse oftentimes *void*.[4]

Thine truly
J. G. Whittier

Manuscript: Huntington Library, San Marino, California. Published, in Part: Pickard, *Life*, p. 344.

1. The reference is to something that Fields could not decipher in one of Whittier's letters or manuscripts.

2. The prose volume, *Old Portraits and Modern Sketches*, was published by Ticknor, Reed, and Fields in January 1850.

3. Grace Greenwood visited in Lynn that August and saw the Whittiers during her stay in New England.

4. Genesis 1:2.

572. To James Thomas Fields

Amesbury, August 20, 1849

My dear friend.

Wilt it be convenient for your firm to pay the Amt. due me for M. S. Journal $122, or if you will send me a check for it, I will duly acknowledge it.[1]

When I come to Boston I will confer with you relative to the prose volumes. I suppose you have so much on hand that you will not be able to publish it this fall. I can have it ready at any time.

If Sarah J. Clarke calls on you today, please say to her that my sister has written her at Lynn, and expects her as early as Wednesday of this week, if she is not otherwise engaged.

If thee see our friend Haskell ask him to send to the Era an account of the Temperance meeting this Evening.[2]

J. G. Whittier

Manuscript: Huntington Library, San Marino, California.

1. See Letter No. 573.

2. Daniel Haskell (1818–1874) was then serving as a Boston correspondent for the Newburyport *Herald*. In 1853 he became editor of the Boston *Transcript*. Father Theobald Mathew, the Irish temperance preacher, was conducting temperance meetings in Boston at this time, but no account of the meetings appeared in the *Era*.

573. To James Thomas Fields

Amesbury, August 21, 1849

Dear friend.

The check of $122 30/00 in full for per cent on the sales of "Margaret Smith's Journal" has been duly received.

In regard to your Boston Book.[1] I have nothing available on hand for it, either in prose or rhyme. But, some years ago I wrote a story for the N. England Magazine (Buckingham's) called "The Opium Eater"—I have *almost* forgotten about it, and I dare say every body else has *entirely*: which might be made use of "as good as new." You will find it in I think the 3rd. volume—(*for 1832*)—[2] If convenient, look for it. It is wholly unlike anything else of my writing as near as I can recollect.

Thine ever,
John G. Whittier

Manuscript: Huntington Library, San Marino, California. Published, in Part: Pickard, *Life*, p. 344.

1. Fields was then editing *The Boston Book. Specimens of Metropolitan Literature* (Boston, 1849). The book included some original works and reprinted articles from Longfellow, Holmes, Hawthorne, Emerson, and others. Whittier's poem "Kathleen" was included, along with his prose easay, "The Yankee Zincali."

2. "The Opium Eater" was published in March 1833.

574. To Horace Greeley

Amesbury Essex Co. (Masstts.)
August 21, 1849

H Greeley Esq
Dr friend

I enclose a copy of some lines of mine—a feeble expression of my feelings—with the wish that they may appear in the Tribune;[1] and that thou wouldst take pains to send copies of them to the new Italian paper, to Genl. Avessena, and Mr. Foresti.[2] I am not without hopes that they may be translated into Italian, and that the noble hearted Romans may hear on the banks of the Tiber the voice lifted in their behalf on the

banks of the Merrimack. Heartily affirming thy course in
regard to the Roman invasion, I am very truly

thy friend
John G. Whittier

Manuscript: New York Public Library.
    1. "To Pius IX" had appeared in the *National Era*, August 16, 1849. It was a
denunciation of the role played by Pius IX in allowing France and Austria to crush
the republic proclaimed in Rome during 1849. The rebels led by Mazzini and
Garibaldi were finally defeated and Rome was reconquered in June 1849.
    2. Giovanni F. Avesani (1790–1861), an Italian general who fought in the revo-
lution of 1848–1849.
    E. Felice Foresti (1793?–1858), another Italian patriot, was imprisoned and
exiled to America where he became a professor of Italian at Columbia College.

575. To William Sidney Thayer

Amesbury, August 24 [1849]

My Dear Friend,
    I was very glad to get a line from thee, and the poem
enclosed pleased me exceedingly. The concluding verse is
admirable and the whole conception good. I have just sent it
to the "Era."[1]
    Give my best love to thy mother (and father, if he is at
home), and to Sarah and James,[2] and believe me

Very cordially thy friend,
John G. Whittier

P. S. Elizabeth and mother send their love to thee and thine.
We are right glad thou hast so good a friend in Mrs. Lyman,
and still more so that her kindness is so well deserved on thy
part. From my heart, I cannot but thank that woman for
what she has done for thee. God bless her![3]

W.

Source: Susan I. Lesley, *Recollections of My Mother* (Boston, 1886), p. 454.
    Recipient: William Sidney Thayer (1829–1864), the oldest son of Abijah
Thayer, was born in Haverhill and had graduated from Harvard in 1847. He was
connected with the New York *Evening Post*, serving as its Washington correspondent in 1861, and was United States consul general for Egypt where he died
on May 6, 1864.
    1. The poem, "The Fountain of Youth," was published in the *Era*, August 30,
1849. The poem deals with an older Ponce de Leon realizing that the real fountain
of youth is found in "earnest toiling love."
    2. Sarah Thayer (b. 1825) was the first child of Abijah Thayer. James Thayer
(1833–1902) graduated from Harvard in 1852, became a lawyer, and in 1874 was
named a professor of law at Harvard. He was noted for his work on constitutional
law and the law of evidence.
    3. Anne Jean Lyman (1789–1867), then the widow of Judge Lyman of North-
ampton, had befriended the Thayers since their arrival in Northampton. She not
only encouraged both the Thayer boys, William and James, to develop their

intellectual interests, but also she provided money for their education herself and secured support for them from other friends. James later wrote of her: "It is impossible to tell you all that she did for me; I will only say that nothing could have been more strenuous and effective than her efforts in influencing others in our behalf and nothing more constant than the kind offices which she personally did us" (*Recollections of My Mother*, p. 457).

576. To James Thomas Fields

Monday Morn. [October 1849]

My dear Fields.

There is a proof missing—rather an important one—containing the principal part of *Marvel*; and ending at the 112 page—[1] I got but a single proof last week, and this morning I recd. the proof from pages 113 to 128—It is the one before this which I want and must have.

Thine ever.

J. G. W.

Whipple's book is very good. Have sent a notice to the Era.[2]

Manuscript: Huntington Library, San Marino, California.
1. "Andrew Marvell," one of the biographical sketches to be included in *Old Portraits and Modern Sketches*, then in press.
2. *Lectures on Subjects Connected with Literature and Life* (Boston, 1849). Reviewing it in the *National Era*, November 1, 1849, Whittier said: "His style is remarkably direct and energetic, a fitting medium of his clear and sharply defined conceptions—terse, epigrammatic, brilliant, rising at times into true eloquence."

577. To Charles Sumner

Amesbury, November 7, 1849

My dear Sumner.

Wilt thou see that this is in the hands of R R[antoul] *as soon as possible*. If he is not willing to subscribe to the "basis" proposed by S. C. Phillips we must know it. I think he is, although [he] may deny it.[1]

I can vote for no man who is not in favor of that "basis."

In haste thine ever

J. G. W.

Manuscript: Harvard University.
1. Robert Rantoul and Whittier were both candidates on a coalition Free Soil and Democratic ticket as two of the five Essex County senatorial candidates. The coalition was formed on the basis of opposition to the extension of slavery to free territories and succeeded in electing thirteen senators and 130 representatives. Neither Whittier nor Rantoul was elected, though the votes were very close.

578. To Enoch Lewis

Amesbury (Mass) November 10, 1849

To the Editor of the Friend

I send thee herewith two copies of the Boston Daily Transcript containing some strictures upon the unjust representation of the character of William Penn, by Thomas B. Macaulay in his History of England. They are from the pen of *Lucius M. Langcut*, a gentleman well known to the literary and philanthropic public for his cultural taste, learning and talents devoted to the best interests of his fellow men.[1] His "Temperance Tales" have been widely circulated, and have been instrumental in effecting a great amount of good. As the unbiased testimony of a close historical student, whose religious views are widely different from those of our society, I have thought these papers might be worthy of a place in thy valuable journal.[2]

J. G. W.

Manuscript: Central Michigan University.

1. Lucius M. Langcut, the pen name of Lucius M. Sargent (1786–1867), was noted as an antiquary, author, and journalist. His two volumes, *Temperance Tales*, published in 1848, were very popular. He was then writing a column in the *Transcript* entitled, "Dealings with the Dead." Nos. LXIV, LXV, LXVI, published in the *Transcript* on October 20, 27, and November 5, dealt with Macaulay's treatment of the Quakers. Two more numbers on November 12 and 17 finished his examination.

2. Lewis apparently never published these articles (see Letter No. 584).

579. To Francis James Child

Amesbury December 1, 1849

F. J. Child Esq.

It is not without regret that I feel obliged to decline the invitation in respect to the P. B. K. Poem—with which I should have been honored.[1]

The state of my health is such that I do not feel at liberty to enter into any engagement for the future.

Very truly thy friend
John G. Whittier

Permit me to suggest the name of Dr. T. W. Parsons of Boston —who has so ably translated *Dante*.[2]

Manuscript: Harvard University.

Recipient: Francis James Child (1825–1896), the noted philologist and professor, was then an instructor at Harvard. He had already edited *Four Old Plays* (Cambridge, 1848) and had begun his study of language and philology. His 1863 article on Chaucer began an accurate study of Chaucer's metrics, but his main contribution to scholarship was his *English and Scottish Popular Ballads*, which was issued in five volumes from 1883 to 1898.

1. Bayard Taylor was ultimately chosen as the poet, and he recited his "The American Legend" on July 18, 1850, for the anniversary meeting of the Harvard Phi Beta Kappa.

2. Thomas William Parsons (1819–1892), a practicing dentist, was better known as a poet and translator. In 1843 he published *The First Ten Cantos of the Inferno* and published a complete edition of the *Inferno* in 1867. Up to his death he was working on a complete translation of the *Divine Comedy*, but it was never finished.

580. To Moses Austin Cartland[1]

Amesbury December 12, 1849

Dear Cousin,

Et tu Brute?[2] And so thee too want my autograph! I had really thought better of thee, but I see there is no escape for me; I have to "lend my name" to "accommodate" friends oftener than a good natured merchant on Change; The very mail that brought thy note, brought two other polite requests for my name. In short, like John at Patmos, I hear a voice continually crying "*Write!*"[3]

So then thou hadst a glimpse of the old homestead. I'm glad of it; it will be an incident worth remembering. Thy picture of the Mermaid is pronounced a true one by competent judges. Never having seen the creature I can only view it as a work of art in which respect I think highly of it.

I do not often comply with these requests for my name but in thy case, as a sort of family matter, I see no good reason for refusing.

We had a very pleasant visit from thee, and should be pleased to have it repeated whenever it is in thy power. We are so situated that we seldom see any of our relations.

Elizabeth sends her love and with mine I subscribe myself.

Affectionately thy cousin,
John G. Whittier

In the economy of God no effort however small put forth for the right cause fails of its effect; no voice however feeble, lifted up for Truth ever dies amidst the confused noises of time.

John G. Whittier

Manuscript: Central Michigan College.

1. The identification is conjectural, but the familiar tone suggests a correspondent like Moses Cartland.

2. *Julius Caesar*, III, i, 77. Marcus Junius Brutus (85?–42 B.C.), a Roman statesman, was one of the conspirators who murdered Julius Caesar.

3. Revelation 1:9–11.

581. To Ann Elizabeth Wendell

Amesbury, February 8, 1850

My dear Cousin

On returning from Boston a day or two ago I found thy letter awaiting me. I thank thee from my heart for the kind remembrance. I have thought a great deal of thee and thy father of late. I have sincerely sympathized with you in your trials and business difficulties. I hope to see thee in N. E. this summer. Elizabeth is under the care of Dr. Perry of Boston,[1] at her friend Harriet Minot Pitman's with some hope of relief from his skill and care.[2] Mother and I have just returned home, and are living quite in the quiet here, with only a little girl and a cat for company, the one to "do chores" and the other to catch mice. Mother has been staying with Aunt Phebe at Lynn, and I have been in Boston.[3] I went out to Pawtucket last week and spent three days with Gideon and his family and had a very pleasant visit. They all wished thee could have been with us. We had a pleasant ride, first day, to the old Southfield meeting—a house as old as the time of G. Fox, and perhaps he preached in it when he visited America. Mary Eliz. makes a good housekeeper for her father, and Emma is a fine, pretty, half-spoiled child, altogether interesting.[4] The loss of her mother [Mary Whittier Smith], the sense of responsibility and duty, have made Mary E. somewhat different from what she was when at Philadelphia—she is more thoughtful and subdued although still cheerful and warm-hearted as ever.

I send thee with this a little book of mine.[5] I wish it was better, but it is as good as the writer, I fear. Much of it was written under circumstances very unfavorable.

I am sorry to hear of E. L[loyd's] illness. She stays too much at home, alone; she needs society and change. Her mind is too active. I wish she could visit N E with thee, next summer.

I wish I could say anything favorable of my own health. I cannot read or write without pain and weariness. But I will not complain. I have many blessings. I have more than I deserve of happiness. Would that I could make a better improvement of the smiles and chastenings of Him who knows what is best for his erring and unstable child!

Write me, dear Cousin, when thou canst. Remember me affectionately to thy father, to Isaac and Mary and Elisha and Margaret and all who may care to hear from me, and believe me ever and truly thy affectionate Cousin

John G. Whittier

Elizabeth had an excellent letter from E Nicholson, bright and genial as herself.

Source: Snyder, "Whittier's Letters to Ann Elizabeth Wendell," pp. 84–85.

1. Marshall Sears Perry (1805–1859) received his M. D. from Harvard in 1830 and began medical practice in Boston in 1832. He was one of the most popular and successful physicians in Boston and attended Charles Sumner after Sumner had been assaulted in the Senate.

2. Harriet Minot Pitman was then living in Somerville, a suburb of Boston.

3. Phebe Austin Whittier (1798–1871), the daughter of Obadiah Whittier (1758–1814) and sister to Mary Whittier Smith and Anna Whittier Wendell, married Edmund Johnson, a successful farmer. Abby, Caroline, and Mary, three of the Johnson children, as grown women later lived at Oak Knoll with Whittier during his residence there in the 1870's and 1880's.

4. Mary Elizabeth Smith took over the running of the house after her mother's death on May 5, 1849. She later married Frank Pratt. Her sister, Emma (b. 1836), married Henry Smith.

5. *Old Portraits and Modern Sketches*, which was issued in January by Ticknor, Reed, and Fields.

582. To Ann Elizabeth Wendell

[Amesbury] February 15, 1850

My dear Cousin.

I have waited a long time to send a package of books for thee, E. L[loyd] . and E. N[icholson] . but seeing no opportunity I send the enclosed note and could add more to it were I able. My health is greatly impaired. Elizabeth is still in Boston. My best love to all.

J. G. W.

Source: University of Virginia.

583. To Nathaniel Hawthorne

Amesbury, February 22, 1850

N. Hawthorne Esq
Dear friend

I have just learned with regret and surprise that no remittance has been rendered thee for thy admirable story in the Era.[1] Dr. B. wrote me on receipt of it weeks ago, that he had directed his agent in Boston G. W. Light, Cornhill, to pay thee.[2]

The pecuniary affairs of the Era are in the hands of Dr. B. but I was unwilling to leave the matter unadjusted and hasten to forward the amount. It is, I feel, an inadequate compensation.[3]

I am glad to hear of thy forthcoming book. It is spoken of highly by the publishers.[4]

God bless and prosper thee!

Truly thy friend
John G. Whittier

Manuscript: Huntington Library, San Marino, California. Published, in Part: Julian Hawthorne, *Nathaniel Hawthorne and His Wife* (Boston, 1885), I, 355–356.

Recipient: Nathaniel Hawthorne (1804–1864) was then at the height of his powers, having just finished *The Scarlet Letter*. It is doubtful that he and Whittier, though both from Essex County and interested in folklore, colonial history, and supernaturalism, ever met more than once or twice. Whittier had recognized Hawthorne's talent early, reviewing "Sights from a Steeple" with approval in October 1830. Whittier later declared that the "weird and subtle beauty of his legendary tales in [the *Democratic Review*] early awakened my admiration, and rebuked and shamed my own poor efforts in a similar direction" (Letter No. 938). Hawthorne on his part professed to admire Whittier as a man; but in his review of Whittier's *Supernaturalism of New England*, Hawthorne felt that Whittier's moralistic tone and refusal to believe in the tales as an author must believe in his narrative minimized Whittier's achievement. Hawthorne said that Whittier "stoops to the theme with the austere dignity of a schoolmaster at his amusements; a condescension that may seem exaggerated, when we consider that the subject will probably retain a human interest, long after his more earnest efforts shall have lost their importance, in the progress of society." Hawthorne concluded, though: "We like the book, and look upon it as no unworthy contribution from a poet to that species of literature which only a poet should meddle with" (*Literary World*, April 17, 1847, I, 247–248).

1. "The Great Stone Face" was published in the *Era* on January 24, 1850.

2. George Washington Light (1809–1868), a publisher and author, edited many magazines in Boston, including *The Young Men's Magazine* in 1847, and printed a book of poetry in 1851.

3. According to S. T. Pickard, Hawthorne received $25.

4. *The Scarlet Letter* was published in March 1850.

584. To Enoch Lewis

Amesbury, March 4, 1850

I have read, with pleasure, several aritcles, original and selected, in the "Review," in defence of William Penn against the injurious and unjust charges of the historian Macaulay. Enough has, perhaps, already appeared to satisfy any unprejudiced mind, that the picture drawn by Macaulay, of the great champion of religious freedom in the seventeenth century, is altogether erroneous,—a perversion of the actual facts of history, which has scarcely a parallel in the annals of literature. It has however occurred to me, that at the present time an edition of the Life of Penn by Thomas Clarkson,—an exceedingly well written and impartial biography—would find a ready sale, and would be the means of more completely disabusing the public mind, in respect to the gross misrepresentations of Macaulay. I could wish, also, that there might be added to it, by way of notes or appendix, a brief review of Penn's *political life and writings*, showing his hearty sympathy and co-operation with the great Martyr of political freedom, Algernon Sydney,—and that in his support of the tolerant measures of James II. he acted in perfect consistency with his whole life and professions, as a friend of unqualified religious freedom: and that so far from being accountable for the other measures of that monarch, which are justly held in condemnation, he used his influence to prevent and soften them,—and that there is not the slightest ground for charging him with any participation in any act inconsistent with his liberal political principles, and his Christian profession. So much, at least, it seems to me, is due to truth and justice. I have no doubt that such an edition would be soon exhausted, if some one of our large publishing houses would undertake the republication.[1]

While upon this subject, I cannot refrain from expressing my satisfaction in the perusal of a series of papers, published in the Boston Daily Transcript, from the pen of Lucius M. Sargent, who is well known as a writer of taste and discrimination.[2] He enters into a very searching analysis of Macaulay's character of Penn, and exposes its misrepresentation and perversion of facts, with a great deal of acuteness and justifiable severity. His strictures derive additional importance from the fact that the author has no sympathy with the religious opinions of the society of which William Penn was an eminent member.

J. G. W.

Source: The *Friends' Review*, March 1850.

1. Following the letter was an editorial note which stated: "If the writer of the preceding communication would favour the public with notes, or an appendix, such as he has suggested, there can be very little doubt that the additional matter, thus supplied, would greatly enhance the worth of that valuable biography." Clarkson's *Memoirs of the Private and Public Life of William Penn* was reissued in 1849 in London by W. E. Forster with a preface in reply to the charges of Macaulay.

2. See Letter No. 578.

585. To Harriet Farley

Amesbury, March 8, 1850

Dear Friend:—

My friend, J. Aubin, has handed me a line from thee, with a request that I would forward thee the statistics of his corporation which I now enclose.[1] I would add, that the utmost harmony prevails and has always done so, between friend Aubin and his help—a feeling of esteem on one hand and almost paternal care on the other. The girls who have left his employ are among the best housewives in this place and vicinity—and there have been few instances of immoral conduct on the part of the operatives. I think on the whole, that Amesbury is the pattern manufacturing village in New England.

The school spoken of has been well attended. It is under the care of an excellent and competent teacher. The Library will be a good one—the room is neatly fitted up.[2] Wishing thee success in replying to Senator Clemens,[3]

I am, very truly, thy friend,

J. G. Whittier

P. S. I hold myself responsible for the facts here stated. I believe they are entirely correct.

J. G. W.

Source: The *Amesbury Villager*, May 16, 1850.

Recipient: Harriet Farley (1817–1907) had worked in the Lowell mills as a factory girl and edited a periodical, *The Lowell Offering*, containing writings of the factory girls. It attracted much attention, and in 1847 she issued a collection of her writing from the journal entitled *Shells from the Strand of the Sea of Genius*. After her marriage in 1854 she spent most of her life in New York, doing occasional writing and publishing.

1. Joshua Aubin (1789–1867) was the principal agent and superintendent of the Amesbury Flannel Manufacturing Company for over thirty years. He helped found the Amesbury Public Library and contributed over 700 volumes to its collection. In his factory he employed over 220 workers.

2. The company had opened an evening school for girls between fourteen and eighteen, while Aubin's own library of 750 books was used as a basis for the factory library.

3. Harriet Farley published a small pamphlet entitled *Operatives Reply to Hon. Jere Clemens, being a sketch of Factory Life and Factory enterprises, etc.*, which answered the derogatory remarks made by Clemens regarding conditions in New England mills. Whittier's letter and the statistics from Aubin were also published in the pamphlet.

Jeremiah Clemens (1814–1865), a lawyer from Alabama, fought in the Mexican War and served in the United States Senate from 1849 to 1853. During the Civil War he occupied an office under the Confederacy, but eventually came to the Union side in 1864.

586. To An Unidentified Correspondent

Amesbury, March 26, 1850

My dear doctor.

When I had the pleasure of meeting thee last summer, I believe I mentioned to thee the case of a poor sick young woman in Holderness—and I think I mentioned also her name—which I regret has now escaped me. I have been thinking today of her wretched home and desolation and sickness and have felt desirous of knowing something of her condition.[1]

W.

Manuscript: Amesbury Whittier Home.
   1. In a note attached to the manuscript S. T. Pickard states that this is a part of a letter written by Whittier. The letter may never have been sent.

587. To James Thomas Fields

Amesbury. April 6, 1850

My dear Fields,
   I am a little uncertain about publishing my Songs of Labor and other poems, this spring or summer, but perhaps it would be best after all to get them out now. The pieces will make a volume of some 150, or 200 pages, printed in the form of Longfellow's.[1]
   I wish to know upon what terms I can get them published so that the copyright may be mine. How is it with Longfellow, and Lowell and Holmes? What is your interest in their volumes, if any, beyond yr pay for printing and commission on the sales?—Please write me and let me know that I may decide as to my own course.
   In the Era of last week is a take-off of Godey.[2] The printers have spoiled one line by substituting "whistling" for "whirling"—And now business over, let me, in all sincerity, bachelor as I am, congratulate thee on thy escape from single (misery?) blessedness.[3] It is the very wisest thing thee can do. Were I autocrat, I would see to it that any young man over 25 and any young woman over 20 was married without delay. Perhaps, on second thought, it might be well to keep one old maid and one old bachelor in each town, by way of warning, just as the Spartans did their drunken Helots.

Cordially and truly thy fd.
J. G. Whittier

Manuscript: Huntington Library, San Marino, California. Published, in Part: Pickard, Life, p. 348.
   1. Song of Labor, and Other Poems was published in August 1850 by Ticknor, Reed, and Fields.
   2. "Lines on the Portrait of a Celebrated Publisher" (National Era, April 4, 1850) was a satire of Louis Godey, who had dropped Grace Greenwood from his Godey's Lady's Book for fear that her abolitionist feelings would offend southern readers. By a coincidence, Godey's portrait was issued about the same time.
   Louis Godey (1804–1878) started the Lady's Book in 1830 and edited it until 1877, making it the most popular woman's magazine in America. The magazine was noted for its devotion to virtue and moral influence as the special spheres of women.
   3. Eliza Josephine Willard (1831–1851), daughter of a Boston clockmaker, married Fields on March 13, 1850.

588. To James Thomas Fields

Amesbury, May 6, 1850

My dear Fields

I send thee the proof sadly disfigured, for which thank thyself. I have altered some of the rhymes; others I have left to their fate—Heaven help them, I cannot. In the verse commencing:

> "By many a Northern lake and hill"

I don't think I've mended the matter.

> pasture }   water }
> faster }   shorter }   both are

good Yankee rhymes, but out of New England they would be cashiered. Take thy choice. I see no difference.[1]

I have two other songs of Labor but I cannot get the spirit of the early ones, and I think it best to let them go by themselves. I have exhausted that vein so far as I am concerned. I send thee a considerable part of the copy. The rest will be forthcoming.

I humbly thank thee for thy suggestions. Let me have more of them. I had a hearty laugh at thy hint of the "carnal" bearing of one of my lines. It is now simply *rural*. I might have made some other needful changes, had I not been suffering with head-ache all day. I wish to have the pieces in this volume as correct as possible.

The pages are not right I suspect. For I have an introduction in rhyme to precede the body of the volume, of some seven or eight stanzas of perhaps 40 or 45 lines in all. Shall I send it?—it is not copied and I cannot do it today. Or will it not be wanted till the last?[2]

—Kearsarge is pronounced always Ké-ar-sarge—

I send *"Memories"* out of respect to thy opinion and that of our friend Whipple. Is it best to print it?—[3]

It strikes me as best to put all the notes appended to the poems in the end of the book. The page looks better and more uniform.[4]

Cordially thy frd.
J. G. Whittier

Manuscript: Huntington Library, San Marino, California. Published, in Part: Pickard, *Life*, pp. 348–349.
    1. The last verse of "The Drovers," which was finally printed as:

> "By many a Northern lake and hill,
>   From many a mountain pasture,
> Shall fancy play the Drover still,
>   And speed the long night faster."

2. A poem titled "Dedication" was published in the book.

3. Whipple had singled out "Memories" from Whittier's 1843 book, *Lays of My Home, and Other Poems*, as one of his best. It was reprinted in the new volume.

4. The notes were so printed.

589. To William Lloyd Garrison

Amesbury May 13, 1850

Dear friend Garrison:

I have just laid down a New York paper giving the disgraceful details of the outrage upon Free Speech at your late meeting in New York; and I cannot resist the inclination to drop a line to thee, expressive of my hearty sympathy with thee in this matter.[1] We have not always thought alike in respect to the best means of promoting the anti-slavery cause; and perhaps we differ quite as widely now as ever, but when the right to advocate emancipation in *any* shape is called in question, it is no time to split hairs, or to be fastidious in our exclusiveness. Wendell Phillips and Frederick Douglass,[2] and thyself were assailed not because of any peculiarities of opinion which you may entertain on other subjects, but because you were abolitionists and practical believers in the Doctrines of the Declaration of Independence. So understanding it, I thank you for your perseverence and firmness in vindicating rights dear to us all.

The great battle for free speech and free assembling is to be fought over. The signal has been given at Washington, and commercial cupidity at the North is once more marshalling its mobs against us. The scandalous treachery of Webster, and the *backing* he has received from Andover and Harvard, show that we have nothing to hope for from the great political parties and religious sects. Let us be prepared [for] the worst, and may God give us strength, wisdom and ability to withstand it.[3]

With esteem and sympathy
I am very truly thy friend
John G. Whittier

Manuscript: Boston Public Library. Published: Garrison, *William Lloyd Garrison*, III, 300.

1. Garrison had attended the anniversary meeting of the American Anti-Slavery Society in New York City on May 7, along with Wendell Phillips, Frederick Douglass, Francis Jackson, and many others. His speeches and others were interrupted and stopped by a Captain Rynder who had previously organized the Astor Place riot in 1849 in behalf of the actor Edwin Forrest. Rynder and his mob were allowed free reign by city officials and so insulted the speakers and prevented free discussion that Garrison closed the meeting.

2. Frederick Douglass (1817?–1895), an escaped slave, had served as an agent

for the Massachusetts Anti-Slavery Society since 1841. Despite mobbings and personal vilification, Douglass went on to become an outstanding orator. He established The *North Star*, a Negro anti-slavery paper which appeared from 1847 to 1864, and published an account of his life in 1845. During the Civil War he helped recruit Negro troops and afterward served as minister to Haiti from 1889 to 1891.

3. Whittier is referring to Webster's speech on March 7, 1850, in support of Clay's resolutions, which became known as the Compromise of 1850. The final compromise bill admitted California as a free state, organized New Mexico without restriction on slavery, paid money to Texas, enacted a much stronger Fugitive Slave Law, and abolished the slave trade in the District of Columbia after January 1851. Whittier's response to the speech was one of surprise, grief, and outrage, and occasioned his greatest abolitionist poem, "Ichabod," printed in the *National Era* on May 2, 1850, containing these famous lines on Webster's betrayal:

> "All else is gone; from those great eyes
>   The soul has fled:
> When faith is lost, when honor dies,
>   The man is dead!"

590. To an Unidentified Correspondent[1]

Amesbury. May 20, 1850

My dear friend.

This will be handed thee by my friend and townsman James Babson[2] who makes his first visit to Washington—a Whig—but not a Webster Whig. He wishes to see and hear what is notable and desired a note to thee.

I need not tell thee that I heartily and cordially approve thy course, and thank thee for thy noble, though I fear unavailing effort in defense of Freedom.

Thine truly
John G. Whittier

Manuscript: New Hampshire Historical Society.

1. The letter is located in the John H. George papers, but since he was never in Congress and was opposed to abolition, he cannot be the recipient. He was a law partner of Charles H. Peaslee, then serving as Democratic congressman in Washington, so Peaslee may possibly be the recipient (see Letter No. 523, note 2).

2. James Babson (1824–1883), an Amesbury neighbor of Whittier, was a merchant in the drug business and worked with Whittier in the Amesbury lyceum.

591. To James Thomas Fields

Amesbury, May 23, 1850

My dear Fields,

I had only a few minutes yesterday to look at the last proof of my little book. I like the appearance of its title-page, etc.

Is the introductory line worked off yet? If not, I would like to have the heading altered. Instead of To---- which on sober second thought looks rather affectedly mystical, I should have it thus: —

   To A. L. Pennock of Haverford Pa.

The title of the page might be either, "To A L Pennock" or "Dedication."[1] —But I am apprehensive all this is too late—If so let it pass.

   I would not work off a large edition, as I fear that there are some few verbal errors, which I wd like to set right.[2] Two or three of the proofs I have been unable to read over myself, and I cannot vouch for their correctness.

Very truly and cordially thy friend
John G. Whittier

Manuscript: Historical Society of Pennsylvania.

1. The title was left as "Dedication."

2. An edition of 1,900 copies was run off in August and a second printing was done that fall.

592. To James Thomas Fields

Amesbury, May 26, 1850

Dear Fields.

   I think the large type would look better if it were spaced out more, and made as open as the small is. *As it is* I think the latter preferable, although, I might like the large type if it were as open as the other.

   You crowd the page too much, I think. I should strike one line off from the small type, and 2 or perhaps 4 from the large.

   However, as they say in the East "who is my mother's son" that I should presume to dictate to thy superior wisdom? Do as *seemeth* best in thy own eyes, and I shall take it for granted that it *is* best.

   I send thee Godey *done* after my fashion. It was written before I heard of Calhoun's illness, or I should have substituted Foot.[1]

Thine truly
J. G. Whittier

Manuscript: Huntington Library, San Marino, California. Published, in Part: Pickard, *Life*, pp. 349–350.

1. In his "Lines on the Portrait of a Celebrated Publisher," Whittier made a satiric reference to Calhoun, who died on March 31, 1850.

   Henry S. Foote (1804–1880), a Mississippi lawyer, served in the Senate from 1847 to 1852, when he became governor of Mississippi. He supported the compromise bill of 1850.

593. To James Thomas Fields

[May 1850]

Dear Fields.

I promise not to bother you with additions after this, but I could not be satisfied with the Lumbermen as it was. So pray see to the proof as I shall not be likely to have it I suppose.

In the Huskers, the schoolmaster's rhymes should have a name of some sort, and I have called them "The Corn Song"— which may be put in type a little smaller than that which heads the pieces. I am not very particular about it but if it can be done I wd like it. I give in about the "corn-fed girls"[1] — notwithstanding Allan Ramsay[2] or somebody else [who] talks of "kail-fed lassies." Pray continue thy labors of love, and between us we'll make something of the book.

Thine truly
J. G. W.

Manuscript: Huntington Library, San Marino, California.
1. Whittier had originally written lines which read:

"Who will not thank the kindly earth,
    And bless our corn fed girls."

Fields asked him to change it to "farmer girls," which Whittier finally did.
2. Allan Ramsay (1686–1758) had edited a group of Scottish ballads, which edition was popular in the eighteenth century and influenced Robert Burns.

594. To James Thomas Fields

[May 1850]

The doom which to the guilty pair
    Without the walls of Eden came,
Transforming sinless ease to care
And rugged toil, no more shall bear
The burden of old crime, or mark of primal shame.

A blessing now, a curse no more;
    Since He etc

Dear Fields.

Pray get out the book as soon as possible for yr. own sake. I have a terrible propensity after it is too late to see something which I ought to have seen before—

—For instance in the Introductory lines I wish to add a verse before the concluding one, and alter the first line of that also, as above. And still further reflection has persuaded me to strike out "To A. L. P. of etc." and substitute simply *"Dedi-cation."* Can it be done?—[1] Thanks for the English reprint—a neat vol. but what is it to a poor dog of an author?[2] Never mind, I don't go for international copy right, for we Yankees get more than we lose, as yet.

Thine truly
J. G. W.

Manuscript: Huntington Library, San Marino, California. Published, in Part: Pickard, *Life*, p. 350.

1. The verse was inserted for the printed volume and the next line changed. "Dedication" was also left without the "To A. L. P."

2. *Poems by John G. Whittier* (London: G. Routledge, 1850) was a reprint of Mussey's 1849 edition.

595. To James Thomas Fields

Amesbury June 15, 1850

My dear Fields.

As the book is delayed will it be a difficult matter to add the enclosed to it?—It will only be adding three plates more, and an addition of a line to the table of contents. Perhaps, however, the sheets are worked off already, in which case, I will thank thee to send the piece back to me. For particular reasons I wd like to have the piece in the volume; but [I] leave the matter to thy better judgment of what is practicable or expedient.[1]

When will Sumner's book appear?—Grace Greenwood's?[2] I hope she has made a judicious selection of her pieces: She has written some admirable things, and at other times she has been well nigh as careless as thy friend.

J. G. Whittier

P. S. If the sheets are worked off—can you not send me a copy of them?—

Manuscript: Huntington Library, San Marino, California.

1. It is not certain what this poem is, but the last poem listed in the volume is "To A. K. on Receiving a Basket of Sea Mosses," which was not published in the *National Era* until August 22, 1850.

2. Charles Sumner's *Orations and Speeches, 1845–1850* and Grace Greenwood's *Greenwood Leaves: A Collection of Sketches and Letters* were both issued by Ticknor, Reed, and Fields in 1850.

596. To Rufus Griswold

Amesbury, June 21, 1850

My Dear Fr. Griswold: —

I learn from my friend F. W. Kellogg[1] that Alice and Phoebe Cary, of Ohio, are on their way to the East, and would be glad to see them at my place if they come to Boston.[2] Presuming that thou wilt see them in N. Y. I have taken the liberty to invite them, through thee, to call on me. I have been quite ill this spring and my sister also is an invalid, and we see little company, but I should feel sorry to have the "sweet singers" of the West so near and not see them.

Dost ever come to Boston? I should be very glad to see thee at Amesbury. I have a pleasant and grateful recollection of our acquaintance in N. Y. and Boston. I shall be obliged to thee if thou wilt kindly remember me to Tuckerman. I like his last book exceedingly, and shall notice it soon in the *Era*.[3]

Thine cordially
John G. Whittier

Source: Griswold, *Correspondence and Papers of Rufus Griswold*, p. 266.

1. Perhaps Stephen W. Kellogg (1822–1904), born in Massachusetts, who became a lawyer in Connecticut in 1848 and then a judge. He was a prominent Republican in the state and served in the House of Representatives.

2. Alice Cary (1820–1871) and Phoebe Cary (1824–1871), two sisters from near Cincinnati, had obtained popularity with their poems. Whittier helped introduce them to a reading public and had many of their poems published in the *National Era*. He reviewed their first joint volume, *The Poems of Alice and Phoebe Cary*, in the *National Era*, December 13, 1849, with these remarks: "Alice Cary occupies the first and largest portion of the book. Her poems evince the imaginative power of the true poet—the divine creative facility. Her musical talent is seldom at fault, and there is something peculiarly delicate and graceful in the sweet, half-pensive flow of her verse. Phoebe Cary is a stronger and more vigorous writer—she has less of wild fancy than her sister, but her pieces are on the whole more perfect—she less often sacrifices reason to rhyme, and meaning to melody. . . . The moral tone of these poems in unexceptional, and in the freest play of their fancy and imagination the writers never lose sight of Christian reverence and humility." One of the highlights of their eastern visit in 1850 was a meeting with Whittier at Amesbury. Whittier's poem, "The Singer," written after the death of Alice, contains an account of the visit and a characterization of both sisters. In the 1850's the sisters settled in New York, where they continued to write and publish individual volumes of poetry until their deaths in 1871.

3. Whittier reviewed Tuckerman's *The Optimist* (New York, 1850) in the *Era*, July 4, 1850. He especially praised Tuckerman's essays for their "calm, quiet appreciation of the beautiful in common and daily life."

597. To Grace Greenwood

Amesbury July 29 [1850] [1]

My dear friend

We have heard nothing of thee for so long a time that we began to fear that we should, after all, miss of seeing thee at Amesbury.

Why not come up next third day (Tuesday) if fair weather, if not, next day?—And ask your friends Anna Phillips and Miss Scoble to accompany you. [2] We should be very glad to see them.

Ever dear friend
Thine truly
John G. Whittier

The first train reaches here at 1/2 past 9. in the morning—the last leaves here 1/4 before 5. in the afternoon.

Manuscript: Historical Society of Pennsylvania.
1. The year is not certain, but the similarities to Letter No. 599 suggest this year.
2. Anna Hubbard Phillips (b. 1827) of Lynn had achieved some newspaper success with her poems and was included in *Female Poets of America* in 1849. Fields also included some of her poems in his *Boston Book.*

598. To Henry Wadsworth Longfellow

Lynn, August 22, 1850

Dear friend.

Dr. and Margaret Bailey are now at the Ocean House Phillip's point where they will remain two or three weeks. [1] They wd rejoice to know thee and I feel sure that thou wouldst find them most agreeable acquaintances. The Dr. has won the confidence and esteem of all classes at Washington and Margaret Bailey is one of the best specimens of a lady I have ever known. She combines the Southern warmth with the Northern vigor—I know that thou and Mrs. L. will like her exceedingly. [2]

I shall be at Lynn again in a few days, but in the mean time our mutual fd Charles Sumner would be happy to introduce Dr and Mrs B to thee. I shall direct my publisher to send thee my little book, as a poor return for the pleasure I have derived from thy publications, and more especially as a token of the very sincere regard and esteem of thy friend

J. G. Whittier

Manuscript: Harvard University.
1. Margaret Shands Bailey (b. 1812), originally from Virginia, had married

Gamaliel Bailey in 1833. She edited the *Friend of Youth*, a Washington monthly devoted to children, from 1849 to 1852 and after Bailey's death in June 1859, she carried on publication of the *Era* until March 15, 1860.

2. Frances Appleton Longfellow (1817–1861), Longfellow's second wife, married him on July 13, 1843.

599. To Grace Greenwood

Amesbury. August 28 [1850]

Dear friend

My sister wishes me to say to thee that she should be glad to have thee come up the last of this week. Why not come in the train which reaches here at 1/2 past 4. pm on Sixth day, Friday!—We have friends now with us—relatives—but they will leave in a day or two.

I want to talk with thee about thy book and about one that I have in prospect. But we will promise not to trouble thee with literary matters—we want to see thee altogether apart from such "nonsense," as Dr. Noggs would say[1] —we like Grace Greenwood well but we want her to bring Sarah Jane Clarke with her.

Sister says if thy engagements will allow, thee had better come on *Fifth day*, as she wants thee to see Dr. *Weld* who is now in this region and who will leave soon. The old man will be glad to meet thee.

Besides, there's our friend Buchanan Reid,[2] —he must be seen. So come if thy friends at Lynn or Salem have no fishing party or horseback ride in prospect. If they have, we can offer I fear small inducement for thy coming. Ask thy friend Ann H. Phillips if she has not a song for *Mazzini* as well as *Rienzi*.[3]

Ever and truly thy friend
John G. Whittier

Manuscript: Essex Institute, Salem, Massachusetts.

1. Probably Newman Noggs, the eccentric, kind-hearted clerk in *Nicholas Nickleby*, by Charles Dickens.

2. Thomas Buchanan Read (1822–1872) started his career as a painter, but began writing poetry and prose in the 1840's. He published volumes of poetry which achieved some success, edited books, and then in the 1850's returned to painting and lived in Europe. He continued to write and paint until his death.

3. Joseph Mazzini (1808–1872) was of course, the great Italian patriot, while Cola di Rienzi (1313?–1354) was a Roman orator and tribune. Miss Phillips had written a poem, "Nina to Rienzi."

600. To Waldo Higginson

Amesbury September 11, 1850

My dear fd.

I enclose to thee a line from Dr. Palfrey to thy brother, on the subject of a new F. S. paper in Boston. The importance of such a paper and of securing such an editor I am sure thou will fully appreciate.[1]

Be good enough to consult with Sumner, W. A. White,[2] W. Jackson and others on the subject. Dr P.'s suggestion as to the importance of starting the paper before our State Meeting accords with my own views.

In haste, very truly thy fd.

John G. Whittier

Manuscript: Huntington Library, San Marino, California.
Recipient: Waldo Higginson (1814–1894), the older brother of Thomas Wentworth Higginson, graduated from Harvard in 1833 and became a civil engineer, working as an agent for the Boston and Lowell Railroad. He later went into the insurance business.
    1. The *Free Soiler*, a campaign paper, was published that fall in Boston.
    2. William A. White (1818–1856), a graduate of Harvard in 1838, became a journalist and lecturer for both abolitionism and temperance.

601. To an Unidentified Correspondent

Amesbury October 4, 1850.

Dear William

Thine of some days back was recd and I had hoped to be able to answer it by mouth at the Convention but am too unwell.

I did not expect the Democratic Co Convention to be held for some time yet, and was taken by surprise this morning at finding my name in nomination.[1] I cannot be a candidate for any office, whatever. I have written to the Ed. of the Bay State to that effect. The F. S. Convention can easily fill the vacancy. For my own part, I am sick of politics. The Fugitive Slave Act has made me despise Congress,[2] and Judge McLean's decision makes me despise law.

Thine truly
J. G. Whittier

Manuscript: New York Public Library.
    1. The Democratic county convention (which included Free Soilers) was held at Salem on October 2, 1850 (see Letter No. 602). Abner L. Bailey was nominated in Whittier's place at the Free Soil convention on October 14.
    2. The Fugitive Slave Act, part of the Compromise of 1850, passed Congress on September 4, 1850. This act invested commissioners appointed by the federal

courts to decide finally a claimant's rights to an escaped slave, denied the slave a jury trial or hearing before any court, fixed a larger fee for the commissioner when his decision was for the claimant rather for the fugitive slave, and imposed heavy fines on anyone assisting an escaped Negro.

602. To the Editors of the Bay State

Amesbury, October 4, 1850

To the Editors of the Bay State.[1]

I have just learned that my name has been placed on the *ticket* for State Senators by the Democratic County Convention, held at Salem on the 2d Inst. I am grateful for this mark of confidence on the part of that Convention, but must nevertheless decline the nomination. I doubtless sympathise to a great extent with the Convention in respect to the desirableness of *State Reform*, but this consideration alone is, to my mind as dust in the balance compared to the *Senatorial* election by our next *Legislature*. To effect the election of a decided and active Friend of *Human Freedom* to the *National Councils* for the next six years, I would make any exertion or sacrifice consistent with the principles which I cherish and have long publickly maintained. While I have sufficient personal and private reasons for declining any nomination for political office, there is one of a different character, which I may be justified in alluding to. Since the passage of the *Fugitive Slave Law* by *Congress*, I find myself in a position with respect to it, which I fear my fellow citizens generally are not prepared to justify. So far as that law is concerned, I am a nullifier. By no act or countenance or consent of mine shall that law be enforced in *Massachusetts*. My door is still open to the oppressed, whether fleeing from *Austria* or South Carolina.[2]

Thy friend
John G. Whittier

Source: Handwritten copy, Central Michigan University. The copy has written on the outside in Whittier's hand, "Copy of letter to Ed. 'Bay State.' Lynn, Mass."
1. The *Bay State*, a Lynn newspaper, was published from 1849 to 1865.
2. The reference here is to Louis Kossuth (1802–1894), the Hungarian statesman and patriot. Kossuth had led the 1849 rebellion for freedom in Hungary and had been imprisoned and released. He was later to visit the United States on a speaking tour to secure funds for his cause.

The Amesbury Home, exterior

The Amesbury Home, interior—garden room

Joseph Sturge

Elizabeth Lloyd Howell

603. To the Editor of the Essex Freeman

Amesbury. October 10, 1850

My dear friend,

I notified the Editor of the Ny. Port Daily Union as soon as I heard of my nomination on the Senatorial ticket that I could not possibly accept it.[1] It remains for the F. Soil Convention to take such steps as may be requisite in the case, as *I cannot be a candidate for any office*. Please say this for me to the Convention.

Allow me to suggest the names of B. F. S. Griffin of West Newbury, or Abner L. Bailey of Amesbury, or William Carruthers of Salisbury, as each suitable to be upon the ticket. Either of the two first names would accept the nomination beyond a doubt—of Carruthers I am not certain.[2]

I regret that I cannot be with you at the Convention. But I am quite ill, and the attendance of the District Convention yesterday has increased my illness.

Thine truly
John G. Whittier

Manuscript: The University of Pennsylvania.
1. The Newburyport *Daily Union* was published from 1849 to 1853.
2. Abner L. Bailey was nominated in Whittier's place.

604. To James Thomas Fields

Amesbury October 30, 1850

My dear Fields:

My friend Martha Russell of N. Brainford Ct—the author of some very beautiful sketches, and tales, which in my opinion, evince a great deal of talent, has written me in respect to the publication of a small volume of her best productions, and would be glad to have it issued by your house.[1] I think thou wilt agree with me in my estimate of her powers as a writer from the specimens herewith sent, although they are not as good as some others which I cannot now lay my hand upon. When does Grace's book appear?—[2]

Please send by bearer of this the last no. of David Copperfield. *No. 18.*[3] Thine ever and truly

J. G. Whittier

Miss Russell's tales are certainly superior to Fanny Forester's.[4] They are somewhat in the same vein, but there is more thought and intensity about them. The style is simpler and elegant, and every thing is in good taste.

Like a lady's P. S. the important matter of my letter comes
last. By the ac[coun]t forwarded me I find some $60.56 due
me. I am charged in that acct. with $8.20 in books which I
had when the "Lays of Home" were published. As those
books were all I recd. from that publication I thought it might
be suffered to pass. But I yield to yr judgment entirely. Would
it be convenient to send me a check for the balance due?

Yrs.

J. G. W.

Manuscript: Huntington Library, San Marino, California.
   1. Martha Russell, who had contributed her sketches to the *Era*, eventually
published *Stories from New England* with J. P. Jewett and Co. of Boston in 1856.
She published other stories in the 1850's and a novel in 1872.
   2. Grace Greenwood's *History of My Pets* was published by Fields that fall.
Whittier reviewed the book in the *Era*, January 30, 1851, praising her ability to
write sketches about her childhood and animal friends.
   3. *David Copperfield* was published serially in 1849 and 1850.
   4. Fanny Forester, the pen name of Emily Judson (1817–1854), published a
series of conversational and humorous essays based on her personal experience,
Tripping in Author Land (1846), and *Alderbook: A Collection of Fanny Forester's
Village Sketches and Poems (1847).* After her marriage she became a missionary
to Burma.

605. To Henry Wilson

Amesbury, November 18, 1850

My dear friend.
   Thy notification of the meeting of the State Free Soil Com.
and other friends at the Adams' House tomorrow morning
has just reached me, and I should be glad if I could answer it
in person. But as I cannot well be with you, I can do no less
than offer my congratulations upon the measure of success
which has attended the "union ticket"—a ticket to which I
reluctantly assented at the outset, but which has succeeded
thus far beyond the anticipations of those most sanguine in
its behalf.[1]
   I had I confess but a single object in voting it—the election
of a Free Soil U. S. Senator—Give me this and I am willing
that Hunkerdom shall have all our state offices.—I fear however that we are by no means sure of this object—you have
some twenty or thirty Hunker democrats headed by Caleb
Cushing directly in the way. In our town the Dem. Candidate
for town representative openly declared that he preferred
a Webster Whig to a Free-Soil democrat.
   If I were in the Legislature I would demand first of all a
pledge signed by the Democratic members that they would

vote for the Free Soil Senatorial candidate. Without some *positive* assurance of the kind I for one wd never vote for Geo S. Boutwell.[2] I would break off the "union" at once and stick to our own noble and true Phillips.[3]

The "Courier" gives us, with no kind intentions probably, some good advice viz.—not to quarrel among ourselves as to the Senatorial candidate. The first important question is, can a Free Soil man be chosen? This granted, we can then take the man who will best subserve the cause we have at heart. I suppose Sumner, Phillips, Palfrey, Adams, or Allen would, any one of them, do honor to the party of freedom and good service in the Senate. The popular feeling is evidently in favor of Sumner, and many voted the Union ticket solely for his sake.[4] But, situated as these matters are, some deference must be paid to the feelings of our Democratic "allies" in the selection of our candidate.

The Free Soil men of Essex, under circumstances of peculiar aggravation, remained true to their ticket. In our town not a democratic vote was thrown for our three free soil candidates, but we kept our own good faith to a man. It now remains to be seen whether the Democrats in the Legislature will appreciate this course on our part, and fulfill our reasonable expectations in the matter of Senator.

The "Free Soiler" did good service for us.

Thine truly
John G. Whittier

Manuscript: New York Public Library. Published, in Part: Mordell, *Quaker Militant,* p. 163.

1. A coalition ticket of Democrats, Free Soilers, and Conscience Whigs had defeated the election of a Whig governor (which required a majority vote) and secured a considerable majority in both houses of the legislature. The basis for the "Union Ticket" was that the governor and lieutenant governor would be Democrats, while the Free Soilers were to be given an United States senator for a full term. When the legislature met, George Boutwell was elected governor and Charles Sumner was nominated as the Free Soil senator. However, as Whittier feared in this letter, once Boutwell was elected governor, many of the democrats refused to fulfill their end of the bargain. Throughout the winter Sumner's nomination was voted upon, with Winthrop as his chief rival. Finally on April 24 Sumner was elected.

2. George Boutwell (1818–1905), a Democratic representative from Groton from 1842 to 1850, was a leader of the antislavery group of Democrats. He was elected by the coalition in 1851 and again in 1852. He helped organize the Republican party in Massachusetts and served in Congress from 1863 to 1869. Under President Grant he was secretary of the treasury and then a United States senator from 1873 to 1877.

3. Stephen C. Phillips had run as the Free Soil candidate for governor.

4. Whittier had consulted with Sumner at Phillips Beach, Swampscott, in the summer of 1850 about Sumner's being the Free Soil candidate for senator. Sumner was at first unwilling, but under the pressure of Whittier's arguments finally agreed. Whittier, of course, was not the only one urging Sumner to be the candi-

date, but he may have been one of the first to suggest it. Whittier refers to this summer visit and his influence upon Sumner in his poem, "To Charles Sumner" (1854), in which he says:

> "Thou knowest my heart, dear friend, and well canst guess
> That, even though silent, I have not the less
> Rejoiced to see thy actual life agree
> With the large future which I shaped for thee,
> When, years ago, beside the summer sea,
> White in the moon, we saw the long waves fall
> Baffled and broken from the rocky wall,
> That, to the menace of the brawling flood,
> Opposed alone its massive quietude,
> Calm as fate."

See also Letter No. 618 for a further account of Whittier's meeting with Sumner.

606. To the Friend of Youth[1]

November 1850

It may well be questioned whether even Hans Christian Andersen ever wrote anything better adapted to the taste and fancy of children than the following beautiful little poem, which we find credited to the New York Evening Post.[2] It is conceived and executed in the true juvenile spirit of adventure and romance. Whoever the author is, he may be sure of a grateful appreciation, not only on the part of his young readers, but of those, also, whom the poet has not inaptly termed "children of a larger growth."[3]

J. G. W.

Source: The Friend of Youth, Washington, D.C., November 1850.
1. The Friend of Youth, a monthly journal devoted to juvenile literature, was edited by Margaret Bailey at Washington, D.C., from 1849 to 1852.
2. Hans Christian Andersen (1805–1875), the Danish author, was especially noted for his fairy tales. Printed after this note was the poem, "The Wild Horses."
3. John Dryden, All for Love, IV, i.

607. To Elizabeth Lloyd

Amesbury, December 9, 1850

My dear friend,

A letter which I have just read from a mutual friend, W. J. A[llinson], has conveyed to me the painful news of your great bereavement and has filled my heart with deep sympathy with you all in your hour of trial.[1]

I know something of your feelings for I, too, have often felt the solemn sorrow which afflicts you. Alas! the shadow of the cypress falls across all our paths.

From all that I knew of your honored parent, I have ever

regarded him as a true strong man, fine in the performance of
what he felt to be duty, in the church and among his fellow
men at large, and with deep and intense affections, not the
less strong that they were not always demonstrative. Oh, it is
a great loss for you; but his peaceful, triumphant end affords
the best consolation. He has passed away from trial and
sorrow and evil times and tongues of unkindness and is, we
fervently trust, with the great and exceeding peace of God.
We feel that with him it is well.

My dear sister would join me in writing, but she is not well
today. Her love and sympathy are with you.

We think of you all: of thy dear mother, and of Sarah and
Hannah.[2] What can we say but to commend you all to the
love of Him who does not afflict willingly: and to entreat
you to arouse yourselves to the performance of duties which
devolve upon you, as the best means of enduring your loss.
Think of others; think of the suffering and sad, and if you
can make one of these poor ones happier you will feel the
sweet reflection of that happiness in your hearts. But your
hearts will be better suggesters than I: weak, inconsistent,
and erring as I feel myself to be.

Say to our friend William J. Allinson when thee sees him,
that I am truly grateful for his kind letter, and that it is not
the want of time so much as my illness which has made me
seemingly neglectful of his correspondence. He has been a
true and valued friend to me, and I am not insensible on that
score. My love to him and his family.

Thy sympathizing friend.
[No signature]

Source: Denervaud, ed., Whittier's Unknown Romance, pp. 10–11.

1. Isaac Lloyd, Elizabeth's father, had died on December 2, 1850, in his seventy-
second year.

2. Elizabeth Lloyd's mother, Elizabeth Lloyd (1777–1869), married Isaac
Lloyd, a prosperous Quaker merchant who lived at 88 Union Street. The Lloyds had
twelve children. For Sarah and Hannah Lloyd, see Letter No. 291, note 13.

608. To Gamaliel Bailey

[December 1850][1]

I fear I shall be not be able to furnish these papers oftener
than a fortnight, as I shall want to write something else.[2]
[. . .] I shall send in a few days a notice of Sarah J. Clarke's
Poem and her capital little Pet book, also of Sumner's essays.[3]
[. . .]

All is yet uncertain as to the U. S. Senate. But I hope for the best, and that C. Sumner will take the place of the late Daniel Webster. [. . .]

Source: Anderson Auction Catalogue, October 14, 1904, no. 758, p. 81, Haverhill Public Library.

1. Though dated as "1851" in the catalogue, this letter was probably sent in late December, since in the January 2, 1851, *Era* Whittier commented on a poem of Grace Greenwood.

2. Probably "Pope Night" (*Era*, January 2, 1851), which was Whittier's first prose essay in the *Era* since November 28, 1850. He did not contribute any more prose until his literary notices on January 30 and his article, "The Proclamation," on March 13, 1850.

3. Her poem, "The Christ Child," had been printed in *Grahams Magazine*, and Whittier called it a "great lesson of human duty" in his comments on January 2, 1851, in the *Era*. He reviewed her new book, *History of My Pets*, in the January 30, 1851, *Era*. See Letter No. 604, note 2.

Apparently Sumner's *Orations and Speeches, 1845–1850* were never reviewed by Whittier.

609. To Samuel Austin Allibone

Amesbury January 2, 1851

S. A. Allibone Esq
Dr fd.

I have examined with great satisfaction thy Dictionary of English Literature.[1] As a work of reference it will be invaluable. It places before the reader a vast amount of biographical and literary information, giving not only an account of the author's themselves and their publications, but the critical comments of the best judges upon them. The amount of labor and research bestowed upon the work surprises me. If completed as begun it will be a most valuable addition to our literature, and entitle the author to the thanks of all who love books.

Very truly thy fd.
John G. Whittier

Manuscript: Huntington Library, San Marino, California.

Recipient: Samuel Austin Allibone (1816–1889), librarian and bibliographer, was working on his collection, *A Critical Dictionary of English Literature and British and American Authors*. The first volume was published in 1858 and two more volumes appeared in 1871. He worked as a librarian in New York City and wrote articles for Appleton's *Cyclopedia of American Biography*.

1. Allibone had apparently sent Whittier some samples of his entries and asked for his support or commentary on the work in progress.

610. To Samuel Gridley Howe

Amesbury, January 13, 1851

The undersigned cheerfully bears testimony to the marked and wonderful improvement in the boy, George J. Rowell. The change is almost like a resurrection of a mind from death— or, rather a new creation.[1]

John G. Whittier

Source: The Amesbury *Villager*, March 6, 1851.

1. Whittier's letter was printed in the *Villager* along with one from George Rowell's father to Samuel Gridley Howe and the testimony of another neighbor, Sarah M. Bradbury, commenting on the change in the boy. The father, Jacob said this about his son: "When he left to go to your institution, he was in a very helpless condition. He could not articulate words, and was sickly, sometimes having two fits in a night. We had to take care of him and attend him as an infant. There seemed no hope of his learning to speak or read, or take care of himself.

"In this condition he went to Boston. On his first visit home, we saw a decided improvement. On the second, we were both surprised and rejoiced; his health was good, and he could speak and read. We now thankfully trust that he will be able to take care of himself in life with comfort to himself and his friends."

George Rowell (1841–1902) had been sent to the Perkins Instituion and Massachusetts School for the Blind in December 1848. However, he never became mentally normal and had to be cared for until his death. The Rowells were neighbors of the Whittiers.

611. To Charles Sumner

Amesbury, January 16, 1851

My dear Sumner,

Illness—severe and protracted confines me at home, or I should ere this have seen thee.

I have read the message of Gov B. It is, under the circumstances, insulting and monstrous.[1] May God forgive us for permitting his election!

I have watched the balloting with intense anxiety. I see now no hope of our success. I think it is determined by both branches of democracy to defeat our purpose.—[2]

Under these circumstances dear Sumner, I who urged thee to accept the nomination so strongly and imperatively, must now confess I see no other course for thee than to *decline at once*, and Wilson, Knapp, Walker, and the three Councillors, should at once resign their places. Think of a free soiler in Gov B.'s Council!—As the election of one of our own men is hopeless, if I were in the Legislature I would vote Gov G N Briggs right into the U. S. Senate, as an anti-Webster, anti-fugitive slave law candidate.[3] We have done him injustice; and he is at heart right on the great questions in which we feel an interest.

I write, as thou wilt see in haste, and with roused feelings incident upon the perusal of that *detestable message* and the vote in the House. I wish thee to consult at once with our friends, Sewall, Adams, S. G. Howe and others, and with Earle and others in the Leg.

Thus far thy position has been manly and honorable. There is now as it seems to me a new state of things, requiring a new course of action.

Pardon the abruptness of this note, it is the result of *feeling* rather than deliberate reflection.

This will be handed thee by our friend J. P. Bishop Esq.[4] Believe me, dear Sumner, Ever and truly thy friend

J. G. Whittier

Manuscript: Harvard University. Published, in Part: Pickard, *Life,* pp. 352–353.

1. After his election, Boutwell in his January message failed to condemn the proslavery policy of the national government and tried to calm down the public indignation against the Fugitive Slave Law. Boutwell was not inclined to favor such a pronounced abolitionist as Sumner.

2. On the balloting of January 14, 1851, Sumner had received 186 votes to 167 for Winthrop and lacked only five votes for an election. However, in the next three months twenty-six ballots were taken before Sumner was elected.

3. For George Nixon Briggs see Letter No. 458, note 1.

4. Joel Prentiss Bishop (1814–1901) had worked with the abolitionists in New York and came to Boston in 1842, becoming a lawyer in 1844. He published many books on criminal law and the laws of marriage and divorce.

612. To Thomas and Ann Tracy

Amesbury March 10, 1851

My dear friends

I take the liberty of sending you two or three late pieces of mine, which may at least serve the purpose of a friendly re-membrancer, on my part. The longest poem "The Hermits' Chapel" is founded on an incident, beautiful and touching in the works of St. Pierre.[1]

The Stanzas for the Times embody my feelings in regard to the cruel and oppressive Fugitive Slave Law. "Derne" is rather a picture than a poem.[2]

Illness has confined me at home a part of the winter. We are now however quite as comfortable as usual.

In the hope that this will find you both in comfortable health, and with love to you from mother, sister and myself I am as ever

Your friend
John G. Whittier

Mr and Mrs Tracy

Elizabeth wishes me to send a very interesting account of Christmas at the *Rauhe Haus* in Hamburgh, by Elihu Burritt.[3] If you have not seen it we are sure you will like it.

Manuscript: Yale University.

1. Bernardin de Saint-Pierre (1737–1814), a French writer, was especially noted for his romantic tale, *Paul and Virginia*, which Whittier often praised. (See Letter No. 741).

2. All three were published in the *Era:* "Derne" on September 26, 1850; "Stanzas for the Times" on December 12, 1850; and "The Chapel of Hermits" on March 6, 1851.

3. The article, an account of Christmas in the Rauhe Haus at Hamburgh, where juvenile delinquents were trained, was reprinted by Burritt in *Thoughts and Things at Home and Abroad* (Boston, 1854), pp. 197–213, as "Christmas in Germany" and "The Rauhe Haus in Hamburgh."

613. To the Editor of the Commonwealth

Amesbury. March 20, 1851

Dear friend,

I forwarded to Dr. S. G. Howe a list of names from our place.[1] If it is not already printed will thee do me the favor to erase the name of Rev. B. Sawyer from it?[2]

He was alarmed by the articles in the Worcester Spy and Lowell American with regard to the convention; and requests the omission of his name in consequence.

Thine truly
J. G. Whittier

Manuscript: Swarthmore College.

1. A call for a meeting of citizens at Boston opposed to the Fugitive Slave Law was being published in many Free Soil papers. A large number of prominent citizens from various communities had signed the call, Sawyer among them. The *Commonwealth* printed a list of names, including Whittier's, on March 26 and 28. Sawyer's name was not on these lists and on March 27, 1851, Sawyer printed a note in the Amesbury *Villager* stating that he had withdrawn his name from the call. The meeting was changed from March 26 to April 8, 1851, in Worcester.

2. Benjamin Sawyer (1782–1871) had been ordained a minister in 1809 and served a parish in Amesbury from 1814 to 1835. He then removed to Salisbury, where he became pastor of the Rocky Hill Church.

614. To the Editor of Commonwealth

Amesbury. March 22, 1851

Ed. Commonwealth[1]
Dear Friend.

The speech of Horace Mann on the Fugitive Slave Law, ought to be in the hands of every citizen of the Free States.[2] It is calculated to open the eyes of all who are not wilfully blind, to the atrocity of this "iniquity framed by Law."

Enclosed are $4.25, the contributions of a few individuals in this village.[3] Please send as many copies of the Speech as the sum will warrant.

Thine truly
J. G. Whittier

Manuscript: The Historical Society of Pennsylvania.

1. The Commonwealth , a Boston Free Soil paper, was published from 1851 to 1854 and had a variety of editors, including Howe, Palfrey, Sewall, and others.

2. Horace Mann delivered a long speech on the Fugitive Slave Law in Congress, February 28, 1851. The speech was reprinted in Mann's book, Slavery: Letters and Speeches (Boston, 1851), which was published that fall. In his speech he treated at length the unconstitutional features of the Fugitive Slave Law in denying a right of trial by jury, as well as the validity of the whole law.

3. The Commonwealth on March 22 had advertised fifty copies of Mann's speech for a dollar which it had printed as a supplement to its regular issue.

615. To Charles Sumner

Amesbury March 28, 1851

My dear Sumner,

Thy letter—most welcome—was recd yesterday and wd have been answered in person had I been able to leave home.[1] I can only assure thee that were I able to visit Boston just now I should need no other inducement than thy request.

I have watched with deep interest the proceedings in our Legislature, and have I think fully comprehended thy feelings, and sympathize with thee in the peculiar and difficult position in which thou hast been placed.

As matters now stand, I cannot venture to offer advice. I fear there would be no prospect of electing any true man if thou shouldst withdraw as it would somewhat remove obligation from the Democrats to vote with us. On the other hand I should be sorry to have the election thrown upon the next legislature, as the Whigs will be sure of a majority in that body. We could not again unite with the Democrats if this Legislature adjourns without thy election. We could not trust them. It would be folly to think of it.[2]

But, I am talking at arm's length and without data. Need I tell thee that I should be right glad to see thee at Amesbury. Why not come and spend First-day with us! Thou canst go back by the 7 o'clk train on Second day (Monday) morning. I shall expect thee. Do not disappoint me.[3] Thine ever

J. G. Whittier

There are two trains to our place in the afternoon—at 2 1/2 o'clk and 4 1/2.

Manuscript: Harvard University. Published, in Part: Pickard, *Life*, pp. 353–354.

1. Charles Sumner had written Whittier on March 25, 1851, asking Whittier to visit with him to discuss "my duty at the present moment. My situation is one of delicacy and embarrassment. Personally I am entirely resigned to any alternative." Sumner added that he had informed his Free Soil backers that he was considering a complete withdrawal (letter, Essex Institute, Salem, Massachusetts).

2. Whittier's view was shared by most of the Free Soil leaders and Sumner was asked to continue as a candidate.

3. Sumner, however, was unable to visit Amesbury at that time.

616. To James Thomas Fields

Amesbury. April 7, 1851

My dear Fields:

Wilt thou do me the favor to send a copy of my Old Portraits etc to Wm. P. Mulchinock, care of Editor of the Literary World, New York.[1]

If thou hast an opportunity it would oblige me if thou wouldst send a copy of Margaret Smith, Portraits and Songs of Labor to Geo. Gilfallan.[2] I do not know his address. Please address them to him as from myself.

So yr Union-tinkers have really caught a "nigger" at last![3] A very pretty, and refreshing sight it must have been to Sabbath-going Christians yesterday—that *chained* court-house of yours. And Bunker Hill Monument looking down upon all!—But, the matter is too sad for irony. God forgive the miserable politicians who gamble for office with dice loaded with human hearts!

Thine really and faithfully
J. G. W.

Manuscript: Huntington Library, San Marino, California. Published, in Part: Pickard, *Life*, p. 359.

1. William P. Mulchinock (1820–1864), a minor poet, had published his *Ballads and Songs* in 1851. He wrote to Whittier on February 25, 1851, thanking Whittier for his previous help and kind words on his writings (letter, Amesbury Whittier home).

2. George Gilfillan (1813–1873), a Presbyterian minister from Scotland, published literary estimates of living writers. He published *A Gallery of Literary Portraits* in 1845, a second series in 1850, and a third series in 1854.

3. Thomas Sims, a fugitive slave, had been recently arrested in Boston and the

city government used all its forces to protect the agent of the Southern claimant. The officials surrounded the court house with chains, kept a militia in the Faneuil Hall barracks, and furnished an escort to the agent and slave when they were returned on April 12, 1851. Whittier's outrage at the event occasioned his "Moloch in State Street" (*National Era*, May 22, 1851), which satirized the greed and economic motivation behind the merchants who aided in returning Sims. In his head-note to the poem Whittier records that 1,500 of Boston's wealthiest and most powerful citizens, merchants, bankers, and others, volunteered their services to prevent the escape of the imprisoned slave.

617. To Charles Sumner

Second day Morning [after April 24, 1851]
My dear Sumner,

I take the earliest moment of ability after a sudden and severe attack of illness to congratulate thee not so much on thy election, as upon the proof which it affords of the turning of the tide—the recoil of the popular feeling,—the near and certain [d]oom of the wicked Slave Laws.[1]

My heart is full of gratitude to God. For when I consider all the circumstances of this election,—I am constrained to regard it as His work, and I rejoice that thy position is so distinct and emphatic:—that thy triumph is such a direct rebuke to politicians, hoary with years of political chicanery and fraud;—that unpledged, free, and without a single concession or compromise thou art enabled to take thy place in the U. S. Senate. May the good Providence which has overruled the purposes of thy life in this matter, give thee strength and grace, to do great things for humanity.

I never knew such a general feelings of real heart-pleasure, and satisfaction as is manifested by all except inveterate Hunkers in view of thy *election*. The whole country is electrified by it. Sick abed I heard the guns, Quaker as I am—with real satisfaction.

I have written something—of the sort suggested in thy note—but have been too ill to copy it.[2]

Ever and cordially
Thy friend
J. G. Whittier

Manuscript: Harvard University. Published, in Part: Pickard, *Life*, pp. 354–355.

1. Sumner had been elected on April 24, 1851, by a majority of 193 votes, just the number necessary for his election.

2. Probably the poem "Moloch in State Street," which appeared on May 22, 1851, in the *National Era*.

618. To Grace Greenwood

[Amesbury] May 18, 1851

I am slowly recovering from the severest illness I have known for years, the issue of which, at one time, was to me exceedingly doubtful. Indeed, I scarcely know now how to report myself, but I am better, and full of gratitude to God that I am permitted once more to go abroad and enjoy this beautiful springtime. The weather now is delightfully warm and bright, and the soft green of the meadows is climbing our hills. It is luxury to live. One feels at such times terribly rooted to this world: old Mother Earth seems sufficient for us. [. . .] After a long trial and much anxiety, our grand object in Massachusetts has been attained. We have sent Charles Sumner into the United States Senate,—a man physically and spiritually head and shoulders above the old hackneyed politicians of that body. The plan for this was worked out last summer at Phillips Beach, and I sounded Sumner upon it the evening we left you at that place. He really did not want the office, but we forced it upon him.[1] I am proud of old Massachusetts, and thankful that I have had an humble share in securing her so true and worthy a representative of her honor, her freedom, and intellect, as Charles Sumner. He is a noble and gifted man, earnest and truthful. I hope great things of him, and I do not fear for his integrity and fidelity, under any trial. That Sims case was particularly mean on the part of the Boston shopkeepers. I never felt so indignant as when I saw the courthouse in chains.

Source: Pickard, *Life*, pp. 355–356.
1. See Letter No. 605, note 4.

619. To Charles Sumner

Amesbury May 20, 1851

My dear Sumner.

The bit of doggerel on the other page might answer to raise a laugh at our friend Gilbert Gove's party tomorrow evening, which I regret I cannot enjoy in person.[1] Give it, if there is nothing objectionable in it, to friend Burlingame[2] or some one who will be at the party, as the anonymous contribution of a friend who could not be present. My soberer piece was sent to the Era a fortnight ago, but when it will appear, if at all, is uncertain.[3]

I quite approve of thy decision in respect to public speaking

to any great extent.[4] Thy letter of acceptance gives great
satisfaction to all except the inveterate Hunkers.[5] I feel
exceedingly anxious for Palfrey's success, and I do not think
it would be any way improper for thee to speak once or twice
in his District. Yr relationship of personal friendship alone
would justify it. If it wd give him ten votes I think thou
shouldst do it.—say in Cambridge or some other large town.
Think of it, and *act*.[6]

Rantoul will unquestionably be chosen.[7]

I am happy to say that my health has somewhat improved.
I wish thou couldst spend a *first day* with me some time.—

Thine ever and truly
J. G. Whittier

Manuscript: Harvard University. Published, in Part: Pickard, *Life*, pp. 357–358.

1. "What State Street said to South Carolina and what South Carolina said to
State Street" accompanied the letter. As a satiric dialogue between the North and
the South, it presents the merchants of Boston apologizing to South Carolina
and protesting their firm allegiance to the divine law of slavery. South Carolina in
reply scoffs at this declaration for:

> "Just wait till December
> Shall see your new Senator stalk through the Chamber,
> And Puritan heresy prove neither dumb nor
> Blind in that pestilent Anakim, Sumner."

2. Anson Burlingame (1820–1870), a Massachusetts lawyer, served in the Massachusetts Senate in 1852 and was elected to Congress as a Free Soiler from 1855
to 1861. He delivered a stinging rebuke to Representative Preston S. Brooks for
his attack on Sumner in 1856 and was challenged to a duel by Brooks, but the
duel was avoided. He later was a minister to China from 1861 to 1867.

3. "Moloch in State Street."

4. Sumner had written Whittier on May 4, 1851, inquiring about Whittier's
health and expressing his sense of unworthiness at being elected senator. In the
letter he said: "I am pressed to speak at suppers and canvasses, but my true policy,
it seems to me, is for the present, *silence*. The cause is now committed to my
discretion and I feel that I can best promote it by caution and reserve at least until
I take my seat" (letter, Essex Institute, Salem, Massachusetts).

5. Sumner had sent a formal letter of acceptance to the legislature, May 14,
1851, in which he stated his loyalty to the Constitution and his regard for the
Union.

6. Sumner did not speak for Palfrey or any other candidate, but wrote a public letter earnestly supporting him. Palfrey was nominated as the Free Soil candidate for governor and, although losing by a wide majority, helped throw the race
into the legislature, where the coalition candidate, Boutwell, was again elected.

7. Robert Rantoul ran for Congress on the Democratic ticket and was elected.
Sumner praised Rantoul in his letter about Palfrey.

620. To Thomas and Ann Tracy

Amesbury July 10, 1851

My dear friends

I send herewith the second vol of Wordsworth—[1] We were especially interested in the visit paid to W. Scott—just before the great [word illegible] left his house in the vain effort to restore his health. There is something beautiful and touching in the description of the ev[en]ing at Abbotsford,—the daughter singing for him the dear old ballads he so much loved.[3]

Neither E. nor myself have been quite well enough to visit you yet, but we do not give up the idea, some fine day, of dropping in upon you. In the mean time, if dear Mrs Tracy's health will admit of it, I need not say, we should rejoice to see you at Amesbury. My mother and Elizabeth send their love. May Heaven bless and keep you!

Yr friend

John G. Whittier

How touchingly characteristic of the loving and kindly spirit of Wordsworth is the account of the burial of poor Hartley Coleridge— "Let him lie by us: he would have wished it!"[3]

I think you will be interested in the letter of Ellis Yarnell of of Philadelphia—near the close of the volume—[4] It presents a beautiful picture of the poet in his old age.

J. G. W.

Manuscript: New York Public Library.

1. *The Memoirs of William Wordsworth* (Boston, 1851), by Christopher Wordsworth, in two volumes.

2. Vol. II, pp. 234–235, the daughter was Charlotte Sophia Lockhart (1799–1837).

3. Vol. II, p. 514. Hartley Coleridge (1796–1849), eldest son of Samuel Taylor Coleridge, also wrote poetry.

4. Vol. II, pp. 494–510 has a long account of a visit paid by Yarnall to Wordsworth in the summer of 1849. Ellis Yarnall (1817–1905), a Philadelphia Quaker, later wrote a book on Wordsworth, *Wordsworth and the Coleridges* (New York, 1899).

621. To Charles Sumner

Amesbury. August 20, 1851

My dear Sumner

I wish I felt able to take the cars to Boston and hear thy speech this Evening.[1] I was glad to hear of the Meeting, although I greatly fear it is too late to be of any service to poor Hungary. She will be crushed under the avalanche of Russian barbarism, and the sympathies and the congratu-

lations of the friends of freedom abroad will be to her
"like delicates poured upon a mouth shut up, or as meats
set upon a grave."

I wish, either in resolutions or speeches, the disgraceful
conduct of that miserable disciple of Calhoun democracy
and Papal infallibility, R. Walsh, would be noticed as it
deserves.[2] Through him our government commits itself in
favor of the Kings and Priests of Europe in their barbarous
measures for suppressing the growth of free principles. We
are made parties to the usurpations of Bonaparte the Less,[3]
the bombardment of Rome—the bloody rule of Naples—the
atrocious barbarities of Austria and Russia in Hungary. The
miserable fellow would be nothing by himself[,] but as an
official of our government, he can do a good deal to disgrace us.

What will become of the Roman and Prussian exiles, driven
from Malta and Switzerland?—Cannot our government, in
case they wish to emigrate to this country secure them safe
passage to ports for that purpose?

The N. Y. conference ended as I expected after the late
elections.[4] The South always continues to control the North
by throwing itself on the Whig or Democratic side, just as
these parties are inclined toward abolition. For instance,
in 1839 the Whigs talked anti-Slavery at the North. The slave
holders deserted their faithful allies and went over to the abolition Whigs, and the Whigs as in duty bound eschewed abolition: in 1843–4—they set aside V. B. and got a Slave holder
nominated by the Democrats, who was for Texas annexation
with Slavery and voted him into power. He did his work, and
the Whigs, in their exasperation, again threatened to become
abolitionists; and the South silenced them by voting for Gen
Taylor. Now, the Democrats are forming coalitions with
the abolitionists, and the South must change in *their* favor.
This is the way the two parties at the North are managed.

I have been desirous to see thee and other of our F. S.
friends and should have attended the State Com meeting, had
I not been confined at home by illness. I hope to be able to
meet you at Worcester.[5]

Aff thy friend
J. G. Whittier

Manuscript: Harvard University. Published, in Part: Pickard, *Life,* pp. 361–363.
   1. A meeting to express sympathy for Hungary was held in Boston on August
20 and Sumner was expected to make a speech, though no record of the speech
can be found in the Boston newspapers.
   2. Robert Walsh (1784–1859), a journalist and editor, founded the *National*

Gazette in 1820 and edited other journals. From 1844 to 1851 he served as consul general in France.

3. Louis Napoleon (1808–1873) was emperor of France from 1852 to 1870.

4. There had been a meeting of the two sections of the Whig party in Albany, New York, that summer which produced some resolutions stating that they were against slavery. This may be the meeting Whittier is referring to.

5. The annual Free Soil convention to select candidates for governor and lieutenant governor was to be held in Worcester, September 16, 1851.

622. To Charles Sumner

Amesbury September 14, 1851

My dear Sumner,

Thy note has been duly recd and I will write thee in a day or two.[1] The proceedings of the Whig Convention have gone far to reconcile me to the views expressed in thy letter.[2] Still I am not prepared to act: my old Liberty party *impracticability* is difficult to overcome. I want to be in Worcester—but I am not able to bear the fatigue and excitement.

My friend Geo. Turner of this place is authorized to call on thee and if possible to secure thee as a lecturer in our new Lyceum.[3] Do not refuse. I want to see thee before thou leaves for Washington.

Thine ever
John G. Whittier

By Geo. Turner, Esq of Amesbury

Manuscript: Harvard University.

1. Sumner had written Whittier on September 11, 1851: "I distrust myself where I differ from you; but I do most sincerely believe that the good of our cause is most intimately connected with the triumph of the coalition this autumn. And though I covet the entire absorption of the entire Dem. party by our force, yet I am willing to *use them*, and also for other matters to cooperate with them, on the best terms, we can get. Websterized Whigg[e] ry must be defeated. But this can be done only by a coalition, securing to freedom once more the Balance of power in the Legislature. For that balance of power I pray. Help us. Do" (Albree, ed., *Whittier Correspondence*, p. 117).

2. The Whig convention was held on September 10, 1851, at Springfield, Massachusetts, nominating Robert C. Winthrop for governor and electing delegates to attend the national Whig convention. Its resolutions praised Daniel Webster's recent actions.

3. George Turner (1814–1887), an Amesbury trial judge and assessor, served as the manager for the Amesbury Lyceum.

Sumner spoke at Amesbury on November 19, 1851, on "Improvement of Time." See Letter No. 627.

623. To Rufus Griswold

Amesbury October 10, 1851

My dear friend

I was glad to get thy note relative to Alice Carey's book.[1] I think very highly of her genius—I do not think thou hast at all overrated her. Some of her prose pieces are *unique* in their simplicity, beauty and pathos.

I would be glad to aid in the publication of her volume: but am now forbidden to write: indeed I have not been able for months to answer, even briefly, my correspondents. The cooler weather I trust will in some degree benefit me, but I cannot depend upon it.

If my opinion, however, could have any weight with your publishers I have no hesitation in saying that it is not often that so rich and valuable material is offered for an American book, as might be prepared from the prose sketches of Alice Carey.—I am not able to do justice to her or myself, now: and on that ground must decline writing a preface; but I do not think well of such things. The public look upon prefaces of this kind as an attempt to pass off by and of a known name, what otherwise would not pass current. This would be an in-justice to such a writer as Alice Carey. She can stand by her-self—on her own original merit.—Let me know if anything which I *can* do is needed to facilitate the publication.[2]

Very truly thy friend

J. G. W.

P. S. I will call attention to the proposed publication in some of the Boston papers as soon as I feel able to send or go there; or what will perhaps be better I will notice it in the Era.[3] I think, if I were Alice, I wd leave out all poetical quotations— as a general thing they injure and weaken the effect of her admirable prose.

Manuscript: Boston Public Library.

1. Whittier continually misspelled Cary as "Carey."

2. The book, a series of sketches and short stories, was issued as *Clovernook: or, Recollections of Our Neighborhood in the West* (New York, 1852). A second series was issued in 1853, and in 1855 *Clovernook Children* was issued at Boston by Ticknor, Reed, and Fields.

3. Whittier reviewed the proposed volume in the *Era*, October 30, 1851, as follows: "*Recollections of Our Neighborhood in Ohio.*—Under this title, we understand that a New York publisher is about to issue a volume of prose tales by our correspondent, Alice Carey, already known for her poetical writings. We do not hesitate to predict for these sketches a wide popularity. They bear the true stamp of genius—simple, natural, truthful—and evince a keen sense of the humor and pathos of the comedy and tragedy of life in the country." In the January 29, 1852, *Era* Whittier noted the published book.

624. To Charles Sumner

Amesbury October 16 [1851]

My dear Sumner.

Thy line before leaving for Washington was duly recd.[1]

I wish I could agree with you in this matter of coalition; but I confess I cannot see it in the light in which a vast majority of our friends regard it.[2]

I shall oppose no obstacle to the movement of this majority. But, for myself I cannot vote knowingly for an open defender of the Fugitive Slave Law, and such an nomination on Coalition ticket.[3]

About our Lyceum. Do come up and see me and give a lecture. We have kept on thy account our lectures for the *3rd and 4th Thursdays of* November unengaged. Choose either of them, as may best suit thy convenience; *but by all means come.*[4]

Please write and let me know whether we can depend upon thee.

Cordially thy friend
John G. Whittier

Manuscript: Harvard University.

1. Sumner had written Whittier on October 7, 1851, asking Whittier to support the coalition and mentioning a visit with Dr. Gamaliel Bailey. Sumner said: "I do feel that we must not neglect the opportunity afforded by alliances—not fusion—with the Democrats to prevent the Whigs from establishing themselves in the State" (letter, Essex Institute, Salem, Massachusetts).

2. Many others besides Whittier were opposed to the idea of continuing the coalition. Charles Francis Adams, Thomas Wentworth Higginson, and others had reservations. The coalition held together for this election, with Winthrop, the Whig candidate, polling a large plurality over both Boutwell, the Democratic candidate, and Palfrey, the Free Soil candidate. However, since Winthrop failed of the majority, Boutwell was again elected governor by the coalition-controlled legislature. In 1852 the coalition failed of its purpose and a Whig governor was elected.

3. Whittier is here referring to George Boutwell.

4. Sumner came on November 19, 1851, and delivered a lecture.

625. To Edwards Amasa Park

Amesbury October 29, 1851

Prof E. A. Park
Respected friend.

I have not, I regret to say, the book thou inquirest after; nor do I know where it can be found, unless my friend Joshua Coffin, antiquarian and historian of Newbury, has it, or a clue to it.

I know of no other biography of Hopkins than those re-

ferred to in thy letter.[1] I think there is more. I am glad thou
hast undertaken the work of doing justice to the memory of
the great and good man. The biographies of him extant are
not what is required—indeed they seem to me very far from
it. I know of no person better qualified than thyself to delin-
eate the character of this noble old theologian, beneath whose
polemic armor, the tried steel of his intellectual deductions,
beat ever more the great and warm heart of Christian charity
and benevolence.[2]

I thank thee for thy pamphlets. I am no stranger to the
"Discourse on the theology of the Intellect and feelings"—
but am glad [of] another copy.[3] The Election Sermon I have
not before seen.[4]

With regard and esteem
I am thy friend
John G. Whittier

Manuscript: Boston Public Library.
Recipient: Edwards Amasa Park (1808–1900), a professor and theologian, was
one of the noted preachers and orators of his time. As one of the last influential
exponents of the old New England theology, Park taught at Andover Theological
Seminary from 1836 to 1881.
1. Samuel Hopkins (1721–1803), a Congregational minister at Newport, Rhode
Island, was the leading disciple of Jonathan Edwards, on whose philosophy he
based his own "Hopkinsianism."
2. Park published a "Memoir of the Life and Character of Samuel Hopkins"
in the *Works of Samuel Hopkins* (Boston, 1852), three volumes.
3. *A Theology of the Intellect and of the Feelings* (Boston, 1850).
4. *The Indebtedness of the State to the Clergy* (Boston, 1851), an election sermon preached by Park on January 2, 1851.

626. To Ralph Waldo Emerson

Amesbury, November 3, 1851

My dear friend

I am instructed by the Committee of our Lyceum, just
established, to request thee to favor us with a lecture, if convenient, on the 1st. of Jany. 1852.[1]

If not convenient for thee on that day, we should be glad
to have thee come at some future time. Our lecturers are
engaged through this month and December.

We have a population of some 3 or 4,000—and I will promise thee an audience of 500—and by no means wanting in intelligence.

It wd give me great pleasure to have thee make my house
thy shelter while here.

The proper train to reach here in Season for a comfortable
supper before lecture, leaves Boston at 1/2 past 2 P. M. Thou

canst leave next day at 1/2 past 9.

I understand thou art engaged for the Newburyport Lyceum. Their lectures are on Friday evenings: ours on Thursdays. Perhaps we can so arrange it as to have our lecture the day before that at N. Port.

I shall look with interest for thy life of Margaret Fuller.[2]

Thine truly
John G. Whittier

R. W. Emerson

Dr. O. W. Holmes delivered the opening Lecture: Drs. Gannett and Peabody lecture next month.[3] W. Phillips and probably Sumner.[4]

Manuscript: Harvard University.

1. This is the first of six letters that Whittier wrote to Emerson in the winter of 1851–1852 trying to arrange a lyceum date for Emerson. Emerson finally lectured on February 27, 1852, on the subject of "Power."

2. Emerson was the coauthor and coeditor, along with William H. Channing and James Freeman Clarke, of *Memoirs of Margaret Fuller Ossoli* (Boston, 1852), two volumes. The books mainly consisted of excerpts from her letters and journal, along with commentary. Margaret Fuller Ossoli (1810–1850) was a Transcendentalist writer and critic.

3. Holmes lectured in Amesbury on October 30, 1851, his subject being "History of Medicine."

Ezra Stiles Gannett (1801–1871), a Unitarian clergyman, succeeded to the pulpit of William E. Channing. He was coeditor of the *Christian Examiner* from 1844 to 1849 and president of the American Unitarian Association from 1847 to 1851. He lectured in Amesbury on November 6, 1851, his subject being "Conversation."

Andrew Preston Peabody (1811–1893), a Unitarian clergyman, served as pastor of a Unitarian church in Portsmouth, New Hampshire, from 1833 to 1860. From 1860 to 1881 he was a professor at Harvard. He published widely on a variety of subjects and served as an editor for the *North American Review*. Peabody was to lecture on December 11, but missed giving the lecture, and it was rescheduled for May 27, 1852.

4. Wendell Phillips lectured on March 25, 1852, on "Lost Arts."

627. To Charles Sumner

Amesbury November 17, 1851

My dear Sumner.

I am truly glad that thou hast concluded to visit Amesbury— I suppose thou hast been informed that we have agreeably to thy request fixed the evening of the lecture for *Wednesday the 19th.*[1]

In order to reach here comfortably, take the afternoon train at 2-1/2 o clk. which will just get thee here in season for tea. If thou waits till the last train thou wilt only and barely have time to go the Hall.

Thine ever
John G. Whittier

Manuscript: Harvard University.
1. Sumner lectured on the subject, "Improvement of Time."

628. To Charles Sumner

[Before December 12, 1851] [1]

My dear Sumner.

On thy way to Washington pray see W. C. Bryant, Seward or some other leading man—Greeley for instance—and caution them to see to it that the Union savers do not thrust their notions upon Kossuth, and call out from him speeches of the Castle Garden stamp.[2] Naturally he wd deprecate a dissolution of this Union—but he ought to understand that it is not in the slightest jeopardy—the solicitude of the *"Union-savers"* is all for political effect—

I wish he could have a half-hour's talk with Benton.—I do not wish him to be mixed up in *any way* with our domestic matters. He has his mission: we ours.

I hope thou wilt see the great Hungarian's reception in New York, and take a part in it.[3] I have just finished reading his English Speeches, and I am deeply impressed by his ability and wisdom.

God bless thee, my dear friend, in thy new and difficult but glorious position.—The hopes and sympathies of thousands are with thee.

As Ever thy friend
J. G. Whittier

Manuscript: Harvard University. Published: Pickard, *Life,* pp. 363–364.
1. Dated internally by reference to Sumner's leaving for Washington on November 25, 1851, and the large reception held for Kossuth on December 12, 1851.
2. On October 30 at Castle Garden in New York a public meeting of thousands of mercantile and professional men was held to affirm that obligations to the United States Constitution were superior to any political ties. This meeting of Whigs and Democrats, like many others then being held, supported obedience to the Fugitive Slave Law and condemned the abolitionists as disunionists. From this Castle Garden meeting a Union-saving committee of a hundred men was appointed with large financial support to aid in securing the rendition of fugitive slaves. A similar meeting was held later in Boston at Faneuil Hall.
Ironically, Kossuth's first speech after landing in New York and coming to the city on December 5, 1851, was at Castle Garden. In this speech he stressed the fact that he would not interfere with or comment on domestic problems in America.
3. Sumner, however, arrived in Washington by December 1, 1851, while the grand reception in New York was held on December 12, 1851. Sumner's first speech in the Senate, delivered on December 9, was one of welcome for Kossuth and was very favorably received by both parties.

629. To Ralph Waldo Emerson

Amesbury December 27, 1851

Dear friend

Will it be convenient for thee to give us a Lecture some time in February? Our Lyceum time is fixed for Thursday Evg but we can accommodate thee with some other evening in the week. Please drop me a line soon fixing thy own time.

Believe me truly thy friend

John G. Whittier

Manuscript: Harvard University.

630. To Ralph Waldo Emerson

Amesbury January 8, 1852

My dear fd.

I am directed by the Bd of Managers of our Lyceum to say that as a Lecturer from a distance has been engaged for the last of Jany.[1] we shall hope to have thee *on the 26th of Feby.* In the mean time should anything occur which may make it inconvenient for thee to come at that time, we shall still hope that some time in March may suit thy circumstances and engagements.

Very truly thy friend,
John G. Whittier

Manuscript: Harvard University.

1. John Johnston Carruthers (1800–1890), an English minister, after missionary work in many countries became pastor of the Second Parish Church in Portland, Maine, in 1846 and served until 1877. He had a brother, William, then living in Amesbury, who was a personal friend of the Whittiers. He lectured in Amesbury on the subject of "Russia" on January 29, 1852.

631. To Ralph Waldo Emerson

Amesbury February 18, 1852

My Dear friend:

Thine just recd. Canst thou come March 4th? Or if not on the 1st of April?—So I am directed by our Committee to enquire. Please drop me a line *on receipt of this* and state thy prospects and determination. We do not like the idea of losing thy lecture—and we will not—if perseverance can avail us.

In haste as the mail is closing

Thy friend
J. G. Whittier

Manuscript: Harvard University.

632. To Ralph Waldo Emerson

Amesbury Second Day Mg February 23, 1852
My dear fd.

Our lecturer, Hon Mr. Lawrence is engaged for the 26th.
Thursday—[1] but we sometimes have two in a week—So that
it wd. answer our purpose as well if thou couldst *come on the
27th Friday of this week.* Will this do? Let me hear from thee
immediately, so that we can know by the mail of day after
tomorrow.[2]

I am really sorry to trouble thee with writing so many
replies, but I hope this will suit your convenience. It wd be
difficult for us to procure the Hall on the evenings named by
thee.

In haste thy friend
John G. Whittier

Manuscript: Harvard University.
1. Myron Lawrence's lecture, "Duties and Responsibilities of Young Men," was
given on March 4, 1852.
2. Emerson lectured on February 27, 1852.

633. To Ralph Waldo Emerson

Amesbury February 23, 1852
My dear friend

Our lecture is engaged for Thursday the 26th. Canst thou
not come on *Friday the 27th* as well? Please drop me a line
immediately.

I have sent a line to thee at Concord but feared it would
not find thee.

Thine with esteem and admiration
J. G. Whittier

Manuscript: Harvard University.

634. To Grace Greenwood

Amesbury March 10, 1852

My dear friend:

Thy letter was re[ceived] some days ago, when I was unable to write. I take the first moment of ability to answer. I will write forthwith to my friend Sturge and to Chas Gilpin (his nephew)[1] who resides in London and is a Book publisher, having no doubt of their readiness to receive thee kindly and cordially. I shall get a line from them before thee leave. I know thou wilt be welcome for thy own sake as well as mine. We are sorry that we shall not see thee before thy tour; but we shall hope to see thee soon after thy return.[2] I wd like to be in Washington this Spring but am really too ill to think of it seriously. I must content myself for the present to "Sojourn in Meshech and dwell in the tents of Kedar."[3]

I did not like thy apologies for asking of *me* so trifling a favor. I wish I could do far more: it would give me more pleasure than it would benefit thee.

Elizabeth sends her love—Believe me ever and truly thy friend in word and deed,

J. G. Whittier

Excuse my dear friend the brevity of this note. It is the best I can do today and I thought thee might be anxious for an answer.

W.

Geo. William Alexander and his excellent lady would I know be very happy to render thee any service in their power.— They reside a few miles out of London I believe.[4]

Manuscript: New York Public Library.

1. Charles Gilpin (1815–1874), a nephew of Joseph Sturge, owned a book-selling and publishing business in London. He served as a member of Parliament for Northampton from 1857 to 1874.

2. Grace Greenwood was then leaving for England on the first part of an European tour that lasted fifteen months. Throughout the tour she sent letters which were published in the *Era* and ultimately in book form as *Haps and Mishaps of a Tour in Europe.*

3. Psalms 120:5.

4. George Alexander married Catherine Horsnaill (1806–1878) in 1845 and they had one child.

635. To Ticknor, Reed, and Fields

Amesbury April 8, 1852

My dear fd.

Will you send me the second volume of LaMartine's Histy. of the Restoration in France?[1]

Yours truly
J. G. Whittier

Buckingham's auto-biography in 2 vols. I want, also, but fear it will not come within my means.[2]

I have a poem of some 2 or 300 lines—"The Chapel of the Hermits."—which with some 12 or 15 other poems would make a volume of about 80 or 100 pp. I have half a mind to publish it. I fear however you have an over-plus of new books just now on yr hands. I could make it still smaller—, say 75 pages,—and perhaps make the book better for its brevity. If you think favorably of it let me know at yr. convenience.[3]

Thy frd.
J. G. W.

I suppose fd Fields has not returned. I hear of him by way of G. Greenwood in London.[4]

Manuscript: Swarthmore College.

1. Alphonse Marie Louis de Lamartine's *The History of the Restoration of the Monarchy in France* was then being published in four volumes (London, 1851–1853).

2. Joseph T. Buckingham, *Personal Memoirs and Recollections of an Editorial Life*, published by Ticknor, Reed, and Fields in 1852.

3. *The Chapel of the Hermits, and Other Poems* was finally published in February, although the printing was completed in the fall of 1852. The title poem was published along with twenty-five other poems to make a volume of 118 pages.

4. After the death of his first wife, Fields had gone to Europe in 1851 and remained there until the summer of 1852.

636. To Samuel Gridley Howe

Amesbury April 30, 1852

My dear fd:

Truly "the spirit is willing"[1] but I am not well enough at this time to leave, as my illness is aggravated by a cold. It is a grievous disappointment to me—but God's will be done!—

I am at any rate most grateful to thee for the kind invitation. On this wide earth there is but one Kossuth—the true hero of the time. God bless him![2]

Wilt thou be kind enough to give the enclosed note to thy honored guest.

With kind remembrance of Mrs. H. and with heartfelt thanks for thy invitation, I am ever and truly[3]

thy friend
John G. Whittier

Manuscript: Huntington Library, San Marino, California.

1. Matthew 26:41, modified.

2. Kossuth was in New England from April 23 to May 18; he spoke in Faneuil Hall on April 29 and was officially welcomed by the governor and state legislature at a banquet on April 30. He gave two other addresses at Fanueil Hall, besides lecturing throughout New England. Whittier had already published a poem on his arrival, "Kossuth," in the *National Era*, December 4, 1851.

3. Julia Ward (1819–1910), author and reformer, had married Samuel Gridley Howe in 1843. She helped her husband edit the Boston *Commonwealth* and published a popular book of poetry, *Passion Flowers*, in 1854. Her "Battle Hymn of the Republic" became the most famous poem from the Civil War, and after the war Mrs. Howe spent her time in reform and various causes. See Letter No. 689 for Whittier's comments on her *Passion Flowers*.

637. To William Lloyd Garrison

May 1852

It did me good to see thy handwriting, friend William, reminding me of the old days when we fought the beasts at Ephesus[1] together in Philadelphia. Ah me! I am no longer able to take active part in the conflicts and skirmishes which are preparing the way for the great battle of Armageddon,—the world-wide, final struggle between freedom and slavery.—but, sick or well, in the body or out, I shall be no unconcerned spectator. I bless God that, through the leadings of his Providence, I have a right to rejoice in the certain victory of the right.

What a glorious work Harriet Beecher Stowe has wrought.[2] *Thanks* for the Fugitive Slave Law! Better for slavery that law had never been enacted, for it gave occasion for "Uncle Tom's Cabin"!

Source: Harriet Beecher Stowe, *Uncle Tom's Cabin* (Boston, 1879), introduction, p. xvi.

1. 1 Corinthians 15:32.

2. Harriet Beecher Stowe (1811–1896) had published *Uncle Tom's Cabin* serially in the *National Era* from June 1851 to April 1852. It was published in book form in March 1852 and sold over 300,000 copies in its first year to become the most popular American novel and an influential force in molding antislavery feeling. In her later works Mrs. Stowe utilized New England settings for local color stories and novels. For further comments by Whittier on *Uncle Tom's Cabin* see Letter Nos. 649 and 654.

638. To Ophelia Underwood

Amesbury, July 8, 1852

Dear Friend:

I have received thy note of this morning, inviting me to attend the Levee this evening.[1] I regret that I am obliged to decline the invitation, yet I am not the less gratified by it, and the kind terms in which it has been conveyed. So far as intention goes, it does me more than justice, since, in my efforts against the great social and political wrongs of the country, I have not over-looked more immediate evils.

I have long been convinced that the term of daily labor in manufacturing companies should be abridged. I would prefer that it should be done by the voluntary action of owners and directors, but, as this is scarcely to be hoped for, the Legislature must provide a remedy.

If the unpleasant state of things in this place shall have the effect to call attention to the subject, and bring about the Ten Hour system, I am persuaded none of us will regret any temporary inconvenience or loss, in consequence of it. With very few exceptions, the operatives have the cordial sympathy of our citizens. This fact is a strong testimony to their good conduct and respectability. It shows too, that ours is essentially a republican community. We have no privileged class, no petty village aristocracy proud of its worthlessness, and despising the more useful, and, in all practical matters, more intelligent members of society. In this respect ours is a model manufacturing village. Long may it continue so.

With kind wishes for the welfare of thyself and thy friends, and that, in your present position, you may know how to "*overcome evil with good*,"[2] and temper the firmness of principle with charity, courtesy and christian forbearance, I am very truly, thy friend

John G. Whittier

Source: The Amesbury *Villager*, July 15, 1852.

Recipient: Ophelia Underwood, one of the mill girls then on strike in Amesbury, was secretary of the Female Operatives of Salisbury Manufacturing Company.

1. A levee was being held to arrange for the support of recently discharged workers from the Salisbury Manufacturing Company. For years the mills had opened at 5 A. M. and closed at 7 P. M., allowing a half-hour recess for breakfast and an hour for dinner. In addition, the male operatives were permitted a fifteen-minute break in the morning and afternoon. A new agent had abolished these two breaks and on June 1, 1852, when 100 men left the mill for their morning break, they were discharged. After fruitless conferences with the director and agent, the girls employed in the mill also quit work. On June 5 a mass meeting of citizens adopted five resolutions, drawn up by Whittier, asking the management to rehire the discharged workers. Other circulars signed by Whittier started a campaign for political action to cure the evils of unrestricted hours of daily labor

in the factories. The petition supported a bill then submitted to the General Court to reduce the work load to a ten-hour work day. However, the directors and agent remained adamant and most of the old operatives left the town. This resulted in the employment of a large number of foreigners and the character of operatives in Amesbury was entirely changed.

2. Romans 12:21.

639. To Thomas Wentworth Higginson

Amesbury July 13, 1852

My dear Higginson

Thy letter was exactly to the purpose and was read at the Levee, and will be published this week in the "Villager"—[1] Thou will see by the Villager of last week what we are doing about the Ten Hour Law. That must be made a point in our elections this fall—I think we can carry it through the next Legislature.[2]

I hope thou will be able to go to the Dist. Convention at Lowell tomorrow.[3] Our del. is instructed to go for thee as one of the delegates to Pittsburgh. Dont refuse. We should be glad to see thee at any time.

Ever thine
J. G. W.

Manuscript: Huntington Library, San Marino, California. Published: Higginson, *Whittier,* p. 87.

1. Higginson had sent a letter, published on July 15, 1852, in support of the workers, along with some money. He stated that the operatives had a right to combine for their own interests and should not submit to despotic and arbitrary rule.

2. Whittier and others from Salisbury and Amesbury had drawn up a circular which supported petitions for the ten-hour system bill then in the Massachusetts legislature. However, it was not until 1865 that Massachusetts enacted a ten-hour law. Jonathan Nayson, a signer of the petition, was elected to the legislature that fall.

3. A meeting of Free Soil members to select delegates to attend the national Free Soil convention in Pittsburgh on August 11, 1852, for the purpose of nominating a presidential candidate. Higginson, however, was not able to attend and was not selected as a delegate.

640. To William Stevens Robinson

Amesbury, July 14, 1852

My Dear Friend,—

Thy letter of the 7th inst. is before me. I am unable, from illness, to attend the Convention to be held tomorrow, but I cannot withhold the expression of my full and hearty sympathy with its objects. It is fitting that, after the total abandonment of national and republican principles by the two

Conventions lately held at Baltimore, and the adoption by both of a platform sectional, unconstitutional and anti-democratic, the Free Democracy of Massachusetts should assemble and reaffirm the truths of the Declaration of Independence.[1]

So far from being discouraged by the defections of some who have acted with us in New York—a defection, the consequences of which, are likely to prove quite as serious to themselves as to the cause they, to the extent of their power, betrayed—I see ample reason for congratulation and hopeful trust in the further development of events.[2] The places left vacant will be more than filled. What matters it that the Whig and Democratic Conventions resolve the *"finality"* of the Fugitive Slave Law? That Law is dead; its funeral services have been performed in the trial and rescuers of Shadrach and the "rebels" of Christiana.[3] A Law which has been judged and condemned by such a Democrat as Robert Rantoul, Jr., and such a Whig as William H. Seward, and which has been laughed to scorn and trodden into the very dust of the floor of the Congress by Joshua R. Giddings, cannot be galvanized into life by the resolves of Presidental caucuses.

Then again, what a rebuke to our feebleness of faith in the wisdom of the Disposer of events is given by the result of the late Whig and Democratic Conventions. The wheels of Providence are not moved by blind chance; they are full of eyes round about. [4] No doubt one of the candidates at least was well worthy of their common platform; and, for the other, he seems to have adjusted himself to it with military promptness and precision. But, where are the hoary politicians, who have demoralized the Free States by seeking these nominations through base obeisance to Slavery? Unsuspected, unseen, and avenging Nemesis sat in the two Conventions, making of their scheming and selfish members blind and unconscious instruments of the righteous judgment of God. Henceforth the ambition of the North will seek the Presidency by other paths than that trodden by the defeated candidates of the Baltimore Convention. Their example might have been a danger; it is now only a warning.

We have reason, moreover, to rejoice that all disguises are stripped off; that neither Whig nor Democrat can look us in the face, and ask us to vote for their men and platforms. Both parties have made an unqualified surrender to the Slave power. They are slaves; and any attempt at escape on their part would properly come under the cognizance of the Fugitive Slave Law and Commissioner Ingraham.[5] *Our* path is clear—nobody can mistake it.—Should we hesitate to enter upon it, the meanest of our enemies would be justified in holding us up to contempt and derision.

The rallying cry of Liberty has already gone forth from the full heart of the Commonwealth. Let it be echoed by your Convention. Not in vain shall it sweep over our hills and valleys. The day of humiliation for Massachusetts is passed. Even Boston—admonished by the result of her political and mercantile venture in the shipment of Thomas Sims for the Southern market—is in no mood to repeat the experiment.[6] And out of Boston there is not a spot on the broad territory of the State where the Fugitive Law could be executed. You might as well seek to put in force the witchcraft law of 1692, or the edicts of Edmund Andros.[7]

Trusting that tried and faithful friends of Freedom will be selected to represent our District in the National Convention, I am very truly thy friend

John G. Whittier

W. S. Robinson, Esq.

Source: The Amesbury *Villager*, July 22, 1852.

1. The Democratic national convention met at Baltimore on June 1, 1852, and nominated Franklin Pierce for President on a platform accepting the finality of the Compromise of 1850 and affirming opposition to attempts to renew congressional agitation on the slavery question. The Whig national convention met also at Baltimore on June 16, 1852, and nominated General Winfield Scott for President. The Whig platform accepted the Compromise of 1850, condemned further agitation of the slavery question, and affirmed states' rights.

2. Many of the New York Democrats, notably Martin Van Buren and his son, who had been Free Soilers in 1848, returned to the Democratic party and supported Pierce.

3. Both prominent "slave" cases in 1851. Shadrach, a black waiter in Boston, was arrested as a fugitive slave in February 1851. While the plans for trial were being considered, a group of black citizens of Boston overcame the guards and freed Shadrach, who escaped to Canada and freedom. His escape caused a national uproar that forced the President to issue a proclamation for aid in capturing the escaped slave. Five persons engaged in the rescue were brought to trial, but no conviction could be made against them.

The Christiana, Pennsylvania, rebels were a group of Negroes who on September 11, 1851, resisted an attempt to be retaken to slavery and, exchanging shots with the southern claimants, killed Edward Gorsuch of Maryland and his son. The Negroes escaped and an ensuing trial of some Quaker onlookers resulted in their acquittal.

4. Ezekiel 10:12.

5. Edward Ingraham (1793–1854), a Philadelphia lawyer and author, was one of the commissioners appointed under the Fugitive Slave Law. He was an active Democrat, supported the Mexican War, and as commissioner occasioned much criticism for his willing support of southern claimants. He was the commissioner who issued the warrant that resulted in the Christiana killings.

6. See Letter No. 616, note 3.

7. Edmund Andros (1637–1714), the autocratic royal governor of the New England colonies from 1686 to 1688, was driven out by a Boston uprising.

641. To Elizabeth Nicholson

Amesbury July 14, 1852

My dear friend.

Well of all the strange things in this strange world! To think of one so sensible, discreet and worldly wise as thyself, turning author and letting herself down to book-making! And to think of compiling a book, and taking liberties with irritable geniuses, stretching one and lopping another to the iron bedstead of Quakerism.[1] Has thee forgotten how Benj Jones and I got up the North Star? But it's no use talking: "Wilfu' folk maun hae their way"—[2]

But seriously, I like thy plan, and give thee leave to do with me and mine as seems best in thy eyes. I must say however that I quite agree with our dear fd Enoch Lewis, in respect to "My countrymen" etc. [3] I regret—and deeply too—all that I have written which is not in spirit and in the letter consistent with principles, and testimonies which I love and regard as vital to the interests of humanity, and the cause not of Quakerism alone but of "pure religion and undefiled."[4]

I hope therefore that nothing of mine may be published in a book for Friends, which can be construed in any way as adverse to sound doctrine and the "form" even of sound words. I shouldn't quite dare to trust thee alone—but E. L. is a safe counsellor, and I am glad he is willing to aid thee. I have no doubt the book will be an excellent one, as thy good taste, and E. L['s]. clear judgment will be combined.

In omitting or altering any thing of mine, I only stipulate that the original meaning, and wholeness of the piece be not lost. Many of the pieces of prose and poetry of mine are full of mistakes made in copying and printing. I hope thou wilt not perpetuate these. As to the pieces written for the Freeman, I very much doubt the propriety of printing any of them.

I have not been able for a year past to write except at rare intervals, and have suffered much from illness. I should be glad to see Philada and all of my old friends there, but I am not able to undergo the fatigue of the journey.

Sister E. is at home this summer, much as she has been for some time past—She sends her love to thee, and will write soon—With kind remembrance of thy father and sisters and of all enquiring friends, I am as Ever thy fd.

John G. Whittier

Manuscript: Haverford College. Published: Snyder, "Whittier Returns to Philadelphia," p. 155.

1. Elizabeth Nicholson was then editing an anthology of prose and poetry as an advanced reader for Quaker schools. She had asked permission to reprint sixteen poems and four prose pieces by Whittier to be interspersed with pieces by Bryant, Longfellow, Tennyson, and others. Elizabeth Nicholson, Elizabeth Lloyd, and Whittier's sister Elizabeth also contributed poems to the collection. Enoch Lewis wrote the introduction for the volume, which was titled *The Wheat-Sheaf; or, Gleanings for the Wayside and Fireside* (Philadelphia, 1853).

2. Robert Burns, "In Simmer, When the Hay was Mawn."

3. Probably "Expostulation," which opens:

> "Our fellow-countrymen in chains!
> Slaves, in a land of light and law
> Slaves, crouching on the very plains
>   Where rolled the storm of Freedom's war!
> A groan from Eutaw's haunted wood,
>   A wail where Camden's martyrs fell,
> By every shrine of patriot blood,
>   From Moultrie's wall and Jasper's well."

This praise of the Revolutionary War and warriors continues in the next stanza also.

4. James 1:27.

642. To Charles Sumner

Amesbury August 10 [1852]

My dear Sumner.

The sad intelligence of the death of Rantoul has just reached us. I have lost an old and valued friend, and the state and country a strong and noble man. How little did I expect to outlive him![1] I have just read thy tribute to him. It is a relief to me [to] have the right word spoken of my friend.[2]

I am by no means surprised at the refusal of the Senate to hear thee. It is simply carrying out the resolutions of the two Baltimore Conventions. Never mind. The right time will come for thee, if not this session, the next certainly.[3] I think our proper place for speaking now is to the people directly, rather than to Congress. I want thee to put on the harness this fall and do battle as in '48.

Dr. Bailey has just left me for the White Mts. He is anxious that Chase should be nominated at Pittsburg; but the popular feeling is strong for Hale. and I am not sure that he will not do as much to defeat Hunkerism in its disguise of Democracy as Chase.[4]

We want thee to open our Lyceum course here, this fall— Can'st thou not do it?—[5] At any rate I should be right glad to see thee at our place. My health is more comfortable than in the winter and spring. I was sorry to hear of thy own illness.

Ever and truly thy fd.

John G. Whittier

Manuscript: Harvard University. Published, in Part: Pickard, *Life*, pp. 364–365.

1. Robert Rantoul had died on August 7, 1852, at Washington. Whittier published a poetic tribute to him, "Rantoul," in the *National Era*, July 14, 1853, which expressed his hopes for Rantoul:

> "Through him we hoped to speak the word
>   Which wins the freedom of a land;
> And lift, for human right, the sword
>   Which dropped from Hampden's dying hand."

Rantoul had been elected to Congress as the result of the coalition of Democrats and Free Soilers, and it was hoped in the next state election that he would be placed in the Senate.

2. Sumner had delivered a brief eulogy for Rantoul on August 9, 1852.

3. Sumner had been waiting since his entrance to the Senate to speak on the Fugitive Slave Law. He had attempted to speak on the subject July 28, but was not allowed to give his speech, since both Whigs and Democrats wanted no further slavery discussion before the fall election. Sumner finally delivered his Fugitive Slave Law speech on August 26, a few days before the session was to end. In his reply to Whittier on August 13, 1852, Sumner said: "I am grateful for your words of cheer and confidence. I have never desired to come here, as you well know. Since I have been here, our cause has never been out of my mind. In the exercise of my best discretion I have postponed speaking until now. To this course I was advised by friends also. Should I not succeed before the close of the session, I shall feel sad; but I cannot feel that I have failed in a duty. *But I shall speak* on an amendment of the Civil Appropriation Bill. Thus far, whenever I have spoken I have been listened to. On this occasion I may not have the attention; but the speech shall be made. For a long time I have been prepared to handle the Fugitive Slave Bill at length. By the blessing of God it shall be done" (Pickard, *Life*, p. 365).

4. At the national Free Soil convention in Pittsburgh on August 11, 1852, John P. Hale became the Free Soil candidate for President.

5. Sumner, however, in his reply said that he could not make any lyceum engagements for the coming season.

643. To Robert Carter[1]

Amesbury, August 12, 1852

Dear friend

Although a stranger to thee, personally, I venture to ask a favor of thee. My friend Miss Phebe Carey of Cincinnati—whose name as a writer is doubtless familiar to thee [—] is stopping today and tomorrow at the Marlboro. I should take it as a great favor if thou could call on her, and introduce her to some of your literary people—If my young friend William S. Thayer is in town—or at thy office, he would like to see her. [Richard] Hildreth she would like to see—

Allow me to say that I read the Commonwealth with great daily satisfaction—and regard it as the best Free Soil paper we have ever had—

Thy friend
J. G. Whittier

Miss C. would like to see Prof. Longfellow. She was unable when in Boston two years ago to accept an invitation from

him to visit him at Nahant. She is, of course, a Free Soiler—I
regard [her] as a young woman of some genius—

Manuscript: New York Public Library.
1. This is conjectural, but Carter was editing the *Commonwealth* in 1852. See
Letter No. 397, note 4.

644. To Henry Wadsworth Longfellow

Amesbury, August 12, 1852

My dear fd.
    This will be taken Bostonward by my worthy young friend
Miss Phebe Carey of Cincinnati—and as she will be a day or
two in Boston she would be glad to see thee. She has I think
the true poetic "vision and faculty divine"[1] and withal she is
more and better than a poet—a true and pleasant woman. I
hope thou wilt be able to call on her at the Marlboro Hotel
today (Thursday) or tomorrow—

Believe me truly thy friend
J. G. Whittier

Manuscript: Harvard University.
1. William Wordsworth, *The Excursion*, Book I, line 79.

645. To Samuel Fessenden and James Appleton

Amesbury, August 19 [1852]

Dear Friends
    This will be handed you by my friends W. J. and Saml
Allinson of N. Jersey.
    They are staunch advocates of Temperance and freedom
and visit Portland mainly to inquire into the workings of the
Maine law. They wish to see Neal Dow if he is in the city.[1]

Your friend
John G. Whittier

Source: Handwritten copy, Haverford College.
1. Neal Dow (1804–1897), a successful businessman and Quaker, served as
mayor of Portland in 1851. During that time he advocated and secured the passage of a group of severe prohibition laws to stop the selling of liquor, known as the
Maine Law. He devoted most of his life to the cause of temperance and achieved a
national reputation for his temperance reform ideas. During the Civil War he
served as a general, being wounded and captured by the Confederates.

646. To Walter Channing, George Jewett, Moses Grant, and George Washington Bungay

Amesbury, August 19, 1852

The bearers, W. J. and Saml Allinson of N. Jersey, strong advocates of the Temperance cause—wish to see some of the friends of that cause in Boston. I take pleasure in introducing them to you as gentlemen of high-standing and character.

Yrs. truly

John G. Whittier

Dr. Walter Channing
Dr. Jewett
Moses Grant, Esq.
G. W. Bungay

Source: Handwritten copy, Haverford College.

Recipients: Walter Channing (1786–1876), a brother of William Ellery Channing, was a prominent doctor in Boston. He authored many medical treatises and taught at Harvard from 1812 to 1854.

Dr. Jewett is probably George Baker Jewett (1818–1886), a graduate of Andover Theological Seminary in 1842. He had taught around Boston and was a professor of classics at Amherst in 1850. He later became a pastor in New Hampshire, and wrote many books on religious subjects.

Moses Grant (1785–1861), a successful Boston businessman in paper, served on the board of aldermen for Boston and was president of the Temperance Society.

George Washington Bungay (1818–1892) wrote *Crayon Sketches and Off-Hand Takings, of Distinguished Statesmen, Orators, Divines, Essayists, Editors, Poets, and Philanthropists* (Boston, 1852), which contains an account of an interview with Whittier.

647. To William Buel Sprague

Amesbury, August 28 [1852] [1]

I am sorry it is not in my power to comply with thy request in behalf of the G. M. A. of Albany.

I am very truly thy friend

John G. Whittier

Wm. B. Sprague, Esq.

Manuscript: The British Museum, London, England.

Recipient: William Buel Sprague (1795–1876), a Presbyterian clergyman, was pastor of the Presbyterian church at Albany from 1829 to 1869. He was then engaged in publishing his *Annals of The American Pulpit,* the first two volumes of which were published in 1856.

1. The date is difficult to read and might be 1856 or even 1862.

648. To William Ticknor

Amesbury October 3, 1852

Friend Ticknor.

I am ready to send the copy of the little volume I spoke of; but am not quite satisfied whether to publish the poem, "*The Chapel of the Hermits*" by itself, or in connection with other (and perhaps in some respects better) pieces. The poem contains between 3 and 400 lines—

However, if you are ready to print it, I will send the copy at once, as I should like to have it out this season. If my friend Fields has returned he will perhaps give me his opinion when he sees the MS. The whole copy will make some 120 pages as near as I can judge.

Truly thy friend
J. G. Whittier

On second thought I send herewith the principal poem of the collection—If you could let me hear from you soon you would oblige me, as I wish to know when I may expect the proof sheets.

J. G. W.

Manuscript: Huntington Library, San Marino, California.

649. To Harriet Beecher Stowe

Amesbury, October 8, 1852

My dear friend.

I send thee the *first draft* of a piece for the book referred to in thy note. Illness must excuse my not copying it.[1]

Ten thousand thanks for thy immortal book! My young friend Mary Irving[2] (of the Era) writes me that she has been reading it to some twenty young ladies, daughters of Louisiana slave-holders, near New Orleans, and amidst the scenes described in it, and that they with one accord pronounced it true.

Saml Rhoads of Philadelphia can give the information of R. Dillingham.[3]

Address "Saml Rhoads Blockly near Philada."

Truly thy friend
John G. Whittier

Manuscript: Chicago Historical Society.
1. Mrs. Stowe was then gathering materials for her *A Key to Uncle Tom's Cabin* (Cleveland, 1853), which was to answer criticism of her book as being merely a fictional account of slavery. The bulk of the book contained histories and

documents to prove the authenticity of her novel. Chapter XIII of Part I contained an account of "The Quakers," for which Whittier probably supplied materials.

2. Mary Irving, a free-lance writer, had written poems and stories for the *Era*.

3. Richard Dillingham (d. 1850), an Ohio Quaker, had been arrested for trying to help slaves escape on December 5, 1848. He was sentenced to three years in prison, but, after serving a year, died of the cholera. Whittier wrote a poetic tribute to Dillingham, "The Cross," in the *National Era*, February 26, 1852. Mrs. Stowe reprinted Whittier's poem in the chapter, "The Quakers," in *A Key to Uncle Tom's Cabin*, as well as a complete account of Dillingham's arrest and death.

650. To Gamaliel Bailey

Amesbury December 8 [1852]

My dear friend Bailey.

I fear thee think I have forgotten thee and the Era. Far otherwise; but the truth is except at long intervals I cannot write without suffering too intensely to allow me any courage for the task.

I have, however, one or two things nearly ready for the Era, which I will send as soon as I can.[1]

The coalition has failed here and I do not greatly regret it.[2] We shall lose nothing by it. I hope and trust *Adams* will get to Congress.[3] It wd be a noble acquisition. Hood in our (Rantoul's) Dist. is right on the Fugitive S. L. and we hope to elect him.[4]

Thine truly
John G. Whittier

Manuscript: Swarthmore College.

1. Since October 14, 1852, Whittier had published only one brief review in the *Era*, "Waverly Novels." His poem, "The Poor Voter on Election Day," appeared in the *Era*, December 23, 1852.

2. The coalition of Free Soilers and Democrats which had elected Boutwell governor for the past two years failed to gain a sufficient majority in the legislature and John H. Clifford, the Whig candidate, was elected.

3. Charles Francis Adams, running on a Free Soil ticket in his father's district, forced a runoff with the Whig candidate, but lost the election by 550 votes.

5. George Hood (1806–1859) had served several times in the state legislature. Running as a Democrat, he lost the election by only 200 votes. He was mayor of Lynn from 1850 to 1852, having been elected the city's first mayor in 1850.

651. To Ralph Waldo Emerson

Amesbury December 12, 1852

My dear friend.

Will it be in thy power to visit us once more some time this season? Our Lyceum managers wish me to say that they would be glad to have thee choose any evening most agreeable to thyself, in the months of Feby. and March (with the excep-

tion March 3 and Feby. 3). Our lectures are generally on
Thursday Evenings, but if some other evening in the week wd.
suit thee better, we can easily accommodate ourselves to it.[1]

I feel guilty in respect to the *Bhagvah Gita*: but it is too
late to repent: and I will even keep it until I restore it to thee
personally in exchange for Geo Fox. It is a wonderful book—
and has greatly excited my curiosity to know more of the
religious literature of the East.

Believe me truly thy friend

John G. Whittier

An early answer wd. oblige the Managers of the Lyceum.

Manuscript: Harvard University.
1. Emerson agreed to lecture on March 17, 1853.

Part Eight

Poet and Republican

1853-1856

Poet and Republican

1853-1856

The title poem from Whittier's 1856 book, *The Panorama, and Other Poems,* concludes with a revealing analysis of the inner divisions then existing in him. Wearied with his abolitionist role, Whittier records his attraction to summer pastorals and legendary tales and his desire to write sweetly and mildly about these things. At the same time impelled by a "voice and vision," the reformer-moralist in him continues to handle public themes in tones of sharp rebuke and scorn. Finally protesting his love of fellowmen, Whittier breaks off, as if unable to reconcile the conflict:

> But the time passes. It were vain to crave
> A late indulgence. *What I had I gave*.

During these years the poet slowly gained ascendancy over the reformer, and tales of New England and countryside scenes replaced abolitionist pieces. Increasingly Whittier wrote about a summer's day, a gift of a mayflower, or a walk in autumn. The incidents of his youth, the barefoot boy days, the nostalgic memories of a past social order or a lost love furnished the materials for his poems, rather than "public wrongs." Whittier had begun to tap the inner poetic wellspring that produced his best ballads and genre poems. "Maud Muller" and "The Barefoot Boy" typify these pieces. Both are sentimental and tend towards platitudinous moralizing, but both poems touch universal and moving themes: the loss of romantic dreams and the joys of innocent boyhood. A sparse, simple diction and a tightly controlled structure counterbalance the bathos of "Maud Muller"; while the graphic listing of the boy's main activities in "The Barefoot Boy" minimizes its awkward phrasings and conventional imagery.

Poetic and literary topics now occupied the bulk of his time and correspondence. He told Fields that he had made an April fool of himself by reading reviews of his new book;

asked Higginson and Mrs. Stowe to review *The Chapel of Hermits*; and was incensed when a British reviewer ridiculed his "Barclay of Ury." Increasingly his incidental correspondence mentioned literary acquaintances and discussed current literature. His own critical judgments never fully escaped from the moral limitations of his Quaker background nor the popular taste of his age, for he considered a now-forgotten *Passion Flowers* a great book, one which placed its author "at the head of us all." At the same time he thought Thoreau's *Walden* "capital reading but very wicked and heathenish. The practical moral of it seems to be that if a man is willing to sink himself into a woodchuck, he can live as cheaply as that quadruped." He earnestly solicited publication for friends like Lucy Larcom or the Cary sisters, reading their manuscripts and offering suggestions for revisions, as well as following the travels and writings of friends like Bayard Taylor and Grace Greenwood. Conversely, Whittier wrote fewer letters to political figures like Sumner and Winthrop, and his communications to the press almost ceased.

Still, as his ambivalent remarks in "The Panorama" indicate, public events and the political scene retained a strong hold on his poetic imagination. Nearly half the poems from this period were occasioned by topical incidents like the arrest of a fugitive slave in Boston or violence in Kansas. But even these poems forecast the final transformation of the propagandist into poet. "What of the day?" moved with an apocalyptic grandeur unequaled in his earlier verse, while "Letter. . ." blended slang and broad humor to parody pulpit oratory. "The Haschish" cleverly related the effects of a powerful drug to northern dependence on the cotton market, and "The Kansas Emigrants" became the song of thousands of free settlers as they traveled to Kansas. These poems show Whittier experimenting with poetic form and effectively controlling his emotions with understatement and humor. Truly Whittier *had given what he had*, for after 1856 he wrote few abolition or reform poems.

Perhaps the most significant national event, certainly the one that most engaged Whittier's attention, was the passage of the Kansas-Nebraska bill in 1854 and the resulting formation of the Republican party. This bill overthrew the Missouri Compromise by opening all new territories to slavery under a popular sovereignty option. Immediately after its passage a new fugitive slave case occurred in Boston with the arrest and return of an escaped slave, Anthony Burns. The incident raised popular feelings to a fever pitch and even Whittier found it difficult to control his outrage and frustration. He excitedly wrote to Bowditch after Burns's arrest: "That man *must* not be sent out of Boston as a slave. Anything but that! The whole people must be called out, the country must precipitate itself upon the city—an avalanche of freemen. . . . In the name of God let the people be summoned! Send out the fiery crosses without further delay." Spurred by similar emotions, Higginson and others risked their lives in an abortive attempt to free Burns and caused the death of a guard. Recoiling from such actions, Whittier pleaded for nonresistance and decried the use of force. Whittier's dilemma, compounded by his Quaker pacifism, was a painful one. His words and inspiration had fired the emotions of thousands and impelled a lethargic North to action—now this aroused public feeling swelled uncontrollably as the maelstrom of agitation and bitterness pushed the country toward an open civil war. Though deploring the violence, Whittier realistically appraised the situation. He wrote to Winthrop that if popular ferment were not channeled in a legitimate way, the next attempt to execute the Fugitive Slave Law in New England would be resisted to the death in an open-armed revolution.

This outbreak merely foreshadowed the larger national violence soon to occur in Kansas and on the very floors of Congress. In Kansas proslavery "border ruffians" openly fought and killed free settlers, led by northern fighters like John Brown. The refusal of the national government to control these outrages and the proslavery dominance of the two major parties led opponents of the Kansas-Nebraska bill to form a new party. Feeling that both the Whig and Democratic parties had totally surrendered to the slave power and having assisted third-party movements for over thirteen years, Whittier wrote to Emerson: "I care nothing for names; I have no prejudices against Whig or Democrat; show me a party cutting itself loose from slavery, repudiating its treacherous professed allies of the South, and making the *protection of Man* the paramount object, and I am ready to go with it heart and soul. The great body of the people of all parties here are ready to unite in the formation of a new party." This feeling was so widespread that it forced a radical realignment of political forces. A coalition of Whigs, Free Soilers, and antislavery Democrats, united upon the repeal of the Kansas-Nebraska bill and the restriction of slavery, formed the Republican party in 1854. By the election of 1856 it had become a major political force.

The year 1856 was a demanding one for Whittier. He pub-

lished *The Panorama, and Other Poems* in March, helped
organize the new Amesbury Public Library, actively backed
Frémont for the Presidency, and wrote songs and letters in his
party's behalf throughout the campaign. Popular enthusiasm
for the romantic, though politically inexperienced, Frémont
ran high and Whittier himself caught some of the spirit as his
letters pictured Frémont saving the country from slave bondage and restoring peace to bleeding Kansas. But the violence
only increased and a shocked North heard of the brutal and
senseless caning of Charles Sumner by a southern congressman
on the Senate floor. This assault, coupled with the news of the
pillaging of a free settlement in Kansas, galvanized antislavery
feeling in the North. For over three years Sumner's seat remained unoccupied, an eloquent, tangible symbol of northern
opposition to slavery. Personally affected by Sumner's severe
physical suffering, Whittier still strove to direct inflamed public emotions toward a political end. He cautioned his Amesbury neighbors against fruitless indignation: "Let us not be
betrayed into threats. Leave violence where it belongs, with
the wrong doer. It is worse than folly to talk of fighting slavery, when we have not yet agreed to vote against it. Our
business is with poll boxes, not cartridge boxes; with ballots,
not bullets." Though the Republican party failed to win the
election, Frémont had gained 114 electoral votes and popular
support of over 1,300,000. The party had proven its strength
and an undiscouraged Whittier claimed victory had only been
delayed for four years.

Whittier's calm acceptance of his party's defeat rested
mainly in the maturity and certainty of his own personal
faith—that God personally directed human events for his own
ends and that in time the infinite workings of his divine plan
would be unfolded. An 1855 letter sets forth the essence of
his religious beliefs. Stressing his indifference to creeds and
outward forms, Whittier says: "Christianity is the ultimate—
the highest possible ideal—and all lines of human progress,
however widely apart at the outset, converge upon it. I see
nothing in any school of philosophy to compare with the sublime simplicity of its truth, as adapted to the wants of our
nature." Accepting the divine efficacy of Christ's life, Whittier
held that faith in Christ was best manifested by a life of devotion to the welfare of humanity. Another source of Whittier's
security and confidence resided in his attachment to his
Amesbury home and the close association with surrounding
neighbors. As an active participant in town life, Whittier
served a year on the school committee, where he decided not

to force a Catholic student to read the Bible and bought trees
to beautify the school grounds; he helped organize and purchase books for the new public library; solicited and secured
speakers like Emerson, Sumner, and Taylor for the local lyceum; and served as corresponding secretary for an Amesbury
Agricultural Society. His personal correspondence during this
time, like his poetry, showed a definite shift away from political and public events to the more intimate, relaxed topics of
common friends, current books, and household incidents.
These years brought new friends who began to surround Whittier with the social charm and affection that had been lacking
since his Philadelphia years. Lucy Larcom, to whom Whittier
wrote ten letters in these four years, became a frequent visitor
to his Amesbury home and grew especially close to his sister
Elizabeth. He advised her on publication, praised her work in
reviews, and came to regard her as almost one of the Whittier
family. The forming of new relationships, the security of the
Amesbury home, and the gradual withdrawal from active
political involvement freed Whittier's poetic inspiration. He
was now ready to create the ballads and songs of New England
that ensured his poetic fame.

652. To James Thomas Fields

Amesbury, January 8, 1853

My dear friend.
   "*Wo ist Peter Grimm?*"[1] Where's the Hermits?[2] I am sorry
the book is not out: but as Toots says in Dombey and Son,
"it's no sort of consequence—"[3]
   I wrote thee about the poems of Phebe Carey—I think she
has a very marked and beautiful collection of poems—enough
for a small volume, which I hope you will publish. She will be
in Boston soon and you can decide about it.[4]

Thine truly
J. G. W.

I have material for two volumes of prose stories, essays and
Historical Sketches which I might get together under the title
of "*Literary Recreations and Miscellanies.*"[5] I think a considerable portion of them are better than anything I have yet
published. The very titles of some of them will indicate their
character[:] "The Little Iron Soldier," "The Great Ipswich
Fright," "The Boy Captives," "Passaconaway," "Pope Night,"
"Lord Ashley and the Thieves," "The Two Processions,"
"The Better Land," "The Poetry of the North," "A Night on

Mt. Katahdin," "The Proselytes," etc. etc.–What [do you] think of it? I wish to have "The Chapel of Hermits" sent as soon as convenient to Dr. Bowring, W. S. Landor of London, and to Joseph Mazzini, also I believe in London.[6] I want copies sent to Wm and Mary Howitt and to thy friend Mary R. Mitford.[7] (And Geo. W. Alexander and Joseph Sturge, care of Chas Gilpin, Publisher London.) I wd like if it were not too much trouble to have them sent as *from the author.*

Every and truly thine
J. G. Whittier

Manuscript: Huntington Library, San Marino, California.

1. The allusion here may possibly be to Peter Grimes, the reprobate scoundrel of George Crabbe's twenty-second tale of *The Borough.*

2. *The Chapel of Hermits, and Other Poems* was published in February, although its printing had taken place in early fall 1852. Fields replied to Whittier's letter on January 9, 1853, as follows:

"I am keeping the Chapel back as the holidays are past till the row of the New Year is over. In a couple of weeks we shall publish. Touching the vol. of Miss Carey I am afraid we have no place for it. The truth is we have so much to look after we could not I fear do her justice. Your vols. of Literary Recreations I pray you send at once. Bravo! I am so glad you are ready to print again. Just as soon as you choose to go ahead we are ready to print. The Titles sound admirable" (letter, Essex Institute, Salem, Massachusetts).

3. Mr. P. Toots, a wealthy, somewhat dimwitted, student in Dickens' *Dombey and Son.* He uses the expression "it's of no consequence" throughout the novel.

4. Fields, despite his reservations in his reply, published her poems, *Poems and Parodies,* in 1854.

5. The book was published in September 1854.

6. Walter Savage Landor (1775–1864), the English poet and writer.

7. Mary Russell Mitford (1787–1855) wrote poetry and a series of plays, but was most noted for her essays, *Our Village, Sketches of English Life,* which appeared in five volumes from 1824 to 1832.

653. To an Unidentified Correspondent[1]

Amesbury, January 20 [1853]

My dear friend–

I like the idea of thy circular, and have answered it to the best of my ability. In this way, and this way only a true conception of the real available strength of the F. S. party in each town can be obtained and sitting in thy office in Boston thee can see over the whole state, and know exactly whom to call upon in any emergency of the cause.

Ticknor will send a copy of my little book, now ready or nearly so, and I will feel obliged to thee for a notice of it. It is not all I wished to make it, but sickness and sheer inability to read or write except a few minutes at a time prevented me from doing justice to my idea. However, this is no excuse for it. Let it be judged on its own merits.

My blood boils at the treatment of Kossuth and his dying mother.[2] How long, oh Lord, how long![3]

Thy friend
John G. Whittier

Manuscript: Massachusetts Historical Society.

1. The correspondent may possibly be Samuel Edmund Sewall.

2. Kossuth's aged mother and sister had taken refuge in Brussels after the revolution. In 1852 the Austrian government tried to force the Belgium king to deport them back. Only the revelation that Kossuth's mother was seriously ill stopped the deportation.

3. Psalms 94:3, modified.

654. To Harriet Beecher Stowe

Amesbury, January 30, 1853

Dear friend.

If any thing of mine can be of service to thee, I shall be not only willing but gratified to place it at thy disposal. I do not know exactly the plan of thy forthcoming work,[1] but it has occured to me that if facts were needed that a volume of the Penna. Freeman which I edited in '38 and 9 might contain something to the purpose. If it wd be of any use, I wd forward it to thee.

I send herewith a little vol of mine—in advance of its publication—which I would be obliged to thee to notice in the Independent when thou canst find leisure to look at it. I suppose we should not quite think alike on doctrinal matters, but I trust we agree in the orthodoxy of practical Christianity. The book has faults, I am well and painfully aware, but I have been too severely ill to be able to correct them.

I have a pleasant remembrance of meeting Prof Stowe, and it wd give me great pleasure to renew acquaintance with him and make thine. I have been confined at home for the most part for the last 18 months, and am really too much of an invalid to inflict myself upon others.

Does Dr. Stowe ever deliver Lyceum lectures? We have a Lyceum here, and I think our people wd be glad to hear him.[2]

I say nothing of thy book. It needs no words. I bless God for it, as I look with awe and wonder upon its world moving mission.

I have collected some facts in relation to the way in which the Society of Friends relieved themselves of the evil of Slavery, with a view to their publication in some form. I would like to do it in the shape of a letter to some person of another denomination of Christians, who might inquire of me how slavery was abolished in our Society. Shall I use thy name or that of Dr. S. as the querist? I shall confine myself to a simple detail of the facts in the case.[3]

Believe me most truly
Thy fd.
John G. Whittier

Manuscript: Chicago Historical Society.

1. *A Key to Uncle Tom's Cabin* (Cleveland, 1853).

2. Calvin Ellis Stowe (1802–1886), then a professor of sacred literature at Andover, wrote many books on the Bible. Apparently he never lectured in the Amesbury lyceum as he is not mentioned in the list of speakers in its record book.

3. Whittier never wrote this essay, although in Harriet Beecher Stowe's book, Part IV, "The Influence of the American Church on Slavery," she says, "One denomination of Christians has pursued such a course entirely, and in fact, to free every one of its members from any participation in slave-holding. We refer to the Quakers. The course by which this result has been effected will be shown by a pamphlet soon to be issued by J. G. Whittier, one of their own body" (*A Key to Uncle Tom's Cabin*, p. 194). Whittier had previously published a serialized article in the *National Era*, April 8, 15, 22, 1847, entitled, "Quaker Slaveholding, and How It Was Abolished." (See Letter No. 657 for more comment on this project.)

655. To Thomas Wentworth Higginson

Amesbury, February 8 [1853]

My dear Higginson.

I did a very silly thing in asking thee to notice my little book; and for the sake of preserving my own self respect and thy good opinion, I would now fully release thee from all obligation to put pen to paper in that matter. Let it be as if it had not been. As to the Book let it take its chance. I have no desire to trouble my friends with it.

Pierpont gave us his poem last week—well liked.[1] Mary Curzon was over here—a short time ago, but I unhappily missed seeing her—She is a glorious girl: I think thee must miss her and Margy exceedingly.[2]

Every and truly thy fd.
John G. Whittier

Manuscript: University of Virginia.

1. Pierpont lectured for the Amesbury lyceum on February 3, 1853, on the topic, "The Scholar's Hope."

2. Mary Russell Curzon (1825–1911) and Margaret Seale Curzon (1828–1898) lived at Artichoke Mills, a few miles from Newburyport, with their widowed mother. The family was literary and intellectual and had been especially close to Higginson and his wife, Mary Elizabeth, during the years that Higginson lived in Newburyport. Whittier had written a poem to the two girls, "To ——. Lines Written After a Summer Day's Excursion," in 1851 after the girls had taken him on a boating trip on the Artichoke river. It compared the girls to Undine and Diana, "wise in lore of wood and mead."

656. To an Unidentified Correspondent

Amesbury, March 11, 1853

"Yet when the patriot cannon jars
    That prison's cold and gloomy wall.
And, through its grates, the stripes and stars
    Rise on the wind and fall
Think ye that prisoner's aged ear
Rejoices in the general cheer?
Think ye his dim and failing eye
Is kindled by your pagentry?
Sorrowing of heart and chained of limb
What is your carnival to him?"[1]

John G. Whittier

Dr. fd.
  Thy note found me too unwell to comply, in full, with thy request, which backed by a gentleman whom I have long known as a worthy and gifted member of the literary brotherhood, I should have been glad to have answered more to the purpose.

Very truly thy frd.
J. G. W.

Manuscript: Huntington Library, San Marino, California.
  1. The second to the last stanza from Whittier's "The Prisoner For Debt," which he wrote in 1835.

657. To Samuel Allinson

Amesbury, March 12, 1853

My dear friend.
  I am grieved to hear of thy dear and excellent aunt's illness:[1] I have seen but little of her, but that little was enough to assure me that she was one to love and reverence even as a fine and gentle spirit, who though outwardly blind was favored to behold with the inward eye "the beauty of holiness,"[2] and to conform her life thereto. Remember me most affectionately to her and to the dear household at Burlington.
  I thank thee for calling my attention to J. Hepburn's book.[3] I wd really like to see [it] and wd be careful of it. I am writing, or rather am about to write a letter to H. B. Stowe on the way in which slavery was got rid of by our society—a pamphlet of some 50 pages—and the book is just in time. I want also a little book [on] the life of Benj. Lay and that of

Benezet by Vaux I believe.[4] Who has them?—Could thee
obtain them for me and send them to me by mail if not too
large for that conveyance with Hepburn's book?

The Maine Law is safe in Massachusetts! A test vote yesterday in the House of Rep. shows this beyond doubt.[5] We had a
great temperance meeting at Boston day before yesterday. H.
Ward Beecher spoke.[6] Depend upon it Massachusetts *will not
go backwards.*

My mother (who regrets not seeing thee) and my sister
desire their remembrance. My health has been much better
for the last six weeks than when thou wast here.

With affection thy friend
J. G. Whittier

Source: Typed copy, Haverford College.

1. Elizabeth Allinson.

2. Psalms 96:9.

3. Allinson had written Whittier on March 10, 1853, that John Hepburn's book
was the "first direct attack upon Slavery published by a friend" (letter, Central
Michigan University). Allinson owned a copy of the book and offered to send it
to Whittier if he desired to read it. The book was *The American Defence of the
Christian Golden Rule, or An Essay to Prove the Unlawfulness of Making Slaves
of Men*, printed in 1715 by Hepburn, who was an Englishman then living in
America.

4. Roberts Vaux (1786–1836), a Quaker philanthropist, was interested in many
reforms, among them temperance, prison reform, and free schools. His *Memoirs
of the Lives of Benjamin Lay and Ralph Sandiford* was published in 1815 and his
Memoirs of the Life of Anthony Benezet in 1817.

5. An attempt to introduce a bill for the repeal of the Maine liquor law had
been defeated by a vote of 152 to 56.

6. A state temperance meeting was held on March 10 in Boston and passed
resolutions supporting the antiliquor laws. Beecher spoke along with Higginson.

658. To Ralph Waldo Emerson

Amesbury, March 12, 1853

My dear friend.

We shall expect thee next week fifth day, the 17th at our
Lyceum.

It will be well to take the same train thou didst last year,
the 1/2 past 2 o clk from Boston.

Of course thou will come directly to my house.

Thine truly
J. G. Whittier

Bring with thee thy lectures on "Worship" and "The Anglo-
Saxon."[1]

Manuscript: Harvard University.

1. Emerson lectured March 17, 1853, on "Culture."

659. To Ralph Waldo Emerson

Amesbury, March 16, 1853

My dear Emerson.

All's right! Come on in the 5 o clk train and leave it at *East Salisbury*, where thou wilt find a carriage waiting for thee.

I hope there will be time before lecture (half past 7) to get a cup of tea. Am sorry to have thee hurried so.

Ever and truly

J. G. W.

Some of our folks wd like to hear thy lecture on "Worship."

Manuscript: Harvard University.

660. To William James Allinson

Amesbury, March 16, 1853

Dear friend

I am glad to see that thou hast undertaken to continue the Non Slave holder, believing as I do that such a paper is needed—[1] It touches a point of especial interest to the religious society with which we are connected—and in inculcating the particular duty of abstinence from the products of an oppressive system, it leads us also to inquire more closely of ourselves how far in our business, our habits of living and in general intercourse with our fellow men we are directly or indirectly giving aid or countenance to other evils and other forms of oppression.

I was pleased to see in thy first number a notice of Mary Murray's history.[2] I have carefully looked over the book and fully concur in the favorable estimate of it which Judge Jay has so well expressed. It ought to be introduced into all Friends' schools, and I should be glad to see it in all others.

We remember with pleasure the little visit of Samuel and thyself at our place last summer although I was quite too ill to make your visit pleasant I fear. I have I think felt stronger this winter although still unable to write without a great deal of suffering.

My sister and mother desire their love to thee and thy family, and as respects the latter I too wd unite with them, and assure thee that I am as ever thy aff friend

John G. Whittier

Source: Handwritten copy, Haverford College. Published: Snyder, "John Greenleaf Whittier to William J. Allinson," p. 25.

1. *The Non-Slaveholder* had been published from 1846 to 1850 and was again published from 1853 to 1854. It advocated abstinence from any products of slave labor.

2. *History of the United States of America, written in accordance with the principles of peace* (Boston, 1852).

661. To an Unidentified Correspondent

Amesbury, March 24, 1853

Recd of the Adm of the Estate of Jacob Caldwell the share of my ward in eleven shares in the B. and M. Railroad and in eight shares in the Merrimack Bank.[1]

John B. Nichols[2] Guardian of L. H. Caldwell.[3]

If thee agree with us in regard to the sale of the place at that price, I want thee to send the enclosed line to George Ayer as I have forgotten the street in which he lives.[4] If thee know the street and number put it on the letter, and put it in the mail.[5]

Manuscript: Swarthmore College.

1. All of this note save the signature by John B. Nichols is in Whittier's hand. Jacob Caldwell had committed suicide on February 18, 1851, and his estate was then being settled in Probate Court at Newburyport. Whittier had been appointed guardian of his sister's estate.

2. John B. Nichols (1821–1904), a shoe manufacturer, lived in Rocks Village, near Haverhill.

3. Louis Henry Caldwell (b. 1832), the only son of Mary Whittier Caldwell, worked at various jobs without much success. After serving in the Civil War, he married in 1867 and his wife, Adelaide, became quite close to Whittier, often living for long periods in the Amesbury house. The Caldwells divorced in the 1880's and Louis married again. During the 1890's Caldwell lived in New Jersey, apparently working in the appraiser's office of the Port of New York.

4. George Ayer was perhaps a relative of the Ayer family who were the nearest neighbors to the Whittier farm in East Haverhill.

5. The remainder of the manuscript is torn off.

662. To Mary Whittier Caldwell

Amesbury, Sixth Day Mg (March 1853)[1]

Dear Sister

Mother got home well last night, and, I am glad she had a chance to pay a good visit.

She tells me thee think of applying to Esqr [James] Duncan, to go with you to the Probate Court at N[ewbury]. Port. On the whole, I am not sure but it would be the best. If he is not engaged I think I would employ him. He knows the situation of matters as well as anyone and the business will be done right.

I hope to be able to meet thee at N Port. I have been troubled of late with faintness and dizziness and there are some days in which I am too unwell to go out. But, if I *can* I will be there. Cousin George Varney of Newbury will be there; and he would be an excellent man to attend at the auction. I do not know of anybody who would be so useful to thee, in the way of advice and assistance.

Affectionately.

J. G. W.

I have not had time to look up the will of Uncle Moses but I will do it.[2] I think the Judge ought to be inclined to give thee the furniture, but, he might consider that there would be property enough for thee without it.

Manuscript: Essex Institute, Salem, Massachusetts.

1. Dated by reference to the action of the Probate Court on the estate of Jacob Caldwell which was finished on April 19, 1853.

2. Moses Whittier (1762–1824), Whittier's uncle, was the youngest brother of Whittier's father. He and John Whittier ran the Haverhill farm as partners and Moses, a bachelor, lived with the Whittiers until his death. Whittier's warm relationship with Moses and responsiveness to Moses' outdoor interests are well described in *Snow-Bound*:

"Our uncle, innocent of books,
Was rich in lore of fields and brooks,
. . . .

A simple, guileless, childlike man,
Content to live where life began,
Strong only on his native grounds."

663. To James Winchell Stone

Amesbury, May 5, 1853

Dr. J. W. Stone.

Dear friend:

It is a matter of especial regret to me that I am unable to join the friends of freedom today in their well-deserved tribute to the character and services of their distinguished guest.[1] From the first appearance of his Anti-Texas letter to his constituents he has taken "no step backward." He has acted throughout wisely, efficiently, successfully. From his six years probation in the Senate—where he has had to contend not only with principalities and powers and spiritual wickedness in high places, but with wild beasts also, like the apostle at Ephesus,[2] —he has come forth with the universal reputation of a manly, honest and able statesman. Nobody, North or South, distrusts his fidelity to his principles or his ability to defend them. Earnest without fanaticism he has made no blunders; every blow of his has told in the right direction. So much, at least it is fitting should be said, not so much for his sake as for that of the cause he has so well served.

But personal eulogium, however well merited, is not, I trust the primary object of this gathering of the friends of freedom. Liberty has not leisure now for compliments. The signs of the times, although not without encouragement, admonish us that all we have done heretofore is but the preparation for great and final conflict between Democracy and Slavery. We know not in what manner or in what hour that stern crisis will come, nor what trial and sacrifices it may demand of us, but watching and waiting at our posts of duty, let us say with John Quincy Adams, *"Let it come!"*

Truly thy friend
John G. Whittier

Dr. J. W. Stone,
of Com of Arrangements.
Dear Dr.

If the foregoing letter wd. be of any service at the Festival where I regret I cannot be, please to make use of it.

In haste,
J. G. W.

Manuscript: Swarthmore College.
Recipient: James Winchell Stone (1824–1863), who obtained his M.D. from Harvard in 1847, served as reporter and then president of the Boston Reporting Association. He was an active Free Soiler, served in the Massachusetts House in the 1850's, and later became a Republican. He was a member of the committee for arrangements at the Hale dinner.

1. Hale, of course, had been defeated as the Free Soil presidential candidate in 1852, and in December 1852 a Democratic-controlled legislature in New Hampshire selected Charles Atherton to replace Hale in the Senate. Hale had returned home to Dover in March and was on his way to set up law practice in New York City when a testimonial dinner was given in his honor on May 5, 1853, at Boston.

This dinner was attended by 1,500 men and women, including John Palfrey, William Lloyd Garrison, Ralph Waldo Emerson, Charles Sumner, Henry Wilson, Thomas Wentworth Higginson, Cassius M. Clay, Horace Mann, and many others. The affair lasted nearly seven hours and was filled with tributes like Whittier's to the achievements of Hale as senator.

2. I Corinthians 15:32.

664. To James Thomas Fields

May 27 [1853][1]

My dear Fields.

I feel that I owe thee many thanks for the delightful little note from Mary Russell Mitford. Wilt thou see that the enclosed is forwarded to her when thee write next to thy excellent friend?—

My time has been occupied with business of a very unpoetical kind, when I have been able to do anything: I have had the care of a relative's property, involved in suits and difficulties,[2] but it is now pretty much over, and I hope to be able to prepare and get together my Literary Recreations and Miscellanies.[3]

Thine Ever
J. G. Whittier

Manuscript: Historical Society of Pennsylvania.
1. Dated by postmark.
2. See Letter Nos. 661 and 662.
3. *Literary Recreations and Miscellanies* was, however, not published until the fall of 1854. See Letter Nos. 698, 700, and 701.

665. To James Thomas Fields

Amesbury, July 8, 1853

My dear Fields:

I enclose to thee what I regard as a very unique and beautiful little book in MS. I dont wish thee however to take my opinion; but, the first leisure hour thee have read it, and I am sure thee will decide that it is exactly the thing for your publishing list this fall.

I am quite sure that if it was an *English* book of equal merit and beauty, it wd not lack republication here at once,— The little prose poems, are unlike anything in our literature, and remind one of the German writer, Lessing.[1] They are equally adapted to young and old.

The designs, five in number, are by the author herself, and in the hands of an Engraver wd. make effective pictures. The author proposes for her title—"*Similitudes, from the Sea-Side and the Prairie.*" Pray let me know as soon as convenient, what thy decision is,[2] and believe me cordially thy fd.

John G. Whittier

If you have as much on hand as you wish for the season or the MS. appears less favorably to thee than to myself, please return it as soon as possible, and do not mention to other publishers that it has been "in the market."

The author, Lucy Larcom of Beverly, is a novice in writing and bookmaking, and with no ambition to appear in print, and were I not perfectly certain that her little collection is worthy of type, I would be the last to encourage her to take even this small step to publicity.[3]

Thy fd.
J. G. W.

Read "The Impression of Rain-drops," "The Steam-Boat and Niagara," "The Laughing Water," "My Father's House"—etc.

Manuscript: Yale University.
1. Gotthold Lessing (1729–1781), a German critic and dramatist.
2. Fields declined to publish the book and it was brought out by John P. Jewett as *Similitudes from Ocean and Prairie* (Boston, 1854). See Letter No. 666.
3. Lucy Larcom (1824–1893) had begun writing as a mill woker at Lowell, contributing to the magazine of the mill workers, The *Lowell Offering*. Whittier became acquainted with her while editing the *Middlesex Standard* in 1844–1845 and interested his mother and sister in her behalf. She became an especially close friend of Elizabeth Whittier and was a frequent visitor to the Amesbury house. Whittier secured the publication of her poems and prose pieces in the *National Era* and later praised her work as holding in a "rare combination the healthfulness of simple truth and common sense, with a fine and delicate fancy, and an artist's perception of all beauty. Wholly without cant, affection, or imitation the moral tone of the serious poems is noteworthy" (Edwin Cady and Harry H. Clark, *Whittier on Writers and Writing*, Syracuse, 1950, p. 195). She taught school in the Midwest from 1846 to 1848, attended a seminary for four years, and then from 1854 to 1862 taught at the Wheaton Seminary in Norton, Massachusetts. After the appearance of her book, she won a prize for her poem, "Call to Kansas," in 1855.
After the death of Elizabeth Whittier, Miss Larcom and Whittier remained close friends, constantly exchanging visits and letters. He sent her all his books, penned rhymed epistles to her, and in his letters wrote her as if she were a member of his family. From 1865 to 1873 she edited *Our Young Folks*, a very successful juvenile magazine, and in the 1870's edited with Whittier three anthologies, *Child-Life, Child-Life in Prose*, and *Songs of Three Centuries,* books which she mainly compiled. In the 1880's, when Miss Larcom was in need, Whittier raised an annuity for her and in his will left her the copyright of the three books they coedited. She continued to write sketches and poetry throughout her life, and her autobiographical book, *A New England Girlhood* (1889), gave a graphic picture of life in the Lowell mills.

666. To Lucy Larcom

Amesbury, July 28, 1853

My dear friend.

On my return last night from Reading, I found thy letter—which reminded me that I should have written before this time, after carrying off thy MS. in so unceremonious a manner. I read it with great satisfaction, my principal objection being that it was too brief. Have thee not like "the Razor Strap Man"—a *"few more of the same sort"*? If so it wd. be well to add them, as the book will otherwise be rather small. I have seen J. P. Jewett and he is quite ready to publish it.[1] He says he will do his part of the business so well that thou wilt not have cause to complain. I am certain he is the best publisher for it. He will make a handsome little volume of it.

The MS. is now in his hands, and he is ready to commence it, at once. Shall he send the proof to thee at Rochester [New Hampshire] ?

Thanks to thee I had a very pleasant ride to Waters' place
and back.[2] What signifies thy boast of riding with a Poet?
Did'nt I ride with one too, and a Prose-poet in the bargain?
So we are equal, so far as that expedition is concerned. I
drove after leaving thee, Jehu-like,[3] and just reached the cars
in season to jump on.

I saw Harriet Farley about ten days ago. She is still in
Amesbury I believe. She told me she had engaged to write a
book of stories for a New York publisher. She says she had
expected to have thee visit her—

I hope to see thee ere long in Rochester—if my sister is able
to leave home—

Very truly thy friend.
John G. Whittier

Manuscript: Massachusetts Historical Society.

1. John P. Jewett (1814–1884), a Boston publisher, had printed Harriet Beecher
Stowe's *Uncle Tom's Cabin* and many other successful books in the 1850's before
he overextended himself and his publishing firm failed.

2. Richard P. Waters (1807–1887), a Salem businessman and abolitionist, had
established trade with Zanzibar and served as United States consul there until
1844. Upon his return, he lived on a farm and served in the legislature in 1855.

3. II Kings 9:20. Jehu, one of the kings of Israel, was noted for driving his
chariots furiously.

667. To William James Allinson

Amesbury, July 30, 1853

My dear friend
    Enclosed are $2 for eight copies of the Non Slave Holder
to be directed as follows commencing with the number for
the 9th month.[1]

Eliphalet Barnard
Phillip Jones
Moses Huntington Jr
David Challis
Josiah D. Challis
Milton Elliott
Jona. Beede
John G. Whittier

I hope thou wilt be encouraged to persevere in thy good work.

I regretted that I was unable to see our English friends when
they arrived in Boston.[2]

I understand they brought with them two or three large
packages of books and pamphlets; and I have been afraid the

distribution of them in the Southern States might seriously affect the success of their mission. I do not know as they intend to circulate A. S. tracts or books there but if such is their prospect, looking at it from my point of view, I am fearful they will meet with difficulty. If thou has occasion to write them, I wish thee wd offer a word of caution in this matter. After all if as we believe they are rightly engaged here in the Divine Master's service perhaps we cannot do better than leave them to His counsel and direction.

My mother and sister join me in love to thee and thy family.

Ever and affectionately thy friend
John G. Whittier

Source: Handwritten copy, Haverford College. Published: Snyder, "John Greenleaf Whittier to William J. Allinson," p. 26.

1. The following were Amesbury neighbors of Whittier, most of whom were Quakers and all of whom were abolitionists: Eliphalet Barnard (b. 1787); Phillip Jones (1810–1884), who had a brief romance with Elizabeth Whittier; Moses Huntington, Jr. (1809–1899), a farmer and elder in the Society of Friends; David Challis (1801–1887); Josiah D. Challis (1802–1885), who served as a selectman in Amesbury; Milton Elliott (1804–1854); and Jonathan Beede (1803?–1892), who died in Iowa.

2. A group of English Quakers, William Forster, Josiah Forster, John Candler, and William Holmes, brought to the United States *An Address on Slavery and the Slave Trade* from the London Yearly Meeting and presented it to the president, state governors, and other United States authorities. Josiah Forster replied personally to Whittier that they were being very careful and were not carrying any antislavery tracts with them. They met with no violence in their visit, although William Forster died of natural causes in Tennessee.

668. To Charles Sumner

Amesbury, August 2, 1853

My dear Sumner.

I cannot deny myself the pleasure of saying how well I am pleased with thy Plymouth Speech. It is a perfect gem. Its tone and bearing are unmistakable and yet unobjectionable. When I read the toast which called thee up I confess I would see very little appropriateness in it. —In fact, it seemed to me a very compromising text, and I almost feared to read the sermon. I enjoyed it all the better for my misgivings. I can think of nothing more admirably conceived and expressed than the sentence—"Better the despised Pilgrims etc"—[1]

Thou wilt have an invitation (if not already rcd) from our N. H. friends to meet them on the shores of their beautiful Lake at Wolfeboro— which I really hope thou wilt accept. It will be a great gathering, and if I mistake not, a very important one. It may put the ball of a new Revolution in motion, which shall result in the return of John P. Hale to the Senate. The divided state of the Democracy in N. H. renders this not wholly improbable.[2]

But at any rate, the trip will be a pleasant one—and seasonable withal. I hope to be there myself and the prospect of meeting thee will be an additional inducement.

Cordially and truly thy friend
John G. Whittier

Manuscript: Harvard University. Published, in Part: Sumner, *Complete Works,* IV, 73.

1. On August 1, 1853, Sumner delivered an address at Plymouth, Massachusetts, "Finger Point from Plymouth Rock," to celebrate the embarkation of the Pilgrim fathers at Southampton. The toast or sentiment which introduced his speech was "*The Senate of the United States,*—The concentrated light of the stars of the Union." Sumner's remarks on the Pilgrims were a thinly veiled tribute to the pioneers of the antislavery cause. The sentence Whittier alludes to read: "Better the despised Puritan, a fugitive for freedom, than the halting politician, forgetful of principle, 'with a Senate at his heels.'"

2. See Letter Nos. 669, 670, 671, and 672 for further details about this meeting. Whittier's prediction about the possibility of Hale's return proved correct as Hale won reelection to the Senate in 1855.

669. To Moses Austin Cartland

Amesbury, August 11, 1853

Dear Moses,

Thank thee for thy two kind notes. I am glad to find thee wide awake for the gathering on the 24th. I wrote a line to Fogg[1] a week or more ago—not for publication however and I wrote Freeman also as to the expense of him and Burlingame [—] all you have to do is to pay their travelling expenses— scarce $5 apiece. Surely that ought not to stand in the way. Tell Jonathan to increase his faith. A small, timid, half way meeting wd be worse than none.

As to myself, I will do all I can to help you, and will write to the Manchester or Concord paper, perhaps. I hope to be at the gathering, but if I am, it is not worth while to say much about it, for I should be worth nothing to you.

Thanks for thy bugle blast from the Ind. Dem. Keep the pot boiling. I am sure the meeting will come off gloriously.

Thine ever and truly
J. G. W.

I wrote to Tuck today to get a notice of the meeting in the Exeter N. Letter.

Source: Shackford, ed., *Whittier and the Cartlands,* pp. 43–44.

1. George Gilman Fogg (1813–1881), a New Hampshire lawyer and state legislator, edited the *Independent Democrat* at Manchester and Concord from 1846 to
1867. He served as secretary of state for New Hampshire in 1846 and later became
a Republican. From 1861 to 1865, he was minister to Switzerland and served for
a year in the United States Senate.

670. To Anson Burlingame

Rochester, N. H., August 17, 1853
My dear Burlingame,
   Our friends here are anxious to have thee at their Wolfeboro
meeting on the 24th. It will be best for thee and others from
Boston to come up the day before by the afternoon train
which meets the steam boat at Alton and spend the night at
Wolfeboro. Do not fail to come. It will be a great gathering
beyond question.

Cordially thy friend
J. G. Whittier

Manuscript: University of Virginia.

671. To Charles Sumner

Wolfeboro, N. H., Monday, August 22 [1853]
My dear Sumner,
   There is a very great desire on the part of the friends of
Freedom in this place to have thee here at the great F. Soil
gathering on the 24th. and I write at the urgent request of a
member of the Com. of Arrangements M. Varney Esq. to invite thee to be with us.[1] Do not hesitate, but regard this as a
special call,—I should esteem thy coming a personal favor.[2]
   Everything promises a great meeting.

Ever and truly thy fd.
John G. Whittier

Manuscript: Harvard University.
   1. Moses Varney (1810–1886), a New Hampshire businessman, owned a large
tannery in Wolfeboro. He later became a farmer.
   2. Sumner replied from Newport, Rhode Island, on August 26 that Whittier's
letter reached him on the day of the meeting (letter, Essex Institute, Salem,
Massachusetts).

672. To the National Era

Wolfeboro, Lake Winnepiseogee, N. H., August 25, 1853

Will the reader take a seat with me in the cars of the Boston and Maine Railroad, at the Exeter (N. H.) station? It is a dull, foggy, August morning; but as we glide away into the open country, we can see that the river mist is growing thinner, and its gray warp beginning to be woven with a golden woof of sun-beams. The church spire of the ancient town stands out white and clean against the cleaving sky of the east, high over the wet and drooping elm-rows. We glide on, past New Market, sonorous with its manufacturies, through Durham, quite picturesque, unprogressive—and over miles of meadows and woodlands, until we catch brief, flying glimpses of a "steepled city," spreading over a wide surface of hill and dale. This is Dover—one of the brave old border towns of the seventeenth century, whose far-pushed outposts met and broke the strength of Northern invasion—a place famous in the annals of French and Indian Wars, and whose old inhabitants still tell tragic stories of the times when "Cocheco was cut off," and stout old Major Waldron slain in his garrison;[1] a large, thriving manufacturing town—not without special interest to liberty-loving travellers as the residence of John P. Hale, the late Free Democrat Senator from New Hampshire. We pass on over a pleasant farming tract, and enter upon a level wooded country. Here is Pine Grove Quaker meeting-house—a small plain, white structure, set finely in its dark frame of evergreens; and now, over a swell of land to the left, a painted belfrey and clustering chimney-tops indicate the locality of Squaminegonic—abbreviated to "Gonic"—an old Indian camping-ground, now a flourishing little manufacturing village. Onward, and still farther, and here is Rochester, spreading broadly over its low, level plain, overhung with magnificent elms, looking ghost-like in the mist which wreathes thin and gray along the valley. The steeple-house however, lifts its weathervane into a clearer atmosphere; and as we looked northwardly to the scolloped horizon, there is a lift of transparent ether, hard and cool, under which the distant ridges, Blue Job and the Milton Hills, stand sharply outlined.

It needs not Scripture to tell us that "fair weather cometh out of the North."[2] Onward, then into the broadening brightness of the hill country. This village, nestling in its valley below the track of rail-cars, is Farmington. Beyond, to the east, the horizon shuts down upon the border towns of Maine, and now the long land-swells have grown into hills, belted with rock-maple foliage, and bristling atop with fir and hackmatac. What is it that we see over the tree-tops, towards the west and north, rising higher and higher, blue and dark, like heavy shower-clouds? Mountains!—the rugged walls of the inland sea.

We have now reached the end of our land journey—Alton, with its dark hill background. Off to the right, is a glorious reach of blue water—Alton Bay—the southern extremity of Lake Winnepiseogee. We step on board the steamer Dover, which lies waiting for us. The strong bracing north-west wind, which breaks down through the gorges of the hills, has swept away the clouds and mists; and, mounting to the hurricane deck, we look forth upon the ever-varying panorama of sparkling waters, green islands, and mountains starting abruptly from the lake, some clothed in the deep verdure of mid-summer, and others bare-bowed and slide-scalped. Ten miles from Alton Bay, gliding between a long projecting headland and a small island, we enter a broad and beautiful bay, at the head of which lies the village of Wolfeboro,' its dwellings brilliant in white and green, scattered in picturesque irregularity along the fertile slopes of the southward trending hills, looking out over crystal clear waters upon long broken ranges of misty mountains on the opposite shore. Nothing finer than its site can be found in New England. It has two large hotels, a flourishing academy, an orthodox and Friends' meeting house. Two steamboats run regularly between it and Alton, Centre Harbor, and Meredith. The lake itself, some twenty-four miles in length by ten in its widest part, is about 500 feet above tide water, and is walled around by mountains from 800 to 2,000 feet higher. Back of these still loftier summits lean hard and blue against the northern sky—Ossipee, White Face, Chocorua's Peak, Moorehillock; and, misty and dim beyond all, the great Notch mountains.

The Free Soil Convention, which met here yesterday, was a most spirited and successful demonstration. Early in the morning, the steamboats came in, heavily laden with passengers—a fine representation of the strength and beauty of the Free Democracy of New Hampshire. Large numbers had arrived the night before; and land carriages of all kinds, from the neighboring towns, contributed to swell the procession, which moved to a beautiful pine grove, a little distance from the centre of the village. Here a platform had been erected for the speakers in the centre of a sort of natural amphitheatre, well furnished with seats, the ladies occupying the

front, with dark masses of men behind, and on the right and
left. The number present could not have been less than 3,000.
Hon. Amos Tuck, of Exeter, was President of the day, who,
after a few pertinent remarks, introduced Moses A. Cartland,
of North Weare, who called out the enthusiastic cheers
of the multitude by his eloquent and indignant denunciation
of the Fugitive Slave Law. He was followed by Ex-Senator
Hale, who, on rising, was greeted with cheer after cheer, the
waving of hankerchiefs, and every possible demonstration of
applause. It was a noble testimony to the home popularity
of the speaker. He commenced by assuring his friends that he
rejoiced to meet them in that open temple of the Most High,
with no man's device above them, and with nothing to interfere between them and His serene heavens. He rejoiced to
meet them amidst these mountains, which he looked upon as
his old and familiar friends; and beside that beautiful lake,
which the poetical spirit of the indian had regarded as the
"Smile of the Great Spirit," who made the mountain and the
lake for his abode. He rejoiced to meet them all—men, and
women, and children—for he wanted to speak to such alone.
He had spoken to politicians so long, that he was weary of it;
and he thanked God he stood to-day where he could speak
directly to human hearts.

In the course of his remarks, he alluded to the late *fugitive*
case at Smyrna—the seizure of the Hungarian, Kosta, by an
Austrian commissioner and his official kidnappers, and his
rescue by an American officer.[3] His description of the scene
in the Turkish harbor, when the hunted refugee found protection under the shadow of our flag, had a dramatic intensity
that almost hushed the breath of the listeners, until the success of the daring American called forth as hearty cheers as if
the Bay of Wolfeboro' had been the Bay of Smyrna, and the
event transpired beneath their eyes. The news of this rescue,
said the speaker, had thrilled every American heart. All classes
hailed it with pride and exultation. Why was this? It was a
flagrant violation of the Fugitive Slave Law. Kosta "owed
service" to the Austrian Emperor;[4] he had escaped, and the
commissioner had caught him. We had interfered; whatever
we might do at home, we would not see the Fugitive Law
enforced abroad. What had been done at Syracuse and Boston,[5] in spite of Government officials, had been done at
Smyrna by the officials themselves. Yet the whole nation
rejoiced over it. That universal exultation was an index to the
heart of the People. It was the testimony of human nature
in behalf of its own character and dignity, against the false

position in which the people of these States had been placed by the Federal Government on the question of Slavery.

The conclusion of Senator Hale's speech was impressive and eloquent, and told effectively upon the large auditory. If the Fugitive Slave Law must be enforced, he said, he could almost wish that the victim might be seized in the midst of these solemn and majestic forms of Nature. Let us see if the Slave Power can cast its chains around yonder mountain tops, as it did around Boston Court-house. "For one," he said, "I believe that when the Almighty fashioned this beautiful land, He meant it for the abode of Freedom, and not the hunting-ground of slaves. The air which waves the pines above us, was sent forth from His breath for the lungs of freemen, and not of slaves. And when the Great Spirit placed His smile between these hills, He meant that around its peaceful waters no human blood-hound should hunt his prey, but that its shores should be now and forever the home of freedom, virtue, and independence."

Hon. Amos Tuck followed in an able and effective speech. The afternoon session was held, in consequence of rain, in front of the Pavilion, the speakers occupying the balcony. L. D. Mason, Esq., of the New Hampshire Legislature,[6] J. H. Talbot, Esq.[7] —the latter an able lawyer from Maine—made brief and pertinent addresses, and were followed by John P. Hale. In the evening the Convention met in a large tent near the Pavilion, and after two or three hours of animated speaking, principally on the part of the active and working men of the Free Democracy, adjourned in high spirits and with an apparent determination on the part of its members to see to it that through no negligence of theirs the cause of impartial Democracy shall fail of making a strong demonstration at the next election.

The old Democratic or Hunker party of the State is by no means a unit at the present time. In the distribution of "the spoils of office" President Pierce has signally failed to satisfy the clamorous demands of some scores of patriotic applicants for an opportunity to serve the country, to each one of whom, if their own stories are to be credited, he is indebted, directly or indirectly, for his remarkable elevation. The harvest is past, the summer of Governmental patronage well nigh gone, and these disinterested worthies yet lack the salvation of office. So far as they are concerned, President Pierce[8] might as well have hailed from Tombigbee or Opelousas, as from Hillsborough or Concord. For aught that appears to them, his place in the White House might just as well have been filled by General Scott[9] or John P. Hale. Under these circumstances, it is not surprising that his worst foes should be "those of his own household."[10] These gentlemen have found a mouthpiece in the Hon. Edmund Burke, late Commissioner of Patents and an Ex-member of Congress from New Hampshire.[11] In the course of the quarrel, some precious developments have been made relative to the course which the leaders of the old Democratic party in the State have seen fit to pursue on the Slavery question, by no means calculated to raise one's esti- mation of the moral dignity of party politics. Burke is accused of writing letters from Washington in 1848, urging the party to take Anti-Slavery ground, and rivaling even Hale himself in zeal for the Wilmot Proviso; and on the other hand it is more than intimated that certain epistles of similar tenor, from no less a personage than the President himself, may yet be forthcoming. It is understood that no suspicion whatever rests upon either of these gentlemen, of having advocated Free Soil, on the ground of principle, any more than they are now suspected of making their devotion to the Fugitive Slave Law as a matter of conscience. In all this there is hope that the people of New Hampshire—as worthy and liberty-loving as any other on the face of the earth—will have their eyes opened to the true character of the men who have so long abused their confidence and made use of their primary meet- ings, to play, for their own private ends, alternately, the tunes of Free Soil and Pro-Slavery. There is hope for New Hamp- shire. If it is still dark in her valleys, there is light on the moun- tain tops.

From the wharf at Wolfeboro', a neat little steamer, the Lady of the Lake, runs to Centre Harbor, a distance of twenty miles, through clustering islands, under thick wood-shadows, and in view of the piled mountains looming through every break in the neighboring hills. Centre Harbor is a model little village on the northernmost bay of the Lake, nestled under the shadow of steep, wooded hills—a narrow plot of green fertility, sloping quietly to the water, occupied by some twen- ty dwelling houses, a store or two, meeting-houses, and large hotel, commanding from its plaza a view of the entire length of the Lake. Red Hill, 2,000 feet above, looks down upon it. Just in the rear lies Squam Lake—a smaller Winnepiseogee— some eight miles long, picturesque with islands and with the rugged Sandwich mountains for its northern rim; a quiet, slumberous, comfort-promising spot, the tide of fashionable tourists ebbs and flows there annually, and leaves it unchanged. It has no unsightly manufactory, no overworked spinners and weavers, no self-important corporation agent. It enjoys a blessed exemption from that uncomfortable class of persons known as "smart business men," who seem sent into the world to tread upon the toes of sober people, and break up the afternoon nap of quiet waiters upon Providence. To use a Yankeeism, the place don't "progress"; it don't keep step in the march of improvement. It has, or has had, when we were there, a lawyer, to whom courts, cases, and decisions, had well nigh become mythical. Innocent of writs, he seemed well satisfied with his profession, without its practice. Jack Cade, when he hung the lawyers, would have clapped him on the back as a good fellow.[1][2] There was a warm hearted, genial tempered doctor, who (thanks to the pure mountain air) had nothing to do, and did it. Altogether, a quieter and more inviting retreat from the noisome city and the feverish unrest of money-getting, can scarcely be found than the neat, quaint, old fashioned village of Centre Harbor.

But we have lingered overlong by these pleasant waters. The boatbell is ringing, and we must bid farewell to the kind friends who have freely opened home and hearts to us. One last look at the mountains draped and tasseled by the scattering clouds of last night's storm, luminous with the morning brightness, and redolent with the balsamic breath of pines and now, southward to the lowlands, where up the river-valley of home comes the sound of plunging waves, and the horizon towards the sunrise is bright with the dazzling blink of the great sea.

J. G. W.

Source: The *National Era*, September 15, 1853, printed with the caption, "New Hampshire. Free Democratic Convention."

1. Richard Walderne (1615–1689), a pioneer and soldier, was killed on June 1689 in revenge for sending two hundred Indians into captivity. Whittier celebrated another of Major Walderne's deeds, his order to whip three Quaker women from Dover through various New England towns in 1662, in "How the Women Went from Dover."

2. Job 37:22.

3. Martin Koszta, a Hungarian exile who fought in the Revolution of 1848–1849, had lived in the United States for nearly two years and had declared his intention to become a United States citizen. On a business trip to Turkey, he was seized and imprisoned upon an Austrian warship to be returned to Austria for trial. The United States consul protested and, upon the arrival of a United States warship, the *St. Louis*, commanded by Captain Duncan Ingraham (1802–1891), demanded that Koszta be returned. When the Austrians refused, Captain Ingraham threatened them with an attack and Koszta was released. Upon their return to the United States in 1852, both Ingraham and Koszta were received as heroes.

4. Francis Joseph (1830–1916) was emperor of Austria from 1848 to 1916.

5. The rescue of the fugitive slave Jerry McHenry from the courthouse, where he had been imprisoned waiting to be returned South, occurred at Syracuse, New York, in October 1851. In February 1851 Shadrach, a colored waiter from

Boston, was also freed from custody by a group of abolitionists and escaped to Canada.

6. Larkin D. Mason (1810–1903), a businessman and farmer, served in both the New Hampshire Senate and House. He once ran as the Prohibition candidate for governor and after the Civil War was a judge of the Probate Court.

7. His name appeared in the newspaper account as T. H. Talbot, a lawyer from Portland, Maine.

8. Franklin Pierce (1804–1869) served as President from 1853 to 1857.

9. Winfield Scott (1786–1866), an American general, was the Whig presidential candidate in 1852.

10. Matthew 10:36.

11. Edmund Burke (1809–1882), a lawyer from Newport, New Hampshire, edited the *New Hampshire Argus* for many years and served in Congress as a Democrat from 1839 to 1845. From 1846 to 1850, he was commissioner of patents in New Hampshire.

12. Jack Cade (d. 1450) was an English rebel who led a revolution in 1450, during which he killed many justices and lawyers.

673. To Lucy Larcom

September 3, 1853

My Dear Friend,

I thank thee for thy note. The personal allusion would be flattering enough, did I not know that it originated in a sad misconception and overestimate of one who knows himself "no better than he should be."[1] It is a way we have. We are continually investing somebody or other with whatever is best in ourselves. It does not follow that the objects themselves are worth much. The vines of our fancy often drape the ugliest stumps in the whole forest.

I am anxious to see thy little book in print. Whatever may be its fate with the public at large, I feel quite sure it will give thee a place in the best minds and hearts. The best kind of fame, after all.

Thy friend,
J. G. Whittier

Source: Addison, *Lucy Larcom*, pp. 67–68.
1. Francis Beaumont and John Fletcher, *The Coxcomb*, IV, iii, modified.

674. To Edward A. Stansbury, Minthorne Tompkins, Monroe B. Bryant, William McDermot, and George W. Rose

Amesbury, September 23, 1853

Gentlemen,

I have received your note inviting me to attend the meeting of the Free Democracy to be held in New York on the 29th inst.[1]

I regret that the state of my health will not permit [me]

to comply with your invitation. It would give me real pleasure to meet with you on an occasion of so much interest, and under circumstances so full of promise to the cause in which we are engaged.

The late elections in Maine and Vermont have given the balance of power in both of these States to the Free Democracy. A United States Senator is to be elected from each; and none but decided opponents of the fugitive Slave Law have any chance of success. There are strong reasons for hope that New Hampshire will follow their example.[2]

In Massachusetts the cause of Freedom was never so strong as at this hour. Our late Convention at Fitchburg was full and enthusiastic, and our state ticket commands the respect of all parties. Our friends are active and confident of success. If we fail, at least, it will be from no lack of labor and vigilance.[3]

I scarcely know whether the present peculiar position of parties in your state is a cause of regret or congratulation. I profess no skill for solving at this distance the riddle of New York politics. It is your business to stand watchful and prepared; availing yourselves of any turn in the political kaleidoscope which promises directly or otherwise to promote the great object you have in view. One thing you may safely rely upon. Nobody, except the lowest class of official kidnappers supports the Fugitive Slave Law from love for it. The men who swear by the Baltimore platform today will be very glad of a fair pretext for swearing by that of Buffalo tomorrow. Nobody suspects that the priests and politicians who defend the Fugitive Law on Scriptural and Constitutional grounds, at heart believe a syllable of their doctrine. God has not left even a Mammon-loving expounder of commercial Christianity and cotton-market ethics to believe a lie so monstrous.

The late attempts to enforce this atrocious Law at Niagara, Wilksbarre, and Cincinnati have been marked on the part of the official and unofficial ruffians concerned in them by a dastard cruelty and low brutality, which would drive a Bedowin Arab in disgrace from his caravan, and put a Feejee Islander in *taboo* as unfit for the society of respectable cannibals.[4] Where is the priest who dares to lift up his hands to Heaven and pray for the success of such atrocities? Where is the Union-saving Hunker or Castle Garden patriot who can look an honest man in the face, and justify them?—If there be any such they must be in the condition of the trafficker in the German tale, who bartered off his heart of flesh for a cobble-stone.

In truth, whatever party caucuses may resolve, or party

leaders subscribe to, we have the satisfaction of knowing that the heart of the people is with us—that the common instincts of human nature as God made it, are on our side.

—"We have great allies, Powers that work for us, air and earth and skies: Our friends are exultations, agonies, and love, and man's unconquerable mind."[5] Every noble utterance and every brave deed for freedom the world over, redounds to our benefit. The eloquence of Victor Hugo over the graves of his companions in the isle of Jersey,[6] and the rescue of the Hungarian exile in the Bay of Smyrna are part and parcel of our great movement. Thus circumstanced, let us by our vigilance and devotion deserve the success, which must sooner or later crown our efforts.

I am, gentlemen, your friend and co-laborer,

John G. Whittier

Manuscript: New York Public Library. Published: New York *Herald*, October 12, 1853.

Recipients: Edward A. Stansbury was a broker in New York; Minthorne Tompkins (1831?–1869), another broker in New York, served as president of the meeting of Free Democracy in New York City; Monroe B. Bryant (d. 1912) was a jeweler in New York City; William McDermot (d. 1886) was a New York lawyer; and George William Rose (1808?–1884) was a bookkeeper in New York.

1. This meeting of Free Democrats ratified the nomination of state officers and was addressed by John P. Hale. Letters from Whittier, Joshua Giddings, and others were read at the convention.

2. The Whigs had failed to secure a majority in both these states and the coalition of Free Soilers and Democrats thus controlled their legislatures.

3. The Free Soil convention was held at Fitchburg, Massachusetts, on September 15, 1853, and nominated Henry Wilson as its candidate for governor.

4. All these incidents involved the seizure of fugitive slaves by government officials. The Wilkes-Barre affair concerned the violent resistance of a fugitive slave, William Thomas, to the three officials who tried to seize him. After a severe struggle and knife cuts, Thomas escaped. In Cincinnati, a young colored girl, Jane Trainer, was the object of a court trial to determine her parentage and whether she was still a slave.

5. William Wordsworth, "To Toussaint L'Ouverture," lines 10 and 12–14, modified.

6. In exile for his actions against the government, Victor Hugo, the famed French poet and writer, had pronounced two funeral orations for comrades who had also died in exile, one on April 20, 1853, for Jean Bousquet and the other for Louise Julien on July 26, 1853.

675. To Grace Greenwood

Amesbury September 28 [1853][1]

My dear friend.

I went up to Boston, last sixth day expecting to see thee there or at Lynn, when I learned with great regret from Fields of thy severe illness.

I was glad to hear that thou wast recovering and hope that

this note will find thee well once more and that we shall soon
have the pleasure of seeing thee in our home, where I need not
tell thee thou art a good deal more than welcome. We should
have been rejoiced to see thee in the summer with Leander
L.[2] Elizabeth wishes much to meet him. I am sure she will
like him. That he loves thee is a ready passport to our sympathies.

Ah me! how much I have to say, and how idle to attempt
its expression on paper! Come and see us, when thou art
able, and in the mean time take this apology for a letter as an
earnest of something better. Our love to thy mother whom we
love for thy sake.[3]

God bless thee—Ever and truly thy fd.

J. G. Whittier

Manuscript: Yale University.

1. Dated by reference to Leander Lippincott, whom Grace Greenwood (Sarah
Jane Clarke) married in October 1853. The letter may be from a different year.

2. Leander K. Lippincott of Philadelphia helped his wife edit the *Little Pilgrim*,
a monthly juvenile magazine, and authored stories for children.

3. Deborah Clarke, from Connecticut, was the mother of eleven children.

676. To Thomas Tracy

[September 1853][1]

My dear friend Tracy

I am afraid of troubling thee, but I would really like to
have thee and Mrs. T. read the enclosed poem, and suggest to
me any erasure or amendment which may seem to you requisite—And if it wd not be asking too much of thee I would be
glad to have it copied for me in thy plain clear hand, punctu-
ated and capitalized according to thy taste, for the press,
as I am unfortunate in making the printers understand my
writing, and besides the mere labor of copying is now a burden to me, which I am selfish enough to wish to shift upon a
friend's shoulders. The last line of the poem is *almost* literally
from St. Augustine's City of God.[2] Should it be quoted?—[3]

Elizabeth unites with me in love to you.

Ever and truly
J. G. W.

I wd like to get it again by Thursday.—I wd like at the same
time the little collection of poems which I sent some months
ago, if it is at hand. We heard from you the other day by
Mary Curzon, who made us a delightful little visit. Of course
you have seen Dickens "Bleak House."

Manuscript: New York Public Library.

1. Dated by reference to Dickens' *Bleak House*, which, after appearing serially

from April 1852 to October 1853, had been issued in book form in September 1853.

2. St. Augustine (354–430) was an African bishop and writer.

3. The poem, "Summer by the Lakeside," was published in the *National Era*, September 29, 1853. The last line of the poem was: "Be thou the mirror of God's love." Whittier did not put the line in quotations.

677. To Ralph Waldo Emerson

Amesbury, October 24, 1853

My dear friend.

I forgot to mention that the train leaving Boston at 2.45 P. M. is the proper one to take, in order to reach here before dark, and in season to take some refreshment.[1]

What marvelous weather! Amidst the autumnal opulence of the last two weeks, I have lived more than regally. How poor and mean in comparison seem all the pomps and shows of Kings and priests! And what folly to run abroad over the old world when all that is beautiful may be seen from our own door-stone! Munich, the Louvre and the Vatican are doubtless well worth seeing, but I fancy I see all and much more in my painted woodlands. At any rate, I am satisfied. Oh! that I could put into words the hymn of gratitude and unspeakable love which at such a season as this is sung in my heart.

I wish thou couldst have been with us the other day on the Merrimack. We wanted an interpreter of the mystery of glory about us.—

Believe me truly thy friend
John G. Whittier

Manuscript: Harvard University. Published, in Part: Pickard, *Life*, p. 366.

1. Emerson lectured on October 28, 1853, to the Amesbury lyceum, his subject being "The Contrast of English and American Culture."

678. To Ralph Waldo Emerson

Amesbury, October 26 [1853]

My dear friend.

The President of our Lyceum asks me to request thee to bring with thee thy Lecture on England and the English—

We shall expect thee at our place on the 28th. at the arrival of the cars in the afternoon train which reaches here at 1/2 past 4.

Thine truly
J. G. Whittier

Manuscript: Harvard University.

679. To Anson Burlingame

Amesbury, November 2 [1853], Wednesday Mg[1]
My dear Burlingame

Take the train which leaves Boston at 1/4 before 3. o ck
or thee will not get to our place until just before the lecture
commences. The 1/4 before 3 train is here a little before 5.
The next train is often as late as 1/2 past 7.

Ever and truly thy fd.
John G. Whittier

Manuscript: Harvard University.

1. The year has to be 1853 since November 2 was on Wednesday that year, but
Burlingame did not deliver a lecture that fall in the lyceum series, nor in any of
the four fall lyceum lectures from 1851 to 1854 for which there are records. He
delivered two lectures in the spring lyceum series, however, on March 25, 1853
("The Past and the Present") and on March 8, 1854 ("The Valley of the Mississippi").

680. To the Chairman of Essex County Commission for Free Democracy

Amesbury, November 7, 1853.
To the Ch. of Co. Com. of the Free Democracy for Essex

The bearer of this Azor G. Woodman Esqr is the chairman
of the Town Com. of the F. D. for Amesbury, and as such
entitled to cooperate with the Co. Com. in the business for
which it is convened.[1]

John G. Whittier

Manuscript: Essex Institute, Salem, Massachusetts.

1. Azor Woodman (b. 1821) of Salisbury was a maker of organs. He later
worked in an organ plant in Brattleboro, New York.

681. To Charles Sumner

Amesbury, November 15, 1853
My dear friend.

We are defeated as I expected, after Cushing's edict appeared.[1] I knew that we could not cope with the money of
Boston and the patronage of Washington combined.

This must be the end of *coalition* except on anti-slavery
grounds.[2] I wash my hands of it henceforth. It becomes us
now to take our stand on the old platform with *inexorable
firmness*. Let us palter no more: let us lift up the standard
of principle and unite all who are sick of the rule of the slave-

power to join us, in open and manly opposition to it. So doing, I verily believe our defeat will be our gain.

I do hope our friends of the State Committee will see the matter in this light and take bold ground. It wd be worse than folly longer to court our unwilling and wavering old line democracy. Let it go and reap the fruit of its doings. *We* have something worth contending for; let us have faith in our principles and be willing to follow them into a minority for the present. We have lost nothing: we are today what we were yesterday. Courage, faith, perseverance! with these all will be well.

I was glad to see thy bro. George. I liked him much. His lecture was unreservedly admired.[3]

Write me soon and believe me cordially and Ever thy friend
J. G. Whittier

Wilson gets a noble vote—some 1500 or 2,000 more than Hale last year. Up to the time of Cushing's letter I had little doubt of his being Governor.[4]

Manuscript: Harvard University. Published: Albree, ed., *Whittier Correspondence*, p. 279.

1. A convention to revise the Constitution of Massachusetts, especially to readjust the basis of representation in the House of Representatives, took place in June and July 1853. The extensive revision was backed by Free Soilers and Democrats as well as some Whigs and seemed certain of passage in the fall election. In a letter to Whittier of November 21, 1853, Sumner analyzed the defeat as follows: "The loss of the Constitution is a severe calamity to the Liberal cause in this State. I deplore it from my heart. It seems to me that it may be traced to three causes:

"1st. in order of time; the defection of Palfrey and Adams which stimulated the Whigs and neutralized many of our friends.

"2ndly. Cushing's letter, which paralyzed the activities of the Democratic leaders; and

3dly. the positive intervention of the Catholic Church" (Albree, ed., *Whittier Correspondence*, p. 121).

Caleb Cushing, then attorney-general of the United States, had sent a letter assuming to speak for President Pierce, forbidding any further political association of the Democrats with the Free Soilers. Since the avowed purpose of the administration was to crush out abolitionism as a dangerous movement, no association was possible.

2. This defeat ended the coalition movement in Massachusetts and prepared the way for the Free Soilers and abolitionists to join the new Republican party in 1854.

3. George Sumner (1817–1863), a political economist, had traveled for many years in Europe. He assisted Samuel Gridley Howe in many philanthropic projects and wrote articles for the *North American Review* and the *Democratic Review*. He lectured in Amesbury on November 9, 1853, on the French and the effects of the revolutions of 1792, 1830, and 1848 upon the French people.

4. Wilson, the Free Soil candidate for governor, obtained 29,545 votes, while Washburn, the Whig, received 60,472 and Bishop, the Democrat, 35,254. Emory Washburn was then elected governor by the Whig-controlled legislature (see Letter No. 709, note 3 for identification).

682. To Francis Henry Underwood

Amesbury, November 25, 1853

Dear friend.

I am delighted with the prospect of a free Magazine—It will go: The time has come for it, and Jewett is the man for the hour.[1]

I will try and send something on or before the 5th. At any rate I shall be glad to write for it, if my health permits.[2]

Wilt thou say to Jewett that I thank him for his capital getting up of my "Sabbath Scene."[3] The illustrations are admirable,—the best of the kind I ever saw. They do great credit to the artist.

Thine truly
J. G. Whittier

Manuscript: Swarthmore College. Published: Perry, "The Editor Who Was Never the Editor," p. 663.

Recipient: Francis Henry Underwood (1825–1894) had begun his career as a lawyer in 1850 and had served as clerk of the Massachusetts Senate in 1852. Roused by the injustices of the Fugitive Slave Law, Underwood persuaded John P. Jewett to issue a monthly magazine which would print the best writings of northern abolitionists and others. Underwood sent out letters for contributions for the first issue, but Jewett's firm failed and the project was abandoned. Two years later he succeeded in persuading another publisher, Moses Phillips, to back the project, now called the *Atlantic Monthly*, and enlisted the services of all the main writers of the time. Underwood went to Europe in 1857 to arrange for articles from British writers. James Russell Lowell was nominated as editor-in-chief and Underwood was his assistant. He remained with the *Atlantic Monthly* for two years, leaving in 1859 to return to his clerkship. He wrote stories and biographies throughout his career, including studies of Lowell and Longfellow and the first authorized biography of Whittier in 1883. Whittier exchanged scores of letters with Underwood while he edited the *Atlantic Monthly* and during the period when Underwood wrote his biography. His admiration and appreciation of Whittier both as a man and poet are clearly manifest in all their correspondence, and only Underwood's tact and perseverance enabled him to assemble the biographical materials he did from a Whittier who resented any investigation of his private life.

1. The magazine, scheduled to be first published in January 1854, was discontinued when Jewett's firm failed. See Letter No. 687.

2. Whittier sent Underwood a poem, probably "The Haschish," for the first issue.

3. "The Sabbath Scene" had been published by Jewett's firm in book form with an illustration on each page.

683. To Lucy Larcom

Amesbury, November 28 [1853]

My dear Friend.

Excuse me for not sooner acknowledging thy Book and letters. The truth is, I have been unable to answer my letters punctually on account of illness.

The Book is beautifully got up, as it ought to be, for it is

highly creditable to its author. I see it noticed everywhere
with favor. I have written a little notice of it, and shall publish it in the Era or in some other paper.[1] By the by, that last
poem of thine in the Era was like Coleridge's Christabel
"beautiful exceedingly."[2] It is the best thing thou ever did,
and, if Dr. Bailey dont offer thee some substantial token of
appreciation, he will fall short of his duty.

R. P. Waters Esq of Beverly was here the other day, reminding me of our pleasant ride to Ryal Side last summer.
Excuse the haste of this, and believe me

Truly thy friend
J. G. Whittier

Manuscript: Massachusetts Historical Society.

1. Whittier had already noted the book in the Era, September 29, 1853, saying: "Another writer for the Era—Lucy Larcom—has in the Press of J. P. Jewett
and Co. of Boston, a unique and altogether original little volume entitled—Similitudes from the Sea-Side and Prairie—a series of prose poems evincing delicate
fancy and great beauty of thought and expression." The Era printed another brief
announcement of the book, November 10, 1853, and Whittier printed a fuller
review on December 22, 1853, which ran:

"The Era has already noticed the appearance of this beautiful little book, from
the press of Jewett and Co., of Boston. Its real merit induces us again to call attention to it. It consists of some forty brief sketches—prose poems, or parables—
illustrating from natural objects and simple life-incidents, human duty and destiny.
Like Kriemacher, Lessing, and Herder—and often with equal success—the writer
has adopted the method of imparting lessons of truth and wisdom, which forms
one of the most attractive features of Mohammedan literature, and which lends
such picturesque beauty to the old Hebrew poetry and the parables of the Divine
Teacher. The style is chaste, simple, and graceful. Adapted, as it is, alike to old
and young, and grave and gay, we doubt if a more acceptable gift book for the
holidays will be issued this season."

2. "Blessed Be Nothing," a poem dealing with the virtues of poverty.

684. To James Miller McKim

Amesbury, November 30, 1853

My dear friend.

Thy note of invitation to the meeting to be held in Philada.
on the 3rd of next month, in commemoration of the formation of the American Anti-Slavery Society has been received.

It is a matter of real regret that I am not able to be with
you, to take a part in the pleasures and duties of an occasion
of so much interest. Twenty years have elapsed since thou
and I, in the ardor of youth, met for the first time, in the
Convention which formed the National Anti-Slavery Society.
It was my first experience of a meeting of the kind, and my
excellent friend Lewis Tappan with whom I acted as associate
Secretary will doubtless smile as he remembers my awkward-
ness in discharge of novel duties. Every incident of that mem-

orable meeting is fresh in my recollection. I seem to see and
hear again the old familiar faces and voices. Over how many
of these have the Silence and the Shadow fallen! Others, we
can call to mind, who failing to count the cost, in the onset,
grew weary in the after struggle, and left us. I was one of the
sub-committee to whom was assigned the preparation [of] a
paper setting forth our designs and objects; and I well remember how, with our dear friend, Samuel J. May, by lamp-light,
in the grey dawn, in the upper chamber of the house of one
of our colored friends, I heard William Lloyd Garrison read
the first draft of that Declaration of Sentiment—the Apostle's
creed of Anti-Slavery—from which nothing could be taken
and to which nothing could be added.

Since we signed that Declaration twenty years have passed—
years of labor, and trial and baffled endeavor, but relieved and
cheered by unmistakable signs of progress. Thy experiences I
am sure will correspond with mine when I say that I have
never felt a desire to release myself from the responsibility of
that act, and the obligations thereby incurred. I have never
found occasion to regret it. It has cost me nothing which has
not been more than compensated; and now, in view of it, my
heart is bowed in gratitude to the Divine Providence.

Apart from these personal matters, many thoughts crowd
upon me, to which I cannot, at this time, give utterance. I
can only say that, looking back over the events of two decades,
I find no reason for discouragement. Under God, our labor
has not been in vain. We have broken up the criminal apathy
of the nation. We have compelled the Church which, at the
commencement of our labors, seemed utterly blind to the
subject, to look at Slavery as it is, until, with eyes open to all
its enormities, it stands without excuse before God and man.
We have brought Freedom and Despotism, Light and Darkness, Christianity and Heathenism, face to face, for the final
arbitrament of the great question between them. We have
helped to make up the issue, and hastened the long foreseen
crisis. The result is in God's hands and we need not fear for
it, for every Divine attribute is pledged to the side of Righteousness and Truth.

I remain as Ever, thy friend
John G. Whittier

Manuscript: Boston Public Library.

685. To Henry Stephens Randall

Amesbury, November 30, 1853.

Hon. H. S. Randall,

It wd give me great pleasure to receive the Book, referred to in thy note.[1] The vols. may be sent by the Express to Boston care of *David Batchelder* [.] *Amesbury Express.*

I have recd. and read with satisfaction thy decision in the case of Catholic Scholars and the Bible. We have a similar question here, and as one of the Committee I am glad to have thy views on it.[2]

With great respect and esteem thy friend
John G. Whittier

Manuscript: Haverford College. Published: Hewitt and Snyder, "Letters of John Greenleaf Whittier in The Roberts Collection," pp. 34–35.

Recipient: Henry Stephens Randall (1811–1876), an educator and author, was superintendent of public instruction in New York from 1851 to 1853. He also served as secretary of State for New York and later wrote a three-volume biography of Thomas Jefferson.

1. This probably refers to Randall's book, *Sheep Husbandry in the South* (Philadelphia, 1848), which had been reprinted in 1852 and was already the standard book on the subject.

2. Whittier was then serving on the Amesbury school committee, having been elected for a one-year term in the spring of 1853. The Bible formed a part of the course of study, but the parents of a Catholic child objected to his reading of it and Whittier was soliciting opinions from educators about the subject. Whittier's final views on this subject were expressed in Letter No. 686.

686. To Gyles Kelley

Amesbury Mills, December 3, 1853

My dear friend.

On more mature reflection upon the case of the Catholic scholar at West Amesbury, I am induced to believe that it wd be safest to leave the matter very much with the teacher. If he can induce all to read in the Testament it will be well; but, I would by no means have him use any coercion or force. That would be little short of persecution,—and would be a good cause of complaint on the part of our Catholic fellow citizens. If the scholar's parents profess that they cannot conscientiously permit him to read the Bible, we may regret their delusion, but we cannot *compel* their child to read the good Book. I think I shall write Dr. Sears on the subject,[1] and in the meantime I am of [the] opinion that we had better err, if at all, on the side of toleration! At any rate, I would by no means wish the teacher to use any coercion. Perhaps there is no danger of its being done; but it might be well to caution him in that respect.

The question is one of circumstance and perhaps there can be no harm in leaving it in the way I have suggested, until we can hear from Dr. Sears.

As ever, cordially thy fr.
John G. Whittier

Manuscript: Haverhill Public Library.

Recipient: Gyles M. Kelley (b. 1813) lived in the Birch Meadow section of Amesbury and was one of Whittier's students when he taught there in 1827–1828. Kelley was given a book on Latin grammar for his excellence in studies. He became a teacher himself and was then serving on the School Committee with Whittier.

1. Barnas Sears (1802–1880), a clergyman and educator, had taught from 1836 to 1848 at the Newton Theological Institute, besides editing the *Christian Review.* He had been appointed secretary of the Massachusetts Board of Education in 1848, succeeding Horace Mann. He served in that position for seven years, after which he became president of Brown University from 1855 to 1867.

687. To Francis Henry Underwood

Amesbury, December 6, 1853

Dear Sir,—

I regret the failure of the magazine project. I was quite sure of its success.

I sent thee a poem, care of J. P. J[ewett] and Co. which I will thank thee to return to me immediately, and thereby greatly oblige

Thine truly
John G. Whittier

Source: Perry, "The Editor Who Was Never the Editor," pp. 664–665.

688. To Bayard Taylor

Amesbury, December 29, 1853

My dear Bayard,

Give me thy hand! Welcome home again and a Happy New Year to thee! We are fellow-travelers: I have followed thee all the way over the world, without any share of thy expenses, trouble or fatigue. I wish though we could have reached the Snowy African mountains— *Thou* was there, in spirit, however, beyond doubt, as thy splendid poem testifies.[1]

But to the point. Canst thou not steal away for a day or two,—see Whipple, Lowell, Longfellow and Fields—run up and spend a night with me—and talk an hour or so to our Lyceum on what thee saw in Africa or Japan? Don't refuse—there's no need of a formal lecture—our folks only want to see thee and hear thee talk a little.

Don't rank this with a thousand and one applications—but drop me a line and say *yes.*

Our lecturers are engaged except for *February 23.* If it would suit thy convenience better—it could be on the 22nd. or 24th. We pay $20 and $5 for expenses.[2]

Say a good word for Phoebe Carey's Poems and Mrs. Howe's admirable "Passion Flowers" just out from Ticknor's—[3]

Every and truly thy frd.
John G. Whittier

Manuscript: New York Public Library. Published: Pickard, *Life,* pp. 366–367.

Recipient: Bayard Taylor (1825–1878), the popular travel writer and poet, had just returned from two years of travel in Egypt, Turkey, India, and China. His friendship with Whittier began in 1847 when Whittier reprinted his "The Norseman's Ride" with an enthusiastic commendation, though he did know the author. Taylor immediately wrote to Whittier and the two began a correspondence which led to Taylor's visiting Amesbury to meet Whittier. One of the longest literary reviews Whittier wrote for the *Era* was on Taylor's *Eldorado* on July 4, 1850. Whittier noted that the two volumes abounded in "valuable facts and statistics, but they have in a high degree that charm of personal adventure and experience to which we have referred. Bayard Taylor is a born tourist. He has eyes to see, skill to make the most of whatever opens before him under the ever-shifting horizon of the traveler." Writing to Whittier after the review, Taylor remarked: "I have read it with the most genuine pleasure, not on account of the life it will give my literary reputation, but because you seem to have so thoroughly appreciated and enjoyed my work. I care but little for the general praise or censure, but I *do* value that of my friends" (Pickard, *Life,* p. 360). Their friendship remained a deep and satisfying one for both men throughout their lives. Taylor visisted Whittier at his home, lectured in the Amesbury lyceum, and dedicated one of his books to Whittier, while Whittier continued to review and praise Taylor's travel books and poetry. Whittier wrote of his pleasure in Taylor's visits in "The Last Walk in Autumn" and included Taylor as one of the companions in *The Tent on the Beach.* Taylor went on to write a group of novels about his native county in Pennsylvania and translated Goethe's *Faust* in two volumes. At his death he was serving as minister to Germany, and Whittier wrote a poetic tribute to him which read in part:

> "He brought us wonders of the new and old;
> We shared all climes with him. The Arab's tent
> To him its story-telling secret lent.
> And, pleased, we listened to the tales he told.
> His task, beguiled with songs that shall endure,
> In manly, honest thoroughness he wrought;
> From humble home-lays to the heights of thought
> Slowly he climbed, but every step was sure."

1. "Kilimandjaro," which Taylor wrote from the banks of the Nile in 1852.

2. Taylor lectured in Amesbury on February 9, 1854, on the Arabs.

3. Phoebe Cary wrote *Poems and Parodies* (Boston, 1854). For Mrs. Howe's volume, see Letter No. 689.

689. To Julia Ward Howe

Amesbury, December 29, 1853

My Dear Fd.—

A thousand thanks for thy volume! I rec'd it some days ago, but was too ill to read it. I glanced at "Rome," "Newport and Rome," and they excited me like a war-trumpet. To-day, with the wild storm drifting without, my sister and I have been busy with thy book, basking in the warm atmosphere of its flowers of passion. It is a great book—it has placed thee at the head of us all. I like its noble aims, its scorn and hate of priestcraft and Slavery. It speaks out bravely, beautifully all I have *felt*, but could not express, when contemplating the condition of Europe. God bless thee for it![1]

I owe an apology to Dr. Howe, if not to thyself, for putting into verse an incident of his early life, which a friend related to me. When I saw his name connected with it, in some of the papers that copied it, I felt fearful that I had wounded, perhaps, the feelings of one I love and honor beyond almost any other man, by the liberty I had taken. I can only say I could not well help it—a sort of necessity was before me, to say what I did.[2]

I wish I *could* tell thee how glad thy volume has made me. I have marked it all over with notes of admiration. I dare say it has faults enough, but thee need not fear on that account. It had beauty enough to save thy "slender neck" from the axe of the critical headsman. The veriest "de'il"—as Burns says—"wad look into thy face and swear he could na wrang thee."[3]

With love to the Doctor and thy lovely little folk,[4] I am

Very sincerely thy friend
John G. Whittier

Source: Laura E. Richards and Maud Elliot, *Julia Ward Howe: 1819–1910* (Boston, 1916), pp. 138–139.

1. Whittier reviewed *Passion Flowers* in the *National Era*, January 25, 1854, especially praising Mrs. Howe's poems dealing with Italy and quoting long excerpts from two of them.

2. "The Hero" was based on the early exploits of Dr. Samuel Gridley Howe as a fighter for Greek independence in the 1820's. It was published in the *Era*, April 28, 1853.

3. "O Saw Ye Bonie Lesley."

4. At this time the Howes had four children: Julia Romana (1844–1886), who became a teacher; Florence Marion (1845–1922), who became an author and lecturer; Henry Marion (1848–1922), who became a metallurgist; and Laura Elizabeth (1850–1943), who became a biographer and writer of children's stories.

690. To James Thomas Fields

[January 1, 1854][1]

My dr Fields.

Thanks for such choice books as Mrs. Howe's Passion Flowers, Phebe Carey's Poems, and Capt. Reid's Boy Voyageurs.[2]

Mrs. Howe's book is really great—it has as many fine passages as Alex. Smith[3] —and is truer, nobler every way.

Will thou see that the enclosed note goes to M. R. Mitford?— May it find her in health and happiness!

I met Holmes for the first time at Haverhill the other night.— There is rare humor in him, and I suspect he knows it. But I like him.[4]

I enclose to thee a jingle of mine—*not published* and therefore only for thy private reading. It is one of those poems that *make themselves* and come to you uncalled for.[5] "My "Singletary papers" drag their length along—still. I fear they will prove like the German "Story without an End."[6]

Ever thine

J. G. Whittier

I want to see G. Greenwood's book, as soon as it is out.[7] Please send with it Kingsley's "Hypatia"—which is said to be worth reading.[8]

Manuscript: Huntington Library, San Marino, California. Published, in Part: Pickard, *Life*, pp. 368–369.

1. Dated by reference to an enclosed letter to Mary R. Mitford which has the date January 1, 1854.

2. Mayne Reid (1818–1863), an Irish author, had emigrated to the United States, fought in the Mexican War, and published popular romantic novels during the 1850's. *The Young Voyageurs, or the Boy Hunters* was published in London in 1852, where Reid lived after 1850.

3. Alexander Smith (1830–1867), an English poet, was just then gaining popular approval with his *The Life Drama and Other Poems* (London, 1853).

4. Holmes had been announced as a lecturer for the Haverhill Lyceum series of 1853 to 1854, though no account of his talk can be found in the newspapers. The lecture for December 30, 1853, was supposed to have been given by Timothy Bigelow, but he was also listed as speaking on February 17, 1854. Holmes may have spoken on December 30, 1853, as a replacement for Bigelow (see Letter No. 691).

5. Perhaps "A Memory," which was published in the *Era*, January 28, 1854.

6. Whittier had begun "My Summer with Dr. Singletary" in 1851, publishing three installments in the *Era* for January; then two more installments in January 1852; and the last installment on January 3, 1854.

7. *Haps and Mishaps of a Tour in Europe* (Boston, 1854), which Whittier reviewed in the *Era*, February 13, 1854.

8. Charles Kingsley (1819–1875), the English novelist, published his historical romance, *Hypatia*, in 1853. Whittier later met Kingsley during his visit to America and wrote an account of the meeting (see Letter No. 1269).

691. To Mary Russell Mitford

Amesbury, January 1, 1854

My Dear Friend, Mary Russell Mitford,

Permit me to wish thee a happy New Year! I am quite sure that thousands who have been made happier by thy writings will join with me. I wish thou wouldst come over to America, just to see what a host of friends thou hast made for thyself on this side of the water.

I should long before have answered thy kind note, but for the lassitude and disquiet of illness, which often for weeks together make writing of any kind painful and difficult. I spent the latter part of the summer in the wild hill country of New Hampshire, and think I am still all the better for the inspiring scenery and pure mountain air. At any rate, I can again use my pen, and write newspaper articles for the *National Era*, and now and then I indulge in a jingle of song, a specimen of which I enclose to thee, which has never been published. I know the *subject* will commend it to thee.

I also enclose two short poems, commemorative of my sojourn in the hill-country. As a specimen of the quieter mood of a rough reformer and controversialist, they may not be wholly without interest.[1]

Our excellent friend, James Fields, announces two books of thine as forthcoming.[2] Shall we have a new series of the "Literary Reminiscences?"

A little volume of poems, under the title of "Passion Flowers," by Julia Howe, wife of Dr. Howe of Boston, is attracting much attention. I hope thou wilt see it. Ticknor and Fields publish it. It seems to me to have great merit.

My friend Dr. Holmes is lecturing this winter on the English poets—very witty and genial.

We have recently had a delightful visit from Ralph Waldo Emerson. I wish thou wouldst meet him. He is a man not only admired, but loved.

I need not tell thee that I should be exceedingly glad to hear from thee. Thy two notes are among my choice treasures.

Believe me, most cordially thy friend,

John G. Whittier

Source: Alfred Guy L'Estrange, ed., *The Friendships of Mary Russell Mitford as Recorded in Letters from her Literary Correspondents* (London, 1882), II, 117–118.

1. "Summer by the Lakeside," which consisted of two poems, "Noon" and "Evening."

2. *The Dramatic Works of Mary Russell Mitford* (London, 1854) in two vol-

umes; and *Atherton, and Other Tales* (Boston, 1854). Whittier reviewed *Atherton* in the *National Era*, June 28, 1854.

692. To Bayard Taylor

Amesbury, January 16, 1854

My dear friend:

Many thanks for thy willingness to oblige us. We can make the cheque to suit thee—

So then we shall expect thee on the 9th. of Feby. O. Taylor Bey!

Take the train which leaves Boston at 2.45 P. M. and thou wilt get here in time for an early tea.

Ever and truly thy fd.

John G. Whittier

I wish I could have been with thee in good old Chester Co. As old Walton said of the Strawberry, the Lord *might* have made a pleasanter country—*but he did'nt.*[1]

Manuscript: Cornell University.

1. From *The Compleat Angler*, Part I, chapter V, by Izaak Walton (1593–1683), the English biographer and sportsman.

693. To Frank Phelps

[Amesbury, January 24, 1854][1]

It is a matter of real regret to me that I cannot accept the invitation tendered in thy kind letter. My health is in such a state that I dare not make any consignment of the kind. With an expression of highest regard and deepest reverence for the venerable and noble Dr. Nott (in whose honor the celebration is being held.)[2]

Source: Typewritten copy, papers of C. Marshall Taylor, Swarthmore College. Taylor lists it as a letter sold by Swann Galleries on June 20, 1944.

Recipient: Perhaps Franklin S. Phelps (1833–1898), who lived in Lynn. He is not listed among the graduates or former students of Union College.

1. Taylor so dates it, though the correct date may be July 24, 1854.

2. Eliphalet Nott, then completing his fiftieth year as president of Union College, was honored with a celebration attended by 600 of his former pupils and other dignitaries on July 25, 1854. Whittier had worked with Nott in the abolitionist cause in the 1830's.

694. To an Unidentified Correspondent[1]

Amesbury, February 3, 1854

My dear friend.

I thank thee from my heart for thy very kind letter with the accompanying book and poem. My mother, sister and myself have read "Lucretia" with a great deal of interest. It is very true to the Quaker character—as it should be always—and as it sometimes *is*. Hannah is a well drawn picture from real life, I am sure.

I really feel gratified for thy lines—although humbled by a sense of ill-deserving them.

It would give me great pleasure to visit your island home, but my health is such that I seldom leave my residence. Should it improve I should like to try the effect of your sea-air next summer.—[2]

Believe me cordially thy friend
John G. Whittier

Manuscript: Yale University.

1. The recipient may possibly be Celia Thaxter since she and her husband were then living at Curzon's Mills next to the Curzon family whom Whittier knew and visited. However, Whittier's friendship with her did not begin until the middle 1860's and there is no correspondence between them or mention of her by Whittier before 1861.

2. Possibly a reference to Celia Thaxter's home on Appledore Island, Maine, where her father and family ran a hotel for summer guests.

695. To Robert Charles Winthrop

Amesbury, February 4, 1854

Dear friend.

I cannot doubt that the threatened and too probable repeal of the Miss. Compromise, by the Bill now before the Senate, backed by the whole power of the Executive, is as repugnant to thy feelings and convictions, as to my own.[1] Permit me to inquire if something cannot be done to avert this great and terrible evil—a broad, generous Northern movement, not confined to the narrow grounds of party. I know of no one so well able as thyself to take the first step in this movement—no one whose antecedents are so likely to secure a cordial hearing from the whole country. The honored name of Winthrop has ever been dear and sacred to the descendants of the Pilgrims, and, I mean no empty compliment in saying that it has lost nothing in thy profession.

At this crisis I cannot feel or speak as a party man. Would

to God that all our old dissensions could be buried and forgotten and that all who love freedom and the good old ways of the fathers could unite for their preservation. I know that I am not alone in looking to thee at this time. Providence has placed thee in a position to speak and act with effect; and surely the power to do so on thy part involves a duty.[2]

Pardon this abrupt appeal and believe me with respect and esteem thy friend

John G. Whittier

Manuscript: Massachusetts Historical Society. Published: Mordell, *Quaker Militant*, p. 165.

1. Stephen Douglas' bill, which became the Kansas-Nebraska Act, provided for the organization of the Kansas-Nebraska territory on the "squatter principle," that is, these territories could determine for themselves whether they would enter the Union with or without slavery. This bill, which repealed the Missouri Compromise and established the doctrine of congressional nonintervention, was passed on May 30 after three months of bitter debate. The bill was strongly opposed by Free Soilers, Conscience Whigs, Independent Democrats, and abolitionists, and the popular dissatisfaction with the bill led to a realignment of political forces in the East and West that took the name of the Republican party. Sumner, Chase, and others were leaders in the movement and had issued on January 24, 1854, an appeal which condemned the proposed bill as a violation of a sacred pledge and the product of a slaveholders' plot.

2. Whittier appealed to Winthrop as the acknowledged leader of the Whig party in Massachusetts. Winthrop had had a distinguished career in both the House and for a year in the United States Senate before he had been defeated for a full senatorial term by Charles Sumner in 1851. Winthrop, however, held aloof from any new party movement and never responded to Whittier's appeal. Whittier tried once more on June 10, 1854, asking Winthrop to support a new movement opposed to slavery and the Kansas-Nebraska Act (see Letter No. 710).

696. To Charles Sumner

Amesbury, March 9, 1854

My dear Sumner.

If I am late in my congratulations upon thy most successful and every way admirable speech, I am none the less earnest in my admiration of it. It will live the full life of American history.[1]

Its solemn, lofty tone is worthy of thee, and of the great occasion. I am unused to flatter any one; least of all one whom I love and honor, but I must say in all sincerity that there is no orator or statesman living in this country or in Europe, whose force is so great as not to deserve additional luster from such a speech.

A thousand thanks for that most happy illustration of the power of Slavery over Northern politicians—The Black mountain which draws the *iron* out of them! Nothing could be truer or more striking.[2]

I am moving our friends to urge the Legislature, under the pressure of this Nebraska diabolism—to secure to all persons, in cases affecting personal freedom, a jury trial. We must seize the occasion to nullify the Fugitive Law.

Winthrop's speech at the Whig A. Nebraska meeting was a manly one—and gives me a better opinion of him. His declaration of hostility to the "Compromise" was received with the loudest applause.[3] Hillard did well, all things considered. Depend upon it, if Webster were now living, after his experience of Southern faith and gratitude, he would *wake* a "North." The shorn and blinded old giant would make such sport for the slave-holders, as Samson did for the Philistines when he tumbled their temple about their ears.[4] But I must close. God bless thee!

> Ever and truly thy fd.
> John G. Whittier

Honor to Sam Houston![5] His speech shows that he has a heart. Are you not glad of Fessenden's cooperation?[6] I wish we could hope for the defeat of Pierce in N. H. next week.[7] — It is not improbable. The anti-Nebraska feeling there is very strong.

Manuscript: Harvard University. Published, in Part: Pierce, *Memoir and Letters of Charles Sumner*, III, 358.

1. "No Repeal of the Missouri Compromise," a speech given by Charles Sumner in the Senate on February 21, 1854, was an analysis of the background of the Missouri Compromise and the duty of the Congress to prohibit slavery in the territories.

2. This section from the speech read: "It is one of the melancholy tokens of the power of Slavery, under our political system, and especially through the operations of the National Government, that it loosens and destroys the character of Northern men, exerting its subtle influence even at a distance—like the black magnetic mountain in the Arabian story, under whose irresistible attraction, the iron bolts which held together the strong timbers of a stately ship, floating securely on the distant wave, were drawn out, till the whole fell apart, and became a disjointed wreck. Alas! too often those principles which give consistency, individuality, and form to the Northern character, which render it stanch, strong, and seaworthy, which bind it together as with iron, are sucked out, one by one, like the bolts of the ill-fated vessel, and from the miserable loosened fragments is formed that human anomaly, *a Northern man with Southern principles*" (Sumner, *Complete Works*, IV, 131–132).

3. On February 24, 1854, at a meeting held in Faneuil Hall, Winthrop in an impromptu speech spoke against the repeal of the Missouri Compromise.

4. Judges 16:25–30.

5. Samuel Houston, then serving in the Senate, opposed the bill, fearing it would stir up agitation and endanger the Union.

6. William P. Fessenden (1806–1869), a Maine Whig who had served in Congress, had been elected to the Senate in 1854. He delivered his maiden speech on March 3, 1854, denouncing the Kansas-Nebraska Bill. He later became secretary of the treasury from 1864 to 1865.

7. The New Hampshire election proved to be an overwhelming victory for the opponents of the bill; the Democratic party was badly split and a solid group of Conscience Whigs and Free Soilers nearly won control of the House of Representa-

tives. Since this was President Pierce's home state, it was an embarrassing defeat for the administration and its backing of the bill.

697. To Samuel Austin Allibone[1]

Amesbury, March 30, 1854

Dear friend.

Thy favor is just recd. In reply I wd say that I have published as near as I can now recollect besides the Poems by Mussey, The Stranger in Lowell. Boston Waite, Pierce and Co. pp. 156—1845. 2 editions. Margaret Smith's Journal[.] Ticknor, Reed, and Fields. pp. 224.—1849. Old Portraits and Modern Sketches. Tickr Reed and Fields. pp. 304 1850[.] Songs of Labor. Tckr, Reed and Fields. Boston 1850. pp. 127. Chapel of the Hermits and other Poems. Tickr Reed and Fields. Boston 1853. pp. 118.

I have not included in this list pamphlets etc on slavery and other political questions. My attention has been devoted more to political reforms than to literature. What I have written in that line has been uncollected and fragmentary. Ticknor and Co. are about to publish "Essays and Literary Recreations" in 2 vols.

How much we miss Rantoul at this time in Congress! If any man could have arrested this mischief he was the man of all others. The Anti-Nebraska democrats have now no leader.

Believe me with great respect and esteem thy friend.

John G. Whittier

I have given the dates of the publication of the Books.

Manuscript: Swarthmore College.
1. The identification is conjectural. Allibone had already written to Whittier in 1851 about his proposed *Critical Dictionary of English Literature and British and American Authors*, which was published in 1858. The information contained in this letter was exactly the sort that Allibone included in his collection.

698. To James Thomas Fields

Amesbury, Seventh Day Mg [March 1854][1]

My dear Fields.

Would it do to publish my "Literary Recreations and Miscellanies" this spring![2] Or would it be better to wait until Fall. I have enough for three or four volumes of the size of Barry Cornwall's Essays and Tales.[3] But I think 2 vols at a time are quite as much as the public will thank us for. I can send the copy now at any time, when it may be needed. I think I can get up two very readable volumes—perhaps better than anything I have published in the Prose line.

I want to get the New England Magazine for the year 1833— from Jan 1st to July 1st. Who has a set of them?—Can thee put me in way of it?

I meant ere this to thank thee for thy new edition of poems —a gem of a volume. The added pieces are excellent. I like those on Wordsworth and Cromwell exceedingly.[4]

Ever and truly thy friend
John G. Whittier

Manuscript: New York Public Library.

1. The dating is conjectural.

2. See Letter Nos. 664, 700, and 701 for further comments about this volume, which was published in the fall of 1854.

3. Barry Cornwall, the pseudonym of Bryan Waller Procter (1787–1874), was a minor British poet and dramatist. His *Essays and Tales in Prose* (Boston) had been issued in 1853.

4. *Poems, by James T. Fields* (Boston, 1854). "Wordsworth" was the first poem in the new edition; the other poem was "On a Portrait of Cromwell."

699. To William Lloyd Garrison

Amesbury, April 2, 1854

My dear friend Garrison:

Enclosed are $3 for the relief of Stephen F. Weakly.[1] I know of no better way to express my sympathy with him in his sufferings and my hatred of the Fugitive Slave Law which caused them.

I remember that Daniel Webster in a letter to some of his Northern flatterers, boasted of having the support and countenance of the sober and respectable part of the Society of Friends, in his action in behalf of the Fugitive Slave Law. I have no desire to bring a "railing accusation"[2] against these very respectable Friends, but I simply wish a tax could be levied upon them to the full amount of the loss which our friend has sustained in the performance of his Christian duty of feeding the hungry and clothing the naked.

Ever and truly thy friend
John G. Whittier

Manuscript: Boston Public Library. Published: *The Liberator*, April 7, 1854.

1. In 1854 a Daniel Kaufman of Carlisle, Pennsylvania, was arrested for helping a family of fugitive slaves escape. Two friends, Stephen Weakly and Philip Brechbill, were summoned as witnesses and Kaufman was imprisoned. He was then released, but a new suit was instituted naming Kaufman, Weakly, and Brechbill and brought before the United States court in Philadelphia. Though acquitted, Kaufman was fined over $3,000, which Weakly paid and was thus left penniless.

2. Jude 9.

700. To James Thomas Fields

[Before April 30, 1854][1]

My dear Fields.

A severe headache of several days duration has prevented me from sooner sending the copy for my book or books. I shall call it "Essays and Literary Recreations."—The *first vol.* will contain:

Utopian Theorists
Peculiar Institutions of Masstts
Thomas Carlyle on the W. I. Questions
England under the last Stuart
The Two Processions
Evangeline
A Chapter of History
The Shadrach Rebellion and the Proclamation
Fanaticism
The Border War of 1708
The Great Ipswich Fright
Lord Ashley and the Thieves
Mirth and Medicine
The Little Iron Soldier
The Slave Poet of N. Carolina
Alexander Pushkin

II Vol.
My Summer with Dr. Singletary
The Boy Captives
Passaconaway
Pope Night
The Proselytes
Poetry of the North
The Clerical Profession
The Stranger in Lowell etc

I can add, of course to either of the volumes to make it about 300 pages each.

Herewith I send a part of the copy: If you want the rest at once, let me know—I think the volumes will be more readable than "Old Portraits"—At any rate they are nearer my idea of what a book should be. I wish only to borrow the Magazine containing Passaconaway and the Opium Eater.[2] I have included the "Stranger in Lowell"—but have plenty of other matter to take its place which has never been published.[3]

Thine ever and truly
J. G. Whittier

Manuscript: New York Public Library.

1. Dated by similarity of content to Letter No. 701.

2. Both appeared in the *New England Magazine* in 1833. Neither one was printed in the prose volume.

3. The essays from Whittier's *The Stranger in Lowell* were included in this book.

701. To James Thomas Fields

Amesbury, April 30, 1854

My dear Fields.

What is best about these Recreations and Miscellanies?— One vol or two?—The more I think of it, I am inclined to believe that one volume is quite enough for the present. It looks a little audacious to thrust two volumes of this sort into the hands of the public. I am for one volume of say 400 or 450 pages; if it is worth any thing it may prepare the way for another hereafter. If you concur in this: I shall wait a little before sending the rest of the copy in order to know how much will be needed to make up a volume of the size required.[1]

With this I send the last proofs, and a quantity of matter, principally from Supernaturalism of N. England. I also enclose for the printers a list of the articles to follow in their order.

Ever and truly thy fd.
John G. Whittier

Manuscript: Swarthmore College.

1. It was finally printed in one volume and contained 431 pages.

702. To Lucy Larcom

Amesbury, May 14 [1854]

My dear friend.

Thank God the beautiful Spring is here, at last. The fair Freya of the old Norse Mythology is taking her northerly tour over our hills and meadows, and leaves grow wherever she glances and flowers spring up under her footsteps. But, I dare say you saw her in Beverly a week, at least, before she reached Amesbury.

Whenever I take up "Similitudes," or read a letter of thine I am impressed with the notion that thou shouldst write a story of sufficient length for a book by itself. It vexes me to see such a work as the Lamplighter having such a run, when you cannot remember a single sentence or idea in it after reading it.[1] I am sure thee could do better—give pleasure to thy

old friends, and make a thousand new ones—and "put money
in thy purse"[2] if I may be permitted to speak after the manner of a Yankee. Pray think of it—study thy plan well and go
ahead.[3]

I thank thee for thy kindly interest, and assure thee that
I am by no means insensible to the good wishes and sympathies of my friends. I would that I could feel that I deserved
so many good offices.

I have not been as well for the past six weeks as in the winter, and I can not write without paying too dearly for it in
after suffering.

I thank thee for thy invitation to call on thee, and shall be
glad to do so, if I visit Salem.

Believe me as Ever thy friend.

John G. Whittier

Perhaps I have done injustice in some degree to the author of
the Lamplighter—The book certainly has merit: but it is not
to my taste. It is simply a good story.

Ticknor and Co. have in press a book of mine "Literary
Recreations and Miscellanies."—I publish it with many misgivings, but hope thee will find some things in it worthy of
notice.

Manuscript: Massachusetts Historical Society.

1. *The Lamplighter*, published in 1854 by Maria Cummins (1827–1866), was
then a best seller. She wrote other popular, moralistic romances in the 1850's and
became a contributor to the *Atlantic Monthly*.

2. *Othello*, I, iii, 336.

3. See Letter Nos. 716, 722, and 758 for further comments on this proposed
book.

703. To Henry Ingersoll Bowditch

Amesbury, May 26, 1854

My Dear Friend,—

That man must not be sent out of Boston as a slave. Anything but that! The whole people must be called out, the country must precipitate itself upon the city—an avalanche of
freemen! Where are your circulars and your expresses? In the
name of God, let the people be summoned! Send out the fiery
cross without further delay! Tell us what you want and what
we can do! Thousands are waiting for the word from you.

Is it not possible to keep the matter open until next week?
If so, will not some of the Anti-Nebraska pulpits speak out?
I write in great haste, as I have just seen the "Commonwealth,"
and the mail is about closing. If you want the country into

Boston, say so at once. If another man is to be sacrificed to
Moloch, let the whole people witness it.[1]

Thine truly,
J. G. Whittier

Source: Bowditch, *Life and Correspondence of Henry Ingersoll Bowditch,* I,
269–270.

1. Anthony Burns (1834–1862) a fugitive slave from Virginia, had been arrested
in Boston on May 24, 1854, the day after the Kansas-Nebraska Bill had been
passed. Feeling ran very high and a group of abolitionists, including Samuel Gridley
Howe, Thomas Wentworth Higginson, Samuel Sewall, Wendell Phillips, Theodore
Parker, and others, attended a large meeting at Faneuil Hall on May 26 to determine means of freeing Burns. Acting without full assistance of his friends, Thomas
Wentworth Higginson and a few others attempted to free Burns, but failed to
gain an entrance into the courthouse. In the ensuing struggle James Batchelder, a
Boston truckman acting as guard, was killed.

The city was thronged with outside visitors in the next few days while both the
New England Anti-Slavery Society and the Massachusetts Free Soilers held a convention in the city. Burns was kept closely guarded to prevent any further rescue
attempts, and after a hearing Commissioner Loring surrendered Burns to his
claimant. On June 2 Burns was led from the courthouse through the crowded
streets of Boston to a ship in the harbor which took him back to slavery. Whittier's
poem on the subject, "The Rendition," expressed the popular feeling of the time:

> "And, as I thought of Liberty
>   March handcuffed down that sworded street,
>   The solid earth beneath my feet
> Reeled fluid as the sea.
>
> "I felt a sense of bitter loss,—
>   Shame, tearless grief, and stifling wrath,
>   And loathing fear, as if my path
> A serpent stretched across.
>
> "All love of home, all pride of place,
>   All generous confidence and trust,
>   Sank smothering in that deep disgust
> And anguish of disgrace."

Higginson, Phillips, Parker, and others were indicted for their actions in the case,
but all the cases were quickly dismissed. Burns himself was freed in 1855 and
studied at Oberlin. He finally became a Baptist minister and lived in Canada.

704. To Henry Ingersoll Bowditch

Amesbury, 2d Day, Morning, [May] 29, 1854

Dear Friend,—

I am sorry to see such a spirit of violence manifested, as it
is useless and wrong in itself. I wish the demonstration of feeling to be deep and serious, but earnestly pray that there may
be no resort to force. Cannot the man be *bought*? He must be
saved if possible. I regret the use of my letter to thee at a
meeting of our colored friends.[1] Surely no one who knows me
could suppose that I wish to have any violent measures
adopted. Pray see to it that no such impression was left in the

minds of our colored friends. Oh, let them beware of violence! Let them not injure a holy cause by wrong action. God reigns, and if we are true to his laws we shall do more for liberty than by the use of the devil's weapons, of brute force. Nothing but great illness prevents me from coming down to use my influence on the side of freedom and peace. Dear Doctor, act for me, then, and tide back all as far as possible from anything like violence. Beg our colored friends to bear and forbear.

Thine truly,
J. G. Whittier

P. S. Be good enough to obtain possession of my letter to thee and *keep* it. It was written in haste, and should not have been used by others, as I see it was by a paragraph in the "Times."[2] I wished only that the people of Massachusetts could be witnesses of this awful sacrifice, in the hope that the peaceful, moral demonstration might be of service, if not to the poor victim, yet to the cause of freedom. God bless thee, my dear friend, and give thee wisdom and strength for the occasion.

Source: Bowditch, *Life and Correspondence of Henry Ingersoll Bowditch*, I, 270–271.

1. Whittier's letter of May 26, 1854, had been read by Bowditch at a meeting of Negroes.

2. See Letter No. 705.

705. To the Boston Times

Amesbury, May 29, 1854

To the Editor of the Times:

In thy paper of this morning I see a paragraph, stating that at a meeting of colored citizens in Boston, a document was read from me, tendering aid for the liberation of the new victim of the Fugitive Slave Law.[1] As the paragraph stands, it might be inferred that I was in favor of the extreme measures said to have been proposed to the meeting; and I only notice it for the opportunity of saying, that, so far from counselling resistance, I have always and on all occasions deprecated it, and have on the present occasion most earnestly entreated my friends in Boston to abstain from even the appearance of it. That I feel indignant at this new outrage—that I look with horror upon the Fugitive Slave Law, and deeply sympathize with its victims, I need not say. But I regard all violence as evil and self-destructive, and earnestly desire that the friends of Freedom and Humanity may be preserved from it; and if my voice could reach my colored friends, especially, I would say—Be calm, be patient; God rules, and oppression cannot endure forever.

J. G. Whittier

Source: The Boston Daily Times, May 30, 1854. Printed with the note, "We last evening received the following letter from John G. Whittier, the anti-slavery poet. It explains itself."
    1. The paragraph read: "At the West End the colored people held a secret meeting, and passed, it is said, a series of resolutions to liberate Burns, at all events. A document was read from Whittier, the poet, at Amesbury, tendering any aid, by money or muscle, to this end."

706. To Samuel Edmund Sewall

Amesbury, May 29, 1854

My dear friend

I do earnestly hope and pray that no violence or brute force may be resorted to, by the friends of freedom. I would die rather than *aid* in that wicked law: but I deplore all forcible resistance to it. I know the case is an aggravated one—but, in the end forbearance will be best for all parties; I feel sure that thy influence will be on the side of peace; and I beg of thee *to take especial pains with our colored friends to keep them from [a] resort to force*. May God in His mercy keep us from evil, in opposing evil!

Thine Ever
John G. Whittier

Manuscript: Massachusetts Historical Society. Published: Nina Moore Tiffany, Samuel E. Sewall (Boston, 1898), p. 79.

707. To Mary Russell Curzon

[May 31, 1854] [1]

Dear friend.

Of course you will be *discreet* about our fd.[2] I trust there is no great danger of his being troubled. In his brief note he scolded me for counselling non-resistance. I cannot think his injuries were very severe, as he said nothing of them.

I wish we could see you and talk with you about it, but fear it will not be in our power this week.—I hope our noble friend—will himself be careful and avoid the Phillistines, who would be glad to make an example of him.

In haste
J. G. W.

Manuscript: Harvard University.
1. Dated by reference in Elizabeth Whittier's accompanying note to "4th day Morning" (Wednesday).

2. In his attempt to free Burns, Higginson had been cut upon his head. Higginson later returned voluntarily from Worcester to surrender himself at the marshall's office in Boston, once the police had indicted him. His trial, after being postponed for nearly a year, was never held.

In the letter Whittier had written in Higginson's initials, "T W H," and then crossed them out.

708. To William Lloyd Garrison

Amesbury, June 3, 1854

My Dear Friend:

Enclosed are $2 for *the Liberator*. At a time like this, I cannot lose sight of the pioneer paper.

I fully agree with thy remarks at the meeting of the N. E. Anti-Slavery Convention, in respect to the first duty of the friends of freedom.[1] We must do what has never been done, convert the North. We must use this sad and painful occasion for this purpose. We must forget all past differences, and unite all our strength. Our work now is not in Virginia, or Carolina, nor even at Washington; it is here—in Massachusetts—get the people of the State right, and there will be no more of those hateful Commissioner trials; but around every inhabitant will be thrown the protection of just laws.

If I had any love for the union remaining, the events of the last few weeks have "crushed it out." But I do not forget that the same power which is needed to break from the Union may make the Union the means of abolishing slavery. At any rate, what we want now, is an *abolitionized North*. To this end Unionists and Disunionists can both contribute. At least, let us have *union among ourselves*. In our hatred of slavery, our sympathy for our afflicted colored brethren, and in our indignation against the oppressor, we are already united,—and let us now unite, as far as may be, in action. For one, my heart goes out to all, who in any way manifest love of liberty, and pity for the oppressed.

Ever thy friend,
John G. Whittier

Source: The Liberator, June 9, 1854.
1. The annual meeting of the New England Anti-Slavery Society was held from May 30 to June 1, 1854.

709. To John Denison Baldwin

Amesbury, June 5 [1854]

Our New Senator

The brief notice in the Commonwealth of the appointment of Julius Rockwell, of Pittsfield, to fill the place vacated by Gov. Everett scarcely does justice to that gentleman and to the appointing power. In common with the friends of freedom generally, I have felt a good deal of solicitude respecting the appointment. It was every way important that a true man—honest, uncompromising, unseduced and unterrified— should take his place by the side of the noble Sumner. I believe Julius Rockwell to be such a man. I have known him for several years, and feel the utmost confidence in his integrity and genuine love of freedom. He will take his stand with such men as Wade and Fessenden.[1]

There is at this time, moreover, a peculiar fitness in his appointment. He was the mouth-piece of Massachusetts against Texas annexation, and gave her emphatic and eloquent protest at the final passage of the bill in Congress. I was in Washington at the time, in company with my friend, Gen. Wilson, as bearers of the remonstrance of the State against the measure; and the earnest, manly and very able speech of Julius Rockwell, is really the only pleasant and grateful recollection which I retain from that visit.[2] For me, I thank Gov. Washburn for selecting such a man.[3] It is an appointment eminently "fit to be made." Had the choice been left to me I do not know how I could have better satisfied myself than by placing by the side of him, whose most eloquent closing speech against the Nebraska perfidy[4] finds an echo in the hearts of all lovers of freedom, the man who uttered the indignant and solemn protest of his State against a scarcely less disastrous encroachment of slavery.

J. G. W.

Source: The Commonwealth, June 8, 1854.

Recipient: John Denison Baldwin (1809–1883), after graduating from Yale Divinity School in 1834, went into journalism, editing the Charter Oak in Hartford in the 1840's. From 1852 to 1859 he was in Boston and in 1854 edited the Boston Commonwealth, a Free Soil paper. From 1859 until his death he was the proprietor of the Worcester Spy and from 1863 to 1869 served in Congress as a Republican representative.

1. Benjamin Franklin Wade (1800–1878), a Whig lawyer from Ohio, served in the Senate from 1851 to 1869, mainly as a Republican.

2. Julius Rockwell was serving as a Whig representative when he made his speech against the admission of Texas on December 16, 1845. It was the final speech before the House voted for admission.

3. Emory Washburn (1800–1877), a Whig lawyer, served as governor of Massachusetts from 1854 to 1855. He later became a law professor at Harvard and published many books on property.

4. On May 25, 1854, just before the passage of the Kansas-Nebraska Bill in the Senate, Sumner presented his final remarks against the bill. His speech, which lasted only a few minutes, produced a powerful effect upon the public; its ending section went:

"In passing such a bill as is now threatened you scatter, from this dark midnight hour, no seeds of harmony and good will, but broadcast through the land dragon's teeth, which haply may not spring up in direful crops of armed men, yet I am assured, sir, will fructify in civil strife and feud. From the depths of my soul, as loyal citizen and as senator, I plead, remonstrate, protest the passage of this bill. . . . Thus, sir, standing at the very grave of freedom in Nebraska and Kansas, I lift myself to the vision of that happy resurrection by which freedom will be assured, not only in these territories, but everywhere under the national government. More clearly than ever before, I now penetrate that great future when slavery must disappear. . . . Sorrowfully I bend before the wrong you commit,—joyfully I welcome the promise of the future" (Sumner, *Complete Works*, IV, 146–148).

710. To Robert Charles Winthrop

Amesbury, June 10, 1854

Hon R. C. Winthrop
My dear friend.

I have just been reading over for the second time thy admirable sketch of Algernon Sydney,[1] the just and generous sentiments of which confirm my long-cherished belief that thou canst do more than any other Northern man, at this time, to organize the people of the free states, irrespective of party, in opposition to the encroachments of Slavery, and in so doing save our beloved country from utter disgrace and degradation, or the horrors of bloody revolution. I fully believe that the people of New England—the vast majority—are ready to unite in a movement having for its object the restriction of slavery to the states where it now exists, the repeal of the Fugitive Slave Law, and the Nebraska perfidy.

I enclose a little article of mine published a day or two ago in the Commonwealth; and my object in now writing is to ascertain thy views of this proposition.[2] That the Free Soil party are ready in good faith to abandon their organization and support Whigs or Democrats who will go heartily for the measures above indicated, I am quite sure. Doubtless we may have erred in many of our movements—much has been said and written which I regret,—but the great body of the antislavery party have been honest and true men. Let all that is calculated to irritate and divide the Northern sentiment be forgotten and forgiven; and let the strong and wise men of all parties take counsel together to avert the common danger.

The crisis is upon us; we cannot avert it if we would. It must be met, either with the wild violence of popular excitement or the calm and deliberate wisdom of law-abiding but liberty-loving men—

                    With sentiments of real respect and esteem
                                    Thy fd.
                            John G. Whittier

Nothing but the assurance from myself and other friends of peace that a great Northern movement was on foot prevented a fearful outbreak in your city in the case of Burns. If this hope fails—if such men as thyself do not come forward and lead the popular feeling in the safe channel of legal and constitutional action, the next attempt to execute the F. S. law in N. England will be resisted to the death—armed, organized revolution. I am using no idle words. I beseech thee to seriously consider this matter, in the light of personal duty, and in view of the responsibility which attaches to one in thy position.

                                                        W.

Manuscript: Massachusetts Historical Society. Published: Mordell, *Quaker Militant*, pp. 166–167.

1. *Algernon Sidney: A Lecture Delivered before the Boston Mercantile Library Association, December 21, 1853* (Boston, 1854).

2. "A Convention of the People," Boston *Commonwealth*, June 9, 1854. In the article Whittier asked that Whigs, Democrats, and Free Soilers unite to form a great free party of the North and called for a convention to accomplish this.

711. To Samuel Edmund Sewall

                                    Amesbury, July 2, 1854
Saml E. Sewall, Esq.
Dear Friend,

The circular signed by thyself and others of the Boston Vigilance Committee, was read in our meeting-house at the close of the meeting, and the enclosed sum $17.00 contributed.[1]
The sum is not large, but our meeting is small, and some of us had previously forwarded our mite, for the same object.

We deeply commiserate the condition of our colored fellow-citizens exposed to the dangers of the Fugitive Slave Law. The least we can do is to refuse any aid in executing the atrocious provisions of that law, and, to relieve to the extent of our power the suffering it produces.

In behalf of the Society of Friends in Amesbury,
                                    John G. Whittier[2]

July 2, 1854

My dear Sewall,

Please acknowledge in some way the receipt of this. Perhaps the publication of the note might induce other societies to contribute.

Will thee see that circulars are sent to the following persons.[3]

>   Society of Friends in Lynn
>   Care of Saml Boyce
>   Society of do in Salem
>   Care of Stephen A. Chase
>   Society of do in West-Newbury
>   Care of Wm. Rogers
>   Society of do in Worcester
>   Care of Edwd. Earle
>   Society of do in New Bedford
>   Care of Wm. C. Taber.

I have no doubt all these would aid the Vigilance Committee gladly.

C. Sumner has done nobly—has he not?—God bless him.

>   Ever and truly thine
>   J. G. W.

I was very glad to get a line from thee. I fear thy notion of the leading Whigs was a correct one.

Manuscript: Boston Public Library.

1. After the rendition of Anthony Burns, Boston abolitionists and others organized "The Boston Anti-man-hunting League" to prevent any further returns of fugitive slaves. The Vigilance Committee referred to by Whittier was probably a part of that same group.

2. Whittier had written "turn over" below his signature.

3. Samuel Boyce (1801?–1875); Stephen Abbott Chase (1786–1876), a minister in the society; William Rogers (b. 1786?); Edward Earle (d. 1877), who had been a missionary to the Indians; and William C. Taber (1796?–1886), an elder of the Monthly Meeting.

712. To Charles Sumner

Amesbury, July 3, 1854

My dear Sumner,

I will not trouble thee with a long letter; but I cannot forbear to thank thee, in the name of humanity, and our dear old Commonwealth for thy late noble efforts.[1] I have never seen such an effect produced here by any speech in Congress before. Everybody has read the newspaper reports of the

encounter, and everybody save a few desperate office holders
and Hunkers commend thy course in terms of warm admiration. Thy final speech on the Nebraska crime was every where
commended. Indeed, all things considered, I think it the best
speech of the session. It was the fitting word—it entirely satisfied me, and, with a glow of heart I thank God that its author
was my friend.[2]

We shall have a meeting in Boston on 6th day next—of persons specially invited by the Concord committee.[3] I hope
something may be done. What a pity that Winthrop could not
see the path clear before him, to stand forward at this crisis
and bring his party up to the desired point?—It has occurred
to me that a letter from thee—kind, generous, and earnest—
might move him. I know your personal relations—but it is a
time to forget all this. However, I only throw out the hint;
there may be good reasons against it.

Just now the people of Massachusetts will hear and indeed
approve of almost anything against the Fugitive Slave Law.
One more Burns' case would make Hunkerism an unsafe com-
modity in any part of the State.

Ever dear S. thy friend
John G. Whittier

Manuscript: Harvard University. Published, in Part: Pickard, *Life*, pp. 369–370.

1. During the debate in the Senate which followed a petition for the repeal of
the Fugitive Slave Act, Sumner had been assailed by many southern Senators and
personally insulted. Sumner was called a "serpent," "spaniel," "snake-like pol-
troon"; finally on June 28, 1854, he delivered a speech, "Reply to Assailants," in
which he defended his character and his right to resist slavery.

2. See Letter No. 709, note 4.

3. Ralph Waldo Emerson, Samuel Hoar, and others as a Concord Committee of
Correspondence had extended an invitation for a meeting in Boston to bring together men of all parties who were opposed to the Kansas-Nebraska Bill and the
Fugitive Slave Act. This was one of the many similar meetings being held throughout the state and country which helped prepare the way for the new Republican
party. A convention of July 20, 1854, at Worcester adopted the name Republican
and held a state convention of delegates on September 7 (see Letter No. 713).

713. To Ralph Waldo Emerson

Amesbury, July 3, 1854

The circular signed by thyself and others, inviting me to
meet you at Boston on the 7th inst., has just reached me. If I
am able to visit Boston on that day I shall be glad to comply
with the invitation. Your movement I regard as every way
timely and expedient. I am quite sure good will come of it,
in some way. I have been for some time past engaged in efforts
tending to the same object,—the consolidation of the anti-

slavery sentiment of the North. For myself, I am more than willing to take the humblest place in a new organization made up from Whigs, anti-Nebraska Democrats, and Free-Soilers. I care nothing for names; I have no prejudices against Whig or Democrat; show me a party cutting itself loose from slavery, repudiating its treacherous professed allies of the South, and making the *protection of Man* the paramount object, and I am ready to go with it, heart and soul. The great body of the people of all parties here are ready to unite in the formation of a new party. The Whigs especially only wait for the movement of the men to whom they have been accustomed to look for direction. I may be mistaken, but I fully believe that Robert C. Winthrop holds in his hands the destiny of the North. By throwing himself on the side of this movement he could carry with him the Whig strength of New England. The Democrats here, with the exception of two or three officeholders and their dependents, defend the course of Banks,[1] and applaud the manly speeches of Sumner.

Source: Pickard, *Life*, p. 374.
1. Nathaniel Banks (1816–1894), a Democratic lawyer, had served in the Massachusetts legislature and was speaker of the House in 1851. He entered Congress in 1853 and opposed the Kansas-Nebraska Bill. From 1858 to 1861 he was the Republican governor of Massachusetts and later served again in Congress during the 1860's and 1870's.

714. To James Thomas Fields

Amesbury, August 14 [1854]

My dear Fields
    I want two or three copies of my "Chapel of the Hermits." —When will my big book come out?—Thoreau's "Walden" is capital reading but very wicked and heathenish.[1] The practical moral of it seems to be that if a man is willing to sink himself into a woodchuck, he can live as cheaply as that quadruped; but after all, for me I prefer walking on two legs.
                                                                    Thine Ever
                                                                    J. G. W.
P. S. I want a copy of Dickens' new book, as I understand it is published in full.[2] We are to have thee before our Lyceum this winter—with thy new poem.[3] —
    Is there a copy of my "Recreations and Mis" bound yet? If so I should like one, in advance of publication.
                                                                    J. G. W.

Manuscript: Huntington Library, San Marino, California. Published, in Part: Pickard, *Life*, p. 359.

1. Fields's firm had published *Walden* that August. Henry David Thoreau (1816–1862) had been preparing this account of his two years at Walden Pond since the publication of his only other book, *A Week on the Concord and Merrimack*, in 1849. Whittier's response here is characteristic of the mixed reviews the book received, but he did not hold it permanently, for in later years he spoke of that "wise, wonderful Thoreau," of his "rare genius," and in 1886 that he "loved" both Thoreau and Emerson (Edward Wagenknecht, *John Greenleaf Whittier; A Portrait in Paradox,* New York, 1967, p. 112). Apparently the two writers never met.

2. *Hard Times,* which had been issued serially.

3. Fields, however, did not lecture in Amesbury during the 1854–1855 season.

715. To William Richardson Dempster

Amesbury, October 3, 1854

Dear friend.[1]

Some years ago when we had the pleasure of seeing thee at our fireside, if I recollect right thee mentioned having heard Prof Wilson of Edinburgh speak in kind commendation of something of my writing which had fallen under his notice. I recall this now, because in the last number of Blackwood in a review of Mrs. Stowe's book, written by Prof. Aytoun (Wilson's son in law,) I in common with other American writers have been somewhat ungraciously handled.[2] The N. Y. Tribune of last Sept. 30 contains the particulars.

If I am right in my recollection, will it be asking too much of thee to give in a note to the Tribune or N. Y. Evening Post the substance of what Prof. Wilson said of me:—as an offset to the sneer of his son in law and successor?

I wish I could find means to send thee a copy of my last book, "Literary Recreations and Miscellanies" published by Ticknor and Fields. On page 355 in an article called "Yankee Gypsies," I have spoken of thee, and thy Scottish songs, with something of the admiration which I have felt ever since I heard thee.[3]

Excuse this hasty note and believe me

Very truly thy friend
John G. Whittier

Manuscript: New York Public Library.

1. See Letter No. 471, note 2, for remarks on Dempster.

2. William E. Aytoun (1813–1865), an English lawyer, also wrote ballads and poems. He was on the staff at *Blackwood's* for a time and then became a professor of rhetoric and belles lettres at the University of Edinburgh. His article in *Blackwood's,* a review of Mrs. Stowe's *Sunny Memories of Foreign Lands,* was most critical of her and included the following passage on Whittier:

"In like manner she refers to some rubbish of Mr. Whittier, an American Rhymer, as a 'beautiful ballad, called "Barclay of Ury".' We have a distinct recollection of having read that ballad some years ago, and of our impression that it was incomparably the worst which we ever encountered; though, if a naked sword

were at this moment to be presented to our throats, we could depone nothing
further, than that 'rising in fury' rhymed to 'Barclay of Ury'; and also, that
'frowning very darkly' chimed in to the name of 'Barclay.' But it was woeful stuff;
and it lingers in our memory solely by reason of its absurdity" (*Blackwood's
Edinburgh Magazine*, 76 : 316–317, September 1854).

3. In "Yankee Gypsies" Whittier remarked about first hearing Burns's poems
from a wandering Scotsman: "He had a rich, full voice, and entered heartily into
the spirit of his lyrics. I have since listened to the same melodies from the lips of
Dempster, than whom the Scottish bard has had no sweeter or truer interpreter"
(Whittier, *Works*, V, 336).

716. To Lucy Larcom

Amesbury, October 15, 1854

My dear friend.

I expected ere this to have seen thee at Beverly, but company and illness have prevented. I ought to have acknowledged thy letter, however, sooner.

Can I do anything for thee on thy new Book?—If so, let
me know of it. I like thy plan of the book as far as developed
in thy letter. The innocent with his rhymes perhaps had better
be omitted. On the whole I think thou hadst better keep to
thy original plan, and not try to make the heroine speak in
her own person, unless episodically, or by letters to her
friends.[1]

Shall we not see thee during the Indian Summer?—We got
but a glimpse of thee when thee made thy flying visit in the
summer—Excuse the brevity of this and believe me

Ever and truly thy fd.

J. G. Whittier

Manuscript: Massachusetts Historical Society.

1. Lucy Larcom's next book, *Lottie's Thought-book* (Philadelphia, 1858), consisted of the thoughts of a clever child as they were suggested by passing scenes
such as the first snow, a spring morning, and so on. For further comments on the
evolution of this book see Letter Nos. 722 and 758.

717. To Gamaliel Bailey

[Before December 28, 1854][1]

The term "chimney lug" which occurs in this poem refers
to the old custom in New England of hanging a pole with
hooks attached to it down the chimney, to hang pots and
kettles on.[2] It is called a "lug pole." I mention this for fear
the word would not be understood, and taken by the printers
for something else.

Source: Pickard, *Life,* p. 368.

1. Dated by publication of the poem, "Maud Muller."

2. The poem was "Maud Muller," which appeared in the *National Era*, December 28, 1854. The whole line runs: "And for him who sat by the chimney lug."

718. To Elizabeth Lloyd Howell

Amesbury, February 4 [1855]

When I received thy kind letter last winter, inviting me to thy new home, I hoped long ere this to be able to acknowledge it in person, but a wise Providence has seen meet to order it otherwise, and unless some unexpected change takes place in my health, I fear I must forego the pleasure altogether. The winter has been unfavorable to me,—open, damp and changeable, and I dread the coming Spring.

I cannot tell thee how rejoiced I am to hear of thy success in maintaining thy place in our Society. It is a very rare instance. I scarcely know of another like it. Appeals of the kind, whatever may have been their merits, have generally resulted in an endorsement of the subordinate meeting's proceedings.[1]

I hear occasionally from Hannah by way of James' sister, Lydia Rowell.[2] I am glad to know that she enjoys her novel life in the strange land of gold.

Does thee see the reports of our friend Russell Lowell's lectures on the English poets?[3] They are very admirable performances. I must send thee those on Milton and the Old Metrical Romances. The last is full of humor and genius.

Millburn, the blind chaplain of Congress, gave a very eloquent lecture before the Boston Lyceum a few weeks ago.[4] He closed it by reciting thy lines on Milton on his blindness, with very great effect. The Boston papers quote with high terms of eulogy the stanzas of the "Philadelphia Quakeress."[5] I have always regarded it as a really great poem. Why does thee not write more?

We have very quiet winters here and see very little company. My friend Waldo Emerson usually makes me a visit, and I have flying calls from Whipple, James T. Fields, Dr. Bowditch, and others of my Boston friends. We see very few Friends out of our little meeting. I suppose thee knows that Gertrude E. Whittier is engaged to Joseph Cartland. We are in hopes they will settle within the limits of our meeting.[6]

The last arrival brings the sad news of Mary Mitford's death.[7] It was to me very unexpected. I had a long letter from her dated 22, the 11 month [November 22], cheerful and hopeful. Somehow she seemed so full of life and enjoyment, so satisfied with the present, so hearty in her sympathy with all things about her, that I find it hard to think of her as one who has been and is not. Oh, this mystery of Death! How dark and fearful it would be but for our faith in the Divine Goodness.

I am glad to see that thy husband feels an interest in the freedom of Kansas. I enclose a copy of some lines of mine, written, as Ellwood says, in a "drolling style" last summer.[8] President Wayland, of Brown University, in a notice of them said they were worth all the sermons that had been preached on the subject, and that it was the only way to deal with pro-slavery missions.[9] Does thee see or hear anything of Ann Wendell now? I write so seldom that I do not often hear from her. I am sorry to learn that Margaret's husband is quite ill.

Pray write me and let us know all about thee and thine. We do not forget our old friends, and would not have them forget us. It would give me great pleasure to know thy husband (of whom everybody speaks in praise). Farewell, dear Elizabeth, and may Heaven bless thee always.

Ever thy friend,
J. G. Whittier

Source: Denervaud, ed., Whittier's Unknown Romance, pp. 12–14.

1. Elizabeth Lloyd had married Robert Howell (1805?–1856), a Philadelphia businessman, on March 31, 1853. Although he was not a Quaker and Elizabeth was consequently disowned for marrying outside the Society, she asked for reinstatement and was allowed to remain in the Quaker Meeting.

2. Elizabeth's sister, Hannah Lloyd, married James Neall, Jr., (1820–1903) in 1852. Originally from New Hampshire, Neall moved to California, where he lived the rest of his life.

Lydia Neall (1815–1897) married Samuel Rowell, a carriageman and part-time artist in Amesbury. He painted a portrait of Whittier in the 1860's.

3. Lowell and his first wife, Maria White (1821–1853), had lived in Philadelphia from 1844 to 1845, where Lowell had helped edit the Pennsylvania Freeman, Whittier's old paper. They boarded with a Quakeress and moved in the abolitionist Quaker circles which included Elizabeth Lloyd. In January 1855 Lowell gave a series of twelve lectures on the British poets for the Lowell Institute in Boston. The first lecture was delivered on January 9, 1855. See Letter No. 719.

4. William Henry Millburn (1823–1903), a Methodist minister, was totally blind by age thirty. He served as chaplain to the House from 1845 to 1847 and again from 1853 to 1855. He authored many books besides lecturing and later became chaplain of the Senate from 1893 to 1902.

5. Elizabeth Lloyd's "Milton's Prayer of Patience" had been printed in the Wheat-Sheaf in 1852.

6. Gertrude E. Whittier (1822–1911), a cousin of Whittier who was then teaching at the Friends School in Providence, married Joseph Cartland on May 30, 1855. Both Gertrude and her husband served as principals of the school from 1855 to 1860. In later life the Cartlands became very close to Whittier, spending the year 1875–1876 with him in Amesbury and then settling in Newburyport in 1876. Whittier increasingly spent long periods of the winter months with them, as well as vacationing with the Cartlands during the summer.

7. Mary Russell Mitford died on January 10, 1855.

8. "Letter from a Missionary of the Methodist Episcopal Church South, in

Kansas, to a Distinguished Politician" was first published in the *Villager*, October 12, 1854. The poem was a satirical account of a proslavery missionary in Kansas.

9. Francis Wayland (1796–1865), a Baptist clergyman, was the president of Brown University from 1827 to 1855. He was famed for his sermons and skill as an administrator.

719. To James Russell Lowell

Amesbury, February 4, 1855

My dear Lowell.

I don't suppose it will be any great satisfaction to thee, but it certainly will to me, to tell thee how much I have enjoyed the reports of thy Lectures. That on the Metrical Romances, especially. "I like it hugely" as Sterne says. But they are all good.[1]

But what I especially write for now is to beg of thee to devote one lecture to Burns. Somehow I have come to look upon him as the true world-singer—the very Father of Songs as the Orientals would say. The great poets seem to me to be Chaucer, Spenser, Shakespeare, Milton (I had almost said Dryden), *Burns* and Shelley. I know thy appreciation of Burns, and I want to see it in these lectures find a full and free expresion.[2]

Say to thy dear and honored father that his new book of Sermons has given me great comfort while confined at home this winter.[3] May the blessing of our heavenly Father rest on him and his household!

Ever and gratefully thine
John G. Whittier

Manuscript: Swarthmore College.

1. Lowell's lectures had been extensively reprinted in the Boston *Daily Advertiser* by Robert Carter, who used Lowell's manuscript for copy. The lectures were so popular that Lowell had to give each lecture twice, after which it was reprinted in the *Advertiser*. The final lecture was on February 16, 1855. "I like it hugely" is from Laurence Sterne, *Tristram Shandy*, Vol. II, chapter 17.

2. Lowell lectured on the following topics: Definitions, Piers Ploughman's Vision, Metrical Romances, The Ballads, Chaucer, Spenser, Milton, Butler, Pope, Poetic Diction, Wordsworth, and the Function of the Poet.

3. Charles Lowell (1782–1861) had served as pastor of the West Church in Boston from 1806 until his death. He published many of his sermons in 1855, *Book of Sermons, Chiefly Practical* (Boston).

720. To Benjamin F. Ufford

Amesbury, February 8, 1855

Friend Ufford.

Illness must excuse delay in answering thy note, accompanying the gift of one of the best lamps that has been used since the miraculous one of Aladdin.

We have burned it regularly in our sitting room, and thank the donors every time we light it. It is beyond comparison the best lamp I ever used. I have just purchased one for my sister as the most useful present I could make her. With hearty thanks for the gift, I am very truly thy friend

John G. Whittier

Manuscript: Swarthmore College.

721. To William Chambers

Amesbury (Mass.) February 24, 1855

Wm. Chambers Esq.

Permit me to forward thee a copy of a little poem of mine, in which I have expressed the gratitude and admiration which I feel for your great poet—the true World Singer.[1]

However thou might feel constrained to regard the poem itself, I am sure its subject will excuse my sending it. Whatever relates to the crowning glory of Scotland,—her world honored poet, must interest a true Scotsman, and I feel certain that his heart will "warm to the tartan."

With great respect,

John G. Whittier

Manuscript: Central Michigan University.
Recipient: William Chambers (1800–1883), an Edinburgh writer and publisher, established *Chambers Journal* with his brother, Robert, in 1832. They edited the periodical, which lasted until 1888. He and his brother founded the publishing firm of W. and R. Chambers which issued a number of books on Scottish history, biography, and literature.
1. The poem "Burns," which had been published in the *National Era*, February 13, 1854.

722. To Lucy Larcom

March 2, 1855

Dear friend.

I must add a line to my sister's note, thanking thee for thy letters.[1] When I saw the announcement of thy prize song, I was so pleased that I meant to write thee at once, in congratulation, but, something prevented me.[2] It is just what was wanted. The papers all speak of it in terms of praise, and deservedly.

Now, as to that book. The announcement can do no harm, even if circumstances should prevent thee from writing it this year. Don't hurry the matter.—"Take your time Miss Lucy" as the song says.[3]

I judge by thy letter that on the whole, thee like thy situation. It is one where thou canst *do* good, and in so doing *get* good.[4]

I was very much delighted with thy little contribution to Grace Greenwood's paper for January. It was exceedingly happy and graceful.[5]

We shall hope to see thee in thy summer vacation at Amesbury. In the mean time, may Heaven bless and prosper thee,

Ever and truly thy fd.

John G. Whittier

Manuscript: Massachusetts Historical Society.

1. In her letter of February 22, 1855, Miss Larcom had written:

"I wonder if you can guess how frightened I was when I saw the announcement in the Era, that a book of mine would be published this season! I had begun to count it among the impossibilities, my time is so completely broken into little bits here. But when I saw that notice, I said 'Now it *must* be done.' Will it be a 'breach of promise' if I shouldn't succeed in finishing it?

"I doubt my powers as a story-teller, more and more. Still, I am willing to try, and fail, if it must be so, for the sake of experience. I can think of things enough to say, if they could only be made to hang together. And then, when I feel most like writing, a grave 'must not!' rises before me, in the shape of a lesson in Moral Science, or a pile of compositions to be corrected, forty or fifty high. But the thing shall be accomplished, if it is among the possibles. I am somewhat in doubt about returning here another term, unless I can have more time allowed me. And yet I should hardly feel justified in leaving, it is so difficult to obtain a suitable teacher on short notice. The present term closes March 13th, and the next lasts from the first of April to July.

"I am not sorry I came here, for I have found some very pleasant studies in human nature, some agreeable disappointments; besides gaining new knowledge of my own capabilities and disqualifications as a teacher. But I wouldn't like to stay here long; it is too far away from the hills and the sea.

"It was a great surprise to me to hear that my little Kansas song had gained a prize. I wrote it with the simple wish to write something that would do to be sung in so good a cause; not expecting to hear from it again, as it was announced that all the compositions sent in would be retained. It is reward enough, to feel that words of mine will dwell upon the lips, and strengthen the hearts of the westward-bound pilgrims of freedom; but there ought to have been a better song

than that among eighty eight. Indeed, I am more than half sure that mine owed
its inspiration to a previously written one 'The Kansas Emigrants.' I have a great
mind to go to Kansas myself; but I don't suppose they are ready for the school-
mistress yet" (Grace F. Shepard, "Letters of Lucy Larcom to the Whittiers,"
New England Quarterly, 3:501–503 July 1930).

    2. Lucy Larcom had won the fifty-dollar prize offered by the New England
Emigrant Aid Company for her poem, "Call to Kansas," which they judged
would best inspire the settlers with sentiments of freedom.

    3. "Miss Lucy Long," a Negro song.

    4. Miss Larcom had begun teaching at the Wheaton Seminary in Norton, Massa-
chusetts, in the early winter of 1854 and remained there until her health failed
in 1862. She taught history, moral philosophy, literature, and rhetoric, besides
directing the greater part of the compositions.

    5. The *Little Pilgrim*, a juvenile monthly edited by Grace Greenwood, pub-
lished Miss Larcom's poem, "Little Nannie," in January.

723. To Charles Sumner

Amesbury, March 29, 1855

My dear Sumner.

    The bearer of this note, William Williamson,[1] is a very
worthy intelligent youth, who goes all the way from Salisbury
to Boston to hear thee tomorrow Evening.[2] His great admiration of thee can only be satisfied by an interview of a few
minutes, and if thou canst give it to him, I shall esteem it as a
personal favor. Let me thank thee for thy noble midnight
speech against the Fugitive Slave Law and Toucey's monstrous
proposition.[3] It was well and bravely done.

    Mason W. Tappan in a letter written since his election to
Congress from N. H. says that John P. Hale and a Whig occupying the same ground on the Slave question will be elected
Senators. This is well. I hope their influence will not be neutralized by their connection with K. Nothingism. Oh, for a
clear field![4]

    I should not miss of thy lecture if I had health and strength
to hear it. I hope I shall see thee at Amesbury this Summer.

Ever and truly thy friend
John G. Whittier

Manuscript: Harvard University.

    1. William Williamson (b. 1834) lived in Salisbury, Massachusetts.

    2. Sumner's speech, "The necessity, practicability, and dignity of the Antislav-
ery enterprise, with glances at the special duties of the North," was delivered on
March 29, 1855, at the Tremont Temple in Boston and repeated on March 30.

    3. Senator Isaac Toucey, a Democrat from Connecticut, had introduced a bill
on February 23, 1855, to protect officers and other persons acting under the
authority of the United States. This bill would transfer from the state courts to the
federal ones cases arising from trespass and damages under the Fugitive Slave Law.
The debate on the proposed bill extended into the night with Sumner denouncing
the bill as an attempt to bolster up the Fugitive Slave Law and as being in defiance
of the Constitution.

4. Mason W. Tappan (1817–1886), a New Hampshire lawyer, served as a Free
Soiler in Congress from 1855 to 1861. He later became attorney general for the
state. Tappan, along with men like Henry Wilson, joined the Know-Nothing movement in order to further the antislavery cause. Tappan managed Hale's reelection
as senator in June 1855, with the other seat going to a Whig, James Bell, who
also joined the Know-Nothing group (see Letter No. 727, note 5).

The Know-Nothing movement sponsored secret societies to oppose the political influence of foreign-born groups, especially Catholics. The movement had considerable influence on local and state elections and in 1854 became known as the
American party.

724. To Charles Sumner

Amesbury, April 18, 1855

My dear friend Sumner,

The people in this section of the State are anxious to hear
thy anti-Slavery speech and I am authorized by gentlemen
of all parties to request thee to deliver it here.[1] I understand
it is to be given at Newburyport on the 27th inst. Couldst
thou not give us an Evening during this month or the next?—
I need not add that it wd. be a great personal gratification to
have thee come.

We can give $50 and expenses.—

Let me hear from thee at thy earliest convenience.

Ever and truly thy friend
John G. Whittier

Manuscript: Harvard University.
1. Sumner was then delivering his Tremont Temple speech of March 29, 1855,
throughout the state. He replied to Whittier's letter on April 22, saying: "Count
upon me at Amesbury some day next week—probably Tuesday. My special pleasure will be in seeing you." Sumner delivered his speech on May 1 in Amesbury.

725. To the Yearly Meeting of Progressive Friends

Amesbury, Mass., May 12, 1855

Dear Friends:—

I have received your invitation to attend the Pennsylvania
Yearly meeting of Progressive Friends, to be held at Longwood, Chester Co., on the 20th inst.[1] I thank you for this
kindly remembrance. It would give me great pleasure to be
able to revisit the quiet and beautiful locality of your meeting,
and to renew my acquaintance with a people whose social
virtues and generous philanthropy entitle them to the unsec-
tarian appellation of Friends.

I scarcely need say that the testimonies which your organization is designed to promote meet my cordial approbation.

In that ancient Society whose name and order you have to some extent adopted, I have found freedom to advocate them to the extent of my ability, and while I have had to lament over too much conservatism, short-coming and prejudice among its members, I have also met with much encouragement and sympathy; and I rejoice to believe that a better and more liberal spirit is prevailing, and that you are not entitled to an entire monopoly of the term "progressive."

I attach little importance to creeds, forms, professions and outward organizations. But the assembling of ourselves together, in reverent recognition of our dependence upon our Heavenly Father for strength and guidance, seems to me at once a solemn duty and a great privilege. Christianity is the ultimate—the highest possible ideal—and all the lines of human progress, however widely apart at the outset, converge upon it. I see nothing in any school of philosophy to compare with the sublime simplicity of its truth, as adapted to the wants of our nature. Looking over the ages I see nothing higher and holier than its great Teacher. I believe in the divine efficacy of His life and its consummation of sacrifice; and I regard the record of His precepts and example as the true text-book of the reformer. With you, I believe that our faith in Him is best manifested by purity of life and devotion to the welfare of our fellow men.

I have no means of knowing, nor is it necessary in this connection to inquire, how far we might agree upon doctrinal speculations, but be assured that my best wishes are with those who seek to reduce Christianity to practice and promote the true orthodoxy of life. That in our endeavors to this end we may not rely too much upon our own strength and wisdom, but, on the contrary, realizing our natural weakness and frailty, look reverently and prayerfully to the only Source of light and ability, is the desire of your friend,

John G. Whittier

Source: Proceedings of the Pennsylvania Yearly Meeting of Progressive Friends, *Longwood, 1855* (New York, 1855), p. 20.

1. This group of Friends held to no system of theological belief but felt that duty to God was given by lives of personal purity and devotion to the welfare of mankind. Organized in 1853, this group had as its common cause the abolition of slavery and other reform movements and continued its meetings until 1865.

726. To Goold Brown

Amesbury, May 24, 1855

To Goold Brown

So honorably known for his successful devotion to that important department of learning, which, in its promotion of precision of language, and accuracy in expression of thought may be regarded as the handmaid of Truth, this little volume is offered by his friend.

The Author

Manuscript: Swarthmore College, in a presentation copy of *Literary Recreations and Miscellanies.*

Recipient: Goold Brown (1791–1875), a Rhode Island Quaker and educator, published many books on grammar as well as running an academy in New York City for twenty years. His *Institute of English Grammar*, published in 1823, was widely used in schools and in 1851 he published his chief work, *Grammar of English Grammars.* In 1855 he was living in Lynn working on revisions for this book.

727. To Mary Jane Smith Cartland

Amesbury, November 11, 1855

Dear Cousin

I am glad to be able to say in reply to thy kind letter of inquiry that Elizabeth is gaining—slowly indeed, but as fast as could be expected. She has been able to sit up half the time for the past week. Her headaches continue but not so severe as formerly. She was at one time very sick and we have reason for gratitude and thankfulness for her recovery thus far.

Tell Jonathan that if Rockwell had accepted the Whig nomination *I* would not vote for him.[1] Does he know our Whigs have adopted the Pierce platform and are hand and glove with Stringfellow[2] and Cushing? They go farther than the Pierce party in N. H. on the Slavery question. I have known Rockwell for 20 years. A truer man never was a candidate for office. As for Gardner—he and his clique are preparing to go with the South next year.[3] Mark what I say, and see if I am not correct.

Our election comes off next third day. Whatever the result may be this year the Republican party will sweep the state next year.[4] I think, however, Rockwell will be elected.

Lizzy often speaks of her Lee visit—it was very pleasant to both of us. She and Mother send their love to thee and Jonathan.

Your Senator Bell speaks in Boston on the Slavery Question this winter at the Tremont Temple lectures.[5] My Poem will be read there on the 22nd of this month, by Thos. Starr King.[6]

J. P. Hale speaks to-morrow evening in Boston. Sumner spoke on sixth day to an immense audience.[7]

Remember us kindly to Elizabeth Smith, the Demeritts and Danl Emerson.[8]

As to "our House lot" tell Jonathan to hold on to it awhile and let the timber grow. Providence permitting we shall see what can be done another season.[9]

Thine truly
John G. Whittier

Source: Shackford, ed., *Whittier and the Cartlands*, pp. 48–49.

Recipient: Mary Jane Smith (1825?–1858) married Jonathan Cartland in 1855 and lived with her husband in Lee, New Hampshire. They had no children.

1. Julius Rockwell, who had served as a Whig senator, had been nominated by the Republicans as governor and came in second to the Know-Nothing candidate, Henry J. Gardner, who was elected governor for his second term.

2. Benjamin Franklin Stringfellow, a Missouri lawyer, was one of the leaders of the proslavery group who wanted Kansas to become a slave state. A letter of his to the effect that Kansas was ideally suited to slaves had been widely published during 1855. Stringfellow was active in many of the military conflicts in Kansas in 1855 and 1856.

3. Henry Joseph Gardner (1818–1892), a Massachusetts businessman, had served in the legislature from 1851 to 1852 and then, with the sudden rise of the Know-Nothing movement, had been elected by an overwhelming majority as governor in 1855. He won again with a smaller vote in 1856 and in 1857, when he was supported by the Republicans. In the fall of 1857 the Republican candidate defeated him in his bid for a fourth term.

4. Whittier's predictions proved correct, for in 1856 the vote for Frémont, the Republican candidate, was almost 60 per cent and the Republicans gained control of the North.

5. James Bell (1804–1857), a New Hampshire lawyer, had been an unsuccessful candidate for governor before his election to the United States Senate in 1855. His talk was one of a series of lectures on slavery to be delivered at the Tremont Temple during 1855–1856.

6. The first lecture in this series was given on November 22, 1855, by Horace Mann, to be followed by Whittier's poem "The Panorama," read by Thomas Starr King (1824–1864), a Unitarian clergyman and writer. After King moved to California, Whittier wrote a hymn for his new church (see Letter Nos. 1006 and 1026).

7. Sumner was then actively campaigning for the Republican cause and spoke at Faneuil Hall in Boston, November 2, 1855, on "Political Parties and our Foreign-Born Population." He discussed the recent outrages in Kansas, insisting that only the Republican party could effectively oppose such occurrences, and also criticized the irrational methods of the Know-Nothings.

8. Elizabeth Jane Smith (1800–1872), the widow of former New Hampshire governor Jeremiah Smith, was interested in both abolitionism and temperance reform and was then living in Lee, New Hampshire. Mary Jane Smith Cartland was her adopted daughter.

Hannah Cartland, the oldest sister of Moses Cartland, had married Andrew Emerson Demeritt.

Daniel Emerson (1792?–1880) was a farmer in Lee.

9. Mary Jane Smith Cartland had written to Whittier on October 30 inquiring what he wanted done with the timber growing on his "house lot"—apparently some land owned by Whittier in Weare (Shackford, ed., *Whittier and the Cartlands*, pp. 46–47).

728. To Lucy Larcom

November 15 [1855] [1]
Elizabeth has been reading Browning's poem, and she tells
me it is great. [2] I have only dipped into it, here and there, but
it is not exactly comfortable reading. It seemed to me like a
galvanic battery in full play—its spasmodic utterances and
intense passion make me feel as if I had been taking a bath
among electric eels. But I have not read enough to criticize.

Source: Pickard, Life, p. 370.
    1. Pickard dates it as "1855," but when listed in a dealer's catalogue the letter
was dated "1857." Since Browning's book, Men and Women, mentioned in the
letter, was published in 1855, I have put the letter in that year.
    2. Pickard identifies the poem as Men and Women. Robert Browning (1812–
1889), though a significant Victorian poet, was not a favorite of Whittier. In a
review of 1850 Whittier commented about readers being "tortured by Browning's
burlesque of rhythm" (National Era, January 3, 1850).

729. To William Henry Kilby

November 18, 1855
To Wm H. Kilby
    Thy criticism is just. Like Sheridan's ghost "The line is im-
proved the wrong way."

John G. Whittier

Manuscript: Yale University. Accompanying the note, written in another hand,
were two of the last three verses of "The Lumbermen."
    Recipient: William Henry Kilby (1820–1898), a Maine businessman and writer,
served in the Maine legislature and for twenty-five years was an agent of the International Steamship Company.

730. To Samuel Gridley Howe [1]

Amesbury, November 24, 1855
My dear fd.
    I hasten to acknowledge the receipt from thee of one Hun-
dred Dollars for the Poem in the Anti Slavery course of Lectures.
    I am not sure but that thy view is correct of my alteration
in the lines alluding to Rantoul. I am perfectly willing the
original should be restored. [2]
    I enclose a line just recd. from Mrs. Stowe. I am not sure
as I understand her, but I am unwilling to do or consent to
anything which wd interfere with her own plans or interest,
or which might be an injury to Mrs. Webb. [3] I do not wish to

give thee any further trouble about the affair, but I am really at a loss what course to take. I am half inclined to let the poem die after this reading.

Truly thy friend
John G. Whittier

Manuscript: Swarthmore College.

1. The identification is conjectural. Samuel Gridley Howe served as chairman of the lecture committee for the series of lectures on slavery delivered in the Tremont Temple during the winter of 1855–1856. Whittier's poem, "The Panorama," was read on November 22, 1855, by Thomas Starr King. King wrote Whittier on November 30 about the reading:

"I have hardly been in Boston since the evening when my voice was honored, as never before, in being the medium of your genius. I beg you therefore to accept this fact as an explanation of the delay in sending you my thanks for the compliment you paid me in asking my poor service as your interpreter. The poem is admirably adapted to lecture utterance. It is so broad in its plan, so vivid, so stirring, so practical in its appeal, that it needs two thousand ears, and the wide atmosphere of the public heart, to allow the proportions of its power to appear, and its eloquence to find sea room to disport itself. I have heard the heartiest encomiums of it, even from men not specially interested in the anti-slavery cause, who were swept by it. Inadequate as the reading was, I am suspicious that the soul of the piece possessed my voice, and lifted it above its natural poverty. If possible, I shall read it in Worcester, some time during the week. Would that Mrs. Webb might give it wings! Though I think it needs a man's throat and passion" (Pickard, *Life*, pp. 375–376).

2. In the printed version the lines read:

> The nursing growth of Monticello's crest,
> In now the glory of the free Northwest;
> To the wise maxims of her olden school
> Virginia listened from thy lips, Rantoul;
> Seward's words of power, and Sumner's fresh renown,
> Flow from the pen that Jefferson laid down!

3. Mary F. Webb, a Negro dramatic reader from Philadelphia, read Mrs. Stowe's dramatization of *Uncle Tom's Cabin* on November 23, 1855. The lecture committee desired that she read "The Panorama" as well, and Mrs. Stowe apparently objected.

731. To Charles Henry Brainard

Amesbury, November 28, 1855

Dear Friend:—

Thy note dated the 22nd has just reached me. It was directed to *West* Amesbury. My residence is Amesbury.

I have no daguerreotype with me. Indeed but two or three have ever been taken. The one most accessible is at Pawtucket. I can procure it if needed. It was taken 3 or 4 years ago. I have Hoyt's picture from which the book portrait was engraved.[1] It is I think far better than the engraving.

I send this to Washington. Please direct me where to send the daguerreotype and I will attend to it.

I fear the high compliment intended me in thy proposed publication is hardly deserved.[2] I can only say that I have "done what I could."[3]

Very truly
thy friend
John G. Whittier

Manuscript: Harvard University.

Recipient: Charles Henry Brainard (1817–1885), a lecturer and author, was then collecting materials for his *Brainard's Portrait Gallery of Distinguished Americans* (Boston, 1855). He later lectured on authors, delivering one on Whittier in 1868, and authored a biography of John Howard Payne in 1885.

1. Albert Gallatin Hoyt (1809–1856), a New England artist, painted portraits of famous Americans. He did an oil painting of Whittier in 1846 which is presently in the Amesbury home. An engraving of this portrait was used in Mussey's edition of Whittier's poems.

2. A lithograph print of several well-known figures, including Greeley, Whittier, Beecher, Sumner, Hale, Chase, and Seward, entitled "Champions of Freedom," was published by Brainard in 1855.

3. Samuel Johnson in a letter to Lord Chesterfield, February 7, 1755.

732. To Leopold Grozelier

Amesbury, December 6, 1855

L. Grozelier, Esq.

My friend Mr. Brainard of Washington requests me to forward to thee a daguerreotype of myself. I send the only one accessible. It was taken five or six years ago—the likeness and expression are said to be correct—time and illness have since deepened the lines of the face somewhat, and sprinkled the black locks with grey. There is no daguerreotypist here, and I hope this will serve thy purpose.

The attitude of the picture is not good nor natural—too stiff—and this effect is increased by a broad neck stock. The portrait in Mussey's edition of my Poems is nearer the truth in this respect, although, in the main, a poor picture.

I think the daguerreotype with the exception of being five or six years too young—is nearly right, so far as the *face* is concerned. The stiff, unnatural position could be perhaps remedied in the Engraving,—and the hair slightly changed.

Hoyt's picture is in my possession from which the book portrait was Engraved. The Daguerreotype is more animated and life-like than the painting, however.

Please to let me know whether this will answer for an Engraving, and believe me,

Very truly thy friend
John G. Whittier

Since writing the above I have found a daguerreotype taken

at about the same time the other was—it was badly managed
as to the light, and the face is almost lost in the deep shadow.
It has the advantage of a better and easier attitude than the
smaller picture. I send it as it may be of service.

J. G. W.

Manuscript: Haverford College. Published: Hewitt and Snyder "Letters of
John Greenleaf Whittier in the Roberts Collection," p. 35.
  Recipient: Leopold Grozelier (1830–1865), a French artist, came to the United
States and worked in Boston as a skilled lithographer. He did all the engravings
for *Brainard's Portrait Gallery of Distinguished Americans* in 1855 and the lithograph
of "Champions of Freedom."

733. To Joshua Leavitt[1]

Amesbury, December 25, 1855

My dear friend
    I am sorry that I have nothing fit for publication in my
head or out of it. If I *should* happen to find something, I will
remember the Independent[2] though it is opulent in good
things and scarcely needs anything of mine.

Thy frd.
John G. Whittier

Manuscript: Swarthmore College.
    1. The identification is conjectural, but Joshua Leavitt, an old abolitionist
friend of Whittier, served as office and managing editor of the *Independent* from
1848 to 1873.
    2. The *Independent*, a religious weekly with strong abolitionist views, was pub-
lished in New York from 1848 to 1928. Whittier became a regular contributor to
the *Independent* in the 1860's and 1870's when the paper was at the height of its
popularity and publishing leading authors.

734. To Lucy Larcom

December, 1855[1]

Has thee read Tennyson's new book?[2] I have looked over
it and do not like it. It seems affected in style and Alexander
Smithish. It is a real falling off from the sweet and solemn
beauty of "In Memoriam." It is a mawkish, morbid love story,
utterly destitute of lofty purposes.

Source: The *Anderson Catalogue*, January 29, 1906, item 541, Haverhill Public Library.
    1. It was dated in the catalogue as "12 mo 1858" but since the book referred
to is identified as *Maud*, it must be 1855 since the book was published in that year.
    2. Alfred, Lord Tennyson (1809–1892), the famed English poet, served as poet
laureate from 1850 to his death. Whittier greatly admired Tennyson's writings,
often quoted them, and corresponded briefly with Tennyson about a poem honoring General Gordon (see Letter No. 1390, note 3).

735. To James Thomas Fields

Amesbury, January 1, 1856

My dear Fields

I suppose ere this reaches thee the MS of my poem "The Panorama" has been left at your office.

I want it published, if at all, immediately or at any rate, as soon as possible. It contains something over 500 lines. Will you do it? If you cannot, please let me know as soon as convenient.[1]

I wd like to have it printed on a page and type similar to my two small volumes of Poems. Of course it wd be pamphlet bound merely.

Thine truly
John G. Whittier

Manuscript: Brown University.
1. *The Panorama, and Other Poems* was published in March 1856 and bound in cloth.

736. To James Thomas Fields

Amesbury, January 6, 1856

My dear J. T. F.

The wisdom of thy suggestion is very manifest.[1] I have only one objection to it. The "Panorama" is a poem for the *present time*. It's like Pierce's Message—it won't keep.[2] But if it could be put at once through the press, with the other poems it would answer my purpose. Now, if you have nothing better to do, just inform me and you shall have the other pieces at once, as I have them, for a wonder, at hand, including one in MS. which I like better than "Maud Muller." But, I don't think much of my own judgment in such matters, and it may be a very poor affair in reality.[3]

How soon could you get out the volume (say 150 pages at most—perhaps not more than 125)?—I will see that your proofs go back by the earliest mail.

Winter is down on us here in earnest. Bayard Taylor would find Lapland here, just at this time, without taking the trouble to follow in the tracks of "Afraja," over the Lap mountains, as he tells me he intends to do.

Tell Prof. Longfellow that I thank him a thousand times for his "Song of Hiawatha."

Thine truly
J. G. W.

Manuscript: Huntington Library, San Marino, California. Published, in Part: Pickard, *Life*, p. 377.

1. Fields suggested in his reply that "The Panorama" was so late that it could not appear until after the holiday season and had better be postponed to next fall (Pickard, *Life*, p. 377).

2. "The Panorama" was an account of the contemporary slavery crisis written in the fall of 1855 to affect the coming presidential campaign.

3. Probably "Mary Garvin," which was published in the *Era*, January 24, 1856, and appeared in *The Panorama, and Other Poems.*

737. To William James Allinson

Amesbury, January 20, 1856

My dear Wm.

Thy letter informing me of the passing onward to eternal rest, of our fd Stephen Grellet was duly recd.[1]

The loss of such a man seems to be very sad; the world seems darker for the withdrawal of such a light. But wherever he is, in the universe of our Heavenly Father, he is the true and loving spirit: his words of love continue the same, only freed from the interruptions of bodily weakness and pain. He is Stephen Grellett still; and the prayer of my heart is that I may be permitted through infinite mercy, all unworthy as I feel myself to be, to meet him once more where there is no more death.

Let me thank thee (as I suppose is thy due) for a copy of Cortland Van Renselaer's beautiful and worthy tribute to our dear friend.[2] I have read it with great satisfaction. I had thought of writing to the Author to thank him for his labor of love; but I hope thou wilt assure him of my sincere and hearty appreciation of his tribute.

I think I know how to sympathize with thee in the loss of thy dear Aunt. But she has, I trust, entered on a path where there is no more darkness.[3]

Is dear Rchd. Mott in Burlington this winter? If so, I desire my loving remembrance to him. I think of him often and always with affectionate interest, and I should esteem it a great privilege to be near him. Thy brother Samuel is I hear again happily married. Remember me most affectionately to him.[4]

Thy dear mother I am glad to hear from; long may she be spared thee—a true mother in Israel.[5] My own mother is feeble, but she is able to be about the house although seldom to get out to Mtg. Elizabeth has had a very severe illness this fall and winter—typhoid fever and has not fully regained her customary state of health.—For myself I can say but little. I am thankful for the ability which is afforded me to do the

daily duties wh—devolve upon me. My kind love to thy R—
and to thy household, in wh—my mother joins.

Every and affly thy fd.

J. G. W.

Source: Handwritten copy, Haverford College. Published: Snyder, "John
Greenleaf Whittier to William J. Allinson," p. 27.

1. Stephen Grellet died on November 16, 1855.

2. Cortland Van Rensselaer (1808–1860) had served as a Presbyterian pastor
in Burlington, New Jersey, from 1837 to 1840 and then worked for the Presbyterian Board of Education while living there. He wrote and lectured on religious
subjects. His book was *The Fight, Faith, and Crown: A Discourse on the Death
of Stephen Grellet, with a Sketch of his Life and Labours* (Philadelphia, 1856).

3. Elizabeth Allinson. See Letter No. 377, note 2.

4. After the death of his first wife in 1850, Samuel Allinson married Ann
Tatum (1818?–1913), in 1855 and had three children by this marriage.

5. Berenice Allinson (1781–1858).

738. To James Thomas Fields

[Before January 24, 1856] [1]

My dear Fields

I send herewith the following pieces, which please print in
order:—

> Summer by the Lakeside
> Hermit of Thebald
> Burns
> William Foster
> Rantoul
> The Pope and St. Peter
> Tauler—Lines etc
> The Voices
> The Hero
> My dream
> The Barefoot Boy
> Flowers in Winter
> Massachusetts
> Fruit Gift
> Memory
> Kansas Emigrants
> To C. S.

Two others "The Haschish" and "The New Exodus" will be
sent as soon as I can catch them. *"Maud Muller," "The Ranger"* and *"Mary Garvin"* should be together. They are of one
family; I hope to be able to send them in a few days. "The
Ranger" contains *150* lines. Mary Garvin from 80 to 100.

The title, if "The Panorama" is the opening poem, should
be *"The Panorama and Other Poems"*—
On the second page of the Panorama MS. after the line

Tell where Pacific rolls his waves a-land

instead of the two lines following, insert these

From many a wide-lapped port and land-locked bay,
Opening with thunderous pomp the world's highway
To Indian isles of spice, and marts of far Cathay

Towards the close of the MS.—(I am not certain as to the page,)
strike out all between

"A well-meant drag upon its hurrying wheel."
                        and
"True to yourselves, feed Freedom's altar-flame,"
                    and insert
Nor chide the man whose honest doubt extends
To the means only, not the righteous ends;
Nor fail to weigh the scruples and the fears
Of milder natures and serener years.
In the long strife with evil which began
With the first lapse of new-created man,
Wisely and well has Providence assigned
To each his part, some forward, some behind.
And they, too, serve who temper and restrain
The o'erwarm human heart that sets on fire the brain.

I should perhaps make some other changes in the Poem—but
brain and hand are numb with frost. Whatever poetical fancies
garnered up in more genial weather may be left within me,
they are frozen before reaching my fingertips like the tunes in
Munchausen's horn, and I cannot like the voracious hunter
get up a fire sufficient to thaw them out.[3]
   —But go ahead with the Poem, and if anything seems to thee
doubtful or positively bad do me the favor to say so, or at
least append thy (?).

Thine truly
J. G. Whittier

Manuscript: Huntington Library, San Marino, California. Published, in Part:
Pickard, *Life*, p. 378.
   1. Dated by references to the coming publication of *The Panorama, and Other
Poems* and by the last letter referring to these matters, No. 739.
   2. One of the many stories of fabulous adventures collected in *Baron's Munchausen's Narrative of His Marvelous Travels and Campaigns in Russia*, published
in 1785 by the German writer, Rudolph Raspe (1737–1794).

288 Poet and Republican 740

739. To James Thomas Fields

January 24, 1856

Dear Fields.

If not too late I wd like to have the Printers change the title
of one of the Poems in the proof sent this morning. Instead of

*Massachusetts,
on the Rendition of Burns*

let it read

The Rendition[1]

and so oblige thine truly

John G. Whittier

Manuscript: Yale University.
1. The poem was printed as "The Rendition."

740. To Joshua Augustus Dix and Arthur T. Edwards

Amesbury, January 25, 1856

Messrs Dix and Edwards

Let me congratulate you on your admirable book the sheets
of which you have been kind enough to send me. I do not
hesitate to predict for it a wide popularity. It is the most
graphic, life-like picture of a large and interesting portion of
our country I have ever seen,—a store-house of facts for the
political economist, of suggestions to the politician and statesman, and of pleasant and amusing narrative for all classes of
readers. It is the book of the season. North and South will be
alike its readers.[1]

If the ballad, *"The Ranger"* is in the Feby no of your magazine, I will thank you for a copy on receipt of this:—or if it
is reserved for the next month, will you ask the printers to
send me a proof-sheet of it? Messrs Ticknor and Fields are
getting out a volume of my poems, and I wish to include *"The
Ranger,"* and they are waiting for it.[2]

Yrs. truly
John G. Whittier

Manuscript: Harvard University.
Recipients: Joshua Augustus Dix (1831–1894), a publisher, worked for *Putnam's Monthly Magazine* and founded the firm of Dix and Edwards in 1854. In
1857 he relinquished his publishing connections and became a public educator in
Elizabeth, New Jersey.
Arthur T. Edwards was a partner with Dix in the firm of Dix and Edwards and
continued in the publishing business after the firm dissolved in 1857.
1. *A Journey in the Seaboard Slave States* by Frederick Law Olmstead (1822–

1903), a landscape architect and travel writer, was published that winter and reviewed by Whittier in the *Era* on May 1, 1856. In his review Whittier said: "Every phase of Southern life and manners is delineated with a minuteness of detail which leaves no room for critical regrets. . . . Nothing richer in humor can be well conceived than his accounts of interviews with negro-drivers, poor whites, and rough spoken planters, and their shiftless, slatternly housekeepers and helpmates. While, as we conceive, no candid Southern reader can take offense at the author's manner of stating the facts which fell under his observation, no Anti-Slavery man can rise from their perusal without a deeper and more settled abhorrence of the baleful institution, which curses not only slave and master, but the very soil on which they tread."

2. "The Ranger" was published in *Putnam's Monthly Magazine*, February 1856.

741. To Olivia Bowditch

Amesbury, January 28, 1856

My dear friend Olivia,—

I thank thee for thy kind note; and am sure some good angel bade thee write it.[1] I was very glad to know that my "Mary Garvin" gave thee so much pleasure.[2] I know of no better way of being happy than in making others so. And then, too, as an author, I was gratified by thy praise of my verses, because I was sure it was the honest expression of thy feeling. I remember that after Bernardin St. Pierre had written his beautiful story of "Paul and Virginia" (which I hope thou hast not read yet, because in that case there is so much more pleasure in store for thee), he was afraid it was not good enough for publication, and was on the point of laying it aside, when he chanced to read it to a group of children, whose evident delight and tearful sympathy encouraged him to print it, and thus please and sadden the hearts of young and old from that time to this.[3] Following St. Pierre's example, I think I shall print "Mary Garvin" in a book with some other pieces. If my young critics are pleased I can well afford to let the older ones find fault. I thank thee and thy dear father and mother for the invitation,[4] and hope I shall be able to accept it when spring brings back the green grass, the bright flowers, and these wintry drifts are only a memory.

Source: Pickard, *Life*, pp. 379–380.

Recipient: Olivia Yardley Bowditch (1842–1928), the second child and only daughter of Henry and Olivia Bowditch, remained unmarried.

1. In a letter her father sent to Whittier on January 27, she enclosed the following note: "Father read aloud to us, last night your Mary Garvin, and, I was so much pleased with it that I thought I should like to write to you, to tell you so. Father told me in the summer, that you were going out to our place at Weston, and, I felt very much disappointed at not seeing you, but I hope it will not be a long time, before I shall have the pleasure of seeing you" (letter, Amesbury Whittier home).

2. "Mary Garvin" was printed in the *Era*, January 24, 1856.

3. *Paul and Virginia* was published in 1788.

4. Olivia Yardley (1816–1890), born in England, married Henry Ingersoll Bowditch in 1838 and had four children.

742. To Lydia Huntley Sigourney

January 31, 1856

The shy boy is now a man of middle years and his black locks are sprinkled with grey. A quarter of a century lies between me and my Hartford memories.

I thank thee for thy kind words about my "Maud Muller."[1] I do not know how it is but that simple, careless (so far as the mere composition goes) ballad finds more favor than my most elaborate pieces—I am pleased to see that thou are interested in Prison Reform. I do not know whether we should agree as well in respect to abolitionism.

I am living in a quiet way on the banks of the Merrimack with my mother and sister. The state of my health compels me to forego in a great measure my literary prospects.

Source: The Library of Louis J. Haber, Part III, item 383, p. 73, Catalogue, Haverhill Public Library.

1. Mrs. Sigourney had written to Whittier on January 16, 1856:

"Perhaps it is not feasible to restore myself to your recollection; but I have a distinct remembrance of an interesting young man, who some lustrums of years since, succeeded Brainard in the editorial chair, and occasionally, tho' seldom, called at my abode.

"Yet, it is not to quicken obtuse, or obliterated impressions that I write, so much as to thank you for the great pleasure derived from 'Maud Muller,' that exquisite ballad of the purest Saxon,—every stanza of which is worthy of illustration.

"I should have gratified myself by expressing this admiration before, but could not ascertain your locality" (letter, Central Michigan University).

743. To an Unidentified Correspondent

Amesbury, February 2, 1856

Dear friend:

Thy very kind letter came to hand some time ago. Illness has prevented me from sending an earlier acknowledgement of the very great satisfaction it afforded me by the assurance it gave me, that I have not lived altogether in vain, and that the words I have spoken have not been altogether void of effect. From my heart I thank thee for thy words of encouragement and sympathy.

I was deeply moved by the incident related of thy dear departed. May I not, also think of her from henceforth as one of my "friends in Spirit land?" That my writings have afforded consolation and awakened hopes in seasons of trial and bereavement is indeed a cause of reverent thankfulness.

I was interested in thee before receiving thy letter. My very dear friend Sarah J. Lippincott had spoken of thee in warm terms of respect and admiration, and I could scarce look upon thy letter as that of a Stranger.

In a few days I trust I shall have the pleasure of mailing to thee a copy of a little book now in press.

I am glad to find that your State manifests a decided disposition to stand firm on the side of freedom. It is rumored here that Gen. Cass, even, has half a mind to break loose from Slavery's leading-strings and do a good thing for Kansas.[1] I hope it is true.

I have just read Conway's noble discourse at Washington.[2] God bless the man for it! Let us not despair of the South when such men are found rising up in her midst.

Believe me most sincerely
Thy fd.
John G. Whittier

Manuscript: Harvard University.

1. Lewis Cass was then serving as a senator from Michigan. He supported the Fugitive Slave Law and was more interested in preserving the Union than deciding the issue of slavery.

2. Moncure Daniel Conway (1832–1907), then pastor of a Unitarian church in Washington, was dismissed by his congregation for his antislavery views in 1856. He later wrote novels and biographies of literary figures. He remained a spokesman for liberal causes in America and Europe throughout his life.

744. To James Freeman Clarke

Amesbury, March 25, 1856

My dear friend,

Thy remarks at the Tremont Temple Meeting, with respect to the course of our Legislature in repealing the P. L. bill, were so in accordance with my own that I cannot forbear writing thee to inquire if something cannot be done to kill that Repeal in the passage to Engrossment or in the Senate.[1] In view of the murderous doings at Washington and Kansas, I cannot bear the thought of the passage of that Bill for Repeal. What a response for Massachusetts to make to the insolent demands of the Slave Power!—What a requital of the heroic self-sacrifice of Sumner! What aid and comfort to Stringfellow and Co.!

Pray consult with our friends in Boston and bring every

possible influence to bear upon the Legislature. Dost thou know Dr. Phelps the Speaker?[2] Could he not be induced to leave his chair and speak a manly word against this gratuitous and mistimed servility—The members of the Senate should be personally labored with, by all who have any access to them.

The times are dark and evil, but God is over all. "How long oh Lord how long!"[3]

Ever and truly thy friend
John G. Whittier

Manuscript: Harvard University.

Recipient: James Freeman Clarke (1810–1888), a Unitarian clergyman, graduated from the Harvard Divinity School in 1833 and served as pastor in Louisville, Kentucky, for the next seven years. While there he edited The *Western Messenger*. He returned to Boston in 1841 where he organized his own church, the Church of the Disciples, which granted most of its authority to the laity. He served in many public positions and wrote a group of books on religious subjects.

1. The Personal Liberty Bill was an act passed in 1855 by the Massachusetts legislature to protect the rights and liberties of individuals, especially fugitive slaves. A group of legislators on March 22, 1856, had asked for a repeal of the bill, which amounted to a strengthening of the Fugitive Slave Law in Massachusetts.

2. Charles A. Phelps (1820–1902), a doctor, served in the House from 1855 to 1857, and was its speaker from 1856 to 1857. He served the next three years in the Senate and became its president from 1859 to 1860. He later published a biography of General Grant.

3. Psalms 94:3, modified.

745. To James Thomas Fields

Amesbury, April 1, 1856

My dear Fields

I suppose I am indebted to thee for several papers containing notes of my little book. I have made an April fool of myself by reading them. Candor compels me to say that I think, on the whole, the writers have made the best of me. At any rate, I could without compunction '*cut up*' the Quaker poet, myself, in a way, which would admonish all young disciples of Fox to "stick to prose and decency." I would not allow a broad-brim to act the part of Charity and cover a multitude of sins!

I gave a wrong initial in the name of Prof Maurice, when I wrote thee the other day. It should be F. D. Maurice instead of F. A. as I think I wrote it.[1] I want a copy sent to Robt. Chambers of Edinburgh.[2]

Now to business. What is the price of the following works in Bohn's English Library?[3]

Plato 6 vols—
Philo 2 vols.

> Pickeny's Races of Men.
> Norway and its scenery.
> Dante—Wright's Trans—[4]
> Howitts German Experiences[5]
> Hendrik Conscious Tales

I see a new Kansas book advertised in the Atlas. The War in Kansas by G. D. Brewerton.?[6] Please send it to me.

> Very truly thy fd.
> John G. Whittier

Lt. Burton's El Medinah![7] I hear it is a great book. Is it to be reprinted here?—And what would be the cost of the Eng. Ed?

Don't trouble thyself to answer this if thou hast anything else to do—Take thy own time.

Manuscript: Historical Society of Pennsylvania.

1. Frederick Denison Maurice (1805–1872), an English minister and educator, had been professor of English literature and history at King's College in London from 1840 to 1853, when he was dismissed for his unorthodox religious views. He later became a professor of moral theology at Cambridge and was known as one of the founders of Christian socialism.

2. Robert Chambers (1802–1871) was a Scottish publisher and author of books on Scotland and history. He established *Chambers Journal* in 1832.

3. Whittier was then a member of a committee to buy books for the proposed new Amesbury Public Library, which opened in June 1856.

Henry George Bohn (1796–1884), an English bookseller and publisher, issued a series of cheap reprints of standard works from 1846 on. From 1831 to 1865, he ran a most successful second-hand bookstore and publishing house.

4. Ichabod Charles Wright (1795–1871), an English businessman, translated Dante's *Divine Comedy* into English over many years. His *Dante, Translated into English Verse* (London) appeared in 1854.

5. William Howitt's *German Experiences: Addressed to the English, Both Stayers at Home and Goers Abroad* (London, 1844).

6. George Douglas Brewerton (1820–1901), *War in Kansas: A Rough Trip to the Border, among New Homes and a Strange People* (New York, 1856).

7. Richard Francis Burton (1821–1890), the celebrated English explorer and author, was best known for his translation of the Arabian Nights. The book was *Personal Narrative of a Pilgrimage to El Medinah and Meccah* (London, 1855).

746. To Lucy Larcom

Amesbury, April 2, 1856

My dear fd.

We are glad to hear of thee again in our neighborhood, and shall be glad to see thee here tomorrow or next day or next as suits thy convenience.

As to thy complaint of being sleepy and stupid—so much the better. Thee will come to the right place precisely. We are stupid—ye or you are stupid, They are stupid. All is stupid. We shall be excellent company for each other. I should like however to learn the trick of sleeping, and if thee can impart the secret it will be of great service to me.

I hold the pen for Elizth. as well as myself. She might have written a more polite invitation but not more cordial than this of thy friend.[1]

John G. Whittier

Manuscript: Swarthmore College.

1. Miss Larcom visited the Whittiers the next week and wrote a letter, saying that she found his April 2 letter on her return. Miss Larcom invited Whittier to visit her at Norton and commented, "It is one of my woes that I cannot get *un-sleepy* permanently. I would send you some poppies, if I were wakeful enough to gather them" (Shepard, "Letters of Lucy Larcom to the Whittiers," p. 504).

747. To Charles Henry Brainard

Amesbury, April 13, 1856

My dear fd.

I thank thee for a copy of thy new Engraving.[1] As a work of art it is very valuable and the likenesses I think are good. My own is a little improved upon—it indicates more health and robust life than I can boast of. But my mother approves of it and she ought to know.

A neighbor of ours has a little boy 3 years old. We took the picture to him, and asked him if he ever saw the face before. The little fellow eyed it a moment and said he had seen me; it was Mr. Whittier's, pointing with his fingers to the head. So I suppose it must be somewhat of a likeness. Speaker Banks is excellent.

My Post Office address is Amesbury, not W. Amesbury as thy note was directed.

I am glad to hear of the success of the Engraving; and hope thee will lose nothing by thy kind endeavor to gratify public curiosity.

Thy friend truly
John G. Whittier

Manuscript: Harvard University.

1. "Champions of Freedom," a lithograph by Grozelier, printed by Brainard. See Letter Nos. 731 and 732.

748. To Lucy Larcom

Amesbury, May, 1856

My dear fd.

I did not call on thee at thy classic retreat when I went to Providence for the following reasons among others.

1st. It was off the main track.

2nd. The visit of an heretical Quaker might damage thy reputation for orthodoxy; and

3rd. *I did not go to Providence.*
My sister preferred that her little girl should be nearer her and so I placed her at Mrs. Wait's school in S. Reading.[1]

We had a splendid picture of Dante and Beatrice sent us soon after thee left. Our suspicions fell upon thee. Were we correct? At any rate, many thanks to the giver of so welcome a gift.[2]

My health has indeed suffered very much for the past year. I am better now, but the Spring winds have been cruel. My sister's health and spirits have been greatly depressed, and I have been obliged to witness her sadness and suffering without the power to cheer her. I have hopes that the beautiful spring will give her strength and spirit. She needs a new scene and new associations: and for that matter I feel that I do. But Heaven forbid that I should complain. I have blessings beyond my deserts; life, in spite of its care and pain, is beautiful; and my heart is often filled with gratitude towards the Merciful Providence whose bounty I enjoy.

I read thy beautiful contribution to the Crayon. It is not merely a promise of beauty; it is its realization.[3]

We have all enjoyed thy prose sketch sent with the N. Y. Enquirer. I think thee excel in such moral lessons. It is the duplication of sound common sense to poetry.

Elizabeth will write thee soon. Our Quarterly Meeting is held here in a few days, and she is busy in preparing for it, as her health will allow.

Very truly thy fd.
John G. Whittier

Manuscript: Massachusetts Historical Society.

1. Mary Elizabeth Caldwell (1844–1887), Whittier's niece, lived in Amesbury during the 1850's with her mother. She married an Amesbury businessman, Enoch Stevens, who died in 1868, and then Robert Patten, by whom she had three children.

2. In her reply of June 2, Miss Larcom said:

"I saw there [at the Athenaeum] the original 'Dante and Beatrice' of Shoeffer. It is a most beautiful painting, but on the whole I do not like it as well as the engraving. There is a purity and appropriateness in that, which I missed in the draperies of red and pink against the bright blue sky of the picture.

"And yet I hope there will be as much in the beauty of colors to make us glad hereafter as here; I mean I *believe* there will be *more*, because the *soul* only sees subtlest shades of beauty, and the soul's eyes will be fully opened then.

"I am glad you have a 'Dante and Beatrice' and enjoy it. I don't believe I would inquire where it came from, if I were you. If I enjoyed it, I should want to do so for its own sake; and if I didn't, it would be woeful to feel that it was my duty to be grateful to somebody when I wasn't" (Shepard, "Letters of Lucy Larcom to the Whittiers," pp. 506–507).

3. Miss Larcom had sent the Whittiers one of the poems she had submitted to the *Crayon* for publication. In August 1856 the *Crayon* published "What is it?" by Miss Larcom.

749. To John Abbott Douglass

Amesbury, June 2, 1856

My dear friend

Fearing that I may not be able to attend the meeting this Evening, I beg leave, through thee, to say a word to my fellow Citizens.[1] I need not say how fully I sympathize with the object of the meeting, nor speak of my grief for the sufferings and danger of a beloved friend, now nearer and dearer than ever, stricken down at his post of duty for his manly defence of Freedom; nor of my mingled pity, horror and indignation in view of the atrocities in Kansas.[2] It seems to me to be no time for the indulgence of mere emotions. Neither wailing nor threats befit the occasion. It is our first duty to inquire why it is that the bad men in power have been emboldened to commit the outrages of which we complain. Why is it that the South has dared to make such experiments upon us?

To my mind the answer is plain. The North is not united for Freedom as the South is for Slavery. We are split into factions. We get up pitiful and paltry side issues and quarrel with and abuse each other, and the Slave Power, as a matter of course, takes advantage of our folly. That evil power is only strong through our dissensions. It could do nothing against a United North. The one indispensable thing for us is *Union*. Can we not have it? Can we not set an example in this very neighborhood—Whigs, Democrats, Free Soilers and Americans, joining hands in defence of our common liberties?

We must *forget, forgive, and unite*. I feel a solemn impression that the present opportunity is the last that will be offered us for the peaceful and constitutional remedy of the evil which afflicts us. The crisis in our destiny has come; the hour is striking of our final and irrevocable choice. God grant that it may be rightfully made!

Let us not be betrayed into threats. Leave violence where it belongs, with the wrong doer. It is worse than folly to talk of fighting slavery, when we have not yet agreed to vote against it. Our business is with poll-boxes, not cartridge-boxes; with ballots, not bullets. The path of duty is plain; God's providence calls us to walk in it. Let me close by repeating: *Forget, forgive, and unite.*[3]

Thy friend,
John G. Whittier

Manuscript: Alice D. Wells, Amesbury, Massachusetts. Published: The Amesbury *Villager*, June 5, 1856.

Recipient: John Abbott Douglass (1827–1916), an Amesbury doctor, obtained his degree from the College of Physicians and Surgeons in New York City in 1861. He married an Amesbury woman, Helen E. Howarth, and then enlisted in the Union Army, serving from 1862 to 1864. After the war he practiced medicine in Amesbury until 1913 and often attended Whittier.

1. This letter was read at a meeting of citizens of Amesbury and Salisbury on June 2 to express their feelings on the assault of Representative Preston S. Brooks upon Charles Sumner. During the congressional debates on Kansas, Sumner had delivered his "Crime against Kansas" speech, which contained insulting and personal remarks against several senators, including Andrew P. Butler of South Carolina. Butler's nephew, Brooks, then assaulted Sumner with a heavy cane as Sumner sat at his desk in the Senate chambers on May 22. Sumner collapsed under the heavy blows and his health was seriously impaired. For the next three years Sumner was absent from the Senate, trying to recover his health, and his vacant Senate seat served as vivid reminder of the slave issue.

In the North the news of the assault and Sumner's severe injuries created widespread indignation and helped swing many uncommitted voters to the Republican side in the fall election.

2. On May 21, 1856, Lawrence, Kansas, the seat of the Free State party, was taken and sacked by proslavery "Border Ruffians" (a term applied to any member of the administration party during the Kansas troubles). In retaliation, on May 24–25, John Brown executed five proslavery colonists who lived near Pottawatomie Creek, and open civil war began in Kanasa.

3. At the meeting a series of resolutions was passed, condemning Brooks's actions and supporting Sumner.

750. To Charles Sumner

Amesbury, June 13, 1856

My dear Sumner

I have been longing to write to thee, or rather to see thee, (for if I had strength for it, I should now be in Washington) for the last fortnight. God knows my heart has been with thee, through thy season of trial and suffering; and now it is full of gratitude and joy that thy life has been spared to us and to Freedom.[1] I have read and reread thy speech, and I look upon it as thy best. A grand and terrible philippic, worthy of the great occasion,—the severe and awful Truth which the sharp agony of the national crisis demanded. It is enough for immortality. So far as thy own reputation is concerned, nothing more is needed. But this is of small importance. We cannot see as yet the entire results of that speech, but everything now indicates that it has *saved the country*. If at the coming election a Free State President is secured it will be solely through the influence of that speech, and the mad fury which its unanswerable logic and fearless exposure of official criminals provoked. Thank God, then, dear Sumner, even in thy suffering, that *He* has "made the wrath of man to praise Him, and that the remainder of wrath He will restrain."[2]

My heart is full, and I have much to say; but, I will not weary thee with words. Permit me a word of caution. Do not try to go back to thy senatorial duties this session. Avoid, as far as possible, all excitement; get out of Washington as soon as thee is able to travel. I almost dread to have thee come North, the feelings of all classes of our people are so wrought up; they so long to manifest to thee their love and admiration that I fear we should retard thy recovery by our demonstrations. Thy brother George must take care of thee, and prevent thy being "killed by kindness!" My mother and sister join me in love to thee. And now, dear Sumner, I can only say, Heaven bless and preserve thee.

Ever thy fd.
John G. Whittier

Manuscript: Harvard University. Published: Pickard, *Life*, pp. 381–382.

1. Sumner's injuries were at first thought to be minor and Sumner himself expressed a desire to return to the Senate in a few days; a relapse followed, however. After being treated at Washington and Philadelphia during the summer, he visited Boston in November and was overwhelmingly reelected by the state legislature as senator in January 1857.

2. Psalms 76:10, modified.

751. To Ralph Waldo Emerson

Amesbury, June 13, 1856

My Dear friend Emerson.

I see this Mg. that Gov Boutwell is not able to attend the Philada. Convention.[1] I believe thou art one of the substitutes, and I drop this line to urge thee to go in his place. It is a great occasion; the most important public duty which can occur in a life-time. By all means go.[2]

A thousand thanks for thy speech at the Concord meeting![3]

Ever and affy thy friend
John G. Whittier

Manuscript: Harvard University. Published: Pickard, *Life*, p. 383.

1. The Republican national convention was being held in Philadelphia on June

17, 1856. Frémont was nominated on the first ballot as the Republican candidate for President.

2. Emerson did not go to the convention.

3. Emerson had delivered a speech, "The Assault upon Mr. Sumner," in Concord, May 26, 1856, in which he declared that the country must be rid of slavery or lose its freedom. Emerson concluded his speech: "Let him [Sumner] hear that every man of worth in New England loves his virtues; that every mother thinks of him as the protector of families; that every friend of freedom thinks him the friend of freedom. And if our arms at this distance cannot defend him from assassins, we confide the defense of a life so precious, to all honorable men and true patriots, and to the Almighty Maker of men" (*Emerson's Complete Works*, Riverside Edition, 1893, XI, 237).

752. To an Unidentified Correspondent

Amesbury, June 20, 1856

Dear fd.

The crime of Giddings was worse than a crime—it was a blunder: and the Convention's vote was another. The N. Americans were not treated handsomely and you must say as much, excusing it as you best can. We *must not* divide on so small a matter, if as I believe, a frank confession of error, can prevent it.[1]

We shall see that the nomination of Fremont is ratified here.[2] My friends in Maine say he will carry the State by from 10. to 20,000. A gentleman from this place out among the wool growers of Pennsylvania, in a letter written before the Convention met, says that "everybody is for Fremont"—

I fear the Telegraph is a trifle too ready to contend with the Bee and its all-sided conductors.[3] Patience and forbearance just now are especially needed.

Thy friend
John G. Whittier

I impute no ill intention to Giddings. He only looked to one side, when he should have been like the creature in Ezekiel's vision "full of eyes round about."[4]

Manuscript: Boston Public Library.

1. The Know-Nothing or American party had split into factions in 1856: a main body that nominated Millard Fillmore for president and a group of northern seceders who were strongly antislavery. This northern group, "North Americans," met in New York right before the Republican convention, hoping to pressure the Republican convention into accepting a candidate at least agreeable to them. On June 16 the North Americans nominated Nathaniel P. Banks as their candidate and a committee was chosen to confer with the Republican convention. Although North Americans had been invited to attend the convention, their letter in reply, which indicated their willingness to join forces, was laid on the table by the motion of Joshua Giddings. This action was resented by the North Americans, but after Frémont had been nominated, Giddings asked for a reconsideration of the vote about the letter. After a debate, the letter was received and the North

Americans promptly dropped Banks and substituted Frémont as their candidate. Thus the two parties were united.

2. John Charles Frémont (1813–1890), an explorer and soldier, had made three important explorations that earned him the title, "the Pathfinder." He played a leading role in the conquest of California during the Mexican War and had resigned from the army after a dispute. He served briefly as United States senator from California in 1851–1852 and was nominated as the first Republican Presidential candidate in 1856. He lost to Buchanan by 500,000 votes, but gained 114 electoral votes. At the outbreak of the Civil War, he was appointed a major general in the charge of the Department of the West, but his radical policy toward slaveholders caused his removal from this command. Whittier enthusiastically supported Frémont during the presidential campaign of 1856, writing a number of poems about the issues. In 1861, when Frémont issued a proclamation that all slaves of the captured Confederates would be regarded as freemen and was removed from his command for refusing to revoke it, Whittier wrote "To John C. Frémont," which praised his act. The poem opened:

> "Thy error, Frémont, simply was to act
> A brave man's part, without the statesman's tact,
> And, taking counsel but of common sense,
> To strike at cause as well as consequence."

Mrs. Frémont and her daughter visited Whittier in September 1863 and told him what consolation his poetic tribute had given to her husband, and she corresponded occasionally with Whittier after the meeting. Frémont later served as territorial governor of Arizona from 1878 to 1883.

3. The Boston *Telegraph*, a Free Soil and Republican paper, was published from 1854 to 1857, following the Boston *Commonwealth*.

The Boston *Daily Bee* was published from 1842 to 1858, when it merged with the *Atlas* to form the Boston *Atlas and Daily Bee*.

4. Ezekiel 1:18.

753. To Othniel Charles Marsh

Amesbury, July 8, 1856

Respected Friend:

I am truly sorry to be obliged to refuse the request of the P. Soc. of Andover, proffered in thy note of the 7th. inst.[1]

But engagements previously made, and a state of health which compels me to leave undone much that I long to do— must excuse me to thy friends at this time.

Very truly thy friend
John G. Whittier

O. C. Marsh

Manuscript: Yale University.

Recipient: Othniel Charles Marsh (1831–1899), then a student at Phillips Academy at Andover, went on to study at Yale and become a scientist. From 1866 to 1899 he was a professor at Yale and was noted for his work in paleontology.

1. Apparently Marsh had asked Whittier to address a group of students at Andover or read one of his poems.

754. To The Voters of Amesbury[1]

Amesbury, July 10, 1856

1. *Resolved*, That the time has come when the interest as well as the duty of the Free States demands a hearty union upon a single, freedom loving candidate for the Presidency.

2. *Resolved*, That the Divine Providence has not mocked us with this great occasion without the man to meet it: that in John C. Fremont we have the Man for the Hour; and we pledge ourselves to his support, confident that, if elected, his administration will combine the Americanism of Washington with the Democracy of Jefferson.

3. *Resolved*, That, the simple outlines of the history of our candidate,—the poor boy toiling to support his widowed mother, the ardent scholar struggling against many difficulties—the faithful and efficient teacher in the Naval service of his country—the daring and world renowned Explorer forcing the wintry gates of the Rocky Mountains, opening the path to the Golden Land beyond them, and planting our flag on the shores of the Pacific—the far sighted patriot urging for the State of which he was the principal founder, a constitutional prohibition of human Slavery—and, last, but not least, the inflexible opponent of Slavery Extension,—afford ample proof of the wisdom of his instinctive selection by the popular heart as the standard bearer of Freedom: a man without fear and without reproach, possessing in an eminent degree the courage, decision and energy which the crisis demands—a man morally and intellectually equal to any fortune, who has never failed in his enterprises and whose very name is a guaranty of success,—whose romantic achievements stir the blood of the young, and whose modesty, prudence, and sound principles commend him to the favor of the conservative, as one whose middle years are rich in varied experience and to whom wisdom is grey hairs and an unspotted life in old age.

4. *Resolved*, That in view of the downward tendency of the Republic under the present Administration—the insolent brutality of the Slave Power—the horrible crusade against freedom in Kansas—the complete surrender of the so called Democratic party to Black Despotism—the distinct foreshadowing of mightier evil to come in the Buchanan platform at Cincinnati,[2] —and, knowing as we do that the only remedy is to be found in the prompt action of a united North, we pledge ourselves to one another, that no personal preferences or party prejudices, on our part, shall interfere to prevent the unity of freemen for the sake of Freedom.

5. *Resolved*, That in this contest the friends of freedom of

all parties must remember that *without union nothing can be done, with it everything.*

6. *Resolved*, That our thanks are due to our Senators in Congress, Hon. Charles Sumner and Hon. Henry Wilson, and to Hon. Anson Burlingame of the House, for their fearless and faithful defense of the principles and rights of Massachusetts.

7. *Resolved*, That in William L. Dayton of New Jersey we recognize a tried statesman and patriot and a consistent friend of Freedom; and, however an unfortunate misunderstanding may interfere with his support and the harmony of the people's movement against Slave Extension, it arises from no distrust of his principles, integrity or ability.[3]

Source: The Amesbury *Villager*, July 10, 1856. The resolutions were introduced by the following:

"Ratification Meeting

"In pursuance of a call signed by over one hundred legal voters of the two towns, of all the parties heretofore recognized among us, such of the citizens as were favorable to the nomination of Col. Fremont, assembled at Washington hall, on Wednesday evening of last week. A very large and enthusiastic audience, including many ladies, was convened on the occasion.

"The following gentlemen were appointed a Committee on Resolutions: J. G. Whittier, Benj. Evans, Wm. P. Colby, M. Thorndike, Dr. Y. C. Hurd, and Frederick Bagley,

Who reported the following:"

1. Whittier was chairman of the committee on resolutions and it is presumed that he wrote most of the resolves.

2. The Democratic convention met at Cincinnati in June and nominated James Buchanan (1791–1868) for President. Buchanan had served in the Senate and House and held many ministerial posts before being elected the fifteenth President of the United States in 1856. The Democratic platform affirmed the Compromise of 1850 and supported the Kansas-Nebraska Act.

3. William L. Dayton (1807–1864) had for many years been a Whig senator from New Jersey, but lost his seat after opposing the Fugitive Slave Law. He became attorney-general of New Jersey from 1857 to 1861 and then served as minister to France. Dayton's nomination as vice-president had been opposed by the North American party, who wanted William F. Johnston of Pennsylvania.

755. To Moses Austin Cartland

Amesbury, July 15, 1856

Dear Moses.

I see by the Ind. Democrat that thou has not been idle.[1] Ah me! I wish I had strength to do what I see should be done! But, all I *can* do shall be done.

I am not apt to be very sanguine, but I certainly have strong hopes of Fremont's election. I think I see the finger of Providence in his nomination. It appeals to all that is good and generous in young America. It touches the popular heart.

I enclose for thee a slip showing what we are doing here, (or rather would do it if I could find the village paper which I have missed since the first clause of the sentence was written).[2] The paper contains an account of the ratification meeting here. We have a large Fremont and Dayton flag flying across our streets.

The Maple Molasses was a rare treat. Nothing could have been more acceptable. We had the flavor of the free hills of freedom. I never saw any so nice and clear. Many thanks to thee and Mary.

Ever affecty
J. G. W.

Source: Shackford, ed., *Whittier and the Cartlands*, pp. 50–51.

1. Whittier is here probably referring to an account of a rally held in Concord, July 4, which ratified New Hampshire support for Frémont. Over 10,000 people attended the rally.

2. In the Amesbury *Villager* for July 10, 1856, there was an account of the town meeting in support of Frémont in which Whittier's resolutions were printed.

756. To Seth Webb

Amesbury, August 5, 1856

My dear Webb,

I am sorry to have thee obliged to write letters and hunt up music-makers, for my poor song, when there is so much more important to occupy thy time.[1]

I wish to add a verse, if not too late to my song—to precede the last verse:—

> The snake about her cradle twined
>> Shall infant Kansas tear:
> And freely on the western wind
>> Shall float her golden hair.
> Then tell, etc., etc.

My sister—the author of the other song—is not willing to have her name used—if thee can help it. I do not see any use in mentioning mine: should be glad to have it omitted.[2]

Thine Ever and Truly
John G. Whittier

I shall send the text of the Songs to the Era today or tomorrow.[3]

Manuscript: Haverford College. Published: Hewitt and Snyder, "Letters of John Greenleaf Whittier in the Roberts Collection at Haverford College," p. 36.

Recipeint: Seth Webb (1823–1862) of Scituate obtained his M. A. from Harvard in 1843, became a lawyer, and practiced in Boston. An active abolitionist, Webb had helped Higginson in his attempt to free the fugitive slave Burns in 1854. He was then a member of the Republican party.

1. Webb had written to Whittier on August 2 as follows:

"Since writing you I have had both the songs put into the hands of a music publisher who is to take them both at his own risk; and he informs me that they are nearly ready. The last one of course is yours. As to the first one, can't the name of the authoress go on the title-page. Everything goes better with a name, particularly if that name has been heard before.

"Please write to me on this point by return mail and make any suggestions.

"I think, don't you? that the text of the songs might be published now. Why don't you send them to a newspaper?" (letter, Essex Institute, Salem, Massachusetts).

2. Whittier's song was "We're Free" and Elizabeth's, "Who'll Follow." Both were published in sheet music form in August by Nathan Richardson of Boston and set to music by Karl Cora.

3. Both songs were published in the *National Era*, August 14, 1856.

757. To William James Allinson

Amesbury, August 7, 1856

My dear fd William

I have just seen a notice of the decease of thy excellent aunt Elizabeth in the F Review, and it has called up before me the picture of the dear and venerable woman as I remember her in your affectionate household group.[1] What a beautiful example her life presented of Christian patience and cheerful submission to the allotment of Providence! It is sad to think that the outward world was all dark to her—that its pleasant pictures were to her not only stained but obliterated. But the inward light was sufficient to her; a child of that light she walked in it and we may trust that she has found that resting place where there is no need of sun or moon but the Lord God and the Lamb are the light thereof.[2]

What evil times we have fallen upon! My heart bleeds for Kansas. I am grieved at the resort to arms on the part of the free State settlers. Their wrongs have been terrible, but I have no faith in overcoming evil with evil.

Humanly speaking I see no hope save in the election of Fremont and I trust every Friend in N. J. or Pa. will vote for him as a candidate opposed to Border Ruffianism at home and to Robbery and Piracy according to the Ostend Circular, abroad.[3]

Enoch Lewis, Stephen Grellett and Richard Mott! What a loss our Society has sustained—who can take their places!

With much love to thy dear household and to thy bro. Saml—Elizabeth unites with me in love.

I am affectionately thy friend
John G. Whittier

Dost thou know R. Mendenhall of Kansas?[4] The Friends
School I see has been broken up. The Friends in Kansas are
deserving of our sympathy in their season of trial and peril.
May our Heavenly Father give them wisdom and strength and
fortitude. Almost anyone can fight even in a bad cause but the
sublime self abnegation of martyrdom is rarely found.

Source: Handwritten copy, Haverford College. Published: Snyder, "John Greenleaf Whittier to William J. Allinson," p. 28.
1. Elizabeth Allinson died in January 1856 (see Letter No. 737).
2. Revelation 21:23, modified.
3. The Ostend Manifesto (1854) had advocated the acquisition of Cuba, by force
if necessary.
4. Richard Mendenhall (1828–1906), a Quaker missionary, had settled south
of Osawatomie, Kansas, in 1856 with his family and other relatives. He established
the first monthly meeting in Kansas and became an intimate friend of John Brown.
He later became a prosperous banker in Minnesota. Whittier wrote a short account
of Mendenhall's activities and the Quakers in Kansas for the *National Era* on
September 4, 1856, entitled "The Friends in Kansas."

758. To Lucy Larcom

Amesbury August 10, 1856

My dear friend:
Many thanks for thy pleasant note from the Granite hills.
I should like to join your party to the Amherst gathering.
The news from Maine is most cheering.[1] It prophe[s]ies of
greater triumphs to come. I begin to believe that God in his
mercy is willing to grant us a longer probation, and that the
election of John G. Fremont will be the beginning of a national regeneration.
Elizabeth and I attended the great Fremont rally at Exeter
N. H. last week. It was beautiful weather, the meeting was
large and most successful, and we enjoyed it exceedingly.
I think E. will visit Beverly sometime this autumn. Shall
we not see thee here on thy way back?
I am glad to hear once more a word about "*that* book." I
am not sure but that the letter form of narration would be
best. Scott's Redgauntlet is so written, and the story loses
none of its interest in its natural development through the
channels of epistolary correspondence.[2]
Make the most of thy New Hampshire visit—good friends,
fine scenery, glorious weather, and the enthusiasm of a great
and holy cause cannot fail to render it healthful to soul and
body. But I must give Elizabeth a chance to say a word.

Ever and truly thy fd.
John G. Whittier

E. is away, and I send the line without her addition *as* the
mail is closing.

Manuscript: Massachusetts Historical Society.
1. The Maine election was to take place in September and the papers had been
carrying articles about increasing support for Frémont.
2. See Letter Nos. 702, 716, and 722 for other comments on this proposed
book.

759. To George William Curtis

Amesbury Ms., September 19 [1856]

My Dr. fr.

I take the liberty of sending thee a copy of some verses I
have just written, and which will be published in the Era.[1]

I thought it possible that they might fill a niche in some of
thy Pennsylvania speeches.[2]

Heaven speed the right!—

Thy friend and admirer,
John G. Whittier

Manuscript: Swarthmore College.
Recipient: George William Curtis (1824–1892), author and orator, had spent
some time at Brook Farm and then traveled as a correspondent for the New York
Tribune. He published many travel books and in 1856 his book of sketches, *Prue
and I*, gained popular success. During 1856 he actively supported the Republican
party, besides gaining recognition for his lectures on woman's rights, abolitionism,
and civil service reform. In 1863 he became an editor for *Harper's Weekly*.
1. With the letter Whittier sent a copy of his poem "To Pennsylvania," which
was published in the *Era*, September 25, 1856.
2. Curtis and other speakers made an extensive tour of Pennsylvania campaigning for the Republican party before the state elections that October. Curtis proved
very effective as a stump orator, although the Republican party was defeated in
Pennsylvania.

760. To Richard Henry Dana, Jr.

Amesbury, October 20, 1856

My dear fd.

Canst thee not visit Penna before election and speak at
Philada. and perhaps W Chester and Lancaster?[1]

For many reasons I wish thou couldst, but mainly for
the benefit of the *Friends* and the cautious conservative class,
who are repelled rather than otherwise by those appliances
which are generally used.

Consider of it and report thyself ready for the service, if it
is a possible thing.

This is our last chance for national regeneration. To fail now, is forever—Let us act accordingly.

Ever and truly thy fd.
John G. Whittier

Manuscript: Massachusetts Historical Society.

Recipient: Richard Henry Dana, Jr. (1815–1882) won literary fame with an account of a sailor's life in *Two Years Before the Mast* (1840). Afterward, as a lawyer, Dana was active in Free Soil politics and provided free legal assistance to slaves captured under the Fugitive Slave Law. During the Civil War he was a United States attorney for Massachusetts and afterward wrote on international law.

1. Dana had recently returned from a trip to Europe and had not been active in the 1856 fall campaign. Dana offered to make a last-minute speaking tour of Pennsylvania, which had gone Democratic in its state elections, to bolster support for Frémont, but it was finally decided not to use him. Dana replied to Whittier's request as follows:

"I am much gratified by the compliment implied in your note of the 20th, which has not reached me until this moment.

"As soon as I found we were defeated in Pennsylvania, I wrote to the Chairman and Sec. of the Fremont Committee of Philadelphia, and offered to go there and speak, if they thought I could be of any use there. I wrote to Mr. Carey and Mr. Balch. I have received no reply as yet, which rather surprises me. If I am needed, I shall delight in going.

"You are too right. This is the last chance we have a *right* to *rely upon* for freedom. We may have another, but have no right to expect one.

"The worst enemies we have to contend with are such men as Hillard,—the men who carry credit for their generally good impulses and sentiments, but incapable of great and generous action in a crisis, and stand in the way of others—'Neither enter in themselves, nor follow those who are entering to go in.'

"I am rather in fear that there is not enough of *virtus*—that ancient Roman phrase for something compounded of virtue and courage—in the Northern hopes, to resist the domination of an oligarchy.

"If I am not called to Pennsylvania, I have offered myself to Connecticut" (letter, Central Michigan University).

761. To an Unidentified Correspondent

Amesbury, October 24, 1856

Dear Henry,

Taking for granted that thou art heartily with us, I write to say that R. H. Dana, Jr. Esq.—one of the noblest and ablest men of our state—will speak for Fremont and Constitutional Freedom at Philadelphia and perhaps two or three other places in Eastern Pa.—if his services are needed. Please see H. C. Carey and others about it.[1] I have written to C. Gibbons.[2] In great haste ever thy friend,

J. G. Whittier

Source: Typewritten copy, Swarthmore College, papers of C. Marshall Taylor.

1. Henry Charles Carey (1793–1879), a political economist and writer, was in

the publishing business until 1835. He joined the Republican party and was an active supporter of it.

2. Probably Joseph Gibbons (1818–1883), a Philadelphia doctor, who had been active in the Liberty party campaigns and became one of the founders of the Pennsylvania Republican party. In 1873 he became the editor of the *Journal*, a weekly paper devoted to the interests of the Society of Friends.

762. To Charles Sumner

Amesbury, November 12, 1856

My dear Sumner.

If I have not written thee often during the last few months, it has been owing to no lack of interest in thy welfare or of sympathy in thy sufferings for the Good old cause. I have not felt at liberty to trouble thee with letters, of which I feared thou hast far too many for thy comfort. I knew that all I could say would be but a feeble and inadequate expression of the feeling which wells up in my heart whenever I think of thee.

I can understand, dear S, that mere bodily suffering has been but a small part of thy trial. I can well understand, (for in some measure I have long felt it) the pain which an earnest spirit feels when obliged to stand still while the battle for Human Freedom is in suspense. During the late momentous campaign I have been utterly unable to do anything effective, or commensurate with my interest in it. What I could do I have done. And for thyself, thy denunciation of the Crime against Kansas has burdened all the winds—thy very absence has spoken for thee; and, the words of cheer and counsel which have been sent from time to time from thy retirement have been potent instrumentalities in awakening the North.

The result of the election has not disappointed me. It is, in fact, better than I dared to hope. Every way considered is it not better than we had a right to expect? If we can hold what we have gained, our victory is only delayed for four years. For me, so far from repining, I bow in grateful acknowledgment to the Divine Providence which has given me, in this canvas, as from the top of Pisgah, a glimpse of the Canaan of freedom.

My chief present anxiety is for Kansas. All looks dark there, but God is over all; and He can turn and overturn, until His right is established.

It is barely possible, however, that policy may dictate to the managers of the President elect a more decent course of action, as respects Kansas, through fear of losing what little hold they still retain of the free States. Nothing will contrib-

ute more to this than a determination manifested at once by
the friends of freedom, to hold their own, and press forward
to new victories, by reorganizing in every section of the free
States on the principles of the Philada. Platform. We have
found that the name of *Fremont* is a spell of power, and we
must use it. With it we can keep our many-sided host together
—Americans, Republicans, and adopted citizens are united
in his favor.

But, enough of such matters. I want to say a word to thee
as an old friend. Do not leave home for Washington, until thy
health is more fully established.[1] Congress will do nothing for
the first month—and the remaining two will not witness any
important action so far as the Senate is concerned. Massachusetts, God bless her! loves her son too well to require him
to hazard his health, by a premature resumption of his duties.
Patience, patience, then, dear S.—Recall that,

> "They also serve who wait"[2]

Do not trouble thyself to answer this but think of me as
Ever and affectionately thy friend[3]
John G. Whittier

My mother and sister wish to add their kind remembrance

I am delighted with thy eulogy of Wilson.[4] How very
nobly he has borne himself—Burlingame's re-election rejoices
us all.[5]

Manuscript: Harvard University. Published: Albree, ed., *Whittier Correspondence,* pp. 280–281.

1. Sumner had planned to go to Washington in December, but his health did
not permit his traveling until near the end of February. He spent only one full day
in the Senate and, on March 4, took oath as senator for his second term. On
March 7, 1857, he sailed for France in another attempt to recapture his former
health.

2. Milton, "Sonnet. On His Blindness." The line should read: "They also serve
who only stand and wait."

3. Sumner replied to Whittier on December 20th as follows:

"Your letter charmed and soothed me. Every day I thought of it, and chided
myself for letting it go unanswered. Then came your beautiful poem of peace
["The Conquest of Finland"] depicting a true conquest, which made my pulse
beat quick and my eyes moisten with tears. Truly do I thank you for that generous sympathy which you give to me, and also to mankind.

"At last we may see the beginning of the end of our great struggle. The North
seems to have assumed an attitude which it cannot abandon. Meanwhile our duty
is clear, to scatter everywhere the seeds of truth. Never was the poet needed more
than now, and the orator too; for the audiences are now larger and more attentive
than ever. No opportunity should be lost for pressing upon the public mind the
best and strongest statements of our cause and the most earnest exhortations to
support it.

"My chief sorrow for seven months of seclusion has been that I have been
shut out from the field of action. I am sad now that I am discouraged by my
physician from making any present effort. I am permitted to take my seat and be
quiet. My purpose is to leave here for Washington very soon. What I shall do there,

must depend on my health. Oh! I long to speak and liberate my soul. If I am
able to speak, as I desire, I think that I shall be shot. Very well; I am content. The
cause will live. But I cannot bear the thought that I may survive with impaired
powers, or with a perpetual disability.

"If I live till March, I shall hurry to Europe; there in travel to recruit my
system and to forget that I am an invalid. Let me hear from you" (Albree, ed.,
Whittier Correspondence, pp. 128–129).

4. Sumner was tendered a public reception in Boston on November 3, 1856,
and in his speech on that occasion he especially singled out for praise the actions
of Wilson in the Senate.

5. Anson Burlingame had been reelected to Congress against strong proslavery
and business opposition.

763. To Thomas Tracy

Amesbury, November 24, 1856

My dear friend

When the Lord of Life sees fit to call to Himself those
whom we have loved and revered, it has seemed to me that
out of the circle of those who have been privileged to enjoy
the familiar acquaintance and confidence of the dear ones,
the common-place expression of sympathy can never be of
much value, and may even be felt as a positive injury—a pro-
fane intrusion upon the sacred places of our hearts. I hope,
that a word from me, at this time may not be so regarded.
Ever since my first acquaintance with the excellent woman
who has been called away from us, I have been thankful for
the great privilege of reckoning her among my friends. I have
never met with a more beautiful and truthful character; and
by the sense of loss which I feel, I can estimate in some
degree the magnitude of thy own bereavement.[1]

We have read with deep interest the volume forwarded to
us. It is indeed a precious and tenderly beautiful tribute to
the memory [of] a good man. It seems really marvelous, that
the writer, so burthened by sorrow and debility of body,
should have been able so well to perform her grateful task of
affection.

I need not tell thee that we shall be happy to see thee at
our house, at any time, and that I shall be glad to call on thee
when I am in N. Port.

Very truly thy friend
John G. Whittier

Manuscript: Middlebury College.
1. Thomas Tracy's wife Ann had died on September 10, 1856 at the age of
seventy-nine.

764. To Lydia Maria Child

December 6, 1856[1]

Thy book, most welcome of itself, was received a day or two ago, with the kind note accompanying it. I have never received the letter to which thee alluded. The Border Ruffian official, perhaps, withheld it on account of its 'image and *superscription.*'[2] I shall try and find it, however, for I am not willing to lose a word of love and kindness from one I have so long loved and honored. I the more regret the destruction of the letter, as I see by thy note that my silence gave thee pain.[3] God forbid that I should forget or neglect an early and much loved friend! When we have reached middle years, and begin to tread the sunset declension of life, it is not easy to make new friends or give up old ones. Long before I knew thee I had read thy writings, and honored thee for thy noble efforts in the cause of freedom. Since then I have had no occasion to qualify my respect and admiration, or to regard thy friendship as anything less than one of the blessings which the Divine Providence has bestowed upon me—in more than compensation for whatever trifling sacrifices I have made for the welfare of my fellow-men.[4]

Source: Underwood, *Whittier*, p. 278, and Pickard, *Life*, pp. 389–390.

1. Pickard incorrectly dates the letter as June 12, 1856, while Underwood's date of December 6, 1856, fits in with Mrs. Child's reply of January 2, 1857.

2. Matthew 22:20.

3. *The Progress of Religious Ideas, Through Successive Ages* (New York, 1855), three volumes. Mrs. Child sent the books with a brief note asking why Whittier had not responded to her previous letter. Mrs. Child had sent the earlier letter with an antislavery device or motto upon the envelope. These devices gave offense to postmasters, who were mainly proslavery, and senders often complained that their letters were burned or lost.

4. In her reply of January 2, 1857, Mrs. Child said: "Your letter in answer to my last greatly refreshed my spirit. I have so often had delightful communion with you, through your writings, I love and honor you so truly, that a load was taken from my heart, when I found you were not offended with me" (letter, Library of Congress).

765. To the Amesbury Villager

Salisbury and Amesbury, December 9, 1856

The committee appointed by the citizens of Salisbury and Amesbury, to receive and forward the funds raised in these towns, for the aid of Kansas and the suffering Free State men in the Territory, would report, that they have received the following sums from the several districts indicated:

From Amesbury

Mills District	$29.50
Ferry	46.25
Corner	13.00
Pond Hills	12.50
Pleasant Valley	11.50
River District	10.00
Lion's Mouth	9.00
	131.75

From Salisbury

Mills District	$97.88
Allen's Corner	8.00
Rocky Hill	21.00
East Salisbury, District No. 2,	19.50
" " " " 8,	10.00
	156.38
Deduct for expense collecting	2.00
	154.38
Rec'd from Committee on Levee	60.00
Whole Amount Received	346.13

The amount received in goods is included in this sum.

The above sums have been paid over to Patrick T. Jackson, Esq., of Boston,[1] deducting the two dollars paid James Rowell,[2] for collecting in Mills District

It is necessary, in order to obtain a full and complete account of all that has been raised in these towns for this object, to state, that $40 was collected and paid from the Mills District, Amesbury, previous to the present subscription, and also that $20 was paid to the Secretary of the Emigrant Aid Society, from a subscription raised in this village some months ago. These sums added to the amount received by your Committee and forwarded, make the whole amount $406.13.

The committee would gratefully acknowledge the readiness of the people to respond to the call of the needy and suffering in the new and distant Territory of Kansas, and hope that those sections of the two towns not yet heard from, may soon report themselves as liberal and willing [in] response.

J. G. Whittier
B. P. Byram[3]

Source: The Amesbury *Villager*, December 11, 1856.

1. Patrick T. Jackson (1818–1891) worked in the shoe business during the 1840's in Beverly.

2. James Rowell (b. 1775?).

3. Boham P. Byram was pastor of the Baptist church in Amesbury from 1850 to the early 1860's. He wrote a *History of the First Baptist Church, Salisbury and Amesbury* (Salisbury, 1860) and later served as a pastor in Providence.

766. To Lydia Maria Child

[December 1856] [1]

I like the spirit of the nautical figure which expresses thy determination in view of our defeat this fall. I too will "work at the pumps," not without hope. Just think of Massachusetts as she was in the fall of '35 and of what she is now in '56. The seed sown in weakness is springing up in power.[2] My chief regret, personally, is that I cannot do much for the good cause. The state of my health is such that sometimes for many days together I cannot write or read without great suffering.

Let me hear from thee, dear friend, whenever but a word for me, and believe me

as Ever and truly thy fd.
John G. Whittier

Manuscript: Historical Society of Pennsylvania.

1. The date is conjectural and this letter may be a part of Letter No. 764.

2. I Corinthians 15:43, modified.

767. To Mary Curzon

Mills, August 15[1]

Miss Curzon[2]

I regret that illness this afternoon prevents me from going to the Ferry in order to ascertain whether there was any truth in the boy's story about buying doves of an elderly gentleman not far from the landing. I am really anxious to be quite sure on this point, as I would not like to give the boy's parents unnecessary alarm and trouble.

Will it be in your power to ascertain this so that I can know before the stage leaves for Haverhill tomorrow morning. I have to trouble you further, but I cannot well avoid it. If he has had trade of the kind with a gentleman at the Ferry, for a pair of Fantail doves, I shall have no doubt whatever that our suspicions are well founded, and the sooner he is checked the better for him as well as his parents, who will be greatly shocked by the unlucky news of his behavior.

Thanking thee for calling on us and giving us the information, I am truly thy friend

                                                                J. G. Whittier

It has occurred to me that it is barely *possible* that the doves may have flown to some person's premises, who has sold them to the boy without inquiring where they belonged.

Manuscript: The Essex Institute, Salem, Massachusetts.

1. The dating of this letter is quite uncertain. From the handwriting and kind of paper used, it seems to be from the early 1850's. Since Whittier first mentions Mary Curzon in 1853 and wrote her a letter in 1854, I have decided to place it here at the end of the period, 1853 to 1856. Whittier, however, knew the Curzon family from at least the 1840's and had written a poem to the two daughters in 1851; so the letter may be of an earlier date.

2. Roland H. Woodwell believes that the name is "Miss Currier," rather than "Miss Curzon," so my identification is also conjectural.

Part Nine

Atlantic Monthly

1857-1858

Atlantic Monthly
1857-1858

Nothing could be more indicative of Whittier's commitment to literature and the general tenor of his correspondence in these years than his first letter of 1857 to James Fields. The letter opened with a discussion of a new poem, "The Last Walk in Autumn," which Whittier said was written for a few personal friends. After favorably commenting on recent books from Fields's firm, Whittier singled out a new edition of Longfellow's complete poems and wondered if his own poetry could be so published. Fields successfully negotiated with Whittier's previous publishers for rights and in July an attractive, two-volume edition of Whittier's poetry was issued. Commonly called the Blue and Gold edition after its blue cloth cover and gilt lettering, it remained the standard edition of Whittier's poems for the next twelve years. With this publication Whittier was securely placed among the respected authors of his own day, like Emerson and Longfellow. Similarly the bulk of his correspondence dealt with literary topics. Nearly half of the eighty-five known letters from this period were written to three editors, Fields, Lowell, and Underwood, while only three of his twenty-three published poems were directly concerned with slavery or political issues. As a recognized literary figure Whittier was asked to write poems for school dedications and to address literary groups; he received solicitations to anthologize his poems and an increasing number of autograph requests; and he took special care to select the correct picture for the frontispiece of the Blue and Gold edition. One of the most gratifying public acknowledgments of Whittier's litterary status came with his appointment to the Board of Overseers of Harvard College. For Whittier, a district-school boy whose higher education consisted of two brief terms at a local academy, the appointment must have brought great satisfaction.

The event that signalized Whittier's coming of poetic age,

however, was the founding of the *Atlantic Monthly* in 1857.
Initiated by Francis Underwood and with Lowell as its first
editor, the magazine had been sponsored and organized by
Lowell, Emerson, Holmes, and Longfellow. Besides agreeing
to contribute regularly to the magazine, Whittier was present
at one of the many summer dinners held to prepare for the
first issue. Conceived as a free magazine, the *Atlantic Monthly*
intended to print original works as well as critical articles
under the guidance of the highest morality. Though outwardly
nonpolitical, it was thoroughly Republican in its politics and
antislavery in its sentiments. The real strength of the magazine and what secured its immediate success as well as lasting
value lay in the quality of writers it attracted and published.
For the first issue Whittier, Longfellow, Holmes, Emerson,
and Lowell wrote poems; Holmes commenced his "Autocrat
of the Breakfast Table"; Emerson contributed an essay;
Mrs. Stowe, a short story; and John Motley, a historical article. Throughout the next forty years under a successsion of
editors the *Atlantic Monthly* remained America's outstanding
literary magazine, printing not only the best of the established
writers but encouraging the development of native American
talent. Nine of Whittier's poems appeared in the first fourteen
issues, and the success of the *Atlantic Monthly* assured Whittier of a wide reading public along with increased financial
assistance.

The poems Whittier contributed to the *Atlantic* gained him
national popularity and critical acclaim. From such unlikely
materials as an old Gloucester refrain about a treacherous
skipper or the folk custom of draping beehives in black after a
family death, Whittier fashioned the gems of his maturity,
"Skipper Ireson's Ride" and "Telling the Bees." New England
history, local legend, Essex County anecdotes and personages
provided him the materials for his hardy ballads and domestic pastorals. If Whittier came late to the realization of the
poetic values hidden in his own and the historical past, he
fully explored it in these years. As he expressed it:

> "Dear to me these far, faint glimpses of the dual life of
>   old,
> Inward, grand with awe and reverence; outward, mean
>   and coarse and cold;
> Gleams of mystic beauty playing over dull and vulgar
>   clay,
> Golden-threaded fancies weaving in a web of hodden
>   gray."

The extensive correspondence with Lowell and Underwood furnishes an inner glimpse into Whittier's creative process as he revises his verses, responds to criticism, and reworks his final proof sheets. The delicate interplay between editor and poet is distinctly captured by his early letters to the *Atlantic*: Lowell reminds Whittier that the refrain in "Skipper Ireson's Ride" would be more effective in dialect; Whittier wonders if the famed simplicity of "Telling the Bees" weren't silliness instead and better suited for the feebleminded; and Underwood suggests that Whittier write a poem on the laying of the Atlantic cable—which he did. Discussing "The Cable Hymn" with Underwood, Whittier commented that "What occurs to one, in writing upon such a subject, must needs, in whole or in part, occur to all." And this was true of much of Whittier's writing. Responsive to popular taste and assured of a common moral and cultural bond with his readers, Whittier brought his art totally into the marketplace. He gave his audience what they wanted and were familiar with: simple narratives of their historic past, domestic accounts of their rural heritage, earnest statements of their democratic traditions, and lyric expressions of their religious beliefs. The Whittier of "Mabel Martin," "The Old Burying Ground," "The Garrison of Cape Ann," and "The Sycamores" touched the hearts of a reading public who had previously viewed him as radical abolitionist or third-party political propagandist. Longfellow echoed this changed sentiment when, after meeting Whittier at Ticknor and Fields in December 1857, he noted in his diary that Whittier grows "milder and mellower as does his poetry."

As the correspondence demonstrates, the settled routine of a small town life, the daily events of seasonal changes, coming vacation trips, and visits of friends, replaced reform activities and national political interests. Middle age found Whittier secure and content in Amesbury, writing poems for county fairs, purchasing books for the local library, attending temperance rallies, and defending the need of social recreation for Amesbury's young people. Reflecting this sense of well-being and fellowship, Whittier in one letter thanked his townsmen for a gift of fruit and flowers as evincing a desired mutual good feeling and regard. In conclusion he stated: "I place a higher estimate on that which assures me of the esteem of my every day acquaintance, and, that I have a place in the kind thoughts of 'mine own people.'" A local newspaper concurred and noted that "no man in the state occupies a higher position in the affections of the people." Most of the letters

from these years are short, a page or two at the most; sometimes only casual asides thanking a friend for a gift, briefly
commenting on his state of health, or expressing his desire to
see an old friend. These letters foreshadow the pattern and
content of Whittier's correspondence from then until his
death, the hundreds, even thousands, of short notes written as
a famous poet and revered public figure.

Still, Whittier's hard-earned rest and settled existence were
not without emotional shocks. In December 1857 Whittier's
mother died. Bachelor as he was and having lived his entire
mature life surrounded by her devotion and love, Whittier felt
the loss keenly. He wrote to Charles Sumner: "We are stunned
by the great bereavement. The world looks far less than it did
when she was with us. Half the motive power of life seems
lost." His mother's Christian resignation and his own faith
comforted him; and when a friend offered to supply spirit
communications to reassure him of immortality, Whittier
emphatically, though kindly, rejected such material proofs.
Faith, he knew, was deeper than sight or demonstration and
all he desired now was the serene and beautiful childlike trust
which made "holy and pleasant" his mother's death. This
inner trust bulwarked him against future losses and found its
poetic outlet in the famed hymns of acceptance and faith that
he was to write in the 1860's. As these two years closed,
Whittier found himself freed from reform activity, assured of
a responsive public audience, secure from debt and, surpris-
ingly, in good health. Thus for the first time as a poet rather
than an abolitionist Whittier faced the coming years.

768. To James Thomas Fields

Amesbury, January 4, 1857
My dear Fields,

A great many thanks dear F. for thy kind response to my
verses. The poem was written for thee, and such as thee;—for
the friends the good God has given me. I didn't expect the
public at large to see much in it.[1]

I suppose thee noticed the printer's emendations "Hafir"
for "Hafiz"—"Athenian Archer" for "Athenian Archon" and
for "Where'er thy singer's name etc" "Wherein thy singer's
etc"—I wish I could get a correct copy of it but it is too long I
suppose for the city papers.

What is the matter of thy hand? I did not recognize the
writing at all.

I was in Boston a few hours this fall, and wanted to call on thee, but was not able to do so. If I get there again this winter I shall find thee out. The weather deals badly with me and I cannot leave home without suffering a great deal. The worst of it is that a large part of the time I can neither write nor read.

I have read several new books from yr firm. Stoddard's poems are some of them very simple and beautiful.[2] I am delighted with Brooks Faust—.[3] It gives me for the first time an adequate idea of Goethe's genius.

Longfellow's poems are always welcome.[4] I like your new Edition exceedingly and wish that some means could be devised to get my verses into a somewhat similar shape. I wish I could get hold of the Muzzy volume. Perhaps Muzzy would be glad to publish it uniform with an edition of yours under the title of "Later Poems." But I would prefer to have one publisher, of course.[5]

Ever and truly thy fd.
J. G. W.

Manuscript: Huntington Library, San Marino, California. Published, in Part: Pickard, *Life*, p. 392.

1. "The Last Walk in Autumn," which was published in the *Era*, January 1, 1857.

2. *Songs of Summer* (Boston, 1857). Richard Henry Stoddard (1825–1903), a New York poet, was literary editor of the New York *Mail and Express* from 1880 to 1903. During the last quarter of the century Stoddard was a literary arbiter for American taste and his own poetry was very popular.

3. *Faust: a Tragedy translated from the German of Goethe, with notes by Charles T. Brooks* (Boston, 1856). Charles T. Brooks (1813–1883), a Unitarian clergyman, served as pastor in Newport from 1837 to 1871. He was mainly known for his translations from the German, which included *Wilhelm Tell* by Schiller and songs by various lyric poets.

4. *Poems, by Henry Wadsworth Longfellow. Complete in Two Volumes* (Boston, 1857).

5. *Poems by John G. Whittier* had been issued in 1849 by Benjamin B. Mussey and Company. Fields replied to this letter on January 12, saying: "I have been trying for a long time to get that big volume of your poems out of Mussey's hands, with reference to bringing you out complete, as we have done Longfellow. Your poems are now held by Sanborn, Carter, Bazin and Company, the successors of Mussey, and I have failed as yet to bring them to terms. In whatever I have attempted to do, I have had your interest in mind. I am still negotiating, and hope I may yet be successful. You had better not write to them at present on the subject" (Pickard, *Life*, pp. 392–393). For further letters on this subject see Letter Nos. 772, 773, 774, 776, and 777. The result of these negotiations was *The Poetical Works of John Greenleaf Whittier. Complete in Two Volumes*, issued in July 1857 by Ticknor and Fields and commonly called the Blue and Gold edition.

322

769. To William James Allinson

Amesbury January 16, 1857

My dear William

I am always glad to hear from thee and thine. I heartily congratulate thee on the advent of the young gentleman and should be proud to have my name in any way connected through him with the honored one of Allinson.[1] I can only say that I hope the newcomer may prove a better man than his namesake—cultivate his Jersey acres in peace and goodwill and never let himself turn to writing poetry.

I think you were quite right in giving the "wee laddie" an easier child's name than Greenleaf. Tell his dear mother I am much obliged to her for her persistence in the choice of the middle name.

I am truly glad to hear of the labors of the English friends. It is a work eminently "fit to be done" and I believe great good will grow out of it.

Ann Wendell writes me of Elisha Maule's decease and of Margaret's joining the Baptists.[2] I cannot understand how any Friend can ever see any life in the "beggarly elements."[3] But let each be persuaded in his own mind—in her case it may be for the best.

Thou speaks of our dear fd E. L. Howell. Hers has indeed been a heavy affliction. I was greatly pleased with her husband and I do not wonder at her sorrow for his loss.[4]

With much love to all thy beloved household and to Samuel I am as ever affectionately

Thy fd.
John G. Whittier

Source: Handwritten copy, Haverford College. Published: Snyder, "John Greenleaf Whittier to William J. Allinson," p. 29.

1. Francis Greenleaf Allinson (1856–1931), born on December 16, went on to become a noted philologist and classical scholar. He taught at Williams, Haverford, and finally at Brown University from 1895 to 1928. For him Whittier wrote the poem, "My Namesake," which was printed in *Harper's Weekly*, May 23, 1857. In the poem Whittier characterized himself as follows:

> "His eye was beauty's powerless slave,
>   And his the ear which discord pains;
> Few guessed beneath his aspect grave
>   What passions strove in chains."

2. Elisha Maule had died on December 20, 1856. See Letter No. 771 for further comment.
3. Galatians 4:9.
4. Robert Howell died on January 18, 1856.

770. To Lucy Larcom

Amesbury February 20, 1857

My dear fd.

Thy kind letter was very welcome and we thank thee for thy remembrance of thy Amesbury friends. More than this I cannot well do, for I have been and still am too unwell to write more than an apology for a letter. My Sister too is confined to her room. Unable to read or write much, it requires all my philosophy and what little of Christian resignation I may be favored with, to keep up my spirits; and a hearty, healthy letter like thine has something of a tonic efficacy.

I am glad to hear that Mary Blair is with thee at Norton.[1] I owe her a letter, but must throw myself upon her charity for the present. If I am ever able I will try and pay all my debts of this kind.

I will send you Woolman's Journal. It is simplicity itself—a record of a life of plain unambitious goodness. May it give you as much pleasure, and do you as much good as it has me. —nay more, for appreciating and loving such a life, I cannot conform my own to it, or rather to that of the Great Exemplar.

Remember me kindly to my friend Mary Blair, and pardon the poverty of this note, and believe me whether sick or well

Cordially and always
Thy fd.
John G. Whittier

I see nothing of thine lately. I am sure thou must have found something to say in thy own clear simple and beautiful way during this long winter. Does not the Voice say to thee as formerly to the Exile of Patmos *Write!*[2] Has thou seen the new translation of the Book of Job?[3] I like it in many respects; it is clearer and the argument of the grand old poem flows on more uninterruptedly—but the learned Professor has spoiled some of the best passages by the introduction of long "Dictionary words"—and Johnsonian Latinisms in the place of the brief homely and vigorous Saxon of the old translation.

W.

Manuscript: Scripps College, Claremont, California.

1. Mary E. Blair (1824–1909), a teacher of Latin and modern languages, had taught at Bradford Academy and Abbott Academy in the 1850's, as well as at Norton. She returned to Bradford Academy in 1858 and afterward taught at Wheaton.

2. Revelation 1:9-11.

3. Probably *The Book of Job, illustrated with fifty engravings from drawings by John Gilbert, and with explanatory notes and poetical parallels by James Hamilton*, which was published in England in 1857. James Hamilton (1817–1897), a Presbyterian minister, wrote devotional and exegetical works.

771. To Ann Elizabeth Wendell

Amesbury, February 24, 1857

My dear Cousin.

I thank thee exceedingly for thy letter. I had heard a few days before I recd. it of the quiet and happy dismissal of Elisha. I intended then to write to dear Margaret, but all this winter I have been too ill to feel like the effort.

From the tone of a little note from her last year, I suppose she has latterly taken a serious view of life and its duties, and that she looks in her trial and bereavement to the only Source of support and consolation. May He who has seen fit to call to His rest her excellent husband be near her in her altered allotment and cheer her with the hope of a blissful reunion in a better world.

Elizabeth and I often think of thee and thy father, and Isaac and talk over the old times when we were together. Truly dear Ann we are often near you in spirit: and we have learned by our own experience to understand the trials and sorrows of our friends.

My dear mother is still spared us—she is feebler this winter than usual—but quiet, calm and peaceful and as she often tells me she sees "nothing in her way." My prayer is for strength to comfort and support her in her declining years; but I leave all in His hands who will do right, and who knows best what is best for His children.

I had a very kind and beautiful letter from Hannah L. Neall this winter. I was glad to hear through thee from our dear friend E. L. Howell.

I notice what thee says of Margaret's change of views—I was about to say I was sorry—but if she finds peace in the change, it is doubtless for the best. She knows that I am no sectarian. I love the good everywhere.

Mother and E send their love. This is but a mere apology for a letter, but it is the best I can do at this time.

We should always be glad to hear from thee. With love to all the family and our mutual friends, I am as Ever thy aff Cousin

John G. Whittier

Manuscript: University of Virginia.

772. To James Thomas Fields

Amesbury March 5, 1857

My dear Fields[1]

Will send thee tomorrow or the first of next week a copy of the "Muzzy book" with such corrections as occur to me.

I have marked for *omission* some eight or ten pieces—and have a great desire to wipe out others. Indeed if I could have my way I would strike out the long Indian poem. In other words I would kill Mogg Megone over again. I think the poem has some degree of merit, but it is not in good taste, and the subject is by no means such as I would now desire. I have objections to it not merely from an artistic point of view but a moral one also—But, I refer the matter to thee; whether Mogg can be omitted. I yield of course to thy decision.[2]

Of course the Panorama and other poems should go in the volume or volumes.

I send thee with the Poems, a Dag. taken nine years ago, and an Ambrotype which has just been taken in this village— Neither one are good pictures, I suspect—, but may serve to give an idea of the original as he was and is.[3] The last one my friends think an excellent likeness, barring a slight grip of the mouth giving it a little twist by way of variety. Never mind that, twists are natural to "men of one idea."[4] I think a good picture could be engraved from either. The last shows the effect of illness, and looks a little odd from a closer cropping of the whiskers than formerly, but an extra scratch from the engraver would remedy that: and on the whole, it is perhaps to be preferred to the earlier one, although that *was* a good likeness.

I send also four pieces which may take the place of those omitted. I really wd not like to tax thy good nature, but if thou canst get time to glance over the volume—and give me the benefit of thy judgment where it may seem to thee requisite it wd be a great favor. I owe much to thy little criticisms and suggestions in the proof sheets from yr house. Let me hear from thee at thy convenience as to the Pictures and the Poems and in the meantime believe me thy friend

John G. Whittier

Instead of the nine year old Dag. I send a damaged copy of one taken to send away last fall. This is very well, but one eye has too much light in it which gives it the effect of a cross or squint! My sister says yr light style of engraving will not answer for my face.

Manuscript: Huntington Library, San Marino, California. Published, in Part: Pickard, *Life*, p. 393.

1. Fields had written Whittier on February 21 as follows:

"I see you are too ill to *talk* about business, therefore I shall not go to Amesbury, but write you a few lines. We have arranged with Mussey's successors to bring out your poems complete in two little volumes uniform with Tennyson and Longfellow. The expense attending this arrangement, is, of necessity, a very large one, and it may be a very long time before we become wholly remunerated of the numerous difficulties which lay in the way of the business part of the matter. We will talk when I see you. As the poems have for a long time been published, the sale has been materially checked, and you have not had a fair chance in the poetic market. Now we hope you will have a wider hearing. It is very important that we stereotype immediately the two little volumes, and you will greatly oblige me by writing at once, if you wish to make any verbal alterations or other changes in the large volume or the three smaller ones.

"I think it would be an excellent plan for you to add to this new edition everything you have written since the 'Panorama and other Poems' came out, that it may be complete up to this spring. There must be a portrait, of course, in the first volume, and I do not like at all the engraving from Hoit's picture. It is a hard, ungenial gentleman, and not J. G. W.'s face as I have known it. Have you a pleasant daguerreotype of the poet which you could send me at once? You say, in yr note, you will leave the whole business matter to me. You shall be well used" (letter, Essex Institute, Salem, Massachusetts).

2. "Mogg Megone" was retained in the edition. See Letter No. 773.

3. The ambrotype portrait was used in the edition.

4. Spoken by Samuel Johnson in 1770 and quoted in Boswell's *Life of Samuel Johnson.*

773. To James Thomas Fields

Amesbury March 11, 1857

My dear Fields.—

So then I must still carry the burden of my poetical sins?— Is there no way to lay the ghosts of unlucky rhymes. As for Mogg Megone he is very far from pleasant company but I see by thy letter that it is idle to think of shaking the tough old rascal off. Let him ride then—bad luck to the ugly face of him!—I had no business to make him, and it is doubtless poetical justice that he shall haunt me like another Frankenstein. But I *insist* on dropping "The Response," "Stanzas for the Times 1844," "Address at the opening of Pa Hall" and "The Album."[1] Their place is more than filled by the pieces added and sent with the book.

I have some eight or ten pieces written during the last year which I will send as soon as I can get them together. I have I believe all but one, and that I have got track of. They are:—

Moloch in State Street	72	lines
Burial of Barber	72	"
Pass of Sierra	44	"
The Conquest of Finland	68	"

Mayflowers	40	"
To my Namesake	124	"
First Flowers	26	"
Last Walk in Autumn	204	"
A Lay of Olden Time	60	"

On receiving thy letter I called on our Daguer[re]otypist and found him just packing up for "fresh fields and pastures new."[2] I had only a chance to get a sitting or two for the original as it was too late for the Hoit portrait. I send thee the result—the artist thinks the first picture—(the one already sent) the best in some respects as in this last the ambrotype process gives the hair and complexion a bleached look, whereas my hair is black and but sprinkled with grey sufficiently to give me the *external* sign of wisdom.

Both the pictures I have sent are good likenesses and yet they are very unlike each other. My sister says the one with the neck cloth spread out in such a jaunty way, must be sobered in its drapery, if it is used. The other picture is right in that respect. After all it is not of much consequence about the picture. I have no fear but that it will be at least as good as the one in the big book.

Paean—Shipley—To a Southern Statesman, and Pinckney's Resolutions—are to be added to the Voices of Freedom—in the 1st. Vol.

The Crisis—Charter Breakers[,] Slaves of Martinique[,] Knight of St. John and Holy Land may be added to the Miscellaneous poems in the Songs of Labor and other poems in the 2nd Vol. I do not like the way in which Muzzy arranged the table of contents—please see to it. If it is necessary, take any of the miscellaneous poems from the 1st vol. and add them to those of the Songs of Labor in the 2nd.

Very truly thy friend
John G. Whittier

My health will not admit of my going to Boston at present. The bare effort of writing a note is painful and wearisome.

Manuscript: Huntington Library, San Marino, California. Published, in Part, Pickard, *Life*, pp. 393–394.

1. These four poems were omitted in the edition.

2. Milton, *Lycidas*, line 193. The line should read: "To-morrow to fresh woods, and pastures new."

774. To James Thomas Fields

[Before March 18, 1857] [1]

Dear F.

Wilt this answer yr purpose? I could say no less and do not want to say more. [2]

I fear there are a great many inaccuracies of punctuation in the Muzzy book. Be good enough to have an eye to them.

Thine truly

J. G. W.

Give the note such a heading as seems best in thy eyes. I have made two suggestions as thou wilt see.

Manuscript: Huntington Library, San Marino, California.

1. Dated by reference to Whittier's prefatory note of March 18, 1857.

2. This refers to the prefatory "Note by the Author," dated "Amesbury, March 18, 1857," which reads as follows:

"In these volumes, for the first time, a complete collection of my poetical writings has been made. While it is satisfactory to know that these scattered children of my brain have found a home, I cannot but regret that I have been unable, by reason of illness, to give that attention to their revision and arrangement, which respect for the opinions of others and my own afterthought and experience demand.

"That there are pieces in this collection which I would 'willingly let die,' I am free to confess. But it is now too late to disown them, and I must submit to the inevitable penalty of poetical as well as other sins. There are others, intimately connected with the author's life and times, which owe their tenacity of vitality to the circumstances under which they were written, and the events by which they were suggested.

"The long poem of Mogg Megone was, in a great measure, composed in early life; and it is scarcely necessary to say that its subject is not such as the writer would have chosen at any subsequent period."

775. To Joshua Aubin

Amesbury March 20, 1857

My dear friend,

Hast thou any objection to our having Mr. L. Cole paint thy portrait for our Library Rooms? [1] I think he wd. get a good picture. I have seen some very good [ones] of his.

Please let me know at thy earliest convenience.

We all send our love to yr. family. [2]

In haste thy fd.

John G. Whittier

Manuscript: Amesbury Public Library.

1. Joshua Aubin had retired from his position as agent for the Amesbury Flannel Manufacturing Company in 1852 and was then living in Newburyport. He had given nearly 750 books, his own personal library, as a basis for the collection in the new Amesbury public library, which was opened in June 1856.

Lyman E. Cole (1812–1878?), a local painter, had painted signs for the Fré-

mont campaign in 1856. Apparently no portrait was painted at this time, for in
1866 F. K. Clarkson painted the portrait of Aubin which now hangs in the public
library.
    2. Joshua Aubin's wife was Mary Bussey Newell (1798?–1880), whom he
married in 1817.

776. To James Thomas Fields

Amesbury April 23, 1857

Dear Fields.
    I send the last of the copy—How does thee like this poem?
I am half inclined to think it better than those that precede
it. Let me see the sheets of the last volume also. I hope I shall
be able to look them over carefully.
    My sister wishes to know what has become of the portrait?

Thine truly
J. G. W.

Is there anything in my favor on yr. books?—or did the Panorama not sell? If there be anything I am just now in need
of it.
    The Clerk of the Weather, Merriam of N. York, I see is
sick.[1] I don't wonder at it. Nobody could stand the responsibility of such weather as we have had for the last fortnight.

Thine Ever
J. G. W.

Manuscript: New York Public Library.
    1. Ebenezer Meriam (1794–1864), a meteorologist, had a successful business
career and then settled in New York, where he contributed to many New York
papers.

777. To James Thomas Fields

Amesbury April 24, 1857

My dear Fields
    The picture which reached us last Evening is very Satisfac-
tory to my sisters and mother. It seems to me to be good as a
likeness and as an engraving. I suppose the Artist followed
the first Photograph sent thee. The hair seems to have been
brushed for the occasion giving me the appearance of one of
the "sleek headed men *who sleep o' nights.*"[1] I wish the fact
corresponded with the appearance. My mother who ought
to know thinks this the best picture I have ever had.
    My sister thanks thee for sending the engraving at her
request.

Very truly thine
John G. Whittier

Manuscript: Wellesley College.
1. *Julius Caesar*, I, ii, 193.

778. To an Unidentified Correspondent

Amesbury April 29, 1857

My dear friend

I comply with the request of the Pres. of the Michn. State
Agr. College in forwarding to thee the inclosed hoping it may
be in the power of thyself or Prof. Lowell to gratify his wish.[1]
Illness affecting my eyes and head, puts it out of my power
to write at present, otherwise I wd. have made an attempt
myself. It is a very admirable movement of the Young State.[2]

If thou canst not write this to order, please drop me a line
at once.

With heartiest admiration and sincerest respect, always

Thy friend
John G. Whittier

Manuscript: Swarthmore College.
1. Joseph R. Williams (1808–1861), a Harvard graduate and lawyer, had been
in the Midwest since 1835 and was an expert on the valuation and purchase of
western land. He had been a Free Soil candidate for the Senate in the 1850's
and helped found the Republican party in Ohio. He served as the first president
of Michigan State Agricultural College from 1857 to 1859. He later served in the
Michigan legislature.
2. The college, which had been founded in 1855, officially opened on May 13,
1857. Whittier had evidently been asked by Williams to write an ode for the opening services, and his 1850 poem, "Seed-Time and Harvest," was read at the services,
along with poems by Francis Osgood and I. M. Cravath.

779. To James Thomas Fields

May 1, 1857

As thee is not one who wearies in well-doing, let me ask of
thee to see friend Haskell of the "Transcript," and ask him to
help set on foot a subscription for the benefit of [Joshua
Coffin], the historian who is now sick in mind and body, at
W[orcester].[1] A kinder-hearted, quainter, and more genial
man never lived than he. He has done a good deal of good in
collecting material for the future historian and novelist. Let
the subscription take the shape of a testimonial for his eminent
services as historian and antiquarian. If Haskell will act as
treasurer, I will send my subscription to him.[2]

Source: Pickard, *Life*, p. 395.
1. Pickard had deleted the name. For further comments on Coffin and the

subscription see Letter Nos. 781–785. The subscription proved to be a success; Coffin's health improved; and he was able to return to his own home.

Daniel Haskell, then an editor for the *Transcript*, had been born in Newburyport. See Letter No. 572, note 2.

2. Fields replied to Whittier on May 1, 1857:

"I will speak to Haskell to-morrow about poor Mr.____, whom I never saw but once or twice; but as he is your friend, he shall have five dollars from a friend of yours, whose name is synonymous with *Meadows*. I will stir Haskell up to write of him in the 'Transcript,'

> "'And he shall say a good word for him,
>   Igo and ago;
> Else may Old Nick to shoe-strings chew him,
>   Iram, coram, dago.'

Let me whisper to you, if at any time you find your pockets light, it will give me great pleasure personally to shovel in a few 'rocks,' to be returned at any time when most convenient to you—or if they should never come back it would be better still. My hand is still lame, but I can sign a check at any time, if a friend needs it" (Pickard, *Life*, pp. 395–396).

780. To Joshua Augustus Dix

                                                   Amesbury May 2, 1857

J. A. Dix Esq.

Some five or six weeks ago I sent a poem entitled "My Namesake" to the Magazine. I learn by a line from my fd Fields that it had not been recd. some ten days ago. As it may possibly yet stray into thy hands, I write to say that it is now in the hands of Ticknor and Co. and about to appear in a new Edition of my poems and of course it is too late for the Magazine.

                                                   Very truly thy fd.
                                                   John G. Whittier

I have just recd. a note from Fields, in which he tells me the poem will not be wanted by him for some weeks.—I have made some alterations in it, and may possibly send it to yr. Magazine.—At any rate the copy sent you already you will oblige me by throwing aside if it ever reaches you.[1]

                                                   J. G. W.

Manuscript: Harvard University.

1. The poem was finally printed in *Harper's Weekly*, May 23, 1857. Dix was then serving as one of editors of Putnams where Whittier had first sent his poem. See Letter Nos. 784 and 785 for further comments on the poem.

781. To Samuel Edmund Sewall

Amesbury May 5, 1857

My dear friend

Our old friend *Joshua Coffin* is now at the Worcester Asylum suffering under an alienation of mind—induced, as it is thought, by poverty and apprehension of want. It is proposed to raise a sum among his anti-slavery and literary friends to be presented to him as a testimonial due to his character as a man and a scholar and antiquarian. I know thy heart is always right in such matters, and write thee for the purpose of asking thy aid in this effort. The money is to be appropriated to his use, at the Asylum if his health does not speedily mend. It is hoped the token of appreciation may have a good effect upon him.

D. N. Haskell of the Transcript or J. T. Fields will receive anything collected for the object. The old anti-Slavery friends I hope will feel disposed to do something for one of pioneers of the N. E. A. S.

Very truly and affectionately
Thy old fd.
John G. Whittier

Manuscript: Massachusetts Historical Society.

782. To the Editor of the Newburyport Herald

Amesbury [before May 6] , 1857[1]

To the Editor of the Herald:

In common with many others in this region, I regret to hear of the continued illness of Joshua Coffin, Esq.,—so well and widely known as the author of the best and most complete town history, which has yet been given to the public:[2] and whose researches into the ancient records of the Massachusetts Colony, have been of great service to more than one of our popular historical authors. His literary and antiquarian labors,—the great value of which will be better appreciated hereafter,—have been poorly compensated; and his present misfortune is aggravated by the evils of pecuniary embarrassment. It has occurred to me that there are hundreds in this state, who would esteem it a privilege to contribute something by the way of testimonial to the worthy man, scholar and antiquarian. The people of Newbury and Newburyport, owe him such a testimonial, and there are many in other places who will be glad to unite with them.—Hoping that you will look with favor upon this proposition and will lend the influence of your position to it, I am very truly your friend.[3]

J. G. W.

Source: The Newburyport Herald, May 6, 1857. The letter was also printed in the Boston Transcript, May 7, 1857.

Recipients: Joseph B. Morss (1808–1883), the publisher and listed as the editor of the Herald, ran the publishing firm of Morss and Brewster in Newburyport.

George J. L. Colby (1813–1890) also served as an editor for the Herald at this time.

1. The letter was dated as "May" by Whittier, but it was published on May 6, 1857.

2. A Sketch of the History of Newbury, Newburyport, and West Newbury from 1635 to 1845 (Boston, 1845).

3. Following Whittier's letter was this note from the editors: "The above suggestion is worthy of its liberal author. What the circumstances of Mr. Coffin are, we have no special means of knowing, but while the citizens of Newbury would never see him suffer, there are others all about the county, and out of the county who would be glad to contribute to his comfort and benefit, if any person connected with him, should present his case."

783. To James Thomas Fields

[Before May 11, 1857][1]

Dear Fields,

I inclose $5. which please hand friend Haskell. Don't let him use my name in the paper again—however.[2] Thy parody of Capt Grose set me to rhyming when I sat down to write thee.[3]

Tell Haskell that I have seen some of the Newburyport women—Mrs. Smith and Mrs. Spaulding etc.[4] and that they will do something for Joshua.

Thine ever
J. G. W.

> Dear F. we'll take a friendly pride in
> The absent hand and heart confiding,
> And if then any are deriding
>   That plea of Haskell's
> We'll count the cautious robes they hide in
>   As sheer wrap rascals!
>
> Oh, well-paid author, fat-fed scholar,
> Whose pockets jingle with the dollar!
> No sheriff's hand upon your collar,
>   No duns to bother,
> Think on't; a tithe of what you swallow
>   Would save your brother!

More blest is he among the living
Who gives than he who is receiving:
And that last robe which Time is weaving
      To bear us off in
Shall be the lighter for our giving
      A lift to ——.

And now Heaven help the old and poor
And keep the gaunt wolf from his door!
I send for lack of silver ore
      These paper shadows:
Thou'lt add, I'm sure, as many more,
      My dear friend—*Meadows*.

So shall the public crowd and mingle
Where'er thou hangest out thy shingle,
And all the joys the happy ingle
      Of human love yields
Be thine, and blessings never single
      Add Fields to Fields!

Manuscript: Haverhill Public Library. Published, in Part: Pickard, *Life*, pp. 396–397.
    1. Dated by similarity of contents with Letter No. 784.
    2. Fields had shown Haskell Whittier's letter of May 1, 1857, who quoted from it in the *Transcript* of May 7, as well as reprinting in full Whittier's letter to the Newburyport *Herald*, before May 6, 1857 (No. 782).
    3. Fields's lines in Letter No. 779, note 2, were a parody of Burns's "Written on an Envelope, Enclosing a Letter to Captain Grose."
    4. Sarah Jane Parker Tappan (1822–1904), who married Reverend Samuel Jones Spaulding, pastor of the Whitefield Church in Newburyport, in 1851, had been a member of the Brook Farm experiment before her marriage. She was also a teacher and writer and contributed to many magazines.

784. To James Thomas Fields

Amesbury May 11, 1857

My dear Fields
    I thank thee for thy suggestion relative to the Poem "Namesake." I did send it to Putnam's Mage. six weeks ago— It has probably gone to the grand national Morgue—the receptacle of dead letters—ere this. If one of yr clerks could copy the poem, as it is now printed, it might not be too late for Putnam. I feel some hesitation about asking this favor, for I am already conscience-troubled with my obligations to thee. And here I am reminded to thank thee for thy ready sympathy with my project for the benefit of my old friend Joshua. If it is not too late, we will save him from the twin demons of

poverty and anxiety. He shall be made as happy as if he had found the Ms of Goody Morse's witch confession,[1] or Lydia Wardwell's petticoat which she left in John Easton's keeping, when she went through the broad aisle of Newbury meeting house, as Godiva rode through Coventry.[2] I am sure Haskell will do his best with such a terrible imprecation hanging over him as is contained in thy parody of Captn. Grose.

I will take an early opportunity to send back the books thou wast so kind as to lend me.

Ever and truly thy friend
John G. Whittier

Manuscript: Swarthmore College.

1. Elizabeth Morse (c. 1615), the wife of William Morse, a shoemaker in New-bury, was accused in 1680 of being a witch and condemned by a Boston court to death by hanging on May 20, 1680. She obtained a reprieve, but was again tried in 1681 when she was finally released and allowed to return to her home. Whittier utilized the facts about the case found in Coffin's *History of Newbury* for his fictional treatment of the supposed witchcraft in *Margaret Smith's Journal.*

2. Lydia Wardwell, a young wife from Hampton, New Hampshire, was supposed to have appeared naked in the Newbury meeting house in 1663. Her actions were intended to answer those who had accused her of false teaching and to illustrate the wickedness in the church. For her actions she was whipped and fined.

785. To James Thomas Fields

Amesbury May 15, 1857

Dear Fields:

I am most agreeably surprised at thy success in transform-ing my verses into a fifty dollar check which has just come to hand. It beat altogether the tricks of the old Alchymists.[1]

I am rejoiced to hear of the success of the Coffin subscrip-tion. Some ladies from Ny. Port have just called on me with the agreeable intelligence that our courtly old friend has so far recovered as to be able to return to his home. If now we can raise two hundred dollars for him it will enable him to hold the old home where his ancestors for many generations have lived and set the old man on his legs again and warm and gladden his heart. His bodily and mental health seems now very nearly restored and he fully appreciates every kind-ness. Tell Haskell that he has done so well, already I hope he will be able to raise his figure to $100. I felt sure he would be the very man for the object. Thine Ever and gratefully

J. G. W.

Manuscript: Middlebury College.

1. Apparently Fields had gotten *Harper's* to accept Whittier's poem, "My Namesake," for fifty dollars.

786. To Henry Ingersoll Bowditch[1]

Amesbury July 1, 1857

Inscription on Sun-Dial
by
John Greenleaf Whittier[2]

With warning hand I mark Time's rapid flight
From Life's glad morning to its solemn night;
Yet, through the dear God's love, I also show
The light above me by this shade below.

Dear Friend
Pardon my tardy reply to thy note and believe me very truly[3]

Thy friend
John G. Whittier

Manuscript: Brown University.
1. The identification is conjectural.
2. The title and "by John Greenleaf Whittier" are written in a hand different from Whittier's.
3. Bowditch had come into possession of an old silver sundial and had it placed in a large copper dish on which were engraved the signs of the zodiac. In December 1854 he asked Whittier for some verses to be engraved on the copper and received these lines in reply. Writing to Dr. Sparhawk on January 15, 1856, Bowditch said: "The more I read Whittier's lines, the more I admire them. Everybody is delighted with them and I am•obliged to give copies in every direction" (Sparhawk, *Whittier at Close Range,* p. 94). This present letter is probably in answer to a request from Bowditch for another copy of the original verses.

787. To the Salem Young Men's Union

Amesbury July 18, 1857

My dear friend
I am sorry that I cannot comply with the request of the Salem Young Men's Union. A powerful affliction of the head and eyes compels me to decline making any new literary engagements. Hoping that this will not occasion your Society any serious inconvenience I am very truly thy fd.

John G. Whittier

Manuscript: Essex Institute, Salem, Massachusetts.

788. To William Rounseville Alger

Amesbury July 20, 1857

Dear friend

From my heart I thank thee for thy noble Oration.[1] It was the right word in the right place. The stupid "flunkyism" of the "brief authorites"[2] of Boston only serves to give it a wider audience and more permanent influence.

Allow me in this place to thank thee also for the pleasure and profit I have derived from thy selections of Oriental poetry—a book full of wisdom and beauty.[3]

Very truly thy fd.
John G. Whittier

Manuscript: Yale University.

Recipient: William Rounseville Alger (1822–1905), a Unitarian clergyman and author, was then pastor of the Bulfinch Street Church in Boston. He wrote many books on religious topics in the 1850's and was a popular lyceum speaker. He later became chaplain for the Massachusetts House of Representatives and wrote a biography of Edwin Forrest.

1. Alger had been asked to give the fourth of July oration in Boston before the city authorities. But since the speech was a protest against the slave power of the South and proslavery supporters in the North, the city authorities refused to vote him the customary thanks or publish the address.

2. *Measure for Measure,* II, ii, 118. The line reads: "But man, proud man, drest in a little brief authority."

3. *The Poetry of the East* (Boston, 1856) was reprinted many times.

789. To William James Allinson[1]

Amesbury July 20, 1857

My dear William

I send according to thy request—making an exception in favor of one who has such vouchers as Sumner and thyself—although quite agreeing with Chas Lamb in the general question.

I did not see the article thee refer to on "the Sycamores." Send it if convenient.

I am glad to hear of thee in the old E[vening] Post[2] again. I was fearful I should have to write an elegy for thee after the fashion of Lycidas substituting for water Nicaraguan need.

Very cordially thy fd.
John G. Whittier

Manuscript: University of Virginia.

1. The identification is conjectural and based on the salutation, "My dear William."

2. The reading is uncertain.

790. To Mary Esther Carter

Amesbury Second Day Mg August 17, 1857

My dr fd.

Elizabeth wishes me to say that she intended to answer thy favor today, but as mother is quite ill with a billious attack, she does not feel able—She is greatly obliged for thy letters. We feel a great deal of sympathy for Daniel—[1] It is sad for him to lose his mother in such a way—but to her it may be a blessing.

We had a pleasant visit from Lucy Larcom last week—Bro. Franklin was here on Sixth day on his way to Boston—will be back tomorrow or next day.

The country about us never looked so beautiful as now— We went to the Salisbury pine woods yesterday after meeting —I never saw such perfect and glorious effects of light and shadow—such perspectives of green earth and blue sky—such grottoes and labyrinths of verdure, barred at the entrance by solid beams of sunlight, like golden gates. At such times I wish I were a painter.

We miss thee not a little and shall be glad to see thee again in Amesbury.[2]

I saw the Aubins last week—they spoke of thee and their Rehoboth friends—

We have had the famous Moncure Conway the late Unitarian minister at Washington. He came over last week with the Curzons.

Mother and E and Mary send their love—

Ever and truly thy fd.

John G. Whittier

Manuscript: Wellesley College. Published, in Part: Sparhawk, *Whittier at Close Range*, pp. 26–27.

Recipient: Mary Esther Carter (1817–1903), the daughter of a Newbury sea captain with an independent income, lived in Amesbury for twenty-five years. Her friendship with the Whittiers, especially Elizabeth and Mrs. Whittier, began in the 1840's when a spiritualist circle led by Miss Carter was formed. Whittier, his mother, and Elizabeth sometimes attended these meetings along with other neighbors who hoped to receive messages from the dead. Whittier wrote her a valentine in 1849 which ran in part:

> "Long have I sought and vainly have I yearned
>   To meet some spirit that could answer mine;
> Then chide me not that I so soon have learned
>   To talk with thine."

Whittier's friendship with her deepened during the 1850's and she remained closely associated with him and Elizabeth in the 1860's. At this time Miss Carter's house was a social and cultural center for Amesbury residents. In her later years she lived in Boston.

1. Mary Carter's cousin, Daniel Maxfield (1843–1927).
2. Miss Carter was then residing temporarily in Boston.

791. To Lucy Larcom

Amesbury August 18, 1857

My dear friend.

Agreeably to my promise I return the MS. with many
thanks for the perusal. A great many of the poems were new
to us—"The Chamber called Peace" is really one of the sweetest
poems of Christian consolation I ever read. It is worthy of all
praise as a work of art too.—I do not see a very fine poem of
thine published in the Era—a splendid autumnal painting—
as I remember it. Was it called *"Indian Summer?"*—I have
marked on thy list of contents with a + those I liked best.
In the 2nd verse of "Eureka"—I don't like the sound of "laurels and *gore"*—The thought and general execution of the
piece are too good to be spoiled by a poor line or two. "The
old Sabbath Days" is good—I would not publish many of the
earlier pieces. The volume will be better. They have done
their work—let them pass. I would not like to see a large volume. I would restrict it to 100 or 125 pages at the most.[1]

I intended yesterday to have seen thee at N. Port—but my
mother was taken quite ill on First day night—and has been
confined to her bed ever since. It is a billious attack but it
alarms us—at her age and in her weak state, she can bear but
little—Well—we are all in God's hands and He is good. May He
give us strength to meet all His dispensations and faith to look
beyond present shadows to the Eternal Light!—

Elizabeth sends her love.
Ever and truly thy friend
John G. Whittier

Manuscript: Massachusetts Historical Society.

1. Whittier wrote Miss Larcom again about her manuscript and received this
reply on September 22:

"I thank thee for thy note, and for the kind criticism of my little poems it
contained. And first of all, I want to tell thee what I have done about them.—One
may be excused for using Friends' language when one is *friendly*, mayn't she?—

"Well, I called on Mr. Jewett, and asked him if he wanted to read some poetry.
He replied that poetry was rather 'out of his line,' and suggested Ticknor and
Fields. So last week I wrote to the latter gentlemen, and have just received a reply,
which I enclose with the inquiry whether your opinion agrees with theirs. If it
does, I will put the MS. to sleep for this winter, if not longer. There is no reason that I
know of, why I should want them published *now*; and it may be much better
to let them rest awhile. I said to myself, when looking over the pieces after I had
arranged them to the best of my ability, 'Rather slender, if you call this *poetry*.'
And perhaps, if I wait, something will come to me which will put more stamina
into the volume—if there ever is one.—If I have begun to see my deficiencies, that
ought to be one step forward. I have found great enjoyment in trying to speak out
my thought thus far, though 'with stammering lips and insufficient sound,' as
Mrs. Browning has it. I long and am ready to strive for nobler thoughts and more
worthy utterances:—but the thought must come by inspiration,—and the utterances too, if genuine. After all, it is only to *live* the highest there is in one, and

then speech, and all that is external, will take its most beautiful form. I cannot conceive of a conceited poet—is there such a phenomenon. Or indeed I might ask, is there conceit in any true thing?

"But I am wandering from the matter about which I began. I should prefer Ticknor to any other publisher, and regard his opinion on these matters highly. But he does not hint that he would *ever* be willing to examine my 'specimens'; why he should say 'good as they are,' I don't understand, when he probably knows nothing about them. But I used your name, as you gave me leave to do, and perhaps he thought that an equivalent for their merits" (Shepard, "Letters of Lucy Larcom to the Whittiers," pp. 507–508).

Whittier continued to urge publication of her poems, writing personally to Fields on October 8, 1860 (Letter No. 953). An edition of her poems was finally published by Fields in 1868.

792. To an Unidentified Correspondent

                    Amesbury Fourth Day Morng September 23, 1857
My dear friend

I am under real obligation to thee for thy package and thy letter enclosing one to thyself from Mattie Griffith.[1] I take the latter, of course, with due allowance for the writer's imagination ascribing to my writings the beauty and significance which they borrowed from her own mind and heart. Still it gives me deep joy to believe that I have not wholly written in vain, and that I have contributed somewhat to the happiness of others.

I fear thy friend would not thank thee as cordially as I do, for the kind act of sending me her letter. It would have given me pleasure to have seen her.

I have been reading that wonderful book of St. Augustine's. My own heart melts in the warmth of the great-hearted African. There are passages of very great power—a power combined always with tenderness and beauty. His account of the loss of his early friend and the effect of the bereavement upon his sensitive nature, is a deeper and profounder "In Memoriam," than Tennyson has sung.

It was very kind in thee to send the "Pinnain Syrup." With but small faith in medicines, I shall give it a fair trial. This cool wet weather affects me very much, and makes even the writing of a note painful.

                              Very truly and sincerely thy fd.
                                    John G. Whittier

Manuscript: Cornell University.

1. Mattie Griffith (d. 1906), a Kentucky woman who emancipated her slaves, had published a book of poems in 1852. She married Albert G. Brown (1835–1891), who later served as an editor for various New York papers.

793. To William Currier

[September 24, 1857]

To the Editor of the Villager:—

I have learned with much surprise, that a resolution adopted at the late Temperance meeting in this place, has been
objected to, as liable to be understood as favoring a class of
social amusements by no means calculated to promote the
moral health of the community.[1] As the author of the resolution in question, permit me to say, that neither the language
of that resolution, nor the tastes, habits and well known opinions of its writer, justify any such inference. It recognized
the fact of the desire of the young for excitement and amusement, and that that desire was too often gratified at the expense of sobriety and sound morality. The sole aim of the
resolution was to induce those more experienced and better
established in the principles of morality to direct that natural,
but too often perverted desire, to objects in themselves innocent and rational;—to watch over and regulate, in a spirit of
kindness and sympathy, the amusements and social pleasures
of the young, discountenancing everything inconsistent with
the maxims of a morality strict without ascetism, and Christian rather than Pharisaical. I do not believe in the propriety
of leaving the young to the unrestricted and unregulated
exercise of their love for recreation and social enjoyment, nor
on the other hand, do I believe in the wisdom or practicality
of its entire repression and crushing out. But I do believe in
such a combination of authority and sympathy, of wise
restraint where necessary, and genial encouragement and
guidance within proper limits,—as may be made, under Him,
who can alone give success to human effort, an important
means of promoting the temperance and moral health of the
young and inexperienced. I would throw open, as far as possible, to this class the curious and beautiful in Art, Science and
Literature—the telescopic revelations of Astronomy—the
wonders of Geology—the lithography of the Eternal finger on
the primal formations. I would open to them new sources of
enjoyment in the studies of Natural History and Botany, and
show them the almost magical results of Experimental Chem-
istry. I would give them every opportunity to listen to lectures
and discourses from variously-gifted orators and thinkers. I
would encourage reading circles—healthful sports and exer-
cises, and excursions amidst the serene beauty of Nature, so
well calculated to exalt the mind towards that which St.
Augustine speaks of as the "Eternal Beauty always new and

always old." I would promote Libraries and Debating Clubs
[—] whatever, in short, promises to unite social enjoyment
with the culture of the mind and heart and the healthful
enjoyment of a sound mind in a sound body. I do not under-
value other instrumentalities, especial the higher ones of a
religious nature. But at the same time I believe that a cheerful,
social Christian is better than a sour and ascetic one. That
good old Puritan, Richard Baxter,[2] used to regret his own
melancholy and gloomy temperament, arising mainly from
bodily infirmity, and in the latter part of his life strove to
introduce a more cheerful disposition among his religious
friends. "True religion," he says, "is not a matter of fears,
tears and scruples: it doth principally consist in obedience,
love and joy."[3]

For myself, so far from advocating laxity of moral disci-
pline, I strongly deprecate the increase and weak indulgence
which prevail at the present time. I believe in law and order—
parental authority—the unescapable responsibilities of the
adult members of society in respect to the younger. But wisdom is profitable to direct; and it is by no means wise to
disregard, even for a good object, the natural laws which
govern mind and matter. Unnatural repression in one direction is sure to lead to a corresponding protuberance of deformity in another. The folly of the Flathead Indian mother
who binds with bark the forehead of her infant until the
frontal portion is forced backward in idiotic prominence,
finds a parallel in all efforts at moral reform which overlook
the great laws of our being.

· J. G. W.

Source: The Amesbury *Villager,* September 24, 1857.

Recipient: William H. B. Currier (1828–1903) was editor and publisher of the
Essex Transcript and the *Villager* for thirty-five years. He was also editor of the
Amesbury *Daily News,* which began in 1888. He held many prominent town
positions in Amesbury, besides serving in the Massachusetts House of Representatives.

1. A meeting of the Essex County Temperance Society was held on September 16, 1857, in Amesbury. Whittier, along with others, helped write a series of
five resolutions, the fifth of which read: "As the natural but often misdirected
desire of the young for excitement and amusement, is a great cause of the use of
intoxicants on their part, we regard the innocent gratification of that desire by
rational recreation—the establishment of Lyceums, Reading Rooms and Libraries
and the encouragement of pleasant social re-unions and gatherings, participated
in by the elder parties of the community, as efficient agencies for the promotion
of Temperance and moral Health."

2. Richard Baxter (1615–1691), a Presbyterian divine, was a voluminous
writer on religious subjects. Whittier wrote a long essay on Baxter, "Richard
Baxter" (reprinted in Whittier, *Works,* VI, 146–183).

3. Quoted by Whittier in "Richard Baxter" (Whittier, *Works,* VI, 151).

794. To Francis Henry Underwood[1]

Amesbury September 24, 1857

Dear friend.

I enclose a little poem written by Lucy Larcom of Norton. The sentiment is one which the universal heart responds to, and it seems to me that there is a beautiful simplicity in its thought and expression.[2] At any rate I should have been glad to call such a poem my own—I send it to thee, in the hope that it may find a place in your new Magazine to which I wish all manner of success—[3]

Very truly thy fd.

J. G. Whittier

Manuscript: New York Public Library.

1. The identification is conjectural; it is based on the allusion to the "new Magazine," the *Atlantic Monthly*, in the letter.

2. "Across the River," which Miss Larcom had sent Whittier on September 22, 1857. On October 30, Miss Larcom wrote Whittier: "I received, a few days ago, the poem 'Across the River,' with a 'respectfully declined,' from the office of the new Maga. I was not at all surprised, only that I did not certainly know that you had sent it. With all deference to the judgment of the gentlemen editors, I think it is quite a decent little poem, with the changes you made; and it is a much greater pleasure to me, to know that you liked it, than it would have been to see it in print among acknowledged seers and songsters. But I am sorry you had your trouble for nothing" (Shepard, "Letters of Lucy Larcom to the Whittiers," pp. 510–511).

3. The *Atlantic Monthly*, a magazine of literature, art, and politics, had been initiated in the summer of 1857 at a dinner given by Moses Phillips, the publisher. Longfellow, Emerson, Lowell, Holmes, and others were present when Lowell was nominated as editor-in-chief and Francis Underwood as his assistant. Holmes suggested the name, the *Atlantic Monthly*, and the first issue was planned for November. Soon after that meeting Lowell wrote Whittier on August 10, 1857:

"I write to you in behalf of the editors of the new Magazine to be published in Boston, to ask you to contribute to it. They hope to have you for a regular contributor, and will make the terms of payment agreeable to yourself. The Mag. I understand will be a free one, and on the right side. Emerson, Longfellow, Prescott, Motley, Holmes, Hawthorne, Whipple and others are, *I know*, to be contributors. I hope that no engagements will stand in the way of your writing [for] it.

"I take particular pleasure in executing this commission, because it gives me a chance to thank you for a poem of yours (The last walk in Autumn), which gave me a special thrill of delight—so much so, indeed, that I thought of writing to you at the time. Nor let me forget the Sycamores in my thanks.

"Should you send anything, address

"F. H. Underwood, care of Phillips, Sampson and Co., Boston" (Albree, ed., *Whittier Correspondence*, p. 130).

795. To Caroline Tallant

Amesbury, Mass. October 22, 1857

My dear fr.

Thy letter took me almost as much by surprise as the entrance of the veritable Hugh himself would have done.[1] When I wrote the poem in question I never expected that a fair descendant of the Milesian Treeplanter would be called up. In fact Hugh Talent was to me a pleasant myth, a shadowy phantom of tradition only.[2]

Since receiving thy letter I have ascertained for a certainty that the Hugh of my ballad and thy gr. grandfather are one and the same. I am not sure of the date of the planting of the trees, but in the early part of the 18 Century certainly Hugh at that time was a resident of Haverhill on the Merrimack now a town of some 10,000 inhabitants. The trees, 20 of which are now standing, he planted on the river bank before the mansion of Col. Richard Saltonstall, br. of Gov. Saltonstall of Conn.[3] The tradition of him is pretty correctly given in the ballad. After leaving Atkinson, then a part of Haverhill, he moved to Pelham or Windham, became a considerable landowner, and was noted for his love of fun and lawsuits. He took the Tory side in the Revolution—, was outlawed, shot at and driven off by his neighbors, but soon managed to return. These latter facts I have just learned. I wish that I had had them as well as those of thy own letter, when writing "The Sycamores."

The trees are about 12 miles up the River from my residence. I should like to show them to a descendant of the merry troubadour who planted them. I give the name as it stands in the Haverhill records, *Talent*. I presume it should be Tallant. Of course thou art at liberty to alter it in the poem.

The incident of Washington is true.[4]

Very truly thy friend,
John G. Whittier

Source: Typed copy, Essex Institute, Salem, Massachusetts. Published: Pickard, *Life*, pp. 399–400.

Recipient: Caroline L. Tallant (1830–1877), the daughter of a Nantucket family, taught high school in Hartford in the 1850's and died in Boston, unmarried. In 1857 she had a small pamphlet printing of Whittier's poem about her great-grandfather, Hugh Tallant, "The Sycamores," issued as a Thanksgiving souvenir for family and friends.

1. Miss Tallant's letter to Whittier and her response to his letter are printed in Pickard, *Life*, pp. 397–398 and 400–401.

2. In the original printing of the poem (*National Era*, June 11, 1857) Whittier spelled the name "Talent." It was later changed to "Tallant."

In Mirick's *History of Haverhill* the following account of Hugh Tallant (1685

or 1687–1795), on which Whittier based his poem, is given: "About this time, the syca-
more-trees, now standing before Widow Samuel W. Duncan's mansion, were
set out. The work was done by one Hugh Talent, a wanderer from the green fields
of Erin and who was a famous fiddler. He lived with Colonel Richard Saltonstall,
in capacity of a servant, and tradition says that he frequently made harmonious
sounds with his cat-gut and rosin for the gratification of the village swains and
lasses" (Pickard, *Life*, pp. 401–403).

3. Richard Saltonstall (1672–1714), a Harvard graduate, served as a representative from Haverhill in 1699 and was a colonel of the local regiment.

His brother Gurdon Saltonstall (1666–1724) was governor of Connecticut
from 1708 to 1724.

4. In the poem Washington is described as remarking, on a visit to Haverhill,
that he had never seen a fairer prospect.

796. To James Russell Lowell

[Before November 4, 1857] [1]

My dear Lowell

Yr first number is excellent.[2] I send for December (I hope
in season)—a bit of a Yankee ballad the spirit of which pleases
me more than the execution.[3] Will it do? Look at it, and use
the freedom of an old friend towards it and its author.

J. G. W.

The incident occured sometime in last century.[4] The refrain
is the actual song of the women on their march. To relish it
one must understand the peculiar tone and dialect of the
ancient Marbleheads.

Manuscript: Harvard University.

1. Dated by reference to "Skipper Ireson's Ride" and Lowell's letter of November 4, 1857, in response to Whittier's query.

2. The first issue of the *Atlantic Monthly* was in November.

3. "Skipper Ireson's Ride" was printed in the December number of the *Atlantic
Monthly*. See Letter Nos. 797, 799, and 800 for further comments on the poem.

Lowell wrote to Whittier about the poem on November 4: "I thank you
heartily for the ballad, which will go into the next number. I like it all the better
for its provincialism—in all fine pears, you know, we can taste the old *pucker*.
I know the story well. I am familiar with Marblehead and its dialect, and as the
burthen is intentionally provincial I have taken the liberty to print it in such a way
as shall give the peculiar accent, thus:—

> "'Cap'n Ireson for his horrd horrt
> Was torred and feathered and corried in a corrt.'

That's the way I've always 'horrd it'—only it began, 'Old Flud Ireson.' What a good
name Ireson (son of wrath) is for the hero of such a history!

"You see that "Tritemius" is going the rounds. I meant to have sent you the
proofs, and to have asked you to make a change in it where these four rhymes
come together (assonances, I mean)—'door,' 'poor,' 'store,' 'more.' It annoyed
me, but I do not find that any one else has been troubled by it, and everybody
likes the poem. I am glad that the Philistines have chosen some verses of mine
for their target, not being able to comprehend the bearing of them. I mean I am
glad that they did it rather than pick out those of any one else for their scapegoat.
I shall not let you rest till I have got a New England pastoral out of you. This last
is cater-cousin to it, at least, being a piscatorial. . . . The sale of Maga. has been

very good considering the times, and I think you will find the second number better than the first" (Pickard, *Life*, p. 407).

4. As with so many of his narratives and ballads, Whittier was mistaken in his facts, for it was skipper Ireson's crew, not the skipper himself, who were responsible for sailing away from a sinking ship. See Whittier's headnote to the poem in Scudder, ed., *Complete Poetical Works*, p. 55.

797. To James Russell Lowell

Amesbury November 4, 1857[1]

My dear Lowell.

I send thee a night piece which if not as good as Parnell's—has at least the merit of presenting American ideas—and the philosophy of Christian democracy.[2] It pleases me—but, that is no reason that it should anybody else. If it can have a place in the Mage for Decr it is at thy service—if not please return it.

What is thy decision as to Capt Ireson? It occurs to me that the line in the first verse

Mahomet mounting on Al Borák.

should read

"Islam's prophet on Al Borák."

Is it not matter of thankfulness that Massachusetts Know Nothingism has gone down at last to its place!—[3]

Ever and truly
J. G. W.

Manuscript: Yale, University. Published, in Part: Pickard, *Life*, pp. 410–411.
1. Dated by Pickard as October 4, 1857.
2. "The Eve of Election," which was finally printed in the *National Era*, January 21, 1858.
Thomas Parnell's poem is "The Night Piece on Death."
3. The Know-Nothing party had failed badly in the presidential election of 1856, though in Massachusetts it elected Gardner for his third term. In the fall election of 1857 the Republican and Frémont Americans elected Banks as governor over Gardner, the Know-Nothing candidate, and ended that party's influence in Massachusetts.

798. To an Unidentified Correspondent

Amesbury November 4, 1857

Dear friend

I have no objection to thy use of my poems, in thy collection. I know they will be in good company, better perhaps than they deserve.

Very truly thy fd.
John G. Whittier

I shall be glad to see Darley's illustration of Maud.[1] Will you
send me a copy?—

Manuscript: University of Rochester.
1. Felix O. C. Darley (1822–1888), an American illustrator, was noted for his
pen and ink drawings. He illustrated the works of Irving, Cooper, Longfellow,
and other American authors.

799. To James Russell Lowell

Amesbury November 5, 1857
My dear Lowell.

I leave the matter of the burthen of my ditty to thy better
judgment as to the spelling. The substitution of "corried"
for "rid" does not suit me so well, but I am not particularly
strenuous about it.

Would it not be well to put it in italics and with quotation
marks, thus:

"Here's Cap'n Ireson etc"

Instead of "was tarred and feathered," it should read as I have
it "Tarred and feathered" and the provincial spelling should
only be used where the women are represented as singing
"Here's Cap'n Ireson etc." Where *I* repeat it, the odd spelling
and the quotation marks should be omitted. At least so it
strikes me.

I had just sent thee a line when I recd. thine. In it I suggest
an alteration of a single line.

I am uncertain what to say as to the money suggestion. All
I know is that such an article as "Cap'n Ireson" would bring
me $50 from another source. It is not worth it perhaps. I
shall set no price upon my pieces but shall leave the matter
to the publishers, who can best judge what they are worth. I
have suffered in my small way in these hard times, and was
beginning to fear that my creditors will not have the christian
grace to forgive my debts. The state of my health—which
makes the writing of a letter a painful burthen—renders it
necessary that I should receive the value of what I am able to
do.

I am glad to hear that the Maga. is doing so well, and thanking thee for thy kind suggestions

I am very truly thy fd.
John G. Whittier

J R Lowell Esq
The "pastoral" shall be thought of. "The Witch's Daughter"—

was an attempt of the kind, but not entirely satisfactory. I
may possibly do better.[1]

Since writing this have recd a line from F. H. U. with the
proof. I have on further consideration adopted your suggestions as to the refrain—and written him accordingly.

W.

Manuscript: Harvard University. Published, in Part: Pickard, *Life*, pp. 408–409.
    1. See Letter No. 796, note 2, where Lowell says: "I shall not let you rest till
I have got a New England pastoral out of you."

800. To Francis Henry Underwood

Amesbury November 6, 1857

Dear Friend

I thank thee for sending the proof of Capt. Ireson—with
thy suggestions. I adopt them, as thou wilt see, mainly. It is
an improvement. As it stands now I like the thing well,
"hugely," as Capt Shandy would say.[1]

As to the pecuniary allusion of thy note, I am sorely in
want of money (as who is not at this time)—but of course
will await your convenience.

The magazine *will, shall, must* succeed. The election of
Banks is a good beginning for it.

Thy friend
John G. Whittier

Source: Perry, "The Editor Who Was Never the Editor," pp. 699–700.
    1. Laurence Sterne, *Tristram Shandy*, Vol. II, chapter 17.

801. To James Russell Lowell

Amesbury November 10, 1857

My dear Lowell

I have no complete copy of the verses I last sent thee, but I
believe there is a grammatical error in the last verse, 3rd line.
If it is to be printed pray for the credit of the maga. look to
it.

Thine Ever
J. G. W.

Manuscript: Swarthmore College.

802. To Mary Esther Carter

Amesbury November 17, 1857

My dear friend.

I should have long ere this answered thy note, but have been uncertain where to direct. Even now, I send to the care of Jos E. Hood, as I suppose he will know thy whereabouts.[1]

Believe me dear friend, thou wast not mistaken in supposing that I should receive thy kind word at parting in the spirit in which it was written.

> "Kind words shall never die
> Saith my philosophy"

and I heartily reciprocate thy own. Yet I cannot but feel that thou hast greatly overrated the benefits derived from my society and friendship. In fact, I feel very much as a debtor in these hard times might be supposed to feel, if his creditor should take occasion to thank him for his indebtedness. The obligation is on my side rather than thine. To me and mine, thou hast been an ever kind and sympathizing friend—one whom we never met without pleasure or parted with without regret. For myself as for them, *my heart thanks thee*. Thou hast cheered us, and helped us in many ways by example as well as words. We have read, thought, hoped, feared, enjoyed and suffered together, and the ties of affection and sympathy so woven from the very tissue of our lives are not easily severed. We miss thee greatly in our little circle; we shall often speak of thee in the dark winter days, and long to see thy familiar face in the light of our evening fires.

What beautiful and serene November days we have had!—The weather now grows colder with keen premonitions of winter. We have been much as usual in health, but I am now suffering from one of my severe neuralgic attacks which has kept me wakeful for several nights, and really unfitted for anything.

There is nothing very new here. Mr. Mott continues to be a prominent topic. Thy cousin Daniel has taken him under his special patronage. We have a new store opened where Uncle Squires traded,[2] which is rather convenient, as Neighbor Young[3] like the wild Highlander in the Baillie's store only "keeps *shop*"—there being nothing in it.

Willie has gone to Washington![4] He started on Seventh day morning. I saw the poor fellow off. There was a prophecy of home-sickness in his face as he left. We shall all miss him—Aunt Dolly especially.[5]

Banks is Govr. by 24,000 plurality. The morning after the election Elizabeth crowned his picture with thy wreath.

Mother sends much love. So does Lizzy. We shall be glad to hear from thee. In the meantime I am Ever

and affectionately thy fd.

John G. Whittier

Excuse this bad penmanship. Head ache and teeth ache must be my apology for that, as well as matter written.

Manuscript: Wellesley College. Published, in Part: Sparhawk, *Whittier at Close Range*, pp. 71–72.

1. See Letter No. 525, note 5. Hood was then living in Springfield where he was one of the editors for the Springfield *Republican.*

2. James Squires (1789–1885), a Quaker neighbor of Whittier, was a cotton spinner in an Amesbury factory. In his later years Whittier organized benefits and celebrations on his birthdays.

3. Benjamin Young ran a local grocery store on School Street where Whittier often spent evenings. He and his daughter also attended the spiritualist sessions at Mary Esther Carter's.

4. William Wallace Colby (1835–1905), an Amesbury neighbor of Whittier, was a local painter.

5. Dolly Currier Osgood (b. 1789), a friend of Abigail Whittier, was a participant in the spiritualist circle of Mary Esther Carter. She had one daughter, who had died.

803. To James Thomas Fields

Amesbury November 24, 1857

My dear Fields

Will thee send me by the bearer of this a catalogue of the Books in the Mer. Library Association—or any other catalogue of a well selected library—We want to obtain something of the kind to make a selection of a few books for our Village Library.

If C. Mackey [Mackay] is in Boston shake hands with him for me, and thank him for his healthful and hopeful songs—[1]

Ever thine

J. G. Whittier

Manuscript: Essex Institute, Salem, Massachusetts.

1. Charles Mackay (1814–1889), an English poet and journalist, was then lecturing in the United States. A book of his songs had been published in 1856 and many of his songs were set to music. See Letter No. 830 for further comments by Whittier on Mackay.

804. To James Russell Lowell

[November 1857] [1]

My dear Lowell

Many thanks for thy suggestions as to my Skipper—I send thee another copy of my verses on Election Eve. I cannot tell what to call it—Pray think of a fitting heading. I believe I called the other "The Eve of Election"—I enclose a little piece of my sister's—against her wish—If it does not answer your purpose please return it *to me.* [2]

J. G. W.

Manuscript: Harvard University.
1. The references in this letter to corrections for "Skipper Ireson's Ride" place it in November, probably near Letter Nos. 796, 797, 799, and 800.
2. "The Wedding Veil" was published in the *Atlantic Monthly* for January 1858.

805. To James Russell Lowell

Amesbury [before December 27, 1857] [1]

My dear fd Lowell.

I am inclined to think that the "Eve of Election" is better adapted, if published at all, to the Natl. Era than to the Atlantic. If thou wilt return it to me I will send in exchange another piece which I like very well, but which, for my own sake as well as that of the Maga. I wish thee and friend Underwood, to return to me, if it seems to you advisable, regarding it as you should do, entirely from a critical point of view. [2] The little piece purloined from my sister's writing desk, be good enough to return also, if not likely to be used, as she misses the MS. and suspects me of some mischief. I was in Boston a day or two ago, but had not time nor health to visit Cambridge as I intended. Why don't you get Fremont to give you a paper on his nomination experiences?—His is a graphic pen and an article from him wd. do something for the Mag.—

Very truly thy fd.
J. G. W.

Manuscript: Harvard University. Published: Pickard, *Life,* pp. 411–412.
1. The tone and contents of this letter indicate that it was sent before the death of Whittier's mother on December 27, 1857.
2. "The Old Burying Ground." See Letter Nos. 806 and 807.

806. To James Russell Lowell

[Before December 27, 1857] [1]

My Dear Lowell.

I thank thee for holding back my Election verses. I send herewith a picture of one of the features of our New England scenery—the old "burying ground." I hope it will meet thy approval, although it does [not] come up to my conception in all respects. The severe sickness of my mother has prevented my giving any thought to it since it was written. I shall be glad to surprise my sister with her printed verses in the stately Atlantic.

Very truly thy fd.

J. G. Whittier

If thou canst lay hands on the "Election" poem please enclose it to me, as I have no copy of it. Do not trouble thyself to look for it, if it is mislaid. [2]

Manuscript: Harvard University. Published, in Part: Pickard, Life, p. 412.

1. Dated by reference to the illness of Whittier's mother, who died on December 27, 1857.

2. Lowell wrote to Whittier on December 30: "Enclosed you will find your poem, which I thought I had already returned.

"I thank you at the same time for the new one which I like very much but which I think would be more effective if shorter. I am frank with you because you can afford it and I am your friend. But you will receive proofsheets and can judge for yourself.

"Everybody likes your Sister's poem and I hope you will Commit more fraternal larcenies on her portfolio. As for you, I defy you or anybody else to write anything so good as Skipper Ireson within the twelvemonth. I hope you will take up my gage and prove me in the wrong" (letter, Central Michigan University).

807. To James Russell Lowell

Amesbury January 1, 1858

Dear Lowell.

The "Old Burying Ground" which I sent thee if published wd be incomplete without the addition of two verses to follow this in the original manuscript:—[1]

"And if we reap as we have sown,
    And take the dole we deal,
The law of pain is love alone
    The wounding is to heal."

Unharmed from change to change we glide,
    We fall as in our dreams;

The far-off terror, at our side
  A smiling angel seems.

Secure on God's all-tender heart
  Alike are great and small;
Why fear to lose our little part
  When He is pledged for all?

The entire piece has now to me a deep and solemn significance.
It was written in part while watching at the sick bed of my
dear mother—now no longer with us. She passed away a few
days ago in the beautiful serenity of a christian's faith.—a quiet
and peaceful dismissal. The mighty bereavement overwhelms
us. May God enable us to bear it, and improve its holy
lesson.—

Ever and truly thy fd.
John G. Whittier

I would like to see a proof of the poem—

Manuscript: Harvard University. Published, in Part: Pickard, *Life,* p. 412.
1. "The Old Burying Ground" was printed in the February *Atlantic.*

808. To James Russell Lowell

January 10, 1858

Nearer, louder, fierce as vengeance,
  Sharp and shrill as swords at strife,
Rose and fell MacGregor's clan call
  Stinging all the air to life.

But, when the far off dust cloud
  To plaided legions grew,
Full, tenderly and blithesomely
  The pipes of rescue blew!

My dear Lowell:
  After the verse in "The Pipes of Lucknow" closing with
these lines:—[1]

    "God be praised! the march of Havelock!—
      The piping of his clans!"

I propose the insertion of the lines above. It is in strict accordance with the facts of the rescue. In the distance, the belea-
guered garrison heard the stern and vengeful slogan of the

MacGregors, but when the troops of Havelock came in view of the English flag still floating from the Residency, the piper struck up the immortal air of Burns, "Should auld acquaintance be forgot." Excuse my troubling thee, and believe me very truly thy friend.

J. G. W.

Manuscript: Swarthmore College. Published: Pickard, *Life,* p. 416, and incorrectly dated as "April 10, 1858."
   1. "The Pipes of Lucknow" was finally printed in the *National Era,* February 4, 1858. See Letter No. 814, note 1.

809. To Henry Brewster Stanton

Amesbury January 10, 1858

My dear Stanton
   I scarcely know anything that wd have given me more pleasure than the sight of thy signature in thy note. It came to me like a kind voice from an old friend, and at the right time. For our dear Mother—(I need not tell thee how good she was) left us on the 28th of last month. It is a heavy sorrow to us as thou mayst well suppose.
   I did not get the paper referred to. It was probably neglected at the office. I should be glad to see it, if I could do so without too much trouble on thy part. Excuse the brevity of this note and believe me ever and truly

thy fd.
J. G. Whittier

My sister Elizabeth sends her love and good wishes.

W.

Manuscript: Rutgers University.

810. To Charles Sumner

Amesbury January 11, 1858

My dear Sumner.
   Many times within the last few days I have been desirous of writing thee. But I have scarcely felt like touching a pen.[1] During the last few weeks I have been watching by the bed side of my dear Mother, following her in love and sympathy to the very entrance of the dark valley of shadows. She is no longer with us. Her end was one of exceeding peace—a quiet and beautiful dismissal. We are stunned by the great bereave-

ment. The world looks far less than it did when she was with us. Half the motive power of life seems lost.

I meant to have seen thee before the session and visited Boston, but unluckily a day or two after thy leaving.—My dear mother, then ill, urged me to go, as she wished me to see thee and Col Fremont who was then in the city.

It pains me to think of thy continual lack of strength. I had hoped that thy restoration was complete. But, with patience and prudence, thou wilt get the better of thy trouble, and be able to atone for thy lost time, by double service in the cause of freedom and Christian progress.

Only think of it—Democracy sided against itself—Douglas against Buchanan!—The father of the Nebraska iniquity shrinking from the consequences of his own scheme![2] Thee can afford to be silent, when the Divine Providence looks, as of old, from the cloud and fire, and troubles the host of the Egyptians and takes off their chariot wheels so that "they drive heavily."[3]

Hoping that I may meet thee erelong, I am ever and aff. thy fd.

John G. Whittier

Manuscript: Harvard University. Published, in Part: Pickard, *Life,* p. 413.

1. On January 10, 1858, Sumner had written Whittier: "I constantly think of you and long for the sound of your voice or at least the sight of your most welcome hand-writing. How fares the world with you? And chiefly, how is your health? I have had for some time disability enough to secure a respite for you. But mine, thank God! is passing away—slowly but surely. Meanwhile I am doomed to silence and repose. This is hard—very hard, and at times makes me very unhappy. God bless you! dear Whittier" (Pickard, *Life,* p. 413).

2. President Buchanan, by supporting the proslavery forces in Kansas who had organized their own government at Lecompton, precipitated a Democratic party crisis. Stephen Douglas (1813–1861), then in the Senate, had come out against the Lecompton group on December 9 and was placed in open opposition to Buchanan. By his continued support of the proslavery faction in Kansas Buchanan lost the support of northern Democrats.

3. Exodus 14:24–25.

811. To William James Allinson

Amesbury January 12, 1858

My dear William

I thank thee for thy very kind letter. All that the sacred word Mother means in its broadest fullest significance our dear mother was to us. A friend, helper, counsellor, companion, ever loving, gentle, unselfish. She was spared to us until her 75th year—and passed away after a sickness of about three weeks in the full possession of her faculties in exceeding peace and with an unshaken trust in the boundless mercy of our Lord. It was a beautiful and holy death-bed.—perfect love had cast out all fear. Fervently do I pray that its lesson may not be lost upon us.

With much love to all the members of your family and much sympathy for thy brother I am as Ever

Aff thy frd.

John G. Whittier

Excuse the brevity of this letter. I am scarcely fit for writing at all. Dear sister Elizabeth is nearly over come with her grief and with the fatigue and sleepless anxiety of the past few weeks. She joins me in love to you.

Source: Handwritten copy, Haverford College. Published: Snyder, "John Greenleaf Whittier to William J. Allinson," pp. 29–30.

812. To Mary Shepard

Amesbury January 13, 1858

My dear friend

Mary Shepard will I am sure be glad to know that her flowers were very grateful to our dear mother. In her name now that she is no more with us, my sister and myself thank thee. Fully understanding and sympathizing with thee, in the great sorrow which we feel in common, the loss of a mother—there is consolation in the thought with them "it is well"—we would not recall our loved ones. In the words of Cowper

> "But no—what here we call our life is such
> So little to be loved, and thou so much
> That I should ill requite thee to constrain
> Thy unbound spirit into bonds again."[1]

Very truly thy friend

John G. Whittier

Source: Currier, Bibliography, p. 277.

Recipient: Mary L. Shepard (d. 1893), a teacher in Salem, was then principal of the Higginson School for girls in Salem. She had taught Charlotte Forten, a Negro girl from Philadelphia (see Letter No. 935, note 2), and the two became close friends, both writing and visiting Whittier throughout the 1850's and 1860's. Whittier wrote Miss Shepard a short poem in 1857 thanking her for a gift of flowers. She later authored books of fiction and short stories.

1. "On the Receipt of My Mother's Picture out of Norfolk," lines 84–88.

813. To Mary Esther Carter

Amesbury January 18, 1858

Dear friend.

Elizabeth suffers so much from exhaustion and headache
that she has not been able to answer thy kind letters. Thy
sympathy and tender solicitude have been fully appreciated
by us. But, at this time our sorrow can find little alleviation
even in the words of affection and friendship. It must wait
for time, and trust and christian faith to do their offices for
it. Nor can we derive anything of substantial consolation
from the spiritual philosophy. For myself, I do not feel the
need of it to assure me of the continuity of life—that my
mother still lives and loves us. All I now ask for is the serene
and beautiful child-like trust which made holy and pleasant
the passage of our dear mother. I no longer ask for *sight*—I
feel that *faith* is better. But I can only speak for myself.
Others may find solace and comfort in what appears to them
to be a communication, direct and certain, with the loved
ones who have entered into the new life.[1]

We have had with us our cousin Mary Hussey from Somer-
worth and yesterday our fd Mrs. Pitman left us. Our neighbors have been very kind and considerate—God forgive me—if
I have ever distrusted their kindness and sympathy! The
world is better than we sometimes think.

We miss thee, however, very much, especially these long
evenings, when it is very hard for us to sit alone with our
thoughts. Elizabeth seems quite overworn and exhausted, but
I hope is slowly gaining—and for myself, I have been little
better than sick for the last six weeks. But I am very thankful
that I was able to be with my mother to the last.

The weather here is like March—clear, warm and pleasant.
We have had no sleighing—save 2 days—this winter. I suspect
you are deep in drifts by this time. I hope so for thee will
have [words cut out] the Doctor as [words cut out].

Remember me very kindly to thy fd. Mansfield.[2] He has no
right to depreciate and underrate his fine "Up county" letters.
If he "is virtuous" he must let other folks have their "cake
and ale."[3] But, I suppose I sympathize a good deal with his
present *feeling*, if not with its *manifestation*. I find no real
consolation in anything short of a prayerful submission to the
Divine Providence—Aunt Dolly is well. I believe Willie writes
in good spirits from Washington—he has found Dr. Breed and
his wife—our cousins—and likes them very much.[4] Mr. Stevens

is in Baltimore.⁵ Dr. and Mrs Sparhawk frequently speak of
thee with great interest.⁶

Remember me to thy Bro⁷ and believe me Ever and truly
thy
[signature cut out]
Elizabeth sends her love and hopes soon to write thee herself.

Manuscript: Wellesley College.

1. Mary Esther Carter had written to the Whittiers on January 12, 1858, offering consolation for the loss of their mother. She went on to state that through a
belief in spiritualism they could still communicate with their mother and that
"she is not lost to us." She concluded by stating: "If you cannot receive this as I
do, you and Greenleaf will I know understand the love and sympathy which
prompts me to give it to you with the earnest hope of its imparting some comfort"
(letter, Essex Institute, Salem, Massachusetts). In the same letter Miss Carter claimed
to have talked with Aunt Mercy and Mrs. Whittier.

2. Lewis William Mansfield (1816–1898) wrote *Up Country Letters* (New York,
1852) and many other books.

3. *Twelfth Night*, II, iii, 124.

4. Daniel Breed (b. 1813), formerly of Weare, New Hampshire, married a
woman named Gulielma and had two daughters. He was still alive in 1888.

5. Enoch Stevens (1821–1868), a successful shoe manufacturer in Amesbury,
was a close friend of Mary Caldwell, Whittier's sister. In 1867 he married her
daughter, Mary Elizabeth Caldwell, and they lived in Amesbury until his death.

6. For Dr. Sparhawk see Letter No. 447, note 4. Elizabeth Sparhawk (1817–
1887), his wife, lived in Newton, Massachusetts, after her husband's death in 1874.

7. Thomas Carter (b. 1810). Mary Carter was then visiting her sister Sarah and
her brother Thomas.

814. To Francis Henry Underwood

Amesbury January 20, 1858

Dear fd.

Some days ago I sent my fd. Lowell a copy of some lines,
"The Pipes of Lucknow." I am not certain what his judgment
was concerning them. If, however, he submitted them to
thee, and there is any probability of their appearance in the
Monthly, I would like to make an alteration in the last four
lines of the first stanza, substituting these:

> Not the braes of bloom and heather,
>   Nor the mountains dark with rain,
> Nor straits nor lake nor firth side
>   Have heard their sweetest strain.

And I would like to *add* the following stanza, after the one
closing with

> "Dinna ye hear it?—'Tis the slogan
>   Will ye no believe it noo?"
> Like the march of soundless music

> Through the vision of the seer,
>   More of feeling than of hearing,
>   Of the heart than of the ear,
>   She knew the droning pibroch,
>   She knew the Campbell's call:
>   "Hark! Hear ye no MacGregor's—
>   The grandest o' them all?"

If friend Lowell however thinks the lines not quite up to the subject or to his estimate of my ability, he is a true man and a true friend, and will act accordingly.[1]

Very truly thy fd.
John G. Whittier

Source: Handwritten copy, Harvard University. Published, in Part: Pickard, Life, pp. 415–416.

1. Lowell replied to this letter on January 23 as follows: "Till Mr. Underwood told me last evening of your note to him, I was under the impression that I had written to you. I devoted a forenoon to bringing up my correspondence, and you were on my list, and how it came that I neglected you, I can only explain by the constant distraction of the printing-office. I am responsible for Maga—; all questions are brought to me about corrections and the like. So you will easily see that with my classes and recitations in College, I am pretty thoroughly employed. So do, pray, keep forgiving me, and I will keep promising to be a good boy. What I tell you of my connection with Maga, is confidential, for I should be overwhelmed by young authors, if they knew anything about it.

"When I received your last poem, I had already got in type another poem on the same topic, so that yours was out of the question, and therefore the more reason that I should have written. I hold out my hand for the ferule like a man. Do let your writing and saying you will send another poem soon, be my punishment.

"I think you will like No. 4 almost as well as No 3.—and on the whole, I can't help feeling that we have made the promise of a good magazine.

"Don't you ever write prose nowadays? Suppose you try your hand on something for us. You see how I am corrupted already and begin to regard filling up.

"On reading your poem over again in print, I take back what I said about its being long. I think it beautiful and quite short enough. I don't pretend to understand a thing fully in Ms; I am so fagged (Albree, ed., Whittier Correspondence, pp 131–132).

815. To James Thomas Fields

Amesbury January 29, 1858

My dear Fields:
  Will you send me Dr. Livingstone's African Travels

  Parthenia by Mrs. Lee
  Bayard Taylor's Norway etc if out
  Dr. Kane's life by W. Elder[1]

Please send a bill of their cost with them.
  Is Atkinson's "Oriental and Western Siberia?" republished here yet?—If so send it also—[2]

I am more and more delighted with Dr Holmes' "Autocrat." Is not the last number admirably fresh, and suggestive?— He will make a great thing of it if he holds out as he has begun.

Ever and faithfully
J. G. Whittier

Manuscript: Property of a New England collector.

1. David Livingstone (1813–1873) was the African missionary and explorer. The book was Missionary Travels and Researches in South Africa (London, 1857).

Eliza Buckminster Lee (c. 1788–1864), a New Hampshire writer, published Parthenia, or the Last Days of Paganism (London and Boston) in 1858. She also wrote a series of tales about New England.

Bayard Taylor's Northern Travel (New York) was published in 1858.

The Biography of Elisha Kent Kane (Philadelphia, 1858) was written by William Elder (see Letter No. 429, note 1).

2. Thomas W. Atkinson (1799–1861), an English traveler and writer, published Oriental and Western Siberia (London) in 1858.

816. To an Unidentified Correspondent

Amesbury February 3, 1858

My dear fd.

It has long been the wish of my sister and myself as it was of our dear Mother[,] now no longer with us, to have thee make us a visit at our home when it might suit thy convenience. We hoped this might be brought about when our mother was living as she had a great desire to see thee. But is it not in thy power to ride up here and spend a few days in our quiet house?—It wd. be a sheer act of charity on thy part, for I am too much of an invalid to be very entertaining to visitors, and my sister as well as myself deeply feel the loss of our mother.

We are only about two hours by the cars from Boston: a branch of the Eastern R. R. runs to this place, twice a day— leaving Boston at 1/2 past 7 in the Morning and at 5 in the afternoon.

Believe me very truly thy fd.
John G. Whittier

Manuscript: Central Michigan University.

817. To Samuel Joseph May

Amesbury February 6, 1858

Dr. Friend.

Enclosed is the letter referred to by thee.[1] The Editorial comments explain it. I notice that some have said that the "General" wrote the letter in his shirt. This is hardly correct. He wrote it under a "deep concern," in haste in the morning twilight—to save his election. He was badly scared, but, I think unnecessarily so. There was not anti-slavery enough in the District to defeat his election. The long letter to which he refers was published in the Salem papers of the time, and may be easily found.[2]

The Resolutions of the Legislature may be looked for in the Liberator of the years 1837–8.—

Very truly thy fd.

John G. Whittier

I do not wish my name unnecessarily connected with the "Hon Gentleman," especially I am unwilling to have the "night-gown" story told on my authority. It may answer for a figure of speech but it is not literally true.—

Manuscript: Boston Public Library.

1. The reference is to letters by Caleb Cushing about the 1838 congressional election in Essex. In his first letter Cushing had refused to give the abolitionists specific pledges, but under pressure from Whittier he dictated a more favorable letter which gained him abolitionist support. A full reprinting of Cushing's letter and an account of Whittier's activities may be found in Letter Nos. 213, note 1, and 214.

2. Cushing's first letter, which was sent to the abolitionist convention in Salem, November 7, 1838, and which proved unacceptable to them (see Letter No. 214).

818. To Francis Henry Underwood

[February 12, 1858][1]

Dear fd.

A lady friend of mine, Mrs Randolph of Philada. sends me the enclosed to hand over to thee if I think best.

I believe there is something due me—but I wd not mention it were it not for the fact that, in common with most others, I am at this time sadly "out of pocket."

Dr. Holmes' "Autocrat" is thrice excellent and the little poem at its close is booked for immortality.[2]

Very truly thy friend

J. G. W.

Give us more papers like "N. E. Ministers."[3]

Manuscript: Brown University. Published: Perry, "The Editor Who Was Never the Editor," p. 672.
    1. Dated in another hand.
    2. "The Chambered Nautilus," which appeared in the February *Atlantic.*
    3. An article which appeared in the February *Atlantic.*

819. To James Russell Lowell

February 16, 1858

Dear Lowell

I send thee a bit of rhyme which pleases me, and yet I am not quite sure about it.[1] What I call simplicity may be only silliness and my poor bantling only fit to be handed over to Dr. Howe's school for feeble-minded children. But I like it: and hope better things of it. Look it over and let me hear from thee, if but a line.

Thy frd.—
J. G. W.

Manuscript: Harvard University. Published: Pickard, *Life*, p. 414.
    1. Enclosed was "The Bees of Fernside," printed as "Telling the Bees" in the April *Atlantic.* See Letter Nos. 822 and 823 for further comment on this poem.

820. To an Unidentified Correspondent

Amesbury, February 16, 1858

Dear Fd.—

I enclose the lines asked for. They are from a poem of some length—"Questions of Life."[1]

Very truly thy fd.
John G. Whittier

Source: Handwritten copy, Swarthmore College.
    1. Enclosed with the letter were the lines beginning with "On Aztec ruins, dark and lone" to "Shall glorify the coming night," twenty-one lines in all.

821. To Joseph Parrish[1]

Amesbury, February 20, 1858

I regret that I have nothing of my own suitable for the occasion, but it gives me pleasure to send the enclosed written by my Sister last evening, with the exception of two or three lines supplied by myself.[2]

May the God of the Poor bless it for his Work of love.

John G. Whittier

Source: Currier, *Bibliography*, p. 85.

Recipient: Joseph Parrish (1818–1891), the son of Joseph Parrish (see Letter No. 148, note 6), was, like his father, a doctor from Philadelphia whose family Whittier knew. He was then superintendent of the Pennsylvania School for Feeble-Minded Children. After the Civil War he established a sanitarium for the treatment of alcoholics.

1. Parrish had written Whittier on January 28, 1858, asking him to write some verses to be sung by children in the Pennsylvania School for Feeble-Minded Children. This was to be part of an appeal to the public and the legislature for funds for a new building (letter, Essex Institute, Salem, Massachusetts). It is on this basis that Parrish is listed as the recipient.

2. Sent with the letter was the poem, "Charity."

822. To James Russell Lowell

Amesbury February 22, 1858

Dear fd.

I believe there was a grammatical error in the poem "The Bees of Fernside." If it is printed I will correct it in the proof.

In transcribing it a verse was omitted immediately following that ending thus:

"On the little red gate and the well-sweep near."
I give it that it may go with the rest;—
I can see it all now:—the slantwise rain
  Of light through the leaves,
The sundown's blaze on her window pane
The bloom of her roses under the eaves

I wish to hear from thee in regard to the piece—if thou hast any doubts about it, send it back to me.—without troubling thyself to explain why and wherefore. I shall be sure that it is for good and sufficient reason.

But at any rate let me hear from thee in some way. If thee fail to do this, I shall turn thee out of thy Professor's Chair—by virtue of my new office of "Overseer!"—[1]

Thine Ever and truly
John G. Whittier

Manuscript: Harvard University. Published, in Part: Pickard, *Life*, p. 414.

1. In February 1858 Whittier had been elected an overseer of Harvard College and remained a member of the board until 1871. In March he was appointed chairman of the examining committee on modern languages. During these years he was present at only four meetings.

823. To Francis Henry Underwood

Amesbury March 1, 1858

Dear Fd.

I thank thee for thy suggestion and have altered the line in question. I have at Lowell's hint changed the title to "Telling the Bees" as more directly to the purpose of the ballad. I have also added a verse for the purpose of introducing this very expression, "telling the bees" etc.

I think the printers need not overrun—they can make space at the head of the piece a trifle less so as to get two lines of the 4th verse on the page:—or the note of the preceding article may be *un-leaded*.[1]

Who wrote "Eben Jackson"? Admirable rendering of the Yankee dialect!—and everyway a good story.[2]

"The Nest" has some very striking verses—Holmes is good, but not quite equal to the paper before—[3]

I like this little thing of mine the best of anything I have written for a long time—But I am no judge of my own.

Thy fd.

John G. Whittier

Source: Jean Downey, "Whittier and Cooke: Unpublished Letters," *Quaker History* 52:33 (1963). The owner of the manuscript is listed as Phelps Soule of Swarthmore, Pennsylvania.

1. As printed in the *Atlantic* for April, the story, "Who is the Thief," with a long footnote at the end, preceded Whittier's "Telling the Bees." The verse with the phrase "telling the bees" was not added.

2. Rose Terry Cooke (1827–1892), a Connecticut short-story writer and poet, was the author of the tale which appeared in the March *Atlantic*. She specialized in local color stories and homely incidents of rural life and corresponded with Whittier throughout the 1880's.

3. References to a poem in the March issue and Holmes's continuing "The Autocrat of the Breakfast Table."

824. To an Unidentified Correspondent

Amesbury, March 5, 1858

I am truly sorry thou hast taken so much pains to get a line from me.

Source: Anderson Catalogue of Whittier material sold on March 5 and 6, 1903, Haverhill Public Library, item 604. It was listed as a note signed with an envelope in Whittier's hand.

825. To Thomas Bayley Lawson

Amesbury March 25, 1858

Dr. fd.

My sister is ill, and may not be able to go to N. Port until the first of next week. If thou hast, any wish for her to see the picture, in its present stage, perhaps thou canst suspend work upon it a day or two. My sister will bring with her a cap, and she can judge better than any one else about the dress.[1]

Very truly

J. G. Whittier

Manuscript: Yale University.

Recipient: Thomas Bayley Lawson (1807–1888), a portrait and miniature painter from Newburyport, had been in business in Boston before becoming a professional painter. From 1841 on he lived in Lowell, although he maintained a studio in Newburyport.

1. Whittier and his sister Elizabeth had commissioned Lawson to paint a portrait of their mother for $40 and the picture was finished that spring. It now hangs in the parlor of the Whittier home in Amesbury.

826. To Daniel Haskell

Amesbury, Mass., April 3, 1858

To the Editor of the Transcript:

I was glad to see the contradiction in the Evening Transcript of the statement that this admirable periodical had passed out of the hands of its veteran editor and proprietor.[1] I know of no periodical in this country or in England, which affords so comprehensive and so satisfactory an idea of the literature, politics, and the science of the time, as this rightly-named Living Age. It has been conducted with remarkable tact and judgment, which wisely mingles the grave and learned disquisitions of the English Quarterlies with the lighter essays, tales and poetry of Blackwood's and the English Monthlies. It gives me great pleasure thus publicly to express my obligation to the editor for the rich and varied weekly entertainment and instruction of his magazine, and to add thereto the hope that he may long continue to cater "wisely and well" for the benfit of the reading public, and that a growing subscription list may give him assurance that his meritorious labors are appreciated.

J. G. W.

Source: Boston *Evening Transcript*, April 5, 1858.

1. Eliakim Littel (1797–1870), an American editor and publisher, had edited the Philadelphia *Register and National Recorder* from 1819 to 1844. He edited

the *Living Age* from 1844 until his death, reprinting the best of foreign periodicals. The journal lasted until 1941.

827. To the Editors of the Congregationalist

Amesbury April 22, 1858
Editors of "Congregationalist"
    You will oblige me by copying the lines on the other page
in yr. able and interesting paper.[1] Whatever may be thought
of the poetry, the tribute to Dr. Cheever is well merited.[2]

Very truly yr friend
John G. Whittier

Manuscript: Swarthmore College.
    1. Enclosed with the letter was a copy of "To George B. Cheever," which had
been published in the *National Era*, April 1, 1858.
    2. George Cheever (1807–1890), then pastor of the Church of Pilgrims in New
York, had written many tracts on temperance and abolitionism. In 1857 he had
published an attack on slavery entitled *God Against Slavery*. In his poem Whittier
compared Cheever to one of the Old Testament prophets who "smite with truth
a guilty nation's ears."

828. To an Unidentified Correspondent

Amesbury April 26, 1858
    I want a copy of the account rendered by me to the Pro-
bate Court April 19, 1853 as Guardian of the Estate of Mary
E. Caldwell—with the inventory of the Estate at that time.[1]
    Let me know the expense and I will forward it on receipt
of copy.

John G. Whittier

Manuscript: Swarthmore College.
    1. See Letter Nos. 661 and 662.

829. To Francis Henry Underwood

Amesbury May 5, 1858
My dear fd. Underwood
    I fear this will come too late for the June no—I hope not
for I like it and hope it will strike thee favorably. Let me
know what thee think of it.[1]

Very truly thy fd.
John G. Whittier

Manuscript: University of Virginia.

1. This letter followed a copy of the poem, "The Swan Song of Parson Avery," which was printed in the *Atlantic Monthly*, July 1858.

830. To William Ticknor and James Thomas Fields

Amesbury May 18, 1858.

My dr fds Ticknor and Fields:

You will scarcely understand how much I mean, when I say that I am exceedingly sorry I cannot avail myself of yr kind invitation.[1] I can well conceive that I am missing a rare opportunity. There are very few living men whose faces I have not seen for whom I entertained a feeling so nearly akin to the warmth of personal friendship, as I do for your honored guest. As one of that class of Americans who really believe in the Declaration of 1776, I must needs love and honor the man who in his "Good Time Coming" has given us the music of the march of Human Progress;—[2] and, who, in his fine lyrical panorama of "Steaming down the Mississippi," while depicting the meanness and splendors, the gloom and glory of the Father of Rivers, has shown himself in a few vivid and pathetic touches, true to the instincts of humanity in view of a lingering relic of barbarism, abhorrent alike to gentlemanly culture and christian benevolence.

Honor then to the true man and love for the genial singer! Let me beg of you, my dear friends to add to your parting salutation, as he leaves our shores, one hearty "God bless thee!" for

Your friend
John G. Whittier

Manuscript: Historical Society of Pennsylvania.

1. Ticknor and Fields had arranged a reception for the English writer Charles Mackay, who had been lecturing in the United States since October 1857. He left for England in June. See Letter No. 803, note 1.

2. His most famous song, which sold over 400,000 copies.

831. To James Russell Lowell

[May 1858]

> And the preacher heard his dear ones,
>   Nestled round him, weeping sore:
> "Never heed, my little children,
>   Christ is walking on before
> To the pleasant land of Heaven
>   Where the sea shall be no more!"

I suppose the *"Parson Avery"* piece was too late for June.
If so, please add the above verse, after the verse beginning
"Blotted-out was all the coast-line." I send with this some
lines suggested by Fields' book. They were hastily written, but
my sister thinks them worthy of type.[1]

Very truly thy fd.
J. G. W.

Manuscript: Harvard University.
1. "To —, on receiving his 'Few Verses for a Few Friends' " was published in
the *Atlantic* for August. Fields's book of poems was privately printed for his
friends. Whittier later titled the poem, "To James T. Fields, on a blank leaf of
'Poems printed, not published.' "

832. To the Amesbury Villager

[Before June 10, 1858]

The number of subscribers for the first six months of the
year was 127; for the last 169. Received by subscriptions etc.

	147.92
Balance in the Treasury of last year's subscriptions	42.16
Total amount	190.08
Expended for new books	86.69
For Librarian	50.00
Re-binding books	6.30
Covering and Repairing	5.38
Oil	7.95
Fuel	.75
New Shelves	2.29
One ream of paper for covers	8.38
Painting (last year's bill)	3.50
Soliciting subscribers	2.00
Miscellaneous expenses	.68
Total of expenditures	173.82
Leaving in Library	16.16

At the commencement of the year just closed there were in
the Library 1170 volumes. Since then there have been added
by purchase 98, and by donation 13 volumes—in all 111.
Present number of volumes, 1281. There are, in addition, a
large number of unbound volumes, magazines, and pamphlets.

The addition of new books includes on its list nearly all the
really popular and valuable publications of the year, in the
several departments of philosophy, history, biography, travels,
and fiction.

In view of the very depressed condition of the business of

the village during the past year, the steady progress of the
Library is a cause of congratulation. The promise of the
Report of last year of one hundred added volumes has been
more than realized; and we now have a library of 1300 volumes. We have no reason to doubt that the close of the present year will show a corresponding increase.

An examination of the books shows that they have been,
in the main, carefully treated, and some improvement in this
respect is manifest as compared with the year previous. But
two books are missing, one which is small and of little value.

In conclusion, the Committee would suggest to those of
our citizens who are blest with the means and the disposition
to do good, that the Library has strong claims upon their
attention, and that donations of money or books are especially
needed at the present time. One hundred dollars over and
above the annual subscription would suffice to make our list
of standard works of English Literature so nearly complete
as to enable us to devote the entire sum received from subscriptions, after defraying needful expenses, to the purchase
of books of interest and value fresh from the press. Apart
from the very obvious benefit to ourselves at the present
time, and the credit which it reflects upon the taste and habits
of our own community let us remember that no better legacy
can be left to those who take our places than a large and well
selected Library, though the use of which we find access to the
world's intellectual treasure house, and become heirs of the
great and good in all ages.

John G. Whittier ⎫
James H. Davis[1] ⎬ Committee
Benjamin Evans[2] ⎭

Source: The Amesbury Villager, June 10, 1858.

1. James H. Davis (1819–1892), an Amesbury teacher, conducted a private
school in Amesbury during the 1840's and 1850's. Later he became principal of
the Amesbury Public High School. He served as secretary of the Amesbury Public
Library from 1856 to 1878 and held other town offices.

2. Benjamin Evans (1812–1883), a former teacher then in business in Amesbury, was one of the trustees of the books given to the library by Joshua Aubin.
He served in the Massachusetts House of Representatives in 1857 and in the
Senate from 1858 to 1859. He later became superintendent of the Reform School
at Worcester, Massachusetts.

833. To Robert J. Davis

Amesbury, June 14, 1858

Dear friend

Enclosed is the report of our Library.[1] We have worked it up to its present position, with a good deal of hard labor. I thought as thee are a Po Hill boy thee might like to lend us a helping hand. A trifle in the way of books or money would be gratefully received and thankfully acknowledged. Almost all our Salisbury and Amesbury born sojourners abroad have done something.[2]

Elizabeth joins me in love to thee and Anna, and the young folks. Mary E. C. is at Newburyport.

Ever and truly thy fd.
John G. Whittier

Manuscript: Central Michigan University.

Recipient: Robert J. Davis, the son of John and Sarah Davis of Amesbury, was then living in Fall River, Massachusetts where he was an active Republican. The identification is conjectural.

1. See Letter No. 832.

2. The public library report for 1859 lists Robert Davis as having given five dollars and a number of books.

834. To Francis Henry Underwood

Amesbury June 26 [1858]

Dear fd.

Do you publish such *incendiary* pieces as this? And if so, can it go in the August no? If not, it will be too late; and I must beg of you *return it at once.*[1]

If Prof Lowell approves of it—and I am sure he will like the spirit of it, whatever he may think of its merits in a merely literary point of view—and you can give it a place in your Aug. no.—I shall be pleased. If not, it is just as well. Could it not take the place of the poem now in type?—[2] That could afford to wait another month, or you could return it to me—

Thine truly
J. G. W.

Manuscript: Swarthmore College.

1. Enclosed with the letter was "Le Marais du Cygne," a poem based on the wanton killing of five free settlers and the wounding of others near Marais du Cygne, Kansas, in May 1858. The following stanza is indicative of its emotional tone:

Wind slow from the Swan's Marsh,
   O dreary death-train,

> With pressed lips as bloodless
>> As lips of the slain!
> Kiss down the young eyelids,
>> Smooth down the gray hairs;
> Let tears quench the curses
>> That burn through your prayers.

The poem, however, was not printed until the September issue. See Letter Nos. 835 and 836 for further comments on the poem.
    2. "To ___, on receiving his 'Few Verses for a Few Friends.'"

835. To Francis Henry Underwood

Amesbury July 5, 1858

My dear fd.

I am heartily obliged to thee for thy kind suggestions. But see what has been the result of them! Is the piece better or worse? Who knows? My sister thinks *she* does, and that I have altered it for the better. I hope it will strike thee and Lowell in the same way. The sweep and rhythm please me, but I have had hard work to keep down my indignation. I feel a good deal more like a wild berserk than like a carpet minstrel "with his singing robes about him,"[1] when recording atrocities like that of the Swan's Marsh.

I want a proof sheet of it as soon as may be to send to Charles Sumner in advance of its publication.

Ever and truly thy fd.
John G. Whittier

There is not a dull page in the last Atlantic. If it could only be kept up to that point it would take precedence by right of all magazines on either side of the Atlantic.

Source: Handwritten copy, Harvard University. Published: Pickard, *Life*, p. 417.
    1. John Milton, *Reason of Church Government*, II, i. The complete phrase reads: "A poet soaring in the high region of his fancies with his garland and singing robes about him."

836. To James Russell Lowell

Amesbury July 10, 1858

My dear friend

I am glad to know that my poem still strikes thee so favorably. There *is* a lack of clearness in the lines quoted by thee. I do not know as it can well be made plainer. Would this be any better?—

Free homes and free altars
　By prairie and flood;
The vale of the Swan's marsh
　Whose bloom is of blood![1]

As respects the name. I purposely put it in the singular—a liberty I think perfectly allowable.

I was pained to hear of the death of C. W. Philleo.[2] He was a writer of admirable promise. The turf should not close over him without a good and kind word from the Magazine with which his name was connected.

Very truly thy friend
John G. Whittier

Manuscript: Harvard University.

1. The poem was printed without this revision.

2. Calvin W. Philleo (1822?–1858), a Hartford lawyer, had published *Twice Married: A Story of Connecticut Life* (New York, 1855) and had written three installments of a new work for the *Atlantic* when he died. The September issue of the *Atlantic* carried a brief obituary notice.

837. To Lucy Larcom

Amesbury July 20, 1858

My dear fd.

We were glad to hear from thee by the Ann. Catalogue of thy school as at Beverly once more. Can thee not run up and make us a little visit of a few days this fine weather?—I ask it for E's sake as well as mine—our home is rather a lonely one —but we would give thee a kind welcome to it. We think some of going into N. H. and should be sorry to miss seeing thee.

Very truly and cordially thy fd.
John G. Whittier

Let us hear from thee, and whether we may expect thee [and] when.[1]

Manuscript: Massachusetts Historical Society.

1. Miss Larcom responded on July 23, saying that she could not come until after next week (letter, Harvard University).

838. To John Hickod

Amesbury July 20, 1858

Dr. fd.

Of course, I can have no objection to the use of my anti-slavery poems in the manner proposed by thy note.

Very truly thy friend
John G. Whittier

Manuscript: Historical Society of Pennsylvania.

839. To Pliny Earle

Amesbury July 26, 1858

My dear friend.

Thy first note was recd when I was too ill to answer, and it was mislaid for some time. I was just about to reply to it when I got thy second. I am very sorry for the delay.[1]

The article on thy brother Thomas was written I think in the spring of 1840 and published either in the Emancipator or the Pa. Freeman.[2] I have no copy of it and cannot supply the deficiency, without some further guide.—I am glad the noble and self-sacrificing traits of thy bro's character are to be called to remembrance. He was a wise, earnest reformer, very faithful to his convictions—a democrat in word and deed. Of course thou hast W. H. Burleigh's lines in the Pa. Reform Convention in which thy bro's noble stand for the colored man's rights is eulogized.—

Very truly thy fd.
John G. Whittier

I wrote only what I believed of Thomas.—I do not remember what I said, as to particulars.—if there be anything in thy view extravagant, or in bad taste please omit, or change it.

Manuscript: American Antiquarian Society, Worcester, Massachusetts.

Recipient: Pliny Earle (1809–1892), a doctor and psychiatrist, had been a teacher and principal at the Friends School in Providence. After becoming a doctor in 1837, he worked with the insane in Philadelphia and New York, retiring to Leicester, Massachusetts in 1855. From 1864 to 1885 he was superintendent of the state lunatic hospital in Northampton. In 1888 he published a family genealogy, *The Earle Family.*

1. Pliny Earle's letter of July 5 (Essex Institute, Salem, Massachusetts) said that he had been asked to gather material for a biography of his brother and that he wanted a full copy of Whittier's letter written about Thomas.

2. The letter was written on October 10, 1840, and published in the *Massachusetts Abolitionist* (see Letter No. 295).

840. To Francis Henry Underwood

August 10, 1858

Dear fd.

Thy suggestion which reached me yesterday I have acted upon today and send thee the result.[1] Is it not too late for the Atlantic Monthly? I have no time to look it over. If printed, let me see a proof, if possible.

Thou wilt see that the 4th and 5th verses are to be transposed.

Thine truly
J. G. Whittier

Manuscript: Haverhill Public Library.

1. Underwood had written Whittier on August 9: "If you feel an electric thrill some of these fine mornings, pray take your pen and let it write the lyric of the Atlantic Cable. We shall have a plenty of verses on the event—the greatest since Columbus landed—but it occurred to me that your sounding lines would most fitly celebrate the triumph of science—the triumph of peace and good will to men."

Enclosed with the letter was Whittier's poem celebrating the completion of the Atlantic cable, then entitled "The Great Wire." The poem was printed in the October issue of the *Atlantic* as "The Telegraph," but Whittier finally titled it "The Cable Hymn." For further comments on this poem see Letter Nos. 841, 843, and 844.

841. To Francis Henry Underwood

Amesbury August 10, 1858

Dear fd.

In my haste yesterday I omitted an idea which seems to me necessary to my little poem on the Great Wire.

After the 5th verse add the following:

> Through Orient Seas, o'er Afric's plain
>   And Asian mountains borne,
> The vigor of the Northern brain
>   Shall nerve the world outworn.
>
> From clime to clime from shine to shine
>   Shall thrill the magic thread,
> The new Prometheus steals once more
>   The fire that wakes the dead!

I take it for granted that the Augt. no of the Mage. is stereotyped; but you reserve a few pages to notice recent events, and perhaps my little lyric may serve to close yr article on the great event of the Age—If so, as I suppose I cannot see the proof, please look to it carefully.

The value of a poem like this depends upon its timely publication. Please drop a single line to inform what I may expect.

Cordially thy fd.

J. G. W.

Perhaps

> "Space mocked and Time outran"
>   would be better than
> "And Space and Time outran"

Manuscript: University of Virginia. Published, in Part: Pickard, *Life*, pp. 417–
418. Pickard printed with this excerpt a section from the letter to Underwood
of August 28, 1858 (No. 844).

842. To Charles A. Barry

Amesbury August 12, 1858

My dear fd.

I am glad to hear so favorable a report of the picture. Of
course thou art entirely at liberty to do with it as thou wilt.
It is pleasant to know that any one cares enough for the
original to take the trouble and expense of such an Engraving.[1]

Did thee get a line from me through W. W. Caldwell of
N. P.?[2] I sent it a few days ago. It contained some verses on
thy picture of "The Motherless"—rather commonplace I fear.[3]

My sister desires [to send] her love to thee. We remember
thy little visit with pleasure.

Very truly thy fd.

John G. Whittier

Remember us kindly to Mrs. Barry—

Manuscript: University of Virginia.
Recipient: Charles A. Barry (1830–1892), a portrait and genre painter from
Boston, worked in both Boston and New York City. His picture, "The Motherless," a crayon drawing, was exhibited at the Athenaeum Gallery in 1858 and was
said to be one of his best works. He did a crayon portrait of Whittier in the summer
of 1858.

1. Barry planned to make an engraving of the crayon sketch he had done of
Whittier.

2. William Warner Caldwell (1823–1908), a Newburyport druggist, had published a book of poems in 1857 and was a translator of German verse. He had
exhibited Barry's portrait in his drugstore during August.

3. "The Sisters. A Picture by Barry," which was published in the *National Era*,
August 12, 1858.

843. To Francis Henry Underwood

                                        Amesbury August 17, 1858
My dear fd.

I fear that if my lines are delayed until next month, I shall
be accused with some show of justice of stealing from a
thousand and one intermediate rhymes. What occurs to one,
in writing upon such a subject, must needs, in whole or in part,
occur to all.

The "Autocrat" I shrewdly suspect will recite some of his
verses on this topic, and I should be sorry to enter into competition with him.

I have pretty much concluded to send my piece to the
"National Era."—But, as its suggestion is thine, I take the liberty of sending it first to thee, begging thee, to glance over it,
as it now stands, and if any thing occurs to thee in the way of
change or improvement be good enough to let me have it
with the MS. as soon as possible. I have scruples about troubling thee, but it will learn thee to hesitate, in future, before
giving hints to a versifier.

After all, the real difficulty in saying anything on this
wonder is the magnitude and vastness of the theme. I feel like
one who holds a farthing dip against the sun.

                                        Ever and truly thy fd.
                                        John G. Whittier

F H Underwood Esq

   Manuscript: Swarthmore College.

844. To Francis Henry Underwood

                                        Amesbury August 28, 1858
My dear friend.

At the risk of calling to mind "Mons. Tonson come again"[1]
—I venture to suggest for the verse in my poem, closing with
the line

      "Clasp hands beneath the sea"

the following as more clear and definite:

      And, one in heart as one in blood
         Shall all her people be;
      The hands of human brotherhood
         Shall clasp beneath the sea.

The last no. of yr Magazine is "excellent well" as my Lord

Bacon somewhere says.—Every body admires thy Kinloch Estate.[2] "Ann Potter's lesson" is one of the best of Yankee stories—a better sermon than has been preached from half the pulpits of Christendom for the last year.[3] Emerson is outdoing himself, and the Autocrat is better and better.[4] The love passage between him and the sweet school-mistress is inimitable. Boston Common is henceforth classic ground.

Very truly thy fd.
John G. Whittier

Manuscript: Yale University. Published, in Part: Pickard, *Life*, p. 418, as part of the letter of August 10, 1858 (No. 841).

    1. An imaginary character in a farce, *Monsieur Tonson*, by William Thomas Moncrieff.

    2. "The Kinloch Estate, and How It Was Settled," a long narrative, had appeared in the *Atlantic* for July, August, and September, when it was concluded.

    3. "Ann Potter's Lesson," a short story, appeared in the September issue.

    4. Emerson's essay, "Eloquence," was the lead article in the September *Atlantic.*

845. To Lydia Maria Child

Amesbury September 2, 1858

My dear fd. Maria Child

My sister wishes me to remind thee of thy promise to visit us at the close of the Summer. I think of leaving home myself on a short journey, but as the time for doing so is not particular, I shall wait to hear from thee.

I wish thee could be with us at this delightful season. Why not come at once?

If thee have any writing to do we will give thee quiet and leisure for it here, as well as elsewhere.

We shall hope to hear from thee soon, and in the meantime as ever

Thy friend
J. G. Whittier

My kindest regards to thy husband. I remember him in the old anti-Slavery days, as one of the few and fearless advocates of the cause of freedom.

Manuscript: Massachusetts Historical Society.

846. To the Editors of the
        Atlas and Daily Bee

                              Amesbury, September 11, 1858
To the Editors of the Atlas and Daily Bee.

I was glad to see in your paper of yesterday a reply to an
article in the Boston *Post* intimating that the disposal of a
resolution offered in the late Worcester Convention with reference to Charles Sumner, was significant of a desire for
that gentlemen's resignation, as his place was wanted by
another.[1] I think, however, that a more decided and emphatic
refutation of a charge, not now for the first time insinuated,
would have been well. As one of the early friends of the cause
which is now dominant in the State, and as a personal as
well as political friend of Charles Sumner, I confess that I am
pained by any intimation of this nature from any quarter.
Sure I am, that no true son of Massachusetts can so far forget
what is due to the honor and dignity of his State, to the
cause of Freedom at home and abroad, and to the claim which
he who suffered for others has upon their gratitude, as to
allow himself to speculate upon the chances of the resignation
of such a man, under such circumstances or to allow private
aims and personal ambitions to outweigh the consideration of
justice, duty and delicate regard for the feelings of one who
has made so great a sacrifice to the cause of human Freedom.
Senator Sumner is now abroad seeking health through terrible
processes of pain, with the fortitude and heroic endurance
characteristic of his noble and manly nature. The result is
doubtful, but there is reason to hope for his permanent
recovery. Be that as it may, sick or well, if he is willing to
"stand and wait"[2] where he now is—silent and yet most eloquent—where is the man who, by virtue of his talents, personal
worth, services and sacrifices, has a right to ask for his place?
Massachusetts is content with her Senatorial representation,
just as it is. She never had more reason to be proud of it.
Henry Wilson has proved himself equal to every emergency;
and the interests and honor of the state were never entrusted
to abler hands, while the reputation of his colleague as scholar,
orator and christian statesman, won in defense of her cherished principles, is wide as the civilized world.

Massachusetts needs no change and asks none. What Charles
Sumner himself, in view of his state of health, may decide to
do, is another matter. Should he feel it his duty to resign a
post to which he has been called by an almost unanimous vote,
it will be time enough for us to sadly acquiese in the necessity,

and look over the list of our truest, ablest and worthiest fellow citizens for his successor. The mantle of Charles Sumner must fall upon no ordinary man. In the mean time let there be no forestalling—let no individual be forced by his enemies, or by his friends from whom he should pray to be delivered, into the unenviable position of a graceless heir waiting with ill-disguised impatience for the patrimony of death. The heart of Massachusetts is sensitive on this point. She will allow no one to thrust himself between her and the man who more than any other is entitled to her sympathy, her love and her gratitude.

J. G. W.

Source: The Atlas and Daily Bee, September 13, 1858.

1. On September 9 the Boston Post published an article entitled "Senator Sumner Snubbed by the Banks Party." In discussing the resolutions passed by the Republican party convention at Worcester on September 7, the article said that one of the resolutions was a veiled hint for Charles Sumner to resign. The resolution stated that representatives and senators should be in constant attendance in the session. It went on to suggest that Governor Banks wanted Sumner's post. The Atlas and Daily Bee printed a refutation to the article on September 10.

2. John Milton, "Sonnet. On his Blindness." The line reads: "They also serve who only stand and wait."

847. To Josiah B. Gale

Amesbury September 30, 1858

To Dr. J. B. Gale, President of the A and S Agricultural and
         Horticultural Association.

Permit me, through thee, to thank the contributors to the late successful exhibition, for the gift of a choice selection from the products of their gardens and orchards.[1]

It will always be a source of gratification to me that the slight service I have been able to render to the festival, has been thus appreciated; and I shall think all the better of my poor and homely rhymes since they have come back to me transmuted into rich fruits and beautiful flowers.[2]

Very truly thy friend,
John G. Whittier

Source: The Amesbury Villager, October 7, 1858.

Recipient: Josiah B. Gale (1803–1877), a graduate of Brown University, had practiced medicine in Amesbury from 1825. He served as the first president of the Amesbury and Salisbury Agricultural and Horticultural Association, which sponsored its first annual fair in 1858.

1. Whittier had entered some pears in competition and won first prize for his Flemish Beauties and second for his Beurre de Capiaumonts.

2. The fair included a religious service on September 28 at the Congregational church, and Whittier wrote a hymn to be sung there called "A Song of Harvest." For his contribution he was sent a gift of fruit and flowers.

848. To Charles Cleveland

Amesbury October 10, 1858

My dear fd.

Illness has compelled me for a long time to abstain from even letter writing, or I should long ago have thanked thee for a copy of thy excellent Com of Am Lit.[1]

I have seen little or nothing to find fault with. I notice some omissions. Chas Brockden Brown—H. W. Beecher, Dr. Chapin, S. Grimke, Jas A Hillhouse, whose fine poem of "Hadad" is worth preserving,[2] two Danas, Richard H. and R. H. Jr.

Please omit in the next edition the extract on Byron. It is a fragment and in too ambitious a style for me.[4]

I am glad to see that the Comp is a success in spite of pro-slavery criticism.

Our old friend J. Coffin was better in health the last I heard from him.

Excuse the brevity of this and believe me very faithfully thy friend

John G. Whittier

Manuscript: University of Virginia.

1. Cleveland had published his *A Compendium of American Literature* (Philadelphia) in 1858. He wrote to Whittier on April 14, 1858, asking Whittier to glance over the proof sheets of the article on Whittier and suggest correction for a future edition of the book (letter, Essex Institute, Salem, Massachusetts). For Whittier he reprinted the following pieces: "Palestine," "Clerical Oppressors," "Leggett's Monument," "Ichabod," "Maud Muller," "Democracy," "The Wish of To-day," and two prose fragments, "Milton" and "Lord Byron."

2. James Hillhouse (1789–1841), a minor American poet, published *Hadad: a Sacred Drama* in 1825 and authored many other romantic verse dramas.

3. Richard Henry Dana (1787–1879), a Massachusetts poet and journalist, founded the *North American Review*. He published an edition of his poems and prose in 1833.

4. The Byron fragment was as follows:

"I admire the sublimity of his genius. But I have feared, and do still fear the consequences—the inevitable consequences of his writings. I fear that in our enthusiastic admiration of genius, our idolatry of poetry, the awful impiety, and the staggering unbelief contained in those writings, are lightly passed over, and acquiesced in, as the allowable aberrations of a master intellect, which had lifted itself above the ordinary world, which had broken down the barriers of ordinary mind, and which revelled in a creation of its own: a world, over which the sunshine of imagination lightened at times with an almost ineffable glory, to be succeeded by the thick blackness of doubt, and terror, and misanthropy, relieved only by the lightning flashes of terrible and unholy passion.

"The blessing of that mighty intellect—the prodigal gift of Heaven—became, in his possession, a burthen and a curse. He was wretched in his gloomy unbelief, and he strove, with the selfish purpose which too often actuates the miserable, to drag his fellow beings from their only abiding hope; to break down, in the human bosom, the beautiful altar of its faith, and to fix in other bosoms the doubt and despair which darkened his own; to lead his readers—the vast multitude of the beautiful, the pure, and the gifted, who knelt to his genius as to the manifestations of a new divinity—into that ever darkened path which is trodden only by the lost to hope—the forsaken of Heaven—and which leads from the perfect light of holiness, down to the shadows of eternal death.

"Genius! the pride of genius! What is there in it, after all, to take the precedence of virtue? Why should we worship the hideousness of vice, although the
drapery of angels be gathered about it? In the awful estimate of eternity, what is
the fame of Shakespeare, to the beautiful humility of a heart sanctified by the
approval of the Searcher of all bosoms? The lowliest taster of the pure and
living waters of *religion* is a better and wiser man than the deepest quaffer of the
fount of Helicon: and the humbler follower of that sublime philosophy of Heaven,
which the pride of the human heart accounteth foolishness, is greater and worthier
than the skilled in human science, whose learning and glory only enable them
'*Sapienter ad infernam descendere*!'

849. To Josiah B. Gale

Amesbury, October 16, 1858

To Dr. J. B. Gale, Pres[iden]t, etc.

Dear Friend,

Thy note in behalf of the Amesbury and Salisbury Agricultural Association, with the elegant Fruit Basket accompanying
it, has just been received.

I accept it, not without some feeling of diffidence, and a
consciousness of scarcely deserving so valuable a gift, trusting
that it may be in my power hereafter to make some adequate
return for it in the service of the Association, which has
done itself so much honor by its first exhibition.

I value this testimonial all the more, that, coming from my
immediate neighbors, it evinces the fact of mutual good feeling and regard. A token of approbation even from strangers is
not unwelcome; but I place a higher estimate on that which
assures me of the esteem of my every day acquaintance, and,
that I have a place in the kind thoughts of "mine own
people."[1]

Very truly thy friend,
John G. Whittier

Source: The Amesbury *Villager*, October 21, 1858.
1. II Kings 4:13.

850. To Gamaliel Bailey

[Around November 11, 1858][1]

Who is Gail Hamilton?[2] That last poem was a very fine
one.[3]

Thine truly,
J. G. W.

Source: Dodge, *Gail Hamilton's Life in Letters*, I, 191.

1. Dated by reference to Gail Hamilton's poem which was published on November 11, 1858.

2. Gail Hamilton, the pen name of Mary Abigail Dodge (1833–1896), a brilliant essayist and poet, was a distant cousin of Whittier and met him in 1859. Her wit, effervescence, and tart humor made her unique among Whittier's friends and their relationship is typified by Whittier's comment in 1865 upon receiving one of her letters: "I was a little blue this morning, but thy letter was just the tonic I needed. If anybody is out of sorts and hypped I shall prescribe for him a course of thy letters" (Letter No. 1057). Her letters to Whittier throughout the 1860's and 1870's are a mixture of whimsy and exuberance, as she addressed him as "Dearly beloved," "Dear Angel," "My dear Sheikh," teased him about his preoccupation with ill health, and both flattered and shocked him with her audacious remarks. Their correspondence forms one of the most amusing and charming aspects of Whittier's later years. Whittier relished her essays and books, while she was a constant visitor to the Whittier home before and after his sister Elizabeth's death. Even when she engaged in a bitter controversy with Fields over royalty payments, her friendship with Whittier remained firm, although he disapproved of her actions and the resulting publication of her *A Battle of Books* in 1870. She herself best sums up what their friendship meant when she wrote after receiving an inscribed copy of *The Tent on the Beach*:

"I have not read it [the book], but I know the best part of it is what he has written on the fly-leaf. I suppose the great mass of persons in the world are really incapable of friendship. Not otherwise can I account for the clouds that seem to hang over so many. I am as far as possible from believing that friendship should, or can, encroach upon love. It seems to me they may run in parallel lines forever, since parallels never meet. I have a very great scorn for the notion you often find afloat that propinquity is the—what do the theologians call it?—predisposing cause of love? It may be a sufficient cause for that bread-and-butter sentiment which keeps the pot boiling, and, of course, if two substances have the natural affinity the coming together is all that is necessary, but the natural affinity is the very thing in question" (Mordell, *Quaker Militant*, p. 229).

During her lifetime, Gail Hamilton published numerous collections of her essays, besides editing *Our Young Folks* from 1865 to 1867. After 1870 she made her residence in Washington.

3. "Terra Incognita," a poem of longing for paradise, was published in the *National Era*, November 11, 1858. Its last two stanzas read:

"But I stand without, alone, alone,
        Crying forevermore—
Oh, who shall roll me this mist away
        From the beautiful unseen shore.

"O Soul of my soul! whither wanderest thou?
        Reach hither thy certain hand,
And lead me crowned and exultant hence
        Into the Mystic Land."

851. To James Thomas Fields

                                        Amesbury November 21, 1858
My dear Fields.

I must write a line to say that I cannot quite make up my mind to be made a "marble statue" of. I liked the Artist [name illegible] exceedingly and, if I was going to be a graven image I should have him do the metamorphosis. I must write him soon, but in the mean time, let him know how I feel about the matter.

Now for a bit of business. Send me for our Library.[1]

> Dr. Barth's new volumes
> Peasant Life in Germany
> Carlyle's Fred. the Great
> "Agnes" by author of "Ida May"
> The New Priest of Conception Bay
> Autocrat of B. T.
> Exiles of Florida
> Longfellow's M. Standish
> Kingsley's Essays
> Robinson Crusoe
> Miss Bremer's New Novel "The Sisters"
> The Cruise of the Betsey[,] Hugh Miller
> Life of Admiral Blake by Hepworth Dixon

Of course you will put them as low as the times and the conscience of your pockets will allow—

Excuse this bad writing. My head aches inordinately, and I can scarcely see what I have written.

Thine truly

John G. Whittier

Manuscript: University of Kansas.

1. The full titles and authors of the books are as follows: Heinrich Barth, Travels and Discoveries in North and Central Africa (New York, 1857–1859); Anna C. Johnson, Peasant Life in Germany (New York, 1858); Thomas Carlyle, History of Frederick the Great (New York, 1858); Mary Hayden Pike, Agnes, A Novel (Boston, 1858); Robert Traill Spence, The New Priest in Conception Bay (Boston, 1858); Oliver Wendell Holmes, The Autocrat of the Breakfast Table (Boston, 1858); Joshua Giddings, Exiles of Florida (Columbus, 1858); Henry Wadsworth Longfellow, The Courtship of Miles Standish (Boston, 1859); Charles Kingsley, Miscellanies (Boston, 1859); Daniel Defoe, Robinson Crusoe; Frederika Bremer, Brothers and Sisters and Other Stories (New York, n. d.); Hugh Miller, The Cruise of the Betsey (Edinburgh, 1858); and Hepworth Dixon, Robert Blake: Admiral and General At Sea, based on Family and State Papers (London, 1852).

Heinrich Barth (1821–1865), a noted German writer and traveler, explored central Africa; Anna C. Johnson wrote travel books about Germany; Mary Hayden Pike (1824–1908), an American novelist and abolitionist, wrote a number of romantic novels; Robert Traill Spence (1816–1871); Daniel Defoe (1659?–1731) was the famous English essayist and novelist; Hugh Miller (1802–1865), an English stonemason, wrote autobiographies and books on geology; and William Hepworth Dixon (1821–1879) was a British explorer and historian.

852. To Richard Henry Stoddard

[November 22, 1858] [1]

My dear fd.

I thank thee for thy kind letter on receiving which I made search for the note previously written and found it among other letters and papers which came when I was too ill to attend to them.

I have no need to look for thee on the Publisher's list. Thy "Songs of Summer" are on my table, and I have long recognized thee as a true singer. [2]

I am really not strong enough to copy the entire poem Maud Muller, and can only send thee a few verses from another piece. [3]

Thee speak of B. T[aylor]. Give him and his the love of my sister and myself. Tell him we expect him to bring us some relic from the land of *Afraja* as he promised.

With respect and esteem
Thy fd.
J. G. W.

Manuscript: Swarthmore College.
1. Dated by Whittier's own dating after the poetry quotation which accompanied the letter.
2. The *Songs of Summer* (Boston, 1857).
3. Accompanying the letter were eight stanzas from "My Namesake," beginning with "The cant of party, creed and sect."

853. To Francis Henry Underwood

December 8, 1858

Dear fd.

I enclose a new poem which my sister thinks is good; and I always defer to her judgment,—when it is agreeable to my wishes. [1]

Source: Handwritten copy, Harvard University. Published, in Part: Pickard, *Life*, p. 420.
1. The poem may be either "The Great Awakening" or "The Voyageur on the Red River," See Letter No. 856. Pickard in his partial reprinting of the letter incorrectly identifies the poem as "The Double-Headed Snake of Newbury."

854. To Bayard Taylor

Amesbury, December 12, 1858

Can thee not make us a call before leaving New England? We want a lecture from thee, and that old pocket-book, which thee remembers was so ostentatiously displayed at the close of thy lecture some years ago, is good for $40. But lecture, or none, come and see us. Our dear mother can no longer welcome thee, but sister and I shall be glad to see thee. Elizabeth expects the feather-pocket from Lofoden![1]

Source: Pickard, *Life,* p. 419.
1. Taylor replied to the letter on December 12 as follows: "As for lecturing, it is quite out of the question. I have not a single evening vacant between now and the middle of April. But I am coming to Amesbury to see two friends whom I thought of many a time on the fjelds of Norway and among the Lofoden Isles. I shall run down on Tuesday or Wednesday and am only sorry that my visit must be a very short one, as I have to lecture in or around Boston every night. But come I must, if only for an hour. My northern tour would almost seem to have been made in vain, if I should not see you and Elizabeth after it" (letter, Cornell University).

855. To William James Allinson

Amesbury December 21, 1858[1]

My dear William

By a paper just received as I suppose from thee, we have learned of the recent removal of thy dear and excellent mother to a better inheritance.[2]

Our own great loss is so recent that we can truly sympathize with thee in this dispensation—and yet so tempered with mercy and the consolation of a blessed hope. Thy dear mother has left a precious and excellent name behind her and as she rests from her labors her good works follow her—and instead of murmuring at our loss, does it not become us rather to be thankful exceedingly for the blessing of such mothers, spared to us so long and for the priceless memory they have left us.

With much love to thy Rebecca and the household including the green leaf of the family tree, in which Elizabeth joins, I remain as Ever

affectionately thy fd.
John Greenleaf Whittier

Remembrances kindly to thy dear Brother Samuel.

Dear William

It is too late for thy repent—the devil—*Printer's* of course—has got it—and the only thing I can do in thy premises is to

give thee the assurance that *I* am satisfied with it—and vouch
for the readers of the Book that they will be not only satisfied but *gratified*. I am sorry I do not feel able to see the right
—Very truly thy fd.[3]

J. G. W.

Source: Handwritten copy, Haverford College. Published: Snyder, "John
Greenleaf Whittier to William J. Allinson," p. 30.

1. Snyder printed the date as February ("2 mo.") and it is so written in the
copy at Haverford, but since Mrs. Allinson died on November 12, 1858, February
is clearly wrong and I have conjectured the date to be "12 mo." or December.

2. Berenice Allinson.

3. This may be another letter, but it was copied on the same sheet as the December 21 letter. The manuscript appears somewhat garbled, but probably Allinson
was trying to recall something he had sent to Whittier for publication.

856. To James Russell Lowell

Amesbury December 29, 1858

Dr fd.

I send herewith "The Doubleheaded Snake of Newbury."
If it is suited to yr meridian use it:[1] As to the other two pieces,
"The Great Awakening," and "The Voyageur on the Red
River" do me the favor to return them to me by the bearer
of this, the Expressman between yr city and Amesbury. I want
them immediately.[2]

Mrs Stowe's story opens admirably.[3] I wish however, she
wd. give more local coloring and atmosphere to her picture,
so that we may know what part of the world we are in, in
what age, as respects costume etc, and what climate. In other
respects the tale is very striking in its promise.

Very truly thy fd.
John G. Whittier

Manuscript: Harvard University. Published: Pickard, *Life*, p. 419.

1. "The Double-Headed Snake of Newbury" appeared in the *Atlantic* for March
1859.

2. "The Great Awakening" (later titled, "The Preacher") appeared in The New
York *Independent*, December 29, 1859, while "The Voyageur on the Red River"
(later titled, "The Red River Voyageur") was printed in the *Independent*, January 20, 1859.

Whittier's connection with the *Independent* began with the acceptance of his
poem "The Prophecy of Samuel Sewall" by the *Independent* in December and its
publication in the January 6, 1859, issue. During 1859 and 1860 Whittier published
more poetry in the *Independent* than in the *Atlantic*, presumably because they
were willing to pay him a hundred dollars a poem, or twice the *Atlantic* price.
Theodore Tilton's letter to Whittier of December 11 explains the association as
follows:

"The publisher of The Independent, who is at present absent from the office,
will forward to you on his return (within a day or two) the sum of one hundred
dollars, for your poem, 'The Prophecy of Samuel Sewall.'"

"I take occasion to say that your offer has been very cheerfully accepted.

"I hope that your health will permit your writing, during the course of the year, more than the 'two or three poems' of which you speak in your note. The circle of our readers embraces a far larger audience than the Atlantic Monthly, and includes the best minds of the Country interested in the progress of Freedom. Our readers will be as much in sympathy with you, as your own personal friends could possibly be.

"I shall take the liberty of mentioning your name together with that of Mrs. H. B. Stowe and Rev Henry Ward Beecher, as among—not *regular* but *special* contributors to The Independent—from whom contributions may be expected during the coming year" (letter, Central Michigan University).

3. This was *The Minister's Wooing*, which started in the December *Atlantic*.

857. To John S. Tyler

Amesbury December 30, 1858

Dr fd.

At the request of my friend Wm. Carruthers Esq (whose father followed Burns to his long resting place,[1] and who was himself at the laying of his cor. stone of the Mt at Dunfries)—I write to inquire what are the terms of admission to the Club; and the Dinner on the 25th at the Parker House! Would it lessen the expense to join the club?

My fd. C. Would like to be at the Festival—he is a gentleman of intelligence and worth—was a member of the late Constitutional Convention of the State.

Yielding to none in admiration of Burns, I hope yr. festival will be worthy of the occasion. Nothing but the state of my health will prevent me from enjoying it.[2]

Very truly thy fd.
John G. Whittier

Manuscript: Swarthmore College.

Recipient: John S. Tyler (1796–1876) had started in a Boston merchant business at fourteen and ultimately became a partner in the Long Wharf Adjusting Company. He was a member of the Massachusetts constitutional convention of 1853 and served in the state legislature for four years. He also served in the state militia from 1812 to 1837 and was made a general of the Boston Light Infantry in 1840. He was then acting as president of the Boston Burns Club.

1. James Carruthers, a Scottish minister, came to America in 1813 where he settled and died in Portland, Maine.

2. A special celebration had been planned to observe the centennial anniversary of Burns's birth. Whittier, along with Lowell, Holmes, and Emerson, had been asked to attend and to contribute to the meeting. Emerson lectured on the "Memory of Burns," while Whittier, Lowell, and Holmes read or sent original poems. William Carruthers not only attended the dinner but gave an address on Burns which was well received. See Letter Nos. 860 and 861 for further comments on the dinner and Whittier's contribution.

Part Ten

Elizabeth Lloyd Howell

1859-1860

Elizabeth Lloyd Howell

1859-1860

The year 1859 remains a significant one in Whittier's life because of his emotional attraction and love for Elizabeth Lloyd Howell. Of the fifty-eight known letters written this year, twenty-three were addressed to her, furnishing an intimate account of their mature love and final decision not to marry. Whittier's acquaintance with Elizabeth Lloyd Howell dated back twenty years to his editorship of the *Pennsylvania Freeman* in Philadelphia where she was one of his many female friends. A strikingly beautiful Quakeress with social poise and a cultivated mind, she was both an amateur artist and poetess, besides being a sympathetic abolitionist. For a time after the death of Lucy Hooper in 1841 their mutual attraction deepened, but Whittier's removal to Amesbury and wide political and literary interests led him to neglect and finally stop their correspondence.

After acquiring some poetic reputation, Elizabeth Lloyd married in 1853, only to become a widow three years later. In 1858 her sister Hannah wrote Whittier of the changes that sorrow had made in Elizabeth and asked him to visit her in Philadelphia. By the spring of 1859 Whittier acted on this invitation and spent five weeks in Philadelphia, where they renewed their former friendship. Whittier was then fifty-one, in a period of comparative good health and freed from the burden of political activity, while Elizabeth was four years younger. Both had recently suffered family losses and were responsive to the exchange of sympathy and comfort. Their frequent meetings reawakened their former attraction and this ripened into an emotionally fulfilling and mature love. On the days Whittier could not see Elizabeth, he wrote her that their time together was sweet and golden, two precious for even a single moment to be lost. He demanded a portrait of her, claiming it was worth more than a whole gallery of Old World madonnas, and wrote upon leaving Philadelphia that the "sweet remembrance of our communion . . . dwells with me—a dear and sacred possession." Once back in Amesbury Whittier wrote openly that she had won his heart and brought him more happiness than he ever expected in this life. With the enthusiasm and ardor of a young lover he begged her not to injure her eyes by writing to him for "the very blank paper which thy hand has folded for my sake will be dear to me." Throughout the spring, Whittier wrote similar letters, both revealing the depth of his love and hinting that his memories were perhaps of equal importance to any future marriage plans.

In May Elizabeth went to New York for a water cure, and that June Whittier attended a Quaker meeting in Newport, Rhode Island. After this the first serious rift in their relationship occurred, for Elizabeth expressed harsh criticism of the pettiness, odd mannerisms, and limited culture of Quakers. Although admitting particular flaws in the Society, Whittier was disturbed by her full condemnation, for he sincerely believed that the philosophy underlying Quakerism remained the purest and best the world had ever known. As he wrote: "My reason, my conscience, my taste, my love of the beautiful and the harmonious, combine to make me love the society." This religious difference suspended whatever thoughts of marriage they might have entertained. Whittier could never renounce his Quaker beliefs or accept the rituals of the Episcopalian faith which now interested Elizabeth. Coupled with this divergence were the problems of their physical separation, Whittier's long years of bachelorhood, and still uncertain health. In August, perhaps hoping to force a reluctant Whittier to some decision, Elizabeth wrote that the tone of his letters had changed. For his answer Whittier wrote a full analysis of his inner feelings and tactfully, but definitely, precluded any future hopes for marriage. "I have grown old," he said, "in a round of duties and responsibilities which still govern and urge me; my notions of life and daily habits are old fashioned and homely . . . . Thee lives in a different sphere." He feared that her fine artist's nature would suffer and be diminished by his bleak way of life and added that he never intended his love to replace the memory of her deceased husband. No abrupt bitter break followed this letter, but their relationship had clearly changed. Now their letters stayed on the safer topics of new books, travel, health, old friends, and daily activities. During the winter Whittier wished to dedicate his new volume of poetry to her and sent her a dedicatory poem for her approval. After some delay and fearful of the resulting publicity, she declined, an act that put the final seal on their love relationship—although they continued to correspond until the mid 1860's.

Significant as this love affair was for Whittier's emotional life, it had little effect on his social or literary activity. The rest of his letters, for example, followed the pattern of previous years, short notes mainly dealing with the external events of his life and current writing. He initiated correspondence with younger women writers like Edna Dean Proctor and began his lifelong friendship with Annie Fields. His few brief forays into the sophisticated social world of the *Atlantic Monthly* dinners led him to comment wryly: "I do not think I ever had any gift for such occasions in my best estate, and time and illness . . . have improved me the wrong way." Reluctantly, Whittier accepted the limited social and emotional life which his delicate nervous system dictated. Changes in climate severely affected him and any extra emotional or physical exertion prostrated him with headaches and stomach trouble. Twenty-eight poems were written in these years. Many of them were occasional and incidental poems, written for the celebration of Burns's centennial, for an Amesbury fall festival, for the dedication of Kenoza Park in Haverhill, or for the memory of Joseph Sturge. A few ballads and pastorals continued to explore New England's past, while a group of religious lyrics demonstrated his mature, serene acceptance of God's will. Whittier gathered the poetry of the late 1850's into a volume, *Home Ballads and Poems*, in 1860, and the caliber of his late poetic flowering caused Lowell to remark that Whittier was "on the whole, the most representative poet New England has produced. He sings her thoughts, her prejudices, her scenery."

As in previous years, few of Whittier's poems or letters dealt with the growing national crisis that swept the Union toward a civil war. After some deliberation, Whittier wrote two editorials on Harper's Ferry, pleading for an end to violence, but blaming the South and slavery for causing Brown's rash and insane act. His poem, "Brown of Ossawatomie," expressed his sympathy for Brown, while condemning his act as harmful to freedom. The return of a healthy Charles Sumner to the Senate in 1860 gave Whittier a personal link with national events, and during the presidential campaign Whittier canvassed Amesbury to insure votes for Lincoln. Though not a strong Lincoln supporter, Whittier felt that Lincoln's "conservative, cautious and moderate" approach would preserve the Union. The Republican victory elated

Whittier and he hoped that southern secession threats were
only words, but his political instincts warned him that there
might be no peaceful solution to the slavery question. Pro-
phetically, he wrote to Elizabeth Lloyd Howell: "It is perhaps too much to expect that so great a wrong should pass
away without convulsing the nation which has so long cherished it." Torn by his Quaker belief in nonresistance and by
his outrage at the moral wrong of slavery—even critical of
his poetry for it gave words instead of action to freedom's
cause—a divided Whittier faced the coming Civil War.

858. To Gamaliel Bailey[1]

Amesbury, January 1, 1859
My dr fd.
  I thank thee for the pictures as does my sister.—
  In regard to an alteration of the piece as suggested, I hardly
think it best.[2] Dr. Robinson and other good authorities have
no belief that the Jordan flowed at the base of Mt. Hor and I
thought it unsafe to take the fact for granted.[3]
  I find that Robinson calls the place El Ghor—At any rate,
its precise locality is marked in the poem by the allusion to
Mt. Hor and Petra.
  I do not like the measure so well as that of Palestine[4] —but
I feared to make a mere parody of the latter poem.

Very truly thy fd.
J. G. Whittier

Manuscript: University of Virginia.
  1. The identification is conjectural.
  2. "The Rock in El Ghor" was printed in the *National Era*, January 6, 1859.
  3. Edward Robinson (1794–1863), a philologist and geographer, was a professor
of biblical studies at Andover Union Theological Seminary. His main work,
Biblical Researches in Palestine, Mount Sinai and Arabia Petraea (London, 1841)
established him as a leading biblical scholar. He published a revision of the book in
1856.
  4. "Palestine" was printed in the *United States Magazine and Democratic
Review*, October/December 1837.

859. To James Russell Lowell

Amesbury, January 21, 1859

My Dr fd.

By a line from Ed. Spencer of Baltimore Co. Md. I learn that he has sent, or is about to send, a story to the At. Monthly.[1] He wishes me to call attention to it, and secure for it, if possible, an examination. I only know him as a rather brilliant writer for the Natl. Era. The story "Jasper," which he is publishing in that paper is very popular. His story sent to the Atlantic is I believe called "Tristan."[2] It may be worthy of a place in the Mage

Very truly thy fd.
John G. Whittier

Manuscript: Harvard University.

1. Edward Spencer (1834–1883), a playwright and author, published stories in the *National Era* and in 1867 published *Tristan; a Story in Three Parts.* He later authored a memorial volume on Baltimore and a biography of Thomas F. Bayard, senator from Delaware.

2. "Tristan" was never published in the *Atlantic.*

860. To John S. Tyler

Amesbury, January 22, 1859

John S. Tyler, Esq.
President of the Boston Burns Club
Dear Friend:

I gratefully acknowledge, through thee, the invitation to the celebration of the centennial anniversary of the birthday of the poet whom I have long regarded as the truest and sweetest of all who have ever sung of home, and love, and humanity.

As I may not be able to be with you, I venture to offer a few lines, which, however inadequate to the occasion, attest a sincere tribute to the great World Singer.[1]

Very truly thy friend,
John G. Whittier

Source: Celebration of the Hundredth Anniversary of the Birth of Robert Burns, by the Boston Burns Club, January 25, 1859 (Boston, 1859), p. 61.

1. See Letter No. 857, note 2 for an account of the celebration. Whittier sent for the occasion the poem, "Lines for the Centennial Celebration of the Birthday of Robert Burns, 25th 1st. mo., 1859" (later titled "The Memory of Burns"), and the poem was read by Ralph Waldo Emerson, as Whittier did not attend the celebration. The poem was published in the *Atlas and Daily Bee*'s account of the dinner and also in the *National Era,* January 27, 1859.

861. To John S. Tyler

Amesbury, January 24, 1859

J. S. Tyler, Esq.
Dr fd.

I have been requested to furnish the Atlas and Bee with a copy of my poem, and I enclose one to thee, slightly altered. I have sent the same to Mr. Emerson, but if he has not got it, let him have this:[1] And, if it is not asking too much, be good enough to correct the MS. previously sent by this, and let the Atlas folks have it.

Very truly thy fd.
John G. Whittier

Manuscript: Essex Institute, Salem, Massachusetts.
1. See Letter No. 860. Emerson was to read Whittier's poem, "Lines for the Centennial Celebration of the Birthday of Robert Burns, 25th 1st. mo., 1859," at the dinner.

862. To an Unidentified Correspondent

Amesbury, February 1, 1859

I wish copies of the will of Moses Whittier of Haverhill whose estate was administered upon in 1824.[1]

Also of John Whittier of Haverhill in 1830.—[2]

Send a bill of the expense of making copies.

John G. Whittier

Manuscript: Essex Institute, Salem, Massachusetts.
1. Whittier's uncle. See Letter No. 662, note 2.
2. Whittier's father. See Letter No. 221, note 6, and Whittier's comments on his father in Letter No. 864.

863. To Daniel Haskell

Amesbury, February 4, 1859

(For the Transcript)

You ask a merrier strain of me,
The shepherd pipe of Arcady,
The vintage hymn, the hunter's horn,
The reaper's carol from the corn!—

Ah! small the choice of him who sings
What sound shall thrill the smitten strings;

Fate holds and guides the hands of Art,
And lips must answer to the heart.

In shadow now, and now in sun,
As runs the life the song must run;
But, glad or sad, to God's good end
Doubt not the varying streams shall tend.[1]

J. G. W.

Dear Haskell.

I see you sometimes publish little fragments of verse, and
perhaps the above may fill a niche in the Transcript, which
I have come to regard as a familiar friend who drops in daily
to chat with me. But don't put my name in full to the verses
[—] let them go as I have written them.

J. G. W.

Manuscript: Pierpont Morgan Library. Published, in Part: Currier, Bibliography,
p. 317.

1. These verses were published in the *Transcript* on February 5, 1859. The
verses were later revised and published with five stanzas under the title "Overruled"
in 1878.

863A. To an Unidentified Correspondent[1]

Amesbury February 11, 1859

My dear fd.

Let me thank thee for doing such a good service for my
poor Maud. I think the figure, attitude and expression of
Maud in thy picture is excellent. It is a better poem than
mine.[2]

I suppose we are to thank thee for a photograph from thy
picture of my face. It is very finely done.

Thy friend R. S. Spofford was here the other day in the
midst of a Snow Storm which wd. have been creditable to
Siberia or Spitzbergen.[3] I suppose thou wilt see him frequently
as he is in the Legislature.

Elizabeth joins me in love to thee and thy wife.

Very truly thy fd.
John G. Whittier

Manuscript: Swarthmore College.

1. This letter may be to Charles Brainard, who frequently corresponded with
Whittier about portraits and pictures of Whittier's works.

2. Whittier is, of course, referring to his poem, "Maud Muller," which had been
published in 1854. It was later issued as a separate volume, *Maud Muller by John
G. Whittier*, with illustrations, in 1867.

3. Richard Spofford (1833–1888), a Newburyport lawyer, served in the state legislature and worked as an attorney for the railroads. He and his wife, Harriet Prescott Spofford, lived at Deer Island on the Merrimack River and were close friends of Whittier. At Spofford's death Whittier wrote "R. S. S. at Deer Island on the Merrimac" in his memory.

864. To William Lloyd Garrison

Amesbury February 14, 1859

Dear Friend.

For thy sake I could have wished thee a better subject for thy Lyceum lecture, but for myself I feel greatly complimented by thy choice.[1] I do not think it worth while to dwell too much on my boyhood. The date of my birth I find by reference to the old record which has just come to light was 12th mo. 17 (Dec. 17, 1807). My birthplace was the old homestead where thee found me when thee astonished me by a visit. My father's name, John Whittier, my mother's Abigail (Hussey) Whittier. My grandmother on my father's side was a Greenleaf of Newbury.[2] I had no schooling except about ten or twelve weeks in a year—the school distant a mile through drifts and storms. Joshua Coffin was my first teacher. I have tried to describe him in "Lines to My Old Schoolmaster." No books except a few Quaker journals, etc. When I was about 16, Master Coffin lent me Burns' Poems. I sent a piece of verse to thee by the carrier of the paper when about 17. The rest is well known to thee. My father did not oppose me; was proud of my pieces, but as he was in straitened circumstances he could do nothing to aid me. He was a man in advance of his times, remarkable for the soundness of his judgment, and freedom from popular errors of thinking. My mother always encouraged me, and sympathized with me. I learned the shoemaker's trade to get the means of education, worked about two years and then went to school to Haverhill Academy for one year. Kept school a while, and then went to Boston, and from there to Hartford. Stayed two years, returned and published my first pamphlet on Slavery in the spring of 1833. Carried on the farm after my father's death till 1836. I have thus given a rude outline of the facts; but I do not see any necessity of using them to any extent. One thing I wish thee would do, if thee read any of my anti-slavery pieces, I would like thee to read my lines on the passage of the Personal Liberty Bill.[3] They were written under the impression that the bill would put an end to slave hunts on our soil, and will be applicable to the present time. I hope thee will not edify the Newburyport folks with any extended recitation of my *first things*. I don't think they are worth reviving. I enclose one of my latest anti-slavery pieces, addressed to Dr. Cheever.[4] It would gratify him I think to hear thee refer to it. Let me call thy attention to "The New Exodus." Do me, as I am sure thou wilt, the justice to note that I have not lived merely for a literary reputation—that what I most desired was to do my duty as a *man*—all else was incidental and subordinate. Heartily thanking thee for thinking of me as a fit subject for thy lecture, and remembering gratefully thy early encouragement, I am ever and truly thy friend

J. G. W.

My father's family lived respectably and in tolerable comfort, but the farm was burdened with debt, and frugality and persistent industry were indispensible. The children as well as their elders had to work indoors and out. The young boys had only ten or twelve weeks of schooling in a year. My early verses indicate scanty opportunities for reading and study.[5]

Source: Handwritten copy, Harvard University. Published, in Part: Pickard, *Life* (1894), I, 52.

1. With his copy of the letter Pickard included the following note: "In 1859, William Lloyd Garrison was invited for the first time to deliver a lecture in his native town, Newburyport. He had previously lectured *without invitation*, and had received the usual honor of a 'prophet in his own country.' He accepted the invitation and chose for his theme the life and services of his Amesbury friend, John G. Whittier. He wrote to Whittier asking for information in regard to his early life, and Whittier replied under date of 2nd mo. 14, 1859." Garrison delivered his talk on February 25, 1859.

2. Sarah Greenleaf (1721–1807) of West Newbury married Joseph Whittier (1716–1796) in 1739 and settled in Haverhill, where they had eleven children.

3. Pickard inserted another note here which read: "'Arisen at last,' written in June 1855 when the Massachusetts Legislature passed a bill to protect the rights of the people of the State against the Fugitive Slave Act." The poem was published in the *National Era*, June 7, 1855.

4. "To George B. Cheever," printed in the *National Era*, April 1, 1858.

5. This postscript had a notation "To F. J. Garrison" and Pickard indicated that he wanted it inserted after the sixth sentence in the letter which ended, "a Greenleaf of Newbury." Though this might therefore be a later comment of Whittier to Francis Garrison, the son of William Lloyd Garrison, I have retained it as a part of the letter.

865. To William Lloyd Garrison

Amesbury, February 23, 1859[ ]

My Dear fd. Garrison

I was pained by the circular signed by thee and W Phillips and Maria Weston Chapman relative to an old and noble fd Geo. Thompson.[1]

I wish I was rich for his sake. As it is, I can only offer the

enclosed $2.00, with fervent desire for his restoration to
health and happiness.

Thank W. P. for his noble speech before the Legislature
Committee.[2] It is one of his best, and that is saying much—

Ever and truly
J. G. W.

Manuscript: Boston Public Library.

1. George Thompson had been lecturing in India in 1856 where he was prostrated by the climate and returned to England apparently a hopeless paralytic.
Garrison and others conducted a personal campaign to secure funds for Thompson
during the winter of 1858–1859 and were able to send sufficient money to
restore his mental and physical well being. By 1860 Thompson became an active
and salaried agent for the American Anti-Slavery Society in England.

2. On February 17, 1859, both Thomas Wentworth Higginson and Phillips had
appeared before a legislative committee to petition for the passage of a law which
would abolish slave hunting in Massachusetts. Their full speeches were reprinted
in *The Liberator*, February 27, 1859.

866. To Robert Charles Winthrop

Amesbury, February 26, 1859

Dear friend.

I thank thee for the privilege of reading the enclosed note,
and the excerpt from the N. Y. paper, but more especially
for the kindly interest manifested in thy own letter.[1] It has
been a matter of real pain to me to feel compelled to differ
in some respects, upon public matters, with thyself and others
whom I greatly esteem. All we can do, in these conflicts of
opinion is to season our dissent with charity, and emulate
the forbearance of Sir Thomas More who could "hear here-
sies talked and yet let the talkers alone."[2]

When thou has an opportunity I beg of thee to assure W. H.
Bogart of my very grateful appreciation of his kind words.[3]
As respects Henry Ward Beecher, I do not know him personally, but I regard him as a man of real genius, and I naturally
sympathize with him in his hatred of oppression and love of
liberty.[4]

With great respect and esteem I am
Very truly thy fd.
John G. Whittier

Hon R. C. Winthrop

Manuscript: Massachusetts Historical Society.

1. Winthrop had written Whittier on February 22, 1859, sending him a note
he had received from William Bogart which expressed Bogart's enthusiastic admiration for Whittier, and also an article from a New York paper about Whittier
(letter, Essex Institute, Salem, Massachusetts).

2. Thomas More (1478–1535) was an English statesman and author who was executed in 1535.

3. William H. Bogart (1810–1888), a New York author and reporter, contributed articles on historical subjects to the New York *World* and the New York *Courier and Inquirer* under the pen name of the "Sentinel." He also authored a life of Daniel Boone and a book of historical reminiscences.

4. Whittier met Beecher that spring. See Letter No. 877.

867. To Charles Warwick Palfray

Amesbury, March 13, 1859

Dr. friend:

Enclosed is an article on the Fugitive S[lave] law Question now before our Legislature which I should like to see copied into the Register.[1] I do not, of course, ask thee to endorse its opinions; but I feel anxious to get the matter before the people in some shape or other.

Very truly thy fd.
John G. Whittier

Manuscript: Essex Institute, Salem, Massachusetts.

Recipient: Charles Warwick Palfray (b. 1813), a graduate of Harvard Law School, served as editor of the Salem *Register* from 1838 to 1893. Four times a member of the state legislature, he also was collector of customs for the port of Salem from 1869 to 1873.

1. The Salem *Register*, a semiweekly newspaper, was published from 1800 to 1893 in Salem, Massachusetts.

868. To Elizabeth Hussey Whittier

528 Spruce Street, Philada., April 18, 1859

My dear sister.

I write a line just to let thee know that I am safe in this city.[1] I have been here ever since a week ago seventh day. I have had a bad cold, but otherwise am about as usual. I have seen almost all my old friends in the city. I am staying with Hannah J. Newhall, 528 Spruce.[2] I have been often to see Ann Wendell, and Margaret. Margaret is a widow and keeps a Boarding house. Ann is in very poor health, and is not in very comfortable circumstances.

I have been beset on all hands with invitations, and have seen a great deal of company. I try to keep as quiet as I can.

A young miss, daughter of W. D. Parish of this city called on me day before yesterday.[3] She has been at Providence and wanted to know if Mary was going next term. She sent her love to her. I saw another one in the cars who had been to Providence. I think her name was Alderson—[4]

If I do not get home by the last of the month (as I think of doing) I shall be glad to have the garden seen to—Spline to dig it up[5] and Uncle Whitcomb to plant it. But I hope to see to it myself. If Boardman can paint the front and west end of the House and the kitchen and woodshed, with the *blinds* I should like to have him do it.[6] It must be done right away if at all. Will thee send to him and see. [Remainder of letter missing.]

Manuscript: John B. Pickard.

1. Whittier had received many invitations to visit Philadelphia and in March made plans for going to the city. A year earlier, Hannah Lloyd Neall had especially wanted Whittier to visit Elizabeth Lloyd Howell, still in mourning over the death of her husband and greatly changed by her sorrow. Also the hope of avoiding the cold east wind must have influenced Whittier, but at any rate in early April he left Boston, visited a while in New York, and came to Philadelphis on April 9, where he remained until May 14. It was during this period that Whittier and Elizabeth Lloyd Howell renewed their friendship and found their mutual affection turning into love. Their letters over the next six months record the course of a deep, mature love.

2. Hannah J. Newhall (1803?–1883), a Philadelphia widow, had been a friend of Whittier during his editorship of the *Pennsylvania Freeman*. Whittier was friendly with her two young daughters, Abby and Mary.

3. Probably Hannah Miller Parrish (1842–1920). She married William Pearsall in 1861.

4. Probably Anna Maria Alderson, the daughter of Harrison Alderson, a Quaker from Burlington, New Jersey. She married William Wistar in 1864.

5. Perhaps David Spline, who was employed at the Amesbury Mills Manufacturing Company.

6. William J. Boardman (1802–1882) was a painter from Salisbury, Massachusetts.

869. To an Unidentified Correspondent

Anti-Slavery Rooms April 19, 1859

My dear friend

I find that it will not be in my power to comply with thy kind invitation for tomorrow. I have become entangled in a network of dinners and suppers—and should need the "good digestion which waits on appetite,"[1] to eat my way out.

With many thanks for thy kind attention and hoping thee and thine a pleasant trip to the old Dominion I am very truly

thy fd.

John G. Whittier

Manuscript: Yale University.
1. *Macbeth*, III, iv, 38.

Charles Sumner in 1846

Engraving by Hezekiah Wright Smith after a crayon by Eastman Johnson

528 Spruce Street

Philad^a 18th 4th mo 1859

My dear Sister,

I write a line just to let thee know that I am safe in this city. I have been here ever since a week ago seventh day. I have a bad cold, but otherwise am about as usual. I have seen almost all my old friends in the city. I am staying with Hannah J. Newhall, 528 Spruce. I ~~shall~~ have been often to see Ann Wendell, & Margaret. Margaret is a widow & keeps a Boarding house, Ann is in very poor health, and is not in very comfortable circumstances.

I have been beset on all hands with invitations, & have seen a great deal of company. I try to keep as quiet

No. 4:   Letter to Elizabeth Whittier, April 18, 1859

870. To Unidentified Correspondents

528 Spruce St April 25, 1859

My dear fds.

I have been looking forward with pleasure to a visit at
Germantown and hope to be able to go out on Sixth day next.
I would say tomorrow, but an illness of two days duration
which entirely prostrates me, makes it doubtful whether I
could do so with safety.

Very cordially and truly
John G. Whittier

Manuscript: Syracuse University.

871. To an Unidentified Correspondent

528 Spruce St Fourth Day Mg April 27, 1859

Dear Friend.

I find that some friends are to be here this Evening who
will be disappointed if I am absent. Under the circumstances
I shall not feel at liberty to accept thy kind invitation. I trust
I shall have an opportunity to see thee before I leave the city.

With great esteem
thy fd.
J. G. Whittier

Manuscript: University of Virginia.

872. To Elizabeth Lloyd Howell

528 Spruce St. [May 2, 1859] [1]

Dear Elizabeth,

I was sorry I did not get thy note until yesterday afternoon,
when I could not get away from company. To-day I am not
well enough to go out in the rain, or I should not content myself with writing. I shall, if possible call on thee to-morrow
afternoon. I cannot bear the thought of losing these golden
moments of opportunity for communion with thee. Life is
too short for ceremony among friends. Deeply grateful to the
kind Providence which has permitted us to meet once more,
I feel that I am not at liberty to neglect the blessing.

I know thee will congratulate me when I tell thee that I
have fairly eaten my way through my dinner and supper table

engagements, and am free from all demands of the kind, and mean to keep so for the present.

I will be ready to go to [Ellis] Yarnall's[2] when thou art ready to accompany me. I hope thy eyes do not trouble thee again. I wish I could cure them as thee did my head, the other day; perhaps if thy faith were as strong as mine was, I might do so.

Affectionately,

J. G. W.

Source: Denervaud, ed., *Whittier's Unknown Romance*, p. 15.

1. Miss Denervaud dated this letter as November 2, which is clearly incorrect. I have conjectured May 2 as the correct date.

2. Miss Denervaud had written here "Edna," but a search of Quaker records reveals no such name. Since Whittier mentions visiting Caroline Yarnall, Ellis Yarnall's wife, in a note following (Letter No. 874), I have conjectured "Ellis" as the correct reading.

873. To Elizabeth Lloyd Howell

Second Day [before May 14, 1859][1]

Dear Elizabeth

As I am not allowed to step over thy threshold to-day, I must needs write to enquire what prospect there is of my having that "counterfeit presentment,"[2] which I assure thee will be worth more to me than a whole gallery of Old World Madonnas and saints. I meant to have spoken of it yester-day but in the presence of the original, I entirely forgot the picture. If I possibly can, I will see Andrew Longacre to-day and ascertain about it and report upon it to thee this evening.

Aff—

J. G. W.

Source: Denervaud, ed., *Whittier's Unknown Romance*, p. 16.

1. The date may be Monday, May 2, since Whittier left Philadelphia on May 11, a day after he planned to go (Tuesday, May 10).

2. *Hamlet*, III, iv, 54.

874. To Elizabeth Lloyd Howell

Fourth Day [before May 14, 1859][1]

Dear Elizabeth,

As I cannot well get an opportunity to see thee this morn-ing, I must tell thee how thoroughly I enjoyed my visit last evening. Thy friend Caroline Yarnall, surrounded by her agreeable family, seems to me to be a very lovable woman.[2] She has great delicacy of refinement, and I was agreeably

disappointed in her liberal tone and feeling. She received me
more like a brother than a stranger, and I shall always remember my visit with pleasure. I wish thou couldst have been with us.

Ah me! these days glide on, and I shall soon have to set
my face towards the sunrise. I shall carry with me many
regrets, but many sweet and precious memories also.

Affectionately,
J. G. W.

Source: Denervaud, ed., *Whittier's Unknown Romance*, pp. 16–17.
1. The date is probably May 4.
2. Caroline Yarnall (d. 1894), the wife of Ellis Yarnall.

875. To Elizabeth Lloyd Howell

Burlington Seventh day Mg. [May 14, 1859][1]

Dear Elizabeth,
I did not leave Philada. on Third day. Ann Wendell came
to H J N[ewhal]l's and I stayed until the next Mg. I had a
longing desire to see thee again, but I knew it wd. be wrong
to attempt it. I went to this place Fourth day Mg., attended
meeting on Fifth day, and heard a beautiful discourse from H.
Alderson.[2] Eliza Gurney was silent, much to my disappointment.[3]

Rode out with her and spent the day, and had a very delightful visit. E P Gurney spoke of thee with much affection
and with a tenderness of sympathy, which really made me
love her.

We have called on Dr Taylor, H Alderson and the Smiths.[4]
Yesterday I was with thy dear Sister Ann. I only wished thou
couldst have been with us. It is now 6 ock and in an hour
I start for N. Y. on my way home. My thoughts dear E. have
been with thee, and if my prayers have not been availing in
thy behalf they have been, at least, fervent. The sweet remembrance of our communion during the past three weeks, dwells
with me—a dear and sacred possession. I am better and happier
for it—rich beyond my hopes.

God in His mercy dear E. keep, comfort, strengthen thee!
I have no time to say more. Thou wilt hear from me from N. Y.
or Boston. In the meantime ever

Affectionately,
J. G. W.

Source: Currier, ed., *Elizabeth Lloyd and the Whittiers*, pp. 128–129.
1. Dated by postmark.

2. Harrison Alderson (d. 1871) was a minister in the Society of Friends at Burlington, New Jersey.

3. Eliza P. Kirkbridge (1801–1881), a Quaker minister, had traveled throughout the United States doing missionary work. In 1841 she married Joseph John Gurney and after his death returned to the United States and lived in Burlington, New Jersey.

4. Joseph Wright Taylor (1810–1880), a Quaker philanthropist and doctor, had been associated with Haverford College and was instrumental in founding Bryn Mawr as a school for Quaker women.

Susan D. Smith (1808–1875), a Quakeress, lived in Burlington.

876. To Elizabeth Lloyd Howell

Amesbury May 17, 1859

Dear E.,

I write thee a single line to say that I arrived home last night, and found my friends well as usual.

I have thought much of thee, Dear E., in thy lonely retreat, and long to know how it is with thee, yet I do not wish thee to write more than a line or two. Fatigue and a basket full of letters to be answered, as well as other duties, oblige me to be brief this morning. In a day or two, I will make amends for this. Elizabeth sends her love—of mine, thee needst no assurance.

Ever affectionately,
J. G. W.

Source: Denervaud, ed., *Whittier's Unknown Romance*, p. 17.

877. To Hannah J. Newhall

Amesbury May 17, 1859

My dear fd.

Did I promise to tell thee how and when I got home? I think so: at any rate, I must do so. I reached here this day (17th): and found Elizabeth expecting me. She and Sister Mary are about as usual in health:[1] I hope E. is the better for her absence, although I do not see much change as yet. I had an excellent visit to Burlington: Went to meeting 5th day; and then to E. P. Gurney's to dinner and tea—Susan Smith[,] Dr. Taylor[,] W. J. Allinson and others were present

We called on H. Alderson, and at the Smith's sixth day. I dined and spent most of day with Ann Lloyd, that was.

I had a charming visit to E P. G. and brought away some very beautiful things as presents.

Seventh day I went to New York—took tea with some of

my literary friends, and on First day went to Staten Island to Elizth Neall Gay's (sister of Danl Neall.) Geo. Curtis, author of Prue and I, was with us.

Went back and took tea with a friend and Second day Mg Henry Ward Beecher gave me a break-neck sort of drive over the city with his spirited team of horses—We went to see Church's wonderful picture of the Andes, among other things.[2] In the afternoon took the boat to Stonington, were roused up at midnight, and got in the cars, reaching Providence at 1/2 past 3. A. M. I wandered half over the city before I could find the "City Hotel," cold, tired and vexed with myself for taking such a route. I went at 8. to the F. Y. B. S. [Friends Yearly Boarding School] saw Ger. and Jos. and my two nieces—and at 11—started for home.[3]

I am too tired now to write further. Let me only say how very grateful I feel for thy kindness and that of thy whole family. I almost felt when I left as if going from home. Tell Abby that I wished she could have been with me at E P. Gurney's.[4] It wd. have been better than our Darby expedition. Elizabeth is pleased with the collar and sends her love. My sister Mary who remembers thee, sends her love. Remember me to George and Mary[5] —Tell Ann Wendell I shall write her soon.

Aff. thy fd.
J. G. W.

Manuscript: Westtown School, Pennsylvania.

1. Whittier's sister Mary had been living in Amesbury with her daughter, a few houses away from the Whittier home.

2. Frederick E. Church (1826–1900), a New York landscape painter who studied under Thomas Cole, specialized in subjects of natural grandeur, like Niagara Falls, icebergs, and mountains. He had visited South America in 1853 and 1856 and brought back many pictures, of which "The Heart of the Andes" was the most famous. See Letter No. 883 for Whittier's comments on this picture.

3. Joseph Cartland and his wife Gertrude were then serving as principals for the Friends Yearly Boarding School in Providence, Rhode Island. The two nieces were Mary E. Caldwell (see Letter No. 748, note 1) and "Lizzie," Elizabeth Hussey Whittier (1845–1902). In the late 1850's when her father, Matthew Franklin Whittier, and his wife were separated, Lizzie spent a good part of her time at the Whittier Amesbury home. During the 1860's she was educated at the Ipswich Female Seminary and from the death of her aunt in 1864 until 1876 she served as the head of the Whittier household. After the Civil War she spent three years in the South as a teacher of Negroes in Virginia and South Carolina. In 1876 she married Samuel T. Pickard, later to become Whittier's official biographer, and moved to Portland where her husband edited the Portland *Transcript*. During the 1890's the Pickards moved to Boston and Mrs. Pickard undertook the restoration and preservation of the Whittier birthplace in Haverhill.

4. Abigail Newhall (1839–1930) wrote a history of Friends in Philadelphia.

5. George Newhall (1836–1886) and Mary Newhall (1845–1899).

878. To Elizabeth Lloyd Howell

Amesbury May 18, 1859

Dear Elizabeth.

I liked thy letter (most welcome I assure thee) but feared
that thy eyes might be suffering while I was enjoying it. Do
not, dear E., feel obliged to answer my letters. Write when
thou canst—one word or ten,—the very blank paper which
thy hand has folded for my sake will be dear to me.

I thank thee for thy words of sympathy, and for the thought
of meeting me on the threshold of my home, with a word of
kindness. It seemed to me that I *felt* thy sympathy—all things
seemed brighter, and all the new burdens and cares which I
took up lighter and easier for thy sake.

Elizabeth, I have been happy—far more so than I ever expected in this life. The sweet memory of the past few weeks
makes me rich forever. What Providence has in store for the
future I know not—I dare not hope scarcely,—but the past is
mine—may I not say ours—sacred and beautiful, a joy forever.
Asking nothing of thee,—and with the tenderest regard for
thy griefs and memories, I have given thee what was thine by
right—the love of an honest heart—not as a restraint or burden
upon thee,—imposing no obligation and calling for no solicitude on thy part as respects myself. Nobody is a loser by
loving or being loved.

I feared thou wouldst be sadly tired and sick on reaching
Elmira, after so hurried a departure.[1] I hope ere this reaches
thee thou wilt be better. I sometimes think it wd. have been
as well for thee to have spent the summer with us. Our country here is then beautiful—cool and bracing with sea-air; and we
could have given thee a large, pleasant chamber looking over
the Northwestern hills. We have fine drives—Salisbury Beach
is only 4 miles away—and we might have had a delightful
season. But it is probably best as it is.

Yesterday I attended our little meeting, cordially welcomed
by our friends. It was pleasant to sit once more with "mine
own people."[2] Bird-songs floated in upon us from without
on breezes sweet with the odors of the greening spring:—the
irreverent bob-o-link adding his rollicking "Negro melodies."

The picture is safe in its handsome oval, velvet case. Meade
and Co., who put it up, pronounced it "a beautiful face, beautifully painted." How much pleasure it will give me!

Dear sister Lizzie is not well—tired out with getting the
girls off to Providence, and with company which has thronged
us of late. She sends her love, and has a grateful sense of thy

sympathy.

Don't try to write much if it pains thee to do so.

I will write whenever I can. I have been very busy and am very tired. Heaven bless, and keep thee!

J. G. W.

Manuscript: Facsimile reproduction, Denervaud, ed., *Whittier's Unknown Romance*, after page 18. Published: Denervaud, ed., *Whittier's Unknown Romance,* pp. 18–20.

1. Elizabeth Lloyd Howell went to Elmira in May for a "water cure." See Letter No. 883 for further comments on her treatments at Dr. L. O. Gleason's sanitarium.

2. II Kings 4:13.

879. To an Unidentified Correspondent

Amesbury May 18, 1859

My dear fd.

I have just returned from a visit to Philada. and Wilmington Del. of some weeks, and have this instant found thy letters. Fearing the delay I instantly sent the *four verses* to F. H. Underwood. Will that do?

I thank thee from my heart for giving me a place in thy charming book—as I am sure it must be—

With the highest respect and esteem
Ever and truly thy fd.
John G. Whittier

Manuscript: University of Virginia.

880. To George Wrightson

Amesbury May 18, 1859

Dr fd.

I have just returned from Philada where I have been trying to escape the East winds for a few weeks. I find thy letter among others reaching me and also one from Mr. Frothing-ham.[1] I thank the association for the invitation, and wish I could accept it.[2] But, illness and a pressure of cares at this time, compels me to decline anything of the kind. Regretting the delay in my answer I am very truly thy fd.

J. G. Whittier

Manuscript: Essex Institute, Salem, Massachusetts.

1. Edward Gilman Frothingham (1811–1876) was the publisher and editor of the *Essex Gazette*, a Haverhill newspaper. He edited the paper from 1843 until 1869 and was an active abolitionist.

2. This request may well have been regarding the building of a clubhouse and organization of a public park along the banks of the "Great Pond" in Haverhill. Whittier was asked to find a name for the park (see Letters No. 891 and 899) and then wrote a poem, "Kenoza Lake," for the dedication of the clubhouse and renaming of the lake, Kenoza. The poem was printed in local papers and in the New York *Independent* on September 8.

881. To William James Allinson

Amesbury May 21, 1859

My dear fd. William

In the midst of a hurry of things[1] to be done in doors and out, I drop thee a line just to let thee know of my safe arrival in my old home. I did not leave N. Y. until second day, dining on first day with my old fd Elizabeth Neall Gay on Staten Island, with Curtis the author. Second day I had a long and pleasant drive with Henry Ward Beecher: and that night went to Providence, spent the forenoon with Joseph Cartland and Gertrude, and got home the same evening, sadly tired but on the whole far better than when I left.

Never mind the overshoes. As to the spoon, give it to my namesake. Elizabeth sends her love to thee and thine. I hope Rebecca's cold is well, and that thy dear Aunt is also comfortable.[2] Do give my love to *all* our friends in Burlington, and assure them, that I have a very pleasant recollection of my brief visit.

Say to thy brother Samuel that it is one of my regrets that I did not see more of him. I wanted to see him at his own house.

How [droll][3] it was that such a story should get to Philada of my being "very sick" at your house. Tell Dr. Pugh he will have the credit of doing a wonderful cure, in my case.[4] I am sure the Dr. did me good if his medicine didn't.

Affly thy fd.
J. G. Whittier

Source: Typewritten copy, Essex Institute, Salem, Massachusetts.
1. After "things" the typewritten copy had "doings and." I deleted the words "doing and" to make the sentence intelligible.
2. Mary Allinson. See Letter No. 905.
3. The typewritten copy has "dull."
4. Perhaps Elijah Pugh (1800–1887).

882. To Abby Newhall

Amesbury May 23, 1859

My dear fd. Abby.

I was heartily glad to hear from you all at my old home in
Spruce Street. It was a droll mistake about my being sick at
Burlington. I was not very well, but sufficiently so to enjoy
my visitings exceedingly. It probably all grew out of my
asking Dr. Pugh after he had prescribed for R. Allinson, what
he could do for me, half in joke. But I am none the less grateful for the kindness which prompted you to inquire personally
into the rumor; and I hope thee and Mary are none the worse
for your errand of mercy to Burlington. I know you must
have enjoyed it. Tell thy mother I saw Josiah and Ruth Challis
on Fifth day and also today at meeting.[1] They were glad to
hear from you. I took with me today to meeting an aid of
Capt. Montgomery the Free State fighter in Southern Kansas.[2]
He says he was two months in the saddle, scarcely, during
that time, sleeping under a roof.

It has rained *every day* since my return and the end is not
yet. I can't plant my garden; nor trim my vines, nor do anything out of doors, of any consequence. As a lazy man
should[,] I resign myself to the will of Providence and wait.
Quarterly meeting is just at hand; and our meeting house is
as clean as a Shaker parlor for the occasion. I wish you could
be with us.

I can fancy your yard looks pretty now with its abundant
rosebloom. *Here* no roses show themselves—even our lilies
of the valley are only buds, as yet. Our pear trees are in bloom.
But we have many very beautiful wildflowers all about us,
and we can make them serve our purpose. I found two boxes
of flowers sent during our absence, withered and faded, but
still welcome as tokens of friendship and love. I notice what
thee mention of friends calling after my departure. I trust I
feel grateful to the kind Providence that has blessed me with
friends, and with kindness far beyond my deservings. I am
glad thy mother saw Grace Greenwood. She is a noble woman,
generous and self-forgetting in her regard for others. If thou
sees E. Nicholson tell her that she must come to N E. Y. M.
and bring with her for Elizth and I a copy of her Book on
Cooking.[3] I may possibly meet her there, if not, we shall
send a delegation from Amesbury. I am glad to hear thee has
made matters right with Deborah Williamson.[4]

Elizth likes the dresses very much and thanks thee and thy
mother for the trouble of getting them. She joins in love to
you.

Very truly thy fd.

John G. Whittier

Tell thy mother her cousin David's outer man is not improved.[5]

Manuscript: Westtown School, Pennsylvania.

1. Ruth Jones Challis (1806–1879) was an elder in the Seabrook, New Hampshire, Quaker meeting.

2. James Montgomery (1814–1871) was one of the military leaders of the
Free-State men then fighting in Kansas. He fought many battles with proslavery
forces and served throughout the Civil War as a colonel.

3. Elizabeth Nicholson's What I Know; or, Hints on the Daily Duties of a
Housekeeper (Philadelphia, 1856) contained suggestions and receipts on cooking,
preserving, ironing, needlework, gardening, and other household tasks.

4. Deborah Williamson (1801?–1876), a Philadelphia Quakeress.

5. II Corinthians 4:16. The phrase reads: "But though the outward man perish,
yet the inward man is renewed day by day."

883. To Elizabeth Lloyd Howell

Amesbury June 2, 1859

Dear Elizabeth

I read last night thy welcome letter with its vivid description of thy new home. It is one of the compensations merci-
fully provided for the minor miseries of life, that we can
look back upon them, and find amusement in all our by-gone
perplexities and disappointments. In this way thy sad, first
night's experience may be worth something to thee.

I am glad thee finds favor with Pat, as an offset to Zipporah.
Not but that I quite agree with the latter in her democratic
notions of equality, although I dare say I might be tempted
to make an exception of thy case, for radical as I am, I think
I can see a difference between liking every body in the abstract
and loving somebody in the concrete. But, in point of fact,
Zip is right. I respect her sturdy democracy, and admire her
pertinacious adherence to principle, against the wrath of thy
friend Kimber, and thy still harder-to-be-resisted mute appeal
for special favor. She must be an extraordinary woman.

Thy description of the "women-kind" in the parlor of yr
establishment alarms me. Will Zipporah, with the decision of
her ancient namesake, make thee like unto them? Will she cut
thy hair off? Will she put thee in Bloomers? Instead of writing
to my old friend, with her sweet Quaker proprieties, shall I
have to address myself to one of the strong-minded, discours-

ing at the breakfast-table on dietetics and physiology? Must
everything suffer a water-change? And, just now it occurs to
me that good old Dr. Woeselheft of Brattleboro had a theory
of the water-cure that it consisted in the entire washing away
of the "old man" of the flesh, and substituting a new one altogether?[1] If this be true, in what shape will thee emerge from
Elmira? How shall we identify the butterfly in bloomers with
the chrysalis in skirts? I give thee fair warning. If thee comes
out of Dr. Gleason's laboratory transmuted and metamor-
phosed into anything more or less than the identical Lizzie
Lloyd of old times, I for one, am not going to like thee at
all.[2] Red republican as I am, I am terribly conservative in that
respect.

I think I understand, now, thy whereabouts, and home-
fixings. Thy room I am sure is a very pleasant one, and I can
imagine how the sunset glorifies thy mountain pictures. By
the way, in New York I went with Beecher (H W.) to see
Church's great painting "The Heart of the Andes." Imagine a
table-land seven thousand feet above the sea, rich with vege-
tation—with blue glimpses of a lake, through tropical green-
ness. Far away beyond rises, dark and vast, a huge mountain
range, and beyond all, through a gorge in the near mountains,
you see cold, strange splendors of snow and ice, and you
follow up—up, into the very heart of the heavens, the "motionless torrents and silent cataracts."[3] White, cold, terribly beautiful, the ghost of a mountain! Above all is the wonderful
transparence of sky and the clouds raking the splintered summits, are like perfect photographs from Nature, rather than
pencil imitations. It is a great picture, and I am glad to hang
it up in my memory as a joy forever.

From what thee says I think it will be quite safe for thee to
trust thyself to the worthy Dr's discretion. Of course, as thy
friend Pat wd. say, he will have his cold water *warm* until
thee can bear the ice-cold liquid from the North side of the
pump. It is best to take things as comfortably as we can, and
if one has to go a pilgrimage with peas in the shoes, it is safer
to have them *boiled*. A degree of stoicism is, however, at
times, necessary. I sent thee today Dana's "Cuba"—the new
book which is so popular in Boston.[4] Get somebody to read
it to thee. I know it is good although I have not read it. I have
just finished planting my potatoes, etc.—rather late, but, if
there is not a crop I shall hold thee partly responsible. I need
not tell thee, dear E., how glad I am to get a line from thee.
Have had some interesting pilgrims here—and some I could
have done without. We are now all alone—only Charlie[5] and

the girl, but the next train may bring somebody, as the weather is so fine. Do get into the air as much as possible. I live out of doors now, when I am not driven in by the headache.

I suppose thou has heard of the death of my old and dear fd Jos Sturge. It is a great loss to his family—to our religious Society and to the world.[6] He lived very closely to the Divine Pattern—a life of eminently *practical righteousness*. So they pass—one after another—and we are spared yet a little longer.—May God enable us to so live that death may be a glad surprise!

The mail is just closing—The dear Lord have thee in his keeping always!

Aff—

J. G. W.

Source: Currier, ed., *Elizabeth Lloyd and the Whittiers*, pp. 130–133.

1. Robert Wesselhoeft (1796–1852) was a pioneer in the practice of hydrotherapy in America and established a water cure in Brattleboro, Vermont. He also espoused the cause of homeopathy and wrote a reply to Oliver Wendell Holmes's *Homœopathy and Its Kindred Delusions.*

2. Dr. L. O. Gleason was the director of a water cure sanitarium in Elmira, New York.

3. Samuel T. Coleridge, "Hymn before Sunrise in the Vale of Chamouni." The line should read: "Motionless torrents! silent cataracts!"

4. *To Cuba and Back* (Boston, 1859).

5. Whittier's pet parrot.

6. Joseph Sturge died on May 14, 1859.

884. To Elizabeth Lloyd Howell

Amesbury, June 9, 1859

Dear Elizabeth,

I am half sick to-day and have been so for two or three days past, unable to do anything but inflict myself upon somebody else. And, as I cannot get to thee in person, what better can I do than send my shadow? It was taken this spring by a wandering peddler in our village. I thought to send it to my dear friend Joseph Sturge, but delayed doing so hoping to get something better until it was too late. I don't think much of it: and I fear thee will not, but there may be times when even such a "counterfeit presentment"[1] of thy friend may be welcome—or as Mrs. Stowe's Candace would say, "better than nuffin."

I fear, dear, thou art suffering a great deal; indeed I seem to know it. May our dear Lord comfort and sustain thee with a feeling that His chastening is to heal! Dear E., let us try to

trust all to Him, and in pain and trial think of our many blessings, and in comparing our lot with that of others look down
instead of up. How many suffer bodily pain as we do, without the compensations and alleviations which we have!

I thought somewhat of attending the Yearly Meeting, but
unless I am better I shall not. If I go, I shall leave to-morrow
or next day.

Excuse the brevity of this note. I will do better when I can.

Ever affectionately,

J. G. W.

Source: Denervaud, ed., *Whittier's Unknown Romance*, pp. 20–21.
1. *Hamlet*, III, iv, 54.

885. To Elizabeth Lloyd Howell

Fillmore House, Newport June 12, 1859

My Dear Elizabeth,

Here I am at Y. M. I started yesterday morning with my
sister Mary, who wanted to take her girl with her from the
Island to Providence School. We got here last night at a quarter past six. The house is full of Friends, and a very social,
pleasant time they seem to make of it. A jollier set than these
sober-dressed Quakers I never saw. The old Providence scholars have a festival here to-morrow, and those who have been
separated for twenty years or more now meet for the first
time. Some Philadelphia people are here—M. Cole and wife,
Jane Pettitt, John Horton and wife, E. Nicholson, and others.[1]

I was not mistaken, then. Thee was sick. Indeed, I felt
that it was so. Sick and sad, and I could not take thy hand;
nor to speak a kind word to cheer thee, or, that failing, to
sorrow with thee! How I wish that my prayers were availing
ones! I can understand thy feeling for I have known sorrow
and trial, and loss, and I have a temperament very much
like thy own, keenly sensitive and alive in every move. How I
wish thou couldst be here to-day—this sweetest of early Summer Sabbaths—beautiful as that immortal in the verse of
Herbert—"The bridal of the earth and sky!"[2] My friend D. A.
Wasson is here.[3] Does thee remember some beautiful lines of
his entitled "All's Well" in the Atlantic Monthly?

By the by, dear E., thee and Elizabeth Nicholson must get
over that difficulty somehow. Thee can afford to forget and
forgive all, and thee will be happier to do so, and make all
allowance for her temperament, habits of thought, and speech,

etc. Do think of it. No matter how wrong she may have been,
there is a greater opportunity for Christian magnanimity on
thy part. E. Nicholson never has said anything to me about
your separation except that you were no longer as you had
been. I must have written this in the midst of noise and talking
all about me. When I can get a quiet hour, I will write again,
and I hope, better.

My health is better than when I wrote last, but I am still
suffering a good deal of pain in my side, and had a sleepless
night last night. Courage, dear Elizabeth. All will be well,
for all is in God's good hands. If thee writes within a few
days, direct to me at the "Marlboro Hotel," Boston.

Affectionately,
J. G. W.

Don't try to write long letters if it pains thee.

Source: Denervaud, ed., *Whittier's Unknown Romance,* pp. 21–23.

1. Perhaps Reuben Cole (1798?–1869), who died in Maine; John Horton (1790?–1865), and Maria W. Horton (1800?–1872).

2. "Virtue," *The Temple* (1633).

3. David A. Wasson (1823–1887), a liberal clergyman and writer, had parishes in both Boston and Worcester. He had a posthumous volume of poetry published in 1888 and his poem, "All's Well," appeared in the *Atlantic* for December 1858.

886. To Elizabeth Lloyd Howell

Amesbury, June 24, 1859

My Dear Elizabeth,

Will thee excuse my long silence? I would have been glad
to have written from Newport again: but really I had no
opportunity. I left the Island on fifth day afternoon, with
Gertrude and Joseph Cartland and Sarah Whittier,[1] and
went to the School, where I remained until yesterday morning. Of course I did not get thy letter until yesterday afternoon I found it awaiting me at the "Marlboro" and was truly
glad to hear again from thee.

What does thee mean by talking as thee does about Friends?
Does thee really think there are no good and worthy and interesting and refined people in the Quaker fold? Thee has surely
too much good sense and conscience, and too delicate a
sense of justice to be swayed by prejudice. Why, dear E., thou
art a Quaker, and those who love thee best have learned to
love thee as such. Thee owes too much to thy Quaker training
and culture, to disown and deny us at this late day. I, as thee
knows, am no sectarian, but I am a Quaker, nevertheless, and
I regard the philosophy underlying Quakerism as the truest

and purest the world has ever known. I care little for some of
our peculiarities: but I love the principles of our Society, and
I know that it, with all its faults and follies, is, at the moment,
in the very van of Christendom: that among its members, at
this very hour, are the best specimens of Christians to be
found in the wide world. My reason, my conscience, my taste,
my love of the beautiful and the harmonious, combine to
make me love the society. I cannot understand thy feeling: I
am only very sorry for it. I am well aware how the conduct of
certain individuals, and the general condition of things in
Philidelphia, might affect thee, but thy noble and generous
nature could not include all in thy condemnation. Oh, dear
E., let us cultivate charity, let us forget and forgive. Think
how the dear God bears with us—how his infinite pity follows
us, rebuking our ingratitude with blessings!

I saw many pleasant people, Friends and otherwise, at
Newport and Providence. My friend D. A. Wasson was at the
hotel where I stayed at Newport. We visited Mrs. Ames (wife
of the painter), and saw her nobly modeled heads.[2] That of
Voltaire was wonderfully expressive of the character of the
man. At Providence I had a visit with Gertrude and Sarah
Tobey[3] at Dr. Wayland's. I do not know when I ever met with
so cordial a reception. I met also, Rowland G. Hazard,[4] the
intimate friend of Dr. Channing, and a man of great intellectual power, Charles S. Brooks, the best English translator of
Goethe's Faust, and others.

The meeting of the old scholars and teachers of the Providence School held during the Y. M. week, was a very spirited
and creditable affair. The Boston Daily Advertiser, the organ
of New England respectability, says that the speeches would
have done credit to any college in the country. I was very sorry
that [. . .] was not with us.

Gertrude speaks of thee with much love and admiration.
Joseph, thee knows, was always one of thy admirers. I have
read Rush Plumley's "Compensation."[5] It is really a beautiful
poem—oriental as a palm tree. There are some exquisite lines
in it.

I note what thee commands about my health. I should find
it difficult to obey thee right off, however, for Dr. Bowditch
is just now floating in the shadow of the Nubian temples on
the waters of the Nile. He will be back again in a few weeks. I
will try to take care of myself as well as I can.

I hope thee is better thyself and that sunshine is compen-
sating for thy "cloudy days." Ah me! how poor and weak we
seem when we cannot make those happy whom we love!

I shall write to Hannah Sturge.[6] How I thank our Heavenly Father for the privilege of knowing and loving and being beloved by such a man as her dear husband!

Whatever may be thy own recollection of Newport, I find, dear E., that thou wast kindly remembered. I am sure if thou hadst been with us at the Fillmore House, thou wouldst not have found it difficult to be pleased.

I am sorry the picture wasn't better, but the sun is no flatterer, and I rather think it is truer to the original at this time than the one thee alludes to in the large book.

Ever affectionately thy friend
J. G. W.

Source: Denervaud, ed., *Whittier's Unknown Romance*, pp. 23–27.

1. Sarah E. Whittier (b. 1836), an attractive cousin of Whittier, married Amos C. Weeden of New Hampshire.

2. Sarah Fisher Ames (1817–1901), a sculptress, was noted for her heads of Lincoln and Grant. She was an abolitionist and served as a nurse during the Civil War. Her husband, Joseph Ames (1816–1872), was a portrait painter and illustrator.

3. Sarah Fry Tobey (1807?–1894) was the wife of a Rhode Island doctor.

4. Rowland G. Hazard (1801–1888), author and abolitionist, wrote books on language and theology and published essays on Channing.

5. Benjamin Rush Plumley (1816–1887), a Pennsylvania abolitionist, published many of his oriental poems in the *Atlantic Monthly*. He later served in the Civil War and settled in Texas.

6. Hannah Dickinson (1816–1896), the second wife of Joseph Sturge, married him in 1846 and they had five children.

887. To Elizabeth Lloyd Howell

Amesbury, June 29, 1859

Dear Elizabeth,

Thy letter and the sunshine, after a week of rain and mist, came together. I am thankful for both. I greatly enjoyed thy description of thy morning excursion, and the evidence it afforded of renewed health and spirits. I constantly find myself wishing for thee in my outgoings, and incomings: I want thee to see what I see and hear what I hear. Outward nature seems more beautiful to me than ever, and the frail tenure by which I hold it is very apparent to me. I have been sad over the sudden death of my old friend and associate Dr. Bailey.[1] I have just written a letter of sympathy to Margaret Bailey. Her loss is a very great one, for he was one of the kindest and truest of men.

I wish, dear E., it was in my power to visit Elmira. But home duties of an imperative kind now detain me, and I fear my health is not at this time equal to the fatigue of the journey. But the thought is often with me, and, if possible, I may see thee before the summer is over. Shall thee not return to Philadelphia in the fall?

I am almost sorry I said anything to thee about E. N., for I fear it gave thee pain. It is a feeling—weakness perhaps—of mine that I must be on good terms personally with everybody, good or bad, pleasant or indifferent, and I want those I love to have the good will of every one too. It comes of my intense longing for harmony, and a strong need of approbation, which extends to my friends, who are a part of myself.

We have all been "hydropathists" here for the last two weeks. "The rain, it raineth every day."[2] To-day, however, it is fresh and bright as Eden before Adam's unlucky bite of the apple. I enjoy it, but somehow miss *some one* and *somebody* to enjoy it with me. To-morrow we go over the river to a picnic at the "Laurels"—one of the most charming river views in the world—with a select company from Salem, Lynn, and Newburyport.[3] How happy and proud I should be to have thee with us!

My poor old friend Joshua Coffin, "my old schoolmaster," who has been ill in mind and body for some time, is spending the day with me. He fears he is not one of the elect. I tell him God will do the best thing possible for him and everybody else, that he never deserts us, and that his love is always about us. But there is no "ministering to the mind diseased."[4]

I enclose the two items which I cut from the daily papers, both presenting me in a rather novel light to the public. The coupling my name with Robert and Sarah is droll enough.[5]

Joshua is impatient and I must talk with him. Do let me know how thou art in health, and what the water is doing for thee. The dear God love and keep thee!

Affectionately,

J. G. W.

Source: Denervaud, ed., *Whittier's Unknown Romance,* pp. 27–29.

1. Gamaliel Bailey had died on June 5, 1859, and Whittier wrote an article about him, "Gamaliel Bailey," which appeared in the *National Era* of July 7. In it Whittier said that "Bailey was a gifted and dear friend. . . . He was one of those who mold and shape the age in which they live. . . . None but those who knew him well, and understood his social and genial nature and his strong love of approbation could estimate how much it cost him to maintain under circumstances to which a weaker man would have yielded as to destiny, his perfect loyalty to truth."

2. *Twelfth Night,* V, i, 401.

3. The "Laurels" was a natural amphitheater near the Newburyport shore of the Merrimack River where William Ashby and his friends had an annual party when the laurels were in bloom. At first the parties were small but by 1859 guests came from as far away as New Bedford. Whittier attended many of the laurel parties and wrote a poem for the twentieth and last anniversary, "The Laurels," in 1870.

4. *Macbeth*, V, iii, 40, modified.
5. Robert Lindsey (1801–1863), a Quaker minister, traveled widely throughout the world in the interests of his Society. In 1857, together with his wife,
Sarah Crossland (1804–1872), he visited remote parts of North America, the
Sandwich Islands, and Australia.

888. To Elizabeth Lloyd Howell

Amesbury June 31 [1859]

Dear E.,

From the golden threshold of this glorious day I cannot
fail in greeting thee. How is it with thee? I hope for the best.

We found on Third day a large gathering at the Laurels, on
the riverside. The company were from Boston, New Bedford,
Salem, Lynn, and Newburyport—a little too fashionable and
conventional for that comfortable lapse into savage freedom
that a picnic implies, but there were many of the true kind.
The day was intensely hot, but river, trees, and flowers were
never more inviting. We spent the early evening with our dear
friends Margaret and Mary Curzon, on the Artichoke, watching
the sun go down through the great oaks, transforming the
water into a river of light. How I wished for thee! I would fain
have all I enjoy with thee.

I have only time to try to say good morning! The blessing
of our Father's love be with thee!

Ever and truly thine.
J. G. W.

Source: Denervaud, ed., *Whittier's Unknown Romance*, p. 30.

889. To Wendell Phillips Garrison

Amesbury July 5, 1859

Dear fd.

Thy letter is just recd. I think well of the petition, and, if
present, shall cheerfully *vote* for it.

But such is my health at this time that it is not certain that
I can be at the meeting of the Board;—and, if there, I should
not feel like attempting to speak. It wd. be better, I think, to
place the petition in some other person's hands. Whatever
I can do to promote its object shall be done.[1]

Be pleased to remember me affectionately to thy father—
one of my oldest and dearest friends.

May God bless thee, my young friend, and unite in thee the
distinctive qualities of those whose names are joined in thine—

the sweet persuasive power of the one, and the lofty integrity and loyalty to truth of the other.

Thine truly
John G. Whittier

Manuscript: University of Rochester.

Recipient: Wendell Phillips Garrison (1840–1907), then a freshman at Harvard, graduated in 1861 and then served most of his life as the literary editor for the *Nation*. He published with his brother Francis a four-volume life of his father, *William Lloyd Garrison, 1805–1879,* in 1885 and authored many books of translation and verses for children.

1. The only summer meeting of the board of overseers was held on July 20. Whittier was not present and the only business transacted was to give assent to the degrees for the coming commencement. The next meetings of the board were an adjourned special meeting and a regular annual meeting on January 26, 1860. Whittier was not present then, but at that meeting a petition from 179 students concerning the regulations for church attendance on Sundays was received.

890. To Elizabeth Lloyd Howell

Marlborough Hotel, Boston July 9, 1859

Dear Elizabeth,

Soon after getting thy long letter—too long, for thy eyes are of more consequence than our notions upon the matters treated therein—I had to come to this wicked little city, leaving a line to thee unfinished at home.

I see we cannot think alike about Friends. I am sorry, but it cannot be helped. Heart and soul, I am a Quaker and, as respects forms, rituals, priests, and churches, an iconoclast, unsparing as Milton or John Knox. But I am not going to discuss the endless subject. I shall not make a red republican of thee, nor will thee convert me to a belief in Bishops, reverend fathers, and apostolic succession. I don't see any saving virtue in candles, surplices, altars and prayer books. At the same time I am but an indifferently good Quaker—I take my own way, and Friends theirs. I don't well see how I could be any more free.

We have just got through with an Atlantic dinner at the Revere House. Let me give thee the names of our company: Dr. Holmes sits one side of me, Prof. Stowe on the other; next to him, Wyman, one of the editors;[1] next, Edwin P. Whipple, the essayist; next, Underwood, another editor; then comes Mrs. Stowe; by her side is Lowell; opposite her is Longfellow; next him is Stillman, the artist and poet;[2] then comes Wentworth Higginson; and opposite me sits Miss Prescott, etc., etc.[3] Holmes has been in the Autocrat vein. Mrs. Stowe has come out wonderfully. We have discussed literature, manners, races, and national characteristics—not omitting theology, for we are Yankees. It was a pleasant gathering, lasting from 3 to 6. When I left, Longfellow, Holmes, Quincy, Lowell, and Whipple were lingering over their claret and cigars. Emerson wrote us that he had sprained his ankle on Wachuset mountain, and was on two sticks like the hero of Le Sage's novel.[4] For myself, I don't much like those dinners. At such times when I break through my natural reserve I am liable to say more than I mean—to be extravagant and overstrong in my assertions. I dare say that I have said a good deal to-day that I ought to be sorry for, but luckily my conscience does not bring any specific charge against me.

I wish I could write more, but I am so weary. I will write when I get home, I hope more to the purpose.

That beautiful evening thee speaks of was lovely here also. We both enjoyed it, unconscious that the other shared it.

God bless, comfort, and direct thee dear E. Has Dr. Neidhard written thee?[5] I suppose he knows how thee gets along with the water treatment.

Ever affec.,

J. G. W.

Source: Denervaud, ed., *Whittier's Unknown Romance*, pp. 31–33.

1. John C. Wyman, an assistant editor of the *Atlantic Monthly*.

2. William James Stillman (1828–1901) was noted for his landscape paintings and in 1858 founded the *Crayon*, a journal of the graphic arts. After 1860 he devoted himself entirely to writing and became a reporter for the London *Times*.

3. Harriet Prescott (1835–1921), a Newburyport writer best known for her romantic short stories, had recently published a story, "In a Cellar," in the *Atlantic*. She continued to write novels and poetry throughout her life, and after her marriage in 1865 to Richard Spoffard, purchased a home on Deer Island on the Merrimack. During the 1870's she became quite friendly with Whittier and he referred to her "June on the Merrimac," besides writing a poetic tribute to her husband, "R. S. S. at Deer Island on the Merrimac."

4. Asmodeus, the dwarf spirit in Le Sage's novel, *Le Diable Boiteux*, had the legs of a goat and used two sticks to walk with.

5. Charles Neidhard (1809–1895) was a doctor and professor of clinical medicine in the Homoeopathic Medical College of Pennsylvania.

891. To Elizabeth Lloyd Howell

Amesbury, July 14, 1859

Dear Elizabeth

I have been wishing to write ever since my return from Boston, but have been troubled so much with pain in my head and eyes that I have not ventured to do so. Even now, I must only say a word. I have been so troubled and perplexed with my brother's affairs, and some other matters of late that if I was writing to anybody but thyself, I am afraid I should have been inclined to pick a quarrel by way of relief.[1] We are having delightful weather here, and I hope it extends to Elmira, and that thy health and spirits are improving under its influence.

My dear sister Elizabeth is quite feeble this summer in bodily health, and still suffers under the deep depression which I mentioned to thee. I feel very anxious about her. How hard it is to leave some things to Providence! To trust our nearest and dearest wholly and unreservedly to the love and pity of our Father!

I was amused by thy description of Newport and Y. M. I don't wonder at thy unfavorable impression. I am sure it would have been different this year if thou hadst been there.

I saw Hannah Shipley's husband, Joel Bean, at Y. M.[2] He has a good deal of native delicacy and refinement. I got a line from Hannah on the eve of her marriage. I could not but smile at thy remark about the food of your Sanitarium among the hills. I am far from indifferent to the good things of life, but I could live, if necessary, on the black broth of Sparta, or the oatmeal porritch of the Scotchman. I didn't board with Joseph Healy, with Sarah Jonathan for cook, so long for nothing. Henceforth I defy the fates in the shape of cookery. With the Scriptural injunction I "eat what is set before me, asking no questions."[3]

I had a droll matter to settle this morning. The good people of Haverhill have bought and ornamented a large tract of land on the margin of a beautiful pond known as Great Pond. They wanted a name for it and couldn't agree among themselves, and finally voted to leave it to me. I have been hunting over Indian vocabularies, and have heartily learned to pity Adam, who had so many things to find names for.[4]

I shall set thee an example of brevity in this letter. Enclosed is a notice of Dr. Bailey. "Seen and Unseen" is not mine.

Take care of thyself, dear E. Let me hear from thee, but don't write another long letter.

Affectionately,
J. G. W.

Source: Denervaud, ed., Whittier's Unknown Romance, pp. 33–35.

1. Matthew Franklin Whittier was then separated from his second wife and for a time his children were kept at the Whittier home in Amesbury. Lizzie Whittier remained there throughout a good part of the 1860's and permanently after her Aunt Elizabeth's death in 1864, while her brother Charles and sister Alice resided with their mother in Portland. By the early 1860's Matthew Franklin was living with his third wife, Mary Waite Whittier, near Boston, where he was a clerk in the Boston custom house.

2. Hannah Shipley (1830?–1909) the daughter of Thomas Shipley, a Phila-

delphia Quaker philanthropist and abolitionist, had married Joel Bean (1825?–
1914) in 1859.
    3. I Corinthians 10:27, modified.
    4. See Letter No. 880, note 2.

892. To Elizabeth Lloyd Howell

Amesbury, July 14, 1859

Dear E

    Thy welcome letter has reached me. I am glad to know that
thy sister is to visit thee.[1] Thee do not say what Dr N. thought
of the water treatment.[. . .]

    I think the saddest part of life is to see things going wrong
within us and without us, and yet feel unable to right them.
The inability to do! Yet this painful solicitude has its uses and
compensations.

    Did thee ever think what a dull place Heaven must be if the
popular notion of it is correct. A state of sheer spiritual lazi-
ness—nothing to do because everything is *done*—nobody to
help—nobody to pity—nobody to pray for—no employment
but to sing hymns!

    I enclose a tribute to the memory of the best man I ever
knew.[2] I don't think I have said too much, but, I fancy I hear
him say: "No—no, John; I am nothing but a living testimony
to the mercy and compassion of God."

    We have had gloriously bright summer weather for two
weeks—To day the rain is falling—quietly and thunderless—a
sweet and unalloyed blessing.

    Excuse me, dear fd, for speaking of my troubles and vexa-
tions. I know thou hast enough of thy own without any addition from others. If I were a stronger man and a better
Christian, I should not let them disturb even myself. As it is,
I feel sure that *somehow* all will be well—and my confidence
in the Divine Goodness is unshaken. Come what may let us
trust in that. At times, I feel all that I have expressed in "My
Psalm" in the Atlantic Monthly.[3] I have so much to be thankful for that I ought always to feel so, but the spirit is willing
often when the flesh is weak.[4]

    Do you have any pond lillies at Elmira?—Here, our little
lakes are white and sweet with them. I wish I could send thee
a fine cluster of them fresh from the water. They recall
Tennyson's verse,

    "White lillies of eternal peace
      Whose odors haunt my dreams."[5]

My little sheet is full. Ever and affectionately

J. G. W.

Source: Currier, ed., *Elizabeth Lloyd and the Whittiers,* pp. 133–135.

1. Hannah Lloyd Neal, then living in California. She did not come as expected, but arrived in December (see Letter No. 912).

2. "In Remembrance of Joseph Sturge."

3. "My Psalm" appeared in the *Atlantic*, August 1859.

4. Matthew 26:41, modified.

5. "Sir Galahad," lines 67–68. The first word should be "pure" instead of "white."

893. To an Unidentified Correspondent

[After July 21, 1859] [1]

I thank thee for thy invitation to Berkshire. I wd like exceedingly to look upon that mountain again, but am not well enough now to do so. I have a friend in Pittsfield Julius Rockwell whom I dare say thou hast met.

I am glad thou liked my lines on Joseph Sturge. His eulogy was not exaggerated. He was the best man I ever knew. Thank God for such!

> "Still shines the light of holy lives
>   Like star beams over doubt
> Each sainted memory, Christ-like, drives
>   Some dark possession out." [2]

Believe me very truly thy fd.

J. G. Whittier

Manuscript: University of Virginia.

1. Dated by reference to the poem, "In Remembrance of Joseph Sturge," which was published in the New York *Independent*, July 21, 1859.

2. From Whittier's "William Forster."

894. To Elizabeth Lloyd Howell

Amesbury, July 30, 1859

Dear Elizabeth,

I hope the clearing weather for the last three weeks has been enjoyed by thee. Here we have had no rain except two showers for the whole time. The last shower was very severe, and something of a tornado passed near us.

Unhappily, neither E. nor myself have been well enough for a week past to enjoy the season as we should otherwise have done. I have been unable to read or write, and even now

I must apologize for not writing.

In what a sad condition Napoleon III has left Italy! Her last estate is worse than her first. One cannot but pity the poor exiles and refugees who rallied from all parts of the world for the liberation of their Fatherland; thousands of them are now lying in hospitals, sick, wounded, and despairing. But the good God sees all, and the lie of Priestcraft, and Kingcraft cannot live forever. We have this promise, that He will turn and overturn until He whose right it is shall reign.[1]

Excuse this hasty note. Do not try to answer it, for it is not worth it. I shall write again when I am fit for it.

I have just had a very kind and beautiful letter from Josiah Forster.[2] I believe thee knew him.

Aff.,
J. G. W.

Source: Denervaud, ed., *Whittier's Unknown Romance*, pp. 35–36.
1. Ezekiel 21:27, modified.
2. Josiah Forster (1782?–1870), an English Quaker and abolitionist, had traveled to the United States many times on religious work.

895. To Elizabeth Lloyd Howell

Amesbury, August 3, 1859

Dear Elizabeth,

Thy letter was most welcome, for I had really begun to fear thee was seriously ill.

If there has been any change in the letters, I am sure there is no change in the feeling which dictated them, so far as *thou* art concerned. But I ought to confess to thee that the old feeling of self-distrust, and painful consciousness of all I would be, and of all I am not, and of my inability to make those I love happy, come back to me, the stronger, perhaps, that for a time it was held in abeyance. I have grown old in a round of duties and responsibilities which still govern me and urge me: my notions of life and daily habits are old-fashioned and homely: I could not for any length of time endure the restraints of fashion and society: art, refinement, and cultivated taste please me as something apart from myself. Constantly baffled by illness and weakness, and every way reminded of my frailty and limitation, I can scarcely hope anything, but live in the present: enduring what I must and enjoying what I can, thankful, I trust, for the many blessings which our Father has vouchsafed, and comforting myself with the faith that my trials and crosses are blessings also, in an-

other form. But I cannot, dear E., be blind to the fact that
thee lives in a different sphere—that thy sense of the fitting and
beautiful demand accessories and surroundings very different
from those that have become familiar and habitual to me. I
am sure thy fine artist-nature would pine and die under the
hard and uncongenial influences which make me what I am,
and from which I cannot escape without feeling that I have
abandoned the post of duty, without losing my self-respect,
and forfeiting all right to be loved in return by those I love.
These considerations, and the discouraging influence of illness,
may have affected the tone and spirit of my letters.

But above all—and I know thou wilt pardon me if I touch,
with all tenderness, upon a subject which should be sacred—I
feel that thy instincts were right as respects that very happy
and beautiful episode in thy life—that sweet, calm sufficiency
and fullness of love graciously offered thee for a season,
which, brief as it was, had the length of years in its complete-
ness, and which still blesses thee with the richest legacies of
memory, and with hopes that outreach time and take hold
upon eternity. Knowing myself, I have never felt that I could
ever have been to thee what *he* was, whom the Great Goodness
gave thee. And, if, in the great happiness of meeting thee I
seemed at any time to forget this, I am sure thee understood
me, and knew instinctively that I would not designedly thrust
myself between thee and the memory of such a life and such
love, nor intrude, otherwise than as a loving and sympathizing
friend, upon thy sanctities of sorrow. It was no more than
thy due to know how much thy unconscious influence had
been to me, and how happy I was to meet thee again. I am
sure, in the end, it cannot harm thee or me, to know that
years and cares and sorrows have not estranged us, nor
blunted our mutual sympathies. What the world suffers from
is the *want* of love, not the excess of it. There cannot be too
much of kindness and affection—of that large charity which
will think no evil of its object, but good and good only.

And now, dear E., thou wilt see that if I have doubts or
misgivings, they belong to myself, and not to thee. There
seems, at times, a wide space between us, which I feel I have
no power or right even to cross, and hence, perhaps, something of the kind is manifest in my letters. For myself, I
have ceased to demand what is impossible, or to quarrel with
what is inevitable, for I know that the definite Goodness
must order all things well, for me, for thee, for all: and there
are times when I am, as it were, reconciled to all things—save
my own sins and follies.

This is the last day of summer, and the season goes out in beauty. The air is sweet and clear, and the sky and earth flecked and picturesque with clouds and sunshine. I would like to have thee see how the sunset looks from our hills: glorifying the valley, the river, and dying away in the misty Atlantic. Didst thou see the Aurora Borealis on First day evening? I think I never saw anything so weird, mystic, and wonderful. I wish I could for once annihilate distance, for I want to show thee a marvelous picture—a very large daguerreotype which the artist sent from Boston to Elizabeth to see, and which he values at $1000. It is the most exquisite thing I ever saw—face, attitude, and expression surpassing any dreams of the old painters. The beauty is doubtless a good deal accidental.

Dear sister is not, I think, any better: she cannot walk out much or ride without making her worse: and she has many cares which wear upon her and depress her. For her sake, how I wish that I were strong and well, instead of the constant invalid that I am! It seems to me wrong to be sick, and I dare say it is somehow, for it seems so necessary to be well. I am better than when I wrote last, however.

I am very glad to hear of Hannah's coming back for so long a visit: and hope I shall meet you all at the old home on Union Street, where I used to joke with her in the old times.

Forgive this long scrawl, and do not imitate it in length for thy eyes' sake. I will try to write a more cheerful one next time, but, glad or otherwise.

Affectionately,
J. G. W.

Source: Denervaud, ed., Whittier's Unknown Romance, pp. 36–41.

896. To Elizabeth Lloyd Howell

Amesbury, August 17, 1859

Dear E.,

I believe I wrote thee last when I was too sick to be a very agreeable correspondent. When one can do nothing but complain he should beware of pen and paper. I am still hardly fit for their use.

We have had clearing weather and a good deal of company with it—Judge Aldis and wife of Vermont,[1] Louisa Loring, widow of my old friend Ellis Gray Loring, and her daughter,[2] and William Lloyd Garrison and wife among others. We were glad to see them—especially Garrison, one of our old friends

who knew us when we were children at Haverhill. We talked
over the old times together—of what life had promised us, and
what it had given us,—compared our present views and conditions, and looked forward reverently and trustfully to the
end, near at hand, and the great Hereafter. G. does not believe
as I do on some points, but his faith, such as it is, seems strong
and real. As he grows older he grows gentler and more charitable, and his old love of nature, so long held in abeyance by
his anti-slavery controversy, and mission of reform, comes
back with renewed strength and keenness.

I hope thy sister's visit has been cheering to thee, and not
without enjoyment and profit to her.

The country has lost a great man, and I a very valued friend,
in Horace Mann.[3] How fast they pass away! How strange it
seems that I, the frailest of them all, remain!

I hope to feel well enough soon to go [on] a little journey in
New Hampshire. I shall try to persuade Lizzie to accompany
me, but without much hope of success. I wish we could by a
day's ride reach thy place of sojourn. We are getting ready
for our Horticultural and Agriculture Exhibition, next month.
We had the finest last year in this part of the state, but this
year our apples are few, our grapes less, and our peaches none.
Of pears we shall have a great show, and I am nursing mine
for the premium. My Flemish Beauties have just begun "to
blush on the side that's next the sun."

My letter is dull and stupid as the head that conceives it,
and I can only ask thy indulgence and remain,

As ever, affectionately,

J. G. W.

Has thee seen Tennyson's new book?[4] I have only looked at
it. Full of beautiful, sensuous pictures, but not great and deep
and earnest and loving like In Memoriam.

Source: Denervaud, ed., Whittier's Unknown Romance, pp. 41–43.

1. Asa O. Aldis (1811–1891), a Vermont lawyer, was appointed a judge in the
Vermont Supreme Court in 1857. He later served as the American consul to Nice.
Mary Taylor, his wife, married Judge Aldis in the 1840's and had seven children.

2. Louisa Gilman (1797–1868) married Ellis Gray Loring in 1827, and he died
in 1858. The Lorings had one child, Anna Loring (1830–1896).

3. Horace Mann died on August 2, 1859.

4. Idylls of the King (Boston, 1859).

897. To Elizabeth Lloyd Howell

                                        Amesbury, August 22, 1859

Dear Elizabeth,

I fear thy eyes are worse or that thou art ill, it is so long since I heard from thee.

I have just returned from Lynn and Nahant, and am in hopes I shall feel all the better for the change. I saw Sarah Aldrich at my aunt's.[1] She talked about Hannah and, on the whole, gave a very good idea of her Western home and mode of life. She said Hannah gave her a cane for me, but she was not able to take it with her. We hear that the English friends Robert and Sarah Lindsey have reached San Francisco. It must have been pleasant for Hannah to see them.

At Nahant, Fanny Longfellow showed me some fine marine sketches by the marine painter Kensett, which the artist has left with her husband.[2] One or two from Newport were very true and beautiful—but not as good as one in thy parlor which I remember.

But the pictures out of doors around the rugged coast of Nahant were, after all, more beautiful. A storm far out in the ocean drove the waves high and white upon the rocks, and far up the glimmering beaches, and under the bright summer sun (for on shore it was perfectly fair and clear). If I were a painter I should despair of making a picture of such a scene as I looked at from the outermost crag of Nahant, where the waves rolled in with the mighty force of the Atlantic.

Margaret Bailey is very anxious that I write regularly for the Era. Indeed, she seems to depend upon it. But I really cannot undertake it, as my health is not equal to the exertion, and I am advised against attempting it. I am sorry I cannot materially aid her, but I have done a great deal more in times past for the Era than my health and my interest pecuniarily warranted. In fact, I have been unjust to myself in the matter.[3]

We are having the most perfect summer weather—clear, cool, and dry. For the first time for four years in this part of New England the ground is dry enough to lie down upon with entire safety. My good friend H. J. Newhall and daughters are at Lynn and will visit Amesbury the last of this week.

Has thee read the "Idyls" yet? I have just got Kingsley's new volume, "Good News from God."[4] I see he takes the same view I do of the ultimate triumph of good and the end of all evil. The cross of Christ, he says, is as deep as hell and high as heaven.

I do not wish to tax thy eyes, but shall be glad to hear from

thee if but a line, as I am afraid that sickness prevents thee
from writing.

Ever and affectionately,
J. G. W.

Source: Denervaud, ed., *Whittier's Unknown Romance*, pp. 43–45.

1. Perhaps Sarah Holder Aldrich (1830?–1902).

2. John F. Kensett (1816–1872), an engraver and landscape painter, was best known for his landscapes of mountains and seashores.

3. After the death of her husband Margaret Bailey continued to publish the *National Era* until 1860. Lewis Tappan wrote to Whittier on August 1, 1859, as follows: "Mrs. Bailey, in a letter just recd from her, says: 'If I can carry the paper through the next year, I shall have no fears of its success. I have written to Mr. Whittier to urge him to resume his connection with the paper. Of late, it has been merely nominal. A very little labor on his part would be of great service to me, and I shall be well able to pay him a full renumeration, I have no doubt. If you think well of this, will it be too great a favor to ask you to write to Mr. Whittier and urge or ask him to help me, etc'." (Albree, ed., *Whittier Correspondence*. p. 133).

4. Charles Kingsley, *The Good News of God* (New York, 1859), a collection of his sermons.

898. To William James Allinson

Amesbury August 28, 1859

My dear William,

I was agreeably surprised the other day to get a nice picture of "My Namesake"—really a very [. . .][1] and, taking the *cane* into consideration a striking likeness.

This will be handed thee by William Williamson, who goes tomorrow to the Jersies. He will tell thee how we are.

I hope thee and thy dear wife are well. I felt anxious about her health when I was at Burlington but H. J. Newhall tells me she is better. Remember me to thy excellent Aunt[2] and to Samuel. Elizabeth sends her love—I enclose a picture of Robert Rantoul. I meant to have got one of J. Coffin but was disappointed in it.

With kind remembrances to all Burlington friends I am as ever

Aff thy fd.
J. G. W.

My cousin Sarah Lizzie Whittier will visit Elizabeth Nicholson in the 10th mo. I hope thee will see her. She is the best-looking Whittier in the lot, and I am sure thee would like her.

Source: Handwritten copy, Haverford College. Published: Snyder, "John Greenleaf Whittier to William J. Allinson," p. 31.

1. The word "striking" was written here but then crossed out.

2. Mary Allinson.

899. To Elizabeth Lloyd Howell

Amesbury, Sixth Day [after August 31, 1859][1]
Dear Elizabeth,

I think of starting for a little trip in the country for a few
days, and write a hasty line.

My last letter, was, I am sure, a very weak and foolish one.
But the truth is, I have been too ill to write otherwise; and I
so deeply feel my inability and good-for-nothingness that I
could not help confessing the consciousness.

Hannah J. Newhall and daughters spent a part of two days
with us last week and have just left Lynn for Philadelphia.
Did I tell thee that Cousin Sarah Whittier, of Providence, was
to visit Philadelphia in the tenth month? What is thy prospect
of return to the city? and when does thee expect Hannah's
arrival? I enclose a little account of the naming of my native
park in Haverhill. I could not be present, but sent an apology.[2]
Heaven bless and keep thee, dear E., and think of me as thy
affectionate

J. G. W.

Source: Denervaud, ed., *Whittier's Unknown Romance*, p. 46.
1. Dated by reference to the dedication of Kenoza Park on August 31, 1859.
2. For the dedication Whittier sent his poem, "Kenoza Lake." See Letter No.
880, note 2.

900. To Moses Brown

Amesbury September 6, 1859
My dear friend,

Thy very kind letter was recd. some days ago, but owing to
engagements and illness, I have delayed answering it.[1]

It gave me real pleasure to find myself thus remembered by
thee and thy family. I have a very grateful recollection of
your kindness and hospitality: and would be glad to prove my
words by accepting at once the invitation to Roxboro. But
my own health is at this time quite unfit for traveling, and
my sister I fear will not be able to leave home at all. Indeed I
am very anxious about her. At present I am too uncertain
to be able [to] give any definite answer to thy kind proposal.—

We had last week a too brief but otherwise satisfactory
visit from Hannah J. Newhall and her daughters. Through
them I am indebted to thee for a volume by Prof. Upham.[2] I
have only been able to read a few pages as yet, but, as far
as I have gone, the writer seems to me in the right path. The
standard is indeed very high and difficult, but, like the

Apostle we are to press towards it "not as having attained."[3]
The Divine Ideal must always, I think, be *before* us, never
completely overtaken, for that would be absorption in it, and
the consequent loss of our individuality.

Hoping that I may be able to see thee at thy pleasant country home before the frosts drive thee back to the city; (and
yet, at present, with small ground for the hope),—with much
love to thy wife and Wistar[4] I am ever and truly thy fd.

John G. Whittier

Manuscript: Haverford College.

1. Moses Brown had written Whittier on August 23, thanking him for his
poem in honor of Joseph Sturge and inviting Whittier and his sister to visit him at
his country house for a week (letter, Essex Institute, Salem, Massachusetts).

2. Thomas Cogwell Upham (1799–1872), a writer and professor, taught mental
and moral philosophy at Bowdoin from 1824 to 1867. He wrote many books and
published *A Method of Prayer* (London) in 1859.

3. Philippians 3:12. The correct phrasing is: "Not as though I had already
attained."

4. Mary Wistar was Moses Brown's wife.

Thomas Wistar Brown (1826–1916), Moses Brown's son, became a Philadelphia
banker and broker.

901. To William James and Rebecca Allinson

Amesbury September 25, 1859

Dear fds. Wm and Rebecca Allinson

I ought long ago to have answered your very kind and very
welcome letter, but a multiplicity of cares and a painful
affection of the eyes has prevented me from doing justice to
my kind correspondents.

I suppose Dr. Taylor has told thee that we met at Yearly
Meeting. It was pleasant to meet him, and his friends there.
I hope Rebecca's health is better and that my namesake con-
tinues to do credit to his *verdant* appellation.

Enclosed is a tribute to the memory of our friend Joseph
Sturge. It was published in the New York *Independent*. What
a noble list of worthies England and the world have lost!—
Elizabeth Fry, Joseph J. Gurney, William Allen, William
Forster, Joseph Sturge—Who will fill their places?

Remember me to all the good friends at Burlington and to
thy brother Samuel.

Elizabeth sends her love.

Very aff thy fd.
John G. Whittier

Source: Handwritten copy, Haverford College. Published: Snyder, "John
Greenleaf Whittier to William J. Allinson," pp. 31–32.

902. To Elizabeth Lloyd Howell

                              Amesbury, September 28, 1859

Dear Elizabeth,

This is the day of our annual festival of fruits and flowers—
a bright, glorious autumn day. Our hills and woods never
looked more lovely, and I always wish, when I hear or see
anything beautiful, that thee could see and hear with me. I
enjoy it, although last night was the first for several days that
I have been able to sleep—owing to neuralgic pains and nervous prostration. I am "weak as a yielding wave" bodily and
mentally this morning, but hope to be stronger soon, as the
severe pain has left me. I think of thee and how much thee
must suffer in this way. The mere ache is a trifle, if it did not
affect the nerves and temperament. If one could only keep
the mind serene and calm over all!

Neither my sister or myself are able to go to the exhibition
to-day, but I had the pleasure of aiding in the preliminary
arrangements. I enclose a little piece which was sung at the
Festival. The piece is not very brilliant, but it was luckily
written before I was so ill, or it would have been still poorer.[1]

I suppose thou wilt soon think of returning to Philadelphia.
I hope thy summer sojourn among the hills has really benefited thee, and that thee will carry back with thee to thy
home the warm light and the sweetness of the meadows and
the wild flowers for winter solace.

Thine of the 27th just received. It is as I feared—thee has
been sick. I am glad thee thinks of returning at once to P.
and that Hannah is looked for so soon. Do give my love to her,
and tell her I shall hope to see her erelong, if my health permits. I have not read "Adam Bede" yet or "Bitter-Sweet."[2]
The truth is, my head and eyes have been unfit for reading
much for some time past, and, Lizzie being in the same predicament, we cannot keep pace with the literary novelties. How
well I can understand thy own deprivations now! I will get
the book of Dr. Holland;[3] I know him and like him much as
a man. Emerson has been laid up with lameness this summer,
but is now, I believe, out again. Shall I send him to thee when
he comes to P.?

                              Ever and affectionately,
                                    J. G. W.

Source: Denervaud, ed., Whittier's Unknown Romance, pp. 47–48.
1. "For an Autumn Festival," which was published in the National Era,
September 29, 1859.
2. George Eliot, Adam Bede (New York, 1859), and Josiah G. Holland, Bitter-
Sweet (New York, 1858).

3. Josiah Gilbert Holland (1819–1881) was then associated with Samuel Bowles as an editor of the Springfield *Republican*. He wrote popular novels and poetry throughout the 1870's, and served as the first editor of *Scribner's Monthly* from 1870 to 1881. His *Bitter-Sweet* was a poem in dramatic form.

903. To James Russell Lowell

Amesbury October 10, 1859

Ed. At Monthly.

Some two weeks ago I sent, as I supposed, the enclosed letter to Mr. Underwood, recalling my poem "Rome 1859"— and stating that I thought of publishing it elsewhere. By sheer accident I have just found the letter, which, written during illness, was not put in the P. O. as I supposed. Some days ago I sent a copy of the poem to the N. Y. Independent taking it for granted that all was right as respected the Atlantic, and I fear it is now too late to prevent its appearance in that paper. I have telegraphed to stop it. If however the piece is in type and worked off for the Magazine, and the Independent also, can you not append a note to your last page or cover to this effect.—

"The article 'Rome 1859' forwarded for the October number of the Atlantic was recalled by the author for publication elsewhere, but the letter to that effect, was unfortunately delayed accidentally until the poem was in type."

I am very sorry for the mistake and will cheerfully meet the expense of such a note, as the fault was not yours; I hope, after all, that you have not printed the poem.[1]

Yrs truly,
John G. Whittier

Manuscript: Harvard University. Published, in Part: Pickard, *Life,* pp. 423–424.
1. Whittier's letter to Lowell was in time to prevent the poem's publication in the *Atlantic*, and it was published in the *Independent*, October 27, 1859.

904. To Lydia Maria Child

October 21, 1859

My Dear Friend,—

I was glad to get a line from thee, and glad of the opportunity it affords me and my sister to express our admiration of thy generous sympathy with the brave but, methinks, sadly misguided Captain Brown.[1] We feel deeply (who does not?) for the noble-hearted, self-sacrificing old man. But as friends of peace, as well as believers in the Sermon on the Mount, we dare not lend *any* countenance to such attempts as that at Harper's Ferry.

I hope, in our admiration of the noble traits of John Brown's character, we shall be careful how we encourage a repetition of his rash and ill-judged movement. Thou and I believe in "a more excellent way."[2] I have just been looking at one of the *pikes* sent here by a friend in Baltimore. It is not a Christian weapon; it looks too much like murder.

God is now putting our non-resistance principles to a severe test. I hope we shall not give the lie to our life-long professions. I quite agree with thee that we must judge of Brown by his standards; but at the same time we must be true to our settled convictions, and to the duty we owe to humanity.

Thou wilt see how difficult it is for me to write as thou request. My heart is too heavy and sorrowful. I cannot write now, and can only *wait*, with fervent prayer that the cause we love may receive no detriment.

Source: Underwood, *Whittier*, pp. 227–228.

1. John Brown (1800–1859), abolitionist and Free-State fighter, was a captain in a local Kansas militia and fought from 1856 to 1859 in Kansas against proslavery forces. On October 16, 1859, Brown and a band of twenty-one men seized the Harper's Ferry armory, intending to start an insurrection which would liberate the slaves. He was forced to surrender, quickly convicted, and hanged on December 2 at Charlestown, West Virginia. See Letter Nos. 907, 909, 910, and 911 for further comments on John Brown.

Mrs. Child had written to both Brown and the governor of Virginia, Henry A. Wise, disclaiming sympathy with his method, but avowing her greatest admiration for him personally and her desire to minister to his comfort.

2. I Corinthians 12:31.

905. To William James Allinson

Amesbury October 1859

My dear William.

So then thy dear Aunt [Mary Allinson] has passed away to her rest—Gone to join her sisters and the dear friends with whom she was associated in labors of love. For her sake we cannot mourn—I am thankful for the privilege of knowing and loving her.

I am glad to hear of dear Rebecca's improved health. The picture of "My Namesake" came safe to hand. It is a very life like one.

I had hoped about this time to make a visit to P but my sister does not feel equal to the effort and I have not just now strength or courage for it alone. I suppose cousin Sarah Lizzie is at E. Nicholson's at this time.

Let this serve as a mere apology for a letter. I have been too ill to use my pen for sometime and find it difficult to answer my accumulated letters now I am somewhat better. With much love to thy wife and family, and to all our mutual friends in Burlington, I am as Ever thy aff friend

John G. Whittier

I hear H L. Neall is on her way home. I wd like much to see her.

Source: Handwritten copy, Haverford College. Published: Snyder, "John Greenleaf Whittier to William J. Allinson," pp. 32–33.

906. To Gail Hamilton

Amesbury November 3, 1859

My dear fd.

I am very glad thou hast remembered us, and that thy recollections of our Hermitage are not wholly unpleasant.[1] I don't know what thee expected to find formidable in me: nobody that knows me pretends to be at all afraid of me. I am an abolitionist, it is true, but not of the stuff that John Browns are made of. I enclose for thee the poem thee allude to. Leutze has made a picture from it which he calls "The Puritan," as I see by the last "Crayon."[2]

Thy letter should have been answered before, but I have been suffering too much from illness since the cold weather, to write. My eyes still trouble me greatly. With kindest regards for Mrs. Bailey, I am very truly thy friend,

John G. Whittier

My sister sends her love to thee and Mrs. B.

Manuscript: Essex Institute, Salem, Massachusetts. Published, in Part: Pickard, "A Merry Woman's Letters to a Quiet Poet," p. 7.

Gail Hamilton was then a regular contributor to the *National Era* and residing in Washington with the Baileys. She visited Whittier when she returned to her home in Hamilton.

2. Enclosed with the letter was "Pentucket," a poem written in 1838 by Whittier. Emanuel Leutze (1816–1868) was noted for his historical paintings. He made an etching called "The Puritan" from Whittier's poem.

907. To Elizabeth Lloyd Howell

Amesbury, November 6, 1859

Dear Elizabeth

I was something more than glad to get a line from Sarah,[1] and especially glad to hear so good an account of thy general health. I think the mountain air should have at least as much credit as the water and starvation—the "hunger cure," as I think some German experimenters called it.

I surely sympathize with your grievous disappointment in Hannah's non-arrival. Why did she fail to come? I presume you got some explanation by mail, and trust it is nothing serious, and that she will soon be with you. For myself, I have been quite ill, and am still troubled with pain in my side and head, but am better, and hope to be able to get about and do something. I have not been able to write for weeks beyond a mere note or brief letter. This sad affair of Harper's Ferry has pained and troubled me exceedingly. It is time for all to pause and enquire with what feelings and motives they have acted in the great controversy between Freedom and Slavery. Who ever fans the flames on either side from mere selfishness and for party ends assumes a fearful responsibility. I made several attempts last week to write out my thoughts on the subject, but was compelled to give over from sheer inability to exert mind or body.[2] It seemed to me that nobody said precisely the right thing, and that I could and must say it. I have just got Henry Ward Beecher's discourse, and feel a great relief. It is the right word from the right place. Do read it if thou hast not.

After a long dull season, we are now on the verge of winter, enjoying a faultless day of Indian summer, as warm and genial as May. How I wish I could show thee how lovely our river valley looks in the mellow light. The cold winds and rains have scattered the frosted foliage mostly, but the oaks still retain their many shaded brown leaves, and here and there a rock maple still flowers through the grey nakedness of the woods. It is still as a dream—one of those days which seem specially sent to assure us of the love of God.

The Atlantic Monthly has fallen into the hands of Ticknor and Fields, the right men to publish it.[3] Does thee never write nowadays? I wish thee would let me have something for the Monthly. With such gifts as thine, such powers of expression, how is it possible for thee not to think and write?

Tell Sarah how much I am obliged to her for her kind letter. If thy eyes permit thee I should be glad to hear from thee, if but a line—but a word. From here, in this north-eastern nook, my thoughts are wandering towards Philadelphia, and memory is ever recalling the pleasant picture of the past.

Affectionately thy friend,
John G. Whittier

Source: Denervaud, ed., Whittier's Unknown Romance, pp. 49–51.

1. Sarah Lloyd, her sister.

2. Whittier finally wrote a long article analyzing the situation for the Amesbury Villager of November 17, 1859. Entitled "The Lesson of the Day," it expressed Whittier's doctrine of nonresistance and also admonished the South of the "dangerous nature of slavery—of the insecurity and peril of every community which admits it. It shows that it is not safe for slaveholders, in behalf of their institution, to experiment too far upon the forebearance and patience of those who abhor it. The aggressions of the Slave Power upon Northern rights have a tendency to provoke a retaliation upon slavery. In fact, the moving cause of this miserable outbreak may be distinctly traced to the attempts to extend slavery, which have for years agitated the country. . . . The Eternal Laws cannot be violated with safety. A working population driven by brute force to unpaid toil, must be necessarily unstable, unreliable, and dangerous. But they have it in their power to secure immunity from outward interference. To do this, they must abandon all attempts to extend slavery. . . . Christianity and civilization have placed it in a moral quarantine from which it can only stray at its peril."

3. After the death of Moses D. Phillips, the publisher of the Atlantic Monthly, in August 1859, its publication was assumed by Ticknor and Fields. Fields immediately took charge of the magazine and by the middle of 1861 was its official editor.

908. To William C. Clarke

Amesbury, November 30, 1859

Dear Friend:

Thy note inviting me to attend a meeting in my native town, for the relief of the family of John Brown, I have just received.[1]

It is not in my power to attend the meeting. My sympathies have been strongly moved for the mistaken, but brave man, whom Virginia ought to be brave and magnanimous [enough] to spare. Their families should not be allowed to suffer for the lack of our timely aid.

Praying for the speedy coming of the day when with every evil plant which our Heavenly Father hath not planted, slavery shall be rooted up; and trusting that at your meeting nothing may be said in anger or impatience, but that calmness and Christian moderation may be found perfectly consistent with fidelity to the cause of freedom and humanity, I am very Truly

Thy friend,
John G. Whittier

Source: Haverhill *Tri-Weekly Publisher*, December 3, 1859.

Recipient: William C. Clarke (perhaps 1819–1894) served as pastor of the Winter Street Baptist church in Haverhill from 1858 to 1859. He acted as chairman for a meeting to secure funds to relieve the family of John Brown. He later served as a missionary in Europe and Asia. The identification of Clarke as the recipient is conjectural.

1. The meeting was held on December 2 and Whittier's letter was read.

909. To Lucy Larcom

Amesbury December 2, 1859

My dear friend.

Late as it is, I must thank thee for thy beautiful and thoughtful *"Thirty-five"* which I enclose.[1] It has the true Christian philosophy in it. Thee should not hide it away, for it would do good to many.

What a sad tragedy today in Virginia! I feel deep sympathy for John Brown but deplore from my heart his rash and insane attempt. It injures the cause he sought to serve.

When are we to see something more of the sort of "Hannah binding Shoes" and "Waiting in the Rain"?—Everybody admires these poems.

I have sent the "Hymn" thou wast so kind as to copy to the Editors of the "Hymns of the Ages."[2] It is worthy of a place with the best.

Elizabeth and I often speak of thee and of the very pleasant visit we had from thee; and hope it will soon be repeated.

We had an old fd Grace Greenwood with us for three or four days last week. She has lectured with great success in Boston, Albany, Salem and other places; and really seems to take her place with Whipple, Curtis et al very quietly and naturally.

Isn't it cheering to have C. Sumner come back *well*! Longfellow writes me that he is "as good as new." I wanted to meet him before he left for Washington but was not well enough.

Do let us hear from thee. We are poor correspondents, but our friends must be generous and patient.

Very truly thy fd.
John G. Whittier

Manuscript: Huntington Library, San Marino, California.

1. An autobiographical poem about Miss Larcom's reaching the age of thirty-five.

2. All of the poems mentioned in this letter, save "Waiting in the Rain," were published in Miss Larcom's first collection of verse, *Poems*, in 1868.

910. To Charles Sumner

Amesbury December 8, 1859

My dear Sumner.

How glad I am to hear of thy return with recovered health! Earlier welcomes thou hast doubtless had but none warmer than mine. May God who has restored thee, give thee strength, and wisdom for the crisis which in His Providence seems close at hand.[1]

I enclose a scrap from our village paper in which I have expressed briefly my views of the Harper's Ferry outbreak.[2] I am anxious that our Republican members of Congress should meet the matter fairly and unequivocally condemn *all* fillibustering whether for freedom or for Slavery. I like Trumbull's motion—Harper's ferry is the natural result of the slaveholder's forays into Kansas, and both should be considered together.[3] The distinction should be made clear between the natural sympathy with *the man*, and approval of his mad, and as I think, most dangerous and unjustifiable *act*. The North is sound on this point.—out of the ranks of our Garrison friends. (Garrison himself condemns it)—there are few who approve of the "raid over the Border."

With hearty congratulations and much love and sympathy, I am as Ever

Thy fd.
John G. Whittier

Manuscript: Harvard University. Published, in Part: Pickard, *Life*, pp. 425–426.

1. Sumner replied to this letter: "At last I am well again, with only the natural solicitude as to the effect of work and the constant pressures of affairs on a system which is not yet hardened and annealed. My physician enjoins for the present caution and a gradual resumption of my old activities" (Pickard, *Life*, p. 426).

2. Whittier's article of November 17, 1859. See Letter No. 907, note 2.

3. Lyman Trumbull (1813–1896), a senator from Illinois, served in the Senate from 1855 to 1873 as a Free Soiler and Republican.

911. To Theodore Tilton[1]

Amesbury December 11 [1859]

Dear fd.

I am not altogether satisfied with the piece "Brown of Ossawatomie." It is not what it ought to be and I wd ask the favor if it is not now too late to have the privilege of rewriting it. If however it is in type, it must of course take its chances.[2]

Thine truly
John G. Whittier

Manuscript: Swarthmore College.

Recipeint: Theodore Tilton (1835–1907), New York author and journalist, edited the New York *Independent* from 1856 to 1871. He changed the paper from a Congregational journal to a national newspaper which championed abolitionism and woman suffrage, besides printing some of the best writers of the day. Tilton was also popular as a lyceum lecturer, but his career was ruined in 1874 when he brought suit against Henry Ward Beecher for committing adultery with his wife, Elizabeth Richards. No court decision was reached in the case, but Tilton spent the remainder of his life abroad. He later authored a book of ballads and poems.

1. The identification is conjectural.

2. The poem was printed in the *Independent,* December 22, 1859. For further comments on the poem see Letter No. 919. In the poem Whittier remarked:

> "Perish with him the folly that seeks through evil good!
> Long live the generous purpose unstained with human blood!
> Not the raid of midnight terror, but the thought which underlies;
> Not the borderer's pride of daring, but the Christian's sacrifice."

912. To Elizabeth Lloyd Howell

Amesbury, December 14, 1859

Dear Elizabeth,

I send by to-day's mail Ruskin's Styrian story of "The King of the Golden River."[1] I read it with something of the old boyish feeling of enjoyment, but, like the woman George Fox tells us of who had no stomach for her meat and ale unless she could eat and drink with him, I could not help thinking how much more I should have enjoyed it with thee, and thy sisters. If you have not read it (and I hope you have not) I am sure the story and the fine word-painting of Ruskin and the quaint conceits of his artist-friends illustrating it as a labor of love, will please you.

I enclose with it a photograph from a crayon by Swain, suggested by a little poem of mine, "The Barefoot Boy."[2] It is very good.

And so Hannah is with you, come back to the old home, in health and with richer specimens of California products than the mines have ever furnished. I heard of her through Bayard Taylor, who spent last second day with us, who described her as very bright and witty. How pleasant it must be to you all!

We are having terrible weather here—a wild snowstorm every other day and as cold as Greenland between. My sister and I have both suffered a great deal with the change from the autumn to winter, but hope when the struggle is over between the seasons, and steady cold weather sets in, we shall be better and able to get out more. As we cannot read or write much, these long dark days are very tedious.

Thee does not say how thy eyes are since thy return—better, I hope.

With kind remembrances for Hannah and Sarah, and hoping to see you all in the early spring,

Affectionately,
J. G. W.

Source: Denervaud, ed., *Whittier's Unknown Romance*, pp. 51–52.

1. John Ruskin (1819–1900), the English writer and critic, wrote *The King of the Golden River* (London, 1851), a children's story which was reprinted many times.

2. Cornelia Swain, an artist friend of Mary Curzon, had painted a picture of the barefoot boy based on the poem by that name and on "My Namesake."

913. To an Unidentified Correspondent

Amesbury December 26, 1859

Dr. fd.

Joseph Hooper the father of my friend Lucy Hooper died many years ago.[1] Her mother and sister were living in Brooklyn N. Y. the last I heard from the family. I regret that I am not able to give their address.

Very truly thy fd.
John G. Whittier

Manuscript: Haverford College. Published: Hewitt and Snyder, "Letters of John Greenleaf Whittier in the Roberts Collection at Haverford College," p. 37.

1. Joseph Hooper (1775–1837) was a purser in the navy and then a merchant in Newburyport. He ended his life as a grain measurer in Brooklyn, New York, where Whittier became acquainted with Lucy Hooper, his daughter.

914. To Theodore Tilton[1]

[Before December 29, 1859]

Dear Friend

[. . .] I send herewith a long poem, a sort of companion piece to my "Samuel Sewall" for the New Year. It has cost me a good deal of labor and I shall expect if it is published, the same that I received for the other poem, viz $100.[2]

Source: Typewritten copy, Swarthmore College.

1. A note on the copy says to "Editor, N. Y. Independent."

2. Sent with the letter was "The Preacher," which appeared in the New York *Independent*, December 29, 1859. "The Prophecy of Samuel Sewall" had been published in the *Independent*, January 6, 1859.

915. To Henry Wadsworth Longfellow

[1859][1]

Dear fd. Longfellow

I send by my cousin, Geo. H. Chase, Esq.[2] of Lynn the
Geo. Fox—and a copy of a little book of mine touching upon
some of the old Quaker notabilities.[3]

I also send a photograph from an engraving of Jas. Nayler—
the one which furnished Carlyle with his hints of the personal
traits of Nayler. It was made while he was in prison.

Very truly thy fd.

J. G. W.

I enclose a brief notice of the "Courtship of M. S." which I
gave to the "Natl. Era"—last winter.[4]

Manuscript: Harvard University.

1. Dated by reference to *The Courtship of Miles Standish and Other Poems*,
which was published in 1858.

2. George H. Chase (1826–1888), a shoe manufacturer from Lynn, was postmaster of the city from 1860 to 1868. He was chairman of the Lynn school board,
city auditor and also served in the state legislature.

3. *Old Portraits and Modern Sketches* (Boston, 1850), which contained biographical essays on Thomas Ellwood, James Nayler, and others.

4. An unsigned review of *The Courtship of Miles Standish and Other Poems*
appeared in the *National Era* on December 23, 1858, but its tone and manner
are quite unlike those of Whittier's usual reviews. The review is as follows:

"The reader of the principal poem of this new volume will of necessity call to
mind its beautiful predecessor, the sweet and tender 'Tale of Arcadie'; and, if it
lacks the intensity of interest which pertains to that remarkable poem, he will
charitably ascribe the deficiency to the subject matter rather than to the accomplished artist. The Pilgrim life which it describes was hard and prosaic in the main,
although it had its points of contact with the higher elements of song and romance;
and, in our view, Longfellow has fully sustained his reputation in so successfully
giving malleability and poetic beauty to a legend which we have read an hundred
times, without so much as dreaming of its possible conversion into a puritan
pastoral. Whatever may be said of the fitness of its peculiar versification, none
can deny the art with which it is managed, and its delicate and well-nigh perfect
finish. In this respect, Miles Standish appears to us quite equal to Evangeline,
or to any English translation we have seen of Goethe's Hermann and Dorothea.

"One of the finest passages in the poem is that which describes the departure
of the Mayflower, homeward bound. The white sail rounding the point of the
Gurnet, and meeting the winds of the broad ocean, the little group of pilgrims on
the shore, with the good elder, kneeling in prayer, and that grim, solitary figure
of an Indian, watching from his woods the departing ship, and the diminished
group of settlers behind, altogether leaving a touching and impressive picture on
the memory.

"It would be unwise to complain that in a poem of this kind the writer has
not closely followed the facts of history and the leading of tradition; but in the
matter of language, we expect something like antiquarian exactness of reproduction. We must confess that the replies of the demure little Puritan Priscilla to
the love-making of John Alden in his friend's behalf and his own, do not read to
us very much like quotations from the 'Records of the Colony of Plymouth.'
Now and then they remind us quite too strongly of some of Aurora Leigh's impossible speeches to her lover. They are Orphic utterances, worthy it may be of an
Emerson or Alcott, but ante-dated two hundred years in the Puritan courtship.

"We might also quarrel with an occasional prosaic hexameter, and with one or two figures not entirely apposite. But we are too grateful to the author to dwell on such trifling blemishes. The poem is an honor to our literature. Henceforth the picture of stout Miles Standish will be found in the poetry of Longfellow, rather than in the quaint prose of Winthrop: and the scenery of Plymouth will be the classic ground of romance as well as of patriotism.

"Many of the short poems in the volume are among the author's best productions, and already familiar to the readers of Putnam's and the Atlantic Magazine. We need only refer to such pieces as 'The Two Angels,' 'My Lost Youth,' 'Oliver Basselin,' 'Victor Galbraith,' and 'Sandalphon.'

"Like everything from the house of Ticknor and Fields, the book is faultless in typography."

916. To James P. Nesmith[1]

Amesbury January 2, 1860

Dr. fd.

I was about as much surprised to read that old letter of my boyhood as if I had seen the ghost of my former self.[2] It was a very absurd and ridiculous epistle,—and the utter folly of it, is more striking from the fact that at that very time I was in reality a shy, timid recluse, afraid of a shadow, especially of the shadow of a woman. There is a period in life—a sort of tadpole state between the boy and the man—where any sort of pretense, egotism, and self-conceit—may be expected. Of course, thou will not be likely to present that precious specimen of nonsense, as a fair sample of the grown-up man.

I was glad to hear of thy whereabouts, and shall be happy to call at thy place when I am able to visit Boston. My health is very delicate and I am not able to get about much, but I have great reason for thankfulness for many undeserved blessings.

Wishing thee a happy New Year I am very truly

Thy fd.

John G. Whittier

Manuscript: Swarthmore College. Published, in Part: Pickard, *Life*, pp. 78–79.
1. The identification is conjectural.
2. See Letter No. 15.

917. To James Russell Lowell

Amesbury January 9, 1860

My dear Lowell

I send thee a bit of a pastoral song, which my sister says is very good for me.[1] I am not sure. It is either very simple, or very silly. I leave it with thee to decide.

Bugsmouth hill is a rather remarkable hill in this neighborhood just across the N. H. line.[2]

My Indian has escaped the fire it seems, but the rascal will have to run the gauntlet of the readers of the Maga[3] —I am glad to see that we are to meet occasionally in the N. Y. *Independent.*

Ever and truly
J. G. W.

If thee have any doubts of the enclosed "Eleanor" send her right back by the next mail.[4]

Manuscript: Harvard University.
1. "My Playmate," which was printed in the *Atlantic* for May 1860. See Letter Nos. 918, 921, 922 and 923 for further comments on this poem.
2. Whittier finally changed the name of the hill to "Ramoth." See Letter No. 923.
3. "The Truce of Piscataqua," printed in the February *Atlantic.*
4. The original title for "My Playmate."

918. To James Russell Lowell

Amesbury January 10, 1859

My dear Lowell

In transcribing "Eleanor"[1] yesterday I did not give one verse which I wd like to add now, following the one concluding thus

> "The dusky children of the sun
>   Before her come and go."—

> There haply with her jewelled hands
>   She smooths her silken gown,
> No more the homespun lap wherein
>   I shook the walnuts down.

The verse immediately following I would have read thus

> I linger by her native streams,
>   I haunt her hills of pine,
> And wonder if her gold-brown hair
>   Is thin and grey as mine

Pardon the trouble—and let me have a proof of the piece if it is printed.

J. G. W.

Manuscript: Harvard University. Published: Pickard, *Life,* pp. 426–427.
1. Retitled "My Playmate," when published in the Atlantic.

919. To William Lloyd Garrison

Amesbury January 15, 1860

My dear friend Garrison

In thy notice of my article on "Brown of Ossawatomie" published recently in the N. Y. Independent, thou hast, unintentionally, I am sure, done me injustice.[1] Apart from what thee so well know of my life-long professions and principles, I need only call thy attention to the fact, that in almost every instance, the articles from which thou hast quoted passages containing war-like allusions and figures, contain distinct and emphatic declarations of the entirely peaceful character of the anti-slavery enterprise, and equally emphatic condemnation of war and violence in its behalf. In thy first quotation, the qualifying lines which, in the original, connect the two parts of the extract are omitted:

> "To freedom's perilled altar bear
> The freeman's and the christian's *whole*—
> Tongue, pen and vote and prayer!"[2]

In the article from which thy second quotation is made the following significant stanza is the key-note of the whole[:]

> "Up now for freedom!—*not in strife*
> *Like that your sterner fathers saw,*
> *The awful waste of human life*
> *The glory and the guilt of war*
> But break the chain, the yoke remove
> And smite to earth oppression's rod,
> With those mild arms of Truth and Love
> Made mighty through the living God!"[3]

In the poem entitled "Moral Warfare" (the very title shows its character) the lines quoted by thee, are contrasted with such as these,

> "A moral warfare with the crime
> And folly of an evil time."

> "And strong in Him whose cause is ours
> In conflict with unholy powers
> We grasp the weapons He has given
> The Light and Truth and Love of Heaven!"

The poem "Yorktown" is simply a dramatic representation of the capture of Yorktown and the reinslavement of the fugitive slaves there in the abused name of Liberty. No eulogy of war was intended or given; none can be so understood.

But enough of this merely personal exculpation. No one who knows me, or who has read my writings, can be doubtful for a moment as to my position; utter abhorrence of war and of slavery as in itself a state of war, where the violence is all on one side.

The pledge which we gave to the world at Philadelphia twenty six years ago, when we signed the Declaration of Senti-ments, fresh from thy pen, that we would reject ourselves and entreat the oppressed to reject the use of all carnal weapons for deliverance from bondage:—that we admitted the sover-eignty of the states over the subject of slavery within their limits; and that we were under high moral obligations to use for the promotion of our cause moral and political action, as prescribed in the Constitution of the U. States;—we have since reiterated in a thousand forms and on as many occasions. I have seen no reason to doubt the wisdom of that pledge. Slavery was just what it is now, neither better nor worse, when we made it. If it is right and proper now to use forcible means in behalf of the slave it was right and proper then. If it be said that the Old Testament Christians are not bound by our pledges, and that we are at liberty to applaud them in appeals to the sword, I can only say that I dare not encourage others who have not my scruples to do what I regard as morally wrong. On the contrary I would use even to the slaves, the language of thy own lines:

> "Not by the sword shall your deliverance be,
> Not by the shedding of your masters' blood,
> Not by rebellion, in foul treachery
> Upspringing suddenly like a swelling flood.
> Revenge and Rapine ne'er did bring forth good.
> God's time is best; nor will it long delay.
> Even now your barren cause begins to bud
> And glorious shall the fruit be. Watch and pray!—
> For lo!—the kindling dawn that ushers in the day!"[4]

I am painfully sensible of many errors of feeling and judg-ment, but my conscience bears me witness that I have, at least, honestly striven to be faithful alike to Freedom and Peace. That this is thy own earnest desire I have as little doubt.[5]

Very truly thy friend
J. G. Whittier

Source: The Liberator, January 27, 1860.

1. In *The Liberator* of January 13, 1860, Garrison reprinted Whittier's "Brown of Ossawatomie" and wrote an extended analysis of the poem and Whittier's attitude toward John Brown. Garrison said that Whittier's poem did not express the "same magnanimous recognition of the liberty loving heroism of John Brown which is found in many of the poet's effusions relating to the war-like struggle of 1776." The article went on to quote from Whittier's poetry to show where Whittier had praised warlike activities.
2. From "The Sentence of John L. Brown."
3. From "Expostulation."
4. From Garrison's poem, "Universal Emancipation," stanza 5; the poem was published in the first issue of *The Liberator*, January 1, 1831, and was probably written in 1830.
5. When Garrison printed the letter on January 27, 1860, he commented: "Our friend John G. Whittier . . . wholly misapprehends the point of our criticism, respecting his poetical effusion upon 'Brown of Ossawatomie.' . . . We did not mean to imply that he had departed from his peace principles, in the various extracts, we made from his soul-stirring productions."

920. To James Thomas Fields

Amesbury, January 31, 1860
I am desirous of making some verbal changes in it, to make it more worthy of its place. What has become of Dr. Palmer's long advertised Book of Folk Songs?[1] Is it published and what is its price? What is that of Starr King's White Mountain book?[2] I want both if I can afford to have them.

Source: First Editions, Autograph Letters and Associated Books to be sold at Auction, April 12, 1917, by Scott and O'Shaughnessy, Inc., item 357, page 73, catalogue, Haverhill Public Library.
1. John W. Palmer (1825–1906), a former doctor, lived for many years in California and published books of ballads and poems. His book, *Folk Songs* (New York), was published in 1860 and went through many editions.
2. Thomas Starr King's *The White Hills* (Boston, 1860).

921. To Lucy Larcom

Amesbury [January] 1860[1]
[. . .] I am glad thee have at least a realizing sense of the deference and respect due to a "grave and reverend senior." I have been apprehensive that I was looked upon as a sort of "old boy" by my friends—that the privileges and compensations of age were not allowed me. For the fact is I am on the wrong side of fifty and have a right to be "venerable." But, ah me! If "wisdom is the gray hairs of a man," and an unspotted life old age, I am afraid, nevertheless, that I shall never be old. [. . .] I have sent a poem "The Playmate" to the "Atlantic," which is either very simple or very silly. [. . .] What a terrible kind of story is Dr. Holmes giving us: "Elsie Venner" the Rattlesnake girl!

Source: Catalogue of a Private Collection of First Editions of American Authors. Sold by Anderson Auction Co. N. Y., Jan. 29, 1916, no. 631, page 64, catalogue, Haverhill Public Library.

1. Dated by references to the poem "Eleanor" ("My Playmate") in Letter Nos. 917 and 918.

922. To James Russell Lowell

Amesbury February 3, 1860

My dear fd. Lowell.

From not receiving the proof I presume my little poem will not appear in the next no. of the Atlantic. I would like to see the poem in print before it is irrevocably worked off.

My sister tells me the last verse but one is not in keeping with the others: that I have marred by it the simplicity of the poem—that the idea is not fully explained etc. etc. I think she is right and would like to put the following in its place:—

> The winds so sweet with birch and fern
> A sweeter memory blow;
> And there is spring the veeries sing
> The song of long ago.

Ever and truly thy fd.
John G. Whittier

Manuscript: Harvard University. Published: Pickard, *Life,* p. 427.

923. To James Russell Lowell

[Amesbury] February 18, 1860

My dear fd.

I have made sad work with the enclosed proofs. I have, at thy hint, dropped the old name—taken that of another hill omitting the "Gilead" which is prefixed to it: and to give the thing a local stand-point I have introduced the neighboring woods of Folly mill famous hereaway for their May flowers or ground laurel. I hope it is all the better for the changes. I wish thee to see that the revised proof is all right.

Thine truly
J. G. W.

Manuscript: Harvard University. Published: Pickard, *Life,* pp. 427–428.

924. To Theodore Tilton

Amesbury, February 28, 1860

My dear fd.

I send a poem which if you do not think advisable to publish I hope you will not hesitate to return to me.[1]

It is badly interlined but I hope you can make it out and, of course you will look carefully to the proof.

I am glad Wm A. Butler is writing for you.[2] He is doing a capital thing. I wish he wd write more like his Richmond piece.

Thine ever

J. G. W.

Thank your correspondent "Dean" for her fine poem on the *White Slaves.*[3]

Manuscript: New Hampshire Historical Society.

1. Enclosed was probably the poem, "The Shadow and the Light," which was published in the *Independent*, March 15, 1860.

2. William A. Butler (1825–1902), a successful lawyer, wrote novels and satirical pieces on society.

3. Edna Dean Proctor (1829–1923), poetess and New Hampshire writer, had been publishing her poems chiefly in the New York *Independent*. In 1858 she had edited a book on the life and thoughts of Henry Ward Beecher. Whittier's acquaintance with Miss Proctor began in 1859 with his praise of her "White Slaves" poem and they became regular correspondents and lifelong friends. Her first volume of poetry was published in 1866 and she continuted to write poems and essays about New Hampshire throughout her life.

925. To Elizabeth Lloyd Howell

Amesbury, February 29, 1860

Dear Elizabeth,

It is very long since I have heard from thee. I have been confined at home all winter, too ill much of the time to write,— so depressed, that I feared giving thee more pain than pleasure if I had been able, and unwilling to burden thee with my problem when I knew thou hadst thy own to bear. A complicated nervous affliction, combined with the old trouble in my head and stomach, has rendered me so much of an invalid that the slightest change of weather, any extra physical or mental exertion, or responsibility is sufficient to entirely prostrate me. I am compelled to avoid, as far as possible, all excitement and mental labor as the only condition of preserving anything like quiet and self control, and of obtaining relief from pain. It seems sometimes rather hard—this powerlessness, this protracted hopeless inability to do—not only on

my own account, but of others—but I earnestly try to be
patient and to make the best of my allotment.

It must be that I needed the lesson—that I presumed too
much last year upon my temporary relief from illness. I did
wrong, I now see, in yielding to my feelings so much—in giving pain when I most desired to give happiness. If so, dear
friend, forgive me, and think kindly of me for I can never
think otherwise of thee. Let me, at least, have the privilege of
sympathy in thy efforts to live nearer to our Divine Master,
and to seek the consolation of Him who has been touched
with the feeling of our infirmities.

I want to ask a favor of thee. My publishers wish me to
prepare my recent poems for publication. If I feel able to
prepare and review them, I want the privilege of dedicating
them to thee. If thee feels any objection to it, of course I shall
not urge it, but I do very much wish to. I will send thee a
copy of what I would like to say. I know and appreciate thy
delicacy and unwillingness to invite any unnecessary display,
but somehow I have set my heart upon it—still do not hesitate
to let me know if thee disapprove it. I shall, I dare say, admit
that I am wrong and thee right about it.[1]

Poor Elizabeth has been and still is very much of an invalid.
Of course we are not likely to help each other's spirits. I try
very hard to be cheerful, and sometimes, like Mark Tapley,
in Dickens, I succeed in being jolly "under creditable circumstances."[2] It must be a real comfort to thee to have Hannah
at home, with her ready resources and conversational bril-
liance. She has lived a large, free life, in that wonder-world
on the Pacific, and I am sure she must have much to tell of it.

I send thee the fourth annual report of the Industrial
School for Girls—one of our Yankee notions that I am sure
thee will feel interested in. It is a noble effort in the right
direction.

I am pained to hear of Anna Nicholson's death—poor Elizabeth, her sister, must have felt it very much.[3]

With much love to all, as ever,

Affectionately,
J. G. W.

Source: Denervaud, ed., *Whittier's Unknown Romance*, pp. 53–55.

1. *Home Ballads and Poems* (Boston) was entered for copyright in July but
not put on sale until October. Mrs. Howell hesitated about having the volume
dedicated to her and finally declined after Whittier sent her a copy of the dedicatory poem he had written for her. See Letter No. 929.

2. *Martin Chuzzlewit.* Mark Tapley, Martin's servant whose philosophy was to
be jolly under depressing circumstances, traveled with Martin to America.

3. Anna Nicholson died on November 24, 1859.

926. To William Currier

Amesbury, March 7, 1860

To the Editor of the Villager:—

The sudden death of an honored and esteemed citizen, under most painful circumstances, has cast the shadow of a profound sorrow over our entire community.[1] Long and intimately associated with him, and bound to him by the strongest ties of friendship and affection, I feel too deeply and keenly to do justice, at this time, to his memory; but I cannot permit him to be borne to his last resting-place without a feeble and broken word of tribute. William Carruthers was a native of Scotland,—his grandfather and father having been ministers of the Gospel in his native town.[2] The former had at one time as pupils, two boys, who afterwards became famous the world over—Thomas Carlyle and Edward Irving.[3] His elder brother, John J. Carruthers, D. D., is a minister at Portland, Me.

He came to this place when a young man, poor, unknown, with little or no education, save what he had acquired as a sailor boy and apprentice. By his industry and good conduct he soon provided himself with a comfortable home, and secured the good will and confidence of the community. An active and public spirited citizen, animated by Christian benevolence, he has always been foremost in every enterprise calculated to promote the welfare, temporal and spiritual, of his neighbors and the world. He was an intelligent and steadfast friend of Freedom, in times when it cost something to be so. He took an active interest in Lyceums and Schools, and at the time of his death was President of the Amesbury and Salisbury Library Association. He held the commission of Justice of the Peace, and was a member of the State Convention for the Revision of the Constitution. He was an enthusiastic admirer of his country's great Poet, and at the Parker House Festival, little more than a year ago, made a speech creditable to his head and heart and worthy of the occasion.

His charity was large, and his heart always open to the calls of sickness, and poverty, and sorrow. In the language of the Book whose every precept he loved, "he was eyes to the blind and feet to the lame: the blessing of them that were ready to perish came upon him, and he made the widow's heart to sing for joy!"[4]

He had an extremely sensitive organization; enjoyed keenly and as keenly suffered; the least word of reproach or censure painfully affected him; he was ill-fitted for the trials of his allotment. As Lockhart says of Scott's friend Erskine, "he had the heart of a woman, her enthusiasm, and something of her weakness."[5] To those who knew him most intimately it is not strange that a complication of trials (prominent among which was a distressing family affliction) disturbed at last the balance of his mind, and left him, who had done so much to console others in their suffering, the helpless victim of his own.

Of the manner of his death I can only say that, knowing as I did his condition, mentally and bodily, it excited more pain than surprise; and that it has in no degree affected my estimation of his character as a man and a Christian. Safely may we leave one like him, so tender, so gentle, so loving and so suffering, to the Infinite compassion of Him who "knoweth our frame, and remembereth that we are dust."[6]

J. G. W.

Source: The Amesbury *Villager*, March 8, 1860.

1. William Carruthers committed suicide on March 6. He had broken down under the influence of various troubles, including the insanity of his wife, and hanged himself in the cellar of his store.
2. The maternal grandfather, John Johnston (d. 1812) was a Dissenting minister who conducted a parish school.
3. Edward Irving (1792–1834), a minister of the Church of Scotland, gained fame as a preacher and orator and was a close friend of Carlyle.
4. Job 29:15 and 13.
5. John Gibson Lockhart (1794–1854), writer and son-in-law of Sir Walter Scott, published his *Memoirs of the Life of Scott* in seven volumes. His remarks about William Erskine (1769–1822), an English lawyer who was one of Scott's closest friends, occur in chapter XII of the biography.
6. Psalms 103:14.

927. To Charles Sumner

Amesbury March 9, 1860

My dear fd. Sumner.

My friend Isaac Pitman Esq.[1] wishes to put himself in communication with some one of the members of the British Board of Admiralty, on a matter of cordage manufacture, which his note to thee will explain. If thee can aid him in this I shall esteem it as great favor. He is a gentleman thoroughly reliable, and true on all questions in which we feel an interest. I can vouch for his integrity. His wife (a dear friend of ours, daughter of Judge Minot of Haverhill)[2] is a noble woman, an early and devoted friend of the Anti-Slavery cause.

Any assistance thou canst give him in this matter will be worthily bestowed.

Most cordially and truly
Thy friend
John G. Whittier

Manuscript: Harvard University.

1. See Letter No. 456, note 5 for information on Pitman.

2. Stephen Minot (1776–1861) served as a judge in Essex County from 1811 to 1820 and then returned to his law practice in Haverhill.

928. To William Ticknor

Amesbury March 20 [1860]

My dear fd. Ticknor.

I have prepared a collection of my recent poems. It consists of ten ballads—and some fifteen lyrical pieces—the best, I am sure, I have ever written. It will make a volume of about 120 pages.

Can you publish it this spring?—For many reasons I would prefer to have it printed at this time. If I did not look upon it as rather more to my credit than anything I have ever given you, I should not wish to appear in print again.

Be good enough to let me know thy opinion and decision and oblige

Thy fd.
John G. Whittier

Manuscript: Swarthmore College.

929. To Elizabeth Lloyd Howell

Amesbury, March 20 [1860]

To thee, dear friend, who, when the popular frown
Darkens around a toiler, faint and worn,
In fields which since have Freedom's harvest borne,
Where they who bind the sheaves of party, now,
Have scarce forgiven the rugged breaking plough
And early sowers whom they laughed to scorn,
Wert of the few in all the scoffing town
Who, as his vouchers, spake the words of cheer
Which linger longest on a grateful ear—
Count it not strange, if even now I bring
My tardy gift—no garlands of the Spring,

Woven of tender maple leaves and set
With wind-flower, apple-bloom, and violet,
But Summer's latest flowers and leaves full grown,
And seeded grass, and roses over blown.
Thou, who hast sung for Milton, blind and old,
A song of faith the bard himself might own,
Wilt pardon words of Freedom over bold:
And, not unmindful of the grave discourse
We sometimes dared with reverent lips to hold,
Take up the burden of my serious verse,
And lend thy ear to its low thoughtful tone.[1]

Dear Elizabeth,

Thy kind, noble, generous letter was most welcome. I feel that much of what thee says of my way of living is right, and will try to profit by thy advice and "prescriptions." But I have a very small capital of strength to begin with, and but a limited amount of hope to supply the deficiency. My present illness is only what I have suffered from childhood but I am now less able to bear it. I shall do all I can to regain—not health and vigor, for that I cannot expect—but a condition of ability to be worth something to my friends and the world. I ride out when I am able, and the weather will permit, and hope to profit by it as the season advances.

The day I got thy letter we were dreadfully shocked by the death (by his own hand) of a neighbor and dear friend, to whose kindness and love we owed much. A genial generous, warm-hearted man, the derangement of his wife, and other troubles broke him down and destroyed the balance of his mind. Elizabeth and I had been very anxious about him weeks before. He was greatly beloved: at his funeral the great con-gregation "lifted up their voices and wept."[2] We have not got over the shock: it overpowered me for the time. I believe I sent thee a paper with a notice of him.

Thee sees what I have written—I have withheld much that I would have liked to have said. The book will be divided into two distinct parts—one of local ballads, and the other of my poems and lyrics, which I regard as my best. It is these latter which I wish to associate with thee. Is there anything objec-tionable in the lines? Would thee object to the use of thy name, or the initial of it? I should prefer the name as an open, manly expression of grateful interest. But, of course, I defer to thy better judgement; and if thee has any scruple as to the whole thing,—if it seems to thee not agreeable in any way,— do not hesitate to say so. I rely on thy frankness. I enclose a little poem which I am sure thee will like.[3] After reading it, be good enough to send it to Samuel Rhodes for the Friends' Review. I notice the death of Edward Yarnall.[4] Was he the husband of thy friend Caroline? It must have been a sad bereavement. Will thee remember me to her?

I suppose Spring has reached your favored city. Here there are no signs of her, but her heralds the bluebirds are singing of her coming. The snow has recently gone, and we have had some warm bright days.

I must send thee a poem of mine in the Independent: it may remind thee of some of our conversations.[5]

This is a dull letter: I am ashamed of what may seem like complaining, for God has been good to me, the world has been kind beyond my deserts: better men than I have borne pain and weakness cheerfully and bravely, and I will try to imitate them, holding fast my faith in the Divine goodness, and rejoicing in the love and friendship which blesses me, and the opportunities still afforded me to do good.

I have obeyed thee as to thy letters—reluctantly, but with a feeling that thee had a right to their disposal. Perhaps—in the uncertainties of life—it was best.[6] With much love to thy family,

Ever and affectionately,
J. G. W.

I do not hear how thy health is, or whether thee suffers so much with thy eyes. Do speak of thyself.

Source: Denervaud, ed., *Whittier's Unknown Romance*, pp. 55–59.
1. This poem was never published since Mrs. Howell declined to have the volume of Whittier's new poems dedicated to her with this poem.
2. II Samuel 13:36.
3. Possibly "The Preacher," which appeared in the *Independent*, December 29, 1859.
4. Edward Yarnall (1798?–1859), a Quaker philanthropist from Delaware, was not the husband of Caroline Yarnall.
5. Probably "The Shadow and the Light," which appeared in the *Independent*, March 15, 1860.
6. Mrs. Howell had apparently asked Whittier to destroy her letters to him.

930. To Thomas Chase

Amesbury April 28, 1860

Prof Chase
Dr Fd.

My thanks are due to the Literary Society of Haverford College for the invitation so courteously extended through thee. I heartily wish it were in my power to accept it. But, the very feeble condition of my health, compels [me] to aban-

don, as far as possible, all intellectual exertion of the kind
alluded to. It is true I am under some sort of engagement at
Newport,[1] (I know nothing of any at Yale) but even there I
shall not, I fear, do justice either to myself or the occasion.

I have to thank thee for a very beautiful poem of thine,
read at Haverford, and for thy essay on Schiller and Goethe.[2]

With great respect and esteem
thy fd.
J. G. Whittier

Manuscript: Haverford College.

Recipient: Thomas Chase (1827–1892) had graduated from Harvard in 1848
and was an instructor in Latin at Harvard from 1850 to 1855. He went to Haverford as a professor of classic literature and philology in 1856 and became president
of the college in 1874. He resigned this post in 1886 and was going to write the
official biography of Whittier when he died in 1892.

1. Whittier had been asked to write a poem for the June meeting of the alumni
of the Friends Boarding School in Providence. For that occasion he wrote "The
Quaker Alumni," which was printed in the *Villager*, June 28, 1860, and in Whittier's
Home Ballads and Poems.

2. Chase had delivered an address, "Goethe and Schiller," on November 21,
1859, before the Haverford Longonian Society. The essay had then been published.

931. To the Publisher of the Portsmouth Friend

Amesbury, May 5, 1860

Pub of Portsmouth friend
Dr fd.

My nephew C. F. Whittier thinks of learning the printer's
trade.[1] Have you a place for him in your office. He is in his
17th year, a strong hearty, intelligent boy.

Please let me know at your convenience. If you have a
place for him, please state the terms.

Yrs truly
John G. Whittier

Manuscript: Swarthmore College.

1. Charles Franklin Whittier (1843–1909), the only son of Matthew Franklin
Whittier, served in the Civil War and was an office clerk in the canning business
after the war. He worked with Samuel T. Pickard on the Portland *Transcript* for
twenty-five years and then as an editorial writer for the Portland *Daily Advertiser*
before his death.

932. To William Allinson

Amesbury May 26, 1860

My dear fd. Wm. Allinson

I heartily thank thee for thy excellent lecture. It is worthy of the theme and does credit to the writer's head as well as heart.

I believe with thee that Quakerism is vital—a root of life which underlies all that is true in religious experience—or excellent in practical morality, or efficient in reform and philanthropy.

I should have acknowledged the receipt of it earlier but I have been almost out of practice in writing—the painful affection of my head and eye being so aggravated by the attempt to use my pen that I dread the very sight of it.

I have nearly completed a rambling sort of poem to be read before the Quaker Alumni of Providence School at their meeting next month at Newport. I will try and send thee a copy.

Remember me affectionately to thy Rebecca and family and to all our mutual friends whom I remember with pleasure always. Elizth joins with me in love to thee and thine

Cordially thy fd.
John G. Whittier

Source: Handwritten copy, Haverford College. Published: Snyder, "John Greenleaf Whittier to William J. Allinson," p. 33.

933. To William Ticknor

Amesbury May 30, 1860

Dr fd.

I have seen no proof of the Poems for nearly a week: and I am very desirous to get the last of it, as I must leave for a journey by Friday of next week.

Especially do I wish to have a proof of "The Quaker Alumni" as I have no copy of it, and it is to be read on the 11th of next month. Unless you would have me in the awkward predicament of a parson who gets up to preach, and discovers that his notes are missing, you will see to it that the piece is in type at once.

I send herewith four verses to be added to it, promising not to trouble you with any "more of the same sort."

Ever and truly
J. G. W.

Manuscript: Swarthmore College.

934. To Charles Sumner

Amesbury June 6, 1860

My dear Sumner,

I have just finished reading *the* Speech.[1]

It is all that I could wish for. It takes the dreadful question out of the region of party and expediency, and holds it up in the clear sun-blaze of truth and reason, in all its deformity and with the blackness of the pit clinging about it. In the light of that speech the civilized world will now see American Slavery as it is.

There is something really awful in its Rhadamanthine severity of justice: but it was needed.

It especially rejoices thy personal friends to see in the speech such confirmation of thy complete restoration to health and strength of body, and mind. It was the task of a giant.

Our cause has sustained a great loss in the death of Theo Parker.[2] How he would have rejoiced over thy portraiture of the Barbarism of Slavery!

God bless and keep thee!

Aff thy fd.
John G. Whittier

Manuscript: Harvard University. Published: Pickard, *Life*, p. 428.

1. Sumner's first major speech on the slavery question after his return to his Senate duties was "The Barbarism of Slavery," which was delivered on June 4, 1860.

2. Theodore Parker died on May 10, 1860.

935. To Mary Shepard[1]

Amesbury June 15, 1860

My dear friend

I have been absent for some time past, and my sister ill and occupied or we should ere this have answered thy note.

We shall be glad to see thee and Charlotte [Forten] whenever you can find it convenient to make us a visit.[2] Let it be soon as we think of going away for a while into N. Hampshire, for the sake of the mountain air. Let us know when we may hope to see you. It is a beautiful season for a little trip into the country. By and by, it will be too hot and dusty

Very truly thy friend
John G. Whittier

Manuscript: Swarthmore College.

1. The identification is conjectural.

2. Charlotte Forten (1838–1914) was the granddaughter of James Forten and the niece of Robert Purvis, two of Whittier's Negro friends from Philadelphia. At sixteen she was sent to an unsegregated school in Salem and taught by a friend of the Whittiers, Mary Shepard. During the late 1850's she and Mary Shepard often visited the Whittiers and Charlotte became a close friend of both Elizabeth and the poet. With Whittier's help she obtained a job teaching the freed Negroes at Port Royal in 1862 and remained there until 1863. A published account of her experiences appeared in the *Atlantic*, but ill health kept her from obtaining a permanent job as either a writer or a teacher. Throughout the 1860's and 1870's she corresponded with Whittier and worked at various jobs as translator, secretary and clerk. In 1878 she married a Presbyterian minister and writer, Francis J. Grimke. Whittier sent $50 as a wedding present, noting that Charlotte was a "very worthy and interesting girl, cultivated and intelligent, and with fine and pleasing manners" (letter, April 28, 1878, Haverford College).

936. To an Unidentified Correspondent

Amesbury, Tuesday Noon [June 1860] [1]

My Dear friend

In answer to thy letter just recd. I would say that the cars run up here at 1/2 past nine in the morning, and that the last train from here meets the Eastern train for Portsmouth at East Salisbury.

We should be glad to see thee at our house; but, I fear I may miss thee, as I shall be liable to be called away, at the time thee speak of.—If I could know when to expect thee I think I could arrange it so as to be at home. Can thee not let me know somewhat definitely?—

I am sorry that thy health is not stronger, but glad it is gaining. What a pity that we have to *think* so much! I almost envy the Turk with his pipe enjoying his *Kef*, and letting the world and all that is therein go by as a matter in which he is not concerned.

Very truly thy fd.

J. G. Whittier

My sister remembers thy visit with pleasure and desires to be kindly remembered to thee.

Source: Photocopy, Haverford College. On the copy is the notation that the original letter is located at the Friends Academy, Locust Valley, Long Island, New York.

1. Dated by another hand.

937. To Asa O. Aldis

Amesbury July 2, 1860

Dear fd.

I read with grateful surprise thy kind letter, and that of thy wife to my sister inviting us to your place some time during this month. I would have answered earlier, but I was not certain what to say;—and, even now, while I am compelled to own there seems little probability of our being able to accept yr. invitation, I cannot deny myself the hope that I may be permitted to make a flying visit to Vt. this summer. We thank you from our hearts for remembering us so kindly. My sister wishes me to say to Mrs. Aldis that a powerful affliction of her head and eyes has prevented her from replying to her note.

Remember me to Mrs. A. and rest assured of the grateful regard of thy friend

John G. Whittier

Hon A. O. Aldis

I will write thee if I see any opportunity to visit Vt. In the mean time do not expect me, but make the most of thy interval of leisure. My health will not allow me to *climb* mountains; I shall be only too happy to *see* them.

Manuscript: Yale University.

938. To William Ticknor

Amesbury July 9, 1860

My dear Ticknor.

I regret that I am not able to be at the Dinner tomorrow to join you in welcoming home again my long-ago fellow contributor to the Democratic Review.[1] The weird and subtle beauty of his legendary tales in that periodical early awakened my admiration, and rebuked and shamed my own poor efforts in a similar direction. We all know how the promise of that authorship has since blossomed and borne marvellous fruit— how he has peopled for us the realms of fancy—with what life he has clothed the grim skeleton of old Puritanism—with what richness of coloring he has painted for us the immortal frescoes of his story of Rome and Italy![2] —But why multiply words?—My voice is but the echo of that of thousands who welcome home one who has reflected honor upon us all. I should be glad to take him by the hand; but, for the matter

of a dinner in my present state of health, I must beg to be
excused. I do not think I had ever any gift for such occasions
in my best estate, and time and illness have only, as in the
case of Sheridan's grandmother, "improved me the wrong
way."—

Very truly thy friend
John G. Whittier

Manuscript: Swarthmore College.

1. Nathaniel Hawthorne, returning to America after nearly seven years abroad
in England and Italy, was honored at dinner in Boston that July. See Letter No.
944 for further comment on the dinner.

2. *The Marble Faun* (Boston, 1860) had been published that March.

939. To Theodore Dwight

Amesbury July 10, 1860

T. F. Dwight Esq.

It gives me pleasure to comply with the request conveyed
in thy kind note of the 8th inst. I am very truly

Thy friend
John G. Whittier

Manuscript: Massachusetts Historical Society.

Recipient: Probably Theodore Dwight (1796–1866), a newspaperman and
educator, who taught most of his life in Brooklyn, New York. During the 1850's
he was an active Republican and helped send thousands of Free-State men to
settle in Kansas. He worked on the editorial staff of the New York *Daily Advertiser*
and wrote many history and travel books.

940. To Theodore Tilton[1]

Amesbury July 12, 1860

My dear fd.

I send thee a little poem which, has, at least, the merit of
being a true picture of a sunset scene on the Merrimack, as
well as a simple and truthful expression of the feelings it
awakened.[2]

Let me thank thee for thy words at the Music Hall—nobly
and beautifully said. My heart responded to them.

Very truly thy fd.
John G. Whittier

The transcript is poor: but, I have no doubt thou will make it
out and see that the printers do not blunder. Will thee send
me 3 copies of it?

Manuscript: New York Public Library.

1. The identification is conjectural, but Tilton wrote Whittier on August 17, asking him to send the *Independent* more poems like "The River-Path" (letter, Essex Institute, Salem, Massachusetts).

2. "The River-Path" was printed in the New York *Independent* on July 19, 1860.

941. To Bayard Taylor

Amesbury July 15, 1860

My dear Bayard

I am more than sorry to miss thee in thy northern tour. I have told Elizth. so much about thy Marie that she wants to see her exceedingly.[1]

I hope almost against hope that we shall be able to visit you in your new home this fall, when we will plant our trees of friendship and enjoy ourselves.

I wish I was a better traveller; if I could keep pace with you I would join you at the mountains instead of sending this note. I travel a great deal, however, by proxy. I have had thee in my service for many years, very much to my satisfaction. Dr Barth has been to Timbucto for me, and Burton to Mecca. Atkinson has been *doing* Siberia for me.[2] I think (if thy Marie does not object) of sending thee off again to find Xanadu and Kubla Khan.

Elizth. joins me in love to thee and thy wife. We have just been enjoying thy friend Hans Ch Andersen's charming "Land Hills of Jutland." The "Mud King's Daughter" is almost equal to Undine.

I am glad to hear of thy poems forth-coming.[3] What pleasant Chester County Idyls may we not expect!—

Affectionately thy friend[4]
John G. Whittier

Manuscript: Scripps College, California. Published, in Part: Pickard, *Life,* p. 429.

1. Marie Hansen (1829–1925), the daughter of a Danish astronomer, married Bayard Taylor in 1857. She later published, with Horace E. Scudder, *Life and Letters of Bayard Taylor* (Boston, 1884) in two volumes.

2. For Thomas W. Atkinson, see Letter No. 815, note 2.

3. Taylor's next book of poetry, *The Poet's Journal* (Boston), was not published until 1862.

4. Taylor replied to this letter on August 6, 1860, from his new home in Kennett, Pennsylvania, and said: "Your letter reached me among the White Mountains, but I was too busy, as showman to our friends, to write during the tour. Now it is over, and we are under our own roof, let me say—no hoping against hope! No hope at all! Because hope implies doubt, and we won't hear of that. We look for you with positive anticipation" (letter, Cornell University).

942. To James Thomas Fields

Amesbury July 16, 1860

My dear Fields

Pity my out of the way ignorance!—the first intimation of thy actual presence in Boston reached me in thy own note.[1]

I am glad heartily to know thou art once more at thy post. I stretch my hand all the way to Boston to shake thine.

I had a kind of guilty feeling about my little volume, as if I had taken advantage of thy absence to smuggle it through. I lacked thy "notes and queries" while it was going on: and I was persuaded against my better judgment to make it too large by one third.

As to its time of publication, suit yourselves. I am indifferent about it. I wd. like three or four copies of it for a special purpose—but even that is not of sufficient consequence to cause you any trouble about it.

How much thee have seen and heard!—What pleasant pictures of England and Italy must be living up in thy memory. Well!—since it could not be me, I am glad it was thee. What our friends enjoy is, in some sort, our own.

Bayard Taylor, of course, thee have seen. He writes me on his way to White Mts and Canada. Holmes is doing a great thing with his story in the Atlantic.[2]

With love to thy wife—[3] Ever and truly
Thy fd.
John G. Whittier

I ought to be at meeting of the Overseers of Har. College this week but I am not well enough. The College must take care of itself, and for one I regard it perfectly safe in our friend Felton's keeping.[4]

Manuscript: Huntington Library, San Marino, California.

1. Fields with his wife Annie had been in England and Europe since the fall of 1859 and had returned to Boston in June. On July 16 he wrote Whittier: "Touching the Home Ballads. Will it not be better to publish in a few weeks hence when people are more plenty in town? During the hot season no one feels like the exertion of pulling out 75 cents. September is a much better month for buyers. However, if you have a special reason for the appearance of the volume *now*, it shall come out. . . . The Home Ballads volume is a charming one. I have read it every word" (letter, Essex Institute, Salem, Massachusetts). The volume was finally put on sale in October.

2. "The Professor's Story" (published in book form as *Elsie Venner*) was then appearing in the *Atlantic*.

3. Annie Adams (1834–1915) had married Fields in 1854 and came to be almost as prominent as her husband. She belonged to an old Boston family and her social poise and grace balanced Fields's slight shyness. Under her direction their home on Charles Street became a literary salon and a gathering place for literary people in Boston. She formed many warm friendships with authors like Harriet Beecher Stowe, Celia Thaxter, and especially Sarah Orne Jewett. Whittier,

already a close friend of Fields, became deeply attached to Annie Fields and from
the 1860's till his death he corresponded regularly with her and frequently stayed
at the Fields home while in Boston. An author in her own right, she published a
biography of her husband, as well as reminiscences of Whittier and Stowe. Whittier's
relationships with Annie Fields and Sarah Orne Jewett formed the most lasting
and intimate ones of his later years.

4. Cornelius Conway Felton (1807–1862), a classical scholar, taught at Harvard
from 1829 until becoming president of the college in 1860. (His inauguration was
on July 19, 1860.) He served as a professor of Greek literature and was known for
his editions of ancient texts.

943. To Oliver Wendell Holmes

August 2, 1860

My dear fd.

I thank thee for thy note, and for thy interest in the widow
of our friend Phillips.[1] I wish I could aid you. There is a divine
pleasure in giving: but I have at this time calls among those
providentially in my care, which absorb all my means, so that
I am as safe as Chaucer's poor man who,

> "going by the way
> Beforne the thieves may sing and play"[2]

Have I ever written thee anent thy "Story"!—If not, I have
meant to. It has profoundly interested me. The conception of
Elsie Venner is one of the most striking in all romance. The
moral bearings of her case are deeply suggestive—

The school mistress Helen, I find is a great favorite. I like
the old Dr: he must be drawn from life.

Very truly thy fd.
John G. Whittier

Manuscript: Library of Congress.

1. Moses D. Phillips (1813–1859), a publisher and bookseller, became the
senior partner in the firm of Phillips, Sampson and Company, and was the publisher for the *Atlantic Monthly* until his death. The financial crisis of 1857–1858
severely affected his firm. His widow was Charlotte Foxcroft Phillips (b. 1812).

2. *The Canterbury Tales*, "The Wife of Bath's Tale," lines 1199–1200.

944. To Elizabeth Lloyd Howell

Amesbury, August 8, 1860

Dear Elizabeth,

Thy first day occupation in writing me was pardonable in
view of the most rigid orthodoxy, for, if not a work of necessity, it was of mercy. It was pleasant to get an idea of thy
mountain home and way of life—to follow thee up the side

of Wachuset, and look with thee upon the heart of the old
Commonwealth, throbbing with summer heat below.

I have been looking for Hannah for the last three weeks,
every few days hearing that she was about to come. I am
almost afraid that I shall somehow miss her, as I shall have
to leave home, if I am well enough this week for some days.[1]

I like Thomas Chase and his wife very much.[2] We had a
flying visit from them. Thomas has a great deal of real refinement, and is, I think, far superior to any young man in our
society in respect to talents and culture.

They had a nice little dinner for Hawthorne in Boston the
other day to welcome him home after his long absence. Emerson, Lowell, Whipple, Fields, Longfellow, etc. were present.
I was not able to be with them, much to my regret. Does
Lucy Chase spend much time at Wachuset this summer?[3] She
told me you had such pleasant times together in the early
Spring.

I have been hoping that Elizabeth would be well enough to
leave Amesbury and spend some weeks with her friends Mrs.
Pitman and Mrs. Sewall in Reading and Melrose; but she is very
feeble this summer, and a ride in a chaise of three or four
miles greatly fatigues her. We have two of my brother's children with us, and a good deal of company, strangers mostly,
whose "continual coming"[4] prevents us from having the
pleasure of our friends' visits. "If," as the old song says "they
would only let a body be." One hates to be stared at, and put
on exhibition. I hope to be able to get away, and would like
to look in upon you at some time and sit under the shadow
of Wachuset.

I have been trying, to write some political essays, but my
head and eyes have failed me, and I am now obliged to forego
all reading and writing as far as possible. I can do little more
than sit in the shadows, and enjoy all I can of the abounding
beauty of the season.

In my next I dare say I shall be able to give thee some
account of Hannah. She is now daily expected.

Excuse the brevity of this letter. The thermometer is at 90,
and I am sure if it is as hot at Wachuset thee will have no
more strength to read than I have to write. So goodbye for the
present, affectionately,

J. G. W.

Source: Denervaud, ed., *Whittier's Unknown Romance*, pp. 59–61.
1. See Letter No. 950.
2. Alice Underhill Cromwell (d. 1882) of New York married Thomas Chase in
February 1860.

3. Lucy Chase (b. 1822), the sister of Thomas Chase, grew up in Worcester, near Wachuset. In 1888 she was living abroad, unmarried.

4. Luke 18:5. Alice Greenwood Whittier (1848–1898) married Wilbur Berry in 1867 and had two children, Elizabeth Greenleaf and Charles.

945. To Harriet Minot Pitman

Lynn, August 25 [1860][1]

My dear fd.

Elizth wishes me to say that she intends to visit thee for a few days, if it is agreeable to thee: She will, if she hears nothing to the contrary, go to Reading on Fourth Day (Wednesday).

I wish I could go with her but I must try and get further from the sea, up among the hills. I have been spending a week in Worcester Co.

I want to see thee, at this time of our great National trial. How life is crowded with events!—How fearfully *fast* we live!

Love to Isaac. God bless and keep you!

Aff
John G. Whittier

Manuscript: Yale University.

1. The year is conjectural, but internal references to events mentioned in other letters of this time seem to indicate 1860.

946. To William Warner Caldwell

Amesbury [August] 1860[1]

My dear friend

We want a song or a hymn for a horticultural fair which takes place the last of next month.[2]

Will thee oblige us by giving us one?

I know of no one who has a finer gift as a songwriter. Many of thy little poems sing themselves.

Pray let me know as soon as possible.

Very truly thy friend
John G. Whittier

Source: Typewritten copy, papers of Thomas Franklin Currier, Harvard University.

1. Roland H. Woodwell dates this letter as September 3, 1860.

2. Caldwell was unable to write the hymn for the Amesbury and Salisbury Agricultural Exhibition of September 17, 1860. See Letter No. 949.

947. To Charles Sumner

Lynn September 3, 1860

My Dear fd. Sumner:

I regret that illness prevents me from seeing thee, as I expected to-day. I shall be under the necessity of going directly home.

It has given me real pleasure to see thee; and to know that in thee the will and ability to serve the cause of freedom are once more united. God bless thee and preserve thee!

Shake John A. Andrew's hand for me, in hearty congratulation:[1] Tell him not to trouble himself about the Courier:[2] Let the poor fellows who manage that sheet enjoy to the utmost their privilege of scolding. They can do nothing else.

Thine truly
John G. Whittier

Manuscript: Harvard University.

1. John A. Andrew (1818–1867), lawyer and statesman, served as a delegate to the Republican national convention in Chicago and was elected governor of Massachusetts in 1860 and four times reelected.

2. The Boston *Courier* in an article, August 31, 1860, stated that John Andrew had formerly attended a meeting for John Brown and that Andrew felt that Brown intended good at Harper's Ferry. The article went on to ask if these were the sentiments of the Republican party in Massachusetts.

948. To an Unidentified Correspondent

Amesbury September 10, 1860

I take pleasure in stating that my friend Mr. Franckle[1] has taught very successfully several classes in French and German in this Village.

I regard him as a gentlemanly and competent instructor and as such commend him to those who need his services.

John G. Whittier

Manuscript: Swarthmore College.

1. Jones Frankle (1829–1909) came to the United States from Germany in 1854 and was a school teacher in Merrimac. During the Civil War Frankle rose to the rank of colonel and afterward went into the insurance business in Haverhill.

949. To Harriet McEwen Kimball

Amesbury September 11, 1860

My dear fd.

Thy kind note and the poem came to hand just now.[1] I am delighted with it. It is the very finest Harvest-song I ever read; and I feel as Cpt. Cuttle would say, that I "worked a good traverse" when I set thee to writing it.[2] I can assure thee of the gratitude of our whole community; we give thee from henceforth the "freedom of our city."

I went away with such a pleasant memory of my visit at your house. I have been telling my sister of thy sister's singing.[3] I met her in the street when I was in too much of a hurry to call at Capt. Hovey's before the cars started to allow me to stop and thank her.

I hope that we shall be able to make a visit to P. this fall but do not stay at home on our account if thee art able to leave. My sister sends her love.

Remember me kindly to thy parents,[4] aunt and sister and believe me ever and truly thy friend

John G. Whittier

The entire poem is excellent but I particularly like the last three verses. It is exactly what I wanted. My sister thinks as I do of it.

W.

Source: Weeks, "John Greenleaf Whittier to Harriet M. Kimball," p. 42. Weeks locates the manuscript as belonging to Nancy Hayward, York, Maine.

Recipient: Harriet McEwen Kimball (1834–1917), a poetess and philanthropist from Portsmouth, New Hampshire, issued several volumes of poetry during her lifetime and occasionally corresponded with Whittier.

1. "A Harvest Hymn written for the Amesbury and Salisbury Agricultural Exhibition, Sept. 17, 1860." See also Letter No. 951.

2. Captain Edward Cuttle, a genial old sea captain in Dickens' *Dombey and Son.*

3. Harriet had two sisters, Lucy (b. 1832) and Caroline (b. 1836).

4. David Kimball (1799–1885) and Caroline R. Kimball (1802–1887).

950. To Elizabeth Lloyd Howell

Amesbury, September 19, 1860

Dear Elizabeth,

I have delayed writing a long time in the hope like the Irish letter writer to carry my letter myself.

In the first place I was a delegate to the Worcester State Rep. Convention, and I started to go to it but was so ill at Lynn that I had to return. Afterwards I returned to Lynn, expecting Hannah would accompany me, but could not arrange matters as respected her children, and dared not risk them with the "Mumps" at Princeton.[1] I thought of going on nevertheless with W. Spooner, but a recurrence of illness compelled me to give up the trip.[2] Last week I thought of visiting thee and taking Emerson on with me, but I have been affected with a cold which has settled on my lungs, and I am as hoarse as any raven that ever croaked.

I was not sure till I got thy letter that thee was still at P.[3] I am glad thee liked my "Ballads," and especially my favorite one "My Playmate." Thine is indeed "The sweet approval that is more than fame." Also "The Witch's Daughter" is a tale of our own neighborhood. Hannah will tell thee that I showed her the place where the Witch's house stood, on the margin of the river.

We were so glad to see Hannah. I did my best to make her visit to Amesbury pleasant, but my own and sister's illness prevented me from enjoying it so thoroughly as I should otherwise have done. But it was a very pleasant episode in our life to meet her and talk the old and the new times over, and to show her our streams and hills. If thee comes to Salem I shall see thee. When does thee expect to leave Princeton? I had a pleasant "forgathering" a few days ago with Charlotte Cushman and Miss Stebbins, the artist.[4] Charlotte is a great woman, with a large heart, and a reformer of the better stamp. I wish I could show thee a photograph Miss Stebbins gave me of the "Miner." The statue is a happy mingling of the classic ideal and the homely Yankee reality—Mercury, in cotton shirt and trousers, bearing his pick in place of the Caduceus.

My poem in the forthcoming Atlantic is, I fear, a little complaining, in its tone. I could not well help it at the time. It is not, however, markedly so. Thee will recognize it in "The Summons."[5]

Thee ought to stay to see October throw her crown upon the Wachuset woods. Let me hear from thee, and believe me,

Affectionately,
J. G. W.

Source: Denervaud, ed., *Whittier's Unknown Romance*, pp. 61–63.

1. Elizabeth Lloyd Howell was staying at Princeton, Massachusetts, where there had been an outbreak of mumps.

2. William S. Spooner, an old friend of the Howell family.

3. Mrs. Howell wrote on September 13, 1860, as follows:

"I was particularly glad to receive thy new volume yesterday,—a rainy day— and not a bright one to me in any sense, for I was sick with a cold, and had exhausted my medicines—in the way of books.

"'My Playmate' is as beautiful as 'Evangeline'—and 'The Witch's Daughter' has the sweetness and noble simplicity of the immortal love-story of Ruth. I like 'Trinitas' very much; was it ever in print before?

"Thee has a large number of admirers here, so it will do good to others as well as to me.

"I think the best of all thy Poems of nowadays are Ballads. 'Maud Muller' is an exquisite thing. Did I tell thee we had it in Tableaux up here? Thee should have seen it.

"I shall be left almost alone for a week or ten days. There is to be quite a break up on the 15th but I so much enjoy the country in autumn, that I shall want no other society for the short time of my stay" (Currier, ed., *Elizabeth Lloyd and the Whittiers,* pp. 135–136).

4. Charlotte Cushman (1816–1876), a Boston-born actress, began her career as an opera singer, but soon won great fame as an interpreter of both male and female parts in the theater. She was best known for her Shakespearean roles.

Emma Stebbins (1815–1882), portrait artist and monument sculptress, worked mainly in sculpture after 1857.

5. "The Summons" was published in the October *Atlantic.* In the poem Whittier complains that he loiters idly writing verses when the cause of freedom demands action. The second to last verse reads.

> "Shamed be the hands that idly fold,
>   And lips that woo the reed's accord,
> When laggard Time the hour has tolled
> For true with false and new with old
>   To fight the battles of the Lord!"

See Letter No. 952 for further comments on this poem.

951. To Harriet McEwen Kimball

Amesbury September 29, 1860

My dear fd.

Thy contribution to our Annual Festival was greatly admired.[1] We make thee an inadequate return of thanks and send a specimen of our fruits.

Among them are a big Flemish Beauty pear from my garden, and several varieties of our apples—the "Whittier" sweet apple.

Hoping thou art well enough to enjoy the taste of our fruits as they ripen and mellow, I am, in great haste, very truly

Thy fd.

John G. Whittier

Manuscript: Haverhill Public Library. Published: Weeks, "John Greenleaf Whittier to Harriet M. Kimball," p. 43.

1. See Letter No. 949.

952. To Lucy Larcom

Amesbury, October 1, 1860

I do not quite like the tone of "The Summons" myself now that it is published. It was, however, an expression of a state of mind which thee would regard as pardonable if thee knew all the circumstances. It is *too complaining*, and I hope I shall not be left to do such a thing again.[1]

Source: Pickard, *Life*, p. 431, and *Anderson Catalogue*, March 5 and 6, 1903, item 605, pp. 40–41, Haverhill Public Library.
    1. See also Letter No. 950.

953. To James Thomas Fields

Amesbury October 8, 1860

My dear Fields

I think I spoke to thee some time ago of my friend Miss Lucy Larcom's Poems. I really think them worthy of a place in your catalogue. They are what the Germans call "Folk Songs"—simple tasteful, healthful—a very rare combination of fancy and common sense.[1]

I know how many applications you must have of the kind:— Miss L. herself would be the last person to intrude herself upon your notice.—but I am so sure that her little collection would find popular favor and do good, that I want thee as a personal favor to look over it, and if thy opinion and that of Wm. Ticknor corresponds to mine, I am sure it will be put on your list.

Do thee stay in the city now all the time?—I hope thee will get a glimpse of Nature in her autumn glory. It is worth living the whole year for, and that is saying a good deal in N England where one is compelled half the year like Job's friends to "fill his belly with the East wind."[2] The woods are beginning to look anything but Quakerly in their attire.

Cordially and truly
Thy fd.
J. G. W.

Manuscript: Huntington Library, San Marino, California.
    1. See Letter No. 791 and note 1 thereof. Her poems were finally published by Fields as *Poems* in 1868.
    2. Job 15:2.

954. To Salmon Portland Chase

Amesbury Ms. October 30, 1860

My dear fd.

This will be handed thee by a young friend and townsman of mine Francis Batchelder, a very worthy and ardent republican who is at this time in Columbus.—He would like just to take thee by the hand, and I am sure thou wilt not deem it intrusive on his or my part.[1]

For the first time in my life, I shall vote, I suppose, for a successful candidate for the Presidency,[2] if I am spared to do so. Hitherto I have been in the minority at every election.

I was sorry that I was away when thee was detained at Amesbury. Dr. Sparhawk is well and remembers thy visit with much pleasure.

Believe me ever and truly thy fd.[3]

John G. Whittier

Hon S. P. Chase

Manuscript: University of Virginia.

1. Francis Batchelder (b. 1838) moved to Brooklyn, New York, where he worked in the leather business. In 1898 he was still alive and living in New Jersey.

2. Abraham Lincoln (1809–1865), who became the sixteenth President of the United States, from 1860 to 1865. Like most abolitionists, Whittier was concerned over Lincoln's failure to abolish slavery immediately after the Civil War began, but finally accepted the necessity of Lincoln's actions.

3. Chase replied to this letter and another one Whittier sent later about the Republican election on November 23, 1860:

"We have indeed great reason to rejoice; for the power of the Slave Interest is certainly broken. What use will be made of the victory, does not so clearly appear. Some indications lead me to apprehend that the wisest and best use will not be made. Great efforts will doubtless be put forth to degrade Republicanism to the Compromise level of 1850.

"There are also some serious dangers on the disunion side. I have always regarded the Slavery question as the crucial test of our institutions; and it has been my hope and prayer that a peaceful settlement of this question on the basis, first, of denationalization, and then final enfranchisement through voluntary State action, would establish beyond all dispute the superiority of free institutions, and the capacity of a free Christian people to deal with every evil and peril lying in the path of its progress.

"To this end, all needless irritation should be carefully avoided, and much forbearance exercised. The citizens of the Free States have now to suffer injuries, when travelling or temporarily sojourning in Slave States, which, under ordinary circumstances and upon common principles, would, as between independent sovereignties, justify extreme measures. If extreme measures are not resorted to, it is because the people of the Free States love the Union and prefer to forbear. And this is right.

"On the other hand, however, the Slave States have, regarding matters from their standpoint, some just causes of complaint. The slaveholders undoubtedly think that they have a right to take their slaves, as property, into the territories and be protected in holding them by Federal power, and nearly all jurists and statesmen, North and South, are agreed that the Fugitive Servant Clause of the Constitution entitles them to have their fugitive slaves delivered up on claim. The Republicans insist, however, that the first demand is not well founded in the

Constitution, while some propose what they call a reasonable Fugitive Act in satisfaction of the second, and others, still, refuse to have anything to do with the returning of fugitives, Constitution or no Constitution.

"Now two facts seem clear to me; first, that the Constitution was intended to create, and fairly construed, does create an obligation, so far as human compacts can, to surrender fugitives from service; and secondly, that in the progress of civilization and Christian humanity it has become impossible that this obligation shall be fulfilled. With my sentiments and convictions, I could no more participate in the seizure and surrender to slavery of a human being, than I could in cannibalism. Still there stands the compact: and there in the Slave States are fellow citizens, who verily believe otherwise than I do, and who insist on its fulfilment and complain of bad faith in its nonfulfilment: and in a matter of compact I am not at liberty to substitute my convictions for theirs.

"What then to do? Just here it seems to me that the principle of compensation may be admitted. We may say, true there is the compact—true, we of the Free States cannot execute it—but we will prove to you that we will act in good faith by redeeming ourselves through compensation from an obligation which our consciences do not permit us to fulfil. Mr. Rhett of S. C. once very manfully denounced the Fugitive Act as unconstitutional, but still insisted on the Constitutional obligation which he summed up in these words 'Surrender or Pay.' Now, if we say we cannot surrender, but we will pay, shall we not command the highest respect for our principles, and do a great deal towards securing the final peaceful and glorious result which we all so much desire?

"There would be some difficulties of detail, if the principle were adopted; but none insuperable.

"There is still another plan of adjustment which might be adopted, though I fear that, in the Slave States, and perhaps in the Free States, it would meet with greater objection. It would consist in amendments of the Constitution by which the Slave States would give up the Fugitive Slave Clause altogether, and the Free States would agree to a representation in Congress of the whole population, abrogating the three fifths rule. One advantage of this would be that the Constitution would be freed from all discriminations between persons, and would contain nothing which could, by any implication, be tortured into a recognition of Slavery. Will you think over these matters carefully and give me your ideas upon them?

"I have written in much haste, but I think you will understand me. What I have written is too crudely expressed for any but friendly eyes; and I hope that you will let nobody see this letter, except if you think fit, our friend Sparhawk and your sister" (Albree, ed., *Whittier Correspondence*, pp. 136–139).

955. To Hannah Lloyd Neall

Amesbury, November 8, 1860

My Dear Friend

I told E. that we must write thee to-day, but she is not able to do her part, so I will just say a word to thee merely as a prelude to a letter erelong. We were heartily glad to get thy kind letter and have read it over several times—a proof of our estimate of it and thee. The truth is, thy visit to A. was the pleasantest episode of our last year's life; and I am sure it did Elizabeth good. I was so sorry to be so miserably ill when I parted from thee at Lynn. I should have been more than glad to have introduced thee to Longfellow. By-the bye, Charles Sumner was pleased with thy call on him and evidently enjoyed it, as did also Dr. Holmes. Longfellow I have not seen, but I am sure he thought it all right.

I have been unable to visit Boston for some weeks, but am now better somewhat, and hope to go soon. I spent a pleasant day with Emerson this Fall, in company with Charlotte Cushman, who, apart from her actress vocation, is one of the noblest of women, a warm abolitionist, and friend of all good causes.

I suppose Elizabeth has not yet returned from Baltimore. I was greatly disappointed in not being able to visit her at her mountain eyrie, at Wachuset. E., I fear, was not made for a Quaker, and I cannot find it in my heart to blame her for living out her nature with its love of all beauty and harmony: and I hope and believe she has self-poise enough to sustain her in her newly found freedom. She has a deeply religious nature, but it seeks expression in other forms and symbols than those of her early faith; and circumstances have made her a little uncharitable towards the "plain Friends." Time will correct all that. As she sees more of her new associates, she will discover that human nature is very much the same, in the Episcopal canonicals, as in Monthly Meeting uniform.

I am glad thee did not go away this fall, it must be so pleasant for thy mother and sisters to have thee with them. I wish I could say that sister and I could visit Philadelphia this winter, but I dare not look forward to it as a probability.

Well, the election is over—Lincoln is elected! The slave power rebuked for once. I do not feel like *exulted*: I am not yet sure that we have gained as much as we hoped. But I do feel grateful to our Heavenly Father that he has permitted me to see this day. I enclose one of our ballots, by which thee will see that I am one of the Electors chosen for our State.

My eyes and head forbid my writing much more. Elizabeth will be glad to write thee when she is able. Give our love to thy dear mother and to Sarah and Elizabeth.

> "God bless you!" Our prayer is.
> God keep you, whose care is
> So tender and true:
> Old friends!—We forget not,
> Old friends!—We have met not
> Friends dearer than you!

Ever and affectionately,
John G. Whittier

Source: Denervaud, ed., *Whittier's Unknown Romance,* pp. 66–68.

956. To Edna Dean Proctor

Amesbury November 10, 1860

My dear fd.

Many thanks for thy noble poem. God grant that all it antic-
ipates may be realized.

If I had not many things to teach me lessons of humility,
the kind and flattering words of thy letter might cause me to
overestimate myself and my writings. As it is, there is no great
danger; and from my heart, I thank thee.

I read all thy poems with pleasure and hearty sympathy.
This last is one of the best.

I am sorry I did not see thee when in N. E.

Very truly thy fd.

John G. Whittier

I have to thank thee, in common with thousands of others,
for introducing me to the life and thoughts of Henry Ward
Beecher.[1] I read his sermons regularly and always with deep
interest and general approval. Like Tennyson's Sir Galahad
"His strength is as the strength of ten."[2]

Manuscript: New Hampshire Historical Society.

1. Miss Proctor had edited *Life Thoughts from the Extemporaneous Discourses
of Henry Ward Beecher* (Boston, 1858).

2. "Sir Galahad," line 3.

957. To Edward Gilman Frothingham

Amesbury, November 21, 1860

Dear Friend:—

I regret that I am not able to join you in the celebration of
the Republican triumph, to which thy letter invites me. It
would be an especial satisfaction to meet my old neighbors
and fellow-townsmen, on an occasion of so much interest.
When I "dwelt among mine own people,"[1] many years ago, I
stood, at first, alone on the Slavery question, and I remember
with gratitude the tolerance with which what was regarded
as the fanaticism of a young man, was treated; and the personal kindness of those who differed from me, I have never forgotten. Time and the current of events have brought us nearer
together; for the first time in my life I have voted for a successful candidate, and find myself in strange companionship
with the rejoicing majority.

Avoiding all unmanly exultation over those of our fellow-
citizens who have honestly striven against us—and who have

the same stake in the welfare of the country that we have,—we
have certainly good cause for rejoicing. It is the inauguration
of a new and better era; or rather it is the re-affirming of the
national faith in the doctrines of the Declaration of Independence—the return of our Government, after long and dark
years of apostasy, to the path marked out by the fathers and
founders of the Republic.

A great responsibility is laid upon us. We must prove that
we deserve our success by asking nothing of any class of our
fellow-countrymen, North or South, but what is morally and
legally right, and yielding to nothing which is morally and
legally wrong. We must be firm, but not defiant; we are too
strong in the right and in our majorities to answer railing with
railing. We can afford to be moderate and generous. With
slavery in the States we have no right to interfere, and no
desire to do so beyond the mild persuasion of the successful
example of Freedom; but outside of State sovereignty, Slavery
has no more legal right or constitutional guaranty, than Polyg-
amy out of Utah. Its home is only in the States; everywhere
else it is an outlaw.

I cannot but regard the menace of disunion from the South
as more likely to prove mischievous than really dangerous. It
may do injury to the industrial and financial interests of the
country, but the evil will work its own cure. Business men at
the South will not long indulge in the childish folly of setting
fire to the clothes on their backs, in the expectation that
their neighbors' fingers will be scorched in putting it out. The
clamor that the Union should be dissolved, because slave
extensionists are out-voted, for the first time in twenty years,
is simply ludicrous. It is a quarrel with the census tables and
Greenleaf's arithmetic; figure Three complaining that it is not
equal to figure Five. Never was there so miserable a pretext
for rebellion and treason. The people have chosen, fairly and
constitutionally, a chief magistrate of unquestioned integrity
and patriotism. He stands pledged to follow the example of
Washington and Jefferson, in preventing the extension of
Slavery. This is all. He will leave the Slave States to the enjoyment or endurance of their peculiar institution; but it could
be a stretch of charity to allow that every South Carolinian
carries with him, in his own proper person, the sovereignty of
his State; that he can pull a slave code out of his pocket and
put it in force whenever he pleases, on the slopes of the Rocky
Mountains, or on the shores of the Pacific!

Let us hope that wiser counsels will prevail in the South. And for our part let us see to it that the present difficulties are not aggravated by weak concessions or idle bravado. Taunts, threats and reproaches are not likely to promote peace and good will; yielding to menace and clamor will only act as a premium upon these unworthy expedients. Prudence, patience, firmness, and strict, even-handed justice, are alone required on our part to meet the emergency, and we have no reason to fear that these will be wanting in the Administration about to be inaugurated.

The voice of the people at the late election has declared with unmistakable emphasis that *Slavery shall go no farther.* For this let us rejoice. As respects the rendition of fugitives, it has decided nothing. The same must be said of the position and rights of our colored population. Massachusetts in this matter has set a noble example from which I trust she will not swerve, whatever may be the course of her sister States. God hasten the time when, in the striking language of our Chief Magistrate in his closing State paper, there shall be a "recognition of all men of whatsoever caste, condition or clime, as children of a common Father, and subjects of one universal and incomprehensible destiny."

Truly thy friend,
John G. Whittier

E. G. Frothingham, Esq.

Source: The Amesbury *Villager*, November 29, 1860. Printed with the note: "Last Thursday evening the Republicans of Haverhill had a demonstration in honor of the recent success of their principles. The following letter, written by John G. Whittier and read at the festival, will be read with interest by his fellow-townsmen."

1. 2 Kings 4:13.

958. To Elizabeth Lloyd Howell

Amesbury November 22, 1860

Dear Elizth.

I have been hoping every day since I recd thy kind note, that I should be able to answer it, cheerfully and the genial manner it deserves, but I must not any longer delay my thanks for it, although too ill to be anything but a sorry correspondent.[1] I was called to Portland some four weeks ago, in reference to my brother's family, and what, with mental anxiety and fatigue and exposure, I came home very ill, and have

suffered greatly since. The unsettled weather, vacillating between autumn and winter, had something to do with it. Even
the severe cold of our climate will be better than the changes,
and I hope to be able soon to give a better account of myself.
I have not been able to answer half my letters for the last
month, and I cannot read much, so that I am of not much
use anyhow, and as thee may suppose, I put very cheap estimate upon myself.

I am very grateful for thy kind inquiries, but, I do not think
I ought to take advantage of thy generous offer to listen to
my complaints. I have made too many already; I who ought
to be able to speak words of cheer and comfort to those I love.
I am vexed with myself for my lack of manly firmness,
patience, and endurance. I have trials and perplexities, which
at times very painfully affect my extremely sensitive nervous
organization: but I have much to be thankful for, and I enjoy
any gleam of sunshine that reaches me, and the love and sympathy of my friends, is a constant joy, notwithstanding a
consciousness that I am not quite worthy of it. [. . .]

My sister is more feeble this fall than she has ever been. I
have to be the *cheerful* one of the household, but it is a poor
make-believe sometimes.

What an excitement arises at the South from the election
of Lincoln! I cannot bring myself to look upon it as really in
earnest. Lincoln is a very conservative, cautious and moderate
man; and will do nothing rash or illegal. If South Carolina
dissolves the Union on so flimsy a pretext, she will not carry
anybody else with her. God grant that this awful question of
Slavery may have a peaceful solution! It is perhaps too much
to expect that so great a wrong should pass away without
convulsing the nation which has so long cherished it.

I wrote to Hannah a line not long ago. We heard by the
way of Newburyport that she thought of leaving for home
this fall, but it seems it was a mistake.

Has thee seen Dr Palmer's famous Book of "Folk Songs"?[2]
It is said to be the finest thing of the kind ever published.
Does thee read Dr. Holmes' story?—It fascinates and repels
me, like the evil influence of the snake it describes.

This week is our festival of Thanksgiving. It is a beautiful
institution, gathering under the old roof-tree the scattered and
divided families. It will be a lonely one to us, as we are not
likely to have any of our own family with us. But, I know we
shall nevertheless, have much to be thankful for to the Giver

of all good gifts. You have, I believe, a similar festival in Pennsylvania; it is one of our "Yankee notions" which is worth borrowing, and I wish I could enjoy it with you.

Ever and affectionately

Thy frd.

J. G. W.

Source: Currier, ed., *Elizabeth Lloyd and the Whittiers*, pp. 138–140.

1. Elizabeth Lloyd Howell had written from Philadelphia on November 14, 1860:

"It is so long since I have heard from thee that I am afraid thy illness has been more serious than usual. Send me a line—if thee can write at all, and tell me how thee is.

"If thee is pressed or troubled let me know, for sometimes 'speaking is relief.' And I need not reassure thee that my sympathy is always alive for *thy* needs.

"I begin to think thee did not get my last note from Princeton—first—because it required an answer, and secondly because thee ought to want to know something about me. Then I fall back upon the fear that thee is ill and unable to write. So it would be a great relief to hear from thee—good or evil, whatever may have befallen thee—

"We are all well and have had several heart-warming reunions, at Mother's and in 3d St. It is delightful to be at home again in the midst of kind frds and loving kindred.

"I cannot write much, for my eyes are very painful" (Currier, ed., *Elizabeth Lloyd and the Whittiers*, pp. 137–138).

2. See Letter No. 920, note 1.

959. To James Thomas Fields

[Before November 25, 1860]

I send thee an absurd ballad which I like *for* its absurdity.[1] Read it, and let me know whether thee think it worth submitting to Lowell. It is just what Harper would like, but I would like better to see it in the Maga., if it is proper for it. I am greatly obliged to the writer of the notice of my poems in the last Atlantic,—Lowell, I suppose.[2] [. . .] I have used the Yankee word "woodsy" instead of "woody" in the ballad.

Source: Pickard, *Life*, p. 430.

1. Sent with this letter was "Cobbler Keezar's Vision" which was printed in the *Atlantic* for February.

2. The November *Atlantic* contained a long review of *Home Ballads and Poems* by James Russell Lowell. Part of the review reads: "He is, on the whole, the most representative poet New England has produced. He sings her thoughts, her prejudices, her scenery. . . . Whatever Mr. Whittier may lack, he has the prime merit that he smacks of the soil. It is a New England heart he buttons his strait-breasted coat over, and it gives the buttons a sharp strain now and then. Even the native idiom creeps out here and there in his verses."

960. To James Thomas Fields

Amesbury November 25, 1860

My dear Fields

If my little ballad of "Cobbler Keezar" is to be published, it wd greatly oblige me if thee could get me a proof of it, before it is printed.

Very truly
J. G. Whittier

Manuscript: Harvard University.

961. To Lucy Larcom

[November 1860]

I agree with thee that "hallelujah" is better than "hurra."[1] [. . .] The poem on Whitefield[2] was written long ago. I added an introduction to it, in which I attempted to describe the sunset in the Merrimack valley, which we looked on together from Whittier Hill.[3]

Source: Pickard, *Life,* pp. 432 and 422.

1. Pickard printed this excerpt with the following remarks: "The news of Lincoln's election in November 1860 was received by Mr. Whittier with devout thankfulness. He wrote to Lucy Larcom."

2. George Whitefield (1714–1770) was an English preacher and evangelist.

3. This second excerpt was printed by Pickard with these remarks: "In a letter to Miss Larcom, written in 1860." Although I have tentatively combined these two excerpts they may be from two different letters. The poem referred to is "The Preacher," which was printed in the *Independent,* December 29, 1859.